Jason vanValkenburgh

Anthony Steven

Patrick Grote

SAMS Teach Yourself

Microsoft® Exchange Server™ 5.5

in 21 Days

SAMS

201 West 103rd St., Indianapolis, Indiana, 46290 USA

Sams Teach Yourself Microsoft® Exchange Server™ 5.5 in 21 Days

Copyright ©1999 by Sams® Publishing

International Standard Book Number: 0-672-31525-4

Library of Congress Catalog Card Number: 98-89636

Printed in the United States of America

First Printing: April, 1999

01   00   99   4   3   2   1

Trademarks

Warning and Disclaimer

EXECUTIVE EDITOR
Grace Buechlein

DEVELOPMENT EDITOR
Gregory Harris

MANAGING EDITOR
Brice Gosnell

PROJECT EDITOR
Natalie Harris

COPY EDITOR
Kate Givens

INDEXER
Johnna VanHoose

PROOFREADERS
Billy Fields
M. Steinhart

TECHNICAL EDITOR
John Ray

INTERIOR DESIGN
Erin Howell

COVER DESIGN
Anne Jones

LAYOUT TECHNICIANS
Brian Borders
Heather Moseman
Mark Walchle

Contents at a Glance

Contents

About the Authors

JASON VANVALKENBURGH is a technical architect and infrastructure consultant for Arthur Andersen's Business Consulting practice in Washington, DC. He has been involved in planning, implementing, and supporting Windows NT Server, Exchange Server, and Systems Management Server (SMS) systems for medium- to large-sized companies. Having worked with Windows NT since its beta release, he is a Microsoft Certified Systems Engineer (MCSE) and has detailed experience implementing local and wide area networks in support of UNIX and Windows NT-based Enterprise Resource Planning (ERP) systems such as PeopleSoft and Oracle Financials. He can be reached at jason.a.vanvalkenburgh@us.arthurandersen.com.

ANTHONY STEVEN is a Microsoft Certified Systems Engineer + Internet and a Microsoft Certified Trainer specializing in Microsoft Exchange Server. He was educated at Ampleforth College and Nottingham University, where he took honors in Electrical and Electronic Engineering. After University, he didn't want a real job, so he joined the British Army. Following officer training at the Royal Military Academy, Sandhurst, he was commissioned into the 13th/18th Royal Hussars (Queen Mary's Own). He served in Norway, Cyprus, Denmark, Germany, and Turkey before selection for Special Duties. On retirement from the Army, he started his own business and now is Managing Director of Office Automation Systems Limited, an IT Training and Consultancy company based near Harrogate in North Yorkshire. He is 35, married, with a small and often delightful daughter. You can reach him at Anthony@off-auto.demon.co.uk.

PATRICK GROTE's Microsoft Exchange experience begins with a foundation of Microsoft Mail and is built with hands-on experience with each and every version of Microsoft Exchange. With more than 10 years of networking and email experience combined with Microsoft Certified Systems Engineer status, Patrick sports the experience and knowledge necessary to write an authoritative book on Microsoft Exchange 5.5. A writer for most of his professional life, Patrick authored his own shareware reviews before anyone knew the concept of shareware. He also served three years as a Managing Editor of a regional computing newspaper.

Dedication

To a former boss Wally Abrams, who taught me everything I needed to know: Sometimes the best way to learn is to make a mistake. Just don't make the same mistake twice. Those hot summers of pulling cable really paid off!—*Jason vanValkenburgh*

To my wife, Caroline, for sustaining me and to my daughter, Lucinda, for distracting me.—*Anthony Steven*

Acknowledgments

I'd like to thank the staff at Macmillan Computer Publishing for their patience, support, and advice throughout the completion of this work. Grace Buechline, Gregory Harris, and Dean Miller helped get this work off the ground and flying. Their gentle prods kept me going at sometimes difficult times when my day job kept me busy.

This book could not have been finished by one person (or at least not me!). Anthony Steven and Patrick Grote came through in fine style, adding insight and material that provides color and technical depth to the book. Anthony deserves particular thanks, having written such a substantial portion of the text. His British humor also made reading each chapter of his a lot of fun.

I'd also like to thank the partners, managers, and clients of Arthur Andersen's Business Consulting practice. They've provided the experience and support necessary to be qualified and capable of writing a book like this.—*Jason vanValkenburgh*

Tell Us What You Think!

As the reader of this book, *you* are our most important critic and commentator. We value your opinion and want to know what we're doing right, what we could do better, what areas you'd like to see us publish in, and any other words of wisdom you're willing to pass our way.

As an associate publisher for the Sams Publishing, I welcome your comments. You can fax, email, or write me directly to let me know what you did or didn't like about this book—as well as what we can do to make our books stronger.

Please note that I cannot help you with technical problems related to the topic of this book, and that due to the high volume of mail I receive, I might not be able to reply to every message.

When you write, please be sure to include this book's title and authors as well as your name and phone or fax number. I will carefully review your comments and share them with the authors and editors who worked on the book.

Fax: 317.581.4770

Email: opsys@mcp.com

Mail: Associate Publisher
          Sams Publishing
          201 West 103rd Street
          Indianapolis, IN 46290 USA

Introduction

by Jason vanValkenburgh

In my daily life as a consultant and systems professional, my clients and colleagues are constantly asking me, "Is there a book I can read to learn all of this?" Whether we're talking about networking software, Exchange Server, or how to deploy a system to tens or hundreds of locations, the answer is often "No." There are lots of books that go through the nuts and bolts of configuration. Others cover general project management principles. Few ever present the long-term and strategic approach needed to implement a large infrastructure system like Exchange while also providing a quick-hit solution by covering the technical configuration you need to do to get the job done. You need both skills to successfully implement Exchange server, so why not write a book that covers step-by-step instructions on building an Exchange system while providing a solid conceptual and management foundation to help make your project successful after the configuration is done? Fortunately my co-author, Anthony Steven, and I have been given the opportunity to make such a book a reality.

The audience of this book is any professional implementing or planning to implement Exchange Server in an organization. If you're an engineer, network administrator, project manager, or sponsor, this book will help make your effort successful. Hopefully you'll learn something each day that you can apply to your project and, better yet, take something away that can help on the next project as well—even if it has nothing to do with Exchange Server.

The book starts with learning the basics of Exchange Server: what it is, how it works, and what it can do. Understanding basic Exchange terms and concepts will help you see the meaning and reason behind the check boxes and dialog boxes that appear later in the book. Who cares about a setting being right if you don't understand what the setting actually does?

Every successful project starts with a solid understanding of its goals, objective, and scope. Understanding why you're implementing Exchange and what parts of Exchange you'll use is critical. After that you can start creating your Exchange topology and design. Then you can start building that design, first by installing Exchange Server. Then you configure that server with users, distribution lists and other Exchange objects. After you have a single, functional server you can start connecting that server to other servers and locations.

Exchange Server is just one piece of an Exchange system; typical end users care little for servers and fancy machines. They want an easy-to-use software program to read and send mail. That's why this book covers configuring the different Exchange clients and the basics of Outlook 98.

The best design can go nowhere if getting tools and knowledge in the hands of users is not successful; this book wants you to know how to rollout and deploy Exchange to your locations. This should lay the foundation for managing your desktops and users. Likewise a well-deployed system will fail if the equipment and networks it is built upon cannot handle the burden of your users. Server and network load testing are critical aspects of a mission-critical Exchange project.

Years ago email was an isolated, internal support system that we all used but didn't rely upon. If an email system went down, you'd pick up the phone and call someone instead of sending a mail message. Today nothing is further from the truth: Email is a mission-critical system providing a vital link between employees, customers, and suppliers. The Internet now provides customers with a pipeline straight into your company, often through email. That's why managing, monitoring, and backing up your Exchange system is key to delivering uptime. Providing the knowledge necessary to restore your system and hopefully prevent the failure in the first place is one of the goals of this book.

My last point is that Exchange Server relies upon a lot of other components. That's why this book spends so much time covering topics outside of the core of Exchange Server: the Internet, local and wide area networks, systems management tools, and Windows NT Server. A good Exchange engineer is conversant at all of these levels; a successful Exchange implementation is one that takes all of these into account.

My colleagues and I have enjoyed working on this book, and I hope you enjoy reading it.

WEEK 1

At A Glance

This week, you'll begin by learning the basics of Microsoft Exchange Server. The most important step at this phase is planning your configuration and rollout. You'll also learn how to install and configure the Exchange client and server, and how to connect your server to other sites. By the end of the week, you should know all you need to get started deploying Exchange in your enterprise.

- Day 1, "Introduction to Exchange," helps you learn the basics of Exchange Server and understand its key components and tools. You'll also gain an understanding of the Exchange hierarchy system.

- Day 2, "Planning Your Exchange Implementation," gets you started designing your Exchange system's topology. You'll identify your organizational needs and deciding how to meet them. You'll also explore how to connect your network to the Internet, other networks, and other email systems.

- Day 3, "Setting Up Exchange Server," begins the vital installation process. You'll prepare your Exchange configuration and install the software suite. Along the way, you'll examine other tools and software you'll need to facilitate a smooth setup process. You'll also review the Exchange Service Pack and learn about its added functionality.

- Day 4, "Server Configuration," begins the configuration process. Learn how to add users, create distribution lists, create address books, implement public folders, and configure Information Store properties to control access to these items.

1

2

3

4

5

6

7

- Day 5, "Working with Multiple Sites," shows you how to connect your Exchange server to other sites. Begin by examining the differences between inter-site and intra-site communication. You'll also configure replication of directories and public folders and consider the performance impact of these items.

- Day 6, "Connect Exchange to Other Sites," demonstrates how to link your Exchange server to other systems using a variety of network protocols. You'll see how to choose a network connector and learn how Exchange routes messages.

- Day 7, "Configuring the Exchange Client," teaches you all about the myriad aspects of configuring a variety of Exchange clients. You'll create messaging profiles and configure remote access.

DAY **1**

Introduction to Exchange

By Jason vanValkenburgh

Chapter Objectives

To begin, you'll learn the basics of Exchange Server and its components. After you complete today's lesson, you should be able to answer the following questions:

- What is Microsoft Exchange Server?
- Why would I implement Microsoft Exchange Server?
- What are the different Exchange components?
- What tools come with Exchange to help me implement and manage Exchange?
- What is an Exchange Hierarchy?

What Is Microsoft Exchange Server?

Because this book is about Microsoft Exchange Server, it makes sense to spend some
time explaining exactly what Microsoft Exchange is and what it can do. Having an
understanding of Exchange Server's capabilities will make your implementation of
Exchange easier as well as enable you to spot opportunities to extend Exchange in your
organization beyond simple email.

Messaging

Exchange's core competency and function is that of a messaging platform. This means
that Exchange Server sends, receives, and stores messages in the form of electronic mail.
Messaging covers both handling mail for client personal computers and sending or forwarding mail to other servers on behalf of client computers. Exchange stores electronic
mail for users as well as temporarily storing messages to forward them to people using
other mail servers.

Group Scheduling

By using either Microsoft Outlook or Microsoft Schedule+, you can have Exchange
Server handle group scheduling. You can keep your schedule on the computer, enabling
other people in your company to see your schedule. You can send meeting requests to
other users as an electronic form, automatically placing the meeting on an individual's
calendar as well as tracking whom can or cannot attend a meeting. You can even have
Exchange suggest a meeting time when everyone you need to attend is available.

Groupware and Application Development

Exchange Server offers extensive application development capabilities, which enable you
to create functional enterprise applications that can be accessed via an Exchange or
Microsoft Outlook client. By leveraging Exchange Server's messaging capabilities, you
can create powerful groupware applications. Microsoft also provides sample applications
to help you start programming in Exchange Server.

Working With the Internet

Microsoft Exchange Server enables your company to send and receive electronic mail
with the Internet, as well as supporting Internet mail (POP3 and IMAP4) clients.
Exchange Server can provide the core messaging platform for Internet Service Providers
(ISPs) and provide chat and directory services for the Internet. You can use Exchange to
publish your corporate white pages with LDAP or Exchange Server's extensive Web
integration. You can even use the Internet to connect your company's locations into a

seamless Exchange-based organization, leveraging the availability and low cost of the Internet to deliver affordable enterprisewide electronic mail.

Scalability, Flexibility and Reliability

One of the advantages of Exchange Server is that it's suitable for organizations of any size, from the smallest company to a Fortune 500 corporation. Exchange Server can easily handle companies with tens of thousands of users, leveraging the flexibility and ease-of-use of Windows NT Server with a robust, powerful messaging engine.

Microsoft Exchange Server 5.5 also supports Microsoft's new Microsoft Cluster Server (MCS), available with Windows NT Server 4.0 Enterprise Edition and expected to be a part of the upcoming Windows 2000. MCS enables the services and applications a Windows NT server provides to be made available on another computer in the event of a crash. This can be done without reconfiguring client computers or causing significant downtime. Microsoft Exchange Server 5.5 allows mail service to continue to function even if the server where Exchange normally runs is down.

Security

A solid corporate messaging solution must be secure. Microsoft Exchange Server provides integrated security with Windows NT Server's Domain model, allowing administrators to secure email and other Exchange components, as you will examine further in subsequent lessons. Likewise, Exchange can encrypt email, provide digital signatures, and provide strong encryption to ensure both internal and external mail is secure.

Ease of Use and Administration

Microsoft Outlook and the Exchange Client are powerful, easy-to-use programs. Exchange Server's administrative tools have an advanced Graphical User Interface (GUI) that anyone can learn easily. The ease at which novices can use and maintain Exchange is an advantage for organizations without deep technical skills or experience.

Why Would I Want to Implement Exchange Server?

There are many reasons why you may want to implement Exchange Server in your organization. Identifying why you are implementing Exchange can be a critical aspect of successfully installing and using Exchange Server. Knowing why allows you to think about your Exchange project's goals and objectives. Here are some reasons why your organization may be implementing or evaluating whether to implement Microsoft Exchange.

Capacity of Current Email System

Your current email system may not have the capability to keep up with the email volume your company handles. Migrating from your old email system to Exchange may expand capacity. Looking at the shortcomings of your existing system and how Exchange will address them is a key part of your project's success. Exchange may also present opportunities to use features not available in your old system.

New Company or Organization

If your company is just starting up, you may be looking for an email system you can start with and continue to grow with. If yours is a small company with limited IS resources, you will want to ensure that you implement Exchange in an easy-to-maintain fashion, ensuring that you have also accommodated for growth within your organization.

Opportunity for New Features

Many organizations simply choose Exchange Server because users want more from their current email system. Group scheduling, groupware, Web access, and other Exchange features often drive companies to buy and implement Exchange. For you it will be important to identify the new features your users want from Exchange so that you can be sure to deliver them! It is also beneficial to prioritize these features so that you can manageably and effectively deliver them. Few Exchange projects attempt to support all features at once.

As a Service Provider

Organizations are increasingly looking to outsource the operations of some of their systems, either as a cost-saving or service-enhancing measure. Companies are beginning to offer Exchange hosting services to companies who want to outsource their email system, Internet presence, or both.

Understanding Your Specific Goals and Objectives

Regardless of why your organization is implementing Microsoft Exchange Server, it is critical that you identify your specific goals and objectives for implementing Exchange. Spending the time and energy early in your Exchange project to understand what your company views as its key objectives will help you prioritize and dedicate your efforts on meeting those objectives.

Core Exchange Components

As a complex messaging platform, Exchange Server is broken down into multiple pieces. This section explains the core components that you need for a functional Exchange system, along with how each component interacts with the other Exchange component to form a robust and capable messaging system.

The Directory

The Directory contains information about all of the objects within the Exchange system, including users, servers, sites, distribution lists, and public folders. You could consider the Directory the "brains" of the Exchange system in that all configuration information about the system is in the Directory, especially where all the mailboxes in the system are and who they belong to.

End users will be most familiar with the Directory because they use it to get a list of other system users in the form of their Address Book, which can contain the names and email addresses of users within and outside the Exchange system. Creating the address book for Exchange users is covered on Day 4, "Server Configuration," when you'll begin configuring your system.

Information Store

The Information Store holds all of the messages in the system's mailboxes and public folders. There are actually two information stores, the Private Information Store and the Public Information Store. The Private Information Store holds users' mailboxes and messages while the Public Information Store holds public folders.

In addition to simply storing messages, the Information Stores deliver messages to and from recipients on the same server. The Information Stores also contain views, rules, and storage or age limits pertaining to objects in the Information Store.

The Information Stores use a transaction-based design in order to provide performance, scalability, and fault tolerance. By writing each change or transaction that affects the information store into a transaction log before making the change, any incomplete changes made during a server outage (such as a power or disk failure) can be recovered by applying the transaction log as needed. This Exchange feature makes it similar to database engines such as Microsoft SQL Server in its architecture and use of hardware. These features of Exchange are covered more on Day 16, "Backup and Disaster Recovery."

Message Transfer Agent (MTA)

The Message Transfer Agent sends, receives, and delivers mail between servers within the Exchange System. The MTA sends messages to recipients on other servers to that server. Likewise, the MTA accepts messages from other servers and ensures they are delivered successfully to recipients stored within that server's Information Store. The MTA will also use addressing and routing information to act as an intermediary, accepting messages from other servers and forwarding them to their destination.

System Attendant

The system attendant is a maintenance service that runs in the background and is critical to the smooth operation of Exchange Server. The system attendant generates addressing information, monitors the system, and performs other forms of routine maintenance. One example of this maintenance would be enforcing limits on users' mailbox sizes by scanning the Private Information Store on a nightly or periodic basis.

Taken together, these basic Exchange components link into a complete Exchange system, as shown in Figure 1.1.

FIGURE 1.1

The core Exchange components form the basis of an Exchange system.

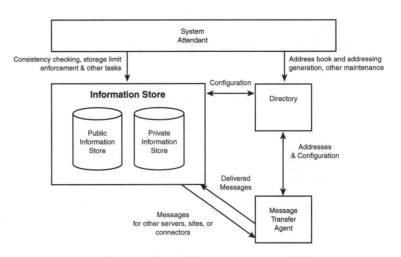

All of these core components are separate Windows NT services, so some Exchange literature or documentation may refer to the Exchange Directory, or to the Exchange Service. Don't be confused—these two terms refer to the same thing. As network services, Exchange components appear in the server's Services Control Panel, as shown in Figure 1.2. Each Exchange component can be stopped and started using the NET START commands used to control any Windows NT service.

FIGURE 1.2

Each core Exchange component is a Windows NT-based service and appears in the Services Control Panel.

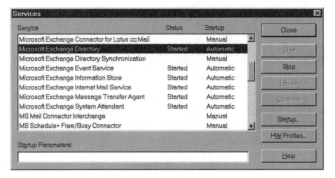

Optional Exchange Components

In addition to the core components previously covered, you will want to know about several additional Exchange components. Depending on how you implement Exchange for your company, you may use some of these optional components.

Internet Mail Service

The Internet Mail Service is responsible for sending and receiving mail messages from other servers and clients via the Internet's SMTP (Simple Mail Transfer Protocol), as well as handling mail requests from POP3 (Post Office Protocol version 3) and IMAP4 (Internet Message Access Protocol, version 4) clients. Known as the Internet Mail Connector in prior versions of Exchange, the Internet Mail Service is the core of Exchange's support for Internet-standards[nd]based mail messaging. You'll cover setting up the Internet Mail Service on Day 12, "Exchange on the Internet."

Site Connector

The Site Connector links Exchange sites, enabling an Exchange Server or site to send and receive messages from Exchange Servers at other locations. Exchange sites and site connectors are covered in detail on Day 5, "Working with Multiple Sites."

X.400 Connector

The X.400 connector links your Exchange Server or site with an X.400 mail system, enabling you to send and receive messages with such a system. The X.400 connector also lets you replicate directory information with that system to enable you to view that system's recipients with the Exchange Address.

RAS Connector

The RAS Connector, known as the Dynamic RAS Connector in early versions of Exchange, enables you to connect your Exchange sites using Windows NT Server's Remote Access Server capability. RAS enables you to use analog modems, ISDN terminal adapters, and other telecommunications devices directly with Windows NT to connect to remote networks; the RAS Connector enables you to use RAS to connect your Exchange sites, server-to-server.

Internet News Service

The Internet News Service enables you to provide connectivity to Internet newsgroups using the NNTP (Network News Transfer Protocol), as well as allowing NNTP client software to view Exchange public folders. The Internet News Service connects to an NNTP news feed and enables your users to view Internet newsgroups as Exchange public folders, sending postings and receiving postings to the Internet from an Exchange client (such as Microsoft Outlook).

Microsoft Mail Connector

The Microsoft Mail connector serves as a gateway between Microsoft Exchange and Microsoft Mail. The MS Mail Connector is used primarily for gradually migrating from Microsoft Mail to Microsoft Exchange. The MS Mail Connector lets you replace the MS Mail Message Transfer Agent (MTA) with Exchange, enabling you to gradually migrate MS Mail postoffices to Exchange until your migration is complete. Migrating from MS Mail is covered more on Day 21, "Migrating from Microsoft Mail."

Schedule+ Free/Busy Connector

Companies that are migrating from MS Mail to Exchange may also use Schedule+, Microsoft's group and personal scheduling software. To facilitate a migration to Microsoft Exchange, Exchange comes with a Schedule+ Free/Busy Connector to enable Schedule+ and Exchange users to view each other's free/busy information. This enables employees of companies that are using both systems to make the integration between Exchange and MS Mail as painless as possible.

Key Management Server

The Key Management (KM) server enables you to use the advanced security features of Exchange Server, such as key-based encryption. The KM Server generates, stores, and issues private and public keys for use inside and outside your organization. You'll learn more about the Key Management Server on Day 19, "Making Exchange Secure."

1

Lotus cc:Mail and Lotus Notes Connectors

Microsoft Exchange Server comes with connectors for cc:Mail and Lotus Notes to allow Exchange to interoperate with these email systems. The cc:Mail connector comes on the Exchange Server CD-ROM, while the Lotus Notes connector can be downloaded from the Microsoft Web site
(`http://backoffice.microsoft.com/downtrial/moreinfo/connectorLotus.asp`).

Microsoft Outlook Web Access

Outlook Web Access enables users to send and receive their mail using a Web-based email client that uses a Web browser, much like Hotmail or Yahoo mail.

Third-Party Add-ins and Components

Third-party vendors have produced a wide variety of supplements and products for Microsoft Exchange, either as server-side components or client-side add-ins. These products range from connectors with legacy email systems (PROFS, for example) to PGP encryption to integration tools for voice mail.

Exchange Clients

It is difficult to talk about Exchange Server without talking about the multiple types of client software used to connect to an Exchange Server. Exchange supports a wide variety of clients, from simple Internet standards-based clients to sophisticated group scheduling and contact management software. Take a look now at the options Microsoft supplies for connecting to Microsoft Exchange Server.

Exchange Client

The Exchange Client is the most basic non-Internet client. The Exchange Client is the natural evolution of the Microsoft Mail client, supporting most significant Exchange features such as forms and public folders. Group scheduling is handled as a separate application, Schedule+. The Exchange client is also the only 16-bit client for Exchange, so it supports Windows 3.1 users. The client also comes in 32-bit Windows 95, Windows NT (Intel and Alpha), and Macintosh versions.

Microsoft Outlook 97/98

Exchange Server 5.5 originally shipped with Outlook 97; the Exchange Server 5.5 Service Pack 1 offers Outlook 98. Outlook integrates email, group scheduling, and contact management in a single client application. Outlook also provides advanced email viewing options, such as previewing unread mail messages. Outlook is Microsoft's unofficially preferred email client for Exchange; most organizations implementing Exchange today use the Outlook client. Outlook is available on a 32-bit Windows 95 or NT platform.

Internet Clients

Exchange Server's support for Internet protocols enables you to connect to an Exchange Server to read mail using a standard POP3 or IMAP4 mail client such as Outlook Express or Netscape Mail. Exchange Server also enables you to use an NNTP newsreader to access Internet newsgroups or Exchange public folders.

With this many clients to choose from, how do you choose the right client? On Day 9, "Deploying Exchange," you'll cover this topic as part of learning about how to deploy Exchange into your organization.

Exchange Implementation and Administration Tools

Microsoft Exchange Server comes with a variety of tools designed to help you implement and manage it. There are also tools that Microsoft provides as part of its BackOffice Resource Kit that help you implement Exchange Server.

Tools Provided with Exchange

Here's a quick rundown of the various tools you'll find available on the Exchange CD-ROM.

The Exchange Administrator

The Exchange Administrator will be your most widely used tool. The Exchange Administrator, shown in Figure 1.3, enables you to configure and administer your entire Exchange organization, including servers at your location in addition to servers at other sites. The tool can add and change users, configure servers and connectors, monitor servers and their status, and ensure that messages are being delivered.

FIGURE 1.3

*The Exchange
Administrator program
is the primary tool
used to configure and
manage Microsoft
Exchange Server.*

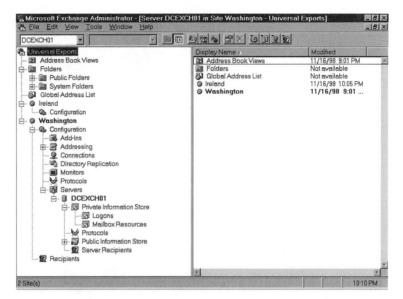

Exchange Administrator can automatically create a Windows NT account for each
recipient as you create mailboxes. The Exchange setup program also integrates Exchange
Administrator with the Windows NT User Manager for Domains, prompting the administrator to create an Exchange mailbox for each user as a Windows NT domain account is
created.

The Performance Optimizer

The Performance Optimizer is a wizard used to find the optimal locations for the various
Exchange files, such as the Public and Private Information Stores, the Directory, and the
Exchange transaction logs. It analyzes the performance of your server's hard disk drives,
placing the different types of files in the optimal location. The Performance Optimizer is
covered in depth on Day 3, "Setting up Exchange Server."

Migration Wizard

The Migration Wizard enables you to import user information and mailboxes into
Microsoft Exchange using a simple wizard interface. As you can see in Figure 1.4, the
Migration Wizard can import mail objects from MS Mail, cc:Mail, Collabra Share, and
Novell GroupWise. The Mail Wizard can also import from specially formatted files that
you can create on your own from another mail system. The Migration Wizard is covered
in depth on Day 21, when you learn more about migrating from Microsoft Mail.

FIGURE 1.4

*The Migration Wizard
simplifies the process
of migrating a user
from an email system
to Exchange.*

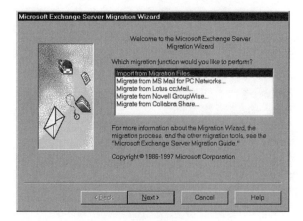

Exchange Version of NTBACKUP

The Exchange Server setup program replaces the version of NTBACKUP that comes
with Windows NT Server with a version that can back up and restore Microsoft
Exchange information stores and directories. This version of NTBACKUP is designed to
perform online backups so that you can back up your databases while the Exchange services are still running.

Information Store, Directory and MTA Utilities

Microsoft Exchange comes with troubleshooting and repair utilities designed to help you
solve problems that crop up with your Exchange databases. These tools include:

- MTACHECK, which verifies the validity and consistency of objects used by the
  Message Transfer Agent to deliver mail. This includes messages that are stuck in
  an outbound or inbound message queue.

- ISINTEG, which checks the structure and contents of the information stores. This
  tool can fix the information store when the information store service will not start.

- ESEUTIL, which can check, repair, and defragment the Exchange directory and
  information stores. This utility replaces the EDBUTIL program found in early versions of Microsoft Exchange, and is cautiously provided by Microsoft (this utility
  is for disaster recovery and is quite dangerous if used incorrectly).

Other Tools and Resources

In addition to the tools provided with Exchange, there are other tools you may want to
obtain. Take a look at them now.

1

The Exchange Resource Kit

The Exchange Resource Kit is a vital set of utilities, tools, and documents useful for implementing and maintaining Exchange. The Exchange CD-ROM comes with a sampler or subset of the full resource kit. You can either purchase the resource kit with full printed documentation at a bookstore, or you can download the Resource Kit tools and files from Microsoft's Web site at `http://www.microsoft.com/exchange/reskit.htm`. I highly recommend obtaining the Exchange Resource Kit, and so would almost every Exchange administrator.

Windows NT Server Resource Kit

Windows NT Server has a Resource Kit that also has utilities useful to anyone implementing Exchange. Anyone using Windows NT Server should obtain this kit and its associated utilities. The kit comes with a Microsoft Technet subscription, can be purchased at book stores, and can be downloaded at Microsoft's Web site,
`http://www.microsoft.com/ntserver/nts/downloads/recommended/ntkit/`
`default.asp`.

The Exchange Topology

Microsoft Exchange Server includes and extends basic messaging principles. Let's first cover the different Exchange terms and what each term means in an Exchange-based messaging environment.

Recipients

The building block of Exchange is the recipient. A recipient is the person (or persons) who describe a particular mailbox in the Private Information Store. For the most part recipients will be your users. Each recipient in Microsoft Exchange uses an Exchange or Internet mail client to access his mailbox stored in the Private Information Store. For this to happen, each recipient needs a Windows NT account, usually (but not necessarily) through a Windows NT domain that both the user and the server belong to.

Exchange can capture different properties of a recipient. At a minimum, a typical Exchange recipient has a system name, and if it's a typical user a first and last name. Exchange can also store phone numbers, office locations, managers, and other information relevant to a particular recipient. Applications written in Exchange can use these properties to their advantage. For example, the Manager or Direct Reports fields could dictate the behavior of a workflow application, such as automatically forwarding items to a manager should a person fail to respond to them in a certain period of time. You can see information on a typical recipient in Figure 1.5.

FIGURE **1.5**

Exchange enables you to capture different attributes of an Exchange user beyond a simple name and user ID.

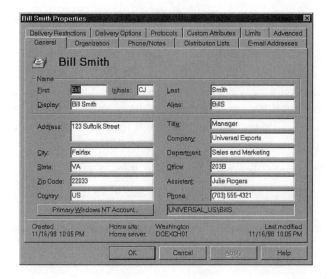

Special Recipients

There are multiple types of recipients: those that represent users with mailboxes in an information store in an Exchange system, and special recipients that represent users outside the mail system. Special recipients are placeholders in the recipients list that allow non-Exchange users to appear in the Address Book.

A possible use of special recipients is to create entries for key business partners in the Global Address Book, such as auditors, consultants, or other individuals who routinely exchange information with people in your company. Some organizations use special recipients to place entries in the address book for home or personal email addresses.

Distribution Lists

A Distribution List enables a single email address to be used to send messages to one or more recipients. For example, you could create a distribution list for each department in your company, so that you could send a message to an address called "Sales" and have that message sent to the entire Sales & Marketing department. Distribution lists can also help with sending mail to individuals based on their role or job in the company. I could send a mail message to "Phones" asking to get a phone set up, and Exchange Server could forward that to the appropriate person in the company. If the person handling phones changes jobs, the distribution list can be updated to send mail to the new person in that job, while end users are oblivious to the change.

1

Public Folders

A public folder is a place for users to share information, either with all Exchange users or with individuals who have explicit security rights. Shared folders work like directories in Windows Explorer, except that the folder contains messages instead of files. Public folders are a great way to share companywide information, such as document templates, the phone list, or Human Resources information. One benefit of public folders is Exchange Server's capability to let users access folders between sites, using either public folder replication or affinity.

Public Folder Replication

Public folders can be replicated to multiple servers. This means that you can have the same folder in multiple sites, with changes made at any one location automatically forwarded to the other folders on other sites. Replication can take place at predetermined times and intervals, so that public folder replication messages can be sent during off-peak hours to conserve network bandwidth and server speed. Configuring public folder replication is covered on Day 6, "Connecting Exchange to Other Sites," when you connect Exchange to other sites.

Public Folder Affinity

Sometimes you don't want to dedicate the messaging overhead and server storage resources to replicating your folders between sites. Another way to allow users access to public folders between sites is to use public folder affinity. With affinity, users see folders from other sites in their Exchange client and connect directly to that folder in its own site. This requires that you have permanent network connectivity between your sites, specifically between the client computer in one site and an Exchange Server at another site.

The Exchange Hierarchy

Exchange groups objects in a hierarchical structure. This structure looks like a tree placed upside-down, with a root at the top and branches flowing downwards into multiple levels. As you can see in Figure 1.6, this hierarchy is similar to that in Windows Explorer.

FIGURE 1.6

*A typical Exchange
hierarchy, as seen in
Exchange
Administrator, consists
of an organization's
folders, address views,
global address list, and
sites.*

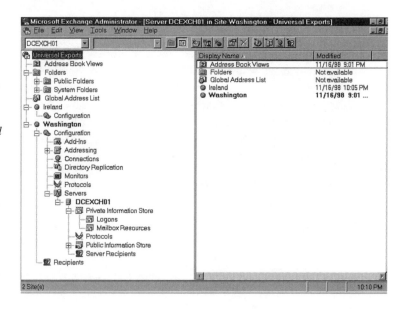

At the highest level is your organization. The organization is the entire company.
Exchange objects that are in the same organization can be managed together in a centralized or decentralized fashion. You can only have one organization on your hierarchy,
which is usually the name of your company, either in its entirety or in a limited fashion.

In the level under an organization there are sites, address book views, folders (both public and system-related), and the global address list.

Address book views control how users are organized into logical collections for viewing
in the address book. You can group users by their recipient's properties, allowing you to
group users by department, location, or any other Exchange recipient property you
choose.

Folders at the organization level include both public and system-related folders. Placing
public folders at this level makes their true physical location irrelevant to users. Users
don't have to know or care where a folder is (at their site or at another site), but simply
how to navigate through the hierarchy of public folders.

The global address list contains a view of all the recipients and distribution lists in your
organization.

A site represents a location where you have users who will use the system. A site is also
another level of Exchange management, and servers in the same site can be managed as a
collective group. As the name suggests, sites usually indicate where your company has

1

offices, for example New York City, Atlanta, and San Francisco. Sites are usually physically separate locations, and as such use different types of network links than systems inside the same building. So if you had two buildings across town from one another, you would typically make them separate sites. But if they were right next door and had a high-speed network link, you might make them part of the same site. You'll cover the technical considerations of when to make a location a site or to make multiple locations a site on Day 2, "Planning Your Exchange Implementation."

Inside a site are recipients and that site's configuration information. The recipients container holds users and user-specific information, such as distribution lists and custom recipients for that site.

Each site's configuration includes add-ins in use at the site, site-level addressing information, connections to other sites, directory replication information, server monitors, the protocols Exchange uses at the site, and the servers at the site.

You'll learn more about each of these parts of a site's configuration on Day 4.

Understanding Messaging and Exchange Concepts

Now that you understand some of the features and capabilities of Exchange, let's spend some time covering basic messaging and Exchange Server concepts. Understanding these concepts will help you design and build a robust Exchange infrastructure, as well as help you understand how electronic mail systems are designed and built.

The Store-and-Forward Model

Microsoft Exchange Server, as well as most other electronic mail systems, uses a *store-and-forward* processing model. A mail system consists of a collection of mail servers, each server holding certain users' mailboxes. When a user sends a message, the server that the user has his or her mailbox on accepts it. The server then looks at who the message is supposed to go to and figures out what to do with it: if the message recipient's mailbox is on that server, the server simply places the message in the recipient's mailbox. If the message recipient's mailbox is on another server, the server forwards the mail message to another server. You can see this process illustrated in Figure 1.7.

FIGURE 1.7

*If a message is sent to
a recipient on the same
server, the message is
delivered. If it is bound
for another server, the
Message Transfer
Agent sends the mes-
sage to its destination.*

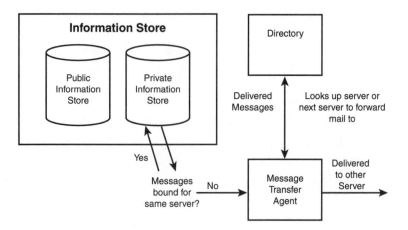

The server that receives this message performs the same check as the previous server: if
the recipient's mailbox is on that server, the message is placed in the recipient's mailbox.
Otherwise, the message is either returned as undeliverable, or the message is forwarded
to another server. A message can potentially pass between many servers until it arrives at
the intended recipient.

The Benefits of Storing and Forwarding Mail

This store-and-forward concept is important in Exchange and today's messaging systems
because it provides some important benefits, especially in the areas of fault tolerance,
performance, and flexibility.

Fault tolerance is of primary importance because the route messages take can vary
depending upon any server or network outages. Servers can re-direct mail to take alternative routes should intermediate servers or network links fail or become overloaded, as
shown in Figure 1.8. Exchange Server enables you to assign preferred and secondary
routes a message can take in order to ensure both good performance when links or
servers are functional and fault tolerance when links or servers fail.

Another benefit is performance from an end-user's perspective. Because the client computer sends the mail to the server to be delivered, the end user and his or her computer is
freed up to do other tasks. The server will ensure that either the message is sent successfully or that a failed mail message (one that cannot reach its intended destination) is sent
back to the sender.

FIGURE 1.8

If a server that normally accepts and forwards messages for another server fails, Exchange can automatically reroute messages through working servers.

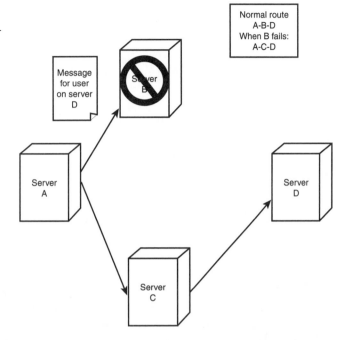

Another performance benefit is that server-to-server message transactions are non-interactive. What this means is that servers are patient: because no end user is waiting for mail delivery with an hour glass holding up a computer, server-to-server email can successfully work with slow or temporary network connections. This can best be shown in the use of relatively slow dial-up connections to the Internet or the use of slow international telecommunications links in cases where costs are typically exorbitant for high-speed links.

Flexibility and integration are other key benefits: each server stop along the way can serve as a gateway to a different type of messaging system, as shown in Figure 1.9. While not as common today due to the prevalence of the Internet and its SMTP mail protocol, it is possible for a mail message to go between multiple formats and systems along its path to delivery. For example, an IBM mainframe user can send a message that then goes to an Exchange Server running Windows NT, which in turn forwards the message to a UNIX server on the Internet, which sends the message to a company using Lotus Notes. Store-and-forward concepts mean that a mail message can take some interesting and unexpected turns! And all of this can be transparent to both the sender and receiver of the mail in question.

FIGURE 1.9

Email gateways enable different email systems to exchange messages and directory information. In Exchange, this is performed by connectors to third-party email systems.

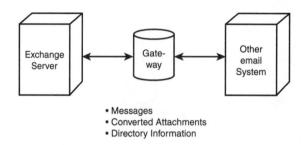

• Messages
• Converted Attachments
• Directory Information

NEW TERM A mail gateway connects two different types of email systems together. An example of a mail gateway would be a server that converts your organization's Exchange messages to Lotus cc:Mail format for delivery to another company's cc:Mail system. Exchange uses the term *connector* to integrate Exchange with non-Exchange systems; the term *gateway* is an generic industry term used to convey a similar topic.

Summary

Microsoft Exchange Server is a complete messaging and application development solution. Exchange Server offers group scheduling, integrated security, scalability, and reliability.

Exchange Server supports the Internet, being able to send and receive Internet mail as well as participating in Internet newsgroups. Exchange also enables Internet POP3 and IMAP4 clients to use Exchange email.

Microsoft Exchange Server's Core and Optional Components

Microsoft Exchange uses core and optional components to create its email solution. All Exchange Servers include the core components; some organizations will choose to implement some optional components to extend Exchange Server's capabilities.

Microsoft Exchange's core components are as follows:

- **The Directory** holds information about mailboxes, sites, and other aspects of your Exchange hierarchy. Most Exchange configuration information is stored in the Directory.
- **The Message Transfer Agent** transfers and accepts mail between servers. The MTA also works with Connectors to ensure mail is sent and received with other Exchange sites and email systems.

1

- **The Information Store**, whose two sections, the Public Information Store and the Private Information Store hold public folders and individual mailboxes respectively.

- **The System Attendant** performs background maintenance tasks, such as generating the address book, handling addressing, and checking information store integrity on a regular basis.

Exchange supports a variety of clients for sending and receiving mail, from the Exchange Client to Outlook 98 to a POP3 or IMAP4 email client. Exchange also supports public folder access using an Internet newsgroup reader using the NNTP protocol.

Exchange Server comes with a variety of tools to help you implement Exchange successfully. The Exchange Administrator is the primary tool for configuring, managing, and maintaining Exchange. The Optimization Wizard enables you to place Exchange files on the best disk drives to maximize performance, while the Migration Wizard helps you migrate from another email system to Exchange.

An implementation of Microsoft Exchange organizes itself in a hierarchical structure, reflecting the structure and geography of the organization it is supporting. At the very top of this hierarchy is the Organization, representing the organization or company running Exchange. This level also holds public folders, the global address list, and address list views. The next level is the site, representing a location or locations where exchange is deployed.

Microsoft Exchange uses a store-and-forward model for email delivery. This design provides performance and reliability advantages, as well as allowing for smooth integration with other emailsystems.

Q&A

Q **My company is evaluating using Microsoft Exchange Server or a standard SMTP/POP3 mail server on a UNIX machine we already use as a database server. Why would I want to choose Exchange?**

A Many companies have existing UNIX systems that come with a free email service called *sendmail*. While sendmail is the email service that runs most Internet servers, Exchange supplies the same functionality in an easy-to-use form. Exchange offers additional functionality such as Web browser support, group scheduling, forms, and integrated directory synchronization not available in standard UNIX application services such as sendmail. Exchange can easily coexist and compliment a sendmail-based email infrastructure.

Q **Exchange uses a store-and-forward messaging model, just like Internet mail. This messaging style is often cited as a reason why Internet email is unsecure and readable to prying eyes. How does Exchange Server address this problem?**

A Microsoft Exchange Server provides extra security by allowing encryption at multiple levels, from server-to-server network traffic to the encryption of individual messages using industry-standard certificates. Although the Internet mail standard does not support encryption by default, you can configure Exchange to use Secure Sockets Layer (SSL) encryption for Internet mail delivery to servers that support SSL.

Q **The Exchange hierarchy looks similar to LDAP structures and Novell Directory Services (NDS) trees that I've seen on some networks. Are they similar to Exchange's directory?**

A LDAP, Exchange, and NDS all use the X.500 directory structure as a starting point. While the X.500 standard itself is not very popular (LDAP is a stripped-down version of X.500), major software companies such as Microsoft and Novell saw an opportunity to adopt its structure and naming convention. While Exchange and NDS have very little in common from a practical perspective, their structure and naming conventions are the same.

Workshop

The Workshop provides two ways for you to affirm what you've learned in this lesson. The Quiz section poses questions to help you solidify your understanding of the material covered and the Exercise section provides you with experience in using what you have learned. You can find answers to the quiz questions and exercises in Appendix B, "Answers to Quiz Questions and Exercises."

Quiz

1. Which Exchange component is responsible for sending from a mailbox on a server to a recipient on the same server?

2. Which Exchange component is responsible for sending from a mailbox on a server to a recipient on a different Exchange Server?

3. At what level in an Exchange hierarchy are public folders managed?

4. What Exchange feature enables users using one Exchange Server to access a public folder stored on another server?

Exercise

Review the diagram in Figure 1.10 that shows four locations linked by email. Sites A,B, and C are all linked directly together, with Site D exchanging mail with Site C. List out the best route taken to deliver mail from Site A to Site D, detailing each "hop" or step along the way. Then repeat the exercise without the link between Site A and Site C. List out each hop mail would take to get between Site A and Site D.

FIGURE 1.10

An Exchange system has sites A,B,C and D connected together. Mail has a "best" route in addition to alternate routes in the event of a link failure between two sites.

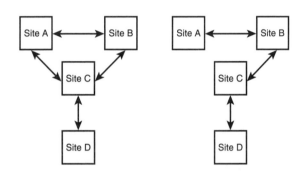

WEEK 1

DAY 2

Planning Your Exchange Implementation

By Jason vanValkenburgh

Chapter Objectives

Today's lesson shows you how to build your overall Exchange topology and design. After you complete today's lesson, you should be able to answer the following questions:

- How do I identify what my company needs from its Exchange implementation?

- How do I control what my project delivers in order to make my project more successful?

- What is Microsoft Exchange's relationship with Windows NT domains?

- How does my organization's business, geographical, and technical characteristics impact my Exchange design?

- How does Exchange affect my company's network and Internet connections?
- What is the best way to connect Exchange to other email systems?

Defining Your Exchange Requirements

The first step in designing your Exchange topology is understanding what your company wants from its Exchange implementation. Do you want messaging? Do you want group scheduling? Do you want Internet mail? What about newsgroups? These are all questions you have to answer to build the best Exchange design for your organization.

Identify Workgroups and Their Needs

While Exchange approaches messaging at the level of an individual mailbox, it is important to realize that few people, if any, work in a vacuum. Look around your organization and find people who often work together or on similar projects. These may be departments or groups within departments. If you've properly identified who these groups are, you can use them as a basis for identifying Exchange requirements, Exchange capabilities, and features that users need or want to be implemented.

Interview Key System Users and Champions

After you have identified the significant workgroups or user populations in your organization, sit down with a representative or typical member of that group. This could be a rank-and-file user, or the leader of the group. The important aspect of interviewing this person is that your goal is to both identify requirements and opportunities for Exchange, as well as champion your project. "Selling" your project to the end-user community by asking questions and then explaining the benefits that Exchange will bring will help open lines of communication and help make your project successful. The most successful projects are those that have end-user support and momentum instead of those driven by an Information Systems or Data Processing department.

In your interviews, ask people how they work and use their computers. If there is an existing email system, understand how people use it. Look for attachments being sent between groups of people; look for what and why messages are sent to the outside, to business partners or customers.

Mobile or Remote Users

Another thing to look for early on in your project is whether some users are in your company's office building and locations, or some travel with a laptop or use a computer at home. Understanding your mobile users and their requirements will have an impact on how you design your Exchange topology, which is covered later in today's lesson.

Identify Other Technical and Managerial Requirements

Some of the requirements for your Exchange implementation will be technical or managerial in nature: they are invisible to users, but play a large impact on how you build the system. Some of these requirements could have to do with support for protocols in use on your existing network, a connection to the Internet, how many administrators you have for managing the email system once it is installed, or how much money you have to build the system. It is important to know these requirements before you start your Exchange design.

Match Requirements to Exchange Capabilities

The next step is to match the requirements you have defined based on interviews and research with the capabilities of Microsoft Exchange. Some of the basic Exchange capabilities should be examined for applicability to your implementation:

- Identify the Exchange mailboxes you need to create. Typically this is at least one per user. There may also be times when you will need to create a mailbox for special purposes; this mailbox might have to be shared by multiple individuals in Exchange.

- Identify the distribution lists that make sense to create. Usually there is a distribution list covering each department or workgroup, so that it is easy for people to easily send messages to everyone they work with on a daily basis. You may also want to create distribution lists for specific projects or purposes. You may even want to create distribution lists of people outside the organization you may want to contact, such as key customers or suppliers.

- Look for opportunities to create public folders. These folders can be organized by topic or department; the best way to identify when a public folder makes sense is if people working together find themselves constantly sending versions of the same document as attachments in an existing email system. A good example of a public folder is an HR/Benefits folder, which contains companywide benefits or payroll information that every employee will want access to.

- Identify whether group scheduling makes sense for your organization. Do your users hold a lot of meetings? Do people spend a lot of time scheduling meetings only to find they can't get everyone together at once? Group scheduling may be a great opportunity to help.

- Exchange forms are beneficial for many organizations. Some basic forms come with Exchange, such as a "While you were out" form to handle missed phone calls. You may want to use some of these basic forms, or create new forms to fit your company. Likewise, you can identify applications you might want to build with Exchange's messaging and programming capabilities.

- Continue these same thoughts on all the other features of Exchange Server, such as custom recipients, delegated mailboxes (for example, a secretary that needs to read and send mail on the boss's behalf), and address book views. You may also have Exchange client-specific requirements. For example, you may identify the need for Outlook to be configured to use Word as its email editor. You may also identify computers that are shared and hence need multiple messaging profiles in order to allow Exchange to be used by multiple people.

Rank and Prioritize Requirements

After you've listed the requirements and how to implement them with Exchange, identify which requirements are high priority and which are low. You can do this by looking at each requirement and its impact on your company and the project. For example, the requirement that all users in the company can send and receive email to each other affects the whole company and is a basic feature of Exchange; this requirement would typically be considered a high priority. However, if one person has a need for an Exchange form, this could be a low priority considering it affects a limited number of people in the company while being more technically complex. When prioritizing requirements, consider the following:

- The applicability of the requirement on the organization. Does this requirement touch everyone, or just a selected few users? Did most of your interviewees mention this requirement, or just one person? If many people mention a particular feature, such as group scheduling or Internet email, you will want to rank it high on your requirements.

- The ease at which you can implement the requirement with Exchange Server. If the requirement is easy to meet, it may make sense to implement. For example, it is simple to delegate mailbox access to a secretary. Likewise, if it is a more complex feature, you may want to hold off on its implementation until after your initial project. A good example of this would be building an Exchange application to track phone calls.

- Whether Exchange is the best tool to meet the requirement. Sometimes Exchange Server is not the best way to meet a particular requirement. For example, if the HR department in your company wants to distribute benefits information, you may have a better solution in place besides Exchange. A good example would be the use of an existing corporate intranet Web site to post benefits information, where users would expect to go looking for the information. Another example would be building a standalone client/server order entry system as opposed to building one in Exchange, because the application could stretch the technical capabilities of Exchange as a development application.

Decide What Requirements You Will Meet and When

A hard thing to realize is that you won't be able to meet all the requirements in the first cut of your implementation. Some of the requirements will have to be either implemented after you've gotten your first pass at Exchange operational, or won't be met at all. Taking your highest priority requirements and focusing on those will help your project be more focused and more successful. The determination of which requirements you will meet in your implementation is part of defining the scope of your implementation.

Defining Implementation Scope

The previous section covered narrowing the functional scope of the implementation by identifying which key requirements of the organization you will fulfill. There are other aspects of scope that depend on characteristics of your organization, including geographic coverage and organizational structure.

Geographic Coverage

It is essential that you clearly define what geography your project covers. This may be easy; if you have only one business location, your scope is that location. If your company has multiple locations, or operates in multiple countries, you must determine how many and which locations your implementation will cover. For example, you may want to start with your corporate headquarters first, and then roll out Exchange to the other offices after that.

Organizational Structure

You may want to limit the groups within your company where you first implement Exchange. For example, if your company is broken out into autonomous business units, you may want to implement Exchange in one business unit, and then tackle the other business unit.

Taking a Phased Approach

You may have noticed that breaking out your implementation by geography or organizational structure could leave your project half-done. What's the benefit of rolling out Exchange to your headquarters without having Exchange in your field offices? What's the benefit of having one business unit use Exchange while the other half of the company has another system? Often the benefits of Exchange are reduced if only part of your company has Exchange. The answer is to break your project into phases of geographical and organizational scope, with each phase having different requirements that will be met. This enables you to break off manageable chunks of work, letting you finish each phase successfully. You also ensure that your goals and objectives for each phase have been met before you proceed to the next phase.

TABLE 2.1   SAMPLE BREAKOUT OF PHASE 1 AND PHASE 2 SCOPE FOR AN EXCHANGE IMPLEMENTATION

Phase 1 (January–April 1999)	Phase 2 (May–September 1999)
All sites have Exchange mail	Group Scheduling
Internet Mail	Custom Forms
Internet newsgroups	Advanced Security (KM Server)
MS Mail connector for migration	Outlook Web Access

Understanding Your Current Networks and Systems

Now that you've defined what features of Exchange you plan to implement, where you will roll out Exchange, and who will be included in your project, the next step is to understand your company's existing systems and networks. Because the network is a shared resource, any application or system on a network must be identified and classified as to how it uses the network. Ensuring your Exchange design takes network capacity, performance, and characteristics in mind will help make your Exchange system function smoothly.

Review Your Network Infrastructure

It is important to undertake a review of your network infrastructure and architecture before you add any application to it. While this book is about Exchange Server, the principles of network planning apply whether you're installing Exchange, Microsoft SMS, or any other network-based application.

The first step is to document your current network architecture, identifying all the network components in the locations where you will be implementing Exchange. It is important to document any wide area network connections that Exchange may use, such as Frame Relay Service, ISDN, or analog modems. Likewise any connections to the Internet should be identified, as well as any relevant firewall or proxy server configurations.

Conducting a Site Survey

Many Exchange Server projects find themselves deploying Microsoft Exchange to multiple business locations. Because it is important to document each location's technical infrastructure, the best way to thoroughly review each site is to conduct site surveys. Site surveys gather important technical information that your team can then use to design its Exchange topology.

Tip Sometimes you have too many sites to visit to conduct a thorough site survey for all the locations. Sometimes building a paper-based questionnaire can get many of your questions answered. If you are adding Exchange servers to some locations, sending a Polaroid or digital camera to each location and having someone take pictures of wiring closets and server rooms makes things easier.

You will want to gather the critical technical aspects of each Exchange location.

Users and Groups Who are the location's Exchange users? Are all users included? It is important to gather the number of users, as well as whether they could be considered heavy Exchange users. Some of this information can be gathered from existing systems.

Use of Existing Email System If there is an existing email system, gather statistics and information that give you a sense of magnitude of how often people use email. Logs and other information can tell you how much mail is intra-site, and how much mail is forwarded via a Mail Transfer Agent (MTA) to another postoffice or location.

Hubs, Switches, and Routers Identify the components of the LAN infrastructure, such as hubs, switches, and routers. Gather capacity information, identifying how many ports are in use versus available ports. This is particularly important for hubs and switches because adding an Exchange server may require an additional port that might not be available without replacing or adding equipment.

It is also important to note LAN speeds, such as 100Mbps switches or 10Mbps hubs. Usually the highest-speed network links are on a server backbone, a place where servers are centralized on the network. Identify the backbone's location and speed; you will probably place an Exchange server here should the location need one.

Network Applications and Servers Because the network is a shared resource (all servers on the network share the infrastructure), you should understand what other servers and applications are on the network. Inventory the servers on the network and what they do. For example, if the location has a Novell NetWare server used for file and print sharing, you will want to know this so that Exchange can smoothly integrate with the network. Likewise, if there is a Windows NT Server machine, you may want to examine the server's applicability to running Exchange; you might be able to save money and effort by installing Exchange on that machine instead of bringing in a new machine.

Network Protocols   While you are examining the servers, you can also document what network protocols are being used to communicate. What protocols are in use will influence what protocol your Exchange server uses. Many networks will either use NetBEUI, IPX, or TCP/IP. Increasingly TCP/IP is the network protocol of choice, with IPX used in existing networks using Novell NetWare. If at all possible, use TCP/IP on your servers. If your network already uses TCP/IP, check to make sure you have enough IP addresses for additional servers and users.

Physical Environment   Many projects overlook the importance of ensuring adequate power and air conditioning for servers. Make sure each location that needs a server has a suitable location for a server, and that the room has air conditioning (preferably with a separate thermostat). Also ensure that the building or office suite air conditioning is not shut down over the weekend. I once found a server room was fine during the week (when staff was there), but weekend temperatures put the room's temperature above 100° F. Most servers would fail under these conditions given that their internal parts generate temperatures far higher than that!

While most Windows NT and Exchange servers do not draw significant power, make sure there is adequate power. Also make sure there is either an existing UPS (Uninteruptible Power Supply) or the capability to add one for the server.

It is also important that any server locations be physically secure. Locking doors are important so no one can get to your server to gain access to its console, reboot it, or otherwise break into it. Most security audits performed by the government and private industry check for means to limit physical access to the server; it is much easier to break into a machine standing next to it versus accessing it from a network.

Cabling   One of my former bosses once told me that 70% of all network problems are caused by bad cabling. At the time I didn't take his advice seriously, but now, after spending hours and hours troubleshooting intermittent problems on various networks, I know this to be true. Make sure that you document the location's network cabling in terms of its location and type. Check for Category 3 and Category 5 twisted-pair cabling. If you can, remove any Category 3 cabling; the cable cannot support speeds above 10Mbps with Ethernet. If you have to add new cable, make sure it is 100Mbps-rated Category 5 cabling. If you are installing new cable, make sure the installer provides printed test reports verifying 100Mbps support. This ensures you're getting your money's worth. And if there's any thin Ethernet cabling around, get rid of it if you can!

End-User PCs One overlooked aspect of an Exchange project is that its success is won and lost at an individual desktop level. Make sure users' PCs are fast enough to adequately run Exchange and other aspects of Windows 95, 98, or NT. Make sure there is enough RAM, processor speed, and disk space for a typical Exchange client such as Microsoft Outlook. A solid Exchange-ready PC would meet these minimum requirements:

- 166Mhz Pentium or above
- 32MB of RAM
- 1GB hard disk drive (100MB free)
- Network interface card (if on network)
- 33.6Kbps or 56Kbps modem (if using dial-up networking)

If there are PCs that do not meet what you consider to be a suitable Exchange-ready PC, you will want to document which PCs need to be upgraded or replaced. It is my experience that replacing a PC is better than upgrading an existing machine, not only because a new machine will be faster, but also because a new PC will be implemented faster while being more stable and reliable.

Analyzing and Summarizing your Site Surveys

Once you have reviewed a site's infrastructure, it is time to analyze each location's infrastructure. Look for opportunities to improve the infrastructure before you implement Exchange at that location. The deployment of new PCs, adding LAN bandwidth through switching, upgrading operating systems, and replacing cabling are all network improvements that can be executed independently of an Exchange project. Starting these improvements while you are designing and testing Exchange will save you time and headaches when you start deployment.

You should be able to generate a series of important documentation that will help you deploy Exchange to that location. This documentation includes the following:

- A wide area network diagram, showing all of your wide area network links and the locations they connect to.
- Physical and logical diagrams of each location's local area network, including cabling, switches, hubs, and routers. The logical network diagram should include any IP or IPX protocol information.
- A list of Exchange users, as well as each user's current PC configuration and its capability to meet your minimum requirements.

You can then use this documentation to determine what changes you need to make at each location, such as network changes or configuration changes to users' PCs.

Your Windows NT Domains and Exchange

Another aspect of your technical infrastructure that you need to consider when you design an Exchange topology is your Windows NT domain structure. Your organization likely follows one of the four Windows NT domain models. Let's review them briefly.

Single Domain Model

In this model, illustrated in Figure 2.1, your organization has only one Windows NT domain, with all users, servers, and other resources maintained as part of a single domain database. This domain model works well for single-location Windows NT installations or those with moderate numbers of users connected with a reliable Wide Area Network. Because Microsoft claims a single domain can hold up to 26,000 user accounts, many organizations with thousands of users choose this domain model. I've seen few organizations with 5,000 or more accounts use this model, although it is theoretically possible.

FIGURE 2.1

The single domain model has all user and servers in one domain. This is the simplest Windows NT domain model.

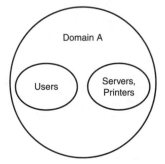

Single-Master Domain Model

The Single Master Domain Model separates your Windows NT network into two or more domains: one holding all user accounts and other domains containing resources that users will access. The resource domains establish trusts with the user account domain, providing distributed management of network resources while allowing centralized administration of user accounts. Figure 2.2 depicts the Single-Master Domain Model.

FIGURE 2.2

The single-master domain model has all users in one domain and servers and other resources in another domain. The resource domain trusts the user account domain.

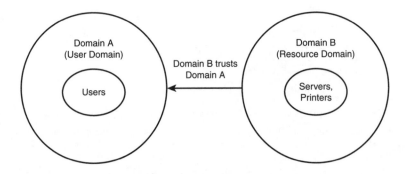

Multimaster Domain Model

This modification of the single-master domain model takes the user domain and splits it into two or more domains, allowing further administrative granularity, allowing business units or locations to administer their own user accounts. Each user domain establishes two-way trusts with the other user domains to allow seamless access to resources, as you can see in Figure 2.3.

2

FIGURE 2.3

The multimaster domain model has users two or more domains, with servers and other resources in another domain or domains. The resource domains trust the user account domains, and the user domains trust each other.

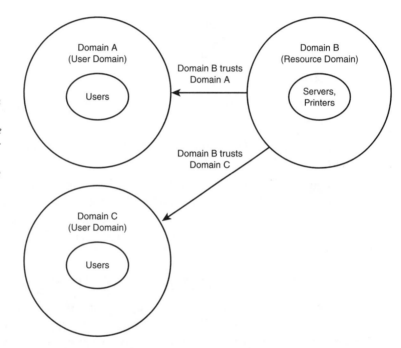

A Windows NT *domain* is a collection of servers, printers, and user accounts gathered together. Items in the same domain are administered and managed together. Microsoft Exchange Server must run on a computer that is a member of a domain; all Exchange users must have Windows NT domain accounts to use an Exchange server.

NEW TERM

A *domain trust* enables users in one domain to access resources in another, or vice-versa. Trusts essentially mean that one Windows NT domain "trusts" the users of another domain to use its resources. For example, a branch-office domain might trust a headquarters domain so that headquarters personnel could access servers that belong to a branch-office's domain. Trusts are either one-way (one domain trusts another), or are two-way (two domains trust each other). Two-way trusts are created by establishing two one-way trusts.

NEW TERM

Don't confuse Windows NT domains with TCP/IP domains. Windows NT domains dictate how Windows NT manages its users and resources, whereas TCP/IP domains typically indicate how organizations name and advertise their resources to the Internet or other TCP/IP-based networks. While some organizations' Windows NT domains are similar in name and structure to a TCP/IP domain, the two concepts are distinctly different in their objectives and approach.

How Your Windows NT Domain Model Affects Exchange

Once you understand which Windows NT domain model your organization uses, let's look at how this affects your Microsoft Exchange Server design.

Determine Whether You Need to Add Windows NT Domain Trusts

If your organization uses a domain model with more than one domain, you will need to establish Windows NT domain trusts if you have Exchange users in a different domain than the Exchange server. Establishing the trust relationship is covered in Day 3, "Setting Up Exchange Server," when you perform key pre-installation tasks.

Designing the Exchange Topology

The process of designing your Exchange topology includes determining which locations are grouped into sites, determining the network connectivity between your locations, designing connectors between sites and external email systems (including the Internet), and determining the configuration of other Exchange components.

Locations and Sites

You may have noticed that I've used the terms location and site in this book. While in a generic context these terms are equivalent, Exchange has a special meaning for the term site. An *Exchange site* is a collection of one or more Exchange servers, managed together and sharing a collection of users, public folders, and addressing information.

An Exchange site may actually consist of one or more locations connected together with a local or wide area network. All the Exchange servers in a site belong to the same Windows NT domain.

Network Considerations

Mail messages are transferred between Exchange servers in a site using RPCs (Remote Procedure Calls), a means Windows NT can use to communicate between machines. Why this matters to you is because RPCs use more network bandwidth than Exchange Site Connectors. If you are limited in the amount of bandwidth you can afford or provide between locations, more locations will be Exchange sites. If two or more locations have good network bandwidth, you can group the locations together to form a single Exchange site.

Another network consideration is that client-to-server network traffic only uses RPCs if you are using a native Exchange client such as Microsoft Outlook. Using Outlook Web Access or Exchange's POP3 client support can lower the amount of bandwidth your users require by allowing the use of a POP3 client or Web browser to send and receive mail. What users lose by taking this approach is some client and server functionality that only a native Exchange client can deliver.

Functional Requirements

Another factor influencing your site decisions is the functionality that you will deliver as part of your Exchange project. As part of your effort to figure out end user requirements, you may have identified the need for group scheduling, custom applications, the use of large attachments, or other ways people will use Exchange. If you anticipate a location's Exchange usage to be high either in terms of message volume or message size, you will more likely want to break out that location into a separate site. Likewise, a location with only a few casual users may find that joining other locations in a site will deliver acceptable performance.

Staffing and Administrative Considerations

People are often overlooked in an Exchange design. Exchange servers and sites need to be monitored, managed, and maintained. Because servers within a site send messages directly to one another using RPC mechanisms while sites communicate with each other using connectors, more sites mean more connectors that need to be monitored and managed. Exchange connectors, either to other Exchange sites or to other email systems, maintain queues and settings that should be monitored. Having adequate resources at a location level is an important concern. Having more Exchange sites is more feasible if each location has technical staff to help in the implementation and administration of Exchange.

Capital and Ongoing Costs

Although this is a technical book, who has ever been able to avoid thinking about costs or budgets? Let's face it, no one has an unlimited budget, so money is often a constraint that influences how we design and build our systems.

There are two ways your Exchange design could affect costs: one-time capital costs for equipment (servers, routers, and other network equipment), and ongoing costs for telecommunications services (like wide area network circuits or long distance charges), administrative time, and support costs. Sometimes you can save money over time by spending more money up front at the beginning of the project. Other times it makes better sense to use as little money up front and spend more on ongoing service and administrative costs. Although showing how to conduct the cost analysis behind such a decision is outside the scope of this book, it is important to understand how your Exchange design hits your company's bottom line.

Choosing a Topology Approach

The considerations that you've just covered may drive you to one of two main topology decisions: to make each location an Exchange site, or to group locations together to form multiple sites, with fewer sites than locations. Let's spend some time going over the advantages and disadvantages of each approach.

Making Each Location a Site   One topology option is to make each location that uses Exchange its own site. Because each site requires at least one Exchange server, you will have to have each site maintain its own Exchange server.

Advantages   The advantages of this approach is that you minimize network bandwidth utilization by keeping client-to-server network traffic on the location's local area network, giving end users fast response times when communicating with the server. Because LAN bandwidth is essentially free while WAN bandwidth has a cost for higher speeds, this approach lowers your ongoing telecom service charges as opposed to using bandwidth-intensive RPCs across a WAN.

Disadvantages   The downside of this approach is that you must purchase a server for each location, potentially driving up your initial equipment costs and setup time. Because every server needs to be maintained by being monitored, backed up, and serviced, this may add to your technical personnel's work.

Grouping Locations Together into Sites   If you have a robust, high-speed network and your employees are light email readers, you might want to consider grouping more locations together into sites.

Advantages   One advantage of this approach is that you minimize how many servers you need to build and maintain. If you don't have administrators at each location, it is easier to have an administrator at a location manage several locations as site.

Disadvantages   The downside of this approach is that you use more WAN bandwidth, something that may be in high demand and usually has a high cost associated with it.

After you have chosen your preferred approach to how you handle sites and locations, spend some time looking at your connectivity options between locations and sites. Understanding the network technologies that are in your design toolbox will help you decide on location and site designs.

Wide Area Network Technologies

Because your Exchange locations will need to be connected together using a WAN, you should know the different WAN transports available and how much bandwidth each transport can give you.

Analog Modems

The first and most basic WAN technology is the analog modem, operating over normal phone lines at speeds up to 56Kbps. Windows NT and Exchange can use analog modems using Windows NT's Remote Access Service, which Exchange can use as a site-to-site connection option. Standard phone lines using analog modems are sometimes called POTS on network documentation, meaning Plain Old Telephone Service.

A consideration when you use analog modems is their relatively slow speed; for Exchange you would only use modems for site-to-site email transfer or for a single user to dial up into a Remote Access Server to gain access to her mailbox. Another aspect to modems is rated versus actual speeds; using a 56K modem does not guarantee you get a 56Kbps connection. Phone line quality will dictate what speed the modems actually use. Also, using analog modem lines to connect your sites may incur long distance charges.

ISDN

ISDN, or Integrated Services Digital Network, is a popular form of digital phone line. ISDN is popular in areas where it is available for both telecommuting and Internet access. Using special ISDN terminal adapters or routers, ISDN offers speeds up to 128Kbps (two 64Kbps channels joined together) in its most popular form, ISDN BRI (Basic Rate Interface). Often ISDN is usage sensitive, costing a per-minute, per-channel rate, although flat-fee service may also be available. You might also incur long distance charges. ISDN is often used as a backup telecommunications transport for higher-speed technologies such as Frame Relay or leased lines. Recent technologies are threatening ISDN's use for Internet access, but ISDN's greater availability and maturity have slowed the introduction of emerging technologies such as ADSL.

ADSL

ADSL, or Asymmetric Digital Subscriber Line, is a promising technology whose adoption is not widespread but growing. Targeted towards high-speed Internet access, ADSL and its related technologies offer speeds up to 1.5Mbps in one direction while offering slower speeds in another. This is perfect for the Internet (and Exchange!) in that users often receive more from a server than they send. ADSL is a technology to watch, but a lack of standards, vendor interoperability, and widespread availability may limit its applicability to your Exchange project. But its promise of high-speed, low-cost Internet access is one you should consider when you examine how your remote users will access their Exchange mail.

Cable Modems

Cable modems are another emerging technology like ADSL designed to connect homes and offices to the Internet, and by extension to your company through the Internet and your company's firewall or proxy server. Cable modems are not available in all locations, but they can often be a low-cost connectivity option for telecommuting workers.

Leased Lines

A leased line is a dedicated digital phone line connecting two points, usually two business locations. This scheme is illustrated in Figure 2.4. Typical leased lines in the United States operate at speeds from 56Kbps to 1.5Mpbs. Leased lines are often used for dedicated, high-speed Internet connectivity as well as to connect two close locations together. Typical leased line pricing is both bandwidth- and distance-sensitive, which means that you pay more for faster and longer leased lines.

FIGURE 2.4

*Leased lines connect
two locations in a
point-to-point fashion.*

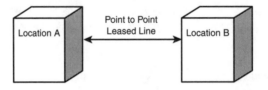

A special consideration with any leased line is its speed. Most leased lines come in three flavors and speeds: 56Kbps, fractional T-1 (64Kbps to less than 1.5Mbps), and T-1 (1.5 Mbps.) A 56Kbps leased line uses different equipment than fractional or full T-1 lines, so watch out not to under-size your lines by using 56Kbps equipment; moving to speeds higher than 56Kbps will require you to change equipment. When in doubt, overestimate the network speeds for locations that may require more bandwidth later.

Because frame relay uses leased lines to provide connectivity between your location and the service provider's point of presence, this caution applies not only to leased lines but to frame relay as well.

Frame Relay Service

Frame Relay is a shared, private network service that enables you to connect several WAN locations into one telecom service. Frame Relay, illustrated in Figure 2.5, is by far the most popular corporate WAN transport. Using a switched and flexible network architecture, a telecom service provider such as AT&T or MCI gives you permanent virtual circuits (PVCs) linking your locations together using a single physical connection to each site. The frame relay "cloud" hides the complex network from you, enabling you to easily add new locations to an existing Frame Relay Service.

FIGURE 2.5

Frame Relay Service enables you to connect your locations with a single connection to a telecom service provider. Frame Relay is the most popular WAN choice for corporate networks.

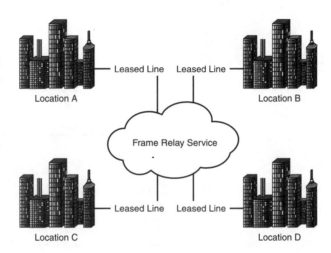

Wireless

Another technology that offers a lot of promise is an entire suite of wireless technologies, from spread-spectrum radio to microwave. Wireless technology relies on line of sight connections between locations, meaning that you have to be able to see one location from another (you can have a lot of fun with weather balloons and binoculars on rooftops to figure out if you have line of sight). Spread-spectrum radio uses a frequency-hopping technology pioneered in the military to deliver speeds from 128Kbps up to 10Mbps; the closer the locations you want to network the greater the bandwidth you can use. Microwave offers speeds up to 45Mbps but requires much more expensive equipment and an FCC license in the United States. Many companies use wireless as a replacement for cross-town leased line connections; some telecom carriers such as Winstar or Teligent offer wireless connections for phone service, Internet connections, and local loop bypasses for Frame Relay Service.

One of the great advantages of using wireless connections that you build is that there are little or no operating costs; bandwidth is essentially free after you spend the capital on implementing the radio equipment, antennas, and towers. You can see an example wireless scheme in Figure 2.6.

FIGURE 2.6

Spread-spectrum, microwave, and other wireless technologies allow for high-speed, low-cost connections between locations that are close to each other and have line-of-sight.

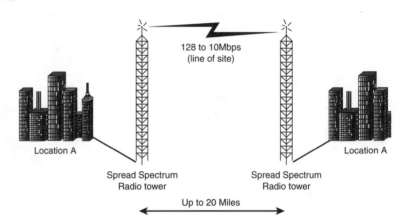

The Internet

The Internet is increasingly viewed as an option for connecting locations using Virtual Private Network (VPN) technology. VPNs enable you to use encryption to allow the Internet to serve as a secure connection between your locations. Some companies are using VPNs to accommodate remote dial-up users who connect to the Internet using an Internet Service Provider (ISP). This option, shown in Figure 2.7, essentially outsources remote access to the ISP, often saving modem management and long distance or toll-free line charges.

Caution

A critical consideration with Internet connectivity is security; Internet connections are open to the world and must be secured using firewalls. Using Exchange with the Internet as a means to send and receive email between your sites should be done cautiously; using available security technologies in firewalls and proxy servers to make sure your information cannot be compromised while it is in transit.

NEW TERM   *Firewalls* and *proxy servers* are computers or devices that secure connections between two networks, usually between a corporate network and the Internet. Running on a server or inside a router, firewalls act as a "traffic cop" between networks, deciding which network traffic to let pass to or from the Internet. Most firewalls use a filtering mechanism, using IP addresses and different traffic types to decide which traffic is allowed or forbidden. A proxy server is a type of firewall that uses more sophisticated software to allow the firewall to act on the behalf of a network device or user; this proxy arrangement provides higher degrees of security for an Internet connection at the price of performance. Many companies use proxy servers to take advantage of advanced features such as Web page caching, virtual private networking, and certificate-based security for access to the corporate network. Popular firewall packages include Checkpoint Firewall/1, TIS Gauntlet, and Cisco PIX.

FIGURE 2.7

The Internet is increasingly used as a replacement for WAN services. This figure shows using Internet-connected firewalls to provide VPN service to multiple locations, including allowing a dial-up user connected to the Internet to access the corporate network at a site.

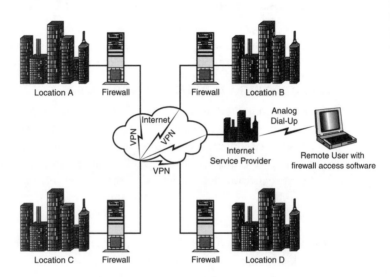

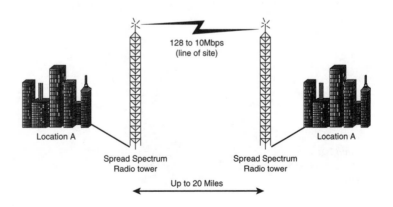

The Internet Mail Service as a Connector Over the Internet   Because
Exchange itself uses messages to perform directory replication and routine communication between sites, some companies use the Internet Mail Service across the Internet to
connect Exchange sites. While the sites may not have direct network connectivity from a
LAN-to-LAN perspective, two locations with Internet email capability can use this to
provide inter-site communications.

Designing Your Exchange Connectivity

After you review your current and planned network links to connect your locations, the
next item to consider is how your Exchange servers will connect with each other and
with the outside world, either to the Internet or to other email systems.

Understanding Exchange Connectors

An Exchange Connector allows Exchange sites to connect to each other or to other systems. Microsoft Exchange Server comes with a variety of connectors, used either for specific network transports (modems, for example) or for specific email systems (X.400
email systems, for example). On Day 1, "Introduction to Exchange," you learned about
the different connectors that come with Exchange; this lesson will review and expand
this topic to help you understand how you implement connectors in your Exchange
topology.

Bridgehead Servers   Exchange connectors work at a site level; a connector is specified to link an Exchange site to another site or email system, as shown in Figure 2.8.
Although connectors are designed at a site level, you have to specify what server actually
handles the Exchange connector. Exchange uses the concept of a bridgehead server to
help simplify linking sites with connectors. Each site has one bridgehead server that is
responsible for handling a particular connector for that site. All mail being sent and
received between two sites on a specific connector flows between each site's bridgehead
server.

FIGURE 2.8

*Bridgehead servers
handle all connections
between sites for a spe-
cific type of connector.
In this figure Exchange
server A and Exchange
server E handle all of
the messages going
between Exchange site
1 and Exchange site 2.*

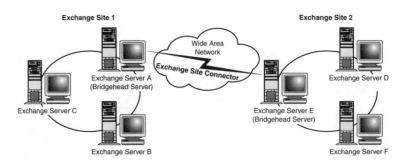

The Exchange Site Connector   An Exchange site connector is used to connect two Exchange sites when there is an existing, permanent network link between one site and the other. This connection could use one of the network technologies covered in the last section of this lesson. This connector is best suited when you have network links between your sites with speeds of 256Kbps or slower. At faster speeds you would consider whether to use site connectors or join the locations into one site.

The RAS Connector   The RAS Connector enables you to use Windows NT Server's Remote Access Server to connect your Exchange sites, usually using analog modems with normal phone lines, as shown in Figure 2.9. The RAS Connector is great for linking your smaller remote offices to a corporate headquarters. One lesson I've learned the hard way from using the RAS Connector is that you should monitor any long distance charges and modem capacity. Make sure that you have enough modems to handle inter-site mail and that any long distance charges don't become so high that Frame Relay or another network technology might be cheaper. If mail volumes grow too high for a modem link running at 33.6Kbps or 56Kbps, mail will constantly back up in your RAS Connector's queues and your phone lines will be in use constantly.

FIGURE 2.9

The RAS Connector uses Exchange servers with Windows NT Server's Remote Access Service to route Exchange messages over RAS devices such as modems connected over regular phone lines.

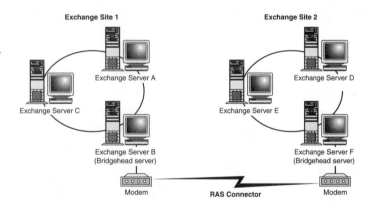

 Caution   Note that the RAS Connector is not used for users to dial-up into your network to access their Exchange mail. While these users may use Windows NT Server's Remote Access Server to connect to Exchange, they are not using the Exchange RAS Connector.

The X.400 Connector   The X.400 Connector enables you to connect your Exchange systems with another X.400 system. In earlier versions of Exchange the X.400 Connector was a viable way to connect your Exchange sites. Exchange Server 5.5's improved

Internet Mail Service along with other connector improvements make the X.400 Connector less desirable for intra-Exchange connections and more suitable for connecting Exchange to external, native X.400 mail systems.

The Internet Mail Service   You can use the Internet Mail Service to serve as a connector between your Exchange sites, either using the actual Internet as your network or using your existing TCP/IP wide area network. This option appeals to organizations whose WANs use firewalls between their locations, because most firewalls and proxy servers have automatic support or sample configurations for SMTP (Simple Mail Transfer Protocol.) A downside of this approach is that the Internet Mail Service on both sites' bridgehead servers consume additional CPU power by converting email attachments and other overhead associated in translating messages between native Exchange formats and Internet mail.

Using Multiple Connectors to Add Robustness   Because each connector has one bridgehead server, you can use different connectors with different bridgehead servers to link your Exchange sites, as shown in Figure 2.10. By giving each connector a different routing preference, you can specify which connector (and hence bridgehead server) is used first to connect your sites; if that server or connector fails you can use another connector as a backup mechanism by assigning that connector a higher weighting in your routing tables. Setting up connectors and assigning routing weights is covered on Day 6, "Connecting Exchange to Other Sites."

FIGURE 2.10

Multiple connectors can be used to allow mail routing to continue should a network link or bridgehead server fail. In this example, if the WAN fails, mail could be re-routed over the RAS Connector's modems.

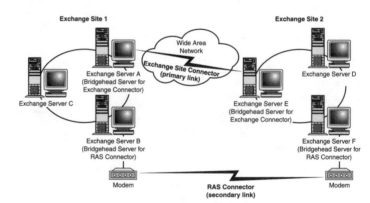

Connections to the Internet

Most of the discussions about the Internet in this book focus on Internet mail. Your Exchange topology may have to take other Internet features of Exchange into consideration, such as Internet newsgroup feeds, publishing your Exchange directory with LDAP, and accommodating remote users over the Internet.

Newsgroups I find that it makes sense to have only one Internet newsgroup feed in your Exchange topology. This makes it simple to control newsgroup security, replication, and other aspects of the newsgroup using Exchange features. It is easier to configure your Internet security as well, because you would open Internet connectivity for one Exchange server. I also find that using one Exchange server for all Internet features, including mail, news, and directory publishing, is easier to manage and secure because only one Exchange server needs to be secured for Internet access.

Directory Publishing with LDAP Like newsgroups, I find that it is logical to have only one Exchange server publishing your Exchange directory to the Internet with LDAP. While you may have some reasons to use LDAP on your Exchange server within your company's networks, I would allow only one server to publish this information outside your company.

Remote Users Over the Internet If you want some of your users to use a Web browser to read their mail using Exchange Server's Outlook Web Access, you will want to make sure that the Web server you configure for Web access is located where Internet connectivity is fastest. You can see this concept illustrated in Figure 2.11. You will also want to make sure that the Outlook Web Access Web server has RPC connectivity to your Exchange servers.

FIGURE 2.11

Remote users can use Outlook Web Access over the Internet to gain access to their Exchange inbox, going though an Internet firewall and accessing a Web server which then connects to an Exchange server

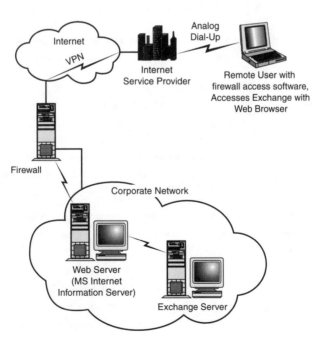

Note

> If you need to use native Exchange Remote Procedure Calls through a fire-wall, you can force an Exchange server to use certain TCP/IP ports for its RPCs, improving your ability to secure and hence allow Exchange RPCs through a firewall. Learn how to do this in Lesson 12, " Exchange on the Internet."

Connections to External Email Systems

One of Exchange Server's benefits is that it comes out of the box with connectors for popular email systems that you may either be migrating from, or that certain parts of your organization may continue to use after you've implemented Exchange.

As a general rule I try to use a particular connection to an email system only once inside an Exchange topology. This makes it easier to manage the connection, having only one place to troubleshoot common problems such as directory synchronization and message attachment conversions.

There are some reasons you may want to use multiple connections to external email systems. One is that you need to establish separate connectors for each email system to connect to; if you have two cc:Mail systems you need to communicate with you will need two connectors. This might not be necessary if both systems can communicate with each other and you decide to use that connection to your advantage; in this case you could create only one cc:Mail connector to one of the email systems.

Connectors as a Migration Tool   Another reason you may want multiple connectors to an external email system is to facilitate your migration from that system to Exchange (see Figure 2.12). For example, many organizations that migrate from Microsoft Mail find that adding an Exchange server at each site where an MS Mail postoffice is located, and then using the Exchange server's MS Mail connector to route mail between MS Mail postoffices, allows for a seamless migration. Individual users can be migrated to Exchange at ease while the MS Mail is gradually phased out of operation.

Directory Synchronization   One thing you will want to decide early in your design is what degree of integration you want between your Exchange system and the external system. If your company controls both systems, you would probably want the level of integration to be high. If the system you want to communicate with is a business partner, supplier, or customer, you may want or settle for lower degrees of integration.

Obviously, a basic requirement for a connector is the successful sending and receiving of email messages. The next level of integration is directory synchronization: Do you want to exchange recipient information between both systems, so that your users can choose users on that email system in an address book, and users in the other system can do the same?

FIGURE 2.12

Placing external email connectors at each site or location where the system allows for a smooth migration to Exchange by using Exchange as the mail routing mechanism. This example shows using Exchange to route MS Mail between postoffices.

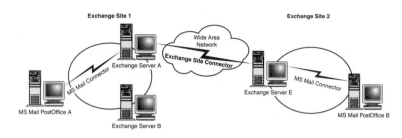

> **Caution**
>
> There are many cases in which an organization will not want to allow directory synchronization for security reasons. You should consult any existing security policies to determine whether you want to establish directory synchronization for an external Exchange connector.

Putting It All Together

Now that you know about the different components you need to consider when you're building an Exchange topology, let's put it all together to get the big picture. Start with your sites, connect them with your network links, put in Exchange site connections, and then connect the Exchange system to the Internet or an external email system. I think the best way to demonstrate this is to give a real-world example of how I've put an Exchange topology together. This case study should give you an example of how the different pieces are put together; I've also included changes that were made in a second phase to address some shortcomings the company came across later in the project. (Some details have been changed to protect the innocent!)

Case Study: Company ABC

Company ABC is an agricultural products maker based out of the United States. The company has a corporate headquarters in Washington, DC, a sales office in New York City, and a variety of farms and plants in Washington State. The Washington State operations center around Seattle, with the company having a main office and a manufacturing plant in Seattle. The Exchange implementation was highly cost conscious, so any opportunity to save money was considered.

Network Connectivity   The locations in Seattle were networked together using spread-spectrum radio, providing a 1.5Mbps link between the locations (this speed is equivalent to a T-1 leased line.) The farms, which only had one user per location, used Windows NT Remote Access Server to connect to the LAN at the main office using 33.6Kbps modems (56Kbps modems were not available at the time).

The Exchange Topology   The Exchange topology shown in Figure 2.13 has three sites: Seattle, Washington, DC, and New York City. Each site used the RAS Connector to send and receive Exchange mail between themselves. Each site used only one Exchange server, with all three servers using the same Windows NT domain (domain synchronization was handled nightly over RAS modem connections). This also means that each server was its site's bridgehead server. Public folder replication was used to replicate a collection of global public folders between all the sites.

Figure 2.13

The first phase of Company ABC's Exchange topology included using the RAS Connector to route mail between the three Exchange sites.

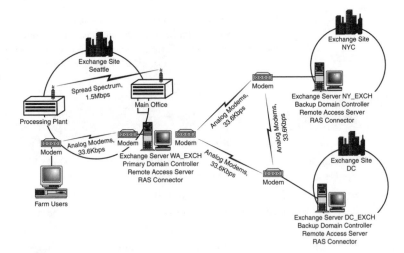

Second Phase Enhancements   The main office in Seattle had by far the most users, and the main office housed the organization's Information Services department. The main office added Internet mail delivery, allowing Internet mail access through a dial-up connection to an ISP. The Exchange server in Seattle ran the Internet Mail Connector.

Another change related to the RAS Connector. Mail traffic volume was higher than expected, so long distance charges between the East and West Coasts were high. The company added Frame Relay Service to interconnect the three main sites, using the Exchange Site Connector to provide Exchange connectivity, as shown in Figure 2.14. The existing RAS infrastructure and connectors were kept in place as backup connectors, so a Frame Relay outage would not result in an interruption of mail delivery.

Figure 2.14

The second phase of Company ABC's Exchange topology included using Frame Relay as the WAN transport and using the Exchange Site Connector to route Exchange mail. The RAS Connector was kept in place as a backup transport (not shown). The company also added Internet mail capability.

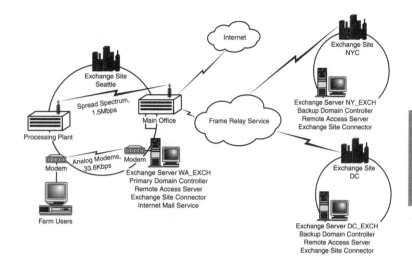

Review

Today's lesson covered how to build an overall Exchange topology and design. You began by defining the requirements for your Exchange implementation. Then you learned how your existing locations, networks, and systems will influence how your Exchange system is designed. Then you went through the steps of designing your Exchange system.

To summarize the main points of this chapter:

- It is important to think about what your users and company needs to achieve for the Exchange project and to document these as requirements for your Exchange design.

- You often can't deliver all the requirements you've found in your interviews and discussions with users. Breaking out your project into phases or parts will make delivering particular Exchange features easier.

- Microsoft Exchange uses Windows NT Server, so the Windows NT domain models your company uses affect your Exchange design. Exchange servers at each site must belong to the same domain. Users can belong to any Windows NT domain if you establish the necessary domain trusts.

- It is important to understand what your Exchange locations have in terms of networks, systems, users, and facilities. Conducting a site survey at each location will help you document what each location has, and then will help you know what changes you need to make to implement Exchange.

- Your Exchange topology will depend on your network connections, cost considerations, technical staffing and support, and other aspects of your project. All of these will affect how many sites you will have relative to the number of locations that use Exchange.

- It makes sense to consolidate certain outside connections and services within your Exchange topology, such as having one server handling Internet mail and newsgroups. Likewise, having a single connector to an external email system simplifies administration and troubleshooting.

Q&A

Q **My company has several Windows NT domains, none of which have any trusts associated between them. They pretty much operate standalone, since each department manages them separately. What's the best domain approach to implement Exchange in this situation?**

A Part of the answer to this question depends on whether your organization plans to consolidate the administration of these domains later, or the status quo is your long-term direction. If you plan to consolidate your domains later, add the Exchange server to which domain holds most other servers (or is the domain where servers will be migrated to), and establish the necessary trusts. If you plan to continue separating your domains, you can either have the server join one of the domains, or add another domain for your server. This would be the first step towards the multimaster domain model (the existing domains would be user accounts domains, and your server would be in a resource domain). Either way you will have to establish the necessary domain trusts to make this work.

Q **My company has Lotus Notes and is in the process of migrating to Microsoft Exchange. My existing Notes setup has Internet mail connectivity. Why wouldn't I just use Internet mail to connect the two systems?**

A This approach would work, although you would have to set up directory information manually because LDAP replication for Internet addresses does not yet fully support replication. Another issue would be Internet mail. If Internet mail addressed to joe_user@mycompany.com gets to Exchange (or Notes), how is the mail sent to the right person? This can be accomplished by setting up specific addressing (like joe_user@notes.mycompany.com), but the amount of work you'd need to do could be saved by using the Lotus Notes Connector that is available for Exchange.

Q My company has several locations that have their own Internet connections and firewalls. Do I want to have the Internet Mail Service at each site?

A It may make sense to have the Internet Mail Service running at each site so outbound mail goes directly to the Internet. If you want incoming mail to come to each site as well, you'll have to configure specific SMTP addressing for each site (joe_user@site1.mycompany.com), and have mail without a site designator (joe_user@mycompany.com) sent to a particular Exchange server for delivery through Exchange site connectors. SMTP addressing is covered in Lesson 12.

Exchange Planning Checklist

In the planning section of this lesson you learned the different things to consider when you're implementing Exchange Server in your organization. The checklist shown in Table 2.2 may help ensure you don't miss anything.

TABLE 2.2 PLANNING CHECKLIST AND STEPS FOR IMPLEMENTING EXCHANGE SERVER

Planning Phase	Steps
Project Planning	Define requirements
	Prioritize requirements
	Define implementation scope
Understand Existing infrastructure	Review network architecture
	Links and locations
	Utilization
	Other applications
	Conduct and analyze site surveys
	Review your Windows NT domains
Design the exchange topology	Review locations and Exchange sites
	Network links
	Physical infrastructure (cabling, room, and so on)
	Review available network options/technologies
	Design Exchange connections
	Define Exchange sites
	Choose connector types
	Connect external email systems
	Connect to the Internet

Workshop

The Workshop provides two ways for you to affirm what you've learned in this chapter. The Quiz section poses questions to help you solidify your understanding of the material covered and the Exercise section provides you with experience in using what you have learned. You can find answers to the quiz questions and exercises in Appendix B, "Answers to Quiz Questions and Exercises."

Quiz

1. If all of your Exchange sites use different Windows NT domains do you have to establish Windows NT domain trusts?

2. What's the first thing you should do when starting to install Exchange for your project?

3. What is the downside of using the Internet Mail Service to connect your Exchange sites?

Exercise

Define an Exchange topology based on Organization A's organizational and technical profile. Organization A is a professional services firm with five business locations spread throughout the United States, with its headquarters in Chicago. Each office has a small technical staff, and a 384Kbps Frame Relay network links all of the sites together (the Chicago site has a larger network connection to accommodate access to a centralized accounting system.) Many of the Organization's users travel and perform work at customer locations or at home using firm-supplied laptops. Some remote employees do not have laptops but instead use customer-supplied and maintained computers with Internet access. Design an Exchange topology to provide email access between the business locations and provide remote e-mail services for traveling users.

DAY **3**

Setting Up Exchange Server

By Jason vanValkenburgh

Chapter Objectives

Today's lesson shows you how to prepare for Exchange and install the product. After you complete today's lesson, you should be able to answer the following questions:

- How big a server does Exchange need? Should I use the server for other applications in addition to Exchange?
- What tools do I need to start setting up Exchange?
- How do I install Exchange?
- What other software will I need to install to build my Exchange server?
- What added functionality will installing the Exchange Server 5.5 Service Pack 1 give me?

Choosing Your Exchange Hardware

While Exchange will run on almost any computer running Windows NT Server that has enough disk space and memory, you will want to consider how Exchange works in choosing the size and kind of computer to use for Exchange. You will also want to think about all the other things your server may do besides run Exchange Server.

Exchange's Minimum Requirements

Microsoft likes to understate all of its applications' minimum hardware requirements. So here's what they say you need:

- Intel Pentium 166Mhz processor or DEC Alpha processor
- 64MB of RAM.
- 300MB of disk space (500 recommended)
- VGA Adapter or better (as supported by Windows NT)
- A network card for connection to the Local Area Network

Keep in mind these requirements are the bare-bones minimum for Exchange to function. Exchange runs on under-powered equipment, although mail delivery, logons, and general connectivity is slow.

More Realistic Hardware Requirements

A larger system more realistic and what I would recommend to someone purchasing a new server (nobody ever complains if a server is too fast). Keep in mind that this is an entry-level system; if you're working on a larger implementation, you'll want to get a correspondingly bigger system:

- Intel Pentium Pro 200Mhz processor or DEC Alpha processor; a Pentium II or Pentium II Xeon of equal or greater speed is better
- 128MB of RAM
- 1GB of free disk space
- CD-ROM drive
- VGA Adapter or better (as supported by Windows NT)
- A network card for connection to the Local Area Network
- A UPS (Uninteruptable Power Supply) with a signaling cable. A UPS is a battery that can keep your server up in the event the server loses power; the signaling cable can tell Windows NT to shut down gracefully so you don't lose data.
- A tape backup unit. Choosing the best tape backup unit and backup software is covered on Day 16, "Backing Up, Restoring, and Repairing Data."

You'll also want to consider some other goodies and tools to help you manage the server after you build it. This applies to any server, not just an Exchange server:

- A 56Kbps modem for the RAS Connector, Internet connectivity to download updates, or for remote troubleshooting.

- Remote-control software so you can access the server console without leaving your desk (or you can use it with the modem.)

Refining Your Hardware Configuration

The key to choosing the best Exchange hardware is to understand how Exchange Server impacts the different parts of a server: the disk drives, processors, memory, network card, tape backup unit, and other peripherals.

Disk Drives and Layout

In Day 1, "Introduction to Exchange," you learned that one of Exchange's advantages is its reliability and performance delivered by its transaction-based database model. Each task that changes an Exchange database (the Directory or Information Stores) results in an Exchange transaction. Before Exchange performs any change to the database, the change is first written to a transaction log. The server then applies the transaction to the database. Should the server or the database's disk fail while the transaction is processed, the server can roll back the transaction, ensuring that the database is in a consistent and safe state. In theory, when the database is started again Exchange can apply pending transactions in the transaction log, and no data is lost.

From a disk input/output perspective, each Exchange transaction results in two disk I/O transactions: one occurs when Exchange writes the transaction to the log, and another occurs when Exchange applies the transaction to the database. An Exchange transaction could be a mail message being delivered, the conversion of an email attachment to go to the Internet, or the pickup of mail messages from users Outbox for delivery to another server. You get the picture: Exchange ends up writing to both the logs and the databases very frequently.

By placing the transaction logs and the databases on different disk drives, the Exchange server can write to both the logs and the databases at the same time. If the logs or database occupy a solid, contiguous part of the disk drive, Exchange can constantly write as the disk drive rotates. If the logs and databases are on the same physical drive, each log and database write results in delays as the disk drive's heads move throughout different portions of the disk drive. This "thrashing" results in both delay and excessive wear-and-tear on the disk drive. That wear-and-tear can result in an earlier disk failure and maybe a long evening of recovering your server!

The bottom line for disk drives is this: plan on using two separate disk drives for your Exchange transaction logs and databases. This is a personal and Microsoft recommendation. Your server will get faster performance and better longevity.

Caution

> The best disk configuration for Exchange is to have two disks, one for your logs and another for the databases. This means you need two independent disk drives—drives that don't operate together as part of a mirror or RAID (Redundant Array of Inexpensive Disks) array. If you mirror, stripe, or use RAID on your disks each "logical" disk operates as a single physical drive from an Exchange or Windows NT perspective. So if you use RAID you will need two separate arrays; if you mirror you'll need at least four disks to fully mirror two sets of disks. One configuration that I've used uses six disks: two drives mirrored for logs and three drives in a RAID array for the databases. With today's hardware RAID arrays you can dynamically expand an array's size by adding disk drives as the Information Store grows. Another tip is to use hardware-based RAID controllers for your mirroring or RAID arrays; while Windows NT supports software mirroring and striping, using a disk controller offloads precious processing time and overhead from your server's CPU.

NEW TERM RAID, mirroring, and striping are all terms for ways to make your disk drives redundant or tolerant in the event of a disk failure. Disks are the most common server component to fail, so time should be spent thinking about mirroring, RAID, or striping to allow your server to stay up if a disk fails. Never implement Exchange (or Windows NT Server, for that matter) without hardware or software-based fault tolerance for your disks. Because a detailed discussion of RAID, mirroring, and striping is outside the topic of this book, I recommend you learn about this in *Sams Teach Yourself Windows NT Server 4 in 21 Days*.

Processors and Memory

Choosing the right number of processors and amount of memory for Exchange really depends on how fast you want your server to be. This is all common sense: the more users you have, the more processors you will want. Because Exchange runs as several separate processes, Exchange takes advantage of additional CPUs. As a rule I try to start with a dual-processor system, and if I need more power I move to a four-processor machine.

Type and Number of CPUs   As for CPU type, I would avoid Pentium Pro machines and choose either Pentium II or Pentium II Xeon-based machines because the Pentium Pro is now officially obsolete for servers. Pentium II machines can only scale to two processors; Pentium II Xeon-based computers can have many more processors, usually two or more.

As a general rule I like to over-size machines for processor speed, so at the risk of offending Microsoft and others who say you don't need a lot of horsepower, I like to use a processor for every 100 to 200 users. No one ever complains if a system is too fast.

Note

> While I like to size servers large for Exchange or any other BackOffice application, I should qualify my position and let you know that I have seen 100 to 200 users supported on small, single 166Mhz Pentium processor machines with 64MB of RAM with no trouble. The only noticeable difference is in the time it takes for the server to pick up mail from your mailbox's Outbox and deliver it. So if you're limited in the size of the machine you can use, go ahead and give it a shot. Migrating to different hardware later is always an option if you find performance to be slow. If you can swing it, always buy a bigger box now because tomorrow you'll be glad for the extra speed.

3

Memory   As for memory, start with at least 128MB of RAM. If you're able to, get more. Extensive Internet mail or newsgroup use, additional applications, or the concurrent number of connections the server has to manage will necessitate additional memory. It is not unheard of to see an Exchange server that supports more than 1,000 users to have 1GB or more of memory. As with any Windows NT Server system, be sure to monitor your server's memory usage after deployment to see if you should add additional memory to prevent paging memory to disk (a time-consuming and performance-degrading event.)

Network Card

The type of network card you purchase will depend greatly on the type and speed of network you already have in place. Today Gigabit Ethernet is becoming more commonplace, although most Exchange and Windows NT Server deployments do not yet need that kind of speed. Emphasis on the word *yet*. Most LAN environments today are Fast Ethernet, so I'll focus this discussion on Fast Ethernet.

If you have a 100Mbps Fast Ethernet switched network backbone, get a 100Mbps Fast Ethernet network card that supports bus mastering and has an on-board processor. This offloads some processing tasks from the server, saving CPU cycles on the server and improving overall speed.

Another word of wisdom: use a name brand network adapter. I can't tell you how many times I've been burned by off-brand or no-name network cards that cause strange, almost untraceable problems with servers. Among brand-name cards there are two brands in which I think you can't go wrong: 3Com and Intel. Most networking professionals prefer one to the other; if your other servers use a particular brand or card, use that model to keep things consistent. It's easier to troubleshoot the devil you know as opposed to the devil you don't.

Tip

If your network is still using 10Mbps Ethernet, purchase a good 10/100Mbps network adapter instead of just a 10Mbps card. This will allow you to upgrade to 100Mbps without swapping out your network card. To move to the higher speed just replace the hub or switch the server is plugged into; the server's network card should automatically select 100Mbps the next time the server is rebooted.

Additional Network Cards   In some cases you may want to install an additional network card in your server. Many new state-of-the-art servers as well as third-party software utilities allow you to define a network card as a spare interface; if the primary card fails, the server can use the second network card. Likewise, there are software packages that allow you to load balance the network load between cards; overall, these work well although there are specific limitations on their effectiveness in routed networks.

Some people like to use a second network card for a "private" server-to-server network or backbone that is used for non-user network traffic, such as Windows NT domain or Exchange directory replication, tape backups across the network, mail routing, or other network services.

Tape Devices

It is important that you think about how you're going to back up your server. While we'll cover tape units in depth on Day 16, it is important to know that you will need to get a tape backup unit. A tape backup unit allows you to back up your Exchange and Windows NT Servers to tape, enabling you to restore your server should it crash or otherwise die.

SCSI Interfaces   Because most tape backup units are SCSI (pronounced "skuzzy") devices, you will need to make sure your server has a SCSI interface or controller card. Most servers use SCSI disk drives, so you can often use the same controller for the tape backup unit. But for the best performance, use a different SCSI interface for your tape unit than the disk drives; this will prevent a bottleneck on that interface. The best thing to do is use either a separate SCSI controller for the tape unit, or the onboard SCSI controller if your server has a SCSI interface on its system board for a CD-ROM drive.

NEW TERM *SCSI, or Small Computer System Interface*, is a standard for disk drives, tape units, scanners, CD-ROMs, and other types of devices to connect to a computer. Although the term SCSI refers strictly to its initial flavor, successive generations of SCSI standards (SCSI-II, Fast Wide SCSI II, Ultra SCSI-3) have emerged, delivering faster speeds and capacities. For the most part these standards have limited interoperability, but you will want to make sure you have the right SCSI-type of interface and connection for both your tape unit and your disk drives.

Considering Other Applications and Uses

One thing to always keep in mind when you're sizing a server is what application or applications the server needs to support. While Exchange sites that must support more than 100 users would probably want to dedicate a server to Exchange, it is quite feasible to place Exchange on a server with other applications.

Windows NT Domain Controllers The first decision you will want to make is whether your Exchange server will be a primary domain controller (PDC), a backup domain controller (BDC), or simply a server in a domain. Microsoft's Exchange documentation steers people away from using an Exchange server as a domain controller; I have had few problems using an Exchange computer as a backup domain controller. Small workgroup installations could easily use an Exchange server as a PDC.

Basic Network Services There are also simple network services that usually have a minimal impact on a server's load. Windows NT Server's DHCP server, TCP/IP printing, WINS, and DNS servers are all examples of often low-intensity services that can be added to a computer running Exchange. Likewise, low amounts of file and printer sharing can be acceptable provided you can ensure adequate performance for both Exchange and file and print users.

Resource Intensive Applications Other resource-intensive applications such as Microsoft SQL Server, Oracle, or Systems Management Server can compete with Exchange Server for system resources; try to avoid running other applications on the same server unless you've invested in a beefy server with plenty of RAM, processor speed, and disks.

Before You Run Setup

No doubt you're itching to start with that Exchange Server CD-ROM and run Setup! But planning your Exchange setup before you begin the actual installation process will help you run setup smoothly, ensuring that you only run it once. Many a time I've installed

3

Exchange, configured everything, and later completed the whole process over again because I made a mistake. So let's cover what tools and information you need before you begin and how to make sure your server is configured well for Exchange.

What You'll Need

Before you run Setup, make sure you have all of the necessary CD-ROM media, downloads, and information. At a minimum you should have all of the following materials at your disposal:

- The Windows NT Server 4.0 CD-ROM
- The latest Windows NT service pack (Service Pack 4), either on CD-ROM (preferred due to its support for strong encryption in the US) or downloaded to the server's disk drive. Even if the service pack is already installed, you will probably want to have it ready.
- The Windows NT 4.0 Option Pack CD-ROM or download from the Internet. The Windows NT 4.0 Option Pack contains Internet Information Server 4.0 (IIS) and Microsoft Certificate Server. If you plan to use Outlook Web Access on this server or plan to use only X.509 V3 security certificates (covered in Day 19, "Making Exchange Secure."), you'll want to install parts of the Option Pack.
- The Exchange Server 5.5 CD-ROM. If you use Microsoft BackOffice, you can use the BackOffice CD-ROM that contains Exchange Server.
- The latest Exchange Server service pack (Service Pack 2). This book assumes you apply Service Pack 1 or later because SP1 and SP2 deliver new functionality such as Outlook 98 and improvements to Outlook Web Access.
- Any third-party software you will install with your server, such as backup software or special device drivers for network cards, modems, or tape drives.

Configuring Windows NT Server

Because Exchange relies upon the foundation of Windows NT Server, it is important to spend some time ensuring Windows NT is installed or configured correctly and that all of the Windows NT–related steps have been completed.

Install Windows NT Server in a Domain

Exchange Server requires that the server you are configuring for Exchange is a member of a Windows NT domain. This means that the Exchange server needs to either belong to a domain you've already created or be a domain controller in a new domain you're creating just for Exchange.

Adding Domain Trusts Depending on your Windows NT domain model (which we covered n Day 2, "Planning Your Exchange Implementation"), you may need to establish domain trusts between your domains. To add the necessary trusts do the following:

1. Determine which trusts you need to establish. Figure out which domain is the trusting domain, and which domain is trusted.

2. Log into each domain as an administrator or a member of the Domain Administrators group.

3. Launch User Administrator for Domains.

4. Under the Policies menu, select Trust Relationships. The Trust Relationships dialog box will appear, as shown in Figure 3.1.

FIGURE 3.1

You can establish Windows NT domain trusts in the User Administrator tool.

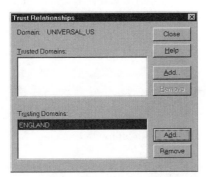

Install Necessary Network Protocols and Services

Because Exchange runs across a network, it is fairly obvious you need to install the network protocols and services you are going to use on your network.

Rules of Thumb for Network Protocols Here are some basic rules that can simplify your Exchange setup and improve performance and maintainability of your Exchange server once it has been built:

- Only install the network protocols you absolutely need. If you can avoid configuring any duplicate or unused network protocols, you could improve the overall health of your network by preventing unnecessary network traffic or broadcasts.

- If you're using any Internet features of Exchange, you have to install TCP/IP. Make sure your server has a static IP address (one that is not dynamically assigned via DHCP). If your server will run the Internet Mail Service, make sure the DNS server setting under the TCP/IP protocol properties has the IP address of a functional DNS server. This will ensure that the Internet Mail Service can use DNS for mail delivery.

- Install any other protocols only on an as-needed basis. If you're in a mixed Novell NetWare/Windows NT network environment, this does not necessarily mean you need to install IPX/SPX protocol support unless your client workstations do not have TCP/IP installed. If your workstations have TCP/IP, use that to connect to Exchange.

- If you're going to use the RAS Connector on your machine you need to install the Remote Access Service. This is covered on Day 10, "Using Microsoft Outlook."

- If you're going to use Outlook Web Access by placing Internet Information Server (IIS) on the same server as Exchange, install IIS. Don't install the SMTP server features as these will interfere with Exchange's Internet Mail Service.

If you follow these guidelines you will save yourself some time by installing and setting up these Windows NT components before you install Exchange. You can always add network protocols or services after Exchange is installed, but it is easier to do this now because you always need to reinstall service packs after you add a protocol or network service.

Install Windows NT Service Packs

The next step after Windows NT is set up is to install the latest service packs. The current service pack is Service Pack 4 (SP4), although Exchange Server 5.5 only requires Service Pack 3 or later.

You can download SP4 from the Microsoft Web page at http://www.microsoft.com/ntserver, you can buy it from Microsoft, or you can find it in the Microsoft TechNet CD-ROM collection.

After you've run the service pack setup, reboot your machine.

Install Windows NT 4.0 Option Pack

If you plan to use Outlook Web Access on this server or plan to use advanced security features of Exchange (security certificates), you will want to install the Windows NT 4.0 Option Pack. The Option pack is available on CD-ROM as part of Microsoft TechNet or it is available on the Internet at http://www.microsoft.com/ntserver. The Windows NT 4.0 Option Pack also comes with Internet Explorer 4.01, which is required for Outlook 98 on client workstations.

If you do not plan to use either certificate-based security or Outlook Web Access on this server, you do not need to install the Windows NT 4.0 Option Pack; you can proceed to the section labeled "Install Hotfixes" further in this lesson.

Which Components You Need to Install   You should install the following items from the Windows NT Option Pack CD-ROM:

- Internet Explorer 4
- Internet Information Server 4.0
- Certificate Server

Running the Option Pack Setup   The Option Pack setup Web page should load automatically when you insert the Option Pack CD-ROM. If it does not, double-click on the file INSTALL.HTM. This should bring up a page where you can select the different installation steps as shown in Figure 3.2.

FIGURE 3.2

The Windows NT 4.0 Option Pack installation page lets you install Windows NT Service Pack 3 (now obsolete), Internet Explorer 4, and the Windows NT 4.0 Option Pack.

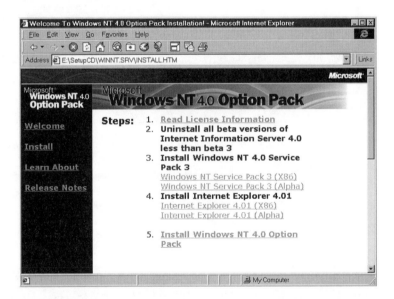

Installing Internet Explorer 4   The main Option Pack setup requires that Internet Explorer 4 is already installed. Click on the option to launch Internet Explorer's setup program. Step through the installation and reboot the machine when Internet Explorer is finished installing.

Starting the Option Pack Setup   After Internet Explorer 4 is installed, in the INSTALL.HTM setup Web page click on the option to launch the Option Pack setup program. Setup will walk you through several pages of information as shown in Figure 3.3; choose which components you want to install.

FIGURE 3.3

The Windows NT 4.0 Option Pack Setup lets you install several additions to Windows NT Server, including Certificate Server and Internet Information Server 4.0.

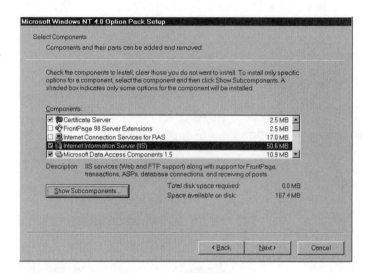

When the Option Pack setup is complete, reboot the machine.

> If you are planning or considering using advanced security like that supplied by Certificate Server or Exchange's Key Manager, you may not want to install Certificate Server yet; waiting until you reach Day 19, "Making Exchange Secure," will provide insight into choosing between your certificate options and configuring Certificate Server properly during installation.

Install Hotfixes

Occasionally Microsoft releases patches or fixes after service packs have been released on its ftp site, which should be applied to your servers. These "hotfixes" usually address serious security concerns or problems; you should always check for hotfixes that you need to install. This is especially the case if your Exchange server will be in any way connected to the Internet. A great number of hotfixes address Internet-related attacks or problems.

To check if there are any release hotfixes to be applied after Service Pack 4, review the files on the Microsoft ftp site under the Windows NT directories, `ftp://ftp.microsoft.com/bussys/winnt/winnt-public/fixes/usa/nt40/hotfixes-postSP4`. There's usually documentation describing what problems the fixes address and whether you should install a particular fix if you don't experience the problem.

Create Exchange Service Account

All of the Microsoft Exchange Server services in a single Exchange site need to use the same Windows NT account to log in to the domain. You need to create a Windows NT account in your domain for Exchange to use.

To create this account, follow these instructions:

1. Log in to the domain as the administrator or as a member of the Domain Administrators group.

2. Launch User Administrator for Domains.

3. Create a new user by selecting New User from the menu at the top of the User Administrator.

4. In the New User dialog box, specify the username, full name, description, and password.

5. Check the boxes labeled User Cannot Change Password and Password Never Expires. This ensures that you don't get any nasty surprises 45 or 90 days later when Exchange can't log in to the server any more. This is shown in Figure 3.4.

FIGURE 3.4

You create an Exchange service account in User Administrator for Domains. Disabling password expiration and preventing a password change prevents later problems with Exchange Server logging into the domain.

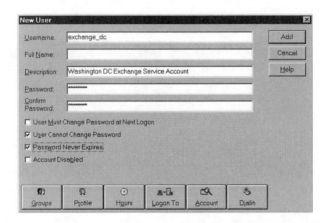

6. Click on the Groups button. Make the user a member of the domain administrators (Domain Admins) group.

7. If your Exchange site will use the RAS Connector you need to allow dial-in permissions to the Exchange service account; other sites will use this account to log in to the network and send and receive mail. To do this, click on the Dialin button and click on the Grant Dialin Permission to user check box, as shown in Figure 3.5. Because multiple sites might use this account, you would not typically set call back

options. If you have only two sites you may want to set a callback number to have the Remote Access Server call back the calling server, raising your level of security.

Figure 3.5

If you are going to use the RAS connector to connect any Exchange sites you will need to grant dial-in permissions to the sites' Exchange service accounts.

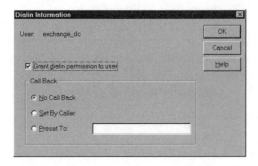

8. To further secure your Exchange site and "lock down" the Exchange service account, you can limit what servers this account can access. By limiting access to only your Exchange servers you lower the exposure this account could have to other servers. This step is only necessary if your site has strong security concerns and is shown in Figure 3.6.

Figure 3.6

Limiting what servers can be accessed with the Exchange service account makes your installation more secure.

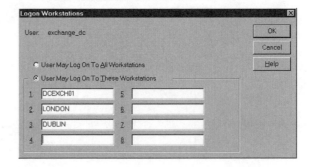

9. Click OK to create the user.

The Exchange Service account, or any account created for an application to use, presents a potential security risk to a Windows NT domain because it typically has strong permissions and a password that rarely if ever changes. To lower this risk, be sure to select a password that is difficult to break, such as a random collection of numbers, letters, and punctuation marks. Do not use the word "Exchange" or any other easy password. Do not use this account to actually log in to administer Exchange. Keep this password safe!

Note

In this text I make the Exchange service account a member of the Domain Administrators group. You do not need to give this account this level of access; I simply do this to help because I always install Exchange Server using this account. You can use any account provided it has the necessary file permissions to the Exchange executables and databases.

Running Exchange Setup

After you've installed, configured, and service packed Windows NT Server 4.0 and created an Exchange service account, you are ready to run the Exchange Server setup program.

Launching Exchange Setup

The Exchange Server Setup program is called SETUP.EXE and is located in either the \i386 or \Alpha subdirectories on the Exchange Server CD-ROM. Launch SETUP.EXE from either directory depending on your server's processor type (\i386 for Intel or Intel-compatible processors and \Alpha for DEC/Compaq Alpha processors).

Choosing the Right Setup Type

The Setup program allows you to perform three different types of setups. Each type installs different combinations of Exchange components or allows you to choose which components to install. The three options are

- Typical. This option installs Exchange Server and the Exchange Administrator program. Setup doesn't install any connectors to external email systems (such as cc:Mail and MS Mail.)

- Complete/Custom. This option allows you to select each component to be installed. By default this is the Exchange Administrator program, the cc:Mail connector, and the MS Mail connector. You can also select Outlook Web Access or choose not to install any of these components, including the online documentation.

- Minimum. This option only installs the Exchange Server software without any connectors or the Exchange Administrator program.

Continuing with Exchange Setup

Once you've selected the install type you want to run, Setup will walk you through the installation process.

If you've chosen the Custom setup you can specify where you want to install Exchange; the default is <drive letter>:\exchsrvr. You can also select which components you want installed, as shown in Figure 3.7.

FIGURE 3.7

The Exchange Setup program lets you select which Exchange components you want to install.

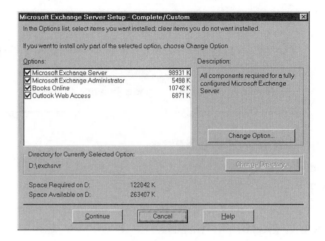

If you choose to install Outlook Web Access you must have either Windows NT Service Pack 4 installed, or have all of the Windows NT Service Pack 3 hotfixes installed. If you have Service Pack 3 installed but do not have the hotfixes installed, you will get an error message like the one shown in Figure 3.8.

FIGURE 3.8

Outlook Web Access requires either Windows NT Service Pack 4 or Windows NT Service Pack 3 with several hotfixes installed. You'll get this dialog box if you don't have all the necessary patches applied.

Agreeing to the Licensing Agreement

The next page asks you to agree to the Microsoft license agreement. Microsoft Exchange uses per-seat licensing, meaning that you need to purchase a client-access license for each user that will access the Exchange Server. Each user also needs a Windows NT client access license, either on a per server basis (such as this server has 100 user licenses) or on a per seat basis (these 100 users have licenses.) Buying licenses in packs of 10, 50, or 100 can lower your cost per user, as well as negotiating companywide licensing arrangements if your company is large and uses several Microsoft products.

If your company uses Windows NT, Exchange, and one or more Microsoft products that come as part of Microsoft BackOffice (say SQL Server or SNA Server), often Microsoft BackOffice server and client licenses cost less. The key with BackOffice is that it usually only makes sense if your users access multiple Microsoft-based applications.

Creating or Joining a Site

The next setup page asks if you want to either join an existing Exchange site or create a new site in your Exchange topology. If this is your first Exchange server, either for this site or your first server ever, you'll want to create a new site. If you're expanding an existing site, you will choose the option to join an existing site.

Joining an Existing Site   When you choose to join an existing site, simply select the radio button labeled Join an Existing Site. Then enter the name of a server in your site.

Creating a New Site   If you're creating a new site, select the appropriate radio button, and then enter the organization and site names for the server, as shown in Figure 3.9. Choose short, descriptive organization and site names.

FIGURE 3.9

You can create a new Exchange site when you build your server or you can join an existing site.

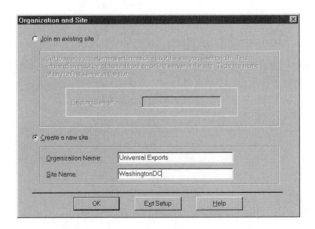

Specifying an Exchange Service Account

If you're creating a new site you need to tell Exchange what Windows NT account to use for the Exchange services. The default service is the account you're currently logged on as; you will want to change this to the Exchange service account you created earlier, as shown in Figure 3.10. Click on the Browse button, select the user account, and click Add. Then click the OK button. After you've returned to the Setup page labeled Site Services Account, enter the Exchange service account's password. When you click OK, Setup will try to use this password to log in to the server.

FIGURE 3.10

Exchange setup asks which Windows NT account to use as its service account; this account is used by all Exchange servers in a site to communicate with each other.

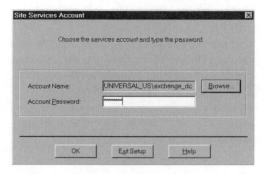

After the account username and password are validated, special rights are added to the account so that Exchange can use the account. These rights are shown in Figure 3.11 in a dialog box that appears after the rights have been added to the account.

FIGURE 3.11

Exchange setup adds special login and access privileges to the Exchange service account.

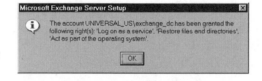

Copying Files and Starting the Services

The next step for Setup is the copying of all of the Exchange files to your server. When this is complete, Setup starts each of the Exchange services and performs some configuration. For example, you will see a message indicating that the Directory service is being started and that directory objects are being created.

After this step you will see a dialog box indicating that Exchange Setup ran successfully. At this point all of the core Exchange components have been installed and are running. You will be prompted to either end setup or run the Exchange Server Optimizer I, as shown in Figure 3.12. You should always run the Optimizer after Setup is complete. I'll explain why in the next section.

FIGURE 3.12

When Exchange Setup is finished you can either end setup or run the Exchange Optimizer.

Running the Exchange Optimizer

After Exchange is successfully installed you should run the Exchange Optimizer Wizard. This program looks at how you intend to use your Exchange server and then automatically performs some basic tuning and configuration to help the server perform well. You should run the Exchange Optimizer after you've first run Setup and after you change how your server is used or the number of users has changed.

> **Caution**
>
> The Exchange Optimizer requires the Exchange services on your server to be shut down. This is usually not a problem after you've just installed your server, but you may find yourself running the Optimizer once your server is actually in use. Make sure that you notify your users that Exchange will be down; the best time to run this Optimizer is after hours when the interruption to your users is minimal.

Defining How Your Server Will Be Used

After you've started the Exchange Optimizer and run past the first welcoming page, the Optimizer presents you with a detailed page with questions related to how your server will be used. You can see this page in Figure 3.13.

FIGURE 3.13

The Exchange Optimizer asks how your server will be used, analyzes the server, and tunes Exchange's configuration.

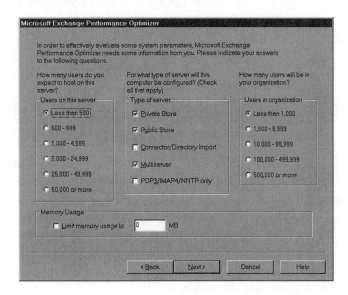

Number of Users

The first question in the upper-left corner is How Many Users Do You Expect to Host on This Server? While you may believe this to mean the total number of users, this question is actually means the number of concurrent users, which is usually a fraction of the total user base. I like to use an assumption that 50% of users will be connected; you can use a lower percentage if you're an Internet Service Provider or host a large number of dial-up users (users who are only occasionally connected).

Type of Server

The next question is For What Type of Server Will This Computer be Configured? You are presented with a number of choices that include the following:

- Private Store. This means that the server will hold individual user mailboxes. A server that a user logs into directly will probably fill this role.

- Public Store. This server type means that the server will have public folders or Internet newsgroups.

- Connector/Directory Import. Check this option if your server will have any Exchange site connectors, including the RAS Connector or connectors to third-party email systems or MS Mail.

- Multiserver. This server type should be selected if your server is part of an Exchange site that contains other servers or has connectors to other systems. This box should always be checked unless the server only handles client connections.

- POP3/IMAP4/NNTP Only. This server type should be selected if you are using your Exchange server to provide Internet or Intranet services using POP3, IMAP4, or NNTP clients and you are not using native Exchange (MAPI) clients for any users.

Choose the appropriate server types for your Exchange Server. For the most part the default settings will fit most companies, so if you're not sure you can always rerun the Optimizer later.

Users in Entire Organization

The next question asks about the size of your organization and in inference how big your Exchange directory will be. Answer the question How Many Users Will Be in Your Organization by choosing the number of total users throughout your Exchange topology. If you're using Connectors such as the MS Mail or cc:Mail connectors to perform directory synchronization (users from other email systems will appear in your directory), you will want to count these users as well.

Memory Usage

The last part of the Optimizer questions relates to memory usage. By default Exchange Server uses all of the available memory in your system. If your server is running other resource-intensive applications such as Microsoft SQL Server or another BackOffice product, you may want to limit the amount of memory Exchange Server uses while it is running. To do so, check the box labeled Limit Memory Usage To and enter the amount of memory you want Exchange to be limited to. This number can be as low as 16MB, but 24MB is the practical minimum; 32MB is a better minimum.

Note

If you're adding Exchange Server to an existing server which runs other applications in addition to Exchange, you may want to limit Exchange's memory usage. How much memory should you use? The answer is use as much as you can. If you're not planning on adding more memory, launch the Task Manager by hitting Control+Alt+Delete and choosing Task List. Look on the Performance page; use a size less than the Available amount under the label Physical Memory (K). Remember to divide this number by 1,024 to get the right number of megabytes. Using this amount or less should help prevent your system from using virtual memory, which moves "pages" of memory to and from disk, a process called paging. Paging can slow your system down dramatically. If the amount of physical free memory is less than 32MB of RAM, consider adding additional RAM to your system.

Note

If your Exchange server uses Internet Information Server (IIS) or any other Web development tools, you will likely want to limit your Exchange Server memory usage with more available free memory. Many Web application environments that use database connectivity, including Outlook Web Access, Active Server Pages, Cold Fusion and others, use memory to buffer data sets and other information. These sets grow and shrink dynamically, so leaving extra free memory ensures that a large query or transaction does not cause virtual memory paging and slows down overall performance.

After you have completed this page, click the next button to start the Optimizer's next step.

Analyzing Disk Drive Performance

The next thing the Exchange Optimizer does is analyze your server's disk drives and how each drive performs relative to another. As you may remember, an optimal

Exchange configuration uses separate physical drives for logs and databases. The Optimizer looks at the disk drives to determine the best location for the information stores, directory, and logs. After the Optimizer is done with this step you will be asked to proceed to the next page.

Locations of Exchange Files

After the Optimizer has learned how your Exchange server will be used, how many users you will have, and how your server's different disks perform, the Optimizer determines the best locations for the different types of Exchange files. The Optimizer will provide a dialog box similar to the one in Figure 3.14 with its recommended file locations.

FIGURE 3.14

The Exchange Optimizer analyzes the server's disk configuration and performance.

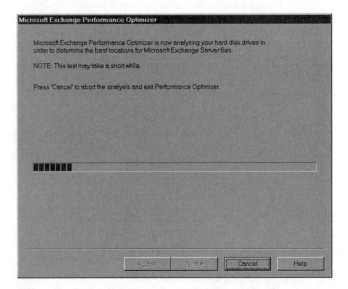

> **Note**
>
> You can either accept the Optimizer's suggested locations or fine-tune them by changing them on this page. I usually accept the recommendations, although the Optimizer does not recognize the difference between physical and logical drives if your system only has one disk, drive mirror, or drive array (a group of disks acting like a single disk.) This means that sometimes the Optimizer will place files on two different drive letters, even though both letters refer to partitions on the same physical disk. In this case, having the files on the two drive letters provides no benefit, so it makes sense to put them on a single drive letter.

Moving the Exchange Files

The next Exchange Optimizer page actually moves the Exchange files. As Figure 3.15 shows, the page allows you to check whether you want the Optimizer to automatically move the files for you. I wouldn't suggest doing this yourself, so don't uncheck this box. Just click Next to move the files.

FIGURE 3.15

The Exchange Optimizer uses its questions and analysis to determine the best locations for the different Exchange files.

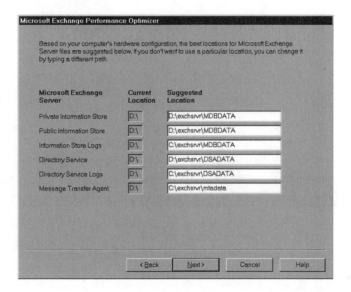

3

> **Caution**
>
> You will notice on the Optimizer page that moves files a warning to make sure you have a backup of your Exchange databases and files. Do not take this warning lightly! Every time you stop, start, or reconfigure an Exchange service there is a risk of damaging your databases. Having a good backup will make your life easier if something should go wrong.

Restarting Exchange

The next page allows you to restart the Exchange services after the Exchange files have been moved and Exchange has been reconfigured. You can check the box labeled Do Not Restart These Services to choose services you don't want started; clicking Next will restart all the services and complete the Optimizer Wizard. You can see this page in Figure 3.16.

FIGURE 3.16

The Exchange Optimizer can move the Exchange files to their new locations automatically.

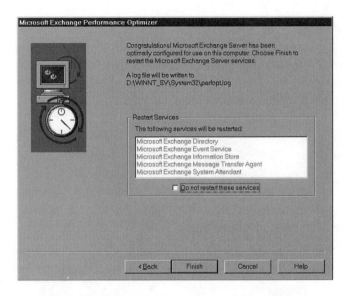

Installing the Exchange Server Service Pack 1

Exchange Service Pack 1 has enhancements and bug fixes that you will want to apply to your Exchange installation. Service Pack 1 includes the following:

- Improved HTML forms support by allowing Outlook forms to be converted to HTML and Active Server Pages for use by Outlook Web Access.

- Functional enhancements to Outlook Web Access, including Contacts folder support, the ability to change your password, and the addition of a Check Names button on messages.

- The addition of Outlook 98 to replace Outlook 97. Outlook 98 provides functional and performance enhancements that make it the better choice over Outlook 97 for new Exchange implementations.

- Improvements to the Exchange Administrator program, allowing you to select messages in user mailboxes to be deleted based on age.

- A Move Server Wizard that allows you to move servers to other sites, establish new sites with a server, and merge servers within a site. The Move Server Wizard is not on the Exchange SP1 CD-ROM but can be downloaded at http:// backoffice.microsoft.com/downtrial/moreinfo/Ex55sp1wizard.asp.

- The ability to use Certificate Server to generate user certificates instead of Exchange Server's Key Manager.

Running Service Pack Setup

To install the service pack, launch the program UPDATE.EXE in the appropriate directory where the Service Pack files are located. (If you downloaded SP1, speak English, and have an Intel-based server, the files will be in the \ENG\SERVER\i386 directory relative to where you extracted the setup files.)

Because you've already installed Exchange Server the first time you should be familiar with Service Pack 1's setup. When you have service packed your Exchange Server you are ready to begin configuring your Exchange server.

Summary

At the end of this lesson you should have an installed Exchange Server. Along the way you learned:

- The tools that you may need to install Exchange, including the Windows NT Server 4.0, Windows NT Service Pack, Windows NT 4.0 Option Pack, Exchange Server, and Exchange Service Pack CD-ROMs.

- Exchange Server needs a machine with at least a Pentium 166Mhz processor, 64MB of RAM, a network card, and 200MB free disk space.

- It is important to install Windows NT service packs and hotfixes to make your Exchange server stable, as well as being able to install Outlook Web Access.

- Exchange Service Pack 1 provides enhancements and patches to add to Exchange Servers manageability and functionality.

Q&A

Q I already have Internet Information Server (IIS) version 3 installed on a Web server on my network. Can I use this Web server instead of setting up another for Outlook Web Access?

A Yes. While this lesson covered installing IIS 4.0, you can use previous versions of IIS that support Active Server Pages, like version 3.0. The server that runs Outlook Web Access does not have to have Exchange Server installed on it; there simply needs to be network connectivity between the Web server and the Exchange server. That said, IIS 4.0 has some performance enhancements that may make it worth your while to upgrade your Web server.

Q **We already have some of our users using Outlook 97. Exchange Service Pack 1 comes with Outlook 98. What is the impact of some people using Outlook 97 and some people using Outlook 98?**

A Apart from user training, the two applications are very similar technically. There should be few if any technical issues with some users using one version and some using another.

Workshop

The Workshop provides two ways for you to affirm what you've learned in this chapter. The "Quiz" section poses questions to help you solidify your understanding of the material covered and the "Exercise" section provides you with experience in using what you have learned. You can find answers to the quiz questions and exercises in Appendix B, "Answers to Quiz Questions and Exercises."

Quiz

1. What is the minimum Windows NT service pack level required for Exchange?

2. Why do you need a Windows NT service account for Exchange Server?

3. What events would cause you to want to run the Exchange Optimizer?

4. What's the best network protocol to use for Exchange Server?

WEEK 1

DAY 4

Server Configuration

by Jason vanValkenburgh

Chapter Objectives

Today's lesson shows you how to set up your Exchange server after it is installed. You will learn the basics of setting up Exchange, including the following:

- How to add users, distribution lists and custom recipients to your site.
- How to easily add large numbers of users from an existing Windows NT or Novell network without re-typing each user.
- How to set up Address Book views to make finding users easier in the Exchange Address Book.
- How to create public folders for your site as well as how to control individuals abilities to view, edit, and delete postings in public folders.
- How to configure Information Store properties so that you can control who has the ability to create top-level public folders.

Starting the Exchange Administrator

The Exchange Administrator program is the primary tool for administering your Exchange system. Launch the Exchange Administrator from the Start menu by choosing Microsoft Exchange, Programs.

Specifying a Server to Connect To

When the Exchange Administrator launches, the program asks you what Exchange server to connect to; this dialog box is shown in Figure 4.1. Enter the name of your server and click OK. If you either don't know the name of the server or you want to connect to another server, select the Browse button and navigate to the server you want to connect to.

FIGURE 4.1

The Exchange Administrator's Connect dialog box enables you to chose what Exchange server to connect to.

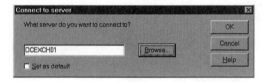

Note

Connecting to a particular Exchange server with the Exchange Administrator lets you administer that server, but also lets you administer any aspects of your Exchange topology, including managing other Exchange servers than the one you're connected to. When you're connected to a particular server, changes you make that affect that server take place immediately. For example, adding users to a server that you are connected to happens when you click OK. Changes that affect other servers or sites happen differently: The Exchange server you're connected to sends email messages to the affected servers and sites to make the changes. That means that it is possible given your site and connector configuration that changes that appear to be immediate may take some time to be reflected and implemented at other sites. The Exchange site and server you are currently connected to show up in **bold** in the Exchange Administrator.

Creating Users

The most basic and important thing you use the Exchange Administrator for is to create and modify user mailboxes. To add users, navigate down the hierarchical structure shown in the left pane of the Exchange Administrator structure down to your site and through to the Recipients container. Your site's Recipients container holds user mailboxes, custom recipients, and distribution lists. First I'll show you how to add a single user and then you'll see how to add many users at once.

Adding an Individual User

To add an individual user, select the File menu and then choose New Mailbox. A dialog box showing user properties will appear with the General tab, shown in Figure 4.2, active by default.

FIGURE 4.2

The General Properties tab for a recipient enables you to specify attributes such as a user's name, address, phone number, and Windows NT account.

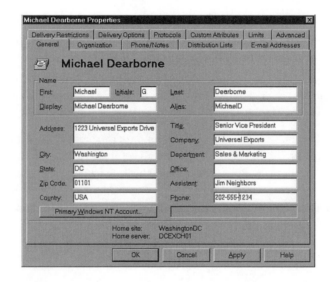

General Properties Tab

The General tab enables you to configure the following properties:

- First Name, Initials, Last Name. Enter the first name, middle initial(s), and last name of the user. This information will be used to generate the next two properties, the display name and the alias.

- Display. This is the name as it appears in the Recipients container and in the default Exchange Address Book view. The Exchange Administrator automatically builds this field from the first and last name, although you can change it to whatever you would like the display name to be.

- Alias. The alias is the name of the Exchange account itself; each user has a unique alias in a particular Exchange recipients container. Like the Display field, this field is automatically generated from the first and last name, although you can change it.

The default way to build this alias is to combine the first name with the first initial of the last name. Later in the lesson, I'll show you how to change this default.

- Address, City, State, Zip Code, and Country. This is the user's business address, including street address, city, state, zip code, and country.
- Title. The user's formal job title.
- Company. The company the user works for. This may or may not be your company.
- Department. The department where the person works.
- Office. The primary office number or location of the user.
- Assistant. The name of the user's assistant, if any. You can also add a phone extension if you want.
- Phone Number. The primary phone number of the user. You can add other phone numbers in the Phone/Notes tab of the User Properties dialog box, which we'll cover later in this lesson.

Obviously there are a lot of properties for a user. You don't have to fill them all out, as long as you provide a display name and alias. It also makes sense to fill out the first and last name because the display name and alias can be generated by Exchange Administrator by using the name fields. Depending upon the naming standards you choose you will need to fill out some of these properties. One consideration to determine how much information you want to fill out is that every Exchange user will have access to this information through the Address Book in an Exchange or Outlook client.

Primary Windows NT Account

The Primary Windows NT Account button is how you select what Windows NT account this mailbox uses. Each mailbox must have a Windows NT account associated with it.

When you click the Primary Windows NT Account button, you are prompted with a dialog box like the one in Figure 4.3, asking whether you would like to use an existing Windows NT account or create a new account.

FIGURE 4.3

Each Exchange recipient must have a Windows NT account associated with it; you can choose an existing account or create a new account for a mailbox.

If you choose to create a new account, you are shown a dialog box that enables you to choose the Windows NT domain to use for the account as well as the account name. This dialog box appears in Figure 4.4. The options will default to the domain that contains your Exchange server and the Exchange account's alias. Click OK to create the user, which will have a blank password until the user first logs in, at which point he will be prompted to change passwords.

FIGURE 4.4

When you create a new Windows NT account for a user you can specify what domain the account should be created in. When you click OK, the account is created and given a blank password.

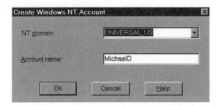

Organization Tab

The Organization tab enables you to select who the user reports to (the user's Manager) as well as people who work for the user (Direct Reports). You can specify each of these properties by clicking the Modify button and selecting other Exchange users from the Recipients container.

This tab, shown in Figure 4.5, can be used by custom Exchange applications to define workflow rules and other features of the application. You can also use this information as a simple way to publish your organizational chart. But the bottom line is that Exchange doesn't really use any of this information; most Exchange administrators leave this tab blank.

Phone/Notes Tab

The Phone/Notes tab, shown in Figure 4.6, enables you to expand upon the phone number listed on the General tab. Here you have the option to add phone numbers, such as a fax, home, mobile, or pager number. You can also enter notes, either about this tab or about the individual as a whole.

Distribution Lists Tab

This tab, shown in Figure 4.7, enables you to specify what distribution lists the user belongs to. If you want to add the user to a distribution list, select the Modify button.

The Organization Properties tab lets you specify who the user reports to and who reports to this user. This can be used by custom Exchange applications to control workflow escalation rules.

The Phone/Notes tab lets you specify phone numbers and administrative notes for the user.

If you click the Modify button, the dialog box shown in Figure 4.8 appears, enabling you to choose additional distribution lists. The list box on the left shows the available distribution lists in the container selected from the Show Names From The list box in the upper-right corner of the tab. To add the current user to a distribution list, choose the list in the left-hand list box and click the Add button. When you're finished, click OK to return to the Distribution Lists tab of the Properties dialog box.

FIGURE 4.7

The Distribution Lists tab lets the recipient join Exchange distribution lists.

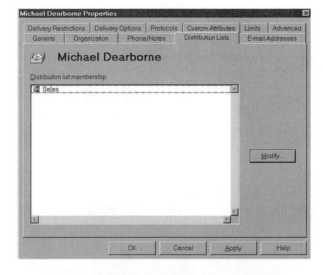

FIGURE 4.8

Clicking the Modify button on the Distribution Lists tab lets you choose Distribution Lists from the Exchange Address Book.

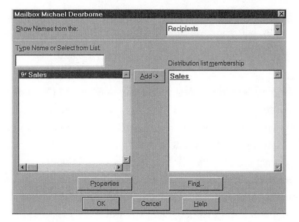

Email Addresses Tab

The Email Addresses tab, shown in Figure 4.9, lists the different system email addresses for this user, including cc:Mail, Microsoft Mail, SMTP (Internet or intranet) mail, and X.400 addresses. If you don't use all these systems (few of us do), you can ignore the ones you don't need.

If you use Internet mail (that is, your Exchange system uses or will use the Internet Mail Service), make sure this address is correct. If your Exchange topology uses only one connection to the Internet, you may want to use the SMTP address format, like

userid@organization.com

The Email Addresses tab shows all the email addresses for this user.

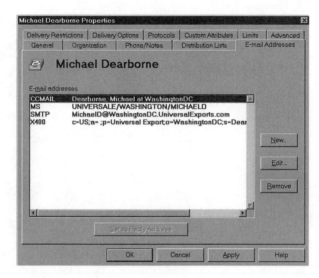

The Exchange default is *alias@site.organition*.com. We'll cover changing this default later in the lesson, but if you do not like the user ID or organization name, you can change it for this user.

If your organization plans to use multiple Internet Mail Services spread throughout your Exchange topology, you may want to use the default SMTP addressing template. This will allow mail to be sent directly to the sites that use the Internet Mail Service. But you probably still want mail to be delivered to *alias@site.organition*.com. If this is the case, click the New button, select the address type SMTP, and enter in the additional SMTP address. This gives the user two SMTP addresses, one which will be delivered directly to the site and another which will be delivered to the entire organization's main entry for Internet mail (this is where the Internet's Domain Name Service comes in, covered in Day 11, "Communication Protocols and the Internet.")

If you have more than one address for a particular address type, you can click the Set as Reply Address button so that sent messages have the return address you want.

Delivery Restrictions Tab

Exchange enables you to control what mail is accepted and rejected for a user within Exchange. The Delivery Restrictions tab shown in Figure 4.10 tells Exchange who to accept messages from for this user. Likewise, you can tell Exchange to reject messages from a particular user.

FIGURE 4.10

The Delivery Restrictions tab lets you control how Exchange accepts and rejects messages delivered to this user.

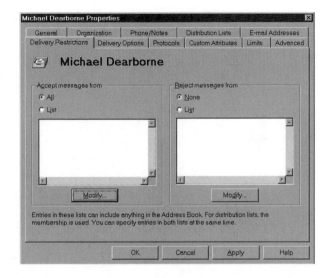

The default settings are to accept messages from everyone and reject messages from no one. Clicking the Modify button under either list box enables you to add people to either accept or reject mail from the Exchange Address Book.

Delivery Options Tab

Sometimes you would like to allow someone else to send mail on your behalf. For example, an administrative assistant or secretary might want to send mail for the boss. Exchange's security model enables you to delegate Send On Behalf Of privileges to another Exchange user. Someone with Send On Behalf Of privileges for a mailbox can send mail as the user of that mailbox. To specify someone to have this ability for the current user, click the Delivery Options tab and then click the Modify button shown in Figure 4.11 to add people from the Exchange Address Book.

You can also designate an alternate recipient for an Exchange mailbox. Mail sent to this mailbox can either be sent to another Exchange user, or can be copied to an Exchange user. To specify a user as an alternate recipient so that all mail delivered to this mailbox is forwarded, select the radio button next to the text box at the bottom of the Delivery Options tab and select the Modify button to choose an Exchange user. Check the box labeled Deliver Messages to Moth Recipient and Alternate Recipient if you'd like mail delivered to both this user and the alternate recipient.

FIGURE 4.11

*Send On Behalf Of
privileges enable
someone to send mail
that appears as if it
came from another
user. This is useful for
enabling
administrative
assistants to send mail
on behalf of their
bosses.*

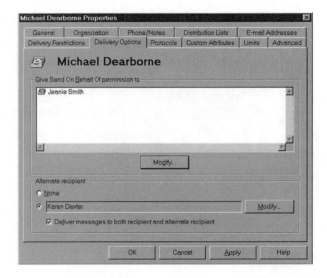

Protocols Tab

In earlier lessons, you learned about Exchange's support for Internet protocols to use
Exchange. The Protocols tab enables you to control different protocol settings for this
user. Because each of the protocol settings' defaults can be controlled at an Information
Store level, this tab is designed to override your defaults and manage these protocol
settings on an exception basis.

The Protocols tab, shown in Figure 4.12, lists all the protocols Exchange supports and a
summary of the current settings. For example, you can see whether each protocol is
enabled for the recipient (Recipient Enabled), activated for this server (Server Enabled),
and if the protocol's settings (if any, or None) are the defaults for this server (Defaults)
or customized (Custom).

Selecting each protocol and clicking the Settings button enables you to customize the
settings for each protocol. Take a moment now and review the different protocol types.

HTTP   The HTTP settings for mailboxes are to simply enable or disable Web access for
this mailbox. Web access lets the user send and receive mail using Outlook Web Access
and a Web browser.

IMAP4   The IMAP4 Protocol settings dialog box, shown in Figure 4.13, first allows
you to enable or disable IMAP4 support for this user (as you'll recall from Day 1,
"Introduction to Exchange," IMAP4 is used for receiving mail).

FIGURE 4.12

The Protocols tab lets you control individual Internet protocol settings for this mailbox.

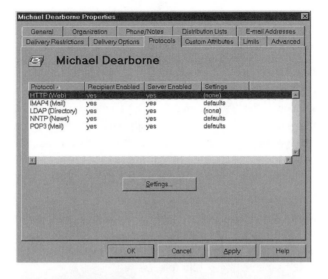

FIGURE 4.13

The IMAP4 Protocol dialog box lets you control IMAP4 protocol settings for this mailbox.

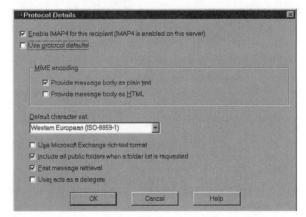

If you uncheck the Use Protocol Defaults check box you can change the IMAP4 protocol defaults. The IMAP4 settings enable you to change how Exchange handles email message formatting, what character sets to use, and how to improve IMAP4 performance. The options on this dialog box that you can change after you've unchecked the Use protocol defaults check box are:

- MIME Encoding. You can specify to encode your mail messages as either plain text or as HTML using the Multipurpose Internet Mail Extensions (MIME) encoding standard. Plain text allows for the most interoperability, whereas HTML enables you to retain more text formatting, such as bold or italic text.

- Default Character Set. This dictates the character set to default for this user. This set and the sets available for you to choose depend upon the languages installed on your server. If you only have one language installed, the default shown should work for you.

- Use Microsoft Exchange Rich Text Format. If the IMAP4 client in use supports Exchange's Rich Text Format (RTF); you can use this option to retain formatting features of your; Exchange Server appends a special formatting attachment to each Exchange Rich Text Format message. Currently this feature is intended for future versions of Microsoft Outlook; no IMAP4 clients that support Exchange Rich Text are available. Therefore, you should leave this setting deselected unless you're using an IMAP4-compatible client.

- Include All Public Folders When a Folder List Is Requested. This option is designed as a performance enhancement by enabling you to turn off the listing of public folders when the IMAP4 client requests a list of folders. Deselect this check box to disable listing public folders.

- Fast Message Retrieval. The Fast Message Retrieval option speeds the downloading of messages by having Exchange estimate the size of the download to the client instead of calculating the total download size. This is a simple way to improve performance; few users will notice the impact of enabling fast message retrieval. I recommend you activate this option.

- User Acts as Delegate. This option enables an IMAP4 delegate user to use this account to access public folders in another user's mailbox.

LDAP   If LDAP is enabled on this server, there is no configuration needed for LDAP support.

NNTP   The NNTP Settings tab, shown in Figure 4.14, allows you to enable or disable NNTP protocol support as well as specify how Exchange handles message attachments. Use these settings to control how Exchange handles Internet-based newsgroups.

In this case, you have two options for message encoding: MIME or UUENCODE. MIME is a newer, more advanced encoding scheme; UUENCODE is used more frequently on the Internet. If you're not sure what to use, choose UUENCODE.

If you choose MIME, you can elect to use plain text or use HTML to show formatting in your documents. If you choose UUENCODE, you can choose to use BinHex, an encoding standard popular on Apple Macintosh computers.

FIGURE 4.14

The NNTP Protocol tab lets you control NNTP protocol settings for this mailbox.

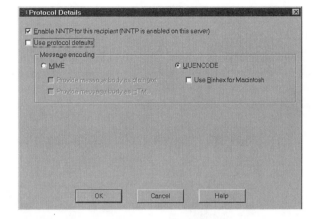

POP3   The POP3 protocol tab enables you to enable POP3 access to this user's Exchange mailbox. In this dialog box, shown in Figure 4.15, you can choose to use the default settings for the server or you can select from a number of options. For example, you can choose how to encode attachments, how to format the body of MIME-encoded messages, select a default character set, and whether to use the Exchange Rich Text Format.

FIGURE 4.15

The POP Protocol tab lets you control POP3 protocol settings for this mailbox.

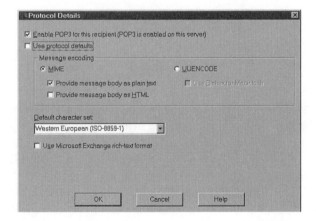

Because each of these settings are explained in previous protocol configuration pages, I'll simply cover the difference between the settings you are now familiar with and the POP3 settings. The only real difference is in POP3's use of Exchange Rich Text Format: because Outlook can be used as a POP3 client, using the Exchange Rich Text Format now actually may make sense.

Custom Attributes Tab

The Custom Attributes tab enables you to enter information about your user that Exchange may not capture. These are basically presented in a plain list of text fields. While most implementations don't use any of the custom attributes shown in Figure 4.16, you may find them useful when you're building custom applications in Exchange. Otherwise, feel free to leave them blank.

FIGURE 4.16

The Custom Attributes tab lets you capture any attributes about this mailbox that Exchange does not normally track.

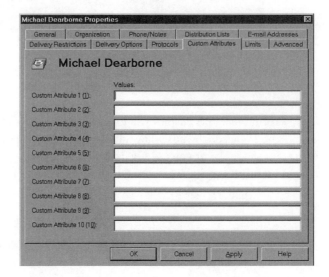

Limits Tab

One of the key things that you'll want to control and monitor as Exchange is in use at your organization is growth. Exchange Server lets you control and manage growth by determining how long you retain deleted items, how large a user's mailbox becomes, and how large sent and received messages can be. The Limits tab enables you to override the Information Store defaults and set these properties for an individual mailbox. Take a second to examine some of the individual settings.

Deleted Items Retention   When a user deletes a message, the message is actually moved to the Deleted Items folder in the user's mailbox. Unless the user explicitly empties this folder, deleted messages will be retained for a certain period of time. You set this time in the Use This Value (Days) text box. You can also specify that items in the Deleted Items folder are not completely deleted until the Information Store has been backed up.

Information Store Storage Limits   You can limit or enforce mailbox sizes by simply warning the user through an email, stopping the user's ability to send new messages, or preventing new mail from being delivered. To set each of these parameters, which are shown in Figure 4.17, simply check the box next to each option and enter the size the mailbox needs to be before the option takes effect. Usually you set the Issue Warning option at a size smaller than the Prohibit Send and Prohibit Receive settings.

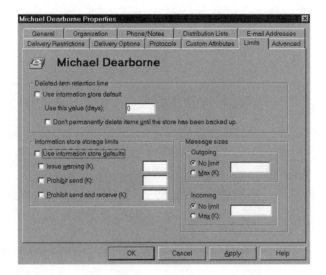

FIGURE 4.17

The Limits tab lets you control and manage the resources consumed by this mailbox by limiting mailbox size, message size, and deleted items retention.

4

Note   These limits and constraints on mailbox size only apply to the size of the mailbox in the server's information store. Depending upon your client configuration, active or archived messages can be downloaded to a .PST file on the client workstation. In this case those messages are not considered when calculating the mailbox size.

Note   Setting the right limits for an individual's mailbox is often a sensitive issue: too little, and users may be seriously hampered in their ability to use mail; too large a limit (or none at all) may cause your Exchange servers to consume disk space like crazy. My advice is to avoid user-level storage limits and set them for the Information Store, and then change them as you need. I'd start with a reasonable mailbox limit, such as 10MB or so. This may sound high, but remember that one PowerPoint presentation could easily be several megabytes in size.

Message Sizes   The Message Sizes group enables you to set limits in kilobytes on individual message sizes for sent or received mail. These settings are especially important if you have a geographically spread out Exchange system, as large messages (often because of attachments) can choke your wide area network.

Advanced Properties Tab

The Advanced Properties tab lets you specify details about this mailbox for directory, Outlook Web Access, and X.400 use. You can see this tab in Figure 4.18.

FIGURE 4.18

The Advanced Properties tab lets you configure Web access, directory, and X.400 settings for a mailbox.

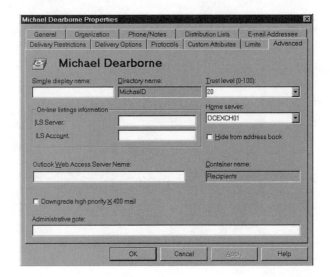

The Simple Display Name text box lets you specify a different display name for external systems that do not support complex display names (for example, some systems may have a length or special character limitation that may require you to specify a different display name for that system).

The Trust level setting lets you establish a trust level for this mailbox. Specifying a lower trust level than the mailbox's recipients container will prevent the mailbox's directory entry from being replicated during directory synchronization.

The Online Listings Information Settings group lets you specify a Microsoft Internet Locator Service (ILS) machine and account to allow Microsoft NetMeeting users find each other and arrange for electronic meetings.

The Home Server text box shows the server where this mailbox resides. To change a mailbox location, you use the Move mailbox command under the Exchange Administrator Tools menu.

The Hide From Address Book check box enables you to specify whether you want this mailbox to normally appear in the directory and Address Book (you can show hidden mailboxes by selecting the Hidden Mailboxes option under the View menu in Exchange Administrator). This is useful for mailboxes you use for administrative purposes and that general users do not need to see. For example, I use hidden mailboxes for sending tape backup logs to a special system administrator account; I don't want people to see this mailbox when they browse the Address Book.

Note

When you're setting up a messaging profile on a user's PC for the first time, the Mailbox Setup Wizard checks the account information you provide before enabling you to use the account for the first time. If you are going to hide a mailbox, uncheck the Hide from Address Book option first, set up the messaging profile and use it once, and then check the Hide From Address Book option.

4

NEW TERM Sometimes you don't want all users to be able to be seen throughout your Exchange system, or when you use directory synchronization with external email systems. *Trust levels* enable you to control whose mailboxes appear during directory synchronization. Setting a mailbox trust level lower than the container trust level prevents synchronization, whereas an equal or higher trust level allows synchronization for this entry. Usually you don't have to change trust levels, but the increasing use of LDAP and opening up your Exchange directory to the Internet makes looking at trust levels more important.

The Outlook Web Access Server Name text box is where you specify the Web server that this mailbox uses for Outlook Web Access. Exchange uses this setting to build URLs (Uniform—or Universal—Resource Locators) that get inserted into messages for POP3 and IMAP4 users. If you don't specify a server here, Exchange will use the default Outlook Web Access server specified in the Private Information Store Properties dialog box. If that too is blank, Exchange won't be able to insert forms and meeting request URLs for Outlook Web Access.

Note

You might see URL spelled out as Universal Resource Locator or Uniform Resource Locator. While both are technically correct, the Universal usage is a bit dated. Currently, the standard usage is Uniform Resource Locators—of course, most people just say URL anyway.

The Downgrade High Priority X.400 Mail setting enables you to automatically remove the high priority flag for messages to X.400 systems coming from this mailbox.

Creating the User

After you've reviewed each of the different property tabs for this user and made the appropriate changes, you can click on the OK button to create the user. If for some reason you forgot to specify a Windows NT account for this mailbox, you'll be prompted to fill out this information.

Changing Exchange Administrator Defaults

One nice thing about Exchange Administrator is that it automatically builds the display name and account alias for each user as you fill out the General Properties tab. But Exchange's default format may not be the way you'd like to generate these properties. Likewise Exchange Administrator defaults to particular Windows NT domain settings, file formats, and other properties. Exchange Administrator easily enables you to change these defaults. Simply select Options from the Exchange Administrator Tools menu . The dialog box shown in Figure 4.19 will appear.

FIGURE 4.19

The Options dialog box under the Tools menu lets you change Exchange Administrator's way of building alias and display names.

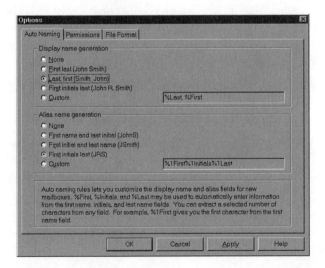

Changing the Display Name and Alias Defaults   The first tab of this dialog box that appears, labeled Auto Naming, enables you to specify how the default display name and alias is chosen. The top section of this tab controls display names. You can choose first name plus last name, last name plus first name separated with a comma, full name with middle initial, or your own custom method. You can use the variables or formulas %First for first name, %Last for last name, and %Initials for the middle initials. You can also preface each variable with a number indicating how many characters to use. For example, %1First gives you the first letter of the first name and %6Last would give you the first seven letters of the last name. The formula %6Last%1First for user "Trudy Johnson" would have the alias "johnsot."

You use the same syntax in the Alias Name Generation section of the tab. Exchange offers the options of first name with first letter of last name, first letter first name plus last name, and the user's initials.

Changing Windows NT Domain and Permissions Defaults   The Permissions tab shown in Figure 4.20 enables you to specify a default Windows NT domain for a user when she is created. You can either specify a domain or have Exchange Administrator choose the domain of the server you're connected to.

FIGURE 4.20

The Permissions tab of the Options dialog box lets you change Exchange Administrator's default Windows NT domains and specify whether Windows NT accounts are deleted when mailboxes are deleted.

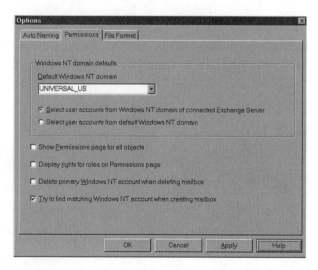

You can also specify whether to display the Permissions tab for each object. The Permissions tab enables you to specify how and who can modify Exchange objects; this topic will be covered more in Day 19, "Making Exchange Secure." You can also specify to show roles, or types and groups of users, and their rights on the Permissions tab.

The Permissions tab also lets you specify if the associated Windows NT account are deleted when a mailbox is deleted, as well as having the program automatically search for a matching Windows NT account from the default domain when creating a mailbox.

Changing File Formats   If you are importing and exporting users you can use the File Format tab, shown in Figure 4.21, to control how fields are separated in your files. You can also specify what character set to use. Typically all these defaults will work for you; I would not change them unless you have a reason. I'll cover importing and exporting users in the next section of this lesson.

FIGURE 4.21

The File Formats tab lets you change Exchange Administrator's default file format for importing and exporting directory information to text files.

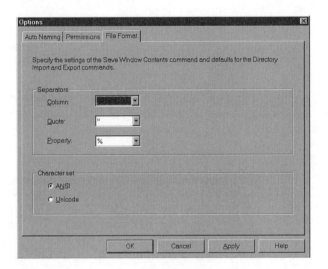

Adding Lots of Users

You may have picked up that adding a user to Exchange can be both a simple and time-consuming task. Fortunately, if you have a Windows NT or Novell NetWare network, Exchange can extract a list of accounts and then bulk import them into Exchange.

The process of adding users in bulk to Exchange Server consists of several steps:

- Creating a template mailbox (optional) that has properties that you'd like set in the added mailboxes but that aren't extracted from the network.
- Extracting a list of users from your Windows NT or NetWare server to a text file (or you can create your own extraction file from another system.)
- Importing the text file into Exchange.

Let's walk through each of these steps in detail.

Creating the Template Mailbox

When Exchange extracts account names from a Windows NT or Novell NetWare server, only basic properties such as the name are imported. Other details, such as company name, address, and other details are simply left blank. Creating a mailbox to use as a template enables you to specify default values for important properties such as company or mailing list. If your network servers or domains were set up along location or department rules, you could use a template to define fields for the extracted users. For example, if you were extracting Novell NetWare account names from the server for your London sales office, you could specify the London office's address and the Sales department as properties for your template mailbox so that all the users you import into Exchange have these properties filled out.

You can either create a temporary mailbox with all the properties that you want to fill out, or you can simply identify an existing mailbox that you'd like to use as the template.

Extracting From Windows NT Networks

If you're pulling your network account list from a Windows NT-based network, select the Extract Windows NT Account List option under the Exchange Administrator Tools menu. The dialog box that appears is shown in Figure 4.22.

FIGURE 4.22

The Extract Windows NT Account list lets you extract a Windows NT account list to a text file for later importing into Exchange.

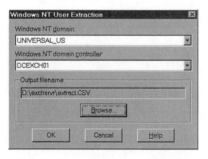

Choose the Windows NT domain you'd like to pull the account list from in the drop-down list box. Then select either a primary domain controller (PDC) or backup domain controller (BDC) for the domain.

Click the Browse button to select where the output from the account extraction will go. Navigate in the window to the directory where you want the file to go. Then enter the name of the file in the filename text box. Exchange defaults the extension of the file to .CSV; there's no real reason to change this. Click the Save button to enter this path and name into the Output File text box in the Windows NT User Extraction dialog box.

Click the OK button to start the extraction process. A window will appear showing progress as the extraction takes place; very large domains could take some time to run.

After this process is complete you can import the output file into Exchange.

Extracting From Novell NetWare Networks

If you'd like to extract a user list from a NetWare server, select the Extract NetWare Account List option under the Exchange Administrator Tools menu. The NetWare User Extraction dialog box appears, as shown in Figure 4.23.

FIGURE 4.23

The Extract NetWare Account list lets you extract a NetWare server's account list to a text file for later importing into Exchange.

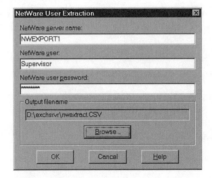

Enter the Novell NetWare server name, username, and password. The user specified must have supervisor rights on that server.

Note

To run the account extract on a Novell NetWare 4.x or later server (including IntranetWare and IntranetWare version 5), you must have bindery emulation enabled on your server and have the bindery context set on the server to the part of the NDS tree where accounts you want listed are. Remember that when you log in to a NetWare server running NDS using a bindery (version 3 or lower) connection as an administrator, give the username SUPERVISOR instead of Admin.

Note

For you to extract from a Novell server you must have connectivity to the NetWare server. This means having a NetWare client installed such as the Microsoft Client for Novell Networks or Novell's IntranetWare client. Because of this requirement I recommend running this process on a user workstation as opposed to the running this process at the server's console. This saves the trouble of installing NetWare connectivity software on the server for this simple task.

Click the Browse button to select where the output from the account extraction will go. Navigate in the window to the directory where you want the file to go. Then enter the name of the file in the filename text box. Exchange defaults the extension of the file to .CSV; there's no real reason to change this. Click the Save button to enter this path and name into the Output File text box in the NetWare User Extraction dialog box.

Click the OK button to start the extraction process. A window will appear showing progress as the extraction takes place; very large account lists could take some time to run.

After this process is complete you can import the output file into Exchange.

Importing the Users Into Exchange

To launch the Directory Import dialog box, select Directory Import from the Tools menu. The resulting dialog box is shown in Figure 4.24.

FIGURE 4.24

The Directory Import option under the Tools menu lets you import an account list from a text file into Exchange.

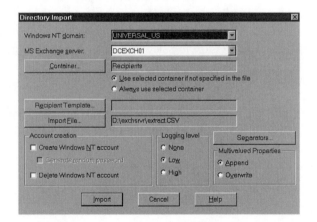

As you can see, the Directory Import dialog box has several fields and settings:

- Windows NT domain. Select the Windows NT domain where you'd like the users added. This defaults to the Windows NT domain that the Exchange server belongs to.

- MS Exchange Server. Choose the Exchange server where you'd like the user mailboxes placed. This defaults to the server you're currently connected to.

- Container. This is the default Recipients container where you'd like the Exchange mailboxes for the user accounts created. Usually this default works fine. You can navigate through the Exchange directory to find the container you'd like by clicking on the Container button. The import file can be edited to specify a Recipients container to use; you can select to use the container specified in the import file or override that setting to always use the container you've specified.

- Recipient Template. If you would like to use a template mailbox, click on the Recipient Template button to choose the template mailbox from the directory.

- Import file. Use the Import File button to find the file you created when you performed the Windows NT or Novell NetWare account extraction.

Note It makes sense for you to edit the import file with a text editor like WordPad to remove any accounts that you don't want set up in Exchange, such as the Administrator's account, service accounts, and the Guest account.

Creating Distribution Lists

As you may remember, a distribution list is a special Exchange object where members of a distribution list are sent mail that is addressed to the distribution list. For example, you could create a Sales distribution list, make members of the Sales and Marketing Department members of the distribution list, and then send mail to all of the list's users simply by addressing a message to Sales. This saves people the time and effort of identifying who should receive a particular message. You can also create a distribution list to simplify services that a department or group within your organization provides. I use the distribution list Help Desk to make sure that email is sent to the correct people for end-user support; if the support staff changes I simply change the distribution list. No user knows that I've made the change.

Adding the Distribution List

Navigate to your site's Recipients container and choose New Distribution List under the File menu. The Distribution List Properties dialog box appears, as shown in Figure 4.25. The title of the dialog box will be the name of your list plus *Properties*. The dialog box has multiple tabs that enable you to specify general properties, distribution list membership, email addresses, delivery restrictions, custom attributes, and advanced options.

General Properties

The General Properties tab lets you specify the distribution list's display name. You must specify both a display name and an alias name.

You can also specify an Owner for this distribution list. The owner is a person who can administer the list by adding and dropping members. While leaving this text box blank would require someone to be an Exchange administrator to administer the list, specifying an end-user as the owner of the list enables you to off-load some administrative work.

FIGURE 4.25

*The distribution list's
General Properties tab
lets you specify basic
attributes of a
distribution list.*

You can also specify the expansion server for this distribution list. You can either specify
any server in the site, or a particular server.

NEW TERM An *Expansion Server* is the server where a message sent to a distribution list is
expanded into individual messages to each distribution list member. Sometimes
you would want to specify an expansion server for this list if the list's membership was
large and you wanted to specify an expansion server that had enough capacity or horsepower to perform the expansion.

To specify who belongs to the distribution list, select the Modify button below the
Members list box on the right-hand section of the tab. Choose the members you would
like added to the list and click OK to return to the General Properties tab.

Distribution Lists Properties

NEW TERM Exchange Server allows a distribution list to actually belong to other
distribution lists. Called a *nested distribution list*, messages sent to distribution
lists shown on this page are also sent to this distribution list. For example, if a list were
called US Employees and belonged to a distribution list named Global Employees, messages sent to the Global Employees list would also be sent to members of US
Employees. This example is shown in Figure 4.26.

Email Addresses

The Email Addresses tab, shown in Figure 4.27, lets you modify the email addresses for
this distribution list. You can click the New button to add an address, the Edit button to
edit an address, and the Remove button to delete an address.

FIGURE 4.26

The Distribution List tab lets you create nested distribution lists so that messages sent to one distribution list are sent to member distribution lists.

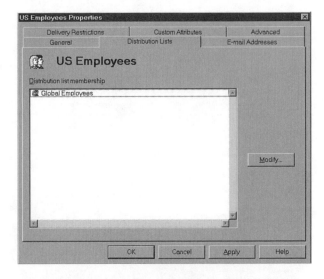

FIGURE 4.27

The Email Addresses tab lets you change the email addresses for a distribution list.

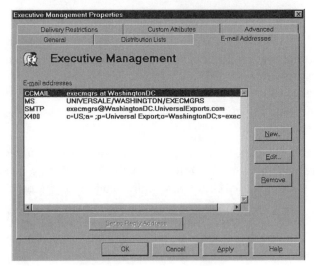

Delivery Restrictions

The Delivery Restrictions tab, shown in Figure 4.28, is similar to the Delivery Restrictions tab for an individual mailbox. You can specify who the distribution list accepts messages from, and who the distribution list will reject messages from.

FIGURE 4.28

The Delivery Restrictions tab specifies who can send messages and who cannot send messages to a recipient.

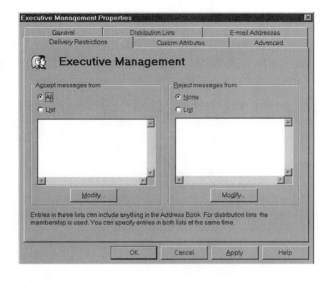

Custom Attributes

The Custom Attributes tab, shown in Figure 4.29, works just like the Custom Attributes for a mailbox. You are free to use these attributes, or not, as you wish.

FIGURE 4.29

The Custom Attributes properties tab captures attributes that Exchange does not normally retain.

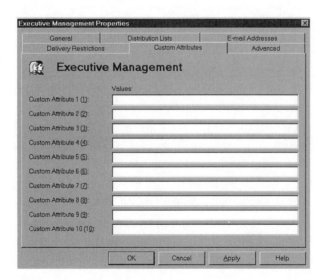

Advanced Properties

The Advanced Properties tab is shown in Figure 4.30. It enables you to control how this distribution list is displayed in external email systems, message limits, reporting, and Address Book options.

FIGURE 4.30

The Advanced Properties tab for a distribution list lets you configure Address Book settings, storage limits, and other configuration information.

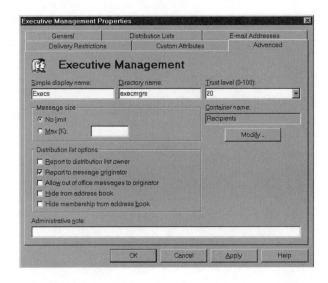

The Simple display name, Directory name, and Trust level options are all properties that apply to distribution lists the same as they apply to recipients.

The Message Size parameter lets you specify a limit, in kilobytes, for the size of messages the distribution list will accept. Because large distribution lists are often expanded before being sent to other sites, you may want to consider setting a limit on the message size in order to keep your servers and networks from being overly burdened.

In the Distribution List section of this tab you can specify how Exchange handles receipt confirmations, out of office messages, and how distribution lists and their members appear in the Address Book. This section has the following options:

- Report to Distribution List Owner. This option tells Exchange to send receipt confirmations or delivery failures to the distribution list's owner as opposed to the person sending the message to the list.

- Report to Message Originator. This tells Exchange to send receipt confirmations for each recipient on the distribution list back to the original sender.

- Allow Out of Office Messages to Originator. This option allows out-of-office replies to be sent to the message originator for individual distribution list members.

- Hide From Address Book. This option hides the distribution list from the Address Book. Administrators can see the list if the Hidden Recipients option is selected in Exchange Administrator.

- Hide membership from Address Book. This option prevents Exchange users from seeing who is a member of this list in the Address Book. If you select this option, the Report to Message Originator option is ignored so that the secrecy is maintained.

After you have filled out all the distribution list's properties, click the OK button at the bottom of the dialog box to create the list.

Creating Custom Recipients

Microsoft Exchange enables you to create a special recipient called a Custom Recipient that enables you to place an entry for an individual in the Exchange directory, even if the recipient is not actually an Exchange user.

To create a custom recipient, select New Custom Recipient under the File menu. The first dialog box, shown in Figure 4.31, asks what address type the recipient is. Depending upon the external connectors your Exchange topology has in place, you select the appropriate address type.

FIGURE 4.31

Exchange lets you create custom recipients that are directory entries for external email users. You can create SMTP, MS Mail, cc:Mail, and X.400 custom recipients.

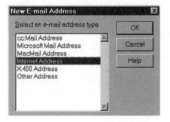

After you've entered the address type you will be presented with a dialog box asking for the address. This dialog box will vary depending upon the address type. Figure 4.32 shows the General Properties tab of an Internet (SMTP) address.

On the Advanced Properties tab of the Internet address dialog box, shown in Figure 4.33, you can override the default Internet mail properties and specify how Exchange encodes attachments.

This tab has several options in the Message Format section:

- MIME. This option uses MIME to encode messages with attachments. If you select MIME you can also choose to format the body of the message with plain text, plain text with HTML, and HTML. If this person also uses Exchange or an advanced email client, selecting MIME makes sense so that the person receives better formatted text and attachments.

FIGURE 4.32

After selecting the type of address used for a custom recipient the Exchange Administrator prompts you to enter the email address. This figure shows entering an SMTP (Internet) email address.

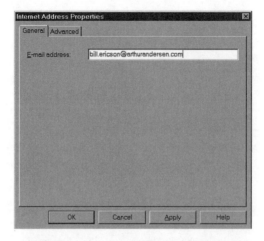

FIGURE 4.33

The Advanced Properties tab for the email address of Custom Recipient lets you control content settings such as how attachments and Rich Text Formatting is handled.

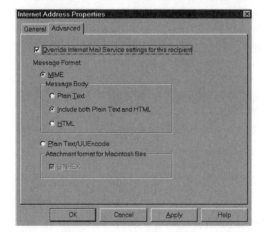

- Plain text/UUENCODE. This option has Internet messages sent with plain text; message attachments are sent using the Internet-standard UUENCODE format. If the person uses a Macintosh, check the BINHEX option. Selecting plain text and UUENCODE is the safest choice if you don't know what kind of email reader this person uses.

After you have reviewed the Advanced Properties tab, you can click OK at the bottom of the dialog box to proceed to the Recipient Properties dialog box.

Recipient Properties

The Recipient Properties dialog box, shown in Figure 4.34, is remarkably similar to the normal mailbox properties dialog box you're already familiar with. The only difference is the Email button at the bottom of the General Properties tab, which enables you to change the Email address properties that you entered in the section just covered.

FIGURE 4.34

The General Properties tab for a Custom Recipient is similar to the General Properties tab for a normal Exchange mailbox.

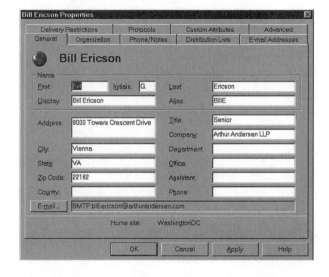

After you've entered all the Custom Recipient properties, click the OK button to create the custom recipient. Custom recipients appear in the Exchange Address Book with a Globe icon next to the display name.

Working with Addresses

You may have noticed from adding Exchange users and mailboxes that Exchange generates an address for each Exchange object. Each Exchange object has several addresses: a cc:Mail address, an MS Mail address, an Internet (or SMTP) address, and an X.400 address. Exchange uses these addresses to allow messages to be sent and received from these objects; the address tells Exchange where in the Exchange topology (for example, what site the object belongs to) the object resides. The addresses also serve another purpose: to tell non-Exchange users how to send messages to the object or recipient.

Each mailbox has an Internet address. When you added each user, the Addressing Properties tab (shown in Figure 4.35) built default email addresses. You can easily change how Exchange Server builds these addresses and how Exchange figures out how to route messages through the Exchange topology by changing the site's addressing properties.

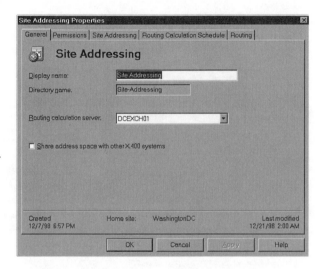

FIGURE 4.35

The Site Addressing Properties dialog box lets you change how site addressing is handled, such as interaction with X.400 email systems and default email addressing schemes for Internet mail.

Changing the Site Addressing Properties

To change the site's addressing properties in the Exchange Administrator, navigate through the hierarchy shown in the left page to your site. If you choose the Configuration item while it's in the left-hand panel, a list of configuration areas appears in the right-hand window. At the bottom is an area labeled Site Addressing Properties. If you double-click on this item, the Site Addressing Properties dialog box, which you saw in Figure 4.35, appears.

General Addressing Properties

General addressing properties, shown in Figure 4.35, include the display name, the routing calculation server, and how Exchange interoperates with X.400 systems sharing addressing information. Let's discuss each of these settings:

- The Display Name setting controls how this dialog box appears in the Exchange Administrator. There are few reasons to change this setting.

- The Routing Calculation Server setting is a server within this site that generates the Exchange routing table for this site. The routing table is used by Exchange to figure out where messages get delivered to depending upon their addressing. Routing between sites is covered in more detail in Day 5, "Working with Multiple Sites." Usually the selected server is just fine; I wouldn't change this setting.

- The Share Address Space With Other X.400 Systems setting enables you to have Exchange share the same addressing space with other X.400 email systems that Exchange is connected with. This is useful when you're migrating to Exchange from an X.400 system by allowing both systems to share the same addressing configuration. You do not have to create separate organizations or organizational units for Exchange and your other X.400 system.

Permissions Properties

The Permissions Properties tab shows the permissions and Windows NT security settings for this Exchange object. Because the default settings here usually work fine (and security is covered in Day 19, "Making Exchange Secure"), we'll move on to the next tab. Figure 4.36 shows the Permissions tab.

FIGURE 4.36

The Permissions tab of the Site Addressing Properties dialog box lets you control who can configure Site Addressing properties.

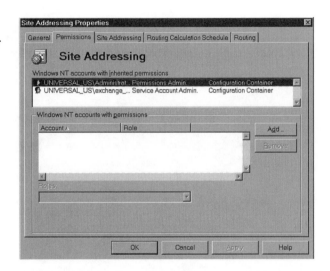

Site Addressing Properties

The Site Addressing tab, shown in Figure 4.37, is the real heart of your site's addressing scheme. If there was any part of addressing that you would want to tweak, this is the place to make changes. The Site Addressing tab enables you to change the template or address Exchange automatically generates for objects in this site.

You can disable the generation of any of the different address types for newly created Exchange objects by simply double-clicking on any address type. Note that Exchange requires SMTP and X.400 addresses for all objects, so these cannot be disabled.

If your site is connected to the Internet you might want to change the SMTP addressing for this site. The default is *alias@sitename.organizationname.com*. If you want all your users to simply have *alias@organizationname.com* you can do this here. Select the SMTP Address line and click the Edit button. An SMTP Address dialog box appears like the one shown in Figure 4.38. You can edit what address is appended to the end of each object's alias or short name.

FIGURE 4.37

The Site Addressing tab of the Site Addressing Properties dialog box lets you choose how email addresses for the site are configured; this tab is important to configure Internet email addresses.

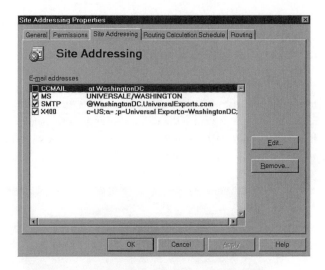

FIGURE 4.38

The Edit button on the Site Addressing tab of the Site Addressing Properties dialog box lets you change site addressing properties for each address type. This figure shows changing SMTP addressing properties.

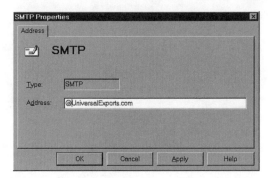

Routing Calculation Schedule

Exchange rebuilds its routing table for this site on a periodic basis regardless of whether there are any changes. (Events that change the routing table such as adding connectors or changing addressing settings trigger Exchange to automatically rebuild the routing table immediately.) As you can see in Figure 4.39, you can change what time of day Exchange generates the routing table. Because Exchange generates the table if you make changes, you should not have to change this setting. If you do, the options are to never generate the routing table, always generate it (which means generate it every 15 minutes), and to generate it on a weekly calendar shown at the bottom of the tab.

Routing

After Exchange Server has generated the routing table you can view it on the Routing tab, shown in Figure 4.40. Because we haven't connected our server to another site, this routing page is empty (you'll have to wait until Day 6, "Connecting Exchange to Other Sites.") The page shows each route in terms of address type, what addresses are sent to this route, and the cost of the route. If you want Exchange to rebuild the routing table immediately you can choose the Recalculate Routing button. You can also view the route's details by selecting the Details button.

FIGURE 4.39

The Routing Calculation Schedule tab of the Site Addressing Properties dialog box lets you specify when the Exchange routing table is rebuilt.

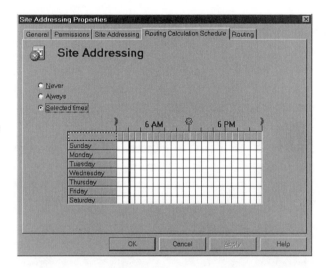

FIGURE 4.40

The Routing tab of the Site Addressing Properties dialog box lets you review the Exchange routing table.

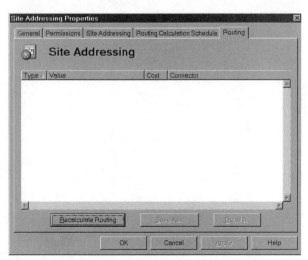

4

NEW TERM   Exchange uses costs for each route to determine the best way to send messages through the Exchange system. Each route is assigned a cost; routes with lower costs are chosen over routes with higher costs if the lower-cost route is available. Costs also ensure that messages take the most direct path to deliver mail because indirect routes to other sites automatically carry higher costs than routes that represent a direct connection. Multiple routes to the same sites help ensure mail delivery if a direct route should fail. Route costs are covered more in Day 6.

Creating Address Book Views

Exchange Server enables you to create Address Book views to help you organize and manage your Exchange recipients, as well as to help end-users navigate through long lists of users. Address Book views make Exchange easier to use and administer, so creating Exchange views is a "no-brainer" means to improve Exchange's productivity in an organization.

Address Book views group users by properties of the recipient. You'll remember from adding recipients that you can enter properties such as Company, Department, State, or Country. You can group recipients with the same properties together to help you find individuals.

To create an Address Book view, select New Other under the File menu, and then select Address Book View from the resulting pop-up menu. The resulting dialog box is shown in Figure 4.41.

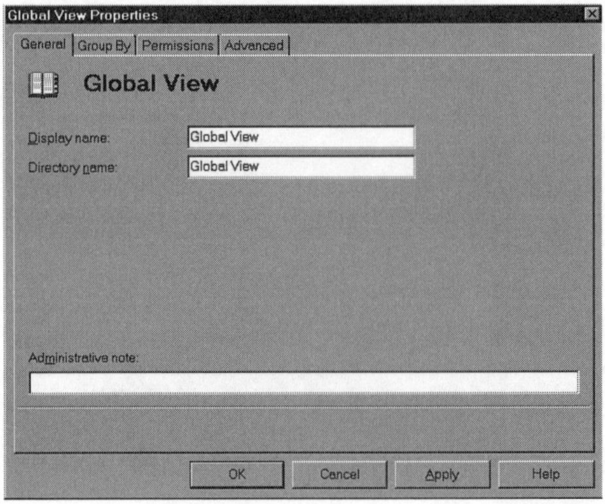

FIGURE 4.41

The General tab of the Properties dialog box for an Address Book view lets you specify the view's name.

General Properties Tab

The General properties tab enables you to set the display name and directory name for this view; I usually use the same name for both to keep things simple. You can enter any name that describes this view; in my example I used Global View, indicating that the view I'm creating enables users to navigate through Universal Export's mail directory by location, starting with countries at the highest level. The final result is shown in Figure 4.42.

FIGURE 4.42

Address Book views appear in the Exchange Administrator and let you drill-down through various Exchange properties to find a recipient.

Group By Tab

The Group By tab lets you specify the different Exchange properties you would like to organize your view by. In the example shown in Figure 4.43, I've selected multiple view levels, starting with Country and proceeding to State and then City.

Advanced Properties Tab

The Advanced Properties tab, shown in Figure 4.44, enables you to control how Exchange shows recipients within address views. The Promote Entries to Parent Containers setting enables lower-level recipients to appear in higher-level views. As you may have noticed in Figure 4.42, the view at a high-level group in the hierarchy includes all the recipients who have that property; selecting US as the country shows all the US users, not just the states. Unchecking the Promote Entries to Parent Containers option prevents lower-level recipients from appearing.

FIGURE 4.43

The Group By tab for an Address Book view lets you specify the grouping order for the view based on different Exchange properties.

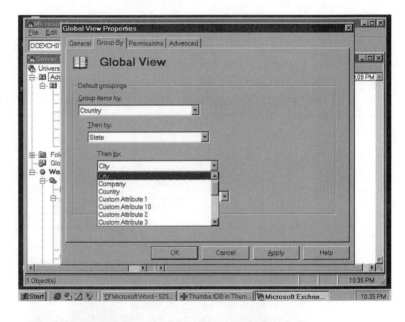

FIGURE 4.44

The Advanced Properties tab for an Address Book view lets you specify how the view appears in the Address Book.

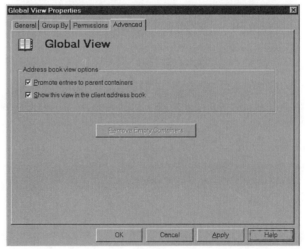

The Show This View in the Client Address Book setting controls whether end-users see this view.

When you're done setting up the view, you can click the OK button to create the view.

Tip

When you select a level in an Address Book view and select the New Mailbox menu item, a dialog box appears to let you add a new user. The nice thing is that the properties that you've grouped your view by are already filled in. That makes it easy to add users without having to type in the properties for this user.

Creating and Managing Public Folders

One of Exchange Server's first capabilities beyond the simple sending and receiving of mail messages is the ability to create "bulletin boards" or public folders. Public folders are shared areas for people to post and review messages or other types of mailbox objects (with Outlook, these objects can be things like contacts or tasks).

Note

One of the key benefits to using public folders is the potential to save server resources through the prevention of using a lot of attachments in Exchange's Information Store. Even though a message with an attachment sent to multiple people results only a single copy of the attachment being stored in the Exchange database, multiple messages with different versions of the same document are stored separately. If people save these messages in their mailboxes, the server's Information Store can become quite large. Educating users about the benefits of Exchange Public Folders and the best ways to use them can make your like as an administrator a lot easier.

Creating Public Folders

Users can easily create public folders; by default Exchange Server enables all users to create public folders (although most Exchange administrators prefer to keep this ability under some form of control or oversight.)

Although you can create a public folder with the Exchange client or with Microsoft Outlook, I'll show you how to create a public folder with Outlook:

1. Start Microsoft Outlook and log in to your Exchange Server.

2. After Outlook is completely started, enable the Folder List view by selecting the Folder List option under the View menu. Exchange and Outlook folders will appear in a window in Outlook, as shown in Figure 4.45.

FIGURE 4.45

Enabling the Folder List option in Outlook lets you navigate through the folder structure to the Public Folders item.

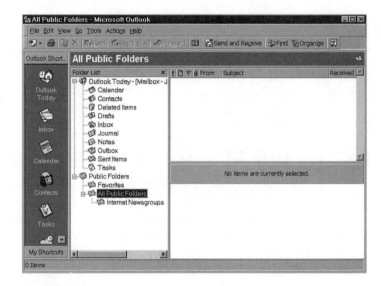

3. Navigate through the Exchange folder hierarchy to the Public Folders item. Now select the Outlook File menu, choose Folder, and select the New Folder command.

4. You are presented with a dialog box that asks you what to name the folder, what the folder contains, and at what level in the Public Folders hierarchy to create it. In the example shown in Figure 4.46, I created a top-level public folder called Universal Employees Reference. This folder is designed to hold Universal Export's Human Resources and benefits information in the form of mail messages—things that a typical employee may want to know about!

5. Click OK to create the folder.

FIGURE 4.46

The Create New Folder dialog box lets you create a new public folder.

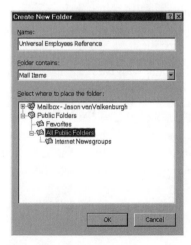

> **Tip**
>
> Because public folders can contain mail messages, tasks, contacts, appointment items, or notes, there are a lot of possibilities when it comes to using public folders. Take for example sharing corporate contact information or a phone list, which many companies either manage with a separate system or with word processing documents. With Exchange public folders you can create a public folder that contains contact items, and then easily share it through your organization. You can even use Outlook Web Access to allow people on your organization's Intranet to look at the list!

Posting to Public Folders

After a public folder is created people can post messages to the folder. If you navigate through the folder structure while you're in an Exchange client, you read and post messages to the folder (provided you have permissions, which I'll cover in a minute). To post a message, select the folder and then select the Post in This Folder menu item when you click on the small push-pin icon in the upper-left corner of the Outlook window. This menu item is shown in Figure 4.47.

FIGURE 4.47

The Post in This Folder menu item in Outlook lets you post a new message to a public folder.

The resulting dialog box will appear like the one shown in Figure 4.48; you can enter whatever subject line and text you'd like in the posting. You can also attach documents that are relevant to the folder subject. In our example we've added an Employee Benefits Guide as a Microsoft Word document.

After you've posted the message to the Public Folder, users with the appropriate permissions can look at and review your posting. They can choose to reply to you, or they can post a message themselves. Figure 4.49 shows what the posting looks like after its been added to the public folder.

FIGURE 4.48

The New Posting window lets you enter a message to go into a public folder. You can enter a subject line and include message attachments.

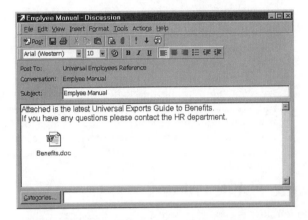

FIGURE 4.49

Messages appear in a public folder using the type of object the folder contains. This figure shows a public folder that contains mail messages.

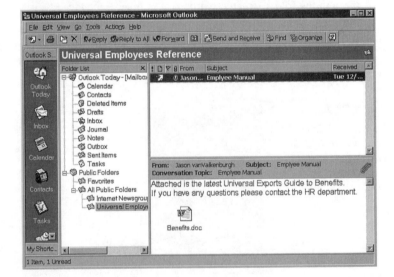

Managing Public Folders

After a public folder is created you can change its properties, including which people can access the folder and what level of access they have to view, change, or delete messages in the folder. You can also manage how old messages can be before they're deleted and enforce limits on the size of messages.

To start managing individual public folders, open Exchange Administrator and navigate to the Public Folders item in the Exchange hierarchy under the Folders item. Drill down through the list until you find the public folder you'd like to manage and double-click on it.

General Properties   The Properties dialog box for the public folder appears, showing the General Properties tab first. Figure 4.50 shows this tab for the Universal Employees Reference folder created earlier in this lesson. The General Properties tab has the following properties that you can change:

- Folder name. This is the name of the folder as it appears to users navigating though the Public Folder hierarchy.

- Address book display name. This is the name as the folder appears in the Address Book. You can select to use the folder name or specify a different name by selecting the Use This Name radio button and entering the Address Book name in the text box to the right.

- Alias Name. This is the Exchange alias name in the Exchange directory. The alias name can be used to send mail to the folder from the To: line in an email message. This defaults to the folder name; usually there are few reasons to change it.

- Limit administrative access to home site. This option prevents Exchange administrators from other sites than where the home version of the folder is from changing the folder's properties. Using folders between Exchange sites is covered in Day 5, "Working With Multiple Sites." The public folder's "home site" is shown at the bottom of the Properties dialog box.

FIGURE 4.50

The General tab of the Properties dialog box for a public folder lets you specify its name and set administrative options.

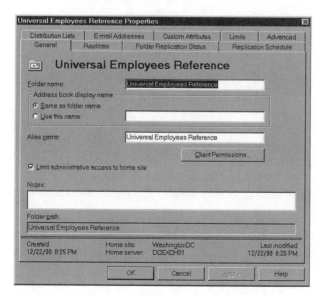

NEW TERM A folder's *home site* and *home server* indicate where a public folder physically resides in an Exchange hierarchy. The folder is stored within the Information Store on the home server, which is in the home site. When you implement Public Folder Replication, covered in Day 5, there will always be a home server and site that represent the "master" copy of the public folder.

Defining the Folder's Security   You may have noticed the Client Permissions button on the General Properties tab; this button is used to control what users have access to the folder and with what permissions. Clicking on the button will result in a Client Permissions dialog box appearing like the one in Figure 4.51.

FIGURE 4.51

The Client Permissions dialog box lets you specify what abilities users have in using a public folder.

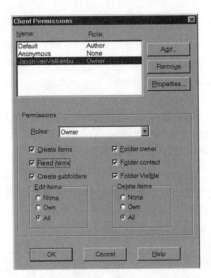

The Client Permissions dialog box enables you to define user rights using a role-based model. Users are assigned a role that defines what level of access they are allowed. The Client permissions tab also has entries for default users (people you do not explicitly define on this tab) and for anonymous users (users who are not authenticated and do not have any particular Exchange account associated with them. These people are usually Internet Newsgroup users.)

In the Name list box you can add users from the Exchange Address Book to explicitly define their security rights by selecting the Add button. The Remove button, not surprisingly, removes people from the list.

Caution   Do not remove the Anonymous and Default properties. If you want to disable access to these users, select the None role to limit access.

The Permissions section of the dialog box controls permissions for the user that is currently selected in the Name list box. The Permissions section begins with a drop-down list box for roles; defining user security by role simplifies managing individual rights. Each role you select presents a different combination of these rights:

- Create Items. This enables you to post items to the public folder.
- Read Items. This enables you to look at items in the folder.
- Create Subfolders. This option enables users to create subfolders within this public folder.
- Folder Owner. This is the owner of the folder; the owner can assign security permissions to the folder.
- Folder Contact. This person is sent administrative messages by Exchange, such as replication warnings or messages.
- Folder Visible. This allows the folder name to be seen in the Public Folders hierarchy.
- Edit Items. This enables a user to edit or change no items in the public folders (None), only items posted by that user (Own), or all the items in the folder (All).
- Edit Items. This enables a user to delete items in the public folders (None), only items posted by that user (Own), or all the items in the folder (All).

A complete list of roles and rights is shown in Table 4.1.

TABLE 4.1 PERMISSINS, ROLES, AND RIGHTS

	Owner	Publishing Editor	Editor	Publishing Author	Author	Non-Editing Author	Reviewer	Contributor	None
Create Items	√	√	√	√	√	√		√	
Read Items	√	√	√	√	√	√	√		
Create Sub-Folders	√	√	√	√					
Folder Owner	√								
Folder Contact	√								
Folder Visible	√	√	√	√	√	√	√	√	√
Edit-None							√	√	
Edit-Own				√	√				
Edit-All	√	√	√						
Delete-None							√	√	
Delete-Own				√	√	√			
Delete-All	√	√	√						

Replicas, Folder Replication Status, and Replication Schedule Tabs   These tabs are covered in Day 5 because they deal with public folder replication, something which is irrelevant for single-site Exchange implementations. You can ignore them for now.

Distribution Lists   The Distribution Lists tab allows the public folder to belong to a distribution list; all messages sent to the distribution list are also sent to the public folder. This feature is useful as a means to archive or record messages sent to the list; it also allows a means for users with a casual or intermittent interest in the distribution list's content to periodically review a list's messages.

Email Addresses Tab   This tab lists the different email addresses for this folder; messages sent to the addresses on this tab will appear in the folder.

Custom Attributes Tab   Just as in the case of recipients, this tab enables you to enter information about the folder into fields that you can use any way you want.

Limits Tab   This tab enables you to set how long deleted items from the public folder are retained, how much storage in the Information Store is used, and how long messages are kept in the folder. This tab, shown in Figure 4.52, has these options:

- Deleted Item Retention Time. This time is the number of days messages are retained once deleted. You can specify the number of days or choose to use Information Store defaults.

- Information Store Storage Limits. This option enables you to specify how large the public folder can become in kilobytes before administrative warnings are sent to the public folder's contact (usually the public folder's owner). You can choose to use the Information Store's default storage limits.

- Age Limits. This option enables you to age postings in the folder to have messages older than the number of days in this box. After a message has been aged it is deleted. This option is useful for public folders with a high message volume and where old messages have little intrinsic value.

Advanced Properties   The Advanced Properties tab, shown in Figure 4.53, enables you to control the public folder's home server, the importance of replication messages, and whether or not to show the folder in the Address Book.

The simple display name, directory name, trust level, and container names are all similar to the same properties for a recipient. The properties that are unique to public folders include:

- Home Server. This is the server whose Information Store holds the master copy of this public folder.

- Replication msg Importance. This enables you to set the level of priority set for messages sent between sites for public folder replication. If this is a low-priority public folder you can potentially improve performance for other messages by downgrading the importance of replication messages. Likewise if this is a critical folder, setting a higher priority may help ensure that replicated folders are kept more up to date.

FIGURE 4.52

The Limits tab for a Public Folder lets you manage the resources consumed by the folder by setting size and age limits for messages.

FIGURE 4.53

The Advanced Properties tab for a Public Folder lets you specify the Public Folder's home server and the importance of replication messages.

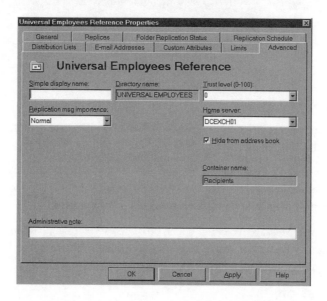

Configuring Site-Level Folder Properties

Exchange Server manages some properties for public folders at a site level. This includes defining security for creating top-level folders, determining when warning messages are generated, and what sites can access the folders in this site via public folder affinity. Because public folder affinity is covered in Day 5 when you connect Exchange with other sites, we'll focus on folder creation and storage warnings.

To review or change a site's Information Store configuration, select the Exchange hierarchy item under your site labeled Configuration in the left-hand panel in Exchange Administrator. You will see the item Information Store Site Configuration in the right-hand panel; double-click on it to bring up the Information Store Site Configuration Properties dialog box like the one shown in Figure 4.54.

FIGURE 4.54

The Site Configuration Addressing Properties tab lets you configure message tracking and where public folders appear in the Address Book.

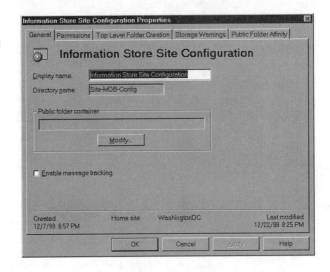

General Properties

The General properties tab enables you to specify the display name for the Information Store site configuration (you really don't need to ever change this).

You can also configure the location of the public folders in the Address Book (the default is the home site's Recipients container.) To choose an alternate location select the Modify button and navigate to the new location in the Address Book.

The Enable Message Tracking check box allows you to enable the tracking of individual messages; you can use this as a diagnostic measure when troubleshooting replication or other types of public folder issues.

Permissions

The Permissions tab is similar to the tab shown for recipients or distribution lists. Permissions are covered in Day 19.

Top Level Folder Creation

By default, Microsoft Exchange Server enables any user to create a public folder. Exchange differentiates between top-level folders (those that are one level below Public Folders) and subfolders. The default enables anyone to create top-level folders, whereas subfolders can only be created by individuals with the rights to create subfolders using the top-level folder's permissions. Often enabling anyone to create a top-level folder is less than desirable. The Top Level Folder Creation tab, shown in Figure 4.55, enables you manage who creates top-level public folders.

FIGURE 4.55

The Top Level Folder Creation tab lets you control who can and cannot create top-level public folders.

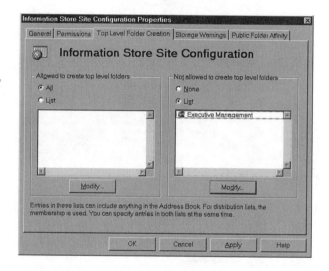

The Top Level Folder Creation tab has two large list boxes similar in format at function to the Delivery Restrictions tab you saw for mailboxes or distribution lists.

The left text box labeled Allowed to Create Top Level Folders enables you to specify who can create top-level folders by enabling you to give everyone (All) the ability to create folders or to specify individual users after clicking on the Modify button.

The right text box labeled Not Allowed to Create Top Level Folders enables you to specify who can't create top-level folders by enabling you to prevent no one (None) from creating folders or to specify individual users who can't create folders by selecting them by choosing the Modify button.

Storage Warnings

The Storage Warnings tab shown in Figure 4.56 lets you configure at what time storage warning messages are generated; usually the default time is acceptable. You can choose to never generate the warnings (Never), generate them every 15 minutes (Always), or specify a specific time (Selected Times).

FIGURE 4.56

The Storage Warnings tab lets you specify when storage waning messages are generated.

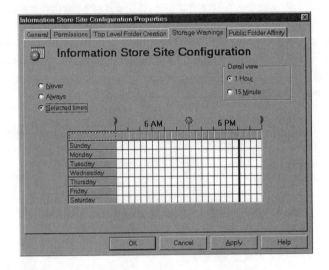

Public Folder Affinity

This tab is relevant for Exchange implementations after you've added additional sites; this is covered in Day 5.

After you have set all the Information Store Site configuration properties you can click OK to let the changes take effect.

Summary

In today's lesson you learned how to set up your Exchange server after it is installed. You learned the basics of setting up Exchange, including the following:

- How to add users, distribution lists, and custom recipients to your site using the Exchange Administrator program.

- How to easily add large numbers of users from an existing Windows NT or Novell network without retyping each user. This is accomplished with the Extract Account List menu items and the Directory Import menu item under the Tools menu.

- How to set up Address Books views to help make finding users easier and simpler in the Exchange Address Book. You can use Address Book views to organize recipients based on any Exchange property. The most common properties for Address Book views are Company, State, City, and Department.

- How to create public folders for your site as well as how to control individuals abilities to view, edit, and delete postings in public folders. Users have rights to public folders based on several basic roles that define the abilities to read, edit, and delete postings in a public folder. Public folders can contain mail messages, contact items, tasks, appointments, notes, and other Outlook items; this presents interesting options for how to use public folders in your organization.

Q&A

Q I am extracting an account list from a NetWare 4.11 network server and I have multiple NDS contexts from which to pull accounts from. How do I get Exchange to pull users from multiple NDS contexts?

A Because the Exchange account extraction process is only bindery-aware, you need to set the server's bindery context to each NDS context from which you want to pull users from. You can set multiple bindery contexts in IntranetWare 4.11 and IntranetWare 5.0 servers to prevent you from manually setting bindery contexts and running the extraction process for each NDS container.

Q I'd like to set more properties than simply the first, last, and display names when I import a large number of users. How can I do this?

A The Directory Import command accepts a comma-delimitated file that contains an individual line for each mailbox or Exchange object. The file that a NetWare or Windows NT account extraction generates has a minimal number of fields defined. If you want to add fields to the file, review Appendix D in the Exchange documentation for a list of the different properties Exchange supports. You simply add columns to the text file for each additional property; the first row in the text file defines which properties are defined in the text file. Remember that fields that aren't in the text file can be added by using a mailbox as a template for imported users.

Q I find that the Client Permissions roles for controlling public folder access don't meet all my security needs. For example, I don't want users to see folders they cannot access. How do I control this?

A The roles that the Client Permissions dialog box in a public folder's properties tab uses are simple suggestions. If you'd like, you can specify that Anonymous or Default users don't see the folder by unchecking the Folder Visible box. The role will change to Custom, reflecting that you've changed the rights from a predefined role to rights you've specifically identified.

Workshop

The Workshop provides two ways for you to affirm what you've learned in this chapter. The "Quiz" section poses questions to help you solidify your understanding of the material covered and the "Exercise" section provides you with experience in using what you have learned. You can find answers to the quiz questions and exercises in Appendix B, "Answers to Quiz Questions and Exercises."

Quiz

1. What would the results be if you used the formula `%5Last%2First%1Initials` to generate your default user aliases for the following individuals:

   - William J. Clinton

   - Paul McCartney

   - Jason G. Lo

2. You have created a new user for an Exchange site that you manage remotely. That is, you manage your building's Exchange site in addition other remote Exchange sites.) Afterwards you see the user in the Address Book, but the user can't log in. What is a likely cause for this problem?

3. A user with two SMTP addresses, one being `johnsonj@universalexports.com` and `johnsonj@washingtondc.universalexports.commailto:johnsonj@washingtondc.universalexports.com`, send mail to a colleague over the Internet. The Reply-To field on the message says `johnsonj@washingtondc.universalexports.com`. You want it to be the other address. How do you fix this?

Exercise

1. Review the User Properties dialog box shown in Figure 4.57. This user is not showing up in the Address Book in a system connected with an email gateway. Other users appear fine in the other system's directory, so something is wrong with this user account. What setting has to be changed?

FIGURE 4.57

This user is not appearing in an external email system's Address Book. What setting needs to be changed?.

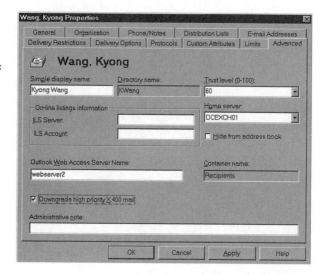

4

DAY 5

Working with Multiple Sites

By Anthony Steven

Chapter Objectives

So far, you have been considering Exchange single-site installations. In today's lesson, you will look at the issues behind installing separate Exchange sites. Separate sites and the different messaging connectors give Exchange the capability to scale into an enterprisewide messaging system spanning the world. However, there are a number of complex issues behind setting up such an arrangement.

You will be covering the following topics:

- Defining a site.
- The differences between intrasite and intersite communication.
- Directory Replication between sites.

- Configuring directory replication.
- Public folder replication.
- Performance considerations in public folder replication.

If your Exchange installation is in a single location with a permanent, high-bandwidth network, you don't need to think about separate sites. However, most companies tend to grow offshoots, and these remote locations usually connect over some form of Wide Area Network (WAN). After you get low-bandwidth links into your networking layout, you are probably going to need to install separate sites.

But first, I will take you on what might seem a small digression. Bear with me, though, because you'll see this knowledge will pay off later in the lesson.

Site Concepts and Basics

In Day 2, "Planning your Exchange Implementation," you looked at the factors in designing your Exchange sites. Now you're going to see what happens when an Exchange server joins a site.

When you add an Exchange server to an existing site, the new server automatically integrates itself into that site. It becomes part of the messaging and directory structure of that site.

Through directory replication, all other servers in the site become aware of the new server. Directory replication also makes each server in the site aware of what is on all the other servers. Mailboxes, public folders, connectors; this information is all freely traded between servers.

Within a site, this passing of directory information is almost instantaneous. Servers within a site can make a Remote Procedure Call (RPC) connection to any other server in the site at any time—in fact, they expect to.

This means that all servers within a site must have a permanent, high-bandwidth connection to all other servers within that site. They expect to connect immediately using RPCs, and the network must let them do that.

 Note Within a site, you must allow about 56kbps of network bandwidth for each server in the site.

Defining a Site

With this knowledge, you can begin to define a site.

A site must have the following attributes:

- The site must provide permanent, high-bandwidth links between Exchange servers.
- The server-to-server links must be capable of supporting Remote Procedure Calls.
- Each server-to-server connection requires a minimum of 56kbps.

So far I have only considered the networking requirements. Nevertheless, Exchange sites will also be collections of mailboxes, and mailboxes mean people. If you have 2MB links all over the country that support RPCs, there is no practical reason why you can't have one site. However, your users may find it a bit strange if your New York and Los Angeles personnel are all lumped together in the same site.

Considering another scenario, you could have two large office complexes, owned by the same company, right next to each other. There could be more than 1,000 users in each building. Again, you may want to make each one a separate site, even though there may be gigabyte fiber-optic links between the buildings.

 I define a *site* as a geographically and organizationally separate location with a permanent, high-bandwidth network capable of supporting Remote Procedure Calls.

Having defined the site, I will now take you through the factors that you need to consider in order to get your sites to work together.

Communication in a Multisite Environment

At this point, it would be useful to contrast the different communication methods used in intrasite and intersite communication.

Single Site Environment   In a single-site environment, an Exchange server talks directly to an Exchange server. There is no routing and the Message Transfer Agent (MTA) is responsible for providing the bulk of intrasite communication. The exception to this rule is that directory service talks directly to directory service.

Hence, if the System Attendant (SA) on one server wants to talk to the SA on another, it sends a message via the MTA. As the System Attendant has a mailbox, the message originates from the Information Store. The message passes to the MTA, which then binds directly to the MTA on the target server using RPC. The MTA sends the message to the target server, where the receiving MTA directs it to the Information Store. The Information Store then delivers it to the System Attendant.

5

The directory service speaks directly to the directory service on all other servers. This process is independent of the MTA, and happens whenever the directory database changes, for example, by adding a mailbox or changing the configuration of a connector.

Figure 5.1 shows the process of intrasite communication. The system attendant is invoking the MTA to deliver a message to the MTA on the other server.

FIGURE 5.1

In a single site environment, the directory services speak to each other, and the MTA does the rest.

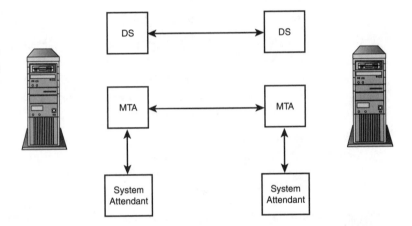

Multisite Environment   With multiple sites, *all* communication is message-based. Thus, any information, wherever it comes from, travels to the other site as a mail message.

The MTA sends these messages over a connector. Now, the MTA no longer has to deliver the message directly or connect via RPC, as the connector does this job. In addition, because all the information sent between sites now consists of mail messages, Exchange can make much better use of bandwidth.

Hence, in moving from a single to a multisite environment, there is a noticeable change in the method that Exchange uses to move information between servers. The MTA can now hand the actual connection process over to a connector, thus removing the requirement for the MTA to bind directly to the remote server via RPC.

The other change in an intersite environment is that the directory service also uses the MTA to communicate. So now, DS-to-DS communication is also message-based. This means that as far as the Exchange servers are concerned, there is no requirement for RPC connections to the remote servers.

Therefore, in a multisite system, the communication process looks like the diagram in Figure 5.2.

Note Just because the Message Transfer Agent and the Directory Service no longer need RPCs to talk to each other in a multisite environment, don't think that RPCs don't feature in links between sites. The Site or Exchange connector uses RPCs to join sites, as you will see in Day 6, "Connecting Exchange to Other Sites."

FIGURE 5.2

In a multisite environment, the MTA sends messages over the messaging connector but no longer has to bind over RPC. The Directory Replication connector also uses the messaging connector to send directory information.

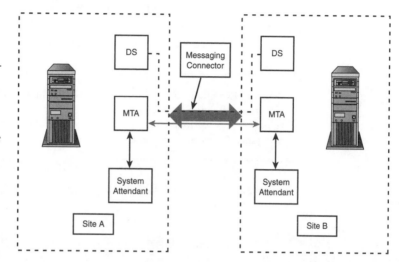

With this change away from RPC-based links (although the Site connector is a special case) towards a message-based system, you are now freed from the bandwidth and connectivity issues that you had in a single site. These mail messages can now travel over any suitable mail connector, whether it be X.400-based, SMTP, or via a dial-up link.

Messaging Connectors

There are four types of messaging connectors:

- Site (or Exchange) connector
- X.400 connector
- Dynamic RAS connector
- Internet Mail Service connector

Each has its own particular strengths and limitations. Wherever you have multiple sites, you will need to install one or more of these messaging connectors.

I will be discussing these connectors further on Day 6.

5

Messaging Bridgehead Servers

When you implement a messaging connector, you will probably have to consider the implications of messaging bridgehead servers. A messaging bridgehead server is a server in one site that handles all the messages destined for a remote site over a specific connector. In other words, bridgehead servers channel the communication between the two sites.

The X.400, Dynamic RAS, and Internet Mail Service connectors all use bridgehead servers. This is because you install these connectors on a specific server, and that server then becomes responsible for all the messages over that connector.

Note   The Site (Exchange) connector does not require the use of bridgehead servers as, by default, any server can connect to any other server in the remote site. Nevertheless, you can configure the Site connector to use bridgehead servers if you want.

Figure 5.3 shows an example of a messaging bridgehead server.

FIGURE 5.3

A bridgehead server channels all communication between two sites.

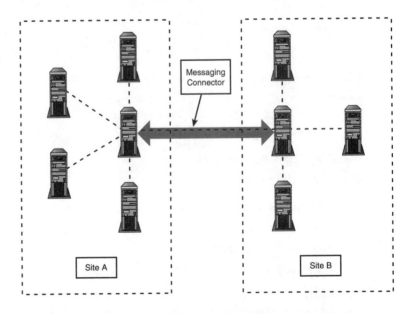

Bridgehead Servers and Resources   Because bridgehead servers are funneling the messages between sites, they will have an extra loading, depending on the volume of messages. Hence, you need to allow extra resources (RAM or additional CPU-power) on messaging bridgehead servers.

Another option is the use of dedicated messaging bridgehead servers. These are servers whose only job is to receive and send messages. They have no public or private information stores and do not expand distribution lists.

Multiple Messaging Connectors

Rather than use dedicated messaging bridgehead servers, you could use multiple messaging connectors. With the exception of the Site connector, you can add multiple messaging connectors of the same type between sites. This gives you the ability to load-balance your servers.

You could also have multiple types of connector linking sites, providing redundancy. I will discuss this further on Day 6.

Directory Replication

Directory replication is the process by which Exchange servers make each other aware of the directory information that they hold. Directory information is a wide remit, and it includes everything that you can see in the Exchange Administrator, as well as quite a few things you can't (unless you run Exchange Administrator in Raw mode).

Directory Replication Basics

You are probably familiar with the idea of directory replication already. After all, you know all about NT domains and how the Primary Domain Controller (PDC) updates the Backup Domain Controllers (BDCs). You don't? OK, a bit of a digression, then.

Directory Replication under NT Windows NT uses replication to synchronize the directory information on user accounts, passwords, and so on, throughout the domain. This is an automatic process, and happens on a regular basis.

If you are adding an account to Windows NT, you do so using User Manager for Domains. User Manager connects to the IPC (Inter-Process Communications) share on the PDC using RPC over Named Pipes. You add the account, specify a password, and click OK.

The PDC then waits for a little while, to see if you are going to make any more changes. After five minutes, assuming no further changes have been made, it calls up to ten BDCs and announces "I have changes." The BDCs then connect to the PDC and update their directory databases. The domain is back in synchronization again.

This is a master-slave arrangement because the PDC has the master copy of the database and the BDCs only have a copy. All the changes happen on the PDC and then disseminate through the system. NetWare 3.x used a similar principle.

5

> This is *not* the same as NT's Replication Service, which you can configure to export logon scripts and system policies from server to server.

Directory Replication Under Exchange   Under Exchange, directory replication happens in a very different fashion. Exchange 5.x uses multimaster replication, where each Exchange server is a master, and operates with all the other servers on a peer-to-peer basis.

Exchange 5.5, Windows 2000, and Active Directory Services (ADS)

The computing world in general is moving towards multimaster replication of directory databases. NetWare 4.x uses multimaster replication, implemented as Novell Directory Service (NDS). Microsoft has replied with Active Directory Services (ADS), scheduled to appear in Windows 2000.

One of the essential components of both ADS and NDS is the concept of multimaster replication. This copes with large organizations by spreading the loading on the servers that hold a copy of the directory. NT 4.0 has a hardware limit of about 40,000 directory objects (that is, users or computers), which is why you have to set up multiple domains with large numbers of users. Windows 2000 is planned to cope with a directory containing more than 1,000,000 objects.

Exchange 5.x was the test bed for the implementation of multimaster replication, which ADS uses. Therefore, if you are familiar with Exchange 5.5's directory replication, you already have a good idea how it works on ADS.

The next release of Exchange, code name PLATINUM, will integrate the Exchange directory with the ADS. However, it is not expected until after Windows 2000 is released and well bedded-down. Just in time for the Millennium bug! (Of course I'm only kidding—Like Exchange 5.5 Service Pack 2 and NT 4.0 Service Pack 4, Windows 2000 will be fully Year-2000 compliant.)

Directory Replication and Messaging Connectors

Directory replication is totally dependent on messaging connectivity. You must define a messaging connector before you can set up directory replication. You can use any of the four messaging connectors I listed earlier.

> Always set up and check your messaging connectivity before you try installing a directory replication connector. I *guarantee* that directory replication will not to work if messages cannot get through.

See Day 6 for more information on installing and configuring messaging connectors.

Directory Replication Topologies

One major difference between configuring your messaging connectors and setting up directory replication is that your directory replication does not have to follow your messaging topology. In fact, unless your site is very simple, it is very probable that it won't.

The way it works is this:

Your sites must all have only one source of directory replication data.

In other words, no loops.

So, while your messaging connectors can be set up in a veritable cat's cradle of interconnections, your directory replication structure should be very simple. Generally, this will be in one of two forms—linear or star. Figure 5.4 shows an example of a star and a linear arrangement.

FIGURE 5.4

The star topology has a central site and is the preferred method of connecting Exchange sites.

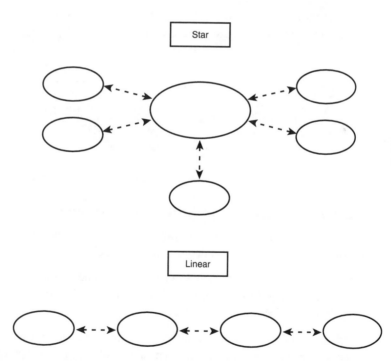

5

> **Star or Linear Topology?**
>
> Really, there is only one choice—the star arrangement. The only time that a linear arrangement is as effective as a star is when there aren't actually enough sites to make a star.
>
> The reason for this is that in a linear arrangement, directory replication changes have to propagate from site to site. If you have four sites, and make a change to site A, it must propagate to site B, which must propagate to site C, and then on to D. Normally, each hop takes up to 15 minutes, meaning that a complete directory update could take up to 45 minutes.
>
> Making this into a star arrangement means that whenever you update a site, its directory information will only take two hops to get right the way around the organization.

For most organizations, this should not present too much of a problem. Generally, the HQ has the best communications links to all the other sites. When designing your directory replication, it is worth looking at the messaging connectivity as well. Then you could make the directory replication connectors run along your fastest messaging links.

 Caution

> Always check your directory replication topology to make sure there are no loops.
>
> Looping causes problems because a site finds that it is receiving directory information about the same site from two different sources. Therefore, if you have any loops in your directory replication connectors, directory replication will fail.

Directory Replication Bridgehead Servers

Directory replication always uses directory replication bridgehead servers. You always install a directory replication connector on a specific server.

Where you have multiple directory replication connectors to several sites, you should consider installing the directory replication links for the different sites on different servers, where possible.

Another option is to install the directory replication connector on the server that has the messaging connector for that site. Whichever solution you go for, don't forget to monitor the loading on your directory replication server.

Controlling Directory Replication

Within a site, directory replication is an automatic process, requiring no manual intervention at all. When you add a mailbox or change a configuration setting on an Exchange server, you connect to any machine in the site. After you have made the change, that server notifies the other ones that there has been a change in the directory structure, and the remote machines then download the changes.

But what if someone else has made a change on another server at the same time? Read on for the answer.

Update Sequence Numbers   The way that Exchange handles updates to the directory is through update sequence numbers (USNs). These are not time dependent, but machine to machine dependent, so each machine keeps track of the updates that it has received from the other Exchange servers. Hence, by keeping track of the USNs on all other machines, Exchange sites keep their directories synchronized.

Figure 5.5 shows this process in action.

FIGURE 5.5

Update sequence numbers make sure that the Exchange site's directory structure is consistent between servers.

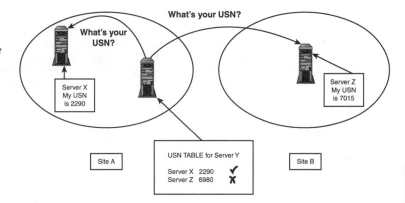

Exchange also uses update sequence numbers to keep track of changes between sites.

Manual Intrasite Directory Updates   Although intrasite directory replication is largely an automatic process, it is not immediate. So what can you do if you want to force directory replication within a site?

Let's say the scenario is that you have just added a large number of users and you want the information on their mailboxes to propagate to all Exchange servers in your site:

 Note   Note that I am forcing the update on the *other* servers in the site; that is, the ones that don't yet know about the new mailboxes.

1. Start Exchange Administrator and select your site in the left pane. Click on the site object to expand it and then double-click on the configuration container object. In the right pane, select the servers object.

2. Double-click on the servers object and then double-click on one of the other servers, *not* the one on which you added the mailboxes.

3. In the right pane, double-click on the Directory Service object. You will now see the dialog box shown in Figure 5.6.

FIGURE 5.6

The directory service dialog box at the server level enables you to force a directory update within a site.

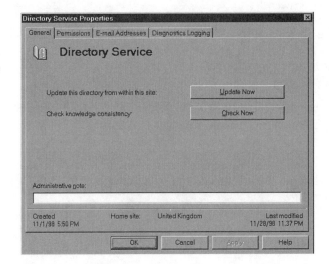

4. Click on the button marked Update Now.

5. A prompt will ask you to select whether you want just recent changes or whether you want to force a complete resynchronization.

> **Caution**
>
> In a large and complex site, complete synchronization can take several hours. This is not something you would want to do during busy times. Usually, you would select to download only the changes since the last update.

6. Your server will now check all the other servers in the site to see if there have been any changes to the directory service.

7. If there have been any changes, this server sends out an update request to the remote machine.

I will cover intersite manual directory updates later in this lesson.

Knowledge Consistency Checker (KCC)   The Check Now button activates the Knowledge Consistency Checker (KCC), which provides a similar service to the one the Update Now button provides, except at a higher level. Update Now works on changes to the directory structure, whereas the KCC looks for new servers and sites.

In normal operation, the KCC runs daily, but there are occasions where you will need to run it manually, for example after you have just joined two sites or brought a server back online.

The KCC works by asking all other servers in the site whether they know about any servers or sites that the requesting server does not know about. This way the requesting server cross-references everything that it knows with everything that all the others know, thus highlighting any discrepancies. Should any discrepancies appear, the requesting server can then request an update from the server that has the information.

> **Tip**
>
> When the KCC runs on a directory replication bridgehead server, it checks the servers in the remote site to see if they know about any sites or servers that the checking server does not know about. Do this whenever you add a new server to a remote site and you want to update the directory database quickly.

> **Note**
>
> If you select the Check Now button, you should update the routing tables. Select the Message Transfer Agent at the server level and click on the Recalculate routing button.

So what do you have to do to get directory replication between sites? Follow the steps I'll outline next to find out.

5

Installing the Directory Replication Connector

Before you install a directory replication connector, here is a quick checklist of what you need to do first.

1. Decide how you want your directory replication topology set up. Factors to consider are how many sites you have, the messaging connectors between them, connection schedules, bandwidth, and so on. Fortunately, you should have already covered most of these topics in Day 2, Planning Your Exchange Implementation.

2. Decide which servers are going to run the directory replication connectors in both the local and remote sites. Do they need upgrading? Are you going to remove any mailboxes and the public information stores from those servers?

3. Configure and test the messaging connectivity. There is no point in attempting to install the directory replication connector until you can get messages to pass between sites. However, you won't be able to click on the To: button, as the remote

site's users won't be listed. In that case you will need to send a message to a recipient in that site using an X.400 address or an SMTP address. You will need to define a custom address of type X.400 in your personal address book and then enter the values shown in the recipient's X.400 email address in their mailbox.

4. When the messaging works okay, you can install the directory replication connector.

The process of installing the directory replication connector is actually very simple. You only need to specify:

- The remote site server onto which you want to install the directory replication connector.
- Whether the remote site is available on the network.
- Whether you want to configure both sides at once.

Follow these steps to set up a directory replication connector:

1. Start Exchange Administrator and click on the File menu. Select New Other and then choose Directory Replication Connector from the menu.

2. Select the target site name.

3. Enter the name of the server in that site onto which you want to install the directory replication connector.

4. Select whether the remote site is available on the network or not. If the remote site is available on the network, you can also choose to configure both sides. Doing so is usually a good idea.

5. You now have three tabs to configure. The General tab lets you change the directory replication bridgehead servers and the display and directory names for this connector. Figure 5.7 shows this screen.

Note   Once you choose a directory name, you can't change it. However, you can subsequently change the display name.

6. The Schedule tab lets you specify a schedule for directory replication to take place. The Selected Times option (every 3 hours) is usually adequate for keeping your directory reasonably up to date. Do not select Always unless you have a permanent high-bandwidth connection between sites. Selecting Never disables directory replication updates. Figure 5.8 shows the Schedule tab.

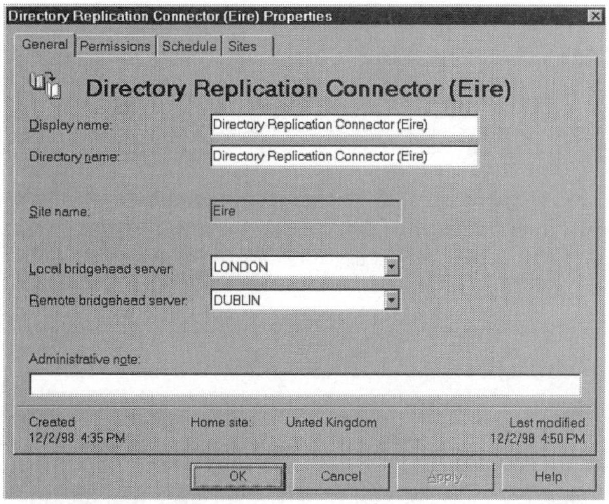

FIGURE 5.7

The General tab on the directory replication connector lets you rename the connector when you install it.

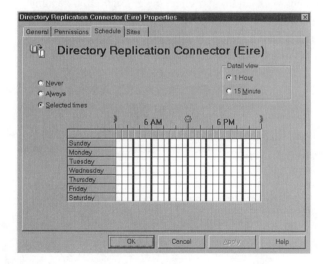

FIGURE 5.8

Use the Schedule tab to control replication frequency.

7. The Sites tab shows you a list of which sites are inbound on this connector and which ones are outbound. You will not see anything here when you install the connector.

8. That's it!

There is no need to specify any security settings because the messaging connector takes care of these.

Over the next few minutes you will see the information from the other site begin to filter across. After directory replication is initialized, the site and configuration container from the remote site appear. However, you won't see the objects in the configuration container immediately. This omission is because Exchange copies across a stub directory and then populates this stub directory over time. This process prevents Exchange from swamping the link between the sites.

Tip

> To speed up the directory replication process, run the KCC on your directory replication bridgehead server in both sites. See the section "Knowledge Consistency Checker (KCC)" earlier in this chapter.

Configuring Directory Replication

After you have set up directory replication, you will usually not have to configure it. However, you might want to force a manual update from a remote site.

To do this, start Exchange Administrator and select your site in the left pane. Click on the site object to expand it and select the configuration container object. In the right pane, select Directory Replication. Double-click on Directory Replication and then double-click on the directory replication connector that you have just created. Click on the Sites tab to see the Properties dialog box shown in Figure 5.9.

FIGURE 5.9

Now that you have set up the directory replication connector, and the sites have replicated, you can see the remote site in the Sites tab.

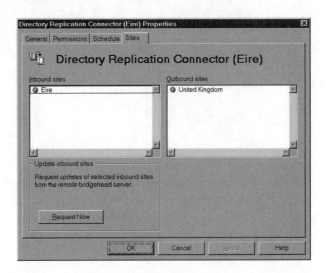

Your local site should appear in the right pane, with the remote site on the left side. If the remote site has links to any other sites, they will also appear in the left pane.

Forcing a Manual Update

To request a manual update, select the relevant site in the left column, and click the Request Now button. You will be prompted to choose between a full refresh or just the changes since the last update, as in Figure 5.10.

FIGURE 5.10

A full refresh could take a very long time!

Again, like at the server level, be particularly careful of requesting a full update across a slow WAN link or a dial-up connection. It could get expensive (in terms of connection time) and take a long time! A progress bar will display, like that in Figure 5.11.

FIGURE 5.11

The progress bar shows how long you have for a cup of coffee.

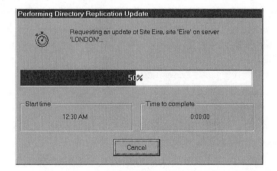

5

> **Tip**
>
> If you are trying to force a change through a number of sites, remember to update the site on which you made the change first. Use the Update Now button in the server level directory service object, as I showed you in the section on Manual Intrasite Directory Updates previously. Then, starting at the site next to the one that you have just changed, *pull* the information through all the other sites.

Now that you are up to speed with directory replication, let's look at the other forms of replication that you get in Exchange.

Public Folders and Multiple Sites

When you configure directory replication between two sites, users in each site can see the other site's public folders in Outlook. However, if they click on these folders, they find that they get a message that tells them that there is no copy of the folder in their site.

There are two ways of making the contents of a public folder available on more than one site. These methods are affinities and replication.

Affinity

With affinity values, no actual replication of data takes place: There is still only one copy of the data. You could also think of affinity as a Windows NT trust relationship.

 Note

> Affinity values are like Windows NT trusts in other ways. Like trusts, affinity values are not transitive. If I configure an affinity between site A and site B, and between site B and site C, there is no affinity between site A and site C.
>
> Again, like trusts, affinity values are also one-way only. So, if I configure an affinity between site A and site B, there is no automatic affinity in the opposite direction, between site B and site A. I would have to configure a separate affinity value between site B and site A.

Let's say you configure an affinity value between the two sites. A user in the site where the folder does not exist then selects the public folder. This time, although there is still no copy of the folder in the user's site, the affinity value allows a transfer of the request to the site that does have a copy. The user can now view and open the messages in that public folder.

Site Connection Order

Affinity is also rather like a cost value on a connector, in that you can assign costs to each affinity connection. Affinity costs work on a simple ranking basis; clients connect to the site with the lowest affinity value first. By assigning lower costs to the links to sites with greater bandwidth, you can control the connection order to remote sites.

In Figure 5.12, you can see affinity values configured between four sites. The affinity values are proportional to the bandwidth. A client in site A will connect to site B first, and then site C. The choice between sites D and E is at random, as they both have the same affinity value.

FIGURE 5.12

*Your clients will con-
nect to the sites with
the lowest affinity val-
ues first.*

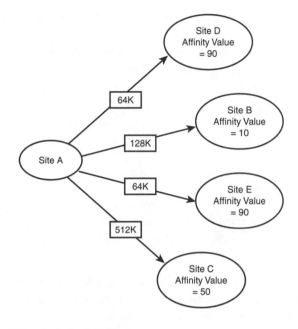

Planning Public Folder Affinity

You should plan public folder affinities carefully. Remember that client connections over these links will probably be slow.

Affinity values work best where there is only occasional access of a public folder from a remote site. The access traffic generated by these requests must be less than the traffic produced by replicating a copy of the folder to the remote site.

Putting it another way, think about how many connections your users are likely to make using affinity values to public folders in other sites. Look at the average size of a message in the relevant public folder and multiply the two to calculate how much bandwidth these connections will use. If this is excessive, you need to look at replicating a copy of the folder instead.

Don't even think about using affinity values across a dial-up connection.

After you have planned any public folder affinities, you are ready to configure affinity values.

Configuring Public Folder Affinity

Configuring public folder affinity is very easy. Start Exchange Administrator and select your site in the left pane. Click on the site object to expand it and select the Configuration container object. In the right pane, double-click on Information Store Site Configuration. You will now see the Properties sheet in Figure 5.13.

FIGURE 5.13

Configuring affinity values between sites is very easy.

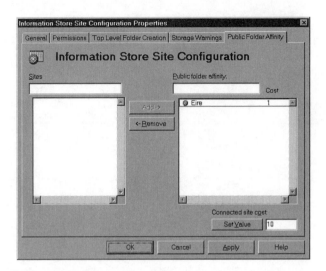

Select the remote site in the left column, and click Add. Set a cost value from 1 to 100 and click OK. It's as simple as that. What is difficult is trying to remember which Properties sheet configures affinity values! Remember, it's the Information Store Site Configuration Properties sheet's Public Folder Affinity tab.

Security Considerations

When you are using affinity values, you have a specific security problem. Let's say that your two Exchange sites are in different domains. The users from each site are in that site's domain. When users connect to a public folder in their site, there isn't a problem, as they authenticate to that domain. However, if they attempt to connect via the affinity value to a public folder in the other domain, Windows NT will refuse them access because they don't have an account in that domain.

There are several workarounds to this problem. You should try to avoid having it happen in the first place by using a proper domain model, like the single master domain. With all the user accounts in the master domain and trusts configured between the resource domain and the master domain, the problem doesn't arise. If you have just two sites, you could get away with using the complete trust model (which is about as far as it realistically scales, despite what some people think).

Replication

Affinity values can't always help us, as bandwidth may restrict their use. However, you can replicate more than just directories in Microsoft Exchange. You can also configure replication between public folders.

Now, this concept is quite interesting because a public folder is a database. Normally, when you think of a database, you think one copy only because as soon as you make two copies of a database and start changing data in each copy, there is no way to re-integrate them again. Yet with Exchange, you can specify that you want to replicate a folder and set up a replica at another site. If you make changes to the original folder or to its replica, they both stay synchronized automatically. Even if you make changes to both simultaneously, there is still a mechanism for resolving any conflicts.

Therefore, like directory replication, public folder replication is also multimaster. In fact, public folders replicate in not one but two different ways: by hierarchy and content.

Hierarchy Replication

The first replication is replication of the public folder hierarchy. A copy of this public folder hierarchy exists on every computer that has a public information store.

Hierarchy replication happens every minute, is not controllable (unless you like hacking around in the Registry), and generally, produces very little network traffic.

Conflict resolution is very easy in hierarchy replication. The last change is accepted. Therefore, if two people make changes to the same branch of the public folder tree, the last person's change will overwrite any previous changes.

Content Replication

Content replication happens entirely separately. With content replication, you manually configure copies of a public folder on other servers that have a public information store.

 Note You can have machines without a public or a private information store. I will be discussing this concept at the end of the chapter.

There are two ways of configuring content replication: push or pull. These correspond to whether you are configuring them to replicate on a per-folder basis, or on an information store basis.

Push Configuration (Replicas)   Push configurations or replicas work on a per-folder basis. They push their contents onto other replicas. You configure replicas from the Replicas tab of the individual public folder in Exchange Administrator, as I will show you later.

Pull Configuration (Instances)   Pull configurations or instances work on a per-information store basis. The public information store pulls the copy of the folder onto the server. You configure instances from the Instances tab on the Public Information Store object at the server level. You will be covering this in the next section.

The Public Folder Replication Agent

The Public Folder Replication Agent (PFRA—sounds more like one of those 1970's terrorist groups) is responsible for ensuring content replication. It monitors folders for changes and then sends out change messages to any other replicas.

Monitoring Changes

The PFRA monitors public folders for changes, like new messages or changes to an existing post. If the PFRA detects a change, it then uses three attributes to coordinate the replication of that message. These attributes are the Change Number, the Time Stamp, and the Predecessor Change List.

The *Change Number* is specific to an information store and a server. It increases sequentially when a user makes a change to an information store's contents.

The *Time Stamp* is just what it says it is. Note that if a message arrives in a store with a time stamp more recent than the server's current time, the original time stamp remains unchanged.

The *Predecessor Change List* is very like the Update Sequence Number in directory replication. It is specific to each link between information stores and again increases sequentially.

Conflict Resolution

Let's say you have two copies of a public folder. If you post a message into one, the PFRA detects the change and then waits a bit to see if you are going to make any other changes. When things have settled down, it contacts the other copy and announces the change. A change message is then sent from the first copy to the second, containing the new posting. The copy of the folder then adds this message to the other public information store. Now you have two messages, one in each copy of the public folder.

If someone else alters the copy of the message (not the original) on the second folder, the PFRA again detects the change and replicates the message back to the original. Because the amended version is more recent than the original, it replaces the one that you first posted.

But what happens if, in the meantime, you altered your original posting as well? Then a conflict arises. You then both get a conflict message, enclosing the two versions of the message and asking you to decide which one to accept. Of course, if you both accept your own version, there is another conflict message.

Planning Public Folder Distribution

You didn't think you were going to get away without any planning, did you? No, I'm afraid you'll have to put a bit of thought into where you put the replicated copies of any folders.

User Locations and Bandwidth

When planning public folders, you need to consider five initial factors:

- How many users will connect to a particular copy of a public folder at any one time?
- Where are those users located?
- How many messages will they read?
- What size are the messages?
- What is the bandwidth of the connection that they will use?

What you are looking for is an estimation of normal usage patterns for a particular public folder. If it's a public folder containing company policy on health and safety, it's probably not going to get that many readers. However, if you have a public folder with a daily Dilbert cartoon, you can bet that the entire company will want to read it at 9:00 a.m. every day.

Microsoft has produced a tool called Loadsim that you can use to simulate real-life loading on an Exchange server. This includes setting up public folders and posting to them. It is available for download from:

```
http://backoffice.microsoft.com/downtrial/default.asp?product=5
```

Performance Considerations

However, your users and the available network bandwidth are not the only factors in the equation. You also need to understand the impact that public folders have on your Exchange servers.

There are four options when it comes to placing public folders on Exchange servers:

- Single server
- Multiple servers, multiple replicas
- Dedicated public folder server
- Multiple dedicated public folder servers

5

Single Server   In a single-server environment, you don't have a lot of choice. In this case, your server will have the public and private information stores. It will also be the routing calculation server, the Internet Mail Service server, the Newsfeed server, the distribution list expansion server, and it will have to make tea for you. Not surprising, this arrangement is prone to overloading.

Multiple Servers and Multiple Replicas   You have multiple servers, all with a public information store on them. You have created a public folder on one and replicated it to all the other servers.

In this case, although each server becomes less of a bottleneck, all your machines will all have other functions, like routing, message bridgeheads, and so on. In addition, you have increased the amount of bandwidth used by the replication process.

Dedicated Public Folder Server   A dedicated public folder server is one that has no private information store. This is only an option in a multiserver site, as you must have at least one instance of a public information store.

You would use a dedicated public folder server in a large site with more than five Exchange servers. They are also useful in situations where users often update the public folder hierarchy.

The drawback with a dedicated public folder server is that with very heavy use, it can become a bottleneck. In addition, if it crashes, you lose all your public folders.

To create a dedicated public folder server, carry out the following steps:

1. Once you add a second server to your site, don't add any mailboxes to it.

2. Carry out a full backup of all your servers.

3. On the non-public folder servers, configure the private information store so that it points to the new server.

4. To do this, start Exchange Administrator and select your site in the left pane. Click on the site object to expand it and select the servers object. In the right pane, select one of the other servers in your site. Double-click on the server and then select the private information store. You will now see the Properties screen in Figure 5.14.

5. Select the public folder server in the drop-down box at the bottom. This will make all mailboxes on this server look to the public folder server first.

6. Repeat this process for all other servers in the site except for the proposed public folder server.

7. Now go to the public information store object on the new server, that is, the one that you have earmarked to be the dedicated public folder server. Select the properties of the public information store and click on the Instances tab.

8. Make sure there is an instance of every public folder in the site on the public folder server, as shown in Figure 5.15.

FIGURE 5.14

The private information store object is where you point to the public folder server.

FIGURE 5.15

Here all the site's public folders are homed on the dedicated public folder server.

5

9. Leave the system for at least an hour to ensure replication of the public folders has taken place. If you have large amounts of information in the public folders, you may need to leave this overnight.

10. Now select the private information store object on the dedicated public folder server. From the Edit menu, choose Delete.

11. Go back to the other servers in the site, and select their public information stores. Again, from the Edit menu, select Delete.

12. You now have a dedicated public folder server. Any new public folders will be homed on this machine.

Multiple Dedicated Public Folder Servers   If your sites are very large (in the order of thousands of users) you will probably need to consider multiple public folder servers. Setting these up is the same as I described above; the difference is that you will now want to replicate the public folders between the dedicated public folder servers.

By keeping a lower number of dedicated public folder servers, you are controlling the replication traffic. The dedicated public folder servers will not be carrying out any other tasks, like message connectivity. Finally, if one dedicated server goes down, you can fall back on the replicas.

Age Limits

Age limits on public folders enable you to set up how long a message will last on a server before expiring. You can use this feature to help control the size of your public information store. If you had a public folder called Next Week's Events, there really isn't much point in the postings existing on that folder for more than seven days. So you can configure age limits so that the information store deletes postings after seven days.

Client Connection Order

Having considered both affinities and replication, I will now show you the order in which a client connects to information stores in order to retrieve a message in a public folder. Let's say you have multiple sites and servers, as shown in Figure 5.16, and you have configured affinity values as shown.

 Note   This process only involves servers that have a public information store.

To start the process, the user double-clicks on a posting or a message in a public folder that he or she would like to read.

Figure 5.16

The client connection order defines how users connect to public folder servers.

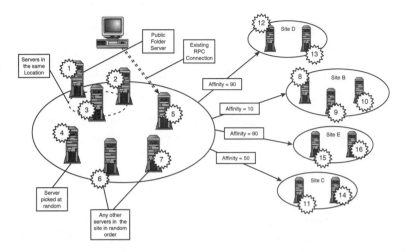

Because the public folder hierarchy replicates to every public folder server, all servers are aware of the existence of the message. In this case, there is only one actual instance of this public folder. Also, because there is a Registry setting of

```
HKEY_LOCAL_MACHINE/SOFTWARE/Microsoft/Exchange/Client/Options/MurphysLaw=0
x1
```

this instance of the public folder will be on the last server that Exchange tries.

Having double-clicked on the message to open it, the user's computer will connect to the public folder servers in the following order:

1. The dedicated public folder server. This is the server listed on the General tab of the private information store containing this user's mailbox.

2. All public folder servers in the same server location. Server locations are defined on the General tab on the properties of the respective servers.

3. A public folder server picked at random.

4. Any server with an existing RPC connection to the client.

5. All other servers in the site at random.

6. A random choice of any server at the site with the lowest affinity value.

7. A random choice of any servers in all sites with equal affinity values.

8. A random choice of servers in the site with the highest affinity value.

9. If the message still does not appear, it must be a Directory Service/Information Service inconsistency. See Day 8, "Troubleshooting Exchange," to learn about fixing DS/IS inconsistencies.

5

Configuring Public Folder Replication

Having planned your public folders, you are now ready to configure them.

By Public Information Store

By far the easiest method to configure your folders is by public information store.

To do this, start Exchange Administrator and select your site in the left pane. Click on the site object to expand it and select the Configuration container object. In the right pane, double-click on the servers object. Double-click on the server you want to configure, and then select the public information store. From the File menu, select Properties to view the properties of the public information store.

Instances   Click on the Instances tab. You can now select the folders that you want to pull onto this instance of the public information store. This is the same dialog box as you saw in Figure 5.15.

Replication Schedule   Here you can define when you want replication to take place. If you have plenty of bandwidth, you can select Always. On very busy networks, you might only want this to happen at night.

Age Limits   On the Age Limits tab, you can configure how long a copy of a message will last on a remote server before it is deleted. Figure 5.17 shows this dialog box.

FIGURE 5.17

You can configure age limits on replicas through the age limits tab.

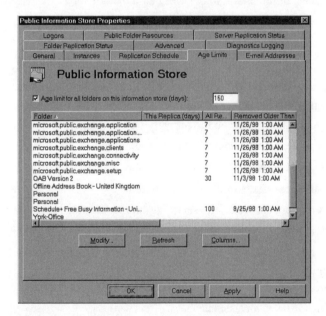

Clicking on the Modify button will show the dialog box in Figure 5.18. Here you can change the maximum age of postings in this replica and on all other copies of a public folder.

FIGURE 5.18

This dialog box lets you configure age limits on all replicas or just this replica.

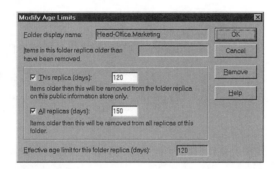

Folder Replication Status   This tab shows you the replication status of all the folders on this information store. Replication status is either local modified (that is, this copy has been modified) or In Sync. Folders not synchronizing over a long time may be indicative of messaging problems.

Figure 5.19 shows the Folder Replication Status tab.

FIGURE 5.19

The Folder Replication Status tab shows just how each folder is replicating.

5

Server Replication Status This shows when your servers last updated. Again, the status should normally be In Sync, and the last received time should be no longer than the Replicate Always interval. Figure 5.20 shows the Server Replication Status tab.

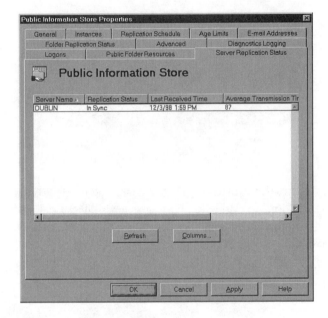

Advanced The Advanced tab has two settings.

The Replication Interval is the frequency with which replication messages appear when you configure Replicate Always in the Replication Interval tab.

> The default setting is usually adequate for most purposes. You should not use a value of less than 5 minutes, as this may prevent the folders from completing replication.

The Replication message size limit is the maximum message size actually used during replication. Hence larger messages split into 300k segments, and smaller messages join into 300k blocks.

Having configured replication at the information store level, I will now show you the settings at an individual folder level.

By Public Folder

Configuring replication by public folder is a similar process. Start Exchange
Administrator and select public folders in the left pane. Expand the public folders by
clicking on the small plus signs in the tree, until you get to the public folder that you
want to configure. Select the File menu and choose Properties. You will now see the dialog box shown in Figure 5.21.

FIGURE 5.21

*You can configure the
properties of a public
folder individually.*

General Tab   The important items on the General tab are the check boxes for Limit
Administrative Access to Home Site and Propagate These Permissions to All Subfolders.

The Limit Administrative Access option will prevent administrators from other sites from
modifying the properties of this folder.

Note   By default, administrative access on a new folder is limited to the home site.

Checking the Propagate These Properties to All Subfolders box and selecting Apply will
produce the dialog box shown in Figure 5.22. You can now select which folder properties
you want to propagate down the folder tree.

5

FIGURE 5.22

Check the boxes to propagate your current settings down the public folder hierarchy.

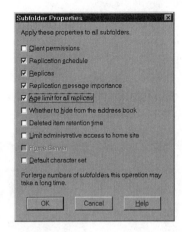

You don't get the Propagate check box at the bottom of the tree—only folders with subfolders below them get it.

To configure replication throughout the subtree, you will want to check the options for:

- Replication schedule
- Replicas
- Replication message importance
- Age limit for all replicas

Replicas Tab   On the Replicas tab, you can select the sites and servers onto which you want to push this folder. Select the servers on the left and click Add. The Site drop-down box at the bottom enables you to select servers in other sites. Figure 5.23 shows the Replicas tab.

Folder Replication Status   The Folder Replication Status tab is like the Server Replication Status tab on the public information store object. It shows the current synchronization status on all servers to which this folder replicates.

Replication Schedule Tab   The Replication Schedule tab gives you an extra option on configuring replication times. You can accept the information store defaults or configure an individual replication schedule for this folder. Again, if you configure this folder individually, you have the options of Always, Never or at Specific Times.

FIGURE 5.23

The Replicas tab lets you configure push replicas of a public folder.

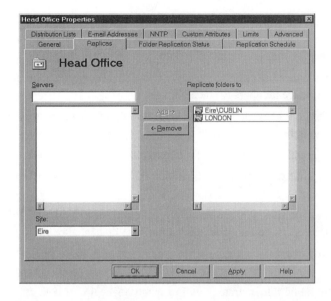

Tip

Let's say you are trying to replicate folders to a site at the end of a slow WAN link. As bandwidth is a major consideration, you would not want to replicate all the folders in the public information store at once. Instead, you should configure the individual public folders to replicate according to an interleaved schedule. Doing so will mean that no two folders are attempting to replicate at the same time, thus preserving bandwidth.

5

Summary

You have now looked at the process of replication within Microsoft Exchange. Directory replication is an important concept to understand, as it is the reason behind Exchange's scalability. Public folder replication enables you to provide fast access for clients connecting to public folders. Directory replication will be a major feature of Windows 2000.

To summarize the main points of this lesson:

- An Exchange site is a geographically and organizationally separate location with a permanent, high-bandwidth network capable of supporting Remote Procedure Calls.

- Within sites, Exchange servers automatically replicate their directory structure with each other.

- To enable directory replication between sites, you must configure messaging connectivity, and then install a directory replication connector.

- After you have configured directory replication between sites, you will be able to see your entire organization in Exchange Administrator. Your users will also see all the other users in their global address book.

- Exchange uses a multimaster concept of directory replication, using update sequence numbers to track changes.

- Public folders also replicate throughout Exchange, and replicate on two levels: hierarchy and content.

- Hierarchy replication is not controllable; content replication is.

- To configure content replication, you must create instances or replicas of a public folder.

- In large sites, you may need to configure dedicated public folder servers. In very large sites, you may even need multiple dedicated public folder servers.

- You can also configure affinity values, which allow clients to connect to other sites to read the contents of public folders.

- A public folder strategy will probably make use of both affinity values and replication.

Q&A

Q My company is located in three separate offices, one in London, one in Glasgow, and one in York. There are about 500 staff at each office. The offices are connected by 2MB MegaStream links, which support RPCs. We are planning to implement our Exchange system as one site. Is this a good idea?

A There's no practical reason why you shouldn't. However, I would recommend that you look at implementing them as three separate sites. Organizationally, your three locations are probably fairly autonomous, so it would probably help your users if there were separate sites for each office. In addition, although the link will support RPCs, having separate sites will make much better use of bandwidth, so clearing your connections for other traffic.

Q I configured directory replication between our two sites a week ago. Yet, when users click on a public folder, they get a message that the folder is unavailable, because directory replication has not taken place. I've looked in the message queues and the messages seem to be flowing correctly between sites. What am I doing wrong?

A What is happening here is that the replication of your public folder contents is independent of the replication of your public folder hierarchy. Hence your users can see the folder hierarchy in both sites, but can only connect to folders that are homed on their site. You need to either configure affinity values between the two sites, or replicate copies of the public folders.

Q I have three sites and I configured site connectors between them all. I tested the messaging connectivity by sending X.400 messages between the sites and everything was working fine. I then installed directory replication connectors over the messaging connectors. However, I'm now getting all sorts of unexpected errors and directory replication doesn't seem to be working at all. What's the problem?

A The problem is that you have probably configured your directory replication connectors in a loop. Just remove one of these connectors, and everything should be hunky-dory.

Q I've just added an Exchange server into one of my sites, but it isn't appearing when I run Exchange Administrator in the other site. How can I make it appear?

A The easy way to do this is to run the knowledge consistency checker on the directory replication bridgehead server in the other site. Go to the server level and double-click on the Directory Service object. Click on the Check Now button. The pop-up box that you see should have a red cross on it, meaning that the new server has been discovered. The new server should appear very shortly. Just keep pressing the F5 button to refresh Exchange Administrator.

Workshop

The Workshop provides two ways for you to affirm what you've learned in this lesson. The "Quiz" section poses questions to help you solidify your understanding of the material covered and the "Exercise" section provides you with experience in using what you have learned. You can find answers to the quiz questions and exercises in Appendix B, "Answers to Quiz Questions and Exercises."

Quiz

1. What must a network be capable of supporting if you want it to function as an Exchange site?

2. What are the four types of messaging connector?

3. What must you install before you can configure directory replication across the Internet?

4. In a single-site environment, which Exchange services communicate directly?

5. Which service in Exchange is responsible for all site-to-site communication?

6. What is a messaging bridgehead server?

7. What is the recommended design of a directory replication topology?

8. What agent is responsible for controlling replication of public folders?

Exercises

1. How do you force a directory update within a site?

2. How do you force a directory update from another site?

DAY 6

Connecting Exchange to Other Sites

By Anthony Steven

Chapter Objectives

Yesterday, you looked at some of the considerations in defining a site, and you saw how to set up directory and public folder replication between sites. However, both directory replication and public folder replication depend on you establishing a messaging route between your sites. Today you will be covering the following topics:

- Sites and messaging connectivity
- The site connector
- The X.400 connector
- The Dynamic RAS connector

- The Internet Mail Service connector
- Choosing a messaging connector
- Messaging connectors and routing
- How Exchange routes a message

Messaging Connectors

In a single-site environment, the MTA and the Directory Service communicate by connecting directly from server to server, using Remote Procedure Calls (RPCs). Using RPCs as a connection method means that Exchange can transfer information in the most efficient way, that is, in message database encoding format (MDBEF). This means that there is no conversion into a standard message body, and that all the data passes around the site in Exchange's internal format.

In a multisite environment, the site-to-site connections are made using messaging connectors, and all data sent from site-to-site goes as mail messages. All Exchange services must send their messages via the MTA, which then carries out the delivery of those messages.

 Note   The site connector is a bit of an anomaly in that it uses RPCs between sites. The Dynamic RAS connector can also connect using RPCs.

In Day 5, "Working with Multiple Sites", I covered directory replication and public folder replication. However, these features all depend on messaging connectivity, so now I will cover how to install and configure messaging connectivity.

There are four types of messaging connectors:

- Site (or Exchange) connector
- X.400 connector
- Dynamic RAS connector
- Internet Mail Service connector

As you will see, each has its own strengths, weaknesses, and particular areas of application. I'll begin by looking at site connectors.

Site Connector

The site connector is the quickest and easiest way to connect two sites. It is also known as the Exchange connector, because it can only be used to connect two Exchange sites.

Characteristics of a Site Connector

Take a look at some of the features, benefits, and disadvantages of the site connector.

Connection Method and Message Format The site connector uses RPCs to connect the sites, and transfers messages in MDBEF, so message translation is not necessary. Thus, a site connector is generally about 25% faster than an X.400 connector.

Address Space The site connector automatically adds an address space for the site to which it connects. You can then add further address spaces as required. The site connector also automatically adds an X.400 address space for the remote site. These appear on the Routing tab in the Site Addressing object. See later in this chapter for more information on routing.

Restrictions on Site Connectors Site connectors have six major disadvantages:

- You cannot schedule site connectors.
- You cannot restrict message sizes.
- You cannot restrict the users who send messages across a site connector.
- You cannot use the site connector on very low bandwidth links.
- The WAN links must support RPCs.
- Site connectors expect to be able to communicate immediately, so they cannot work across a dial-up or dial-on-demand link.

You could think of the site connector as an extension of the RPC-based intra-site communication method that the Exchange MTAs and directory services use to connect to each other within a site.

When Would I Use the Site Connector?

You would use the site connector under the following circumstances:

- You are linking Exchange site to Exchange site.
- You have a permanent WAN link between your sites
- This link supports RPCs.
- You have a minimum available bandwidth of 56Kbs.
- You do not want to restrict user connections, message sizes or activation times across this link.

6

Personally, I would recommend using the site connector whenever you can. It's easy to set up and generally works the first time, unlike the X.400 connector.

Before You Install

Before you install the site connector, it may be worth carrying out the following check of your site-to-site link.

1. Check that your link supports RPCs. Do this by running the RPINGS.EXE (RPINGS_A.EXE for Alpha) file on one of your Exchange servers in the remote site. On the other site, run RPINGC32.EXE on a Windows NT machine. You will now be able to test RPC connectivity between the two sites.

> **Note**　　The RPC Ping tools are on the Exchange Server CD under \Server\Support\Rpcping.

2. Monitor your effective bandwidth over the link. You need at least 56Kbs available most of the time. Occasional blips in demand aren't too much of a problem, but the bandwidth shouldn't dip too much below 56Kbs.

3. Look at your domain layout. If you have a single domain, you don't have any security issues. If you are using multiple domains, and all your accounts are in a central, trusted domain, you still don't have a problem. If, however, your sites are separate domains, and you don't have a trust relationship, you will need to specify a site services account for the connector to use.

Installing the Site Connector

Installing a site connector is very easy. Start Exchange Administrator, select the File menu and click on New Other. Now choose Site Connector, and you will now see the dialog box shown in Figure 6.1.

FIGURE 6.1

Installing a site connector is very easy.

Once you have entered the name of a server in the target site, select OK. You will now see the dialog box in Figure 6.2.

FIGURE 6.2

The site connector General tab lets you specify a name for your connector, a connection cost, and whether you want to use a messaging bridgehead server.

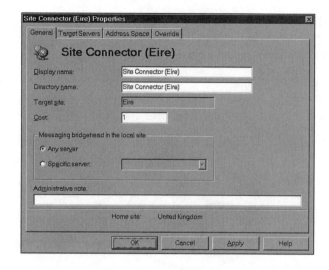

As long as you don't have any inter-site security issues, you can just click OK to have a perfectly functional site connector. That was easy, wasn't it?

Now take a look at the configuration issues.

Configuring the Site Connector

Configuring the site connector isn't very complex, either. Start Exchange Administrator and select your site in the left pane. Click on the site object to expand it and select the Configuration container object. In the right pane, select the Connections object. Double-click on the Connections object and you will now see the site connector. Double-clicking on the site connector will bring you back to the dialog box you saw in Figure 6.2.

General Tab   The General tab is where you can change the display name for this site connector. However, once you have installed the connector, you can't change its directory name.

Cost   You can use costs to control the routes that messages will take between sites. In a complex, multisite environment, you would put higher costs on the slower links. Because Exchange will always route messages over the link with the lowest cost, you can prevent messages from using routes that involve low-bandwidth links.

You can put in a value for the cost of a link from 1 to 100. Costs of zero are not allowed, as this would allow endless message looping over the link. Use a value of 100 if you only want people to use this connector when no other connector is available.

Connectors with equal costs can be used for load balancing. You can also use costs to control the use of different connector types, as I will discuss later.

Messaging Bridgehead Servers By default, site connectors don't use messaging bridgehead servers. In fact, just like with intra-site messaging, any server in one site can connect to any server in the other site over the site connector.

However, you can designate messaging bridgehead servers, and these servers will then be responsible for passing all traffic to the remote site. Figure 6.3 shows the two sorts of configuration.

FIGURE 6.3

With a site connector, you can use messaging bridgehead servers.

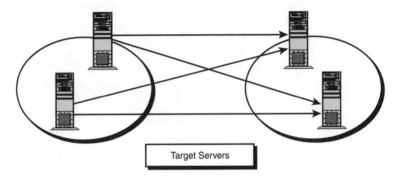

Target Servers

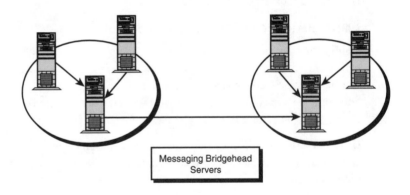

Messaging Bridgehead Servers

Tip

You can get Microsoft Exchange Optimizer to tune a server for use as a dedicated messaging bridgehead server. On the second page of the wizard, click the check boxes for connector/directory replication and then uncheck the boxes for public and private information store and POP3 only. Now complete the rest of the Performance Optimizer wizard.

You might use messaging bridgehead servers in larger sites, where you could designate certain functions to particular servers. When specifying messaging bridgehead servers, you will need to allow for the extra loading imposed by the messaging bridgehead role.

Target Servers   You have already looked at how you can use messaging bridgehead servers on the site connector. However, the normal method of deploying a site connector is to specify target servers. You can then apply values to each target server, allowing you to control the probability of a connection to a specific server. Figure 6.4 shows this process in action.

FIGURE 6.4

Applying values to tar-get servers lets you control the likelihood of a connection from another site.

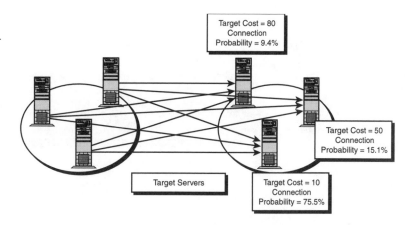

Let's say that in a remote site, you have certain servers that have specific functions and you don't want to load them any further. You would give these servers high target values, which would mean that the site connector would tend to connect to the other servers first.

Note

Target servers use a "weighted average" to determine which server to connect to. Suppose you have two servers—Server A with a target value of 20, and Server B with a target value of 80. The probability that a server in the other site will connect to Server A is 80%, and to Server B is 20%.

Target values can range from zero to 100. A value of zero means always use this server, unless it isn't available. A value of 100 means only use this server if no other ones are available.

Note   Giving a server a target value of zero is not the same as making it a messaging bridgehead server. Messaging bridgeheads apply to the local site; target values are for the remote site.

Address Space   The Address Space tab indicates which types of messages will travel over this connector. You automatically get an address space for an X.400 route to the remote site, as shown in Figure 6.5. You also get an "X.500" address space, which appears in the Routing tab on the Site Addressing object. The address space will be in this form:

```
/O=UNIVERSAL EXPORTS/OU=UNITED KINGDOM
```

FIGURE 6.5

The Address Space tab shows the X.400 address for the remote site.

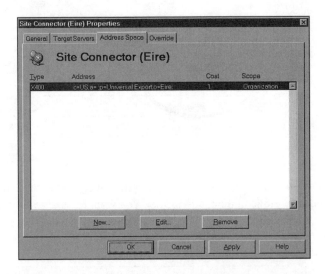

X.500 AND THE SITE CONNECTOR

When you install a site connector, the connector connects to the remote site and interrogates it for a site address. The remote site responds with its directory address, in Exchange's directory services format, which is based on the X.500 recommendations. An X.500-ish routing entry or "address" then appears in your site's routing table, as a route of type EX (such as Exchange).

When you send a message to a recipient in the remote site, Exchange compares the recipient's mailbox address with the entries on the routing table. As it finds a match using the type EX entry, the message goes to the remote site. Thus Exchange uses the X.500 Distinguished Name (DN) to route a message to its destination.

> This is a little strange because X.500 is a definition for a directory service, not a mail protocol. For more information on X.500 and X.400, see Day 11, "Understanding the Internet".

You can add other address spaces to this connector. However, most of the time you won't have to because Exchange will propagate routing information about connectors in other sites via directory replication. For more information on routing and address spaces, see the latter part of this chapter.

Override   The Override tab lets you enter a valid NT user account for the remote domain. You only need to do this if your sites are in separate Windows NT domains and you don't have trusts configured between the domains. Again, good domain planning means that you shouldn't have to specify an account here.

If you need to specify an account, use the Exchange service account in the remote site. Figure 6.6 shows the settings for this tab.

FIGURE 6.6

You only need to use the Override tab if your two sites run in different security contexts.

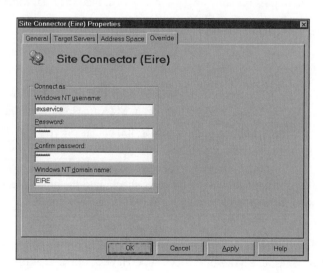

Once you have installed and configured a Site connector, you shouldn't have to configure it any further. My advice is this: Use a site connector whenever possible.

6

X.400 Connector

But what do you do if you can't use a site connector? Or the system you are connecting to isn't an Exchange site? Or if you just think that the site connector sounds a bit too wimpy for someone with the "I TAMED SENDMAIL" T-shirt? In that case, maybe you should look at the X.400 connector.

When Would I Use an X.400 Connector?

This is the connector to use if you have any of the following restrictions:

- You have permanent links that do not support RPCs.
- You are using RRAS and do not want to use the Dynamic RAS connector.
- You need to restrict the users who can send messages over this link.
- You want to place restrictions on the times that the connector is in use.
- You want to restrict the size of messages sent over this link.
- You need to connect to non-Exchange X.400 systems.

If your system falls into any of these categories, then read on, MacDuff!

Before You Install the X.400 Connector

Before you can install an X.400 connector to another site, you must be aware of the following factors:

1. With the X.400 connector, you need to install an MTA Transport Stack first. See the considerations when installing an MTA transport stack later in this chapter.

2. You can't install both sides of an X.400 connector yourself. Hence, you will need someone at the remote site to configure the other end for you. Unless, that is, you can control the other server using Exchange Administrator, which means that you have to be able to make an RPC connection to the other site. (Just remember that one of the reasons for choosing X.400 is because you can't make an RPC connection to the other site.)

Once you have considered these options, you *still* can't install the X.400 connector yet. You have to install a Transport Stack first. Have a look at that process now.

The MTA Transport Stack

X.400 is a standard for message handling systems operating in heterogeneous environments. It is not a means for providing network communication. Hence, to get an X.400 connector to work, you require an MTA Transport Stack.

An MTA Transport Stack is a transport mechanism over which your X.400 connector can work. In Exchange Server, this transport mechanism can run over four types of networking protocols:

- X.25
- TP4
- TCP/IP
- RAS

Tip My bet is that you will want the TCP/IP Transport Stack. Read on to learn why.

X.25 An X.25 Transport Stack uses an X.25 port adapter to route messages across the global X.25 network. If you have the rather obscure and specialized X.25, you will probably know far more about it than I do.

If you are running X.25, you need to install this transport stack before you can install the X.400 connector. The X.25 Transport Stack supports PSTN (POTS) telephone lines (dial-up X.25), X.25 leased lines, the Eicon X.25 terminal adapter, or X.25 via Winsock.

TP4 TP4 is a Connectionless Networking Protocol (CLNP) interface enabling servers using TP4 to communicate over a LAN. It provides an OSI interface in that the TP4 connector allows you to define communication endpoints at different layers on the OSI networking model. TP4 can only communicate with another server running TP4.

Before you can use TP4, you must install it from the NT Server CD. Look in \DRVLIB\PROTOCOL\TP4SETUP. You need to install it as a networking protocol. To do this, select Start, click on Settings and then open Control Panel. Double-click on the Network icon and then click on the Protocols tab. Select Add and then click Have Disk. Go to the \DRVLIB\PROTOCOL\TP4SETUP folder and select OK. The TP4 protocol will now appear as an option. Select OK to install TP4. You will have to reboot your server once you have done this.

The server running the transport stack determines the TP4 network address information. You configure TP4's network service access point (NSAP) address using Windows NT Control Panel.

6

TCP/IP If this is the only acronym that you recognized in the list above, then it's probably the one for you. TCP/IP is the most popular networking protocol, and supports your X.400 connector admirably. However, you have to be running TCP/IP, but I guess you probably are anyway.

RAS This transport stack is not for use with X.400. I will be dealing with the RAS MTA Transport Stack in the next section.

Now you've selected your MTA transport, you can go on to installing the MTA Transport Stack.

Installing the MTA Transport Stack

Installing the MTA transport stack is very easy. Follow along with the steps I describe.

1. In Exchange Administrator, select the File menu and then choose New Other. From the list that appears, choose MTA Transport Stack. You will then see a choice of transport stacks, as shown in Figure 6.7.

FIGURE 6.7

Here you can choose your MTA Transport Stack

2. Select the transport stack that you want to use and click OK. You will now see the properties sheet shown in Figure 6.8.

3. If you have other applications that are using the MTA Transport Stack, you might need to define OSI addressing information. As far as Exchange goes, all you need to do is select OK.

   That's it. You have now installed your MTA Transport Stack. If you need to configure it any further, you can do so through Exchange Administrator. The MTA Transport Stack will show up as an object at the server level, as shown in Figure 6.9.

FIGURE 6.8

Configuring the TCP/IP MTA Transport Stack.

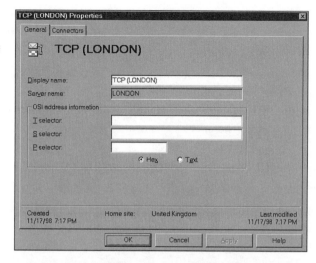

FIGURE 6.9

The MTA Transport Stack is the TCP (LONDON) object in the right pane at the server level.

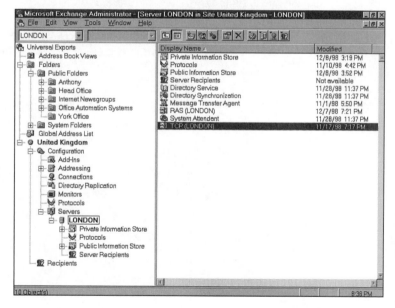

Now that you've installed your MTA Transport Stack, you can install your X.400 connector. Read on to learn how.

Installing the X.400 Connector

As I mentioned before, with the X.400 connector, you install each site separately. I will only cover the basic installation here, and in the next section, I will look at any further configuration that you may want to do.

1. In Exchange Administrator, select the File menu and then choose New Other. From the list that appears, click on X.400 connector. A prompt will suggest that you change to the Connections container. Select Yes.

2. You will then see a list, showing your installed MTA Transport Stacks. Select the transport stack that you installed previously.

3. You now see the properties of the new X.400 connector. Enter a Display name and Directory name. The directory name must be unique.

4. Enter a remote MTA name. With Exchange-to-Exchange site links, this will be the name of the Exchange server in the remote site.

5. Your transport stack will already appear in the drop-down list.

6. If you are connecting Exchange sites, activate the check box that says Remote Clients Support MAPI.

7. Add an administrative note if you require one. Your dialog box should now look like the one in Figure 6.10.

FIGURE 6.10

The General tab of the X.400 connector is where you specify the remote MTA that you want to talk to.

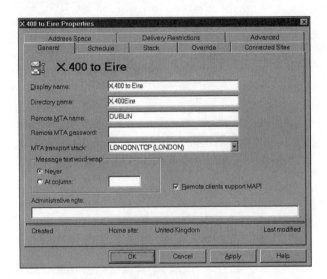

8. Now you need to select the Stack tab. Ignore the OSI address information at the bottom—the part you want is the Address at the top. Here you need to put in either a host name or an IP address. If you use a host name, make sure you can ping that machine by host name; that is, PING HOSTNAME produces a response.

Tip | I usually put an IP address in here, which circumvents any problems of name resolution. However, be aware that communications will fail if the destination server changes its IP address.

9. If you are linking Exchange sites using this X.400 connector, go to the Connected Sites tab and click on the New button. You can now add a site and organization name for the connected site. This adds a routing entry of type EX to the routing table of this site (see "Multiple Sites, Multiple Connectors, and Routing" later in this chapter for more information).

Note | Normally you would be using this connector to link two sites in the same organization. However, you could use it to link two organizations. You wouldn't then be able to link them with a directory replication connector, but you could use it to route messages between sites.

10. Once you have configured the Stack and Connected Sites tabs, click OK. A prompt will remind you that you also need to configure a working X.400 connector in the other site.

    That's it. Once you add an X.400 connector to the other site, you should have a working X.400 link.

What you've done now is to install an X.400 connector to connect two Exchange sites. Now you will look at other configurations, including some of the settings that you might need to make if you are connecting Exchange to another X.400 system.

Configuring the X.400 Connector

The X.400 connector is the most generic connector, and can link Exchange to other X.400 systems. Hence, many configuration options are not required when you are installing the X.400 connector to link two Exchange sites. However, if you are linking Exchange to a foreign X.400 system, you will need these options.

To configure the X.400 connector, Start Exchange Administrator and select your site in the left pane. Click on the site object to expand it and then select the Configuration container object. In the right-hand pane, select the Connections object. Double-click on the Connections object and you will see the new X.400 connector that you installed earlier. Double-click on this object and you will see the General tab that you saw earlier.

6

General Tab   Normally, you will not need to change any settings on this tab. The only possible change that you might want to make is to configure a password for the remote MTA. If you do this between Exchange systems, you need to add a Local MTA password on the Override tab on the MTA in the remote site.

Note   This password appears in clear text.

If you want to, you can also change the display name for this connector. However, you cannot change the directory name, as this is set when you install the connector. To change the directory name, you would have to delete and reinstall the X.400 connector in this site.

Schedule Tab   You have four options for scheduling the X.400 connector.

- Always
- Selected Times
- Remote Initiated
- Never

Use Always if you have permanent connectivity and bandwidth isn't a problem, that is, you can usually guarantee on average about 56Kbps available bandwidth. You can use the X.400 in a lower bandwidth environment, but you may have to adjust some of the connection settings on the Override tab.

Use Selected Times if bandwidth is an issue; for example, if you don't want the messaging connector to be used at certain times of the day, like when everyone logs in at 8 am (09:00 in the UK).

Use remote initiated if you don't want this site to initiate the connection but just to respond when the other site connects. This gives you greater control when you are using scheduled connections because one site is controlling all the connections.

Stack Tab   You should only need to change the Stack tab if the IP address or host name of the remote X.400 system changes.

Override Tab   Use this tab to specify a password or a shorter local MTA name if a remote system does not support longer MTA names. See the section below on connecting to foreign X.400 systems for more information about local MTA names.

Note To see your MTA's current name, you need to go to the server-level MTA object. Double-click on the MTA object underneath your server's name and select the General tab. Here you can enter a local MTA name and password that other MTAs can now use to connect to the MTA on your Exchange server.

RTS Values The RTS (Reliable Transfer Service) values let you specify settings that Exchange uses when it is trying to send messages to another site. RTS ensures that the remote site receives the messages correctly. RTS also acts as a flow control method, requiring periodic acknowledgements of message transfer.

The settings that you specify here override those on the Messaging Defaults tab of the Site level MTA Site Configuration object.

Tip Normally, the defaults work fine. You only need to change these settings if you are running an X.400 connector over a noisy or unreliable link.

RELIABLE TRANSFER SERVICE

The Reliable Transfer Service ensures that messages between MTAs reach their destination. It does this by applying checkpoints and ensuring that it receives acknowledgement of packet delivery.

You could think of RTS as being a bit like TCP sliding windows. Taking the default settings, every 30K of message transfer, the system will send out a checkpoint. The default window size is five blocks. Thus, 150K (5×30K) of data is sent without the sending site requiring an acknowledgement.

The next block of data will not leave until the acknowledgement message from the first block returns. The sending site will wait for up to 60 seconds before giving up and sending all the data again.

The default settings on the X.400 connector are the same as those on the Site level MTA object.

6

Association Parameters Association parameters deal with the associations (a bit like TCP sessions) links made over an X.400 Connector. Normally you do not have to change these values.

Connection Retry Values   These settings go hand-in-hand with the RTS settings. RTS governs what happens when MTAs connect; Connection Retry Values govern what happens when the connection fails or errors occur. The default settings are that the connector will attempt to send a message 144 times before returning it as undeliverable. Once a connection to a remote site is open, the system will attempt two transfers of a message before reporting an error. Between each transfer attempt, the connector will wait 120 seconds. After an error, the connector will wait 600 seconds before trying again.

Normally, you do not have to change these settings.

Transfer Timeouts   Transfer timeouts allow you to configure how long it should take urgent, normal, and non-urgent messages (that is, high, normal, or low priority mail) to transfer to a remote site. Note that these settings allow for the size of the message. Hence a 1K urgent message must have reached the remote site within 1000 seconds (16 minutes) or it will return to the sender as non-deliverable. A 60K message will return as non-deliverable after 16 hours. Hence, the acceptable wait is dependent on both the message priority and the message size.

Note

> Reducing transfer timeouts will not deliver your messages any quicker. It will just mean that should there be a problem with delivery, the messages will return to their sender quicker.

You would only need to change these values if your connector is working across a very low bandwidth link.

Connected Sites Tab   The Connected Sites tab lets you add further Exchange sites and organizations. You can also change the cost of the routes, as I will discuss in the Routing section later in the chapter.

Address Space Tab   The X.400 connector automatically adds an X.400 address space to Exchange. Adding an Exchange site in the Connected Sites tab automatically supplies an Exchange "X.500" address space.

Note

> Between Exchange sites, directory replication will normally take care of the replication of address spaces.

Delivery Restrictions Tab   The Delivery Restriction tab lets you specify which users and groups of users (distribution lists) can send messages over this connector. This is very useful where you have complex messaging systems with different site links. You could configure your X.400 connector so that only people with certain managerial or directorial functions could use the X.400 link. There is an example of this in Figure 6.11.

FIGURE 6.11

Only users in the Management distribution list can use the X.400 connector, except for Roger, who is soon going to be looking for another job.

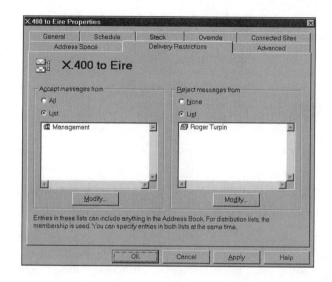

As with previous restriction tabs, the list on the left is much more restrictive than the list on the right. Adding a user to the left-hand list would mean that *only* that user *could* send messages across the link. Adding a user to the right-hand list means that *only* that user *cannot* send messages over the link. Figure 6.11 shows both of these settings configured.

Advanced Tab   Most of the settings on the Advanced tab are for interoperation with Non-Exchange systems, or where you are using X.400 as a backbone between two Exchange sites. For a normal Exchange-to-Exchange site link, you will not need to change any settings on this screen.

The settings that you need to specify here will depend on the foreign X.400 system. See the next section for information on configuring these settings.

6

Note   You can control message sizes over the X.400 connector using the setting at the bottom of the Advanced tab.

That's all you really need to configure for an Exchange-to-Exchange X.400 connector. However, if you need to connect to a non-Exchange system, you will have to do a lot more work! In the next section, you'll tackle those tasks.

Connecting to Non-Exchange X.400 Systems

I am now going to review the same settings that you just looked at in the previous section. This time, however, I will highlight the areas that will be of importance when you are connecting to non-Exchange X.400 mail systems.

General Tab   The three items that you may need to change are

- The Remote MTA name and password
- Message text word wrap
- Remote clients support MAPI

The Remote MTA name and password you should get from the person administering the foreign X.400 system.

The requirement for message text word wrap varies from system to system. Exchange doesn't require it.

Remote clients support MAPI only if you are connecting Exchange sites. However, that can also include when you are using X.400 as a backbone between Exchange sites. If the remote clients support MAPI, messages will be sent in RTF, and attachments are part of the message. If not, messages will be in ASCII text and attachments are separate X.400 messages.

Stack Tab   You may need to change settings for the incoming or outgoing OSI information. These settings must match the settings on the remote system for communication to work.

Override Tab   Here you can specify a shortened MTA name. Some foreign MTAs cannot cope with long MTA names or certain characters, so this tab lets you enter a different MTA name from that entered in the server level MTA object.

You may also want to change the RTS, Connection Retry values, Association parameters and transfer timeouts depending on the reliability of the foreign X.400 system.

Connected Sites   The Connected Sites tab would only be of interest if you are using an X.400 messaging backbone to connect two Exchange sites, as shown in Figure 6.12. This is similar to the way in which you can use the Internet to connect two Exchange sites over SMTP.

FIGURE 6.12

You can use X.400 as a backbone to link two Exchange sites.

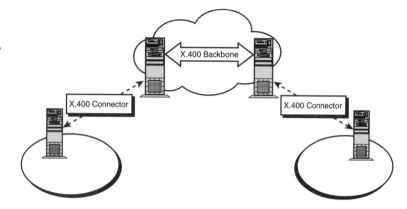

If you are just linking Exchange to a foreign X.400 system, you do not need an entry in the Connected Sites tab.

Address Space   If you want to add any further address spaces to this connector, you can do it here. For example, if you are connecting to a foreign X.400 system, and the foreign system has a connection to the Internet, you could route all Exchange's Internet mail through this connector. To do so, you would add an SMTP address space to this connector. Click New and select SMTP as the address type. To route all SMTP mail through this connector, put * in the email domain. Alternatively, you could add just the email domain for the remote X.400 system.

Once you have added the new address space, your screen will look like the one in Figure 6.13.

FIGURE 6.13

Here I have added an SMTP address space to the X.400 connector.

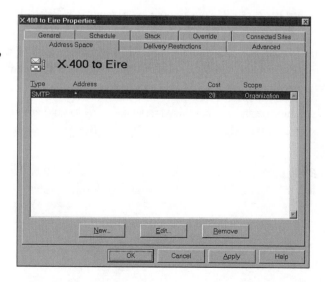

You could add other address spaces—for example, other X.400 systems to which this remote site connects.

Advanced Tab   The bulk of the settings that affect interoperability between Exchange and foreign X.400 systems are on the Advanced tab, as shown in Figure 6.14.

FIGURE 6.14

The Advanced tab settings are mostly concerned with inter-operability with non-Exchange X.400 mail systems.

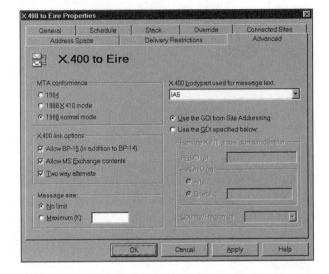

MTA Conformance   The setting you choose here will depend on the X.400 conformance level of your foreign system. Exchange conforms to the 1984 and 1988 standards, but does not fully conform to the 1992 X.400 recommendations.

X.400 Link Options   If your remote system supports BP-15 formatted file attachments, check this box.

If you are using X.400 as a backbone between Exchange servers, check the box for Allow MS Exchange Contents. If you are connecting Exchange to a foreign system, you want to uncheck this box.

Two Way Alternate means that the MTAs take turns to send and receive, a bit like using CB radio, except that MTA's don't say "Breaker, Breaker, one-niner" or drive trailer trucks.

X.400 Bodypart   There are several options for the X.400 bodypart used for message text. Select the choice that works best with your foreign system.

GDI   This setting lets you configure a different Global Domain Identifier (GDI) from the one in your site addressing. You might need this if you are routing over X.400 to your foreign X.400 system, with another X.400 mail system as the backbone. Add the new GDI information in the specified boxes.

Phew! Had enough of X.400 yet? Good, because compared to Dynamic RAS, X.400's a cinch… (Only kidding!)

RAS Connector

The Dynamic RAS connector is one of the most flexible connectors available. You can use this in situations where you cannot use the site or X.400 connectors. In fact, you could use the Dynamic RAS in all dial-up scenarios, using ISDN or PSTN (POTS) telephone lines.

Note

> Due to the increased influence of the Internet, the Internet Mail Service Connector is encroaching on the areas traditionally covered by the Dynamic RAS connector. However, there are still areas where you may want to use a DRAS link. Read on and I'll cover these now.

When Would I Use a Dynamic RAS Connector?

You would use a dynamic RAS connector when the following criteria apply:

- You do not have or do not want a permanent connection between your sites.
- You are using PSTN (POTS) telephone lines, ISDN, or dial-up X.25.
- Your remote sites do not have Internet access.
- A telephone call from RAS client to RAS server is only a local telephone call.

ROUTING AND REMOTE ACCESS SERVER

Microsoft's Routing and Remote Access Server (RRAS) is an add-on to Windows NT server that enables you to set up dial-on-demand routing using NT Server. Once you have installed RRAS, you can use the Internet Mail Service or the X.400 connector to link Exchange sites.

You can download RRAS from Microsoft's Web Site. For further information see:

```
http://www.microsoft.com/ntserver/nts/downloads/winfeatures
➡/RouteRASNT.asp
```

Don't forget to apply Service Pack 4 after you've installed RRAS!

6

Before You Install a Dynamic RAS Connector

Before you can install a Dynamic RAS connector, you need to set up NT's Remote Access Service. There is no point in attempting to configure a Dynamic RAS connector if the RAS dial-up entries don't work. What you are trying to achieve, therefore, is a link from a RAS client that dials up and authenticates automatically to a RAS server. Until you have done this, don't bother installing the DRAS connector.

Before this, there are one or two other points that you need to consider.

1. Decide how you are going to set up your sites. Are you going to have spokes radiating from a central hub, multiple hubs, or a more peer-to-peer arrangement, where any site can dial any other? Figure 6.15 shows these options.

FIGURE 6.15

You must decide on your dial-up layout first.

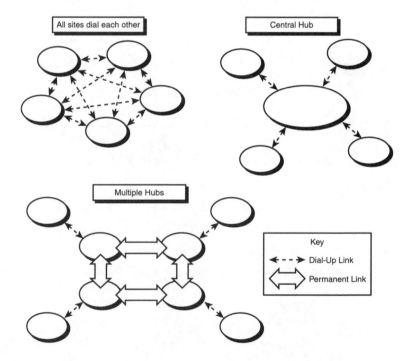

2. What RAS connection method are you going to use? PSTN (POTS), ISDN or X.25?
3. Will one site always dial the other or will two-way initiation be possible?

4. Create an account that will be used to dial-in to the RAS server. This account must have dial-in permission (set through User Manager for Domains) and must have Service Account Admin permission at Organization, Site and Server level. This account should also have a high security password: a fourteen-character, mixed-case, alphanumeric password. See Day 19, "Making Exchange Secure," for more information on setting permissions in Exchange Administrator.

For the purposes of this exercise, I have assumed that you have a two-way setup but you can have one side or the other responsible for initiating communications. I am also assuming that you are using TCP/IP.

Installing RAS

Once you have decided on how you are going to deploy DRAS, you need to install a RAS client and a RAS server. See Day 7, "Configuring the Exchange Client," for more information.

You will need to carry out the following tasks:

1. Install RAS at both sites.

2. On the dialog box resulting from clicking the RAS Configure button, select Dial Out and Receive Calls.

3. On the dialog box resulting from clicking the Network button, select TCP/IP only as the dial-out and server protocol.

4. In the server settings, click the Configure button for TCP/IP. Assign a set of IP addresses for the clients to use. These IP addresses should be from the same subnet as the static IP addresses used for the Exchange servers. However many modems you have set up for RAS, always define one extra IP address. This is because NT uses one IP address for the client and one IP address for the server.

Tip   You can assign static IP addresses to the clients, and let the clients use a static IP address when they dial into the server.

6

5. Make sure that the Exchange servers are using a static IP address for their network cards and select the option to use DNS Enabled for Windows Name Resolution. This will mean that your servers can use a HOSTS file to resolve computer names.

6. On each server, create or edit the existing HOSTS file to include the fixed IP addresses of any other Exchange servers that will connect using the Dynamic RAS connector. You should add lines like:

```
131.107.2.244          EXCHSERVER10
```

where EXCHSERVER10 is a server at a remote site, and 131.107.2.244 is the fixed IP address of its network card. Each server will require the IP addresses of the servers it connects to. So if you are using a hub configuration, each HOSTS file will only have one entry—that of the remote site's Exchange server.

You will find the HOSTS file in

`system32\drivers\etc.`

in your Windows NT directory.

7. Create a RAS phone book entry at each site for the phone number of the other site. Make sure that this phone book entry only uses TCP/IP.

8. If you have a RAS address pool, set up the phone book entry to use a supplied address. If you have gone for the static option, enter a static address for the client connection.

9. Make sure that the phone book entry does not use the remote network as the default gateway.

10. Do *not* use the current user account and password for authentication. You will use the RAS dial-in account that you created previously.

11. Finally, *test* all your dial-up connections. They should all dial in both directions and authenticate automatically (unless you have configured one-way access only).

12. Done all of those? Now it's *almost* time to install the Dynamic RAS connector.

Installing the RAS Transport Stack

Wait for it, you horrible little men! (As they say at the Royal Military Academy, Sandhurst.) You still can't install the DRAS connector because you haven't installed the RAS transport stack yet. So, as you were!

Installing the RAS Transport stack is just like the X.400 version.

1. As with the X.400 Transport Stack, start Exchange Administrator, select the File menu, click New Other, and choose MTA Transport Stack.

2. This time, choose RAS Transport Stack. You will see the properties sheet in Figure 6.16.

3. If you are using callback with this RAS connector, add an MTA callback number. The RAS server will then use this number to call back the site that just dialed in.

4. The RAS Transport Stack will appear in the server level container, that is, the same place as the X.400 Transport Stack.

5. You're now ready to install the Dynamic RAS connector, and you may fire when ready.

FIGURE 6.16

All you need to configure with a RAS transport stack is the MTA Callback number (if applicable) and a display name.

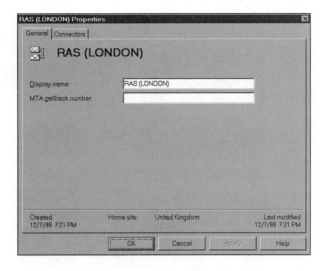

Installing the Dynamic RAS Connector

After all this puffing and blowing to get where you are now, the actual installation of the DRAS connector is very easy. Again, it's rather like the X.400 connector.

1. Start Exchange Administrator, select the File menu and choose New Other. From the list, click on Dynamic RAS Connector.

2. A prompt will ask you if you want to switch to the Connections container. Select Yes.

3. Enter a display name (which you can subsequently change) and a directory name (which you can't).

4. Choose the Phone Book Entry for this link. Select the one you tested earlier.

5. Add a message size limit if you want to set one.

6. Click on the RAS Override tab. Here you need to enter the details of the account that you allocated RAS dial-in permission for earlier. Add this username and password, and the NT domain name. Figure 6.17 shows you the options that you need to enter.

7. If you are using callback, you can specify the MTA callback number (again) and any overriding phone number that should be used instead of the number in the phone book.

8. On the Connected Sites tab, add the Organization and site names of any connected Exchange sites.

6

FIGURE 6.17

The RAS Override tab is where you enter the details on the RAS dial-in account. This account has Service Account Administrator permission in the remote site.

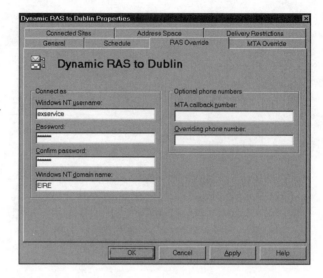

9. On the Address Space tab, add any X.400, MS Mail, or SMTP address spaces that you want routed over this connector.

10. Click OK and a message will tell you that you need to configure a connector on the other side of the link. Well, you knew that, didn't you?

That's all you need to configure for a basic Dynamic RAS connector. Now I will take you through any configuration changes that you might want to make.

Configuring the Dynamic RAS Connector

Most of the DRAS configuration options are identical to the X.400, except that you don't have to muck about with all the X.400 compatibility stuff. Where these settings are the same as the X.400 connector, I will refer back to the previous section.

General Tab   As you saw on the installation phase, this tab lets you change the phone book entry, display name, MTA transport stack, and message size limit.

Schedule Tab   The DRAS Schedule tab is exactly like the X.400 version. The Remote Initiated option is for when you have a remote site that always dials into this site.

Caution   If you use the Always option, expect some heavy phone bills!

RAS Override Tab Use this if you need to change any security settings. Password security is very important with the RAS dial-in account, as this account has a high level of network privileges.

MTA Override Tab Use this tab to override any of the MTA default settings. The values are exactly the same as I discussed earlier in the section on X.400.

Connected Sites Tab Through this tab, you can add any further Exchange sites that connect via this link. However, remember that Directory Replication will propagate routing and addressing information within the same organization. This tab is very like the Connected Sites tab in the Site connector.

Address Space Any additional Address spaces can go in here. The criteria are the same as the criteria I discussed on the Address space tab on the X.400 connector.

Delivery Restrictions This tab is identical to the equivalent tab in the X.400 connector.

That's it for the Dynamic RAS connector.

After all that, is it really worth it? With the introduction of the Internet Mail Service Connector and the growth in popularity of the Internet, you may well find yourself looking at using the Internet Mail Service connector rather than DRAS. After all, most sites will have Internet access, so why go to all the bother of setting up a Dynamic RAS connector? You could even use the X.400 connector with dial-on-demand routing over RRAS as an alternative to DRS.

So if you can't use the Site connector, you don't have a permanent link, and the Dynamic RAS connector sounds like too much hard work, what can you do? Thankfully, the Internet Mail Service connector could be the one for you.

Internet Mail Service Connector

The beauty of installing the Internet Mail Service connector is that you've already done all the hard work by configuring an Internet Mail Service. Actually adding the connector over the top is trivial.

When Would I Use the Internet Mail Service Connector?

You would use the Internet Mail Service Connector when any of the following criteria are in place:

- Your local and remote sites do not have a permanent connection that supports RPCs.

6

- You have a permanent or dial-in connection and you don't want to use the X.400 connector or Dynamic RAS.
- Your local and remote sites both connect to the Internet, either permanently or via dial-up.
- You are trying to connect Exchange sites around the world.

Installing the Internet Mail Service Connector

The main part of installing the Internet Mail Service Connector is the installation of the Internet Mail Service itself. For details on how to install the IMS, see Day 12, "Exchange on the Internet."

Once you have installed your Internet Mail Service and got that working, all you need to do is the following:

1. Start Exchange Administrator and select your site in the left pane. Click on the site object to expand it and select the Configuration container object. In the right pane, select the Connections object. Double-click on the Connections object and you will now see the Internet Mail Service object. Double-click on the IMS object and now click on the Connected Sites tab.

2. Click on the New button. A small dialog box will appear like the one in Figure 6.18.

FIGURE 6.18

Adding a connected site is all you need to do to make the Internet Mail Service into a connector.

3. Add the Organization and site name of the site you are trying to connect to in the General tab.

4. Click on the Routing tab and add the SMTP address of the remote site. This will come from the Site Addressing tab of the Site Addressing object in the remote site. It will be in the form @site.organization.com.

5. Click OK to add that new address as a connected site.

6. Once you click OK on the IMS properties, a message will prompt you to stop and restart the Internet Mail Service.

That's how simple it is!

You can now add directory replication on top of the Internet Mail Service and link your sites across the world. All the directory replication messages travel across the SMTP link, as will any folder replication messages.

Security and the Internet Mail Service Connector

I cover configuring the IMS in Day 12. However, I would like to discuss a few security issues that you might like to consider when you configure an Internet Mail Service connector.

These are particularly applicable if you are not sending email to the Internet but both locations have a direct connection.

1. On the Connections tab, click the Specify by Host button and click the Add button. Enter the IP address and subnet mask of the Exchange server in the remote site, and specify that this host must use encryption and authentication.

2. Under message delivery, specify the IP or host name of the remote Exchange server.

3. On the Address Space tab, remove any address space and enter a new address space of type SMTP, with the domain name of the other site as the address. This will stop this IMS from routing general Internet Mail.

4. On the Security Tab, click Add and then supply the address of the remote site. Select the option for Windows NT Challenge/Response, and then add your Exchange Site Service account as the validating NT account.

5. Now, follow the preceding steps for the other site.

This will mean that the Internet becomes like a virtual private network, and Exchange will encrypt all your email, directory, and public folder replication messages while they are in transit across the Internet. In addition, the Exchange servers will only accept the correct connection type (encrypted and authenticated) from each other.

6

 Note You can integrate this sort of security and still have a connection to the Internet—one way to do this is to have more than one IMS. Each IMS would have to be on a separate server.

Choosing the Right Connector

Now that you've looked at all the connectors, I hope you have an idea as to which one is right for you.

Site Connector

Pros: Quickest, easiest, and automatically recognizes an Exchange site.

Cons: 56K minimum bandwidth, link must support RPCs, can't restrict times, users, or message sizes.

X.400 Connector

Pros: Most generic, can link foreign systems, does not require RPCs, can restrict times, users, and message sizes.

Cons: Requires MTA transport stack, limited protocol support, can be a pain to set up.

Dynamic RAS Connector

Pros: Support for dial-up connections, can restrict times, users, and message sizes.

Cons: Very complex to set up. You have to configure RAS and an MTA transport stack.

Internet Mail Service Connector

Pros: Very easy to set up if you have an IMS already installed. Can link Exchange sites across the world.

Cons: An IMS is not always straightforward to install and you must have an Internet connection at both ends.

Personally, my choices are

- Site connector for LAN/permanent WAN situations
- The Internet Mail Service connector for dial-up and non-RPC WAN solutions.

Now that you've installed all these connectors, how is Exchange going to make sense of them? After all, you could have multiple connectors linking two sites.

Multiple Sites, Multiple Connectors, and Routing

Routing is the process by which Exchange sends a message to its correct destination. It does this by comparing the message's destination address with the information in Exchange's routing tables.

On Day 2, "Planning your Exchange Implementation," you looked at the role of routing in the planning process. Now I want to take a more practical approach to implementing routing and controlling the ways in which Exchange sends messages.

Routing Fundamentals

Routing is an essential component of a multisite messaging system. Without routing, Exchange would not know where to send messages. Thus to move to a true scalable messaging system, there must be a reliable and robust system for routing messages.

Routing Within a Site

In a single site, routing is not an issue, even with multiple servers. This is because every Exchange server can make a direct connection to any other server with the site. As the connections are direct, no routing has to take place. Moreover, as the Directory replicates throughout the site, each server knows instantly about all the other servers, and can make an instant connection to a specific server. Hence routing is not necessary in a single-site environment.

Routing only becomes important when you have multiple sites. Once you install a connector, you can let Exchange know the address of the site at the other end. Once Exchange knows this information, it can match a message's address with the address space for a particular connector. Exchange can then send messages for that site along that connector, as the message address matches the routing address.

Routing and Address Spaces

A connector's address space is where you can specify the routing information for that particular connector. All the connectors that you have looked at in this chapter share an Address Space tab. This tab is where you can define address spaces for the relevant connector.

Distinguished Names and Originator/Recipient Addressing

Exchange generally works on three main types of addressing. One is Distinguished Name (DN) and is X.500-based. The second is Originator/Recipient, based on X.400.

6

The third type is a Domain Defined Attribute (DDA), which includes SMTP, MS Mail, and "other" (such as PROFS, SNADS, cc:Mail) addressing.

Default Address Spaces   Thus, you will normally see four main types of address space in Exchange, and a wild card "other" type. The "other" address type is much less common. The following lists the five types:

- EX or Exchange address. This indicates a remote Exchange site.
- X.400 address for routing to X.400 compatible systems.
- MS Mail address for routing to MS Mail postoffices.
- SMTP for routing to the Internet and SMTP servers.
- Other—for routing to cc:Mail, Lotus Notes, SNADS, and other mail types.

These address spaces are discussed in greater detail in the later section on the GWART.

Exchange uses these address space types in different ways with the various types of connectors.

The Site (or Exchange) connector automatically defines a DN address for the site to which it connects. Because a Site connector can only connect Exchange sites, the sites can interrogate each other and find out the site address. This then appears in the routing table as a message route of type EX, with an address in DN or "X.500" form.

Note   I say "X.500" form because Exchange is not fully X.500-compliant. In particular, Exchange does not support the country attribute defined in X.500. Compare this with Exchange's support for a country attribute in X.400.

Thus when you install a Site connector, you get a routing address of type EX in the form:

```
/O=UNIVERSAL EXPORTS/OU=EIRE
```

This address tells Exchange that any messages that match the Organization Name of Universal Exports and a site name of Eire should go to that site connector.

The Site connector also automatically installs an X.400 address space. Therefore, in addition to the EX entry, you also get an address of the form:

```
c=US;a= ;p=UNIVERSAL EXPORT;o=EIRE;
```

This is an X.400 O/R address, and can be used to route X.400 mail to this connector.

Hence, by installing this Site connector, you get two entries in the routing table or GWART.

With an X.400 connector, by default you only get the X.400 O/R address. However, if you specify a connected site on the Connected Sites tab on the X.400 connector, you also get an EX type address entry, giving the DN of the remote site in "X.500" form.

With the Dynamic RAS connector, you must specify either a Connected site, hence producing an "X.500" Distinguished Name address or you must specify an address space. This address space could be one or more of the MS Mail, SMTP, X.400, or other address types.

The Internet Mail Service connector installs a default SMTP address space for all SMTP addresses (*). However, the IMS can support the other address space types as well.

Thus you can add a connector of whatever type you like, define an address space of any type, and messages will route along that connector.

Routing and Multiple Messaging Paths

In the situation where you have only two sites and one connector, the routing is very easy. However, after you have installed multiple connectors, your messages could take more than one route to get to their destination.

Exchange lets you control routing by assigning costs. You can then specify that particular routes are to be favored over other routes because they are cheaper or do not involve dial-up charges.

Costs

Costs are arbitrary values that apply to any form of Exchange connector, and range from 1 to 100. Costs are cumulative, so each connector increases the cost value of a particular route.

Note   Routing costs are never zero, as this would lead to message looping. A value of 100 indicates "only use this route if no other route is available".

6

Exchange will always send a message via the lowest cost route. If that route is unavailable, Exchange selects the next lowest cost route, and so on. If two routes have the same cost, Exchange will select either of the two routes at random, thus providing load balancing.

You can use costs to control which route Exchange uses in situations where you have different types of connector.

Let's look at a fictional company with two sites, one in Europe, and the other in the United States. Due to the nature of the company's operations, a messaging path between the companies must be available for more than 99.5% of the time.

Hence, the company has two direct links between its two sites—a permanent T1 leased line and X.25 via satellite. Both sites connect to the Internet and both sites have dial-in RAS servers.

The company pays for the T1 line regardless of usage, so it makes sense to use this line in preference to any other. The T1 link supports RPCs.

Nevertheless, what happens if this link goes down? In that case, the next cheapest option would be the Internet Mail Service connector over the permanent Internet connections.

Should the disruption that has taken down the T1 link also affected the Internet, the next option would be the X.25 link. This will not support RPCs and the company will pay for the volume of data that it sends.

Finally, if the X.25 link is also down, a dial-up connection is the final option.

Therefore, our messaging solution looks like the one shown in Table 6.1.

TABLE 6.1 MULTIROUTE LINK SOLUTION

This example is using costs to control how messages reach their destination over different link types.

Connector	Link Type	Cost	Selected
Site connector	T1	1	First
IMS connector	Internet	25	Only if T1 link down
X.400	X.25	80	Only if T1 & Internet down
Dynamic RAS	Dial-up	100	Only if no other link working

Figure 6.19 shows this scheme in action.

Routing and Directory Replication

If you set up Directory Replication, all Exchange sites will become aware of all routes from all the other sites. Hence, if you add an Internet Mail Service to one site, all your other sites will be able to route mail to this connector. The site that does not have the IMS will now get a new route for SMTP:* (where * means all addresses), and can now deliver SMTP mail to this address. The MTA will route SMTP messages to the site with the IMS. This site will then send on these messages to the Internet Mail Service.

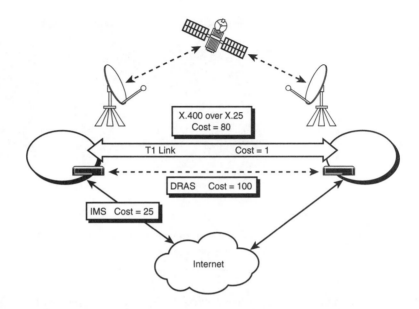

FIGURE 6.19

*In this example, costs
control the message
route selection.*

X.400 over X.25
Cost = 80

T1 Link   Cost = 1

DRAS   Cost = 100

IMS   Cost = 25

Internet

The cost of this route will be the combined cost of the IMS combined with the cost of
traversing the links to get to the IMS.

Controlling Message Routing with Directory Replication   You can control this
effect by limiting the scope of an address space. After all, there may be occasions when
you don't want other sites to dump all their SMTP mail through your Internet connection. *Especially* if you're paying for it and they aren't.

When you add a new connector, you can limit the scope of its address space. You can
also do this when you add subsequent address spaces. Let's use the Site connector as an
example.

To limit the effect of an address space, start Exchange Administrator and select your site
in the left pane. Click on the site object to expand it and select the Configuration container object. In the right pane, select the Connections object. Double-click on the
Connections object and then double-click on the Site connector. Click on the Address
Space tab and then double-click on the existing X.400 address space entry. Now click on
the Restrictions tab and you will see the properties sheet shown in Figure 6.20.

You can now choose to limit this address space to the Site (or server) location. The
default setting is Organization, which means that this address space is spread throughout
the whole organization, and any site can use it to route messages.

6

FIGURE 6.20

The Restrictions tab lets you restrict an address space to a site or a server location.

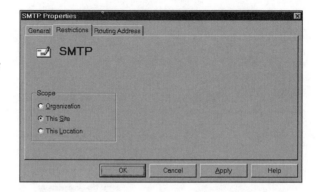

Note

Remember that you can configure server locations through the properties of the *Servername* object.

Having looked at costs and routing, I will now show you how to configure routing.

Configuring Routing

The first part of configuring routing is to add connectors. Assuming you have done this as per the previous sections, you will end up with some default routes. For example, if you add a Site connector you get an X.400 and an X.500(EX) route added automatically. But where do these routes appear?

Site Addressing Object

The Site Addressing object records routing information in Exchange Administrator. This is where you go to view the current site addressing information and routes.

To see the Site Addressing object, start Exchange Administrator and select your site in the left pane. Click on the site object to expand it and select the Configuration container object. In the right pane, double-click on the Site Addressing object, and then click on the Routing tab. You will now see the properties sheet shown in Figure 6.21.

The addressing information itself is contained in the Gateway Address Routing Table (GWART). This is a text file, and you can see it by looking in the \EXCHSRVR\MTADATA directory. There are two versions of the GWART, GWART0.MTA and GWART1.MTA. GWART0 is the current routing table, and GWART1 is the previous
version. If you look at a GWART in Notepad, it looks like the example shown in Figure 6.22.

FIGURE 6.21

The Routing tab in the Site Addressing Object shows Exchange's routing information.

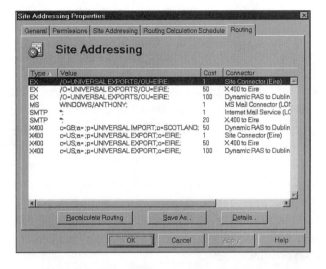

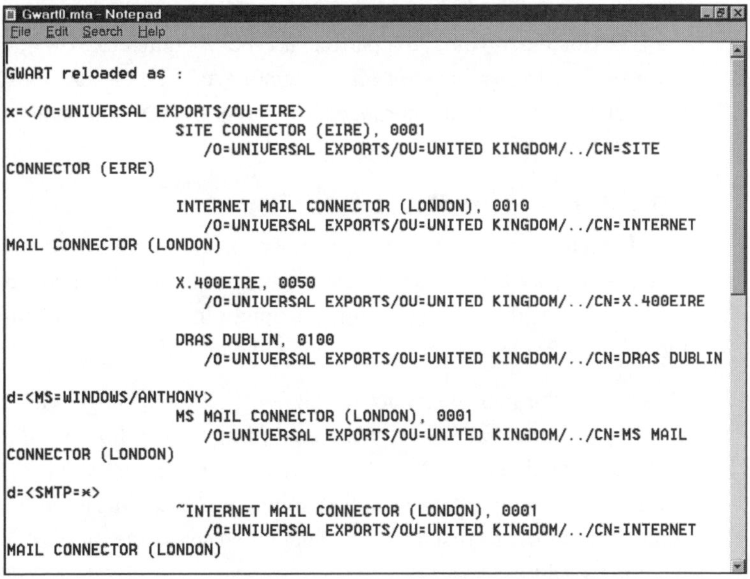

FIGURE 6.22

The Gateway Address Routing Table (GWART) is a text file that Exchange uses for routing messages.

The Exchange System Attendant maintains the Site Addressing object, including the routing information and the GWART.

Understanding the GWART

So what do all these entries in the GWART mean? Looking at the example in Figure 6.21, you can see that there are four types of address showing—types EX, MS, SMTP, and X.400.

These addresses fall into three categories of Exchange address types that I mentioned earlier:

- Type EX is Exchange's internal X.500-type address. This is a Distinguished Name (DN) address and appears automatically if you add a Site connector. You also add an address of this type whenever you specify a remote Exchange site in the Connected Sites tab on the X.400, DRAS, or IMS connectors.

- The SMTP and MS mail addresses are Domain Defined Attributes (DDA). This is because the type of domain that this address routes to also defines the format of the address. By default, you get an MS Mail address whenever you configure the MS Mail Connector, and you get an SMTP address whenever you add the Internet Mail Service.

- The X.400 address is for any X.400 address type, regardless of the connector that defined the address. You get an X.400 address automatically when you add an X.400 or a Site connector.

The important point to understand here is that you get certain address spaces added to the GWART when you add a particular type of connector. However, you can also define *additional* address spaces for *all* connector types, be they X.400, IMS, MS Mail, or Site connectors. Hence, you can route SMTP mail over X.400 connectors, or MS mail over Site connectors.

Routing and Message Delivery

So what happens when you enter an address into the To: field in Outlook and click Send? Outlook sends your message to the Exchange server, and the Information Store receives the message. If the message is for a recipient in that site, Exchange routes the message to the relevant Exchange server and that is the end of it.

However, if the message is not for the local site, Exchange will look in the GWART for a gateway or route that fits the addresses' format. Thus for SMTP mail, the SMTP routes will be selected, and for X.400 addresses, the matching X.400 routes will be chosen. From the list of possible routes that could deliver the message, Exchange selects the route that has the lowest cost. Exchange then sends the message to the connector with the correct address space and the lowest cost.

Adding Address Spaces to Connectors

So how do you add address spaces to connectors?

Each connector that I have described previously in this chapter has either a Connected Sites tab, an Address Space tab, or both.

- The Connected Sites tab lets you add an address of type EX, Exchange's internal "X.500" format. You just specify the Organization name and site name of the remote Exchange site.

- The Address Space tab allows you to add X.400, SMTP, MS Mail, or Other address spaces. Other includes cc:Mail or any type of foreign address system that is, for example, connected to the X.400 system that you have connected to Exchange.

> **Note** You can add additional address spaces to the MS Mail and cc:Mail connectors. If you add the Connectivity pack in the Exchange Enterprise edition, you get the additional Lotus Notes IBM OfficeVision/VM (PROFS) and SNADS connectors, which will add their own DDA addresses to the GWART.

To add an address space to a connector, double-click on the relevant connector in the Connections container. Click on the Address Space tab and click on the New button. You will now see the dialog box shown in Figure 6.23.

FIGURE 6.23

Choose the address type for the address space that you want to add to this connector.

Choose the correct address type for the address space that you want to add and click OK. You will now see a tabbed dialog box that allows you to enter the addressing information for that particular address type. Add the appropriate addressing information and click OK to add the address space to the connector.

Forcing an Update of the Routing Tables

Once you have installed a new connector or added an address space, you may want to force an update of the routing tables. You can do this at two levels, the Site level or the Server level. I'll discuss each in turn.

Site Level At the Site Level, you can force an update of the routing tables through the Routing tab on the Site Addressing object. Go to the dialog box shown in Figure 6.21

previously and click on the Recalculate Routing button. A prompt will tell you that it will take a few minutes for this routing information to replicate across your site.

You can save your routing table as a text file by clicking on the Save As button. This might be useful if you are comparing routing tables from different sites.

By default, the System Attendant recalculates routing tables according to the schedule in the Routing Calculation Schedule tab. Options are Always, Never, or Selected Times.

Server Level   You can force a manual rebuild of the routing information at an individual MTA level. To do so, go to the MTA object at the server level. Double-click on the MTA object and click on the Recalculate Routing button.

Forcing a Complete Routing Update

To force a complete routing update throughout your Exchange organization, carry out the following steps:

1. Add the new connector or address space.
2. On the server where you installed the connector, click on the Recalculate Routing button on the server level MTA object.
3. Go to the Site Addressing object and click on the Recalculate Routing button on the Routing tab.
4. On any other servers in the site, click on the Update Now button on the General tab on the server level Directory Service object.
5. On all the other sites, go to the directory replication connector that links that site to the site to which you have just added a new address space. On the Sites tab, click the Request Now button and force an update from the remote site.
6. On all the servers in the site that are not running the directory replication connector, force an update on the server level directory service object, as you did in step 4.
7. Finally, on the remote site's Site Addressing object, click on the Recalculate Routing button on the Routing tab, as you did in step 3.

Your addressing information will now have propagated to every server in the site. Alternatively, you could just go home for the day. The routing information will propagate overnight, so why make life difficult for yourself?

Summary

In today's lesson, you learned the installation and configuration of the different types of connector. You learned about the factors that affect the deployment of the various connectors. You also learned how to choose the correct connector for your situation. You looked at the routing implications that come from having multiple connectors and address spaces and saw how to add additional address spaces to connectors.

To summarize the main points of today's session:

- Exchange Server uses four types of messaging connector to link Exchange sites: the Site connector, X.400 connector, Dynamic RAS connector, and the Internet Mail Service Connector.

- Each connector is suitable for different situations, although there are occasions where more than one connector may be suitable.

- The Site connector is the easiest to use but can only link Exchange sites across permanent links that support RPCs.

- The X.400 connector is the most generic, allowing you to link any X.400-compliant mail system to Exchange.

- The Dynamic RAS connector is best for remote dial-up sites with no Internet Connection.

- The Internet Mail Service connector is a cheap and effective connector if both sites have a link to the Internet. You can also use the IMS where you have a low-bandwidth WAN running TCP/IP.

- Each type of connector adds an address space to Exchange's routing tables. Exchange then routes mail according to the entries in the routing table.

- You can add address spaces in SMTP, MS Mail, X.400, or other formats to any sort of connector.

- You can control the use of address spaces and connectors by assigning costs or by restricting an address space to a particular site.

- If you add or change addressing information, you can force an update of this information throughout your Exchange organization.

6

Q&A

Q I am deploying Microsoft Exchange at two sites and I want to link them. However, the company cannot afford a leased line, and needs to control the cost of any connection. We have an Internet Mail Service installed at one location. What sort of connector should I use?

A You have a number of options here. You could use the Dynamic RAS connector and dial from one site to another. You could use the X.400 connector and implement RRAS as a dial-on-demand router between the sites. On the other hand, you could install a second link to the Internet and use the Internet Mail Service connector to link your two locations.

Q I have a permanent link between three of my sites over a private WAN running TCP/IP. The link speed is 30Kbps, although the available bandwidth sometimes drops to 10Kbps. Which connector should I use to link my sites?

A In this case, you have two choices. You can't use the Site connector because of the bandwidth restrictions. However, you could use the X.400 connector over TCP/IP. The other option is to use the Internet Mail Service connector. You can schedule both connectors, which lets you stop the connectors running when the bandwidth is in use by other applications.

Q I've just connected two sites using the Site connector. The other site has the Internet Mail Service installed. I have also configured Directory Replication between the sites. Looking in my routing tab on the Site Addressing object, I see that I have three entries, one of type EX, one X.400, and one SMTP. Where have these come from?

A As the site connector always links two Exchange sites, it installs an address space of type Exchange or EX. A Site connector also automatically installs an X.400 address for the remote site. The SMTP address has come from the IMS in the remote site. Knowledge of this connector propagates to your site via directory replication. If you look at the costs of the SMTP address, it will have a cost value of at least 2. This comes from the combination of a cost of 1 on the IMS and a cost of 1 on the Site connector.

Q I'm having problems setting up a Site connector between two Exchange sites. I attempted to install the connector but I get a message about an invalid account. What am I doing wrong?

A My guess is that your sites are two separate NT domains and that your Site connector cannot validate in the remote domain. Use the Site connector's Override tab to specify an account in the remote domain that the connector should use to validate to the remote NT domain. The Exchange site service account will do fine.

Workshop

The Workshop provides two ways for you to affirm what you've learned in this chapter. The Quiz section poses questions to help you solidify your understanding of the material covered and the Exercise section provides you with experience in using what you have learned. You can find answers to the quiz questions and exercises in Appendix B, "Answers to Quiz Questions and Exercises."

Quiz

1. What are the four types of messaging connector in Exchange 5.5?

2. Which connectors can you use on an NWLink-only network?

3. On which connectors can you set a connection schedule?

4. Which connectors can use the global X.25 network?

5. What is the GWART?

6. What are the three types of routing address in Exchange?

7. What is a cost value?

8. What is the effect of having two routes with the same cost?

9. How do you prevent knowledge of a particular route from disseminating throughout your organization?

Exercises

1. You have just added a new connector to your Exchange site and you want this new address space to propagate around your site in the shortest possible time. What do you need to do?

2. How would you configure an Internet Mail Connector to work across a private WAN running TCP/IP but does not support RPCs?

6

DAY 7

Configuring the Exchange Client

By Anthony Steven

Chapter Objectives

So far, I have concentrated on the installation and configuration of Exchange Server. Now it's time to turn your attention to the creation and management of messaging profiles for use with our Exchange client. You will also look at the use of Microsoft Exchange in a mobile environment, such as your sales team using laptops or staff who work from home.

Today you will learn about the following topics:

- Messaging profiles
- Creating a messaging profile
- Adding the Exchange Server service
- Using Personal Stores
- Using multiple profiles

- Mobile considerations
- Offline folders
- Downloading the Address Book
- Remote clients
- Exchange over Remote Access Service

Exchange Client and Messaging Profiles

In this first section, you will look at what is meant by an Exchange Client and a messaging profile. You will then look at the creation and configuration of messaging profiles. Believe me, these apparently simple dialog boxes contain a vast array of options. But on with the lesson.

What Is an Exchange Client?

An Exchange client is the software that enables users to send and receive messages from your Exchange server. In other words, the client is the program that the end user interacts with. Bearing in mind that the prime functionality of an Exchange server is messaging, it makes sense to have some means of getting messages into and out of the system.

Outlook 98, Outlook 97, Outlook for Windows 3.x and Macintosh, Microsoft Mail, and Exchange Client for DOS are all examples of Exchange clients. See Day 9, "Deploying Exchange," and Day 10, "Using Microsoft Outlook," for further details. No matter which client—Outlook or Exchange—you elect to use, you must configure a messaging profile for that client so it can function correctly. These messaging profiles are interchangeable between Microsoft Outlook and other Exchange clients.

When the first user logs on using one of these clients, Exchange Server creates a profile for him automatically. All subsequent users must create their own profile using the New Profile wizard. You'll see how to do so in a moment.

WHAT THE CLIENT DOES

Exchange is a client/server messaging system. In a client/server environment, the job of the client is to provide a user-friendly interface to the active processes running on the server. Hence the client provides the Graphical User Interface (GUI) for the Exchange server, making the messages easy to work with. The client and server themselves communicate using raw data that the server will then process as necessary. When the raw data message arrives at the client, the client then reassembles it to make it readable.

What Is a Messaging Profile?

A messaging profile is a set of addressing, information, transport, and messaging services configured for a specific user.

Before you can use an information or email service such as Microsoft Exchange, you need to have configured a messaging profile. This profile provides a standard interface to the Exchange server and, optionally, to other messaging services.

Standard Information and Messaging Services

There are a number of different messaging services that you can add to a profile, many of which will be available automatically when you install Outlook or the Exchange client. To view these services, select the Start menu, choose Settings, and click Control Panel. When Control Panel is displayed, double-click the Mail icon. The dialog box shown in Figure 7.1 will appear.

FIGURE 7.1

Selecting the Mail icon from the Control Panel as described shows the current profile's properties and any messaging services installed.

Click the Add button, and you will see the list of available messaging services, as shown in Figure 7.2. Selecting a service and clicking OK will add it to your messaging profile.

FIGURE 7.2

From the range of addressing and messaging services, you can select the service you want to add to a profile.

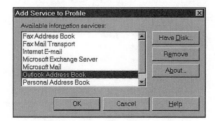

7

Depending on how your system is configured, you may not see all the
information services shown in Figure 7.2.

The default services that should be available to all your network's workstations are
described in the following sections.

Microsoft Exchange Server   This provides connection to a Microsoft Exchange
server for addressing, information storage, and message delivery functions.

When you first install Outlook or the Exchange client, make sure you select
the option for Exchange Server support. Doing so will enable you to use
Exchange's advanced functionality, such as server scripting and folder property pages, on the client.

If you forgot to do this when you first installed Outlook, just re-run the
setup and select the option for Exchange Server support.

Microsoft Mail   This messaging service enables you to send and receive mail directly
from an MS Mail postoffice. Do not confuse this service with using Exchange Server to
connect to MS Mail postoffices via the MS Mail connector! See Day 21, "Migrating
from Microsoft Mail," for more information.

Personal Address Book   This enables you to define a personal address book file
(.PAB). Although they can be useful with the Exchange client that comes with Windows
Messaging on NT or 95 or the Exchange 5.0 client, Personal Address Books are largely
redundant in an Outlook environment. With Outlook they have been replaced with the
Outlook Address Book. The only use I have found for Personal Address Books with
Outlook is for building personal distribution lists.

Outlook Address Book   This is an addressing service for the Outlook client that
enables you to designate folders containing Contact items as Outlook Address Books. By
default, the Contacts folder is automatically added. I'll cover adding folders to your
Outlook address book later in this lesson.

Tip

> If you want to create a personal distribution list, select Address Book from the Tools menu in Outlook (keyboard shortcut Ctrl+Shift+B). Then select New Entry from the File menu or click the New Entry icon.
>
> You now get a choice of new entry types. Select Personal Distribution List and click OK. Give your distribution list a name and add some members. Note that you can add members from Exchange's Global Address List, Outlook Address Book folders, or your Personal Address Book. When you have added all the names, click OK to save your distribution list.
>
> To send a message to this new list, create a new message and click the To button. In the Show Names from Box select your Personal Address Book. You can now add your new distribution list to the list of addressees for that message.

Personal Folders   A Personal Folder is a file with the extension .PST (Personal Store) that can contain email messages, contact items, journal items, and so on. These folders can be located on the user's local hard disk or on a network share. Additionally, they are used for the AutoArchive feature of Outlook.

I'll discuss personal folders in depth later in the lesson.

Internet Email   This is a standard POP3/SMTP client that enables Outlook/Exchange client to collect mail from RFC-compliant Post Office Protocol 3 (POP3) servers and to deliver mail directly to Simple Mail Transfer Protocol (SMTP) servers. In other words, this client lets you send and receive Internet email. I use this service at home to connect to my Internet Service Provider. You may want to consider this as an alternative connection method for clients at remote locations.

See Day 9 for more information about choosing the right client.

Note

> You do not need to install the Internet Mail Service on the client if you have installed Exchange Internet Mail Service on the server. This is because Exchange Server will route all your Internet mail for you. All you need at the client end is the Exchange Server service.

7

Other Messaging Services

Besides the ones I just described, you may be able to add other services to your profile, depending on the functionality that you want in your messaging system and your operating system. Examples include Microsoft Fax, CompuServe, MSN, and LDAP support. Read on for details of each.

Microsoft Fax   This service is available on the Windows 9x platform and as an option on Windows NT Workstation. It enables you to use your Outlook or Exchange client to send faxes straight from your desktop using a locally attached modem. Again, do not confuse this with the integrated Fax service that products like GoldFax and Facsys provide. Microsoft at Work Fax is set up under Windows 9x as part of Microsoft Mail. With Windows NT you need to download and install the FAX_I386.EXE file from the Microsoft Web site; doing so will add the NT Fax service to your computer.

You can get the Windows NT Fax Service from the following Web site:

`www.microsoft.com/windows/downloads/contents/updates/ntpersonalfax.`

CompuServe   CompuServe is available as an information service on Windows 95 (not 98 or NT). It enables you to use Outlook and Exchange clients to send and receive CompuServe email.

MSN   The Microsoft Network Service provides similar functionality to the CompuServe service, again only on Windows 95. It enables you to read and send mail from your MSN account via a Web browser. You must access all other ISPs by using the Internet email service.

LDAP Service   With Outlook 98 you can install a Lightweight Directory Access Protocol (LDAP) service to make directory queries (such as looking up personal information) on an LDAP server. Microsoft Exchange can act as a LDAP server, and there are several commercial LDAP servers on the Internet, such as WhoWhere or Bigfoot. The LDAP client is available for download from the following URL given.

Outlook Add-Ons

If you want to add extra features to Outlook, from a new zany Office Assistant to an updated contact management system, visit the URL shown here:

`http://officeupdate.microsoft.com/downloadCatalog/dldoutlook.htm`

Third party add-ons can be found at

`http://officeupdate.microsoft.com/Articles/3rdparty_addons.htm`

Note

You can also query the Bigfoot and WhoWhere LDAP servers using the Windows Address Book that comes with Internet Explorer 4.0. Try looking up yourself!

WhoWhere can be found on

`http://www.whowhere.com.`

Bigfoot is at

`http://www.bigfoot.com.`

Creating a Messaging Profile

Having looked at some of the availableptions, you are probably thinking that to configure each user's profile manually would keep you occupied for a month of Sundays. And you would be right. Thankfully, there are a number of ways that you can simplify this process of profile creation, depending on how your network is currently operating.

The Default Profile

When you installed Exchange for the first time and started Outlook, you were probably not aware that Outlook created a profile automatically. This default profile creation applies only to the first person to login after the Outlook or Exchange client is installed. This default profile is called MS Exchange Settings or Outlook Settings and is configured using a file called DEFAULT.PRF.

Current Profiles

To see the profiles currently set up on your machine, go to the Start menu, click Settings, launch the Control Panel, and double-click on the Mail icon. You will see the Profile Properties dialog box, as shown in Figure 7.3.

FIGURE 7.3

Here the profile shows the Outlook Address Book service that was added in Figure 7.2.

7

Clicking on the Show Profiles button will display the mail profile information shown in Figure 7.4.

FIGURE 7.4

Here you can see all the mail profiles currently set up for this user.

This dialog box enables you to select a particular profile and alter its properties. It also enables you to create and copy profiles. Take a look at how to create a new profile. In this dialog box, simply click the Add button.

Creating a New Profile Using the Wizard

When you click Add to create a new profile from the Mail Profiles dialog box, Windows runs the New Profile Wizard. The process I'm about to describe is exactly the same as the one a second or subsequent user will see when she starts the Outlook client. First, the Setup Wizard's dialog box will appear, as shown in Figure 7.5.

FIGURE 7.5

On the first screen on the Outlook/Exchange Profile Setup Wizard, you can select the information services you want to add to the new profile.

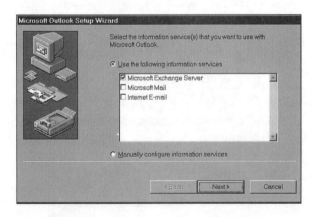

Choosing the Information Services   The first step of the wizard gives you the option to select which information services you want to install. As you are most likely to be using this profile in an Exchange environment, you will probably want to select just the Microsoft Exchange service. However, if you are using the Outlook client at a remote site where the user will be connecting to Exchange via POP3 or collecting his mail from an ISP, you should check the box for Internet Mail. And if you want to configure connections to a Microsoft Mail Post Office at the same time, check the box for MS Mail. However, the combination of using Exchange and MS Mail in this manner is unusual.

When you've selected the information services, click Next.

Naming Your Profile   In the next dialog box, shown in Figure 7.6, you're prompted to give your profile a unique name. It may also be helpful to give it a descriptive name—say, "Master Internet Mail Profile" or "Frank's Exchange Offline Profile." (I'll explain more about these profiles later.) After typing the name you want, click Next.

FIGURE 7.6

*Now you need to give
your profile a unique
name*

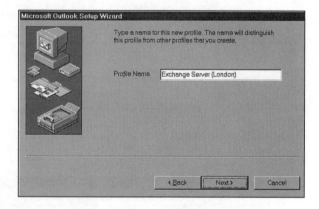

Specifying the Exchange Server and Mailbox Name   Next, you're prompted for the name of the Exchange Server you want to connect to and the name of the Mailbox to open. Let's take a quick look at these elements.

Exchange Server Name   This can be any server in the site where your mailbox is held. Hence, if your mailbox is located on server YORK and you enter the server name LONDON, then as long as YORK and LONDON are in the same Exchange site your profile will be created successfully.

Note

When I refer to *site* I mean the Exchange Server site, as you covered in Day 1, "Introduction to Exchange."

7

Mailbox Name   The mailbox name must be either the user's Display Name or Alias Name (from the properties of that user in Exchange Administrator—see Day 4, "Server Configuration"). Also, to open the mailbox, the mailbox name must match the logon name of the person trying to open that mailbox. You can see a sample dialog box with both these entries in Figure 7.7.

FIGURE 7.7

In this screen, enter the user's name and the name of the Exchange server that her mailbox is on.

To obtain the information needed for this step, you can access that user's mailbox properties in Exchange Administrator. Figure 7.8 shows the properties screen for the user for whom I'm creating this profile, showing his Display Name, Alias Name, and Primary Windows NT Account. The Primary Windows NT Account must match the mailbox name or alias unless you are using groups, as I'll describe in a moment.

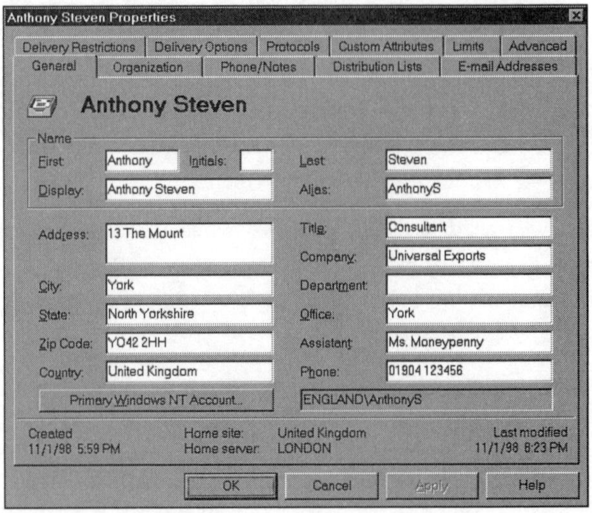

FIGURE 7.8

The properties of user's mailbox screen in Exchange Administrator shows the Alias name and Display name. You can enter either in the mailbox field in Figure 7.7.

When you've obtained and filled in the user's server and mailbox information, click
Next.

Tip

You can make multiple user accounts able to open and use the same mailbox. To do this, make a Global Group the Primary Windows NT Account
(that is, the mailbox's owner). Any members of this Global Group will be
able to add the mailbox to her profiles, and then open and use it.

Use this technique if you have several users who share the same mailbox,
such as workshare employees or shift workers.

Mobile Use   The next screen in the wizard, shown in Figure 7.9, lets you specify
whether you want to add support for mobile users. The Yes option will automatically
install and configure an offline folder (.OST) file, which will make your Exchange
Server folders available while you are not connected to the server. Selecting No will
mean that you will only be able to access your folders when directly connected to
Exchange, either via Remote Access (RAS) and a modem or via the LAN. Click the
radio button indicating your choice, and then click Next.

Caution

Do not select the option for mobile support if you are planning to use the
remote mail functionality of Exchange. Remote mail cannot be used at the
same time as offline folders.

FIGURE 7.9

*Select Yes to use
Outlook with an offline
store, No if you are
using Outlook on a
LAN or with remote
mail*

7

Personal Address Book Path   Although Personal Address Books are not required with Outlook, the Setup Wizard's next step insists on you specifying a location for the .PAB file. You will have to accept a setting and then, if you want, go back and delete the Personal Address Book later (I'll show you how in a moment). Select a location and click Next.

FIGURE 7.10

Here you can specify a location for the Personal Address Book.

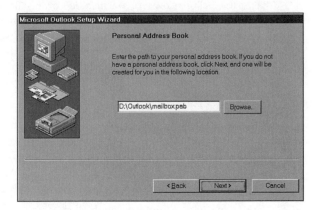

Finishing the Wizard   The final screen, shown in Figure 7.11, displays the services that you have set up. Select Finish to exit the wizard and return to the Profiles screen. The new profile will now appear on the Mail Profiles screen, as shown in Figure 7.12.

FIGURE 7.11

The final screen on the New Profile Wizard shows that the new profile is configured.

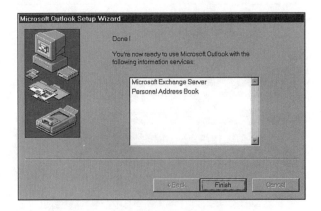

FIGURE 7.12

The new profile is shown in the profiles list.

Configuring a Messaging Profile

After you have created a messaging profile, you will probably want to tweak it further. To do this, open the profile. This can now be done in several ways:

- Select the Start menu, click Settings, choose Control Panel, and double-click the Mail icon in the resulting window.

- Right-click on the Exchange Inbox or Outlook icon (*not* the shortcut icon—it should not have a little arrow on it—and select Properties.

- Start Outlook and then select Services from the Tools menu. Note that if you use this method, you will only be able to configure the active profile; there will be no Show Profiles button.

No matter which method you choose, you'll now be looking at the Properties dialog box for your selected profile, which will resemble the dialog box shown in Figure 7.13. For now, make sure the Services tab is selected. You can use the options here to add and remove services.

Tip

You can view the properties of any item on your desktop by double-clicking on the relevant icon while pressing the Alt key. This works with the Outlook icon as well.

7

FIGURE 7.13

The Properties of your current profile are shown here.

Adding and Removing Services (Services Tab)

Click on Add to install any new services. You will again be presented with the list of available services that you saw in Figure 7.2. Depending on which service you add, you will then be presented with a range of configuration options.

For an explanation of the configuration options on the Internet email client, see Day 14, "Reading Exchange Mail with Internet Client."

Removing services is much easier. Select the service and click Remove. Now, that didn't hurt a bit, did it?

Tip

> You will almost certainly want to add the Outlook Address Book service. Don't worry that you can't specify folders to use as Address Books yet—you will be able to do so later.
>
> If you want, you can remove the Personal Address Book service from your profile. Select the service and click Remove. You will be asked whether you are sure you want to remove this information service from your profile. Of course you're sure!

Specifying Delivery Options (Delivery Tab)

Click on the Delivery tab to specify your delivery options. You'll see the dialog box shown in Figure 7.14. Now it's time to consider the options it offers.

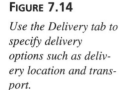

FIGURE 7.14

Use the Delivery tab to specify delivery options such as delivery location and transport.

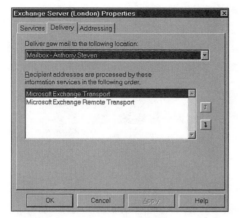

Deliver New Mail to the Following Location This drop-down list enables you to specify the location mail will be delivered to. You can choose between the Inbox in your Exchange mailbox (which is the default) or the Inbox folder in a personal store (if you have added any to your profile). You *must* configure a delivery location—you won't be able to send or receive any mail until you have done so.

Recipient Address Processing You will normally only need to use Recipient Address Processing if you have more than one email service that can process a particular email type. For example, you may have two systems that can process Internet Mail—the Internet email POP3 client and Exchange Server running its own Internet Mail Service. As both can deliver SMTP mail (in the *username@domainname*.com format), you can control the order in which the services process the delivery of this mail type.

Now click the Addressing tab to specify some more options.

Specifying Addressing Options (Addressing Tab)

The Addressing options tab, shown in Figure 17.15, enables you to configure your addressing services. You can specify which directory services the client will query in order to resolve recipient names. Take a closer look at the options this dialog box offers.

Show This Address List First Use this drop-down list to specify which address book appears first when you click on the To button as you're composing messages. In a small organization with only one mail server or a single site, multiple address books are normally not an issue. However, working in a large organization or one with multiple sites may result in a global address list that is too large and cumbersome for easy use. Hence if you have specified additional recipients containers or you are using Address Book Views you may want the first address list shown to be something other than the global address list (your site).

7

FIGURE 7.15

Here you see the addressing options for the current profile.

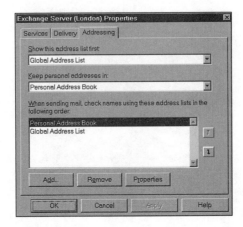

You can also make an Outlook Address Book (that is, a folder with contact items in it) the first address list shown. However, you need to ensure that you have designated the relevant contacts folder as an Outlook Address Book.

Keep Personal Addresses In   If you have deleted the Personal Address Book service from your profile, you will not see an entry for this value. Don't worry, as this functionality is very rarely needed. Having said that, one feature I hope Microsoft adds to future versions of Exchange is to make Contact folders work like Personal Address Books, giving them the ability to store distribution lists.

Checking Address Book Order   The order of address book checking is important—it comes into play with Ambiguous Name Resolution (see sidebar). If you have multiple folders containing contact items set up in your Outlook client (remember that these can be public folders as well), you need to add them as Address Books in this dialog box. Click the Add button to access the dialog box shown in Figure 7.16.

FIGURE 7.16

Here you see how to add an address list to the search list.

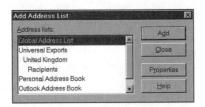

Choose the address list or lists to add and then click OK. After you have added an address list to the Addressing tab you can use the up and down arrows to configure their search order. Make sure your most commonly accessed address book is at the top of the list.

AMBIGUOUS NAME RESOLUTION (ANR)

The Outlook client uses a process of Ambiguous Name Resolution to guess who you are trying to send a message to. To test this process, try entering a partial name, such as "Miles," in the To box. Outlook will either fill in the full name and underline it in black (indicating the name has been resolved) or it will underline it with a dotted green line if it is not resolved (if WordMail option is switched on, you get a wavy red line). To select the correct address manually, you can right-click on the unresolved name and choose the correct name from the list displayed.

If the name is still unresolved when you send the message, a dialog box will appear, presenting a list of possible choices and asking you to clarify who you want the message sent to. If there are no matching names, you have the option to create a new address entry. If you are repeatedly getting failed name resolution, check that all your address lists and contacts folders have been added to the search order using the Addressing tab.

The order in which Outlook searches for a match is dictated by the order specified in the Addressing tab of the properties dialog box belonging to the messaging profile in use. Hence, to speed up ANR, make sure that your most commonly used address book is at the top of your search list.

Copying and Deleting Profiles

The Properties dialog box (which you saw in Figure 7.12) has uses besides adding new profiles. For example, you can use it to copy a profile, making the duplicate available to the same user. This technique is useful when you want to have two profiles with slightly different settings. It's easy: Just select the profile you want to copy and click the Copy button.

Just as when you create a new profile, you must give the duplicate profile a unique name. Having copied your profile, you can now make any configuration changes without affecting the original profile.

In order to use this other profile, you must either set it as the default profile or configure your client to enable you to choose the profile when starting the client. To learn how to do so, see "Using Multiple Profiles" later in this lesson.

7

To delete a profile, just select the profile name in the Properties dialog box and click the
Remove button. You will be prompted for confirmation that you want to delete the profile.

Configuring the Exchange Server Messaging Service

If you need to edit the options affecting your connection to the Exchange server, you can
do so through the profile screen. Choose the desired profile and click Properties. Then,
highlight the appropriate Exchange Server service and again select Properties. The dialog
box shown in Figure 7.17 will appear.

FIGURE 7.17

*This dialog box shows
the General tab from
the properties of the
Exchange Server ser-
vice.*

 Tip

You can also change your Exchange server options for the current profile in
the Outlook client program. Select Services from the Tools menu and then
select the properties of the Exchange service. However, you will need to
select the Exit and Log Off command from Outlook's File menu for the
changes to be implemented.

Let's take a look at the various tabs of the server's Properties dialog box and the options
they provide.

General Tab

As we saw in Figure 7.17, here we can configure the user mailbox account, server name
and connection method.

Exchange Server and Mailbox   This section enables you to check and amend the Exchange Server and Mailbox name. The same conditions apply as when you were setting it up using the New Profile Wizard earlier in the lesson.

Tip

To verify that you have entered a mailbox or server name correctly, click the Check Name button. If the server name and mailbox can be resolved they will be underlined, as they are in Figure 7.17. If the server name is incorrect (or the server is offline) you will get a message informing you that a connection could not be made to the server. If the username is incorrect, the message will tell you that the mailbox could not be found.

When Starting   In this section, you can specify whether you want your Exchange client to use a permanent connection or dial-up networking. If your users are always connected to the LAN, use the Connect with the Network radio button. If you have users permanently based at remote sites, you should configure them to work offline and use dial-up networking by selecting that radio button. Your mobile users with network cards and modems in their laptops and users of offline stores may require the ability to choose the connection type when starting, so you should click this check box when setting up their accounts.

Caution

On a number of occasions, I have found that the options available in the When Starting section do not work. The symptoms are that you lose the ability to choose the connection type on startup. Hence, the profile either connects to the network or stays offline. Usually this happens when you do not log out of Outlook when you exit. Make sure you choose Exit and Log Off from the Outlook File menu before restarting.

Advanced Tab

The Advanced tab, shown in Figure 7.18, enables you to configure a variety of different options, from additional mailboxes to offline folder file settings. These sometimes take considerable planning. An understanding of the effects and consequences of each option will help prevent a plethora of support calls. I'll guide you through the options now and comment on each.

7

FIGURE 7.18

*Changing the proper-
ties of the Exchange
Server service through
the Advanced tab.*

Mailboxes The only option here enables the user to open other users' mailboxes. If you are setting up profiles for managers and secretaries, you will undoubtedly find your-self requiring this feature. Now, this might seem to be somewhat contrary to the princi-ples of good security; surely everyone can then just open each other's mailboxes without so much as a by-your-leave. Well, thankfully, they can't. True, you *can* add another's mailbox to the list of mailboxes to be opened, but if the other user has not given you per-mission, you can see it but not open it. Permissions can only be given by the other user and need to be applied at the mailbox level and to any subfolder that the other user wants someone else to see. They can also be configured using the Delegate Access options in Outlook. I'll show you how to use the latter technique in the sidebar; see Day 19, "Making Exchange Secure," for more information on assigning permissions and config-uring delegate access.

OPENING ADDITIONAL MAILBOXES

When would you need to use this feature? It depends on the size of your organization. In a large corporation, probably quite often and for a variety of purposes.

Managers and secretaries will need to use it so that a secretary can process his or her boss's mail. The manager needs to make their secretary a delegate and to configure dele-gate access appropriately. This process is covered in full on Day 19.

Another situation in which you'd want to access other mailboxes is with resource man-agement. You can set up an Exchange mailbox for a resource, such as a meeting room or an overhead projector. A user in the company could be delegated to oversee the resource's diary and to resolve any booking conflict issues. They would also have the nec-essary permissions to open the Calendar and Inbox folders for that mailbox.

However you configure your system, don't forget that the user attempting to access another mailbox must have at least Reviewer permission on the mailbox itself. See Day 19 for further information on assigning permissions.

Encrypt Information   These settings apply encryption to message packets as they are transmitted from client to server, either over a LAN or over a RAS dial-up link. The encryption is the maximum supported by Windows NT and is similar to that used in encrypted logon sessions between clients and domain controllers.

Note

> This encryption is not the same as enabling advanced security. It simply means that the messages are encrypted in transit. It could still be read by a user who has access to your mailbox. Advanced security provides a digital sealing function that prevents other users from reading a sealed message. Sealed messages can only be read by the intended recipient when they have supplied their own advanced security password. This process will be covered further on Day 19.

Logon Network Security   The three options in this drop-down list govern how the client software checks for Authentication.

NT Password Authentication makes use of the existing system of passwords required to log onto an NT server. Most of the time, you will want to use this system because it is the simplest.

Use the Distributed Password Authentication option if you are working in an environment that supports DPA mechanisms.

If you want people to have to log onto Exchange Client in addition to logging onto the network, use the None setting. You should consider this in cases where you cannot guarantee the physical security of the workstation (for example, with mobile computers or shared workstations) or you are working in a more secure environment and want to implement a further level of network security.

Offline Folder Settings   Click the Offline Folder File Settings button to invoke the dialog box shown in Figure 7.19. Here you'll configure a user's ability to access his or her mail when not attached to the network. Offline folders enable a user to see their Exchange server folders even though they are not connected. We will cover this topic in Mobile Computing later in this lesson.

To enable offline use, enter a path and filename for the offline folder (.OST) file and click OK.

7

FIGURE 7.19

When configuring offline folders, you need to specify a file name, the file location, and the encryption settings.

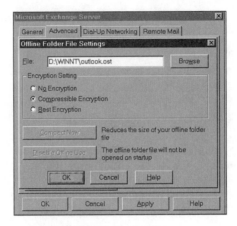

Dial-Up Networking Tab

Click the Dial-Up Networking tab to access the dialog box shown in Figure 7.20. Dial-Up Networking enables you to specify the connection that the client will use to dial in to a Remote Access Service (RAS) server. I'll discuss this topic, and the options contained in this dialog box, more fully in the section on "Mobile Considerations" later in this lesson.

FIGURE 7.20

This dialog enables you to select a dial-up connection to access your Exchange mailbox.

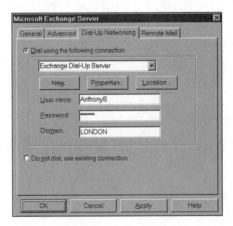

Remote Mail Tab

The last tab you'll examine is Remote Mail; begin by clicking it now. You'll see the dialog box shown in Figure 7.21. Remote Mail enables you to specify on a remote network how often a client will check for new mail. Again, I'll provide more detail in the "Mobile Considerations" section later in this lesson.

FIGURE 7.21

The remote mail options enable you to apply filters and schedule your remote mail connections.

Personal Stores

There are many factors that affect your decision to use personal stores (.PST files). The following sections should offer some guidelines to help you with this decision.

What Is a Personal Store?

A personal store is simply a file that can be used for storing messages. Within that file you can create folders and subfolders that can be used to store emails, contact items, ToDo lists, and Journal items. In fact, a .PST file can contain anything that an Exchange Mailbox or public folder can.

When Would I Use One?

In an Exchange server environment on a LAN, personal stores are usually not required. Your clients can use their mailboxes to keep their messages, contact, and calendar items. However, personal stores will be required under the following circumstances:

- You need to set up a client to connect to an ISP using Internet Mail or to work with Exchange using POP3.
- You are configuring a client to work offline using remote mail.
- You want to enable the AutoArchive feature of Outlook.
- You want to use Outlook as just a personal information manager.
- You are concerned about storage space on the Exchange server and want to control the size of your users' mailboxes.

Personally, I think the last reason (although mentioned in the training materials) is somewhat bogus. If you are that concerned about storage space on your Exchange server then

7

you definitely need a new hard disk. And you can limit the size of user's mailboxes using the Exchange Administrator to prevent the information stores from getting too large. But that aside, let's examine more details of the conditions that require personal stores.

When Connecting to a POP3 Server   If you install the Internet email service (POP3 client) without the Exchange Server service, you will need a location to deliver the mail to. You would use this combination, shown in Figure 7.22, either for connecting to an ISP or to access your Exchange inbox using POP3. Remember that Exchange 5.5 can act as a POP3/SMTP server.

FIGURE 7.22

Here is a profile using Internet email to connect to Exchange Server via POP3 and delivering to a personal store.

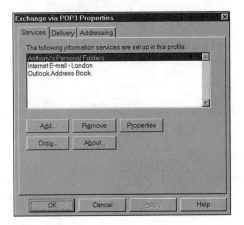

> **Note**
>
> POP3 is simply a collection mechanism. If you are using POP3 to collect mail you will need to use Simple Mail Transfer Protocol (SMTP) to deliver to an SMTP server. To enable the SMTP service on Exchange 5.5 you need to install and configure the Internet Mail Service using the Exchange Administrator.
>
> For more information, see Day 12, "Exchange on the Internet," and Day 14, "Reading Exchange Mail with Internet Clients."

You will be covering how to set up this sort of connection on Day 14.

If you set up this type of profile (by checking the Internet Email option on the New Profile Wizard) you will be prompted to create or select a .PST file.

You will also need to have your delivery options configured so that any new mail collected via the Internet email service is delivered to the .PST file, as shown in Figure 7.23.

For further information on configuring a POP3 client, see Day 14.

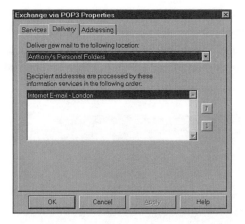

FIGURE 7.23

A Profile configured for delivery to the personal store.

You will probably want to add an Outlook Address Book or a Personal Address Book to the profile for addressing information.

When Using Remote Mail   Another configuration option requiring a personal store is when using the remote mail functionality of Microsoft Exchange. This option enables you to set up a client's connection so that the user can dial in and pick up his mail from a remote location using RAS or dial-up networking (DUN).

Exchange also allows the client to use a remote mail connection even if attached to the LAN. You would use this configuration if you have users at a remote site that has a very low bandwidth link to your Exchange server. I have seen examples where dedicated links have been installed but the available bandwidth for the Exchange client has been in the order of 10Kbps, far slower than most modern modems. Under these circumstances, a direct connection to the Exchange server could not be supported, but remote mail, although slow, allowed for the delivery and receipt of messages.

You cannot use remote mail at the same time as offline folders. Either configure a personal store and connect using remote mail (usually via modem), or use an offline store and synchronize your folders when you are connected to the LAN.

I discuss this concept further in the next section, "Mobile Considerations".

For more information on remote mail, see the next section in this chapter, "Mobile Considerations."

7

When Using the AutoArchive Feature of Outlook Outlook's AutoArchive feature enables you to automatically back up any folders in your mailbox to a .PST file. To configure AutoArchive, select Options from Outlook 98's Tools menu, select the Other tab and then click the AutoArchive button. You will see the dialog box shown in Figure 7.24.

FIGURE 7.24

Here you can see the AutoArchive options configured under Outlook 98.

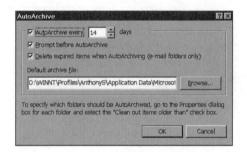

In this dialog box, you can set how often AutoArchiving will run, whether the user will be prompted first, and whether to delete expired items after they have been archived. You can also choose a folder for the AutoArchive. Note that these settings apply only to email items.

A default AutoArchive BACKUP.PST file will be created if one does not exist in the location given.

Configuring AutoArchive on an Individual Folder After you have activated AutoArchiving in Outlook, you can now enable it for individual folders as shown in Figure 7.25. To access this dialog box, right-click on a folder in the folder list in Outlook and select Properties. Then click on the AutoArchive tab.

For each folder, you can now set how old items must be before they are AutoArchived. For the Inbox, the default is three months; for the Calendar, it's six months and for the Sent Items folder, two months. Note that you can set up a different destination file for each folder to archive to.

Note

You can only AutoArchive certain folders. For example, you can AutoArchive your Inbox and Calendar folders but you can't AutoArchive your Contacts folder or any public folders.

FIGURE 7.25

Here you see how to enable AutoArchiving for an individual folder.

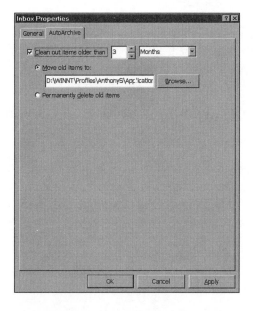

When Using Outlook Without a Messaging Service   Because you have paid good money for a book on Microsoft Exchange, I will not go into great depth on this option because if you're using Exchange you naturally have a messaging service. You can use Outlook as a standalone Personal Information Manager (PIM), in which case you will only require a personal store set up in your profile. The Personal Address Book and Outlook Address Books are no longer required. When using Outlook as a PIM, you'll take advantage of its calendar and contact information options but not its email capability.

Where Can Personal Stores Be Located?

The .PST file can be located anywhere on your network, although you will normally want to place it on a user's hard disk. If you are using personal stores for remote working or with the Internet, you will *definitely* need to place them on the client machine.

Personal stores can also be placed on floppy disks (if they're small enough to fit).

What Else Can I Do with Personal Stores?

Personal stores are very useful when it comes to moving mailboxes from site to site within Exchange or from one recipients' container to another. Although we can easily move mailboxes from one server to another within a site, any other form of move is a somewhat protracted affair. This complexity is because the directory name (such as a X.500 name) of the mailbox object includes the site name and the recipient's container

7

name. As the directory name is fixed when the mailbox object is created, you can't move the mailbox to another site or another recipient's container. Hence you have to export the user's folders to a .PST, delete the mailbox object, re-create it in a new site or recipient's container, and then import the .PST into the new mailbox. See Day 10 for further information on exporting and importing .PST files.

Are There Any Disadvantages to Using Personal Stores?

Yes, there are. As the .PST files are usually stored on the client machine, they will *not* be backed up with the server. Also, as I just obliquely indicated, they can be time-consuming to configure. My approach with personal stores is to inform the users during the roll-out program that the use of personal stores will be supported only for mobile users. Anyone else uses them at his or her own risk. And if they password-protect a .PST file and forget the password, then don't call me.

Adding Personal Stores to a Profile

To add a personal store to a profile, select the Start menu, click Settings, open the Control Panel, and then double-click on the Mail icon. Select Add, and you'll see the dialog box shown in Figure 7.26.

FIGURE 7.26

Here you can select or create a .PST file to use with your profile.

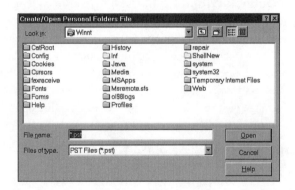

At this point, you can either select an existing .PST file to add to this profile or select a location and a filename to create a new one. You will then be presented with the Personal Folders dialog box, shown in Figure 7.27.

FIGURE 7.27

*These are the options
you need to configure
when setting up a .PST
file for use in a Profile.*

PERSONAL STORES AND OUTLOOK 98

One of the seriously useful enhancements to Outlook 98 is the ability to open and close
.PST files without messing with profiles. To do so, select Open from the File menu and, in
the resulting list, choose Personal Folders File from the Files of Type drop-down list. Find
the .PST file on your computer or on the network, and you can open it just like that!
Closing it is even easier; just right-click the file in Outlook's folder list (you may need to
select Folder List from the View menu first) and select Close *Folder Name* (of course,
you'll see the actual name of the folder for *Folder Name*). Gone!

Let's take a look at the components of this dialog box.

Personal Store Names   The name that you assign the personal store will appear in
Outlook. I usually recommend a descriptive name (such as "Anthony's Personal
Folders") because it helps me to distinguish between .PST files. This is because I tend to
use several at the same time—one for business use, one for personal use, and one for
archiving.

Encryption Settings   The encryption settings are to prevent unauthorized snooping
into the contents of .PST files. However, there is absolutely no point in encrypting the
files if they aren't password-protected.

Passwords   Users can password-protect their personal stores and have the password
added to their password lists. Doing so will mean that when they log on normally and
open their personal store, the password will be supplied automatically, either from their
password list file or from their Windows NT account. A password will only be required
if someone else opens the file or if the user opens it from another logon name. In that
case, if the password is entered correctly, the user can access the store file.

7

> **Note**
>
> You need to warn your users about using passwords on personal stores. If they password-protect their .PST files and then forget the password, you will *not* be able to do some administrator "jiggery-pokery" in the background and magically unlock the file. No—if they forget their password, it's hard cheese. No more data.

You can compress personal stores using the Compact Now button. Doing so will free up space occupied by deleted messages and make it available to store more information.

> **Tip**
>
> Originally, personal stores had a limit of 2GB or 16,000 items but Outlook 8.03 and later (which includes 98) can now use personal stores with more than 16,000 items. However, you cannot then open these larger files with earlier versions of Outlook without splitting them into separate personal stores.
>
> To use larger personal stores, start Outlook, select the Tools menu and choose Services. Double-click on the Personal Folders entry to view its properties and then check the box for Allow Upgrade to Large Tables.

That's it for the options in the Personal Folders dialog box. You've now configured the settings for a single user profile. Now it's time to see what happens when a single user needs more than one profile.

Using Multiple Profiles

We have looked at a number of different profiles that can be set up to cover the many varied configurations of the Microsoft messaging clients. But what do we do if our users need to log in using different profiles at different times?

The Outlook and Exchange clients support using multiple profiles to enable you to log into different combinations of addressing, information storage, and messaging systems. To view the different profiles set up on a machine, you have a couple of options. You could select the Start menu, choose Settings, open the Control Panel, and then double-click the Mail icon. Or you could right-click on the Outlook or Exchange Inbox icon on the desktop and choose Properties.

Either method will take you to the settings for the current profile, as shown at the beginning of the chapter in Figure 7.1. Clicking on the Show Profiles button takes you to the dialog box shown in Figure 7.28, where you'll see a list of all the profiles currently configured.

From this dialog box, you can select the default profile that will be used to start up your client. Additionally, you can configure your system to offer you a choice of profiles at startup. To do this, you have to start the Outlook or Exchange client and select Options from the Tools menu. In Outlook 98, you then need to go to the Mail Services tab, as shown in Figure 7.29. You can then select either a single profile to start with or be prompted to choose a profile when you start the client. In Outlook 97 or Exchange, you select the Email tab in the Options dialog box to accomplish the same purpose. For this example, choose the Prompt for a Profile to be Used radio button. Select OK and then choose Exit and Log Off Outlook from the File menu to implement your changes.

FIGURE 7.28

Here you see multiple profiles configured for use with the messaging client.

FIGURE 7.29

You will need to configure the client to enable selection of messaging profile at startup as shown.

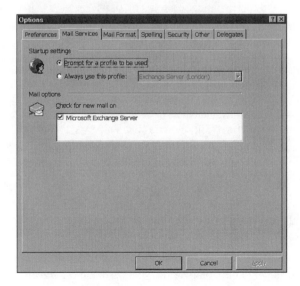

7

When you restart Outlook, you will see the dialog box shown in Figure 7.30.

FIGURE 7.30

Now your Outlook startup screen shows a drop-down list of available profiles.

You can now select which profile you want to use from the drop-down list.

After you select a profile, you may want to be able to choose it in the future without using the drop-down list. To do so, click the Options button in this dialog box; then select the Set as Default Profile check box, and click OK. Clicking OK a second time selects this profile for use by Outlook and also makes the selected profile appear as the default profile on the list when you next start Outlook. It does not remove your ability to select which profile to use; however, you can now accept the default profile simply by clicking OK or pressing Enter.

MESSAGING PROFILES AND ROAMING PROFILES

We have been talking for some time about messaging profiles. Yet you are probably aware of the feature of roaming (not roving!) profiles in Windows NT and 9x. *Roaming profiles* enable your users to log in to any machine on the network and get their individual desktop and configuration settings. You should be aware that these profiles are distinct and separate items!

However, messaging profiles and roaming profiles can be easily integrated. When you create a messaging profile, the profile's settings are stored in the USER.DAT or NTUSER.DAT file at the root of the current user's local profile folders. Copying this local profile to a network share and configuring it as a roaming profile will ensure that wherever your users login, they will receive not only the same desktop settings but also the same messaging profile. Remember that you also need to configure a Profile Path for that user in User Manager for Domains to point to the shared profile.

You can configure roaming messaging profiles for Windows 3.x and DOS, but believe me, you probably don't want to. Windows 3.x and DOS do not support roaming user profiles in the way that Windows 95,98, and NT do.

Mobile Considerations

In this section, I will address the issues of supporting mobile users. Mobile users have become increasingly common over the years as business travelers, roaming consultants, telecommuting workers, and floating troubleshooters proliferated.

Outlook and Exchange server can support mobile users in a number of different ways. However, before you can configure this mobile support, it is important to analyze in which roles your users will operate.

User Roles in the Remote/Mobile Environment

You will probably encounter a number of different user roles in the mobile or remote environment. The following list covers most of the more common variants:

- The Managerial User—This user has a laptop, probably in a docking station. At night, he takes the laptop home and catches up with his email there. On returning in the morning, he wants to be able to connect to Exchange and send all his outstanding messages, and then work normally for the rest of the day.

- The Remote WAN User—This user works at a remote location. This location may be directly connected to your site using either using a modem, ISDN, or a WAN leased line, but the bandwidth considerations prevent the client from using Remote Procedure Calls (RPC) to connect to the Exchange Server.

- The Home User or Telecommuter—This user works at home, using her own PC. She has a modem and a connection to the Internet via an ISP.

- The Mobile User—Usually a member of the sales team, this user comes into the office on an occasional basis, when she needs to connect to the Exchange server. Often she stays in different hotels and needs the ability to connect from multiple locations.

 Note

> You will see several mentions of Remote Procedure Calls (RPCs) in this section. Exchange clients use this method to connect to the Exchange server and that Exchange servers in the same site use to connect to each other. For more information about the role of RPCs in the Exchange Environment, see Day 2, "Planning your Exchange Implementation".

After you have classified your users, it's time to examine the different ways in which you can employ Exchange Server in a WAN/LAN environment.

Exchange Server Roles in the Remote/Mobile Environment

Just as you have a number of different options for your users, there are several different ways in which you can configure Microsoft Exchange server to work with remote users. So next, you need to look at how Exchange server can be implemented.

7

This time your system may fall into more than one of the following categories:

- You have a simple LAN with 10 or 100MB cabling and no Internet connection, RAS server, or remote sites connected via a WAN.
- You have a leased line to the Internet via an ISP.
- You have a routed ISDN or Dial on Demand (DOD) connection to the Internet via an ISP.
- You have a dial-up connection to the Internet via an ISP.
- You have a leased line to your ISP and you are supporting clients logging on using POP3 over the Internet.
- You have a Remote Access Server (RAS) on your network that allows RAS or DUN (dial-up networking) clients to log in.
- You have a RAS server linked to your ISP via a leased line and you are supporting clients logging on using PPTP over the Internet.
- You have remote sites on a WAN employing some form of MegaStream or KiloStream leased line. This connection supports RPC.
- You have remote sites on a WAN connected by a leased line that does not support RPC (Remote Procedure Calls) or the bandwidth is very limited.

Having looked at the client roles and the server deployment choices, you can now investigate the client configuration options.

Remote Client Configuration Options

The client configuration options that you can use to configure the Outlook/Exchange client for remote working are as follows:

- Offline folders
- Remote mail with personal folders
- POP3/Internet email with personal folders

I'll cover use of POP3/IMAP4 and Web browser clients in Day 13, "Building a Web Site Around Exchange," and Day 14, "Reading Exchange Mail with Internet Clients." For now, let's look at the first two configuration options I just mentioned.

Offline Folders

Offline folders can be thought of as a mirror image of a user's Exchange server mailbox. Exchange server mailboxes are only available when a client is directly connected to the server over a network that supports RPC. Offline folders enable you to use your

Exchange mailbox folders as if you *were* connected to the server. However, instead of sending messages to Exchange, they are kept locally in an .OST file and synchronized when you reconnect to the Exchange Server.

Which Users Would Benefit from Using Offline Folders?

Offline folders are generally for one type of user only—the managerial user. As I mentioned earlier, these users will probably have a laptop that can be connected to the corporate LAN when at work (possibly through a docking station) and when they leave for the evening, they undock it and take it with them. Before they leave, they will be able to synchronize their folders and work on any item in them while on the train or at home (hopefully not while driving!). In the morning, they can reconnect to the LAN and their overnight work will be dispatched and their folders synchronized with those on the server.

Which Sites Can Use Offline Folders?

In terms of LAN configuration, offline folders are the only option available if you do not have a RAS server or a connection to the Internet. After all, if you don't have either of these options, how will your remote users connect to you? However, offline folders may not be suitable in a low-bandwidth WAN environment as the synchronization traffic may be unacceptable. Remote mail gives easier control over bandwidth.

What About Public Folders?

Public folders can be configured to be available offline by adding them to your Favorites folder. You will then be able to synchronize them with the folders on the Exchange Server. I will be covering this in detail in step 4 of the following section.

How Do I Configure Folders for Offline Use?

To do this, you have to set up a number of options:

1. Configure your profile for offline folders. In Outlook, select the Tools menu, choose Services, and select the Exchange Server Service and click Properties. On the General tab, check the box that enables you to choose your connection type on starting.

2. Click the Advanced tab and then click on the Offline Folder File Settings button. The settings the resulting dialog box offers, shown in Figure 7.31, are similar to those for personal stores. You can normally accept the default values, although if you have multiple users configured for offline stores on one machine you will need to specify different filenames for each user. However, unlike personal stores, you should *not* put .OST files on a network drive—doing so would negate the point of the offline store!

7

FIGURE 7.31

Here an offline store is being added in the default location.

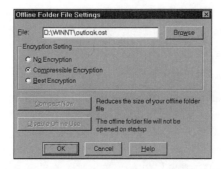

3. After you have configured the profile for offline folders and have confirmed the changes that you have made in the profile, you can right-click on a folder, choose Properties, and then select the Synchronization tab. For all the mailbox folders, such as Inbox, Calendar, and so on. You will see that synchronization is configured automatically.

Tip

When you set up a new profile using the New Profile Wizard and check the option for Do You Travel with This Computer?, an offline store will be created automatically for you in \%WINDOWSROOT%\OUTLOOK.OST and the mailbox folders will be configured for synchronization. The option enabling you to choose the connection type on starting the client will also be checked.

4. To make public folders available offline, you must add the public folders to your Favorites folder. To do this, select the folder in the Folder view pane in Outlook. Then select the File menu, choose Folder and select the Add to Public Folder Favorites command. You will now find that the copy of the folder in Favorites has a Synchronization tab on its Properties dialog box, as shown in Figure 7.32. You can now make this folder available offline or online.

5. After you have configured all your folders for offline use, select Tools, click Synchronize, and select All Folders to update all folders.

6. The final part in configuring for offline use is to download the Offline Address Book (OAB). After you have done this, you will have a copy of your Exchange Global Address List available for offline use. Select the Tools menu again, click Synchronize, and this time choose Download Address Book. You will see the dialog box shown in Figure 7.33.

FIGURE 7.32

The Synchronization tab on a folder enables you to switch synchronization on and off and to filter which items will be synchronized.

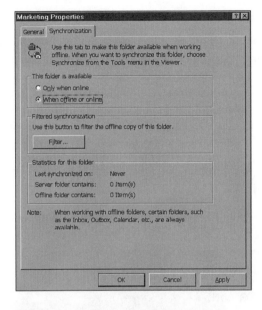

FIGURE 7.33

This dialog box shows the download offline address book options.

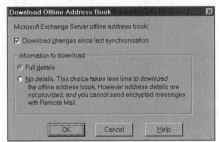

7. Choose the appropriate download options for the Offline Address Book and select OK. You have now successfully configured your client for offline use.

Note

Downloading an Offline Address Book (OAB) will not work until Exchange has generated it. To make this happen, start Exchange Administrator and double-click on your site in the left pane. Now select Configuration. In the right pane, you should now see an object called DS Site Configuration. Double-click on this object in the right pane and you will see its properties. Select the Offline Address Book tab and click the Generate Now button to force generation of the OAB. You can also add recipient containers to the list of containers that the OAB gets recipient information from.

By default, the OAB is generated automatically every 24 hours at 03:00.

See Day 15, "Maintaining Exchange," for more information.

7

Working Offline

Now that you've configured the client to work offline, doing so is easy. Simply log out of Outlook and disconnect from the network. When you log in again, you will see a dialog box giving you the option either to connect to the network or to work offline. Select Work Offline and you will see your Outlook mailbox as usual. The differences are that you can only see the public folders in your Favorites folder that you have configured for synchronization. Also, when you click the To button to address a message, you will see a new Global Address List (Offline) entry, which should contain all the entries from your Global Address List.

Remote Mail and Personal Folders

If you are trying to set up Exchange in a low bandwidth WAN environment or you want your users to connect using RAS, you won't be able to use RPCs. This is because these sorts of connections don't support RPCs. Instead, you will need to use the remote mail features of your Exchange client.

What Is Remote Mail?

Remote mail is a means of connecting to your Exchange Server and downloading only the message header information to your client. This means that the bandwidth used is minimal—no matter the size of the actual messages, you only receive a few bytes' worth of information about each. After you have decided which messages you want to see, you can mark them for delivery. You can then connect a second time and collect the marked mail. This saves bandwidth even further by enabling you to elect not to download a message with a large attachment, such as the latest "dancing baby" video.

Which Users Would Benefit from Using Remote Mail?

Remote mail is far more versatile than offline folders in terms of its application. However, this versatility comes at the expense of a certain amount of functionality.

Looking at your lists of user roles, all users except for the managerial ones (who are configured to use offline folders) can use the remote mail facility. You now need to look at the method by which the remote client can access your network, which will in turn depend on your LAN configuration.

Analyzing the list of server roles that I described earlier, you might notice that you can condense your list of network options further. The questions then become:

- Do you have a permanent link to the Internet?
- Are you running a RAS Server on your network?
- Are your remote sites connected using a private WAN?

Now, take a look at the possible scenarios arising from these questions.

No Permanent Internet Connection and No RAS Server.   If you have neither a permanent link to the Internet (such as using ISDN Dial on Demand or a modem to connect your Exchange Server to your ISP) nor a RAS server, you will have to use the Exchange Internet Mail Service to deliver mail to your remote users. They will need to have individual accounts with an ISP and unique email addresses, such as fredflinstone@aol.com. You can add these addresses as custom recipients in Exchange Administrator (see Day 4) and then use the addresses to send mail to the remote user. Custom recipients can also be included in distribution lists.

At the client end, you will need to add a personal store and the Internet email service. Configure the users' Internet email service to deliver to their ISP and your remote users will now be able to call in, send, and receive mail.

This solution will work for both the home worker and the sales user. In the case of the sales user, you will want to configure a proper Exchange mailbox as well, and possibly have the user set up rules to cover automatic forwarding of mail and other services.

For more information on configuring the Internet Mail Service, see Day 12.

RAS Server and No Permanent Internet Connection.   If you have a RAS server connected to the telephone lines, your clients can use RAS or DUN to connect to your LAN. They can then access the servers on the LAN as if they were connected locally, but at a much slower speed.

Tip

> If your users only use RAS or DUN to connect to your RAS server, you might consider using NetBEUI as the transport protocol over RAS. It is fast and easy to configure, the RAS server can act as a gateway to your LAN protocol, and you don't have to mess with TCP/IP, DHCP, WINS, DNS, or any other acronyms.

This solution will also work for users at a remote office who connect in via RAS or Dial on Demand ISDN to a RAS server.

This solution will also work for the home worker, but unless your company's RAS server is a local phone call away, they will probably end up paying out more in telephone connection charges than if they connected via an ISP.

No RAS Server but a Permanent Internet Connection   With this configuration, you have a number of new options. First, the remote user can connect into your network over the Internet. With the current state of concern over unauthorized access from the Internet, this suggestion usually has IT managers exploding with rage. However, some

7

elementary security precautions available with Windows NT will make this a feasible option.

These security options include the following:

- Add PPTP (Point to Point Tunneling Protocol) as a networking service on the client.
- Configure the network interface connected to your ISP to allow only PPTP connections.
- Disable IP routing between your external and internal interfaces.
- Working with your ISP, restrict the range of incoming addresses on your router to that used by your external clients.

There are several other security options, such as implementing Routing and Remote Access Service (RRAS) or Internet Information Server (IIS) with Proxy Server.

Obviously, allowing this type of access is not a trivial matter and you will need to ensure that your system is secure. For more information on setting up and configuring security on Internet connections see Day 12.

Once connected into your network, your remote user can use either Exchange remote mail to download headers, as I described earlier, or connect to his or her mailbox using POP3.

Remote Sites Connection via a WAN   If your remote users connect to a private WAN, you only need to answer three questions.

- Does the connection support Remote Procedure Calls (RPC)?
- How many users are at the remote site?
- What is the available bandwidth on the connection?

Here the answers are not so obvious, as the number of users and the available bandwidth will affect acceptable performance.

If your WAN link does not support RPCs, you will have to use remote mail and personal stores. I'll describe how to configure these in a moment.

The standard protocols that support RPCs are TCP/IP, IPX (NWLink in NT), NetBEUI, and Vines IP. There are also local procedure calls (LPC) and Named Pipes. LPCs are used when the client and server are on the same machine. Named Pipes are used in a Windows NT environment and are a secure, guaranteed-delivery API implemented as a file system. However, they still need TCP/IP, IPX, NetBIOS, and so on.

Tip

To check whether your link supports RPCs, use the RPC Ping tools on the Exchange Server CD. You will find these under \Server\Support\Rpcping.

First run the appropriate server component for your processor on the server—RPINGS.EXE for Intel, RPINGS_A.EXE for Alpha, and so on. Then run the client executable file at the remote site. There are versions of RPC Ping for DOS (RPINGDOS.EXE), Windows 3.x (RPINGC16.EXE), 95 and 98, and Windows NT (RPINGC32.EXE).

See Day 10 for further information.

If your connection does support RPCs and you have adequate bandwidth and not too many users, you will be able to connect the users directly to the Exchange server.

If your bandwidth is low, the number of users at the remote site very high, or both, you have two other options. Either configure the users to connect via remote mail or install an Exchange server at the remote location and create another site. Of course, the latter option is expensive, but after all, it isn't your money, is it!

How Do I Implement Remote Mail?

Implementing remote mail is easier than implementing offline folders. However, you will need to create a new profile for each remote user. Here's how to do it.

1. Set up a profile by following the procedure outlined earlier in the chapter, adding Exchange Server as a service. This time, do not answer Yes to the option Do You Travel with Your Computer? That action will configure the profile for offline use, which is incompatible with remote mail. Don't worry, we'll take care of the incompatibility in a moment.

2. After you have created your profile, add a personal store (making sure you locate the .PST file on the machine's local hard disk). Click the Add button and add the personal store as we covered in the section on personal stores previously.

3. Now click the Delivery options tab on your new profile and select the Personal Store as the delivery location for new mail, not the Exchange mailbox.

4. Go back to the Services tab and double-click on the Exchange Server service to see its properties. On the General tab of the Exchange Service properties box, select the check box that enables you to choose whether you are connected to the network.

5. On the Dial-Up Networking tab of the Exchange Service properties dialog box, choose the type of connection that you will be using. You will have the option of

7

using a RAS connection via a modem, in which case you will have to supply connection information, or you can use an existing connection. Select Dial Up Networking if connecting to the remote site via a RAS server. Choose Do Not Dial, Use an Existing Connection for working at a remote site that connects via a low-bandwidth private WAN.

6. You can make additional configuration changes on the Remote Mail tab to control the collection of messages and the times that the client will automatically connect to the Exchange server. I'll cover these setting later in the lesson.

> If you are configuring a user's desktop machine at the end of a WAN link, you could choose the option to always work offline using Dial-Up Networking. You then don't need to check the box to enable the client to choose the connection type on startup, as it is unlikely that he will be lugging his desktop machine to your central office. Portables are a different matter, though.
>
> To do this, click the Start button, select Settings, and then click Control Panel. Double-click on the Mail icon and then double-click on the Exchange Server service. On the General tab, select the offline option.

On starting Outlook, you will have the option to connect to the network or work offline. If you connect to the network (for example, if you were a sales representative on a rare visit to the office), you will be able to access your mailbox as normal.

> You cannot use the remote mail tools when you are connected to the Exchange Server. You will get a message telling you that remote mail is not correctly set up.

If you start up your client machine when offline, you will not be able to open your Exchange mailbox. However, if you open the Tools menu, select Remote Mail, and look in the resulting Remote Mail menu, you will see options like Connect and Disconnect. To make the remote mail tools always visible, either select the Tools menu, then Remote Mail, and then Remote Tools, or right-click on the Outlook toolbar (the one below the Menu bar) and select Remote. You'll see the toolbar shown in Figure 7.34, which you can leave floating or dock with the sides of your window.

FIGURE 7.34

The Remote Tools tool-bar can be floating or docked with the other toolbars.

By selecting Connect from the Remote Tools menu, you'll see a wizard, shown in Figure 7.35. Click Next, and the next step will let you choose the actions that you are about to carry out with an estimation of the time taken to complete them (if known), as shown in Figure 7.36.

FIGURE 7.35

You can specify which information service you want to connect to on the first screen of the Remote Connection wizard.

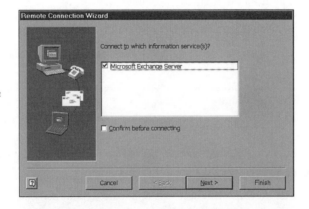

FIGURE 7.36

On the second screen you can specify which actions you want carried out.

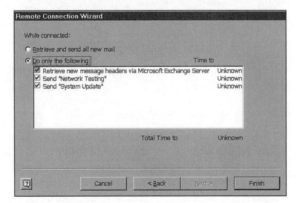

Select all the check boxes and then click Next to continue, and the download process will begin. You now get a very natty display, shown in Figure 7.37, showing your messages being transferred to what looks like a hiccuping globe. (At least to me—it's probably indigestion after swallowing so many letters.)

7

FIGURE 7.37

The remote mail delivery in progress dialog box shows your mail delivery in progress.

On inspecting your Inbox (the one in your personal folders, not the one on your Exchange mailbox), any new messages that you see will be just the headers. You can now select the messages that you want to view and select Mark to Retrieve or Mark to Retrieve a Copy from the Remote Tools toolbar.

 Tip

> You can tell which items are just message headers because they have a tiny shortcut arrow on the message icon.
>
> When you retrieve the full message, the icon changes to the standard message symbol.

Mark to Retrieve will remove the message from the Exchange server and deliver it to your personal store on the client.

Mark to Retrieve a Copy will deliver a duplicate to your personal store on the client, but will also leave the message on the Exchange server.

Should you mistakenly mark a message for retrieval, you can use the Unmark or Unmark All to reset your message markings before downloading it.

After you have marked all the messages that you want to retrieve, you can reconnect to the Exchange server and those messages will be downloaded in full.

 Tip

> If you retrieve a message (removing it from the server) and then decide that you wanted to retain the message on the server, a quick workaround is to forward the same message to yourself. Your forwarded message will then appear back on the server.

Remote Mail Options

If your clients get tired of having to click the Connect button every time they want to send and receive mail, there are some additional remote mail options that you can select.

Open the Properties dialog box for the Exchange Server service in your profile and click on the Remote Mail tab. In the resulting dialog box, shown in Figure 7.38, you can now configure options to govern the behavior of the remote connection.

FIGURE 7.38

This figure shows the options for filtering and scheduling remote mail.

Let's take a closer look at some of the options this dialog box offers.

Remote Mail Connections   This section enables you to specify whether messages are downloaded automatically. For example, if you always want to download messages from your boss, you can select the Retrieve Items that Meet the Following Conditions radio button. Click on the Filter button and you'll see the dialog box shown in Figure 7.39. Here you can specify conditions under which mail will be downloaded immediately, without messing around with headers.

FIGURE 7.39

By filtering your remote mail, you can transfer messages that are important and leave the rest on the server.

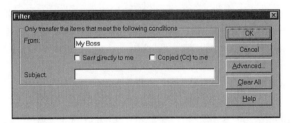

Note   If you do not put any criteria into the filter box then *all* mail will be downloaded. This may be desirable in a WAN environment if the bandwidth available can support the users connecting across it.

7

The Advanced button in the Filter dialog box enables you to specify further criteria as to which messages will be downloaded. You can specify message sizes, dates, importance levels, sensitivity, only unread messages, or only messages with attachments. You can see the Advanced options in Figure 7.40. Select the options you want, and then click OK to return to the Filter dialog box, and OK again to return to the Remote Mail Properties tab.

FIGURE 7.40

The advanced filtering options on remote mail allow you to specify exactly what sort of mail is downloaded as well as completely invert your selection criteria.

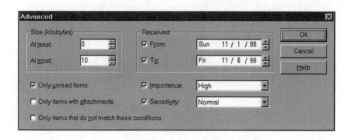

> **Caution**
>
> Note the very innocuous looking check box that says Only Items That Do Not Match These Conditions. This option applies to all criteria set up using the filter dialog and will change the outcome to do the exact opposite of what is specified. Parents will probably understand this function more readily—it's the one that your teenage children are already fitted with.
>
> Hence if you want to download all messages that do *not* have attachments (thus saving bandwidth), check the box for Only Items With Attachments and then the box for Only Items That Do Not Match These Conditions.

Scheduled Connections   Back in the Remote Mail tab, the next set of options is Scheduled Connections. Here you can specify a connection schedule to the Exchange server. Again, this is an option that you are more likely to use in a WAN environment than when accessing the server over a dial-up connection, simply because of the expense that is likely to be incurred if your clients are constantly checking their mail over the telephone lines.

Note that the scheduled connections section also has a Filter button. You can use these options to specify which messages are downloaded in exactly the same way as you do for remote mail connections, which I just described.

Exchange over RAS

You have already looked at a number of issues involved in supporting Exchange in a RAS environment. Now it's time to turn your attention to the server end and look at how you can implement RAS server and thus allow your remote clients to connect to your network.

> **REFERENCE MATERIALS**
>
> For more information on implementing RAS under Windows NT, see Chapters 4–11 of the Networking Supplement Manual, which is published on TechNet. For more information on TechNet, go to
>
> http://www.microsoft.com/technet.
>
> See also the excellent manual *Windows NT 4 Server Unleashed, Professional Reference Edition* by Jason Garms, ISBN: 0-672-31002-3.

What Is RAS?

The Windows NT Remote Access Service (RAS) is Microsoft's implementation of WAN dial-up technology. RAS can support connections over asynchronous modems on the Public Subscriber Telephone Network (PSTN), terminal adapters using Integrated Services Digital Network (ISDN), or X.25 via a dial-up Packet Assembler/Dissembler (PAD) or an X.25 smart card.

 Note
> Some of you may be more familiar with PSTN as POTS—Plain Old Telephone System.

Both RAS server and client are supplied with Windows NT Workstation and NT Server, the difference being that NT Server can host up to 256 simultaneous incoming RAS connections (using a modem multiboard), whereas NT Workstation can only host one.

The RAS client on Windows NT is called Dial-Up Networking (DUN). Windows 95 and 98 have a built-in RAS client, also called Dial-Up Networking.

Windows 95 can act as a RAS server after installation of the Plus! Pack add-on. I don't recommend it, though, as Windows 95 is not secure enough to be a corporate RAS server.

Note
> If using RAS server or client on Windows NT 4.0, make sure you reinstall Service Pack 4 after you have installed RAS.

7

> **ROUTING AND REMOTE ACCESS SERVER**
>
> If you need greater functionality than can be provided by the Windows NT RAS server, you may want to review Microsoft's Routing and Remote Access Server (RRAS). This software gives additional support for IP and IPX routing, as well as filtering based on IP addresses, packet types, and protocols.
>
> It is currently a free download from Microsoft. However, if you choose to implement RRAS, make sure you have the latest patches for this product.
>
> For further information see
>
> http://www.microsoft.com/ntserver/nts/downloads/communications/RouteRASNT.asp

How Do I Implement RAS in an Exchange Environment?

With RAS, you have two deployment options for your RAS server. You can either use one server to run both your RAS and Exchange services, or you can have separate RAS and Exchange servers. Personally, I would always go for the separate option, as this will improve performance and security. The downside is that it costs more, as you will require another server. However, the saving may not be as great as you think because if you run both services on the same server you will need to increase the server's RAM in proportion to the number of simultaneous RAS connections you will be hosting. For the purposes of this book, I will assume you are using separate RAS and Exchange servers.

But before I can get into the nuts and bolts of installing RAS, I need to look at a few more planning issues.

How Can My Remote Clients Connect?

Your clients can connect using three methods, which I'll describe separately in a second. However, you need to assess the best connection method for your situation.

Modem via PSTN (or POTS)   This connection method is the most common. The client needs a modem, a telephone line, Windows dial-up networking service, and an Outlook or Exchange client. At the server end, you need at least one telephone line and a modem. If you require multiple simultaneous access, you will need a modem multiboard (see the "Modem Multiboard" sidebar later in this lesson).

Depending on your modem type and the quality of the telephone lines, you may be able to reach speeds of 56Kbps. However, the reliable two-way communication limit over copper telephone wire is normally 33.6Kbps. Compression can increase this to speeds in excess of 115Kbps.

INCREASING YOUR LINK SPEED

One way to increase the speed of a PSTN modem link is to enable Multilink. This software option allows the RAS client to connect to the RAS server using multiple modems, thus multiplying the bandwidth by the number of simultaneous connections. This solution is one that you would probably only implement where you have a remote site linked in via a dial-up connection and you can't or don't want to implement ISDN.

To use Multilink, you must have two modems at the client end, two at the server end, and two telephone lines. You can then configure each modem to use RAS and then click the Network button on the RAS Service Properties dialog box to enable Multilink. You will then need to add a phone book entry for each modem to connect to one of the remote modems.

Multilink can't be used with the server callback feature of RAS, as callback can only use one phone book entry.

MODEM MULTIBOARDS

If your site requires simultaneous dial-up access by several users, you will need to investigate modem multiboards. These allow multiple (up to 256) modems to connect to an NT RAS server. Several modem manufacturers offer modem multiboards.

More information is available at

`http://www.modemhelp.com/links/Modem_Companies/.`

ISDN Terminal Adapter   Integrated Services Digital Network (ISDN) is another option with the increased access speeds offered. A basic rate ISDN line can connect at 64Kbps. Also, some types of terminal adapter enable you to multiplex two basic rate channels to provide 128Kbps.

Note

I understand that ISDN is not so popular in the USA. If you are interested in looking at the ISDN option, I would suggest that you get your telecomms company to give you the names and telephone numbers of at least three satisfied customers.

You will be paying a premium rate for this service and you should check out your local provider's support facilities.

7

As far as the network is concerned, the ISDN terminal adapter is just another network card. However, its internal operation is similar to a modem, except that is doesn't have to go through the error-prone process of converting the signal from digital to analog and back again. Hence ISDN is usually faster and more reliable than PSTN/POTS. Sadly, in the United Kingdom especially, ISDN is very expensive. Depending on your location, the basic rate you can expect to pay for an ISDN line is $35 to $100.

Use ISDN in situations in which you expect a lot of traffic from your remote site and both locations will support it.

> **Note** Depending on your level of ISDN use, you may find it cheaper to implement a leased line, bearing in mind that it will cost a fixed amount each year and is much easier to budget for.

X.25 The X.25 protocol is a full duplex protocol first standardized by the CCITT in 1976 and then updated in 1978, 1980, 1984, and 1988. The global X.25 network can be thought of as similar to the Internet. However, its functionality is more limited.

 The CCITT (Comité Consultatif Internationale de Telegraphique et Telephonique; or Consultative Committee on International Telephone and Telegraphy), now known as the ITU (Telecommunication Standardization Sector of the International Telecommunications Union), is the primary international body for implementing standards for telecommunications equipment and systems. It is located in Geneva, Switzerland and operates under the mandate of the United Nations.

Implementing RAS over X.25 will usually entail some form of link into the global X.25 packet switched network. This can be implemented as a modem connecting to an X.25 Packet Assembler Dissembler (PAD—Windows 95/98 and Windows NT) or via an X.25 smart card (Windows NT client only).

As RAS implementations over X.25 tend to be very rare, I will not cover this subject any further. If you are currently using X.25, you will doubtless be familiar with its operation and if you are thinking of implementing it then you will need a greater depth of advice than the scope of this book.

How Do I Install RAS on Windows NT?

RAS is implemented as a network service and is configured from the Services tab on the Network icon in Control Panel. Here's how to get started.

1. From the Start menu, click on Settings and then open the Control Panel. Double-click on the Network icon and select the Services tab from the resulting dialog box.

2. Click the Add button and scroll down the list of available services to find the Remote Access Service, as shown in Figure 7.41. Select OK and you will be prompted to supply the location of the NT Server (or Workstation) source files.

FIGURE 7.41

To use remote mail, you will need to add remote access as a network service.

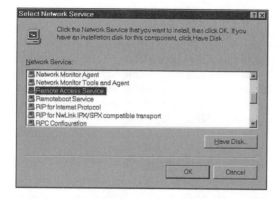

3. If you do not have a RAS-capable device on your client or server, you can add one. Select the Add button from the RAS Setup screen and you will be presented with the dialog box shown in Figure 7.42, which gives you the option to install a Modem or to connect to an X.25 PAD.

FIGURE 7.42

Here you can add RAS devices, such as modems or X.25 PADs.

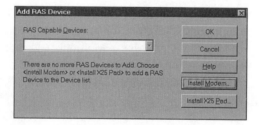

4. Selecting Add New Modem will invoke the Install New Modem Wizard. This will either auto-detect your modem (a reasonably reliable feature, although newer modems won't detect the right driver; you'll need to supply it from the disk provided with the modem) or ask you to choose a specified modem, including using an unlisted or updated driver. Add your modem type and select Next.

5. You will now be asked which communications port you would like the modem to function on. Select the relevant COM port for your machine and select Next. Your modem will now be installed and you will be returned to the RAS setup screen. If you are connecting to an X.25 PAD, you can also install it through this screen.

7

Tip

When configuring modems to use COM ports under Windows NT, you must ensure that the COM port is running at the maximum speed that the modem can use. To do so, select the Start menu, choose Settings, launch the Control Panel, and then double-click on the Ports icon. Select the COM port that your modem is attached to and click the Settings button. Select the Baud Rate from the drop-down list. I use a 28.8Kbps modem with a port speed of 115,200bps.

Caution

In order to support communications in excess of 14.4Kbps on an external modem, your PC must have a 16550 UART chip fitted (check the BIOS). Most PCs made in the last couple of years meet this specification. Internal modems are not affected by this requirement. Be wary of 16550 "compatible" chipsets on cheap serial cards. Compatibility does not necessarily mean equality.

6. After you have installed your modem, you will be returned to the RAS Setup screen and your modem will be shown on the list of devices to use with RAS, as shown in Figure 7.43. If you want to use Multilink, add another modem.

FIGURE 7.43

Here the RAS setup screen shows the modem installed.

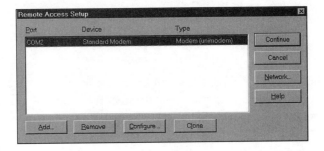

7. In the Remote Access Setup dialog box, click on the Configure button to specify how NT will operate with RAS. The three options are for Dial Out Only (RAS Client), Receive Calls Only (RAS Server), and Dial Out and Receive Calls (both client and server). If you are using the Callback functionality of RAS, you must configure your RAS server to dial out and receive calls, as shown in Figure 7.44.

FIGURE 7.44

You can configure RAS to act as a client (dial out only), server (receive calls only), or both (dial out and receive) by selecting the relevant option.

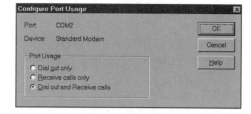

RAS AND THE DYNAMIC RAS CONNECTOR

If you are configuring Exchange to use the Dynamic RAS connector to connect sites, you will normally need to specify that the RAS server (which will also be an Exchange messaging bridgehead server) will work on both dial out and receive calls.

See Day 5, "Working with Multiple Sites," for more information on setting up the Dynamic RAS Connector.

---

8. Click Continue to set up the network configuration of your RAS client or server. Alternatively, you can click on the Network button to set up protocols for use with RAS. Depending on which options you selected for under the Configure button, you will see settings for Dial Out Protocols, Server Settings, or both.

9. Check the boxes for the protocols that you want to enable for RAS, as shown in Figure 7.45. Note that both the server and client settings are shown in this example.

FIGURE 7.45

Check the boxes for the networking protocols you want to run on the client (dial out) or server side.

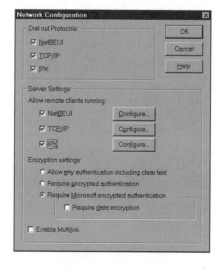

7

10. You can specify the authentication and encryption method used. For Microsoft clients accessing a Microsoft RAS server, use Microsoft Encryption. Other RAS servers can use this functionality as long as they support MS-CHAP (Microsoft Challenge Handshake Authentication Protocol).

11. You can also choose to encrypt all the data that is sent over the link by selecting the Require Data Encryption check box in the lower portion of the dialog box. This will result, however, in slower transmission because all the data has to be encrypted and decrypted.

| | If you are connecting to a non-Microsoft server and you appear to be having authentication problems, try adjusting the encryption settings to a lower level. |

12. If you are using multiple modems to connect to a remote site, you can enable Multilink here by clicking the check box at the bottom of the dialog box.

13. Selecting one or more protocols for RAS server enables their respective Configure buttons. Clicking on Configure enables you to specify whether RAS will be used as a gateway to allow access to other machines on the network or not. For example, click the Configure button next to the TCP/IP setting.

14. This dialog box, shown in Figure 7.46, lets you configure RAS for TCP/IP. All the other configuration boxes are easier than this one, although the IPX configuration dialog box does require an understanding of using IPX/SPX in a routed environment. With TCP/IP you can either use Dynamic Host Configuration Protocol (DHCP) to allocate IP addresses or you can specify a fixed IP range to be used (a sort of mini-DHCP).

| | Remember that if you are not using RAS over the Internet, NetBEUI is the fastest and easiest protocol to configure for RAS. |

15. Finally, after you have configured your protocols, click OK in the various dialog boxes until you return to the Remote Access Setup dialog box. Select Continue, and the network bindings will be adjusted to add RAS as a client or a server. After the bindings have been set, you will be prompted to reboot your server.

16. Don't forget to apply Service Pack 4!

FIGURE 7.46

When configuring TCP/IP for use with RAS, you can specify a static address range or to use DHCP, which requires you to have a DHCP server already set up on your network.

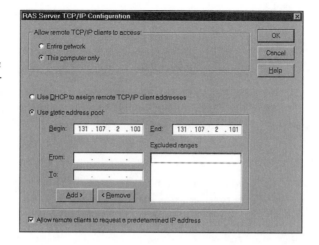

 If RAS and Exchange are on different servers, you must enable the option to access the entire network, no matter what protocol you're using. Doing so enables the NetBIOS gateway or IP/IPX routing as appropriate.

Administration of the RAS Server

Administration of the RAS server is carried out via Remote Access Admin manager in Exchange's Administrative tools. This program enables you to see which users are connected and to grant or revoke RAS dial-in permissions.

You make configuration changes to the RAS service via the Network icon in the Control Panel. Select the Services tab as you did when you installed RAS and highlight the Remote Access Service. Click the Properties button and you can now change the RAS service type, add and remove modems or PADs, and configure protocols. However, you'll have to reboot the machine when you have made these changes.

General Security Issues with RAS.

Now that you have a RAS server implemented on your LAN, anyone could attempt to dial in and access your network. Hence, I'd like to make some suggestions on security:

1. Make sure your passwords are secure. All your service account and administrator passwords should be 14 character mixed-case alphanumeric strings. They should not be based on real names, children's names, pets names, and so on.

7

2. Write down the passwords for your system and place them in your company's fire safe or store them securely off-site.

3. Only grant dial-in access to the users who require it. Configure these permissions through User Manager for Domains or Remote Access Admin.

4. Set an account policy in User Manager for Domains that includes account lockouts, a minimum password length, a password history, and a maximum and minimum password age. To do this, start User Manager for Domains, click the Policies menu, and select Account. You can now configure password restrictions and lockout policy.

5. Rename your administrator account to something else. Remember that this account is very vulnerable to hacking, as there is no lockout on this account.

6. Don't call your Exchange service account something obvious like "EXSERVICE". And *never* use "password" as your password. Or abracadabra. Or opensesame. Or anything else that's easily guessable. Remember the principle of "security through obscurity."

7. Configure Security Auditing to monitor unsuccessful logons.

8. Finally, Check your Security Event Logs regularly!

We discuss these security issues in more detail on Day 19.

Using the RAS Client

To use the RAS client, you need to configure Dial-Up Networking from the Accessories program group. To access it, click the Start menu, choose Programs, select Accessories and then click on Dial-Up Networking. The first time you start this up you will be prompted to create a phone book entry via the New Phone Book Entry Wizard.

You will also be prompted to create a location, as shown in Figure 7.47. Enter some descriptive information in the appropriate text boxes.

 Tip

You can add and edit telephony locations using the Telephony icon in the Control Panel. Telephony locations are particularly useful with mobile users, as they take the guesswork out of whether to include a country or regional code when dialing a number.

FIGURE 7.47

Telephony locations sort out the problem of what area code to dial.

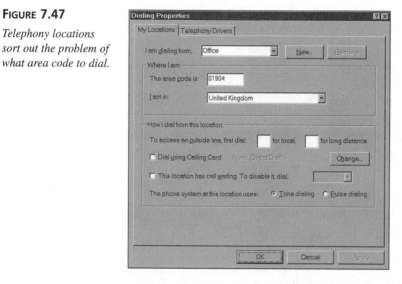

After you have created your phone book entry and clicked OK, you will see the dialog box shown in Figure 7.48.

FIGURE 7.48

Clicking the dial button will connect you using dial-up networking.

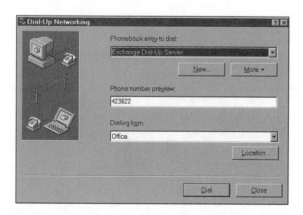

Just click Dial to initiate the RAS connection to your server. That was easy, wasn't it?

Changing Client Configuration Settings

To configure your RAS client further, click on the More button of the Dial-Up Networking dialog box and select Edit Entry and Modem Properties from the resulting drop-down menu. You will now see the dialog box shown in Figure 7.49.

7

FIGURE 7.49

Here you can config-
ure the general proper-
ties of your phone
book entry.

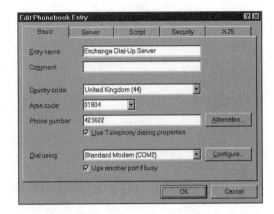

I recommend that you look at the following settings:

1. Click the check box for Use Telephony Dialing Properties.

2. Select the Configure button next to the Dial Using text box.

3. You'll see the Modem Configuration dialog box shown in Figure 7.50. Enable all the options shown in the figure.

FIGURE 7.50

This dialog box shows
your modem properties
under RAS. You can't
change these anywhere
else!

4. Select the Server tab and ensure the enabled protocols match at least one of those that you are using on the server. In the sample dialog box shown in Figure 7.51, you can see that TCP/IP is active, as we configured it earlier.

5. If you are using TCP/IP, you will have to configure an additional dialog box by clicking the TCP/IP Settings button. Again, the settings will depend on how you have implemented TCP/IP. The settings shown in Figure 7.52 are for use with DHCP or a static address pool as configured when setting up the server I described earlier.

FIGURE 7.51

The Server tab lets you configure dial-up protocols and RAS server type.

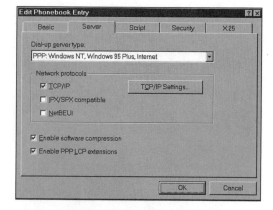

FIGURE 7.52

The TCP/IP options shown here are for a RAS server that issues an IP address, that is, uses a static address pool (refer to Figure 7.46) or DHCP.

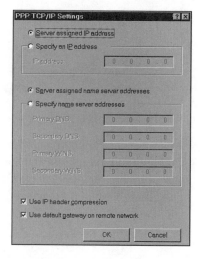

6. The final tab that you will need to configure is the Security tab, shown in Figure 7.53. Generally, you will want to set up this tab as shown. Again, ensure that your encryption settings match those you set up on your server. The option Use Current Name and Password means that the client will log on to your network with the username and password she used to log onto her machine. If you deselect the box, she will be prompted for a username and password again when she logs onto the RAS server. This additional security step makes sense.

7. You will not need the script page for logging onto an NT RAS server the only time you might need this tab is for logging onto an ISP's server, although increasingly they will accept MS-CHAP. You will only need the X.25 options if you are using your modem to log onto an X.25 PAD.

7

FIGURE 7.53

Here you can set up authentication and encryption methods that will be used over the RAS link.

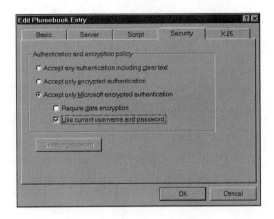

Congratulations! You now have configured your client. Now it's time to fire up RAS for the first time and test it.

Starting Up RAS

After you have added a RAS server to your network and configured a RAS client to dial in and pick up mail, you can then attempt to test your setup. I strongly recommend that you make two telephone lines available wherever you are carrying out the testing so that you can have the client and server next to each other.

Connect the modem on your RAS client and server to the telephone network and make sure the RAS server service is started. Hopefully, when you click the Dial button on Dial Up Networking, you will now be able to connect to the RAS server and log onto the remote network.

AutoDial Manager

The RAS client also installs a service called the AutoDial manager. This program will automatically dial out whenever it receives a request for a resource that is on a remote network. Hence, you do not usually have to dial out on RAS and then click Connect on your Remote Tools in Outlook. Simply click on Connect (or arrange for automatic connection according to your schedule) and you should find that the connection is made automatically.

Troubleshooting RAS

Problems with RAS are usually caused either by security (authentication, account passwords, and so on) or by name resolution on the LAN."

For further information on diagnosing problems with RAS connections, see Microsoft TechNet on

http://www.microsoft.com/technet

or

http://support.microsoft.com/support/.

Summary

In this lesson, you have looked at the creation and configuration of various types of messaging profiles and the different scenarios in which they can be applied. You have also investigated the use of the Outlook or Exchange clients in situations that require support for mobile users. Finally, you looked at how to implement RAS in an Exchange environment.

To summarize the main points of this lesson:

- To connect to Microsoft Exchange using the Outlook or Exchange client, you must first configure a messaging profile.

- Messaging profiles enable you to connect to a variety of information services, not just Exchange.

- You can add Personal Stores (.PST files) to messaging profiles to provide alternative message storage locations, to use with the AutoArchive feature, or for moving messages between mailboxes.

- You can configure multiple profiles and select which profile to use when you start your client.

- Exchange can support your mobile users in a number of different ways, depending on that user's role within your organization.

- Offline folders enable your users to synchronize their folders with the Exchange server and then send and reply to mail as if they were still connected.

- Your users can download an offline copy of the Global Address List for looking up addresses when not connected to the server.

- The remote mail functionality of Exchange enables you to use your mail client with dial-up WAN networking or in situations where bandwidth or line characteristics will not support a full connection.

- You can configure Windows NT to act as a Remote Access server and thus support clients dialing in to your network via PSTN, ISDN or X.25.

7

Q&A

Q **I've now installed Exchange Server and created my mailboxes. What do I need to do to send and receive messages?**

A Assuming you've installed your messaging client, such as Microsoft Outlook, all you need to do now is to get your users to start Outlook, and a messaging profile will be created automatically for them. They will be able to connect to the server and send and receive messages.

Q **When my users start Outlook 97, the profile that is automatically created does not contain the correct information services. How can I alter this?**

A You need to get hold of the Office 97 Resource Kit, which contains an EXCHANGE.PRF file. The resource kit also contains details of how to edit this file. After you have edited it, you can rename it DEFAULT.PRF and place this file in the network share that you are using to install Outlook from. It will then be copied into the Program Files\Microsoft Office\Office directory and used to configure the automatically generated profile.

Q **The automatic generation of profiles works fine for the first person who logs on, but subsequent users are prompted to create a messaging profile. What can I do to ensure that every user gets an automatic profile, regardless of which machine he logs on to?**

A To do this, you need two utilities from the Exchange CD—NEWPROF.EXE and PROFGEN.EXE. If you configure users with a logon script in User Manager for Domains that calls these utilities, you can ensure automatic profile generation for every user. To see the configuration options for these utilities, use NEWPROF /? and PROFGEN /? at a command prompt.

Q **I have implemented roaming profiles on my network. How can I integrate these with messaging profiles?**

A Luckily, a user's messaging profile information is part of his or her local user profile. As long as you copy the local profile with the messaging profile configured to the network share that you want to run the roaming profiles from, the user should get her messaging profile and user profile regardless of what machine she logs on to.

Q My boss has just prevailed upon the accounts department to give him a laptop with a docking station, but it doesn't have a modem. He wants to be able to work at home in the evenings answering and sending emails. Can we support this under our Exchange environment?

A The best option here is probably to configure your boss's machine with an offline store. This will allow him to synchronize his mail store when he leaves work and then reply to those emails at home as if he was connected to the Exchange server. On arriving back in the morning he will be able to synchronize all his folders and deliver the night's batch of messages.

Q I have several remote sites with one or two users who are linked to headquarters. With the other traffic on the link, the effective bandwidth available is less than 10Kbps. Will I be able to use the Outlook client to connect to my Exchange server?

A In this situation, you are not likely to be able to make an RPC or direct connection to the Exchange server. However, you will be able to use the remote mail functionality, which enables your users to download the headers only. They can then decide which messages they would like to download.

Workshop

The Workshop provides two ways for you to affirm what you've learned in this lesson. The Quiz section poses questions to help you solidify your understanding of the material covered and the Exercise section provides you with experience in using what you have learned. You can find answers to the quiz questions and exercises in Appendix B, "Answers to Quiz Questions and Exercises."

Quiz

1. What is a messaging profile?
2. How many messaging profiles can you configure?
3. How can you choose between profiles when starting Outlook?
4. What are the some of the messaging services that you can add to a profile?
5. What mechanism is used to make a connection between an Exchange client and the server?

7

6. What is Multilink and when would you use it?

7. Which is the best protocol to use over RAS?

8. Name two utilities that you can use to configure RAS dial-in permission.

9. What is the normal storage limit on a .PST file?

10. How can you recover information in a .PST file when the user has forgotten the password?

11. What is the purpose of an Outlook Address Book?

Exercises

1. How do you add a RAS device to NT Server?

2. How would you configure your Outlook client to use encryption when communicating with the Exchange server over a LAN?

3. How do you configure Exchange to enable multiple users to open the same mailbox?

WEEK 2

At A Glance

This week you'll learn about the day-to-day operation of
Exchange and its clients, especially Microsoft Outlook. You'll
see how to troubleshoot problems that may crop up, how to
deploy Exchange to your users, set up the Outlook client,
connect to the Internet, and more.

- Day 8, "Troubleshooting Exchange," teaches you
  proven strategies and tools for troubleshooting
  Exchange. See how to track down the source of the
  problem, be it the client, the server, the network or user
  error, and how to cope with the trouble in each case.

- Day 9, "Deploying Exchange," covers how to plan and
  execute your deployment of the Exchange clients.
  You'll review various options for installing software on
  the users' workstations and see how to set up an automatic installation that needs no direct user input.

- Day 10, "Using Microsoft Outlook," demonstrates the
  ins and outs of using the popular Microsoft Outlook
  email client. You'll see how to configure the client, use
  Microsoft word as your email editor, import and export
  information, and create categories for easy message
  sorting.

- Day 11, "Communication Protocols and the Internet,"
  helps you to understand the key protocols used to facilitate communication across the Internet. It covers the
  TCP/IP, SMTP, POP3, IMAP, DNS, NNTP, and LDAP
  protocols, among others. Along the way, you'll consider
  security enhancements for your Internet setup.

- Day 12, "Exchange on the Internet," shows how to link your Exchange server to the Internet to give your users worldwide email capability. You'll see how to configure your connection and decide whether to allow newsgroup access.

- Day 13, "Building a Web Site Around Exchange," shows you how to offer remotes users access to their email via the Web. You'll learn how to link your Exchange server to Microsoft's Internet Information Server and configure security.

- Day 14, "Reading Exchange Mail with Internet Clients," teaches you how to support a variety of Internet-based clients using the POP3, SMTP, and NNTP protocols. You'll also see how to configure LDAP.

DAY **8**

Troubleshooting Exchange

By Anthony Steven

Chapter Objectives

In this chapter, I will cover the area probably closest to an administrator's heart—troubleshooting. You will look at how to troubleshoot Exchange on a number of levels, and how to apply this knowledge to your own system. I will also be sharing a few of the many interesting little issues that I have seen on various consulting projects.

Today you will be covering the following topics:

- Troubleshooting methods
- Exchange-based troubleshooting
- User-based troubleshooting

- Hardware-based troubleshooting
- Network-based troubleshooting
- Tools and techniques
- Further sources of assistance

Troubleshooting Overview

My hope is that you won't need to use this section; experience counsels otherwise. With any complex messaging application like Microsoft Exchange, there are bound to be times when your system doesn't do what it's told. Eventually, you will find yourself faced with a dialog box with a large red exclamation mark, a service that won't start, or, worst of all, some angry users. This is the point at which you start earning your salary.

What I can't hope to give you in this book is a solution for every Exchange problem. Therefore, I am going to concentrate on providing a methodical approach using the Exchange Troubleshooting Model (ETM), and I will highlight some of the more common problems you are likely to see.

Multiple Levels of Troubleshooting

The first part of the Exchange Troubleshooting Model works by categorizing troubleshooting problems into five basic levels:

- User
- Network
- Application
- Operating system
- Hardware

You then apply the troubleshooting methodology described in the next section to each level. However, with experience, you may find yourself jumping straight in at, say, the operating system level, simply because you can immediately identify the characteristics of a particular problem.

I recommend that you start at the user end and work your way toward the server because that is the order in which problems tend to appear. If a user can't log on to Exchange, it could be because of parity errors in the Exchange server's RAM. However, it's more likely to be because the user's made a boo-boo.

Let's look at these levels in detail.

User-Based

The chances are that whatever level of the model is causing the problem, the first warning that you get will be from your users. Now, end users can be simple souls, and tend to frame their complaints along the lines of "I can't log onto Outlook." Generally, they do not say things like "The Exchange System Attendant service has stopped with Error Code 1093" or "DNS Host Name resolution isn't working—again."

The user-based level is the most complex and frustrating part of troubleshooting. The point of user-based troubleshooting is to isolate the problem at the user end—that is, is it something that the user did or did not do. User-level troubleshooting involves looking at user actions, messaging profiles, and permissions.

Network-Based

Having eliminated the problem at the user end, you can now look at the link between the client and the server. At this point, you will be examining the lower end of the networking scale, looking at such issues as whether you have TCP/IP working correctly. When you have proved that the network protocol is working, you can then look at more application-centric questions, like RPC connections.

Network-based troubleshooting also tends to focus on connectivity in different network environments. Usually, these problems appear at the deployment stage, but an alteration to the underlying network could bring your messaging system to a halt. Network-based troubleshooting also covers redirectors, routers, and dial-up issues.

Application

As you have already eliminated the user-based and networking problems above, you can now move to the troubleshooting at an application level. After all, the Exchange application is what you are supporting.

Application-level troubleshooting looks at client-server application connectivity, Exchange services, the message queues, connectors, and Exchange Administrator Objects.

Operating System

Troubleshooting at the operating system level is probably the widest area to cover. It certainly gives you the most number of tools, although you will also be using some of the NT tools to troubleshoot at the application level.

Operating system problems can sometimes be tricky to diagnose. If an Exchange service isn't starting, it could be an Exchange problem or an NT problem. For example, the reason behind the Exchange service not starting could be that the operating system has run out of user heap memory. Now, I bet you thought NT couldn't run out of user heap memory. So did I, once.

Operating System troubleshooting looks at issues like using NT tools, logon validation, network services, and server management.

If all those items check out, it's time to move on to the hardware level.

Hardware-Based

Finally, when you've exhausted all the other options, begin hardware-based troubleshooting. In fact, you may move directly to this stage after considering only one or two previous levels. Hardware faults tend to affect all services equally and immediately. In addition, the smoke pouring out of the back of the machine and a strong smell of burning is usually a bit of a clue.

Troubleshooting Methodology

It's extremely unlikely that you would be reading this book if you are not actively involved in setting up an Exchange messaging system. Unless, of course, you are carrying out field trials on the drug-free treatment of insomnia. As someone already part of the IT industry, and probably a system administrator, I am sure that you have considerable experience in troubleshooting.

It is most probable that you will use an informal approach to troubleshooting, built up through years of practical problem-solving. However, I think it's sometimes useful to have a more formal approach to a troubleshooting methodology.

If you have your own troubleshooting model, I am sure that it will be effective in locating and solving problems with Exchange. However, if you find troubleshooting a bit hit-and-miss, you might like to consider using the following system.

Having defined the five levels at which the Exchange Troubleshooting Model works, you can then apply the troubleshooting methodology shown if Figure 8.1.

The one area in this model that everyone tends to overlook is recording the actions. I cannot emphasize enough the importance of documenting the actions that you take. When I am involved in a consulting project, before I do anything, I take out a large pad and start recording my actions. This log of actions then becomes an Annex in the consulting report, and can be used to track down any issues resulting from the work.

Preventative Maintenance and Service Packs

One area that you should not overlook in troubleshooting is preventative maintenance. This means ensuring that your system has all the latest service packs and patches applied. If you subscribe to TechNet (more about this later), you will have access to the latest service packs. However, Microsoft also post updates or hotfixes to service packs on their public FTP site.

8

FIGURE 8.1

Good troubleshooting methodology follows a logical progression to solve the problem in the minimum time.

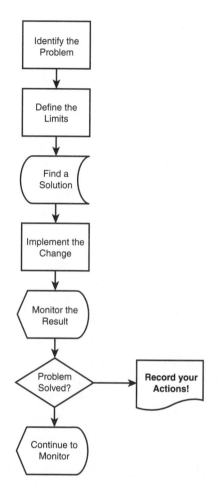

As of January 1999, you should be running Windows NT 4 Service Pack 4 and Microsoft Exchange 5.5 Service Pack 2. In addition, you can find hotfixes to these service packs at the following locations:

```
ftp://ftp.microsoft.com/bussys/winnt/winnt-public/fixes/usa/nt40
➥/hotfixes-postSP4/
ftp://ftp.microsoft.com/bussys/exchange/exchange-public/fixes/Eng
➥/Exchg5.5/PostSP2/
```

Note   You should only apply Post Service-pack hotfixes if you are experiencing the problem described in the Knowledge Base article posted with the Post Service-pack hotfix.

I will now show you some of the different procedures and tools that you can use to solve problems, depending on which level you are operating.

User-Based Troubleshooting

If there is one thing guaranteed to cause a network administrator to groan, it's the thought of having to sort out a user problem. Networks would run really well without users, but then most companies say similar things about their customers. There's no escaping it—at some point you're going to have to deal with people.

If you have more than a couple of hundred users, you may find that it pays to deploy a systems management product like Microsoft Systems Management Server. SMS enables you to view and control a user's desktop from your management console. Most users think this is magic.

To understand if a problem really is user-based, ask yourself the following questions:

- Is this a troubleshooting or a training issue?
- Is he the only user experiencing this problem?
- If so, what could he have possibly changed that might have caused the problem?

If the issue is one of training, you could save yourself a lot of time and avoid considerable frustration by pointing out this training need to your management. After all, how many times do you want to demonstrate this particular procedure to your users? Yes, I would have better things to do as well.

If the system has been working quite happily for the last month, and suddenly this user can't log on, maybe it's something that she's done. However, if the system has been working quite happily for the last month, and suddenly no one can log on, it probably isn't a user issue.

Before you get stuck in the detailed troubleshooting, there is one standard procedure that you need to carry out. Yes, you've guessed—the ritual reboot or, as it's now officially known, the System Hard Reset (SHR).

System Hard Reset

It is part of user folklore that whenever they report a problem to the helpdesk, the first thing the helpdesk operator tells them to do is to reboot the machine. However, unless the reboot happens in a structured fashion, the system may not reset properly.

A System Hard Reset gives you the following benefits:

8

- You perform a proper reset of the system hardware.
- The client machine is starting afresh in a configuration that you know.
- You can monitor any error messages or other information that appears when the machine reboots.
- You can check the user's logon credentials.

I have known machines that fail in such a way that only removing the power lead from the back would reset them. By carrying out an SHR, you are removing this potential source of problems.

An SHR consists of the following steps:

1. Close all applications and save any current work.
2. Close the system down using the Shut Down option on the Start menu.
3. When the system has closed down, power the system off at the power switch.
4. Switch off the processor unit at the mains or pull the power lead out.
5. Wait at least five seconds.
6. Reconnect the power.
7. Switch on.
8. Get the user to log on or log on as the user yourself.

 Note

It is vital that you check the user's logon credentials. There is no point in going into checking permissions and Primary Windows NT Accounts if they are logging on with a different account. You must know which Windows NT account they use.

Having rebooted the client machine in a structured fashion, you can start the troubleshooting process.

Profile Problems

Profile problems are the result of an incorrectly configured messaging (not Windows NT) profile. There are four main areas where errors can arise when you configure a messaging profile and select a mailbox or an Exchange server. These are

- Incorrect mailbox name
- Wrong mailbox

- Incorrect Exchange server name
- Selecting a server in the wrong site

If you try to configure a messaging profile to use a mailbox that does not exist, you will see the message box shown in Figure 8.2.

FIGURE 8.2

You will see this message if the messaging profile is trying to open a non-existent mailbox.

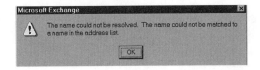

I will cover what happens with the wrong mailbox in the next section.

If you try to connect to a server that does not exist, you get the message in Figure 8.3.

FIGURE 8.3

A non-existent server will produce this message.

In addition, if you configure a profile pointing to a server in the wrong site, a message will appear telling you that the user's mailbox could not be located on that server. The procedure to fix this problem is very similar to that described previously, except that you need to change the server name.

Note This situation should not arise if you have a site connector and directory replication linking the two sites under Exchange 5.5 SP1 with Outlook 98. This is because the site connector automatically re-homes the profile to the correct site.

If the mailbox name won't resolve, you need to look at matching the user's logon credentials to his mailbox, as described later in this section.

If you can't get the server name recognized, you need to check communications, using network-based troubleshooting.

I have already covered setting up messaging profiles on Day 7,—"Configuring the Exchange Client."

Permission Problems

The next level of client problem deals with permissions. As Exchange integrates with Windows NT, users validate to Exchange using their Windows NT account details. Hence, users will be logging on to Windows NT before they log on to Exchange. But what if the user does not have permission to open that mailbox?

You can make users log on to Exchange separately from their workstation logon. To do this, you need to go to the Advanced tab of the Exchange Server service for that user's profile. Select None as the network logon security.

In order to configure permissions on a user's mailbox through Exchange Administrator, you must first make the Permissions tab visible on all objects. To do this, start Exchange Administrator, select the Tools menu, and then choose Options. Click on the Permissions tab and then check the boxes for Show Permissions Page For All Objects and Show Rights For Roles, and then select OK. Now double-click on a mailbox in the Recipients container, and you will see a new Permissions tab.

I have assumed you can see this tab throughout the next section.

Opening a Mailbox

A user can only open a mailbox if she has the correct permissions on that mailbox. That means that either:

- That user's NT account is set as the Primary Windows NT account for that mailbox through Exchange Administrator.

  or

- That user is a member of the global or local group set as the Primary Windows NT account for that mailbox through Exchange Administrator.

  or

- She has User permission on the Mailbox in Exchange Administrator. When you associate a Primary Windows NT account with a mailbox, this should happen automatically.

  or

- The mailbox owner must have given that user at least read permission at the mailbox level using Outlook or Exchange client.

Let's look at these cases and the problems that they generate individually.

Primary Mailbox

Usually, when you create an Exchange user, you associate a Primary Windows NT account with that mailbox. That user account is then given User permission on the relevant mailbox object in the Recipients container in Exchange Administrator.

If these permissions are not set correctly, you will be unable to connect to the mailbox. The symptoms will be that the user won't be able to access his or her Exchange mailbox.

When the user attempts to start Outlook (or another Exchange client), he will see a message informing him that he does not have permissions to open the mailbox. A further message asks whether he wants to open the default file folder instead. If the users select No, Outlook will exit.

To solve this problem, you need to open the relevant messaging profile, and change the username. To do this, carry out the following procedure at the user's workstation:

1. Start Control Panel by clicking on Start and then choosing Settings.

2. Double-click on the Mail icon in the Control Panel window.

3. Click on the Show Profiles button, and you will see a list of all the profiles currently set up on this workstation.

4. If there is only one profile showing, you don't have a problem. If there is more than one, note the entry in the drop-down list at the bottom for which profile to use when starting Microsoft Outlook. Double-click on this profile name in the list of profiles set up on this computer.

5. You will now see the properties of the selected profile. Double-click on the entry for Microsoft Exchange Server.

6. You will now see the properties of the Exchange server messaging service. You should see a server name and a username. Both entries should appear underlined, as shown in Figure 8.4.

7. If the profile's mailbox does not match the user's NT login account, you need to change the mailbox name on the profile to correspond with the NT login name. You can use either the mailbox name (usually *Firstname Lastname*) or the mailbox alias name (normally the Windows NT login name) .

If you have already established that the problem is not due to specifying the incorrect mailbox in the messaging profile, you need to carry out the following task:

1. Check that you know the user's Windows NT logon account. You should have checked this when you carried out the SHR.

2. Start Exchange Administrator, and click on the Recipients button in the toolbar. Find the relevant user in the Recipients container and double-click on her mailbox.

FIGURE 8.4

When a username and server name are resolved, they appear underlined in black

3. At the bottom of the screen is the primary Windows NT account name, which the user must log in as in order to be able to open the mailbox.

4. Now go to the Permissions tab and check that the Primary Windows NT Account has User permission on the mailbox.

Caution

Like Windows NT, changes to Exchange permissions only apply when you log off the Exchange server.

When you are testing permissions, make sure that you get your users to log out of Outlook. To do this, select the Outlook File menu, and then choose Exit and Log Off. If you do not do this, the connection to the server is not closed. Hence, if you restart Outlook, it may reuse the original session with the server, so any changes to permissions will not apply.

Additional Mailboxes In addition to your primary mailbox, you can open additional mailboxes by adding them to your profile. You do this by opening your profile, selecting the properties of the Exchange server service, and clicking on the Advanced tab. Click on the Add button and type in the name of the mailbox that you want to open. Remember that your users can do this as well.

You can add as many additional mailboxes as you like to your profile. However, if you don't have permission to open them, you will get a message like that in Figure 8.5.

To open these mailboxes, you need to have the correct permissions. You can assign permissions for users to open other users' mailboxes in three ways.

FIGURE 8.5

This is the message you see when you attempt to open a mailbox without the correct permissions.

Assigning Permissions using Exchange Administrator To open a mailbox, you must have at least Mailbox Owner permission on the mailbox. To check this, start Exchange Administrator, and click on the Recipients button. In the right pane, scroll down and select the relevant mailbox. Double-click on the mailbox and now click on the Permissions tab. You will now see the Properties sheet in Figure 8.6.

FIGURE 8.6

The Permissions tab lets you configure individual permissions on a mailbox.

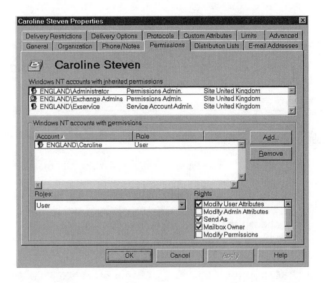

> **Note**
>
> If you can't see the Permissions tab, you haven't carried out the procedure specified earlier, in the "Permission Problems" section.

To open the mailbox, you must add the user's name and either give her the User role, or check the box for Mailbox Owner, which will give her a custom role. When the user now starts Outlook, she should be able to open the additional mailbox.

Assigning Permissions Using an Exchange Client Users can let each other open their mailboxes by configuring the permissions directly in Outlook. However, they must

8

assign a minimum of reviewer role to the other user at the mailbox level. This will let another user see what folders are in their mailboxes. If they want this other user to see items in those folders, the mailbox owner must assign a minimum of reviewer role on those folders.

Note When you assign folder permissions in Outlook, the permissions do not flow down the folder tree. You must configure each folder and subfolder individually. However, if you create a new subfolder, it takes on the permissions of its parent folder.

The usual problem with assigning permissions using the Exchange client is that users forget to assign the reviewer role to their mailbox. To do this, carry out the following procedure:

1. Start Outlook or the Exchange client.
2. From the View menu, check the option for Folder List.
3. Select the mailbox in the folder list. Make sure this says [Mailbox—User Name].
4. Right-click on the selected mailbox and choose Properties.
5. Click on the Permissions tab.
6. Add users by clicking the Add button. Allocate roles to those users by selecting the users and changing the drop-down roles list. You can also apply permissions by checking the boxes for Read items, Create items, and so on.
7. Select OK to accept the changes.

After you have changed permissions at the mailbox level, you also need to change them at the individual folder levels, as you have just done.

Delegate Access You configure Delegate access through the Delegates tab in Outlook 98. For more information on configuring delegate access, see Day 19, "Making Exchange Secure".

All that delegate access does is to configure folder permissions automatically, as you have just covered in the previous section. From a troubleshooting perspective, you should check that the correct delegate access levels apply to the relevant folders (Inbox, Calendar, Contacts, and so on). In addition, check that the delegate has at least reviewer permission at the mailbox level, otherwise the delegate won't be able to open the mailbox.

Access to Public Folders

Problems with access to public folders usually fall into the following categories:

- Authenticated access
- Anonymous access
- Subfolder permissions
- Use of the favorites folder
- Forms

Generally, problems with access to public folders appear as the following message in Outlook:

```
"Unable to display the folder. You do not have sufficient permission to
perform this operation on this object. See the folder contact or your
system administrator."
```

To troubleshoot permission problems from a user's perspective, log in as that user and right-click on the relevant folder. Select Properties and then click on the Summary tab. This shows the contact name for that folder, and the user's current role and permissions. Although your users may not be able to see items in the folders that they do not have permission to view, they can always check on the contact name for that folder.

If you are the owner of the folder, you can control rights and permissions on that folder through Outlook. You can also modify permissions on any folder through Exchange Administrator, as well as cascade these permissions down the folder tree.

 Note Permissions set in Outlook do not cascade down to subfolders. Only Exchange Administrator can do this. Hence, you should change permissions with the Exchange Administrator program.

Authenticated Access The Default account governs authenticated access for all accounts that do not have defined roles. Hence, if you set the default role to None, only users and distribution lists with defined roles will be able to access a public folder.

You can add users or distribution lists, and then give them specific roles. Again, you can do this with Outlook or Exchange Administrator.

Anonymous Access The Anonymous account is for users connecting with anonymous credentials. Therefore, this section is only of interest to organizations that need to grant access to their public folders. Users within your company will be connecting via Outlook, in which case they will be authenticated users.

8

With anonymous access, it depends what method the client is using to connect to a particular public folder. The three connection methods are as follows:

- Newsreader clients via NNTP
- Mail clients via IMAP4
- Outlook Web Access via HTTP

Whichever access method is used, you need to give the anonymous account a minimum of reviewer permission on the relevant public folder.

In addition, you need to check that the following settings in the server level protocols container:

- With NNTP, you have enabled the protocol, enabled client access, and on the Anonymous tab, allowed anonymous access.
- With IMAP4, you must enable the protocol, and on the Anonymous tab, activate anonymous access and add an anonymous account.
- With HTTP, you need to check the box allowing anonymous users to browse the anonymous public folders.

For more information on NNTP and IMAP4, see Day 13, "Building a Web Site Around Exchange," and Day 14, "Reading Exchange Mail with Internet Clients."

Subfolder Permissions   When you change a folder's permissions in Outlook, subfolders are unaffected. However, in Exchange Administrator, you can specify that these permissions should cascade down the folder tree to all subfolders.

Permission problems can arise because this has not happened. The symptoms are that a user can browse a higher level folder but then can't get into any of the subfolders.

You can cascade access permissions from the properties of the relevant public folder in Exchange Administrator. Select the button marked Client Permissions and change the access settings as appropriate. Before you click on OK, check the box marked Propagate These Properties to All Subfolders. When you click OK on the folder properties, this opens a dialog box asking you which properties you want to propagate. Select the option for client permissions and any changes that you made to client permissions on this folder will now flow down the folder tree.

Use of the Favorites Folder   The Favorites folder is a good source of problems for network administrators.

Users don't realize that the Favorites folder they see is just a shortcut to, not a copy of, the original folder. Hence, if a user adds a posting to her Favorites folder, that posting will appear in the original folder as well.

You cannot synchronize public folders with an offline store (.OST file) unless that public folder has been added to the user's Favorites folder.

You can't add a folder to Favorites by right-clicking on it and selecting a menu option. You need to select the folder in Outlook, and then click on the File menu. Choose the Folders option, and then select Add to Public Folder Favorites.

After a user has added a folder as a favorite, the link to that favorite bypasses any file permissions at a higher level. Hence, if you want to change permissions on a hierarchy of folders, you cannot just change the permission on the root folder, using Outlook. You need to change the permission using the Exchange Administrator program, and propagate the permissions throughout the folder tree, as described previously.

Forms   Troubleshooting the actions programmed into forms is a specialist area in itself. See Day 18, "Building Exchange Applications," for more information.

If you have any further permission and mailbox access problems, see the section "Troubleshooting Resources" at the end of this lesson.

Personal Folders

If you are using personal folders, there is a new set of configuration problems to deal with. Personally, I would only recommend personal folders for mobile users and people collecting mail via POP3 using Outlook. My approach is to tell users that I will only support personal folders for mobile users. Everyone else uses personal folders at their own risk.

I have already covered personal folders in depth in Day 7, so I will just briefly remind you of the troubleshooting procedure. For a fuller description, see the relevant sections in Day 7.

Recovering Passwords

Let's deal with the easy one first. You cannot recover the data if a user password-protects a .PST file and forgets the password. There is no administrator work-around for a forgotten password on a personal folder. You should try to impress this fact upon your users in advance.

Repairing Personal Folders

You can repair personal folders that contain a certain amount of corruption in their internal structure. You cannot repair files that become corrupt due to hardware or disk errors.

SCANPST.EXE is the utility that repairs personal folders. To use this, click on the Start button and select Run. Enter SCANPST and click OK. You will see the dialog box shown in Figure 8.7.

FIGURE 8.7

SCANPST *is the repair*
tool for checking .PST
files.

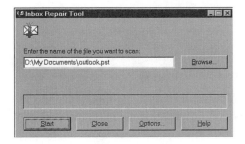

Click on the Browse button and locate the .PST file that you want to repair. If SCANPST finds any errors, you will see a prompt like the one shown in Figure 8.8.

FIGURE 8.8

If SCANPST *finds any*
errors, you will see a
prompt like this.

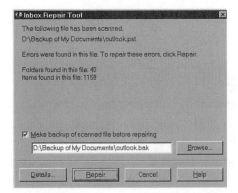

The Details button will inform you of the number of errors found. I recommend that you check the box to make a backup of the file, unless you already have a copy. Click the repair button to carry out the repair. SCANPST will attempt to recover messages and folders, where possible.

After SCANPST has finished running, you should open the rebuilt .PST file in Outlook. Depending on the level of damage to the file, you will see a number of changes:

- Items recovered with their folder information intact will appear in their original folders.

- If there was damage to the folders, you will see new empty folders called Contacts, Calendar, Inbox, and so on.

- With recovered folders, there will be a new folder called Lost and Found. This will hold all the orphaned message items.

- Any irretrievably damaged items will no longer appear.

After you have recovered the .PST file, you should now create a new .PST file and export all the recovered data to the new file. Remember you should not continue to use the restored file.

Compacting Personal Folders

Compacting personal folders will recover any space left from deleted messages. From a troubleshooting perspective, make sure that you run the repair utility before compressing a file. Also, check that you have adequate disk space on the machine where you are compressing the file. You will need more space than the size of the .PST file.

For instructions on compacting .PST files, see Day 7. For any further information, see the troubleshooting sources at the end of the lesson.

Having dealt with most of the more common user-based problems, let's move one level down the Exchange Troubleshooting Model, and look at Network troubleshooting.

Network-Based Troubleshooting

Having eliminated errors caused by the user, you can now proceed along the troubleshooting path. With network-based troubleshooting, you are concerned with connectivity issues between the client and the server.

A messaging system without networking is going to be somewhat limited in scope, as everyone would have to log on to the server. Hence, you need to have a suitable level of network support to use Exchange. Let's examine the different environments that you might find yourself using, and I'll take you through some of the areas to watch.

Exchange in a TCP/IP Environment

With the growth of TCP/IP, the majority of Exchange systems now use this network protocol. TCP/IP isn't the easiest to configure, but it is scalable, routable, platform-independent, and enables you to operate across the Internet. But however many service packs and patches you have applied to Exchange, NT, and Outlook, your brand new TCP/IP-based Exchange email system ain't gonna work if TCP/IP isn't playing.

For more information about TCP/IP, see Day 12, "Exchange on the Internet."

Connection Problems

There are two parts to TCP/IP connectivity. It means one thing if you can't connect by IP address, and it means another thing if you can't connect by Host name. It is important to understand the significance of both forms of communication failure.

Checking TCP/IP Configuration

Before you do anything else, you need to check the TCP/IP configuration on your client and server. You do this using the IPCONFIG utility. On Windows 9x, you should run WINIPCFG instead.

On Windows NT, start a Command Prompt and type IPCONFIG /all. You will see a screen like that in Figure 8.9.

FIGURE 8.9

Use IPCONFIG *to verify your IP address, Host name, and so on.*

```
Command Prompt                                                      _ □ ×
Microsoft(R) Windows NT(TM)
(C) Copyright 1985-1996 Microsoft Corp.

D:\>ipconfig /all

Windows NT IP Configuration

        Host Name . . . . . . . . . : london.off-auto.demon.co.uk
        DNS Servers . . . . . . . . : 131.107.2.200
                                      158.152.1.43
                                      158.152.1.58
        Node Type . . . . . . . . . : Hybrid
        NetBIOS Scope ID. . . . . . :
        IP Routing Enabled. . . . . : No
        WINS Proxy Enabled. . . . . : No
        NetBIOS Resolution Uses DNS : Yes

Ethernet adapter PNPNT1:

        Description . . . . . . . . : Novell 2000 Adapter.
        Physical Address. . . . . . : 00-20-18-34-79-56
        DHCP Enabled. . . . . . . . : No
        IP Address. . . . . . . . . : 131.107.2.200
        Subnet Mask . . . . . . . . : 255.255.255.0
        Default Gateway . . . . . . :
        Primary WINS Server . . . . : 131.107.2.200
```

> **Tip**
>
> There is a graphical version of IPCONFIG that comes as part of the Windows NT Resource Kit.

You must check the following:

- The IP addresses on both client and server are correct.

- The subnet mask is correct. Contrary to popular belief, 255.255.225.0 is *not* a valid Class C address.

- If you are using DHCP, the DHCP client has leased an address. (An IP address of 0.0.0.0 is a bit of a clue that DHCP is up the fabled creek.)

- In a non-routed environment, the client and server should be on the same subnet. When you AND the client's IP address and subnet mask you should get the same number as when you AND the server's IP address and subnet mask.

- In a routed environment, the default gateway's address is correct and *is on the same subnet*. When you logically AND the host's IP address and subnet mask you should get the same number as when you AND the default gateway's IP address and subnet mask.

- In a routed environment, you are using some form of name resolution (WINS, DNS, HOSTS, LMHOSTS, and so on).

Connecting Using IP Addresses

The next phase is to attempt to establish communication using IP address. At the client, first check that the client can PING itself. You can PING the loopback address as follows:

```
PING 127.0.0.1
```

If you receive four successful replies, try PINGing the client's own IP address. Again, at the command prompt, type in something like:

```
PING 131.107.2.200
```

Oh, yes, don't forget to replace 131.107.2.200 with the real IP address of your client, or this last bit won't work at all.

In a routed environment, you could now try PINGing your default gateway. If that is successful, try to PING your Exchange server.

 Tip

You could, of course, cut out all the twaddle and just PING the Exchange server. If that works, everything else works.

Failures at this point are usually due to incorrect TCP/IP configuration, either at the client, the server or on the routers.

 Caution

TCP/IP doesn't work too well if you have duplicate IP addresses on the network. However, NT will warn you if this problem exists by popping up a warning message.

Assuming all is well and you get a PING response from your Exchange server, you can now look at host name resolution.

Host Name Resolution

In fact, most Microsoft applications (including Exchange) use NetBIOS names, not IP addresses to connect to servers. However, establishing a TCP/IP session requires an IP address, not a NetBIOS name. Yet, when you configure a messaging profile, you enter SERVERNAME (or whatever) into the properties of the Exchange Server service, not an IP address. Hence, there needs to be a mechanism for translating NetBIOS names to IP addresses.

8

Windows NT can do this in several ways:

- WINS
- LMHOSTS File
- DNS
- HOSTS file
- Local Broadcast

In a routed environment, broadcast won't work, as routers don't normally forward broadcasts. Hence, most Windows NT networks use WINS or DNS for name resolution.

If your name resolution is working correctly, you should be able to PING the Exchange server by NetBIOS name. Try entering the following at a command prompt:

`PING servername`

If you get a response, name resolution is working. If you don't, yet you can PING the server by IP address, name resolution is failing.

If you don't get a response for a couple of minutes, and then the PING succeeds, the primary means of name resolution is failing, and the client is resorting to broadcast. In this case, run `IPCONFIG /all` again and look at the Node type. If it is Hybrid, you need to check the address of the WINS servers, and then check on the operation of the WINS server. If the option for NetBIOS Resolution Uses DNS is Yes, do the same for the DNS servers.

Note When testing TCP/IP, if you can PING your Exchange server by name, all the other steps must be working.

Integrating Exchange and Novell NetWare

If you are trying to integrate Exchange and Novell NetWare, you certainly have an interesting project on your hands. I will assume a difficult case: you have a number of Novell NetWare servers and several hundred users. Your clients consist of an indeterminate number of Windows for Workgroups, NT, UNIX, Mac, and Windows 95 clients in a big rambling building. Your routed network runs IPX, TCP/IP, NetBEUI, AppleTalk, and MacIP.

The Standard Microsoft method of integrating Exchange with NetWare involves installing NWLink, Gateway Services for Netware (GSNW), and Services Advertising Protocol (SAP) on the Exchange server. You install the Exchange client on the Windows for Workgroups machines, which adds the necessary RPC functionality. Now your IPX/SPX clients should be able to connect to the Exchange server and everything should work fine, right?

Wrong.

Integrating Exchange and Novell NetWare is not as easy as certain training manuals and software vendors would have you believe. The main reason for this is that Novell clients bound to ODI do not like connecting to an Exchange server. You will have to remove the networking client and reinstall it, bound to NDIS. And don't even think about trying to autodetect the frame type with NWLink. It won't work. Have fun.

Exchange-Based Troubleshooting

With a heavyweight messaging system like Exchange, application-level troubleshooting is likely to be complex. If you query TechNet for "Microsoft Exchange Server, version 5.5," TechNet will return 755 topics. If you query the Knowledge Base with the same phrase, you get 731 hits. That's a lot of troubleshooting issue articles to read through, even assuming one covers your specific problem.

I cannot hope to provide more than a basic introduction to the more common errors. However, I would suggest that you continue to apply the Exchange Troubleshooting Methodology.

Problems With Sending Mail

When Outlook is having problems sending mail, the symptom is that your messages remain in the Outbox. This could be due to the following reasons:

- The user is working offline.
- The Exchange server is not responding.
- The address for the message is incorrect.

Assuming you have already eliminated the first reason during your user-based troubleshooting phase, you can now look at the second and third causes.

I have already dealt with connection problems caused by user interaction and permissions. Now you will look at failures caused by the client failing to connect to the Exchange server.

MAPI Error Codes

Outlook and the Exchange client use the Messaging API to communicate with the Exchange server. To do this, the client makes a MAPI call to the server, and the server makes a MAPI response. Here are some of the MAPI error codes:

```
MAPI_E_LOGIN_FAILURE
MAPI_E_DISK_FULL
MAPI_E_INSUFFICIENT_MEMORY
MAPI_E_ACCESS_DENIED
MAPI_E_TOO_MANY_RECIPIENTS
MAPI_E_ATTACHMENT_NOT_FOUND
MAPI_E_UNKNOWN_RECIPIENT
MAPI_E_BAD_RECIPTYPE
MAPI_E_TEXT_TOO_LARGE
MAPI_E_TYPE_NOT_SUPPORTED
MAPI_E_AMBIGUOUS_RECIPIENT
MAPI_E_NETWORK_FAILURE
MAPI_E_INVALID_RECIPS
MAPI_E_NOT_SUPPORTED
```

Any one of these errors can cause a message to fail. Some MAPI codes you can deal with, such as the disk full error. Other MAPI errors result from missing or overwritten files and may require you to reinstall the messaging client and Exchange Server, and reapply all service packs—a hefty task.

RPC Errors

The Exchange client uses MAPI as the language to address the Exchange server. However, MAPI calls happen over a Remote Procedure Call (RPC) connection. If RPC fails, the Exchange client will not be able to talk to the server.

RPC Failure RPC failure occurs under the following circumstances:

- The network transport or link does not support RPC.
- The RPC Service is not loaded.
- The network has failed.
- The network hardware has failed.

You can check RPC functionality using a utility on the Exchange server CD called RPC Ping. You will find it in the \SERVER\SUPPORT\RPCPING folder. There are two parts to RPC Ping: a server and a client component.

 Note RPC Ping has nothing whatsoever to do with the TCP/IP PING command.

The server part is RPINGS.EXE. Alpha (RPINGS_A.EXE) and MIPS (RPINGS_M.EXE) versions exist as well.

There are client versions for Windows NT (RPINGC32.EXE), Windows (RPING16.EXE), DOS (RPINGDOS.EXE), Alpha (RPINGC_A.EXE), and MIPS (RPINGC_M.EXE).

To use RPC Ping, run the relevant server component on your Exchange server. Then go to the client and run the respective client end.

RPC Ping enables you to test RPC connectivity to your server. You can run RPC Ping in two different modes: Ping Only and End Point.

Ping Only simply attempts to establish communication, whereas End Point will connect to the specified service, either Store or Admin. To use RPC Ping, you must specify a server name and a protocol. Alternatively, you can specify all protocols, in which case RPC Ping will report on which protocols successfully connected to the remote server. You can also specify continuous pinging, in which case RPC Ping will keep checking connections until you tell it to stop. This is very useful if you are changing network parameters during the testing process.

Figure 8.10 shows RPC Ping in use. You can select the Security check box if you want to test secure connections to your server using authenticated RPC.

FIGURE 8.10

RPC Ping is a useful utility for checking RPC Connections.

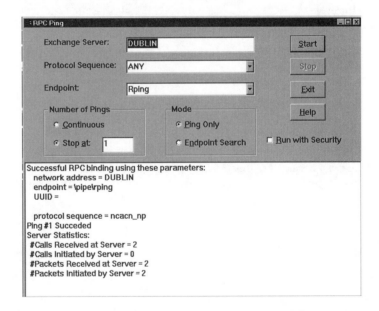

Exchange supports RPC over the following Protocols:

- Local RPC
- TCP/IP
- SPX (NWLink)
- Named Pipes
- NetBIOS (over TCP/IP, NWLink, or NetBEUI)
- Banyan Vines IP

Local RPC is a special case—this is where the client and the server are on the same machine. The remaining protocols are networking protocols. Named Pipes is Windows NT's internal connection-orientated protocol. However, Named Pipes requires TCP/IP, NWLink, or NetBEUI to work.

RPC Binding Order   The various client operating systems use different RPC Binding orders when attempting to connect to an Exchange server. A common client problem is that Outlook can take two or three minutes to start up, but once it has started up, it runs without any problems. One possible reason for this happening is that the RPC Binding Order is not correct.

Tip   The other reason is that your WINS or DNS TCP/IP name resolution isn't working.

RPC Binding Order is the order in which the Exchange client uses the various RPC methods to connect to the server. For efficient operation, the highest protocol in the RPC binding order should also be on the server.

Look at it this way. Suppose you have a mixed Novell/NT network, with Windows for Workgroups clients running the Novell client bound to ODI and TCP/IP32 v1.1b. If you add an Exchange server running TCP only, you will find that the startup times for the Exchange client are very slow. That is because the Windows 3.x client binds to SPX first, and will only try TCP/IP after SPX times out.

So you could either add NWLink to the Exchange server, add SAP and Gateway Services for NetWare, and then go round and reinstall NetWare clients bound to NDIS, or you could change the RPC Binding Order.

So how do you change the binding order?

Windows NT and 9x   In Windows NT and 9x, you can change the RPC binding order either through the Registry or through System Policy Editor. Using the Registry, go to this key:

```
HKEY_LOCAL_MACHINE/SOFTWARE/Microsoft/Exchange/Exchange Provider/
➥RPC_Binding_Order
```

 Caution   Remember that REGEDT32 is the correct Registry editor for Windows NT.

Figure 8.11 shows the default values for Windows NT.

 FIGURE 8.11

You can change the Binding Order through the Registry in Windows NT and 9x.

The default binding orders for the different operating systems are as shown in Table 8.1.

TABLE 8.1   RPC BINDING ORDERS

Windows NT/9x	Windows 3.x	MS-DOS
LRPC	Named Pipes	LRPC
TCP/IP	SPX	Named Pipes
SPX	TCP/IP	SPX
Named Pipes	NetBIOS	TCP/IP
NetBIOS	Vines IP	NetBIOS
Vines IP		

Changing binding orders depends on which operating system you are running.

Caution   When editing Binding Order in the Registry, make sure there is a comma between the RPC Binding Order entries. Also, remember that you can cause untold chaos using the Registry Editor, and if it all goes wrong, Microsoft will not provide support.

To change the RPC Binding Order using System Policy Editor, you need to obtain the policy template (.ADM file) for Outlook under Windows NT or Outlook under Windows 95. You will find this in the Microsoft Office Resource Kit on TechNet.

After you load the relevant .ADM file, you will see a new entry under Default Computer, which lets you change the RPC Binding Order. Because this can generate a system policy file, you can arrange to replicate this policy throughout all your domain controllers. Your Windows NT or 9x clients will then apply this system policy at logon time.

You can also use System Policy Editor in Registry mode, and alter the Registry values through the Local Computer setting.

Windows 3.x   With Windows 3.x, you change the RPC Binding Order via the EXCHNG.INI file.

A typical entry might look like this:

```
[Exchange Provider]
RPC_Binding_Order=ncacn_spx,ncacn_ip_tcp,netbios
```

DOS   Under DOS, you change the RPC Binding order by adding or editing a line in the Autoexec.bat file. The entry is as follows:

```
SET RPC_BINDING_ORDER = ncalrpc, ncacn_np, ncacn_tcp, ncacn_spx, netbios
```

Checking RPC Binding Order With Windows NT or 9x

You can check the speed of the RPC connection with different binding orders using Windows NT or 9x. To do this, open the Registry Editor on the RPC_Binding_Order key as in the previous section. With Outlook started, try changing the binding orders, and then use the name resolution function in Outlook to check the speed of the connection. As long you commit the new values for the RPC_Binding_Order key to the Registry, you will not have to reboot the client machine.

RPC Service Not Loaded

This is an interesting problem that you may not experience very often, but can be a bit perplexing. If you remove (or stop) the RPC service from your Exchange server's networking services, you may get some strange effects. For example, your clients will not be able to send mail nor will you be able to run Exchange Administrator.

If the RPC service fails when you are installing, the installation will halt at the point at which the install program asks you to enter the Service Account name and password. The RPC service is something that you probably assume is always working. However, the RPC service is a network service, like any other, and can fail or be removed. However, this is more of an operating system/networking problem.

Exchange Services Stopped

If Exchange services are not running, you may experience a number of different symptoms. You will see a number of varied effects, depending on which service has stopped. For example, if the MTA stops, outgoing mail will remain in a client's Outbox.

All other services (the Information Store, Directory Service, and System Attendant) will indicate a problem with the server, as shown in Figure 8.12.

FIGURE 8.12

This message can be an indication of a stopped Exchange service.

A stopped Internet Mail Connector may be more difficult to spot, as Internet Mail will still leave the Outbox, but will then queue in the MTA object. You will probably need to use Server Monitoring to identify this problem.

Check that the Exchange services are still running, and that no messages are building up in the MTA queues.

Diagnostics Logging

Exchange comes with a high level of diagnostics logging that you can enable and disable as required. When you have enabled logging, Exchange will then log events into the Application Log in Event Viewer.

Components That Support Logging

The following Exchange components support logging:

- cc:Mail Connector
- Directory Service
- Information Stores
- Message Transfer Agent
- Internet Mail Service
- MS Mail Connector
- Directory Synchronization Service

In addition, the Information Store breaks down into System, Public, Private, and Internet Protocols (POP3, IMAP4, and NNTP).

How to Figure Out Which Components to Enable Logging

More than 100 Exchange components support logging via the Diagnostics tab. The best way to figure out on which components to enable logging is to become familiar with the components within the server object that support logging.

You will also need to understand the role of three of the Core Exchange services—the Directory Service, the Information Store, and the Message Transfer Agent.

Server or Object Level

With protocol logging, you can normally configure logging levels in two areas—either at the object or at the server level. Generally, I find it easier to set logging at the server level. At least you know that all the logging objects appear there.

To configure logging at the server level, start Exchange Administrator, and click on the Servers button. Select the server that you want to configure in the right pane. Now click on the Properties button and then click on the Diagnostics Logging tab. You will now see the screen in Figure 8.13.

FIGURE 8.13

Setting Diagnostic Logging at the Server level is the easiest.

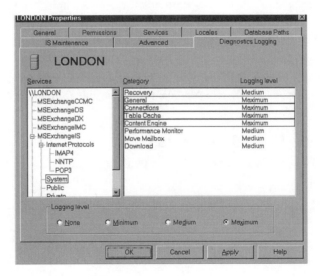

Levels of Logging

You can now expand the branches under the Services window, and the categories will appear in the right window. To increase logging levels, select one or more categories in the left window and increase the logging level to Minimum, Medium, or Maximum.

> **Caution** Do not leave logging levels set to Maximum during normal operation. This is
> because of the heavy performance load that logging imposes.

Setting Logging via the Registry

You can also configure logging via the Registry. In addition, you can enable other types
of logging by editing the Registry directly. For example, the logging settings for the
Private Information Store POP3 Internet protocol appear in:

```
HKEY_LOCAL_MACHINE/SYSTEM/CurrentControlSet/Services/MSExchangeISDiagnostics
➥/9037 Internet Protocols/9038 POP3
```

However, you can configure further POP3 logging by changing the following key:

```
HKEY_LOCAL_MACHINE/SYSTEM/CurrentControlSet/Services/MSExchangeIS
➥/ParametersSystem/POP3 Protocol Logging Level
```

For more information on setting logging through Registry settings, see the Registry
Reference in the Exchange 4.0 Resource Kit.

Message Tracking

Message Tracking in Exchange provides the ability to follow the course of a message
from sender to recipient. You must enable message tracking on the various Exchange
components, and the System Attendant is responsible for monitoring and controlling the
message tracking logs.

Enabling Message Tracking

Before you can use message tracking, you must enable it on a number of different
components.

> **Note** To get the full benefit from message tracking, you must enable it on all
> components on all servers in all sites in your organization. I would recom-
> mend doing this when you first install Exchange.

Information Stores Enable message tracking on the Information Stores if you want
to be able to track the delivery and receipt of messages into the Public and Private
Information Stores.

To enable message tracking on the Information Stores, start Exchange Administrator and
click on the Configuration button in the toolbar. Now double-click on the Information
Store Site Configuration object, and check the box marked Enable Message Tracking.

8

MTA You need to enable message tracking on the MTA object if you have multiple sites. If you do not, the Message Tracking Center will only be able to track the message within your site.

However, MTA tracking is not required if you only have one site, as the messages all route within the Information Stores.

To enable message tracking on the Information Stores, start Exchange Administrator and click on the Configuration button in the toolbar. Now double-click on the MTA Site Configuration object, and check the box marked Enable Message Tracking.

Connectors You can enable message tracking on three connectors. These are the Internet Mail Service, the MS Mail Connector, and the cc:Mail connector. However, once a message has left your Exchange messaging system, you will no longer be able to track the message.

To enable message tracking on connectors, start Exchange Administrator and click on the Configuration button in the toolbar. Now double-click on the Connections container, and then double-click on the connector that you want to configure. Again, check the box marked Enable Message Tracking.

Message Tracking Log Files

Exchange Message Tracking works by keeping text-based log files on individual servers in the EXCHSRVR\TRACKING.LOG directory. If you look in that directory, you will see each log file sequentially as *yyyymmdd*.log (where *yyyymmdd* is the year, month, and day of the file), as shown in Figure 8.14.

FIGURE 8.14

The \TRACKING.LOG directory contains the text message tracking files.

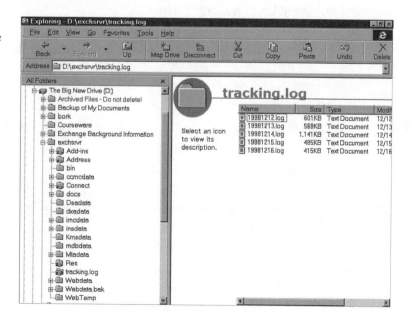

The \TRACKING.LOG directory has the share name of Tracking.log, with
Administrators and the Exchange Service account having full control. The group
Everyone has read access to this directory. The fact that this directory is a shared
directory lets you track a message across multiple servers and sites.

The System Attendant is responsible for the deleting of message tracking logs, which
you can configure on a server-by-server basis. To configure the number of days that message tracking logs are kept, start Exchange Administrator, and click on the Servers button
in the Toolbar. Double-click on the server that you want to configure, and then double-
click on the System Attendant object. You can now change the number of days that message tracking logs will be held before they are deleted.

Note

> You can only track messages sent on a particular day if a message tracking
> log exists for that day.

Caution

> If you select the option not to delete message tracking logs, you will need
> to have a method of archiving and deleting the log files manually. If you
> don't, you will find that the volume holding the log files will eventually run
> out of space.

Using the Message Tracking Center

After you have configured message tracking, you will be able to use the Message
Tracking Center to follow the progress of messages. To use the Message Tracking
Center, start Exchange Administrator, and select the Tools menu. Choose Track Message,
and a prompt will ask you to connect to a server. Choose a server in your site and select
OK. You will now see the screen in Figure 8.15.

It is important to understand that when you start the Message Tracking Center, the opening screen is the Search dialog box.

Note

> Message tracking does not actually allow you to read the messages. To do
> that, you will need to use Message Journaling, which is part of Exchange 5.5
> Service Pack 1.

FIGURE 8.15

The Message Tracking Center Search dialog is where you specify a sender or a recipient.

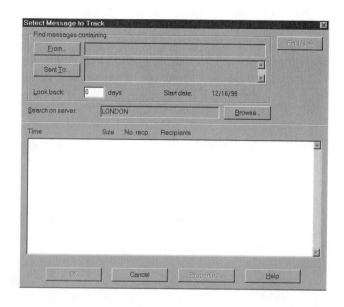

8

Select a sender or a recipient by clicking the relevant buttons. You can choose from Exchange mailboxes, distribution lists, or custom recipients from any site in your organization. Enter the number of days that you want to track back, and click on Find Now. You will see the Message Tracking Center going back through the log files.

Note

You may receive a warning informing you that a message tracking log file is not available. This happens if the Message Tracking Center cannot find a log file for a particular day.

You will now see a list of messages, as shown in Figure 8.16.

Double-clicking on a message will bring up further details on that message, including the recipient and the message size. Figure 8.17 shows an example of this.

If you select an Exchange recipient and click Properties, Exchange will show you the properties of that recipient. If the addressee is outside the Exchange organization, (such as a personal address book entry), you will see a message box stating that the mailbox cannot be opened. Select Close to return to the Search dialog box.

After you have selected the message that you want to track, click the OK button on the Search dialog box. *Don't double-click on the message, as that will take you back to the Properties dialog box.*

FIGURE 8.16

The Search dialog has brought up messages sent over the past seven days.

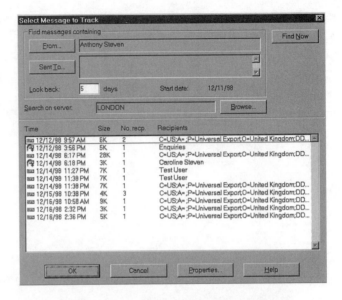

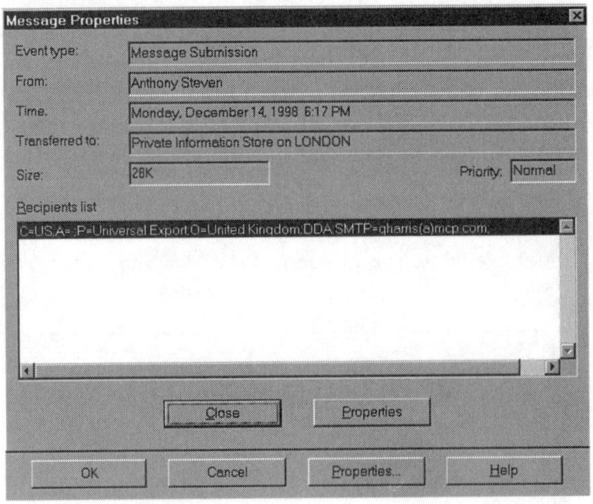

FIGURE 8.17

You can examine the properties of any tracked messages.

You will now be in the main screen of the Message tracking center, as shown in Figure 8.18.

FIGURE 8.18

After you have chosen a message to track and selected OK, you will now use the Track button to perform the tracking action.

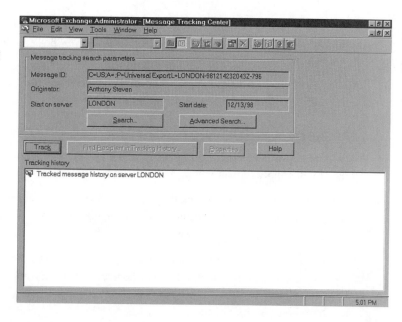

Now click on the Track button, and after a slight pause, you should see the message tracking history start to appear in the box at the bottom of the screen. Figure 8.19 shows what this looks like for a sample message.

FIGURE 8.19

Clicking on the Track button carries out the tracking on the selected message.

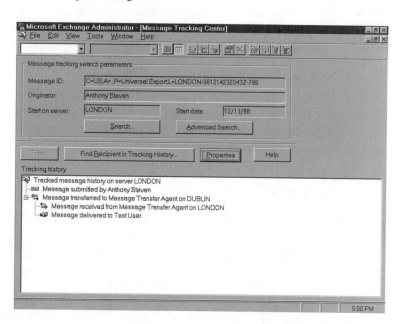

You can expand any of the plus signs in the message tracking history to examine the route that the message took. Endpoints in message tracking are usually either delivered to a user's mailbox or to a connector.

You can configure further searches, or specify advanced searches, which let you search for all messages from a particular server, or transferred to this site.

Message Queue Monitoring

I cover Message queue monitoring in depth in Day 15, "Maintaining Exchange," so today, I will simply look at message queues from a troubleshooting perspective.

Message queues are temporary holding areas for messages awaiting delivery. There are three reasons why you get messages in messaging queues. One is normal, one is acceptable, and the final one is a problem.

- In a normal Exchange operation, messages will appear in the message queues for connectors that have a connection schedule, that is, they are not permanently available. Hence, Dynamic RAS and dial-up Internet Mail Service connectors will often have items in their queues.

- If you have a permanently active connector (not scheduled or non-schedulable), you may see a build-up of messages during busy times. This is acceptable, providing overall performance is not suffering.

- If you have site connectors with significant message queues (more than twenty messages), this is usually a bad sign. Check your network connectivity, RPC links, and security authentication between the sites.

Server MTA Object

The most important place to check messaging queues is the Server level MTA Object. To see this, start Exchange Administrator and click on the Servers button on the toolbar. Double-click on your selected server, and then double-click on the Message Transfer Agent object. Click on the Queues tab, and you will see the dialog box in Figure 8.20.

Drop-down the list and you will see a list of all queues, with the number of items queued. Select an individual queue and you can then manage the items in that queue.

Using Performance Monitor to Monitor Queues

You can use the Windows NT Performance Monitor to help track queue sizes. To do this, you can use the MSExchangeMTA:Work Queue Length counter.

You can use the preconfigured Performance Monitor graph in the Exchange Administrator program group to monitor message queues. To run this, click on the Start button, select Programs, and choose Microsoft Exchange. Now select the Microsoft Exchange Server Queues item. This graph updates every 10 seconds.

FIGURE 8.20

The server level MTA object lets you monitor Message Queues.

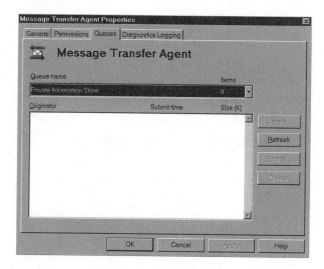

There is an additional preconfigured Performance Monitor graph for the Internet Mail Service queues.

Server and Link Monitors

Server and Link Monitors provide the ability to monitor the services running on Exchange servers and the links between sites. For detailed information on how to deploy and configure Server and Link Monitors, see Day 15.

If the issue that you are troubleshooting cannot be resolved at the application level, the next area to concentrate on is the operating system.

Windows NT-Based Troubleshooting

Having dealt with the user, network, and application levels, I am now going to look at troubleshooting from the operating system perspective. Due to the nature of this book, I only have space to introduce you to some of the Windows NT tools and techniques available for troubleshooting your Exchange system. You will need to use the sources at the end of this lesson for more information. However, you still need to apply your troubleshooting methodology.

There are a number of both built-in and third-party tools for troubleshooting Windows NT. Most of them operate as GUI applications, so generally you're not fooling around with command-line switches all the time.

Task Manager

Task Manager is, without a doubt, one of the most useful tools in Windows NT. I think I must use Task Manager at least twice as often as any other Windows NT utility. Application locked up? Use Task Manager. Something's hogging the processor? Task Manager again. Nice pretty graph of processor and memory usage? Same detail. Tea, toast, and intelligent conversation? Oh, all right, so it doesn't do *everything*.

Terminating Unresponsive Applications

Applications may become unresponsive for a number of reasons, including bugs (very common), incorrect parameters (less common), or operating system failures (usually rare under NT).

To cancel an unresponsive application, start Task Manager by right clicking on the taskbar at the bottom of the screen and selecting Task Manager.

Tip

If your unresponsive application is slowing everything down to such an extent that you can't even get the taskbar to appear, press Ctrl+Alt+Del. You will now be able to click the button marked Task Manager.

After you have started Task Manager, click on the Applications tab. The rogue application probably has Not Responding next to its entry in Task Manager. Select this application and click the End Task button. You will probably receive a prompt indicating that the application cannot respond to the End Task command. You can select to continue and end the task, cancel the request, or wait to see if the application sorts itself out.

The Processes tab shows you the individual applications and services running on your Exchange server. The Exchange services are: DSAMAIN.EXE (the Directory Service), STORE.EXE (the Information Stores), EMSMTA.EXE (the MTA), and MAD.EXE (the System Attendant).

Again, you can select an unresponsive process and click on the End Task button.

Caution

Normally, you would not stop services in this manner. Use the Services Icon in Control Panel to do this.

Checking Processor Usage

You can also find out which applications are hogging the processor. To do this, click on the word CPU at top of the third column. This will order the processes by their use of the CPU. In normal operation, the System Idle process takes most of the processing power.

If you would like a nice graphical readout of the total usage on your processor, click on the Performance tab. You will now see the screen in Figure 8.21.

FIGURE 8.21

The Performance screen in Task Manager isn't just a pretty graph.

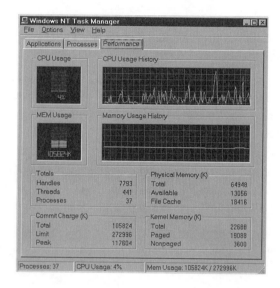

This screen gives some very useful information on memory usage under the Physical Memory and Commit Charge sections. Apart from checking that nobody's nicked your RAM, you can see how the physical memory divides between available RAM and the File Cache. Commit Charge lets you monitor your system's use of the Page File, which also appears on the second graph.

Tip

Double-click on either graph to get an expanded view of processor usage.

Other options on Task Manager are to Show Kernel processor usage on the graph in red, and to add different columns to the display, such as virtual memory size and memory delta (changes in memory usage).

Overall, Task Manager is an excellent application that can get you out of some very difficult problems.

Event Viewer

After Task Manager, Event Viewer is probably the next most useful troubleshooting application. If you have configured Diagnostics Logging as per the earlier section in this lesson, you will have a large amount of data already building up in your Application Log in Event Viewer.

The Log Files

There are three log files in Event Viewer: The System Log, the Security Log, and the Event Log. Each log is a text-based file.

Application Event Log   The Application Event Log holds most of the events generated by applications such as Exchange. It also records events from sources such as the JET database, the License Service, and Dr. Watson. All your diagnostics logging events will appear in the Application Log.

System Event Log   The System Event Log is where NT reports most of its system level events. However, you may see occasional notifications from the Exchange Services, particularly where you are using the Alert view in Performance Monitor to report on Exchange events.

Security Event Log   The Security Event Log will only record events if you have configured auditing. Exchange does not normally use the Security Log, but logs its security information into the Application Log, with a key as the icon for the security event.

Interpreting Events

Events in Event Viewer come in three forms:

- Information (blue)
- Warning (Yellow)
- Error (Red)

Ideally, you want your Event Log to be full of blue entries. However, even within the warning and error categories, there is a range of seriousness. Interpreting events in the Event Logs is one of the great black arts of Windows NT. Even Microsoft isn't always very helpful on this.

First, you need to look at an event's detail. To do this, double-click on the event in the relevant Event Log. You will see a dialog box like that in Figure 8.22.

There is a brief explanation of the event, along with a category, and most importantly, an Event ID. If the explanation given leaves you none the wiser, you can use this event ID to try to discover more information about the problem. The BackOffice Resource Kit (BORK) has a help file on Exchange events. See the section on troubleshooting resources for how to obtain the BORK (it isn't an Icelandic pop star).

FIGURE 8.22

The Event Log details help you to interpret what is happening.

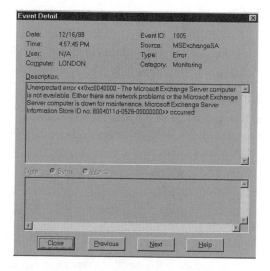

Log File Settings

You can set log file settings through Event Viewer. To do this, select the Log menu and click on Log Settings. You will now see the screen in Figure 8.23.

FIGURE 8.23

Log Settings let you configure the log size and Event Log wrapping.

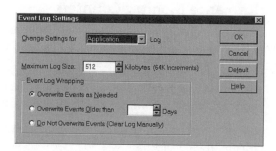

The drop-down box lets you select which log you want to configure.

You can increase the maximum size of the log in 64KB increments, up to the limit of your hard disk space. The log files reside in the %WINNTROOT%\SYSTEM32\ CONFIG directory, as APPEVENT.EVT, SECEVENT.EVT, and SYSEVENT.EVT.

You have three options for Event Log wrapping. If you select none, the Event Log will fill up to its maximum size and then start to overwrite the oldest events.

The Overwrite events older than a set period setting keeps the entries for the specified number of days, and then overwrites them.

The third option is for high security environments, where you have configured auditing. With this setting, if a log file fills up, the system halts. If this happens, an administrator can log on and clear the log file manually. This is to ensure that all NT records all system events.

Archiving Log Files

I would recommend that you set up a system to archive your log files. Luckily, you don't actually have to do it yourself. As long as you have a sidekick who is a member of the Server Operators group, he can do it for you.

To archive an Event Log, select the Log menu and click on Clear All Events. You will see a prompt reminding you to save the log file before you clear it. You can save the log files and then reopen them later using Event Viewer.

Performance Monitor

Performance Monitor is a Windows NT tool that allows you to chart performance, configure automatic alerts, record log files, or wonder what on earth "Report View" is for.

I will cover Performance Monitor in detail in Day 15. Here I just want to bring out its use as a troubleshooting tool.

Exchange Performance Monitor Counters

When you install Exchange, you also install a number of Performance Monitor objects and counters. There are Performance Monitor objects for all the Exchange services, plus a number of ancillary objects as well.

An example of this is the MSExchangeIS: Active Connection Count object, which charts the number of connections that have shown some activity in the last ten minutes.

I would recommend that you spend some time in making yourself familiar with the counters and objects in Microsoft Exchange.

Using Performance Monitor for Troubleshooting

You can use Performance Monitor for troubleshooting in a number of different ways. Firstly, you can use it reactively; that is, you can configure alerts to warn you of excessive queue lengths, server overloading, or even exceeding your license limit. These alerts can supplement server and link monitors, providing early warning of problems.

Note

When I say *early* warning, you may have one or two minutes head start before the world and its uncle start hammering on your door, demanding to know why the email isn't working. At least you will be able to say that you know about it and are working on the problem.

To set up an alert to provide warning of excessive message queues, follow these steps:

1. Start Performance Monitor and, from the View menu, select Alert view.

2. Click on the plus (+) button, and you will see a dialog box showing server name, objects, and counters.

3. Ensure you are monitoring the correct computer. If not, enter \\servername in the field at the top.

4. Click on the Object list, and select the MSExchangeMTA object.

5. From the list of counters, select the Work Queue Length counter.

6. Select Alert If Over and then add 20 as the value. The dialog box should resemble that in Figure 8.24.

FIGURE 8.24

Here I have an automatic alert if the MTA message queues get too large.

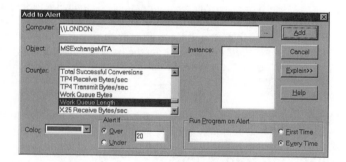

7. Select OK to add the alert.

8. Next, click on the Options button, and you will see the Options dialog in Figure 8.25. Enter a network name for either a computer or a person (which, of course, should *never* be the same) to receive your messages on your desktop. Remember that the Alerting and Messaging Service must be running.

FIGURE 8.25

In Alerting Options, you can specify how you would like your alert.

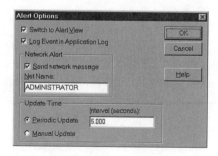

9. Select OK. Now if the messaging queues start to build up, you will receive an alert.

You can also use Performance Monitor proactively. For example, using Log View to record system usage over periods of weeks. You can then use this information to predict increases in resource usage over the next three to six months, thus enabling you to build up a case for purchasing new hardware or other resources.

Windows NT Diagnostics

Windows NT Diagnostics (WinMSD) is a graphical 32-bit version of Microsoft System Diagnostics that comes with DOS6.22. Using WinMSD, you can look at several categories, including System, Display, Memory, Services, and Resource information. However, there are two areas where Windows NT Diagnostics is particularly useful.

Note

Much of the hardware information in Windows NT Diagnostics comes from the HARDWARE key in the NT Registry. The HARDWARE key is itself a volatile key, meaning that it is rebuilt every time the server is booted. In fact, the HARDWARE key comes from the hardware detection routine provided by NTDETECT.COM, which runs as part of the Windows NT boot process.

To start Windows NT Diagnostics, click the Start button, and select Programs. From the Programs group, choose Administrative Tools and then select Windows NT Diagnostics.

Resolving Interrupt Conflicts

Even if you use the Plug-and-Play service on Windows NT, you will probably find yourself grappling with Interrupt Request (IRQ) conflicts. The Resources tab in Windows NT Diagnostics shows you the current IRQ allocations, as shown in Figure 8.26.

Here you can see the serial (COM1 and COM2) ports on IRQs 3 and 4, the sound card is on IRQ10, and the Plug-and-Play network card is on IRQ11. It may be unconventional, but it works fine!

Printing Diagnostic Reports

If you ever need to print a diagnostic report on a server, you can do this very easily through Windows NT Diagnostics. From the File menu, select Print Report. You now get the option to print your report to a file, the Clipboard, or the default printer. You can also select all tabs or just the current tab, and whether you want a summary or a detailed report.

Use WinMSD to print out a diagnostic report after you have installed a new server into a site. You can then file the resultant report with the new server's documentation.

FIGURE 8.26

The IRQ allocations can be invaluable when you are trying to install new hardware.

Server Manager

Server Manager is a graphical utility designed to enable you to control servers remotely. With Server Manager, you can add or remove computers from a domain, administer shares, disconnect users, synchronize a domain, and start or stop services. You can also remotely carry out any of the tasks that you can normally perform from the Server icon in Control Panel on a local machine.

Note

To run Server Manager, the server service must be running and you must log on as either a Server Operator or an Administrator. In addition, in a routed TCP/IP environment, you must have host name resolution configured and an RPC connection to the Primary Domain Controller.

Starting and Stopping Services Remotely

Server Manager is very useful for starting and stopping services remotely. To do this, start Server Manager from the Administrative Tools group, and select the machine that you want to administer. From the Computer menu, select Services. You will now see the screen in Figure 8.27.

You can now stop, start, and pause services, as well as change startup types and service login accounts. You can also obtain an instant readout of the state of the services running on a remote machine.

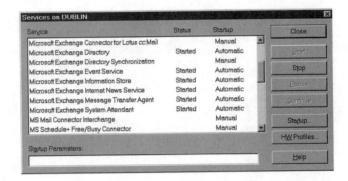

If you want to close down an Exchange Server, you can do this by stopping the Microsoft Exchange System Attendant service. If you want to force a delivery of Internet Mail over the IMS, stop and start the Internet Mail Service.

Disconnecting Users

If you need to disconnect users from your Exchange server, for example, before closing down the server, you can do the following:

1. Start Server Manager which was described earlier.

2. Select (single click) the machine that you want to take off the network. Don't double-click on the server, or you'll just see its properties again.

3. Click on the Computer menu, and choose Send Message.

4. Enter a suitably persuasive, but above all, sensitive and diplomatic message to persuade your users to end their sessions. I find something like "Oi! You! Log off NOW or lose your files!" works well.

5. To close any further sessions with the server that you are rebooting, double-click on that machine's name in Server Manager.

6. You can now disconnect Users, close Shares, or close Resources by clicking on the relevant button and then clicking Disconnect.

7. Sit back, and await the howls of protest.

Having carried out this process, you can now proceed to close down the server.

Hardware-Based Troubleshooting

Sadly, due to reasons of space, I can't go into any detail on this aspect of the ETM. My experience is that hardware faults are the least common and easiest to fix of all the troubleshooting issues that you have to deal with. Yes, totally unlike users. I will leave you with a few tips that I hope will assist you.

8

- Doubling the RAM solves most performance problems with Windows NT.
- After you install any new hardware, run the Exchange Performance Optimizer.
- On large messaging systems, keep your transactional tracking logs on FAT partitions, mounted on separate spindles from the DS and IS databases.
- If all the Exchange services and the Server, Netlogon, and Browser services have not started, your network card may be the problem.
- Black smoke (or excess heat, or an unpleasant odor) coming out of your server means problems. On the other hand, white smoke coming out of the Sistine Chapel means a new Pope.
- Don't forget to arrange a good on-site hardware support contract!

Troubleshooting Resources

Earlier, I said I could write a book on troubleshooting Exchange alone. However, it probably still wouldn't cover the exact problem that you are having at 6:00 p.m. on a Friday evening when you have a "hot date" or two tickets to that evening's ball game. So instead, I will point you in the direction of some excellent resources.

Exchange Administrator

Exchange Server comes with two levels of built-in help. There is the normal help, and there is the online Documentation.

Help

The Exchange Administrator online help system is excellent. It covers nearly all the points that you need to know about the dialog box or button that has flummoxed you. If you are stuck, just press the F1 key.

On-line Documentation

The online documentation is better for looking at the planning and deployment issues. It is set out more like a reference manual, organized into five sections covering Getting Started, Concepts and Planning, Operations, Maintenance and Troubleshooting, and Migration. It uses Internet Explorer to display its information, so I recommend you have IE4, 3.02 or equivalent to view the documentation.

TechNet

If you don't already have this, order it today.

TechNet is the Font of All Knowledge, an invaluable guide to all things Microsofty. You subscribe for a year and it comes out once a month. TechNet can save you thousands on support calls, simply because of the amount of information it contains. Included with TechNet is the Knowledge Base, Service Packs, Option Packs, and Resource Kits. The only downside is that you get about six extra drinks coasters (the International versions) with each issue.

Knowledge Base

The Knowledge Base comes with TechNet. It is more of an archive of troubleshooting issues, but you will find it very useful for the more obscure problems.

BackOffice Resource Kit

The BackOffice Resource Kit consists of a number of very useful utilities, such as Mailstorm, a program that generates mail messages, or ReplVer, a utility that checks public folder replication.

The BackOffice Resource Kit, or BORK, also comes with the following documentation:

- Help on the Exchange Messages found in Event Viewer
- Exchange Server Resource Guide
- Exchange Tools Help
- Help on the Exchange Counters in Performance Monitor

The BackOffice Resource Kit is part of TechNet, so yet another reason to get TechNet.

Microsoft Web Site

The Microsoft Web site has the following areas that will be of interest:

```
http://www.microsoft.com/exchange/
http://www.microsoft.com/technet/
http://support.microsoft.com/support/
```

In addition, there a numerous other private and commercial Web sites devoted (or not!) to Windows NT and Exchange. Visit your favorite search engine, give it the key word "Microsoft Exchange Sever 5.5," and see what you get!

Newsgroups

There are several newsgroups devoted to Exchange issues on Usenet. Under Microsoft.Public.Exchange is Admin, Applications, Clients, Connectivity, Misc, and Setup. They are all busy newsgroups, so if you choose to download them all, you'd have about 600 posts a day to digest. And if you do post there, you might even get a reply from me.

8

Summary

You have now looked at some of the main troubleshooting areas in Exchange. You have seen how you can apply a troubleshooting methodology at different levels and how a structured approach to troubleshooting will reduce downtime and solve problems quickly.

To summarize the main points of this lesson:

- Exchange troubleshooting works on five levels: user, network, application, operating system, and hardware. This process is formalized as the Exchange Troubleshooting Model (ETM).

- At each level, you will benefit from applying a structured methodology to isolate, research, correct, and document problems.

- By working from the user-end towards the Exchange server, you are following a logical pattern of troubleshooting that reflects real-life problems.

- User troubleshooting deals with isolating user-based issues, such as logon validation, access to other folders, and use of personal folders.

- Network-based troubleshooting covers protocol connectivity between the client and server. It also deals with TCP/IP issues, integration with Novell NetWare, and working in routed networks.

- Application-based troubleshooting covers issues such as RPC connectivity, Exchange services not running, message queue monitoring, and message tracking.

- Operating system troubleshooting involves using NT's built-in troubleshooting utilities to monitor and diagnose both operating system and application issues.

- Hardware-based troubleshooting is rarely a problem. If the issue is lack of performance, try adding more RAM.

- If you haven't done so already, get TechNet!

Q&A

Q **For some reason, everyone in my office can connect to Exchange 5.5 using Outlook 98 except one. When I go to the Message Profile and add the username and Exchange name, the Exchange Server service hangs for 30 seconds or so, and then reports an error saying that it cannot connect to the Exchange server.**

It is a mixed environment Windows 9x (this individual is using Windows 98). What's strange is that she can access the servers and map drives. It's only Exchange!

A Applying the Exchange Troubleshooting Model, the initial diagnosis would be that you have a user-based error. What you need to do is to carry out further analysis to discover if this is the case.

Carry out a System Hard Reset and confirm the user's logon details. Then try to add the Exchange Server service to the messaging profile again. Check the user and Exchange Server name and verify that they are correct. If you still get the error message, you can then progress through the troubleshooting levels.

At the networking level, check that you have common protocols on both the client and the Exchange server. Confirm that your client Windows 98 machine can connect to the Exchange server using \\EXCHANGESERVERNAME\TRACKING.LOG. If you can connect to this share (which contains your tracking log files), you have networking connectivity and you can progress to the application level.

At the application level, use the RPC Ping utility to confirm RPC connectivity between the client and the server. Use the Store as the endpoint and connect over the common client and server protocol.

At the operating system level, use NT's Network Monitor to monitor the conversation between the client and the server when you attempt to configure the messaging profile. Use a capture filter on Network Monitor so that you only record the packets between the client and Exchange server.

At the hardware level, you could have an error on the client's networking card. Try removing and reinstalling the networking components, including the network card driver and protocols.

My guess is that you have multiple protocols on your network, and the Windows 98 machine is talking to the other servers using a protocol that isn't on the Exchange machine.

Q After the nightly maintenance routine, I get the following warning in the Event Viewer.

```
Event ID 191
Source ESE97
Type Warning
Category System Parameter
MSexchangeIS ((195)) system parameter preferred version pages was
➥changed from 3744 to 3262 due to physical memory limitation.
```

What's happening here?

A Using the Exchange Troubleshooting Model, you can immediately eliminate the user and network levels, as there are no user-based or connectivity issues at work here. On the surface, it appears to be an application level problem. Researching

ESE97 event 191 in the Exchange Message Reference in the BackOffice Resource Kit will inform you of the following:

"No user action required. If desired, review the system resources. Modify appropriate registry values. You may have to experiment with different settings to find the best configuration for your system. See Microsoft Exchange Server Concepts and Planning Guide, which is on the compact disc."

-Microsoft Exchange Message Reference ©Microsoft Inc.

At the application level, you could try running Performance Optimizer again, which should change the memory settings permanently. Or at the physical level, you could add some more RAM.

Q **I have recently installed an Internet Mail Service to connect Exchange to our ISP. However, I have just received a board-level directive saying that all messages coming in from and going out to the Internet must be traceable. How can I implement this?**

A You don't actually have to do a lot here, except for switching on message tracking on the IMS, Information Store, and possibly the MTA. The IMS keeps copies of all incoming and outgoing messages in THE IMCDATA\IN\ARCHIVE and IMCDATA\OUT\ARCHIVE folders. There will also be copies of all incoming messages in the log files in the IMCDATA\LOG folder.

Workshop

The Workshop provides two ways for you to affirm what you've learned in this lesson. The "Quiz" section poses questions to help you solidify your understanding of the material covered and the "Exercise" section provides you with experience in using what you have learned. You can find answers to the quiz questions and exercises in Appendix B, "Answers to Quiz Questions and Exercises."

Quiz

1. What are the five levels of the Exchange Troubleshooting Model?
2. What are the steps in the Exchange Troubleshooting Methodology?
3. What are the stages in the System Hard Reset?
4. At what level is RPC Communication failure classified?
5. Which tool should you use to change permissions on public folder trees?
6. What utility should you run before you compact a personal folder?
7. What are the two major issues in troubleshooting TCP/IP environments?

8. When users send messages, the messages just sit in their outboxes. No warning messages are received. What could be the problem?

9. Which Exchange components support logging?

10. Where can you change all these logging values in one place?

11. Where does Exchange record diagnostics logging messages?

12. Which service is responsible for the maintenance of tracking logs?

13. Give two ways in which you can monitor message queues.

14. Your server is responding very slowly. How might you find out what is causing it to slow down?

Exercises

1. How would you optimize the RPC Binding Order using Outlook and the Registry?

2. You need a system to warn you if any of the following events occur:

   - The MTA has more than 25 items in the queue.
   - The IMS has more than 50 items in the queue.
   - The Exchange server has more than 100 logged on users.
   - Any Exchange services stop running on the Exchange servers.
   - Any links to other sites stop working.

   How could you implement this?

DAY 9

Deploying Exchange

by Jason vanValkenburgh

Chapter Objectives

Today's lesson shows you how to deploy Exchange within your organization. You will learn the basics of deploying Exchange, including the following:

- How to plan your deployment strategy and identify the correct approach to rolling out Exchange to all of your sites and users.

- How to roll out the Exchange client to your users and how your choice of Exchange clients for your users affects deployment.

- How to use the capabilities of Microsoft Systems Management Server to help in your deployment, from surveying users' PC before deployment to monitoring the success of your deployment while it's in progress.

- How to customize the installation of Outlook 98 to help enforce customization standards and create messaging profiles automatically.

- How to train users to lower your support effort during deployment while helping the success of your project.

Defining Your Deployment Strategy

You may be asking yourself what is meant by "deployment." The answer you get will likely vary from person to person. This lesson uses the term *deployment* to describe the process of installing, configuring, and delivering Exchange to your user community. Deployment includes installing the networks, servers, workstations, and Exchange clients that people will use for Exchange. Deployment is not limited to technical aspects of installing Exchange, but includes end-user training and support as well. Deployment is a far-reaching and broad term describing all the things that need to be done to bring a successful Exchange design to fruition.

A typical Exchange deployment effort is client- (or user-) focused. Let's face it: Setting up one Exchange server per site is a relatively easy task compared to the sheer amount of time and effort required to install an Exchange client on hundreds or thousands of desktops. A user-focused deployment effort has several key stages:

- Distribution. This is the delivery of the software package to the user's desktop. This could be accomplished with a network connection, software distribution tool (such as SMS), CD-ROM, or Web page.

- Installation. This is the actual installation of the client software on the user's PC. This includes copying files to the local hard drive and configuring basic application functionality. The Setup program for the client usually does this step; you can customize the setup program to perform some configuration as well.

- Configuration. This step is the actual configuration of the mail client for a particular user, such as creating a messaging profile with the correct account and server information.

- Support. This is the training and post-installation help that your technical organization supplies to the end user community. Support is a critical, non-technical aspect of deployment that has a large impact on your project's and Exchange Server's success.

These stages are shown in Figure 9.1, along with the key Outlook 98–specific tools and methods available for your deployment. I'll discuss these tools and how they are used later in this lesson.

Defining Your Deployment Scope

One of the parts of defining your project's scope during Day 2, "Planning Your Exchange Implementation," was defining who and where your Exchange users will be. That step typically defines your deployment scope as well, although it is possible to further define your deployment scope by considering how much effort you will be responsible for during deployment. Different organizations may choose to implement Exchange on a national, international, regional, or local basis. Whether you're deploying Exchange globally or locally, the tools and approach should be the same.

FIGURE 9.1

The different stages to deploying an Exchange client, along with the tools available to help your deployment effort.

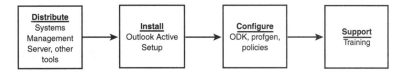

9

Deployment Objectives

You should clearly define the objectives for your deployment effort. Doing so will help you design the best deployment approach and strategy. For example, if you are deploying Microsoft Exchange in conjunction with a migration from Novell NetWare to Windows NT Server, your deployment objectives and scope will be greater than if you are simply deploying Exchange. Likewise it is important to identify other opportunities or objectives beyond simple Exchange deployment; often the effort associated with rolling-out Exchange can be leveraged through the use of tools and techniques whose benefits extend past the initial objective of providing someone with the ability to send and receive email.

Some examples of deployment objectives include the following:

- The installation and configuration of Microsoft Outlook on every user's desktop throughout the company.
- The installation of Microsoft Exchange Server at every site where a server is required.
- The training of all Exchange users in the basic of operating Microsoft Outlook.

Keeping your deployment objectives in mind as you plan your deployment strategy helps ensure that you meet these objectives while remaining on track and focused towards your final goal.

Distributing Exchange Clients

The process of distributing Exchange clients such as Microsoft Outlook to a wide number of users can be a manual and time-consuming task. Software distribution tools, either bought off the shelf or custom-built using login scripts, can decrease the amount of time and human resources dedicated to installing the client software. These resources can then be redirected to often-overlooked areas such as training and support. Microsoft Systems Management Server is a software distribution tool that merits some discussion as a potential tool to use in your project. You can learn more about SMS from Microsoft's Web site at http://www.microsoft.com/smsmgmt/default.asp.

Using Microsoft Systems Management Server

As I just noted, deploying Exchange across an entire organization can be a time-consuming, labor-intensive, and expensive undertaking. Microsoft Systems Management Server (SMS) is a tool that can simplify and streamline your Exchange deployment. I've often been able to implement SMS in conjunction with a Microsoft Exchange or Outlook deployment and justify the SMS implementation costs simply on the merits of a one-time cost savings of using SMS to deploy Outlook to several hundred users or more. Because SMS could easily merit a book in its own right, this discussion of SMS will simply cover what SMS does, how it works, and how you could use SMS to deploy Microsoft Exchange.

What SMS Can Do

Microsoft Systems Management Server is a desktop and PC-server centric management package. SMS focuses on several key capabilities:

- Hardware and Software Inventory Collection. The SMS client can perform hardware and software inventory scans. Each workstation and server that runs SMS client or server software has inventory information collected on a periodic basis; that information then populates a Microsoft SQL Server database. SMS collects hardware information such as each PC's processor speed, memory, network card type, and free disk space. SMS can perform software inventory scans as well; this allows SMS to scan user workstations for specific files indicating a particular software package is installed. The inventory mechanism can also gather a specified text file for collection into the SQL Server database; some installations use this capability to gather AUTOEXEC.BAT and CONFIG.SYS files to assist in troubleshooting.

- Software Distribution and Installation. SMS allows for the remote distribution and installation of software packages. Each distribution task, called a package, can be distributed to SMS servers at other locations or sites; remote workstations are sent a job through the client's Package Command Manager that allows a user to run the package's setup program or script.

NEW TERM SMS uses the term *package* to describe a software distribution task. A package includes the files necessary for the software and information about what command is run to install the program. A package also includes configuration options such as whether the program reboots the PC (or can't reboot the PC) and whether the package is mandatory (the user must install it).

- Remote Control. The SMS Console allows you to use remote control to take over a user's workstation across a network. This capability allows help desk personnel to remotely troubleshoot PC configuration issues as well as walk users through simple configuration tasks such as adding a printer. Because the end user can see the changes a support technician makes, remote control allows for informal training on a specific task over the phone, delivering short-term support and long-term benefit.

- Network Monitoring and Analysis. SMS servers can run the Network Monitoring Agent, which allows for basic network protocol decoding and analysis. SMS can monitor bandwidth utilization, congestion, and network errors, potentially assisting in troubleshooting connectivity or performance problems.

- Software Metering. This capability is slated for Systems Management Server 2.0., due to be released in 1999. Software metering allows companies to monitor concurrent and per-desktop usage of applications. This monitors compliance to software licensing agreements, telling you when you need to buy additional software licenses. (No wonder Microsoft loves this feature!) There are even some cases when you could have too many licenses as well; this is often a key selling point of standalone software metering applications.

Determining Whether You Should Use SMS

Before embarking on the path to use Systems Management Server to deploy Outlook and Exchange, you need to make sure that it makes technical and financial sense to do so. Rushing to implement SMS may let you miss an opportunity to use a tool better suited to your environment or to save money by using "sneaker-net," or walking installation CDs to each desktop. The key is to use the right tool for the right job. Because you figured out what the job was earlier in this lesson, let's figure out if SMS is the right tool.

The decision is not only to use SMS, but to use a systems management tool with software distribution capabilities versus using a manual approach. So your decision is actually two decisions: manual versus tools-based deployment, and then SMS or non-SMS tools.

Manual Versus Automated Deployment   The decision to deploy Exchange and Outlook manually versus automatically is a complex one that needs to take into account your unique requirements. But there are some basic drivers of this decision, most notably:

- Number of Users. A high number of users will force you towards an automated deployment. If you consider how long it takes to install client software at each desktop and multiply that by the number of desktops, installing Outlook could take hundreds of hours for a medium-size company. Considering the hourly cost of your labor, this math alone may justify investing the time, effort, and money to purchase a systems management package.

- Timeframe for Deployment. Because a key benefit of a systems management solution's software distribution capabilities is time savings, an aggressive deadline for a widespread or large deployment will push you towards using automated tools.

- Future needs or applications. If you do not already have a software distribution capability in place and you can justify it with Outlook or Exchange alone, a planned rollout of another application to the same user community may make your use of such tools valuable to other software efforts in the organization. While many projects find that implementing SMS in conjunction with Exchange delivers a one-time cost savings, those savings continue if the organization and other software projects use the infrastructure you've built.

SMS Versus Other Systems Management Packages   If you've determined that it makes sense to use a software distribution or systems management tool to help deploy Exchange and Outlook, the next step is to determine whether to use SMS or another package. Although choosing a systems management package is a detailed and lengthy process, I'll cover the highlights of some of the things that will influence your decision. Several factors should influence your SMS decision:

- The use of or direction towards Windows NT Server throughout your organization. While SMS can function in a Novell NetWare environment, if your long term direction is still NetWare-oriented, you might want to look elsewhere for a management solution. But if your company is fully entrenched with Windows NT Servers as well as other Microsoft products, SMS may be a good fit.

- The use of other BackOffice applications throughout the company. If you already use a SQL Server or SNA Server-based application, you've spent the money with Exchange to move to Microsoft BackOffice. Having done that, SMS's software costs are already paid. Likewise, often the SQL Server component of SMS is a light-duty one; if you already have equipment to put the SMS database on you've also avoided some implementation costs.

- The desire for an integrated, enterprise-level management platform. Let's face it: SMS is not HP OpenView, nor will it ever be. SMS is a desktop-centric management tool, which from Microsoft's perspective is a good thing, given Microsoft's dominance at that level. If you are looking for a solution to integrate with an HP OpenView-type of solution, other solutions may fit the bill better, although SMS can publish SNMP (Simple Network Management Protocol) information to a management console such as OpenView.

Note   HP's OpenView system is a comprehensive management framework and console. HP OpenView itself is not a systems management package, but instead the foundation upon which HP-supplied or third-party applications can build upon. OpenView provides a single console and place to manage network-based components and applications, even if those components are from different vendors. Available HP OpenView-based applications include Seagate NerveCenter, Nortel Networks Optivity (formerly Bay Networks Optivity), and HP Network Node Manager (NNM.)

There are hundreds of specialized software distribution packages available that could meet your Exchange deployment needs, potentially at a lower cost than SMS. The key item to take away from this lesson is not SMS itself but the appreciation that tools like SMS can greatly help your deployment effort.

Ways to Use SMS in Your Exchange Implementation A tool like Systems Management Server can help your overall project be more successful, beyond simple deployment. There are various ways SMS can help your project, including the following:

- Using SMS inventory data to help identify the need for hardware and software upgrades. You can easily query the SMS database to detail how many PCs have to be upgraded, or even how many people need to free up more disk space before installing Microsoft Outlook is possible. This information is particularly useful in planning your project; it helps to know that you'll have to replace PCs early on rather than after you've installed the software and found performance lacking.

- Using SMS to gather configuration information for legacy email systems. SMS can gather specified files from a user's PC; you can use this capability to get configuration information on email systems you're migrating from. For example, you can collect the NOTES.INI file from Lotus Notes users to identify what databases a user accesses. Gathering this information helps you in planning a migration effort.

- Creating a customized Outlook setup package to send to your users and sites. This places the Outlook setup files at each of your Exchange sites and sends the commands necessary to install Outlook to users though the SMS Package Command Manager. You can also use the Package Command Manager as a service on Windows NT computers to allow for completely unattended installations on user workstations on a nightly basis.

- Monitoring the success of automated distribution and installation. You can check the status of each user's installation of Outlook to ensure that the user installed the software and that setup corrected no errors. This is essential to make sure that you don't miss any users.

- Use SMS as a "sales tool" to gain user confidence and trust. Tools that perform software inventorying often ruffle the feathers of users used to "owning" their PCs. Educating users on how SMS can help you support them can address these concerns; remote control, software distribution, and inventorying help you deliver new applications and upgrades to them sooner than before. Hey, we all remember when everybody in our company wanted Windows 95 on their desk the day it came out!

Installing and Configuring an Exchange Client

In Day 1, "Introduction to Exchange," you learned about the different clients that Exchange Server supports. While some may consider the wide variety of clients a benefit, most people implementing Exchange find the choice of client confusing. Understanding the pros and cons of each client and some considerations when choosing a client should clear some of the confusion for you and your users.

As I've noted, there are four basic Exchange Server clients:

- The Exchange Client. This is the original client for Exchange Server, using an interface similar to MS Mail and the Windows Messaging client that comes with Windows 95 and 98. The Exchange client works in conjunction with Schedule+ for group scheduling. Since the introduction of Microsoft Outlook this client is slowly going out of favor, but some companies prefer it due to its less complex interface, lower resource requirements, and faster speed relative to Outlook.

- Microsoft Outlook. Outlook 98 and Outlook 97 are the current "clients of choice" for new Exchange implementations. Outlook uses a single program for email, scheduling, address book, and task management functions. Some people decry Outlook's performance; it is important to note that Outlook 98 is faster than Outlook 97 but still requires a relatively current PC (as a rule of thumb, if Office 97 runs slow on the machine, Outlook will also run slow). Outlook 98 also requires the installation of Internet Explorer 4.0.

- Outlook Express. This client uses Exchange Server's POP3, IMAP4 and SMTP mail support to provide a slimmer, simpler client than Outlook 98. Acting as an Internet mail client, Outlook Express is designed for simpler Exchange implementation; Outlook Express offers a limited email client designed for casual email usage. Choosing Outlook Express as a client is equivalent to choosing another Internet client such as Qualcomm Eudora or Netscape Mail.

- Outlook Web Access. The Outlook Web Access client uses a standard Web browser to deliver basic Outlook functions. This option is appealing for very casual or technically remote email users, or users who need to share a PC in a task-oriented environment such as a manufacturing shop floor or where normal network access is not possible but Internet access is. Outlook Web Access is appealing to many organizations because a Web browser is likely to have already been installed on

PCs. If you use attachments or custom applications you will want to consider another client.

Tools to Automate Installation

There are tools Microsoft makes available to help you install an Exchange client without user intervention. Automating client installation is a prerequisite for using automated software distribution tools, although having a streamlined setup program provides time savings and ensures consistent installations even when you're going from desktop to desktop. Some organizations even find that they can email or post on a Web page a shortcut to the setup program residing on the corporate network to allow users to install their own software!

These installation tools vary in their complexity and flexibility; as Microsoft's management approach and toolset has evolved over the past two years, the Exchange client management tools evolved as well.

The Exchange Client

The Exchange client CD-ROM comes with a tool called the Exchange Setup Editor. This tool allows you to preconfigure a set of SETUP.STF and SETUP.INF files that the Exchange Client setup program uses to control what services or options are installed and in what manner. The Exchange Setup Editor only works for the original Exchange client and is used with the setup program's /Q installation option for an automated or "quiet" installation.

Microsoft also supplies an Exchange Client policy for Windows NT and Windows 95 workstations that preconfigures and locks down common configuration preferences, such as auto-archiving settings. Administrators use the Policy Editor included with Windows NT Server to create a policy template that includes the Exchange client.

NEW TERM Many companies want to standardize how their network's programs and desktops are configured; standardizing configurations are a key component to lowering the effort and cost associated with supporting a network's PC environment common in most organizations. To help with standardizing application and operating system configurations Microsoft created *policies* and *policy templates*. A policy holds basic configuration information for a program such as where files are located or what configuration options are available to the user to be changed. Microsoft supplies a policy template for popular software programs such as Microsoft Office, Outlook, or Windows NT. These templates are combined, edited, and then applied to a Windows NT domain so that the policy is in effect whenever a user logs into the network. "Locked down" policies are combined with automated setup tools to form the backbone of Microsoft's Zero Administration Kit (ZAK) initiative.

Outlook 97

Outlook 97 uses a similar installation method as the Exchange Client, although a "setup editor" is not available to let you control which messaging services and software components are installed. Brave folks may manually edit the client setup configuration files, although I've found that effort time consuming because simple errors can leave the setup unusable. Just as with the Exchange client, SETUP /Q can install Outlook 97 without requiring answers or intervention from an end user; after the setup program starts, it runs to completion and then reboots the PC.

Microsoft also has an Outlook 97 policy template for use with Windows NT security and configuration policies; this template allows you to control many basic configuration options.

Outlook 98

Outlook 98 departs from the standard setup program we're used to seeing; Outlook 98 now uses the Active Setup program that regular users of Internet Explorer 4.0 employ to keep your software constantly up to date. Active Setup provides a lot of improvements over a traditional installation program in that it can analyze for software dependencies and version differences. This is critical because Outlook 98 requires Internet Explorer 4 and Outlook Express to be installed. The Outlook 98 setup program checks to see if these components are already present and installs them if necessary.

Microsoft helps simplify automated and customized installations by providing the Outlook Deployment Kit, which is available on the Exchange 5.5 Service Pack 1 CD-ROM with Microsoft TechNet, Microsoft Select, or Solutions Provider programs. The Outlook Deployment Kit lets you customize the installation of not only Outlook 98 but also Internet Explorer. The Outlook Deployment Kit also combines the customization of installing Outlook as well as configuring policies and restrictions for users after the client is installed.

The Outlook Deployment Kit is the best way for you to deploy Outlook 98. The next section of this lesson covers using the Outlook Deployment Kit to customize the Outlook 98 installation and create the ability to run Outlook 98 setup without user intervention.

The Outlook Deployment Kit

The Outlook Deployment Kit (ODK) lets you tweak, tune, and customize your Outlook 98 and Internet Explorer 4.0 installation to allow you to control vast array of how these programs look and operate. This discussion of the ODK focuses on customizing the core Outlook 98 components that you would be more likely to want to customize; not every customized feature is covered but you should have enough basics to walk through the process and figure out what each option means.

The Outlook Deployment Kit consists of the Outlook Deployment Wizard, policy templates, tools for creating self-extracting Cabinet files, and a variety of utilities used for digitally signing custom components.

Obtaining the Kit

The Outlook Deployment Kit is available with the Microsoft TechNet, Microsoft Select, and Microsoft Solutions Developer CD-ROM subscription products as part of Exchange Server 5.5 Service Pack 1 CD-ROM. If you're not a subscriber to these services, it makes common sense to at least subscribe to Microsoft TechNet; the subscription fee will pay for itself with the first use of this kit if you have hundreds or thousands of clients to roll out.

Note

> Microsoft TechNet is an essential piece of a technical professional's toolkit. You can get a free year's subscription to TechNet by passing a Microsoft Certified Systems Engineer (MCSE) certification. You can also get one-year individual and corporate subscriptions. For more information see TechNet's Web site, http://www.microsoft.com/technet.

Installing the Outlook 98 Deployment Wizard

The Kit's Outlook Deployment Wizard can be installed by launching SETUP.EXE in the \Client\EN\ODK directory on the Exchange Server 5.5 Service Pack 1 CD-ROM. The program launches a dialog box like the one shown in Figure 9.2. Selecting Install the Outlook Deployment Wizard will start the installation process.

FIGURE 9.2

The Outlook Deployment Kit includes the Outlook Deployment Wizard to help you customize the installation of Outlook 98.

The setup program installs the Outlook Deployment Wizard and all of the Outlook program files in the C:\Program Files\ODK directory; this takes approximately 160Mb of free disk space on the C: drive to complete.

Running the Outlook Deployment Wizard

After the installation is complete you can launch the Outlook Deployment Wizard from the Microsoft ODK program group under Start, Programs.

As the opening screen of the Outlook Deployment Wizard shows in Figure 9.3, the Wizard completes five stages or steps to complete your customizations. I'll discuss each stage in more detail in a moment.

- Stage 1 is where you enter basic information such as your license key, language, and target destination for the resulting customized Outlook 98 files.

- Stage 2 analyzes the different components available for you to include in your distribution, as well as providing you the ability to add your own files to the Outlook setup program.

- Stage 3 lets you control the different installation options available to the user when they run Setup, as well as allowing the ability to customize the Autorun setup screen if you place the Outlook distribution on a CD-ROM.

- Stage 4 lets you customize the general configuration of Outlook 98 and Internet Explorer 4.0. You can specify email services, Outlook bar settings, and other settings for both programs.

- Stage 5 lets you control user-specific settings for Internet Explorer and Microsoft Outlook, such as which email editor to use, network security settings, and other options controlled by system policies.

FIGURE 9.3

The first page of the Outlook Wizard outlines the five parts or stages to building a custom Outlook 98 installation package.

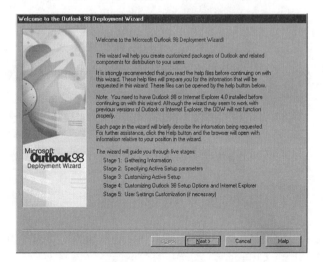

Stage 1—Gathering Information

Stage 1 starts the process by getting license code, company name, language, and output destination out of the way. You'll need to use a license code from your original Outlook or Exchange CD-ROM. These dialog boxes are shown in Figures 9.4, 9.5, and 9.6.

FIGURE 9.4

This page of the Outlook Wizard asks for your company name and license code. All clients installed from this package will have this license code and company name.

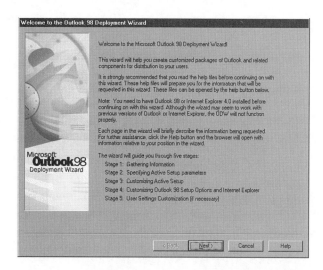

FIGURE 9.5

This page of the Outlook Wizard asks what the primary language used for the package is. This will default to the language used on your PC.

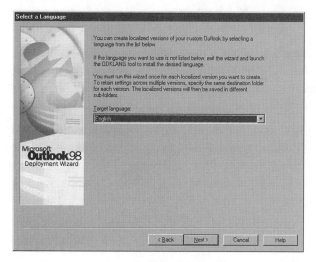

This page of the Outlook Wizard lets you specify where the customized Outlook installation files will be placed. Make sure to specify a drive with 300MB or more of free disk space.

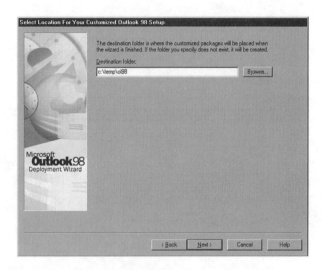

One thing to keep in mind when you're building the customized packages and files is that your installation options may require you to have 200 or more free megabytes of disk space wherever you place the files.

Stage 2—Specifying Active Setup Parameters

Stage 2 first figures out what components are available for inclusion in your package. You are also given the opportunity to add custom components and files to the package.

The Component List page, shown in Figure 9.7, displays the different components included in the Deployment Wizard's files on your hard disk drive. If all of the items show a green check, indicating the component is available, you can simply click Next to proceed to the next page.

The Specify Custom Active Setup Components page, shown in Figure 9.8, allows you to add custom components or files to the distribution package. These components can be self-extracting files (.EXE files) or cabinet (.CAB) files. This page lets you add one or more custom components to the package by clicking the Add button; you need to fill out each component's information text boxes first before you do this. These text boxes include:

- Component. This is the component's name to be used during installation.
- Location. This is the filename and location of the program or cabinet file for this component.
- Command. If you select a .CAB file for your custom component Outlook Active Setup will run a command after the files in the cabinet file are extracted. This is usually the setup or installation program included inside the cabinet file.

- GUID. This is the Globally Unique Identifier for this program. If you don't have a GUID for this component you can have the Deployment Wizard generate one by clicking the Generate button.

FIGURE 9.7

This page shows the available Outlook components that you can install in the package.

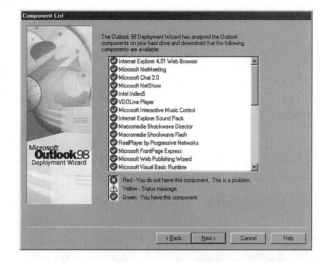

FIGURE 9.8

The Outlook Deployment Wizard lets you include your own customized components to be included in the installation package.

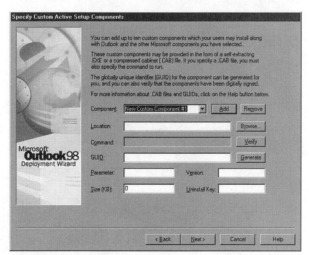

NEW TERM   The *Globally Unique Identifier (GUID)* is based on an Open Systems Foundation (OSF) industry standard algorithm for generating unique identifiers for software programs and components. A GUID ensures that no two software components accidentally use the same registration and configuration information, something that could cause serious trouble on a computer.

- Parameter. This line lets you specify command-line switches or parameters to be passed to the command specified in the Command text box.

- Version. This text box allows you to include a version number for the custom component so that you can track different versions of the component as you roll out subsequent versions of the package.

- Size. This is the size of the program or Cabinet file.

- Uninstall Key. This text box lets you use the Control Panel's Add/Remove Programs applet to launch your component's uninstall program. This text box should include the Registry entry HKEY_LOCAL_MACHINE\SOFTWARE \Microsoft\Windows\CurrentVersion\Uninstall\<component name>\<uninstall command>.

The Verify button on the right side of the page lets you test that the component has been digitally signed; clicking on it will verify the digital signature. The next page in the Wizard lets you specify how you will sign your entire package.

Specifying a Certificate Authority(CA)   The next dialog box, shown in Figure 9.9, allows you to specify what trusted publisher will be used to digitally sign your customized files and the files from the Deployment Wizard. Select the publisher on this page and then click the Next button.

FIGURE 9.9

The Outlook Deployment Wizard asks you what Certificate Authority (CA) will digitally sign your custom components and installation files.

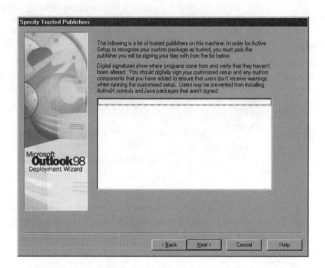

Stage 3—Customizing Active Setup

The third stage of the Outlook Deployment Wizard walks you through customizing the CD-ROM Autorun feature. You can specify which software is included in each setup option as well as adding more available setup options.

Customize the Autorun Screen for CD-ROM Installations   The dialog box shown in Figure 9.10 lets you customize the Autorun program that appears when a CD-ROM is first inserted into the CD drive on a user's PC. This page only applies if you decide to distribute Outlook on CD-ROM. The page lets you specify the following options:

- Title bar text. This is the text that appears in the top of the Autorun dialog box.

- Custom background bitmap location. You can use a customized bitmap (such as your company logo) as the Autorun dialog box's background. If you want to customize this option, click Browse and select the bitmap (.BMP) file you'd like to use.

- Standard text color. This is color of text that isn't part of a link.

- Highlight text color. This is the color of text that is highlighted or part of a link.

- Button style. This lets you control how buttons that install the software or provide more information look. You can choose between three options: standard bilevel buttons, 3D bitmaps (the default), or a custom button image that you can specify using the Browse button.

FIGURE 9.10

The Outlook Deployment Wizard lets you customize the CD-ROM Autorun dialog box's appearance.

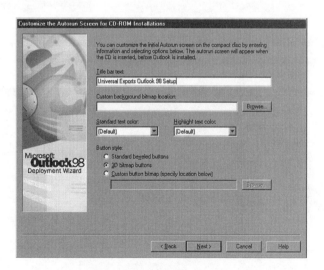

Select Silent Install and Hide Icons   The next dialog box, shown in Figure 9.11, lets you specify a silent installation and hide the Internet Explorer icons on the desktop (provided they aren't already there.)

If you're using the Outlook Deployment Wizard to perform unattended installations you will want to select the Silent installation option by clicking the Install Package Silently check box. The downside to this is that you can only specify a single set of installation options. Because we're focusing on how to deploy Outlook 98 to a large number of users with a software distribution tool, we're selecting the Silent option for this discussion of the ODK.

FIGURE 9.11

The Outlook Deployment Wizard can specify a silent installation, which is required for a fully automated installation of Outlook. You can also hide the Internet Explorer icons from the Desktop and Start menu.

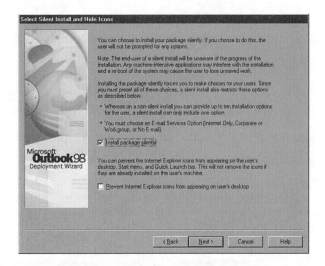

Select Installation Options   The next page, shown in Figure 9.12, lets you select which Outlook and Internet Explorer options you'd like to have installed.

FIGURE 9.12

You can specify which components are included in the Standard, Minimum, and Full installation options. You can also create your own set of installation options.

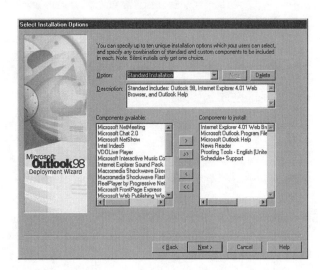

The Option list box lets you choose from three prebuilt installation options: Minimal Installation, Standard Installation, and Full Installation. You can select one of these three to review which components are installed with each.

If you didn't select the silent installation option on the previous page, you can provide additional installation options or selections by selecting the New button. If you don't want to give users the ability to install a specific installation option, click the Delete button to remove it.

If you did select the silent installation option, you can still configure each of these options as you'd like; the choice of installation option is provided when you actually run setup on the user's workstation.

You can customize which components are installed with each option by choosing available components on the Components Available list box on the left and moving the component to the Components to Install list box on the right by clicking the > button. You can remove a component from the Components to Install list box by selecting the < button.

After you've modified the installation options, you can click the Next button.

Select Version Information and Add-on Component URL   The subsequent dialog box, shown in Figure 9.13, lets you specify a version information for your installation package. This prevents users from installing older versions of Outlook packages that you generate with the ODK over newer ones. This is done by using a version number and a unique configuration identifier.

FIGURE 9.13

You can specify a version number and unique configuration identifier. This prevents older versions of your installation package from overwriting newer versions.

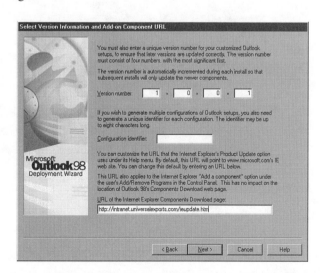

The Version Number text boxes let you specify a version number for this distribution package; this number automatically increments each time you run the Outlook Deployment Wizard successfully.

The Configuration Identifier text box lets you specify a unique configuration name, something you need to do if you're building multiple Outlook packages. This is an eight-digit or letter identifier. This is combined with the company name you specified earlier in the wizard to uniquely identify this configuration.

Because Outlook 98 uses Internet Explorer 4.0 and its components, you have an opportunity to customize Internet Explorer's links to add new components. If you'd like to override the default setting that points to Microsoft's Internet Explorer page, you can specify a different URL in the URL of the Internet Explorer Components Download Page text box.

Specify Where You Want to Install Outlook 98   This page, shown in Figure 9.14, lets you specify where you'd like Outlook 98's files installed. The default is the Microsoft Office directory in Program Files. Choosing this option usually makes sense because technically Outlook is a part of Microsoft Office. Outlook 98 also shares many Office components such as the Office Assistants.

FIGURE 9.14

You can specify where you'd like Outlook 98 installed.

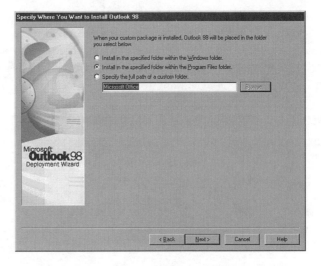

If you'd like to specify a different location, you can do so by specifying a subdirectory under the Windows folder or by specifying a full path to where you'd like Outlook installed.

Integrating the Windows Desktop Update   Figure 9.15 shows the next page in the Wizard that lets you specify whether you want to include the Windows Desktop Update in your package. The Windows Desktop Update includes the Active Desktop and brings Web enhancements to the Explorer, taskbar, and desktop. You can simply indicate your choice using the Yes and No radio buttons. Of course, your end users might get upset if they find their desktops radically altered one morning.

FIGURE 9.15

Because Outlook includes Internet Explorer you have the option to install the Windows Desktop Update.

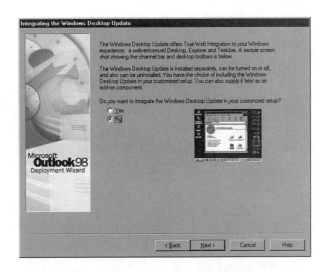

9

Stage 4—Customizing Outlook 98 Setup Options and Internet Explorer

The fourth major part of building your Outlook deployment package is finalizing some Outlook 98 and Internet Explorer options. Because Internet Explorer is included as part of the Outlook 98 distribution, you have the opportunity to customize your Internet Explorer setup.

Choose Email Services Options   Outlook 98 supports a variety of mail services, including the Internet and Microsoft Exchange Server. The page shown in Figure 9.16 lets you specify what types of mail services to install for Outlook 98. You can choose to only install Internet mail support, corporate or workgroup email support, or no mail support. Note that if you're performing a silent installation, you must choose one of these options.

For native Microsoft Exchange Server support, you should select the Corporate or Workgroup option. This option tells Outlook to install MAPI client support (required for Exchange and MS Mail support) and also imports any previous MAPI configuration.

If you choose the Internet Only email option, the Outlook setup program can automatically import email configurations from other programs. You can select these programs from among the radio buttons at the bottom of this page when the Internet Only email option is selected.

Configure Schedule+ Support   The Exchange Client and Office 95 both use the Schedule+ program to provide Exchange Server's group scheduling support. This capability is provided with Outlook, although organizations whose Exchange infrastructure

still uses Schedule+ may want to consider continuing to use Schedule+ for group scheduling for backwards computability.

FIGURE 9.16

*If you select to per-
form a silent installa-
tion you must specify
what type of mail ser-
vice to install with
Outlook. If you are
using Exchange
Server you should
select Corporate or
Workgroup.*

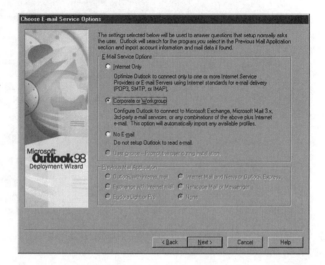

The Configure Schedule+ Support dialog box, shown in Figure 9.17, lets you specify
whether to retain Schedule+ as the group scheduling program should the user already
have Schedule+ installed. If your Exchange implementation is a new one (which it probably is if you're following this lesson), you can answer No to the question Do You Want
to Use Schedule+ for Group Scheduling? Again, if you select to perform a silent installation, you must specify whether to support Schedule+ for group scheduling.

FIGURE 9.17

*If you select to per-
form a silent installa-
tion you must specify
whether to support
Schedule+ for group
scheduling. Most
new Exchange imple-
mentations should
answer No.*

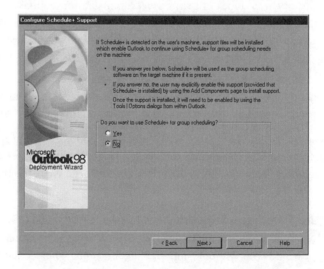

Customize the Outlook Bar and Command Bar Settings   The Outlook Deployment Wizard lets you customize the Outlook Bar that appears on the left side of the Outlook program window. The options to do so are shown in Figure 9.18. This customization is accomplished by changing the file (outlbar.inf) that builds the default Outlook bar; when a user first uses Outlook her Outlook bar is build from this file.

Tip   Although most implementations don't bother with a customized Outlook bar, one thing that you could add to make Outlook easier to use is a Public Folders button to simplify viewing public folders.

If you'd like to customize the Outlook bar, specify your changed `outlbar.inf` file in the proper text box. To find out the file format and how to build this file, look at the sample file and documentation in the \olbin\en\optional directory.

You can also customize the Outlook toolbars by specifying a custom toolbar file, outcmd.dat. This is covered in more detail in the Outlook Deployment Kit documentation, available for download from the Microsoft Web site at

`http://www.microsoft.com/office/98/outlook/documents/o98dkdoc.htm.`

FIGURE 9.18

The Outlook Deployment Wizard lets you customize the Outlook Bar and the Outlook Command toolbar.

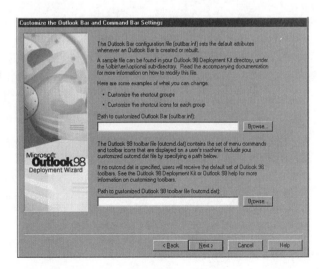

Customize Internet Explorer   The next part of the Outlook Deployment Wizard lets you customize the installation of Internet Explorer.

Note   Because you're focusing on Outlook 98 as part of this lesson (and the customization options for Internet Explorer are immense), you'll choose not to customize the Internet Explorer setup as you walk through the wizard. If you'd like to customize Internet Explorer's settings, you can choose to do so, but we won't cover those steps in this lesson.

Stage 5—User Settings Customization

The fifth and final part of the Outlook Deployment Wizard allows you to customize the user settings for Outlook and Internet Explorer. These settings are the same as those set by Outlook and Windows 98 policies.

Customize User Settings   The page shown in Figure 9.19 lets you specify user settings for the different components of the Outlook package you've built. Major applications, components, and configuration groups are listed in a hierarchical tree structure; you can navigate through the list to change individual settings.

FIGURE 9.19

The Outlook Deployment Wizard lets you customize the user settings, policies, and restrictions for each of the components you've selected for installation.

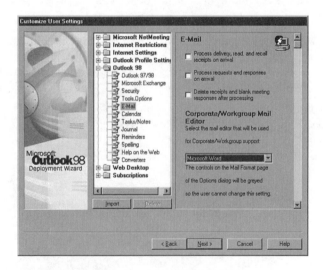

You can also import your own policy and restrictions template (.ADM) file to incorporate any other applications into the package.

Useful Settings   While a thorough discussion of all of the various settings would consume an entire book by itself, knowing what kind of settings you can set may be helpful. Some key abilities include:

- Setting the Mail Editor. You can specify Microsoft Word or Outlook as the email editor.

- Disabling the ability to change Internet Explorer settings. You can lock-down a configuration so that users cannot change content, security, or other settings.

- Specifying a dial-up entry. You can specify a Dial-Up Networking entry that the user can use to connect to Exchange. This option is useful for remote users who connect to Exchange over a modem. These same users benefit from the Outlook Deployment Kit's ability to create a CD-ROM package.

- Specifying default messaging profile settings. The Outlook Profile section lets you specify which services get installed for the initial mail profile, as well as what username and server name to use for Exchange Server users. The Resolve Name at Run Time location lets you use the user's network login name as the Exchange alias name and have a messaging profile automatically created.

- Locking-down Web Desktop features and access. You can hide aspects of the Web Desktop or prevent users from changing settings. You can also hide certain portions of the Start menu and the taskbar.

Note

The Outlook Profile section of the Outlook Deployment Wizard is designed to replace the functionality of the commonly used profgen.exe and newprof.exe tools provided on the Exchange Server or BackOffice Resource Kits. While you can use the ODK's methods to automatically create a profile, the profgen.exe tool remains a viable option to automatically create a messaging profile after Outlook setup or after each user logs into a system. Review the newprof.exe documentation on the BackOffice or Exchange Server Resource Kit CD-ROMs available through Microsoft TechNet.

Add Registry Entries   The Add Registy Entries page, shown in Figure 9.20, lets you add custom Registry entries as part of the setup process. Clicking the Add button brings up a dialog box that allows you to specify the root, data type, key, and key value. This capability is especially useful to add configuration information for custom components.

Copying Files   This is the last page in the Outlook Deployment Wizard. After you've clicked the Finish button on the next page the Wizard will start copying files to your package destination.

Signing Files   The last step to prepare your package is to digitally sign the resulting files in your package if you are distributing your files over the Internet or through a Web browser. The following files should be signed:

- Branding.cab

- Chl<####>.cab

- Desktop.cab

- Folder<#>.cab

- Outcif.cab

- Setup.exe

The Chl<####>.cab means each file that starts with CHL and is numbered (for example, Chl0001.cab and Chl0002.cab). The same convention applies to Folder<#>.cab, representing one or more files starting with Folder1.cab. Folder2.cab, and so on.

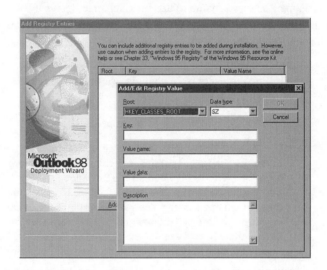

FIGURE 9.20

The Outlook Deployment Wizard lets you add Registry entries to the user's PC after the setup process is complete. This is useful for custom components you've added to the Outlook files.

How to Sign Files   The first thing you need to do is get a publishing certificate from a known Certificate Authority such as GTE or Verisign (if you are using the files internally, you can use your own Microsoft Certificate Server to generate a software publishing certificate(.spc).

If you have a certificate or would like to test signing code, use the tools provided in the ODK\reskit\addons\tools directory. The SignCode.EXE program is used to sign each file; documentation on this program can be found in the Outlook Deployment Kit documentation. It also makes sense to review general background material at Microsoft's security Web site,

`http://www.microsoft.com/security/.`

Distributing the Files

After your Outlook 98 package is built the next step is to distribute it to your users. You have several ways to get your customized Outlook 98 installation to users:

- CD-ROM. This option works best for remote, "casually connected" users, especially if they do not have a high-speed network connection to a corporate network where you can place the Outlook files.

- Network Share. This is simple and easy: give users the ability to run Outlook 98 Setup from a shared folder on the network.

- Intranet page. This option allows users to launch Outlook 98's active setup from a Web page. Specific directions for configuring installation via a Web page is outlined in the Outlook Deployment Kit documentation; further information is available in the Internet Explorer Administrative Kit (IEAK), available from the Microsoft Web site at `http://ieak.microsoft.com`.

- Systems Management Server package. This option is a variation of the Network Share option except that SMS handles creating the directory and other information using its own packaging techniques. The user then launches Outlook setup from an SMS share through the SMS client's Package Command Manager.

Using an SMS Package

If you're using Microsoft Systems Management Server (SMS), the Outlook Deployment Kit comes with a prebuilt Package Definition File (.PDF) in the \odk\tools directory.

After you've created the ability to distribute Outlook or another Exchange client to your users with customized settings and capabilities it's time to take a look at how to train users so that they know how to use the software you've placed on their desk.

Training and Support

One of the most important yet overlooked aspects of implementing Exchange is the necessity to make users, not technical people like ourselves, successful with Exchange. Training can be as simple or as complex as your organization requires.

How Training Fits Into Deployment

As a rule, someone needs to be trained on how to use Exchange before an Exchange client such as Microsoft Outlook is put on the user's PC. This makes the person productive with the system immediately, and prevents a frustrated or confused call to a help desk or support technician.

There are a wide variety of methods available to train people on how to use Exchange. These methods vary on their effectiveness, cost, and complexity but are all better than no training at all.

Formal Classroom Training

Training held in a classroom with an instructor and workshop-like environment can be extremely effective. Classroom training requires a lot of planning and effort; it is common to use professional training organizations for classroom training. This can save an organization money and effort, particularly if the organization is geographically dispersed. The option exists to do the training at your location, a hotel or conference center, or at the trainer's facility. Professional training organizations such as Catapult or AmeriTrain also have additional benefits such as pre-prepared training manuals and retraining guarantees in the event someone feels they didn't learn enough in a training session.

Videotapes

Video training is quickly becoming a viable training option, particularly in situations where only a single person needs to be trained. A good example of this is a new-hire situation; you may not be able to hold classroom training for each new employee so having him view a videotape may be the only option. Something to consider when using videotaped training is the equipment requirements of having a TV and VCR setup. Because the videotapes often can't be viewed in front of a PC, this training is usually less effective than classroom or one-on-one instruction.

Computer Based Training(CBT)

Computer based training usually involves a multimedia CD-ROM or program that interactively walks through various aspects of Exchange. One benefit of CBT training is that its interactivity could force people to walk through the application; the downside is its rather impersonal nature. CBT training is especially useful for refresher training or on-demand training; making the CD-ROM accessible over a network increases its usefulness.

Support Approaches

Because we're talking about training, it also makes sense to also talk about how training fits into an overall support strategy. Approaches to whom you train, how you train, and when you train can all impact the overall support load on the technical staff when the Exchange system becomes operational.

Train the Champion Users   One of the approaches that large, distributed organizations find useful as a training approach includes using "power users" as a means to train rank-and-file users. Semi-technical and enthusiastic people from your user community are given intensive, detailed classroom training. These people then go back to their normal workgroups. When Exchange becomes live, they provide informal ground-level support by answering simple questions and leading the use of Exchange features by example. One caution is not to rely upon these people too much; technical support staff should still provide end-user support for all users.

Time Workgroup Deployment After Training   It is logistically impossible to deploy an application simultaneously across an organization. Training and technical deployment both take place in workgroups or clusters of users. One way to boost the effectiveness of training is to time deployment on an individual basis so that a user has an Exchange client such as Outlook on their desktop as soon as they get out of a training class.

Include Installation or Migration in Training   If you're spending the time and effort to train users on how to use Exchange, take the opportunity to tell and show users how you will install or deploy Exchange. If you're using a new tool for installing Exchange such as SMS or a software distribution tool it makes sense to include this aspect of Exchange in the training curriculum.

Another way to improve the effectiveness of training is to have "delta" training for users migrating from a legacy system to Exchange. This training focuses on the differences between the two systems, saving valuable time by focusing on new features and benefits of Exchange while skipping basic concepts that people already know.

Create a Central Help Desk   It is important to give users a place to call with their questions and problems. Establishing a central help desk with a well-publicized phone number can give users one place to find knowledgeable and competent support.

If your organization already has a help desk, ensure that the support staff are training in Exchange as well as in the methods by which you're using to deploy Exchange.

Summary

Deployment is the most time-consuming aspect of an Exchange Server implementation. Getting an Exchange client in the hands of hundreds or thousands of users can be a difficult task, although Microsoft and other companies provide tools to help make this aspect of your project easier.

Today's lesson showed you how to deploy Exchange within your organization. You learned the basics of deploying Exchange, including the following:

- The considerations and thought required to plan your implementation approach, such as where your users are. Your approach should cover the four stages of deployment: distributing the client, installing it, configuring the mail client for a particular user, and supporting the client after it is in the hands of users.

- The methods available to rollout and customize your Exchange client rollout, such as a software distribution tool and customized setup tools from Microsoft such as the Outlook Deployment Kit (ODK).

- How to use the capabilities of Microsoft Systems Management Server to help in your deployment, from surveying users' PC before deployment to monitoring the success of your deployment while its in progress.

- How to use the Outlook Deployment Kit to customize the installation of Outlook 98 to help enforce customization standards and create messaging profiles automatically.

- How to pick the training method you will use to train users. This along with a help desk can lower your support effort during deployment while helping the success of your project.

Q&A

Q What's the point in a project at which it's too late to consider automated deployment tools such as SMS and the Outlook Deployment Kit?

A Both Systems Management Server, the Outlook Deployment Kit, and any other tool for that matter take a lot of time and effort to use and get the hang of, there isn't a specific point where it is too late. The key is to look at the effort ahead relative to how much time these tools could save: even if it takes several weeks or months to get the tools working but it saves you six months of deployment, the effort is well worth the delay.

Q One idea that we're considering is having users install their own email client. This saves us the effort of attempting to automate the setup or visit each computer. Does this make sense?

A Lots of projects have taken this approach. Things to consider are the sophistication of the users (if they're technically savvy, why not?) and the amount of documentation you can provide. Consider at least using the Outlook Deployment Kit to keep users from choosing between a wide variety of installation options.

Q Can we build our own software distribution mechanism with network login scripts and batch files?

A This option works well provided you test the solution and carefully monitor its progress (just like SMS or any other tool.) A downside to this that you're batch files and scripts can become quite complex; this approach may meet an immediate need but could become cumbersome to manage and change over time. Because any management strategy includes software distribution, the hundreds of commercial tools could be worth the price in terms of simplicity and manageability.

Workshop

The Workshop provides two ways for you to affirm what you've learned in this lesson. The "Quiz" section poses questions to help you solidify your understanding of the material covered and the "Exercise" section provides you with experience in using what you have learned. You can find answers to the quiz questions and exercises in Appendix B, "Answers to Quiz Questions and Exercises."

Quiz

1. The Outlook Deployment Wizard does not show all of the components that you would like to install in the Component List shown in Figure 9.7. What could a possible cause of this be?

2. You are distributing Outlook 98 clients to hundreds of users who will be using Windows 95 and Dial Up Networking to connect to Exchange over 56Kbps modems. What is the best method to get Outlook working for these users?

3. What feature of the Outlook Deployment Wizard prevents users from installing older versions of your package on top of newer ones?

Exercise

1. The Outlook Deployment Wizard allows you to create a customized messaging profile as it is run. This is important for you, as you have many laptop users who will need to have their clients configured for mail to be stored on the local disk drive. This allows them to compose mail offline. In Figure 9.21, are the right settings selected and configured to support this?

FIGURE 9.21

The Outlook Deployment Wizard's profile settings. Does this picture show the right settings if you want mail stored on the user's hard disk drive?

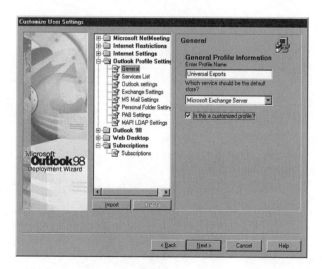

WEEK 2

DAY 10

Using Microsoft Outlook

By Anthony Steven

Chapter Objectives

So far, you have looked at the operation of the Exchange Server. However, email is about giving users the ability to send messages to each other. This requires an email client, and the client best suited to exploit the capabilities of Exchange Server is Outlook 98.

Today you will be covering the following topics:

- Capability and features
- Configuring the Outlook client
- Interoperability with the Exchange client
- Using Microsoft Word as your email editor
- The Rules Wizard and Out of Office Assistant
- Importing and exporting information

- Configuring views
- Find and advanced find
- Using categories

Introduction

Microsoft Outlook first appeared in late 1996 as a component of Office 97. Its original incarnation was as version 8.0 (to fit in with Office 97, which has Word 8.0), and evolutionary rather than revolutionary changes took it through to version 8.04 with Office 97 Service Release 2 in autumn 1998.

Microsoft released Outlook 98 in the summer of 1998 as a Web download, and it is still more of an evolutionary development of the original Outlook. If you are familiar with using the earlier versions, you should have no problems in converting to this latest release.

 Note
> Throughout this lesson, I will be using the latest release of Outlook 98 as of January 1999. This is version 8.5.5603.0 that came with Exchange 5.5 Service Pack 1.

The majority of the visible changes to Outlook 98 are in the Options dialog box, where the configuration interface is significantly different. Areas like Advanced Security have changed noticeably with the introduction of S/MIME support in Exchange 5.5 Service Pack 1. However, the majority of the changes in the Options dialog are interface rather than functionality changes.

Having used Outlook 98 for a few months now, I have found it easier to use than the previous versions, and certainly the best email client to use with Microsoft Exchange. Whether Outlook 98 is the best in a non-Exchange environment is not so clear-cut, although there have been some noticeable improvements here as well.

This next section is more of a Reviewer's guide. I have attempted to put in here some of the features and benefits that could help you write a business case for deploying Microsoft Outlook 98. I certainly don't intend to reproduce the huge feature list of Outlook. If you want more information, see the articles on "MS Outlook 98 Features and Configuration Guide," "MS Outlook 98 Enhancements Guide," and "What's New in Outlook 98" in TechNet. Alternatively, you could look at:

`http://www.microsoft.com/outlook`

Outlook Specifications and Features

Microsoft Outlook 98 is a multipurpose application, combining a fully featured MAPI client with a Personal Information Manager (PIM) that can function in a variety of situations. Outlook 98 fully integrates with Office 97, and can run on Windows NT 4.0, Windows 98, and Windows 95.

You can use Outlook 98:

- As a full MAPI client to Microsoft Exchange.
- As a MAPI client to third-party messaging systems, such as Lotus Notes, Novell GroupWise, CompuServe, Hewlett-Packard OpenMail, and Digital's All-IN-1.
- As a POP3/IMAP4 client either with Microsoft Exchange-based or ISP's POP3 or IMAP4 server.
- As a standalone PIM without any messaging functionality.

Messaging Profiles

Outlook 98 requires that you set up a messaging profile before it can function in a messaging environment. Outlook can use the following addressing, messaging, and storage services:

- Exchange Server Service, for connection via MAPI to Exchange server for message delivery and addressing purposes. The Exchange Server service can also use all gateways attached to the Exchange Server, such as Fax, MS Mail, cc:Mail, SMTP, and X.400 connectors.
- Microsoft Mail Service, for direct connection to MS Mail Post Offices for addressing and mail delivery.
- Internet Email, for message delivery to SMTP servers and collection from POP3 or IMAP4 postoffices.
- Fax Mail Address book, for storing fax numbers.
- Fax Mail transport (dependant on platform).
- LDAP client, for querying LDAP servers for addressing information.
- Outlook Address Book, to make Contact folders available as address books.
- Personal Folders, for storing all types of Outlook messages on local or network drives.
- Personal Address Book, for storing addressing information and personal distribution lists.

Outlook 98 implements these services differently than previous versions. For example, Outlook 98 uses the Corporate or Workgroup messaging service to provide connection to

Exchange Server and POP3 mailboxes, but has a separate Internet Email service for use as a dedicated POP3 or IMAP4 client. You cannot use the two services simultaneously.

For more information on configuring messaging profiles and the various information services, see Day 7, "Configuring the Exchange Client."

Integration with Microsoft Exchange

Outlook 98 is particularly suited for harnessing the features of Exchange Server, and supports the following Exchange-specific features:

- Exchange Events service, enabling the triggering of scripts when certain events take place.
- Creation and management of, and publishing to, Public Folders.
- The Exchange Forms environment, allowing you to create and publish form-based applications to public folders or to the Organizational Forms library.
- Synchronization of Free/Busy information, enabling several users to set up meetings when they all have free time.
- Deleted Item recovery, for those users who love to delete things (twice) and then want them back.
- Delegate Access, letting users grant access to their own folders to selected delegates.
- Support for Remote Mail and Offline working.

Outlook 98 connects to Exchange via the Messaging API (MAPI), which in turn requires a connection over a link supporting Remote Procedure Calls (RPC). In a low-bandwidth environment or where there is no support for RPCs, Outlook 98 uses Remote Mail connectivity.

Outlook with Internet Email

In an Exchange environment, the only reason you might be interested in Outlook in Internet Email configuration would be that you are using Outlook to access your Exchange server via POP3 or IMAP4. In Internet Email mode, Outlook 98 enables you to use the following Internet-specific functions and protocols:

- POP3/IMAP4 for mail collection
- SMTP for mail delivery
- LDAP for addressing
- Sending of contact details via vCard
- Coordinating diaries via vCalendar
- S/MIME digital signatures and encryption

However, Outlook 98 in Internet Email configuration will make a suitable client if you have remote users who connect to your organization over the Internet.

 Note | Outlook 98 has improved support for Internet operation. Outlook 97 was not so convincing in this role, as it would only function as a POP3 client.

Personal Information Management Features

If you use Outlook 98 just as a Personal Information Manager (PIM), I guess you wouldn't be reading this book. However, using Outlook 98 either with or without the messaging functionality, you will have access to a number of standard folders with a several different uses. These folders are as follows:

- Outlook Today
- Calendar
- Contacts
- Deleted Items
- Inbox
- Journal
- Notes
- Outbox
- Sent Items
- Tasks

Take a look at these types now in a little more detail.

Outlook Today   The Outlook Today folder is at the root of your Exchange Mailbox or Personal Folders. It provides a weekly view of your Tasks, Calendar items (appointments), and any unopened messages in your Inbox. You can also find a contact directly in your Contacts folder, and you can elect to have Outlook Today appear as the first folder when you start Outlook 98. (By default, it's the Inbox.)

Calendar   Calendar is a diary or appointments folder that you can use to organize personal, departmental, or resource scheduling. Multiple users can open Calendar folders and use them for coordinating team activities. Secretaries can open their bosses' calendars and make or reschedule appointments as necessary. You can also associate calendar folders with resources such as meeting rooms or equipment like projectors. Bookings for these resources will trigger a check against the resource's availability, thus preventing two groups booking the same meeting room for the same time.

Contacts   The Contacts folder can store any form of addressing information, with multiple locations, telephone numbers, and email addresses for each contact. Additional information such as managers, spouse's name, and contact's birthday make this a basis of a powerful contact management system. Users with modem-equipped workstations can autodial straight from Outlook, or you can send an email directly to a selected contact.

Deleted Items   The Deleted Items folder guards against accidental deletion by providing a temporary storage location for any deleted Outlook item, much like the Windows Recycle Bin. You can then empty the Deleted Items folder manually or automatically.

Inbox   The Inbox is the most important of your folders. Outlook works on the principle of the Universal Inbox as a central receptacle for all your emails and faxes, regardless of their source. You can then apply rules to your Inbox that will move, forward, copy, or delete messages depending on their source or content.

Journal   The Journal folder is for tracking your activities using Outlook. You can monitor your interactions with a particular client, or the Office documents on which you have worked. This lets you use Outlook as a document management system, providing a friendly user interface to documents saved in many different locations.

Notes   Notes provide an electronic version of the yellow sticky notes that people love to use to clutter up their workspace. You can forward these notes to other people, which has the advantage that it doesn't leave glue on their computer screen.

Outbox   The Outbox is where items remain until Outlook can deliver them. If you are working online using the Exchange Server service, items do not remain in the Outbox for long. If you have some form of dialup messaging service, or you are working offline, you can edit your message, and re-send it while the message is still in the Outbox.

Sent Items   The Sent Items folder keeps a record of all your sent messages. It's very useful if someone is claiming not to have received a message.

Tasks   The Tasks folder is a basic to-do list, enabled for workgroup use. Thus, you can issue tasks to employees, and get them to report on a regular basis on the progress of the task. There is add-on support for Microsoft Team Manager, which provides you with tools for managing a larger team. However, it is not Microsoft Project, and the Tasks Folder is not suitable for planning the construction of a second Channel Tunnel.

Categories

You can group most of your Outlook items within folders using user-definable categories. This makes searching for information considerably easier. There are a number of standard categories, but you can add categories to the master list. You can then use this to generate a list of your hot leads, suppliers, ad hoc team members, or bad debtors in an instant.

Outlook Shortcut Bar

Outlook provides a bar with shortcuts to all the standard folders. You can customize this by dragging any other folder onto the Outlook bar, thus providing single-click access to any folder. You can also view files and folders, even to the point of starting applications from inside Outlook.

Views

Views let you apply different ways of looking at your data. This includes sorting, grouping, and filtering of the information in a specific folder, as well as which fields appear in the view. There are a number of standard views, and you can edit or add new views as necessary.

Views in Outlook 98 are simpler than in the previous version, with the aim of making them more usable.

Integration with Office 97

Outlook 98 is more tightly integrated with Office 97 than its release number might suggest. Outlook 98 can track documents opened with any Office module, wherever that document is located on the local system or network. You can use the development environment of Outlook 98 to build complex collaboration applications using multiple Office 97 modules.

Support for Collaboration Applications and Forms

In addition to the support provided for integration with Office 97 applications, Outlook supports designing and building collaboration applications using the Forms Development environment.

Interoperability

Outlook 98 will quite happily work alongside earlier versions of Outlook and the Exchange Client. The main provisos against interoperation are that while Outlook can use the compiled Visual Basic forms from the Exchange client, the Exchange client cannot use forms produced in Outlook 98. In addition, earlier versions of Outlook or the Exchange client cannot use S/MIME digital signing and sealing.

10

If you are using Schedule+ from the Exchange Client, you will either need to add Schedule+ support to Outlook, or configure Outlook users to use Schedule+ instead of the Calendar folder.

 Tip

See if you can upgrade your Exchange client users to Outlook for Windows 3.x. It looks very much like the Exchange client, but it has the Calendar module from Outlook, which means you can scrap Schedule+.

Outlook 98 can interoperate with all industry standard POP3 and IMAP4 servers and clients in LAN, WAN, or Internet environments.

Advanced Security

Outlook 98 can use both Exchange Server's Advanced Security, as provided by the Key Management Service, or S/MIME support, using either Exchange's KMS or external certification authorities, like Microsoft Certificate Server or organizations like VeriSign. For more information on using Outlook with Advanced Security, see Day 19, "Making Exchange Secure."

Assuming that you like the look of Outlook 98, and have decided to proceed with a trial, or you've said, "What the heck, I'll take it anyway," you'll need to choose an installation method. Read on to learn more about this procedure.

Installing Outlook

Installing Outlook 98 has changed significantly from previous versions. You can now deploy Outlook 98 in three ways:

- From the Exchange 5.5 SP1 CD.
- From the Microsoft Internet site.
- From your intranet, a shared folder, or a custom CD using the Outlook Deployment Kit (ODK).

Installing from the CD gives you the fastest installation time, and you will need the CD if you are using the Outlook Deployment Kit. The CD that I am referring to here is the Exchange Server 5.5 Service Pack 1 CD that comes with TechNet.

The Installing from the Internet method is really only applicable to single installations for private users. You could not realistically use this for deploying a large number of clients.

Installing from your private intranet is the most powerful and complex method of deploying Outlook 98. Here Outlook 98 shows some of its integration with Internet Explorer 4.0, as the Outlook Deployment Kit (ODK) has more than a passing resemblance to the Internet Explorer Administration Kit.

For more information on installing using the Outlook Administration kit, see Day 9, "Deploying Exchange."

From the CD

If you have a small number of clients to deal with, you can use the CD to install Outlook 98. To do this from a network share, you can either share the directory on the CD, or copy the files onto a partition and share the folder from there.

The CD installation no longer supports the command-line switches that Outlook 97 did. Hence you can no longer use /Q /B1 for a quiet typical installation. All installation options are now part of the Outlook Deployment Kit.

10

Before You Start

Before you start to install Outlook 98, you must carry out a few actions first:

- You must be running Windows 98, Windows 95 SR1, or Windows NT 4.0 with at least Service Pack 3 applied.

- Outlook 98 will only run from a local installation. If you have installed Office 97 to run from the CD or from a network drive, you will have to uninstall Office and reinstall it locally.

- If you are installing Outlook 98 onto your Exchange server, you must stop the Exchange services first.

- Check the README.TXT file in the same directory as SETUP.EXE.

Running the Installation Routine

After you have carried out all the prerequisites, you are now ready to start the setup routine. To install Microsoft Outlook 98, carry out the following task:

1. Place the Exchange Server SP1 CD into your CD player and change to the \CLIENT\EN\OUTLK98 directory. Double-click on SETUP.EXE file. You will see the startup screen shown in Figure 10.1.

2. Select the Install Outlook 98 option, and you will start the Outlook Installation Wizard. Setup will warn you that this version of Outlook will replace previous versions. Select Next to continue.

FIGURE 10.1

The startup screen for Outlook 98 deployment.

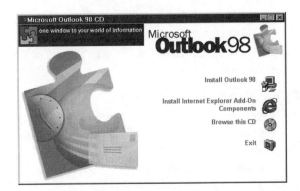

3. The License Agreement screen will inform you that Outlook 98 is licensed in different ways, depending on how you will deploy it. If you are really interested, you can read all the licensing stuff. Otherwise, just select the option to accept the agreement and click Next to continue.

4. The next screen will ask you to enter a username, company name, and CD key, as shown in Figure 10.2. The Exchange CD does not have a CD key printed on it, but you should be able to use the CD key from your Office installation.

FIGURE 10.2

You will need a valid CD key to get past this screen.

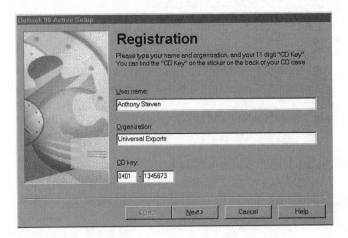

5. The Installation option screen gives you the option to install one of at least three different installation types. In Figure 10.3, you can see the three standard options available.

FIGURE 10.3

Here the three standard options of Minimal, Standard, and Full are visible. When you select a particular option, the components installed with that option are visible underneath.

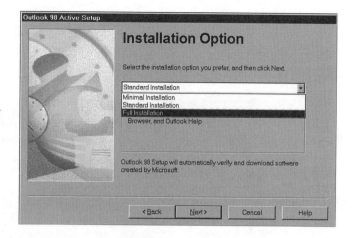

Note

If you are using this machine as a basis for producing a deployment package with the Outlook Deployment Kit, you will probably need the full installation. Like IE4, you cannot include a component in the ODK that you have not already installed.

6. The Email Upgrade Options screen detects any other email clients installed on your client machine, as shown in Figure 10.4. If you do not want to import settings (email servers, connection types, and so on) from these programs, select None of the Above.

FIGURE 10.4

Here the Email Upgrade routine has detected the Outlook Express installation. Selecting Outlook Express will import all mail and directory accounts into Outlook 98.

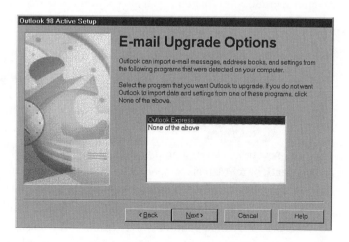

7. The Email Service Options screen is the most important screen so far. This is where you decide what sort of email accounts you will support. You have three options: Internet Only, Corporate or Workgroup, or No Email. Figure 10.5 shows this screen.

FIGURE 10.5

Decision time for messaging support. In an Exchange environment, the choice is straightforward— select the Corporate or Workgroup option.

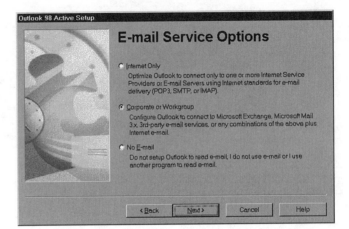

8. If you are setting up a client to connect to an ISP, choose the Internet Only option. This will give you the maximum support for Internet standards, including POP3, IMAP4, and LDAP. However, this option will not let you connect to Exchange, MAPI-compliant servers, and other non-Internet mail systems.

9. In an Exchange server environment, select the Corporate or Workgroup option. You should also select this option if you are connecting to MS Mail postoffices or any MAPI-compliant server. Note that you can still connect to POP3 (but not IMAP4 or LDAP) servers with the Corporate or Workgroup option.

10. If you are not using messaging, select the No Email option. In that case, with respect, why are you reading this book? Oh, yes, you're taking part in that trial for the drug-free treatment of insomnia.

11. Your next choice is for the installation directory. Normally, this will be C:\Program Files\Microsoft Office.

12. You will now probably see a prompt asking you if you want to upgrade only newer components, or reinstall all components. Reinstalling all components takes longer but may be desirable if you are trying to get your installation back to a standard state.

13. The Outlook Active Setup progress bar will now appear. You will see the various components of Outlook 98 installing. After a few minutes, you will see a prompt reminding you to close all applications and save your work before clicking OK.

14. When you click OK, your machine will reboot. When you log in again, you will see a message box announcing "Setting up Outlook 98."

15. You have now installed Outlook 98.

After you have logged on, you can double-click on the Outlook icon and the Outlook Setup Wizard will appear. See Day 7 to learn how to configure a messaging profile.

If you selected the option for Internet Email, on starting Outlook 98, you will see the Mail Account creation Wizard. This is identical to that in Outlook Express. For more information on configuring mail and LDAP accounts, see Day 14, "Reading Exchange Mail with Internet Clients."

From the Internet

Installing Outlook from the Internet has sections that are very similar to installing from the CD. However, to start with, you need to have a connection to the Internet.

When you have a connection to the Internet (the faster the better), go to the following URL:

`http://officeupdate.microsoft.com/downloadDetails/outlook98detail.htm`

After you have connected to this URL, you now need to carry out the following task:

1. Click on the link for Download Now, and you will see a list of download sites. Select the site that is nearest to you from which to run the initial Setup program.

2. After you click on the suitable site, a prompt will ask you whether you want to download the file or run it from its current location. Select the option to run from its current location.

3. You will see the license screen as in the CD version. Accept the terms and continue.

4. The next screen is the Registration screen. However, you should not see a field for the Registration Number at this point.

5. You have the same choice of installation options as with the CD version and you can specify the destination folder as before.

6. The Download Location screen is different from the CD. This lets you select a location from where you want to download the Outlook source files.

Note

This can be a different location to the one from which you ran the setup program.

10

7. Figure 10.6 shows this configured for the European download sites:

FIGURE 10.6

Here I am selecting Demon Internet as my download location. However, I ran the setup routine from a server in California because it was cooler.

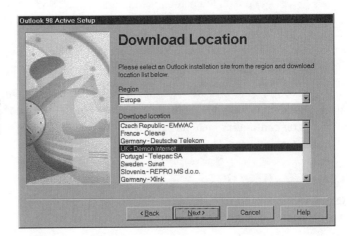

8. Select Next to continue, and the installation routine will then ask whether you want to upgrade just newer components or reinstall all components, as before.

9. The installation routine will then proceed, again forcing a shutdown on your system when Outlook installs successfully.

10. On rebooting, the final configuration will take place, just as with the CD version. You can now start Outlook 98 and create a messaging profile.

The Outlook Deployment Kit

But what do you do if you have a thousand copies of Outlook to deploy? Even if you place the source files on a network share, it is still going to take a long time to go round each machine and install the software. Even if you do each machine in less than ten minutes, your rollout could take up to 20 days.

The Outlook Deployment Kit is a development of the Internet Explorer Administration Kit. It uses a wizard-based interface to collect all the necessary files into compressed .CAB files. You can then deploy Outlook 98 by copying the files to your intranet and connecting to the relevant URL.

Using the Outlook Deployment Kit is covered in Day 9. For more information, see TechNet or Microsoft's Outlook Web site on:

```
http://www.microsoft.com /outlook
```

Using Outlook 98

Now you've installed Outlook 98, and created a messaging profile to connect to your Exchange server, you are ready to start using Outlook. In this section, you will cover how to use the program, with a few hints and tips from the Administrator's point of view.

Starting Outlook 98

After installation, an Outlook icon appears on your desktop. Double-clicking on this icon will start Outlook, and the splash screen will appear.

> **Tip**
>
> If starting Outlook is taking a long time—more than 30 seconds—you could have a problem with your RPC binding orders. See the Section on RPC Binding Orders in Day 8, "Troubleshooting Exchange," for more information.

If you have only one messaging profile configured, Outlook will start using that messaging profile. If you have configured multiple profiles, and have selected the option to choose the profile at startup, you will be able to choose the profile to use. You can also create a new profile from this screen, as shown in Figure 10.7. I will be covering these options later in this lesson.

FIGURE 10.7

This screen lets you choose a profile to use when starting Outlook.

> **Tip**
>
> You can add new profiles via the Outlook icon on your desktop. Either right-click the icon and select Properties or Alt+double-click on the icon. This shows you the properties of the default messaging profile. Clicking on the Show Profiles button takes you to a screen displaying all the currently configured profiles. See Day 7 for more information on creating and configuring profiles.

10

If you have configured the option to choose your connection type on startup, you will see a screen offering you the choice of connecting to the server or working offline. Select Connect to connect to the Exchange server. You would use the Work Offline option if you are not connected to the network and are using offline stores.

Outlook will appear and you should now see the screen that you specified in the User Settings in the Outlook Deployment Kit. Normally, this will be either the Outlook Today screen or the Inbox. If you are not looking at the Outlook Today screen, click on the relevant icon in the Shortcut bar on the left-hand side.

Note

Before I proceed to describe the parts of the interface, I would like you to select the View menu, and check the option for Folder List, or click the Folder List button on the toolbar.

After you have selected the option to view the folder list, your screen should look something like that in Figure 10.8.

FIGURE 10.8

The Outlook Today screen is designed to be your first port of call when you open Outlook.

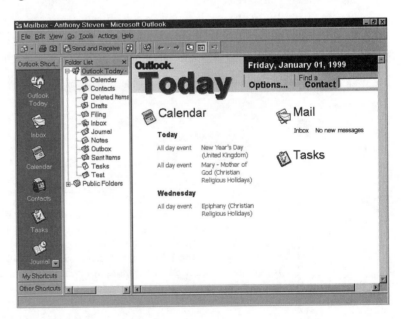

The Outlook Interface

I will now run through the names of the different parts of the Outlook interface. My apologies if this is old hat—in that case, skip to the next section.

The title bar at the top of the screen shows the Application Name and the currently selected folder.

The Outlook bar is the gray area with the icons along the left-hand side headed Outlook Shortcuts. There are two other shortcut bars by default—My Shortcuts and Other Shortcuts at the bottom of the screen. Click on these boxes, and the shortcut bars will appear. Other Shortcuts shows your computer's filing system.

Caution

Note that this lets users run applications direct from local or remote drives.

You can customize these shortcut bars and add extra bars by right-clicking on the shortcut bar areas. This displays the shortcut bar menu. You can also drag-and-drop folders from the Folder List view onto the shortcut bars.

The menu bar is just below the title bar, and changes according to the currently selected folder. If you have any folder from your mailbox or public folders selected, you will see options for File, Edit, View, Go, Tools, Actions, and Help. If you select the Other Shortcuts bar from the bottom left of the screen, and then choose My Computer from the Outlook bar on the left, the Actions menu disappears, and the Tools menu changes significantly.

Note

The contents of the menus and toolbars are context-sensitive, and changes according to which folder you select.

The toolbars are immediately below the menu bar. There are two built-in toolbars—Standard and Advanced. To switch both these toolbars on, select the View menu, choose Toolbars, and ensure that both the Standard and Advanced toolbars are checked.

Tip

You can drag the toolbars and the menu bar about and have them free-floating or dock them at the sides or bottom of the screen. To do this, click and drag on the two raised bars at the left-hand edge of each toolbar. If your users say that they can't read their menus, they've probably dragged them to the side of the screen.

Assuming you switched on the Folders view above, the section to the right of the Outlook bar will be the Folders view. Here you can see all the folders in your mailbox and in the Public Folders. If you have the correct permissions, you can create and administer Public Folders through the Outlook client.

 Caution   Be careful here. Do you really want all your users able to create public folders? I thought not. See Day 19 for more information on securing public folders.

To the right of the Folders view is the folder contents area. This is where the contents of the selected folder appears, as modified by the folder view currently in force. You will see a number of columns (From, Subject, Received, and so on) at the top of this list. I will cover changing the columns in the next section.

 Tip   Click on a column heading to sort by that column. Click again on the same column again to reverse the sort order.

At the bottom of the screen is the status bar. You can switch this on and off from the View menu.

 Tip   You can administer the currently displayed folder by right-clicking on the icon situated at the far right hand side of the screen, just below the toolbars.

Using Folders

Let's now go through some of the standard folders in Outlook, and cover some of the basic operations.

Outlook Today

Outlook Today (refer to Figure 10.8) is the new view of your top-level mailbox folder. It is not really a folder, but a specialized view that lets you see your appointments, unanswered mail messages, and tasks at a glance. In addition, you can search for a contact in your Contacts folder, or any folders that you have designated as Outlook Address Books.

Showing Outlook Today   To go to Outlook Today, either

- Click on the root mailbox folder in the Folder List.
- Click on the Outlook Today button in the Advanced toolbar.
- Select Outlook Today from the Go menu.

You will now see the Outlook Today screen, with your week's appointments, any to-do items, and any unopened email listed on the screen. Clicking on any of the three icons (Calendar, Inbox, or Tasks) will take you to that folder.

Making Outlook Today the Default Startup Folder   To make Outlook Today the folder that Outlook displays on startup, select the Tools menu and choose Options. Click on the Other tab and choose the Advanced Options button. Under General settings, you can now select Outlook Today as the folder to view when Outlook starts, as in Figure 10.9.

10

FIGURE 10.9

This dialog lets you choose Outlook Today as the default startup folder.

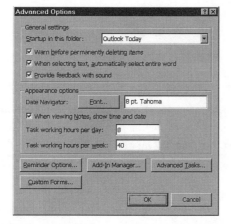

You can also configure this through Outlook Today options.

Changing Outlook Today Options   To change the way that Outlook Today looks, click on Options. You will now see the screen in Figure 10.10.

You can choose how many days' appointments and events to show in the Outlook Today view, as well as make this the default view when you start Outlook. You can make the tasks displayed either today's tasks (depressing) or all outstanding tasks (even more depressing).

FIGURE **10.10**

FIGURE **10.10**

You can customize the
Outlook Today view
in a basic fashion.

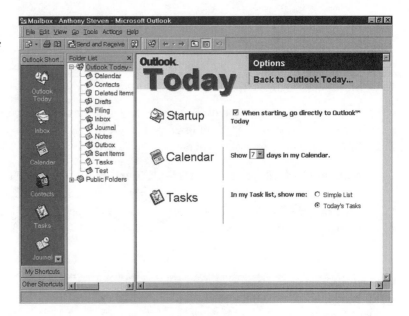

The Mail section only tells you how many drafts and unopened items of mail you have.
It doesn't tell you who sent them.

To search for a contact, type the contact's name into the Find box and click Go or press
Enter. If more than one contact with that name appears, you will be able to select the
entry that you want. Selecting an entry takes you to that person's details in your Outlook
Address Book.

Inbox

The Inbox is likely to be the folder in which your users spend the most time. The Inbox
is the destination for all your incoming messages, and unless you have rules configured
or you move items out of the Inbox manually, this is where those messages will remain.

The first problem that this causes is that the Inbox tends to fill up, and users
don't know what to do with all the messages. You need to teach them how
to use the Rules Wizard (more about this later) or to drag-and-drop messages into folders.

To go to the Inbox, either click on the Inbox icon in Outlook Today, select Inbox from
the folder list, choose Inbox from the Go menu, or press Ctrl+Shift+I together. You will
now see the screen in Figure 10.11.

FIGURE 10.11

The Inbox is where all your messages arrive, regardless of their source.

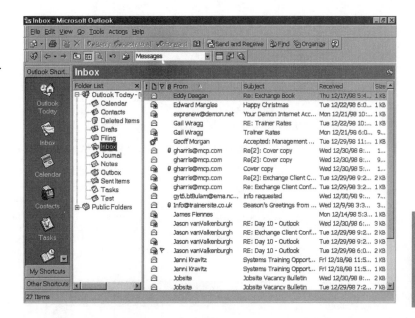

> **Note**
>
> If you have a personal folder as part of your profile, you can configure Outlook to deliver to the Inbox in this personal store instead of the Inbox in the Exchange mailbox. To do this, choose the Tools menu, select Services, and click on the Delivery tab. Change the Delivery location to the personal folder or the Exchange Mailbox as appropriate.

Using the Inbox   The following actions are available when you are in the Inbox and all mail folders:

- Send a new mail message
- Send a new message with a flowery background
- Reply to sender
- Reply to all addressees
- Forward a message
- Flag messages for follow-up
- Add mail to your junk mail lists
- Find related messages

Send a New Mail Message To send a new mail message, either:

- Select New Mail Message from the Actions menu.
- Press Ctrl+N.
- Click on the New Mail Message button on the left-hand side of the Standard toolbar.
- Select the File menu, choose New, and select Mail Message.
- Double-click anywhere on the whitespace on the right-hand side of the Inbox.

You can now add your addressees and carbon copy addressees, enter the message subject and text, and click the send button.

Sending a Message Using Stationery Rather than just sending a boring old plain message, you can liven things up by using stationery. To do this, select the Actions menu, and choose the option for More Stationery. You will now see the screen in Figure 10.12.

FIGURE 10.12

You can choose a flowery background for your messages.

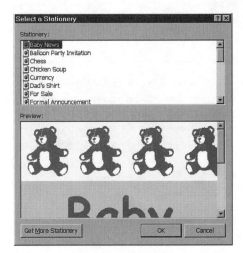

Clicking on the Get More Stationery button will take you to Microsoft's Outlook Update Web page.

Replying to the Sender When you receive a message into the Inbox, you can reply to the sender in a number of different ways:

- Click on the Reply button
- Right-click on the message and select Reply

- Select Reply from the Actions menu
- Double-click on the message to read it, and then click the Reply button, or select Reply from the Actions menu.

After you have composed your reply, click on the send button.

Reply to All   The Reply to All button replies not only to the sender, but to all recipients, including the carbon copy addressees. I would not recommend using this option if you have just received an "all staff" message complaining about over-use of the "all staff" distribution list!

Forward   This lets you send a message on to a recipient or distribution list. *Very* useful for passing the buck.

Flag Message for Follow Up   If you receive a message, and think "I must ring them about that on Monday," you can use the Flag for Follow Up feature to do just that. Select the message, and either right-click and select Flag for Follow Up or choose Flag for Follow Up from the Actions menu. Alternatively, if you double-click on the message to view it, there is a button with a little flag on it, which does the same thing. Whichever option you choose, you will see the screen in Figure 10.13.

FIGURE 10.13

Flag for Follow Up lets you configure an automatic reminder at a set time.

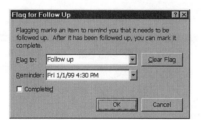

Choose the follow-up action from the list, and if necessary, select a date.

Note   Although you cannot immediately configure the time, you can set a reminder for the relevant day. This will automatically set a time of 5:00 p.m. Now you can change the reminder time to a more suitable figure, if necessary.

Add Senders to Your Junk Mail Lists   To do this, right-click on a message, and from the menu, select Junk Email. You can now add the message to the Junk Senders list or to the Adult Content list.

> **Note**   For the Junk Email settings to work, you must turn on the facility through Organizer. I'll cover this later in this lesson.

Find Related Messages   This is a way of automatically invoking the Find function. Right-click on a message and select Find All. Then choose either Related Messages or Messages from Sender. Whichever option you choose will then fire up the Find dialog box, with Advanced Criteria to match exactly the sender's name or the conversation topic. This function is also available from the Action menu.

> **Tip**   If you have replied to a message, and you want to track any replies, this is very easy to do. Open the message, and at the top it will say `You replied on date/time`. Click on this sentence, and the Find all Related Messages routine will run, thus tracking down all items related to the one that you are looking at.

Calendar

The Calendar is likely to be a popular folder as well. Here you can start organizing your life, or better still, delegate the organizing to someone else. You can use Calendar as a personal diary, but you can also create Calendar-based public folders, and thus create departmental diaries.

One specific use of the Calendar is to keep a diary for a resource, such as a meeting room, or for items of equipment, like projectors. I will cover this at the end of this section.

At a basic level, you can use the Calendar to keep a record of your own appointments and daily events. However, you can also use Calendar to schedule meetings with people, book rooms, and reserve equipment.

Calendar has four basic views—Daily, Weekly, Monthly, and new for Outlook 98, a working week view showing five days. In addition, there are a number of other views, including Active Appointments, Events, Recurring Events, and so on.

Adding an Appointment   The easiest way to add a new appointment is to double-click on the appointment time. This will create a new appointment, with the start time set to the time that you selected.

You can now enter a subject of the appointment, select or enter a location (all locations are saved), and further configure the start or end time. You can even make it an all-day event, if required.

> **Tip**
>
> I would recommend that you set yourself a reminder that gives yourself enough time to prepare for the appointment or to get there. As far as I'm concerned, five-minutes notice of a meeting is as much use as a chocolate fireguard.

You have four options as to how you classify the time spend spent on the appointment. Options are Free, Tentative, Busy, or Out of Office.

If your appointment is recurring, then click the Recurrence button. You will now see the screen in Figure 10.14.

FIGURE 10.14

You can configure recurring appoint-ments for every day, week, month, or year.

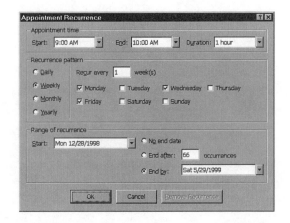

> **Tip**
>
> Married Men: Enter your wife's birthday and your wedding anniversary into your Calendar folder. Make the event recur every year and give yourself at least two day's notice to get a present. You'll never find yourself locked out of the house again!

Click OK to add the recurrence details.

After you have finished editing your appointment details, click Save and Close to enter the appointment in your diary.

Arranging a Meeting   If your appointment is with people in your company, or even with people from outside the organization, you can schedule meetings using Outlook.

10

The big IF here is "if other people keep their diaries up to date."

To do this, click on the Actions menu and then select New Meeting Request. Enter a start time and a finish time, a subject and a location. Select the time as busy and configure a reminder. Leave the To: field empty. Now click on the Attendee Availability tab.

This tab shows the Free/Busy information for your delegates. Click on the Invite Others button and select the names of those you would like to attend. You will see their Free/Busy times appear on the chart. You can now use the AutoPick function to find the next time that all the attendees are free, as shown in Figure 10.15.

FIGURE 10.15

Organizing meetings can be fun—as long as people keep their diaries up to date.

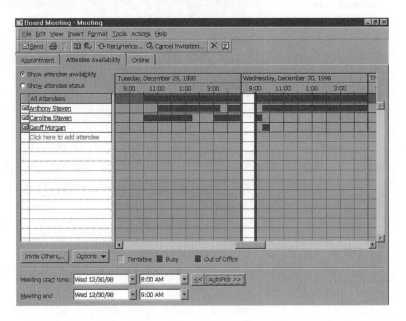

After you have found a suitable time, you can now return to the Appointment tab, where the delegates will be showing on the To: line. Add any details about the meeting and click Send.

Your delegates will receive a message with buttons for Accept, Tentative, or Decline. These responses will appear in your Inbox and will automatically update the meeting item itself.

To view the current delegate status, open the Meeting item and click on the Attendee Availability tab. You will now have a new view, showing delegate status. This will list the delegates with their response to the meeting.

Plan a Meeting   Another way to organize a meeting is to use the Plan a Meeting function from the Actions menu. This works in a similar way as the previous section, except you start by finding out the free times of the other delegates. After you have found a suitable time, just click the Make Meeting button, add the detail on your meeting, and click Send.

Online Meetings   You can arrange and host online meetings in a similar fashion using Microsoft NetMeeting via Outlook 98. To be able to check an Internet user's availability, her mail client must support the vCalendar standard. To configure an online meeting, select New On-line Meeting Request from the Actions menu.

Contacts

You can use the Contacts folder in your own mailbox as a flat-file Address Book. I find this a very useful way of keeping track of my business and personal contact information.

However, one problem with the Contacts folder is that of access. Unless you have configured delegate access, it is difficult to share your personal address information around the organization. One way of overcoming this is to have a public folder containing contact items as your company address book. You can then replicate this information around your organization.

The Contacts folders cannot carry out one important function that the Personal Address Book can. You cannot store personal distribution lists in the Contacts folder.

Adding Contacts   You can add a new entry by double-clicking on the empty space in your Contacts folder, or by selecting Ctrl+N. When adding Contacts, note that you can support multiple addresses, for Work, Home, and Other. You can add up to three email addresses and you can configure up to 19 telephone numbers.

In the Details tab, you can add information like your contact's birthday (which then appears in your diary), manager's name, spouse's name, and even a nickname.

In the All Fields tab, you can add user-defined fields to this item or to the entire folder. These fields can have a range of types, like text, number, logical (Yes/No), Duration, Integer, or Formula. These fields are useful when designing forms or expanding the capabilities of Outlook. For more information on the Forms environment, see Day 18, "Building Exchange Applications."

10

Adding a Contact From Another Company   When you are managing a sales account with a client company, you are constantly meeting other people who work for the same company. Rather than re-type all the company details in again, you can select New Contact from the Same Company, either from the Action menu, or by right-clicking on your current company contact and selecting it from the menu. Now add the name and title of the new contact, and save the record.

Sending a Message to a Contact   If you have an email address or a Fax address (assuming you have support for sending faxes) for a contact, then you can send a message directly to that user. Again, use the Actions menu, or right-click and select, or click on the relevant button in the toolbar. A new message form will appear. Add the subject and the text of your message, and click Send.

AutoDialling a Contact   If you have a modem attached to your workstation, you can AutoDial a contact. Right-click on the contact's name and select AutoDialer. You will now see the screen in Figure 10.16.

FIGURE 10.16

The AutoDial function makes it easy to dial numbers.

Click on Start Call to begin dialing the contact. You will see another dialog box, where you can click Talk as soon as you are connected.

If you checked the box to create a journal item, a new telephone call Journal item will appear, with the time already logging.

New Meeting with Contact/Plan a Meeting   You can create new meetings in the same way that you did with the Calendar module previously. However, most of the time these meetings will not be using Exchange's Free/Busy information, as your contacts will be external to your organization.

New Letter to Contact   You can send a letter to your contact by selecting your contact's name and then choosing Send Letter to Contact from the Actions menu. This takes you to a wizard that starts Microsoft Word, and takes you through a number of steps to generate your letter.

Note You must have Microsoft Word installed to use this option. This is not the same as WordMail.

Forward as vCard   vCard is the emerging Internet standard for electronic business cards. You can send contact information as a vCard to other users on the Internet, and their vCard-aware applications will be able to import this information.

You can import vCard data using the Import/Export function in the File menu.

Task List

The task list can be used as a to-do list for yourself. More importantly, you can use it to delegate tasks to other people. As well as delegating tasks, you can also keep track of the current position on the task.

Creating a New Task   When creating a new task, you enter details of the task, a start and finish date, task status, priority, and the percentage complete. You can make a task recurring by selecting the Recurrence button, as for Calendar items.

On the Details tab you can enter the completion date, the amount of time spent on the task, and any other billing information. Clicking on the Save and Close button will add the task to your list.

After you have added a task to your list, you can mark the task as complete by checking the box next to the task. Alternatively, you can make the task 100% complete.

Assigning a Task   A much better option is to find some other poor soul to lumber with this task. You can do this either by selecting New Task Request from the Action menu, or by clicking on the Assign Task button. Now you can select the unfortunate individual who is going to be lemoned with this little job (unless he can palm it off onto someone else).

Clicking on the Cancel Assignment button will return the task to yourself.

If you have been given a task, you can send a status report by right-clicking on the task and selecting Send Status Report. This status report will detail the amount of time that you have spent on this task, plus any further information about the task's progress. You can also configure your options so that if you complete a delegated task, a status report is sent automatically to the person who gave you the task.

10

Organizing and Displaying Information

In this next section, I will show you some of the methods with which you can organize and display your information. Outlook 98 has some significant improvements over previous versions, and if you are not familiar with this client, this section may save you embarrassment when trying to explain a feature to a user.

Preview Pane

The Preview pane applies to most folders, and lets you preview the contents of the message, contact entry, or calendar item. To switch on the Preview pane, select the View menu and choose Preview Pane. Your folder will now look like that in Figure 10.17.

FIGURE 10.17

The Preview pane lets you see the contents of a selected message.

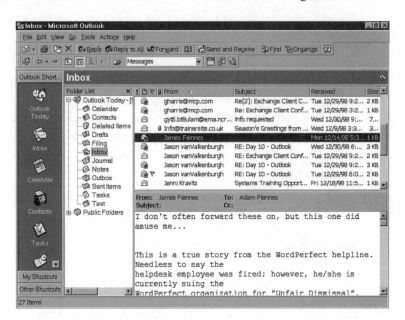

> **Note**
>
> You can configure options that will mark a message as read if you are using the Preview pane. See the section at the end of this lesson on Options for more information.

AutoPreview

The AutoPreview function is not the same as the Preview pane, and applies only to message folders. AutoPreview will display a brief preview of each message in blue just underneath the message header. AutoPreview applies whether a message is read or unread.

> **Note** This is also different from the "Messages with AutoPreview" view, where the AutoPreview applies only to unread messages. I'll cover views in a moment.

You can switch on AutoPreview for each folder by clicking the AutoPreview button on the right side of the Advanced toolbar. Figure 10.18 shows this in action.

FIGURE 10.18

Here I have switched on the AutoPreview function on the Inbox folder.

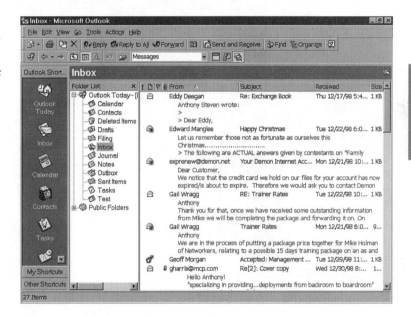

You can also switch on the AutoPreview function from the View menu.

Organize

The Organize function is new to Outlook 98. This feature lets you organize your folders in the following ways:

- Using folders
- Using colors
- Using views
- By junk email

The options available vary, depending on the type of folder.

To use the Organize function, select the folder that you want to organize. Then either click on the Organize button in the toolbar or select Organize from the Tools menu. The options that appear will depend on the folder that you are organizing, but for the Inbox, you should see a screen like that in Figure 10.19.

FIGURE 10.19

The Organize pane applied to the Inbox gives the full range of options.

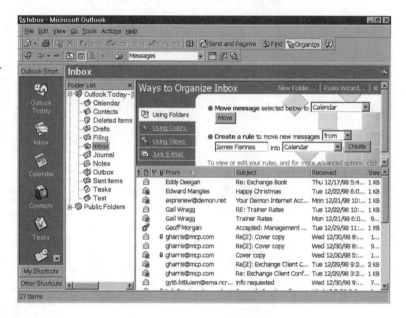

Using Folders When organizing using folders, you can select multiple messages and then use the Move Messages function to move the items to the chosen folder.

> **Tip**
>
> Multi-selecting messages works like other Windows list box. The Shift key lets you select a block of messages; the Control key lets you select individual items that are not in order. Remember that you can sort messages by sender by clicking the From column heading.

You can create a simple rule through this interface by selecting a message from a particular person and then specifying what should happen to this message.

> **Note**
>
> This is only a subset of the full functionality of the Rules Wizard. If you want to start the Rules Wizard, click on the button at the top right of the Organize window.

After you have created a rule, this rule will then fire every time a message from that person arrives in the Inbox.

Using Colors   Organizing using colors simply involves selecting a message from a particular sender, and applying a color to that message. Now all messages from that user will appear in the selected color. In addition, you can apply another color to messages that named you as the sole recipient.

Note   The colors that you select only apply to this view.

Using Views   Using views lets you select a view from the list. The views shown will be all those available for this folder, either preconfigured or user-defined. I'll be discussing views in the next section.

10

Junk Email   The Junk Email setting lets you carry out a specific action on junk or adult content mail. You can either color the junk mail or move it to a specific folder, like the Deleted Items folder.

To do this, select move or color from the actions list, and then select either a folder or a color. Finally click the Turn On button, and mail from get-rich-quick schemes and smutty Web sites will be summarily dispatched into oblivion.

Note   Processing will not happen until you turn on the feature using the button above.

Tip   To add a sender to your junk mail or adult contents sites, right-click on a message from that source and select the Junk Email option at the bottom of the menu. Select the option for junk email or adult content from the smaller menu. Now the Organize feature will process all messages from this source according to the rule that you set up earlier.

Folder Views

Folder views let you configure ways of viewing information according to a number of different criteria. This is particularly useful if you need to categorize your mail quickly.

Predefined Views   Each folder comes with a number of predefined views. These depend on the type of information held in the folder, and automatically appear when you create a new folder. If you are in a calendar folder, you will see views for Day/Week/Month, Active Appointments, Events, and so on. If you are in a message folder, the predefined views will include Messages with AutoPreview, By Sender, By Conversation Topic, and the like.

Applying Views   You can apply views in a number of different ways.

- Select the view from the drop-down list on the Advanced toolbar.
- From the View menu, select Current View, and then choose the view that you want to apply.
- When you are defining a view, you can apply that view to the folder.

Creating Views   You can create your own views from the Views menu. To do this, follow this next task:

1. From the View menu, select Current Views, and then choose Define Views. You will now see the dialog box in Figure 10.20.

FIGURE 10.20

This screen shows a list of the currently defined views.

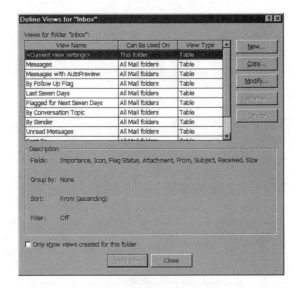

2. This shows a list of all views that you can apply to this folder. This includes views that you created specifically for this folder or the default views that apply to all mail folders.

3. To create a new view, click on the New button to see the screen in Figure 10.21. You should now select the view type from the selection shown. The options are

Table (best with messages), Timeline (for Tasks or opened files), Card (Contacts), Day/Week/Month (Calendar), or Icon view (messages). You can also restrict who can use this view, and if you want this new view to apply to all mail folders, you can set that here.

FIGURE 10.21

Here you can select what type of view you want.

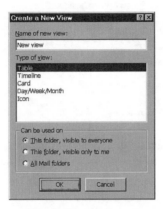

4. The next screen that you see will depend on which option you chose for view type. In this example, I will use the Table view, as this gives you the maximum number of options. In this case, the next screen that you will see looks like Figure 10.22.

FIGURE 10.22

This screen shows the options that you can set in a Table view.

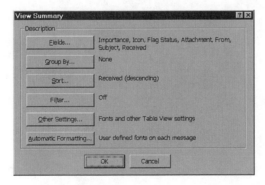

5. Click on the Fields button, and you can now add and remove the fields that will appear in your view. You can select any field using the drop-down list at the bottom left, or you can create a new field using the new field button. When you have chosen the fields that you want to display, your screen will look like that in Figure 10.23. After you have finished adding fields, click OK.

FIGURE 10.23

FIGURE **10.23**

*Here I have added
the required fields to
the view.*

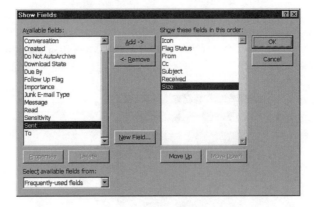

6. The Group By button lets you group your messages according to certain criteria.
   You can select and nest up to four categories of grouping. Hence, you could group
   by sender, then by conversation and then by date. Figure 10.24 shows this set up.
   Again, like with fields, you can select the fields to group by from all available
   Outlook fields.

FIGURE **10.24**

*The Group By screen
lets you create a hier-
archy of groupings.*

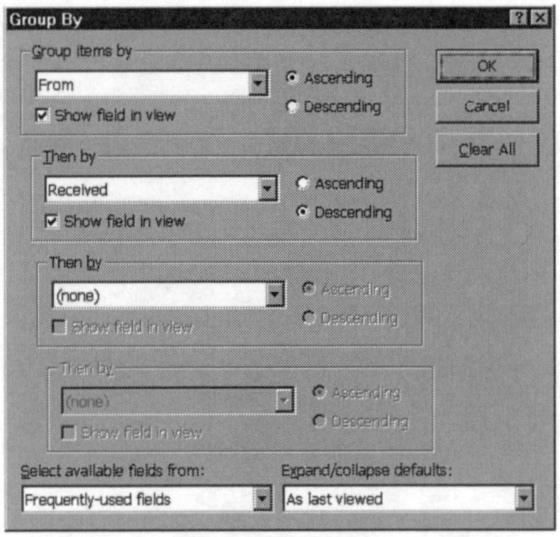

7. You can now sort the items in your view into a specific order. In previous versions of Outlook, you could only sort on fields that appeared in the view. This restriction is no longer in place, and you can sort on any field. If you are sorting on a field that does not appear in the view, a prompt will ask you if you want to add it or not. Again, there are four nested levels that you can sort by, as shown in Figure 10.25.

FIGURE 10.25

You can sort by four levels as well.

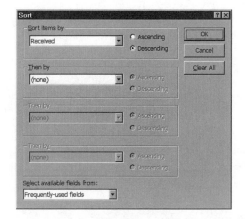

8. Filtering lets you include or exclude messages from your view based on certain criteria. The criteria are quite considerable, but include words in messages, messages from or to someone, and time information, all of which are located on the Messages tab. Figure 10.26 shows an example of this.

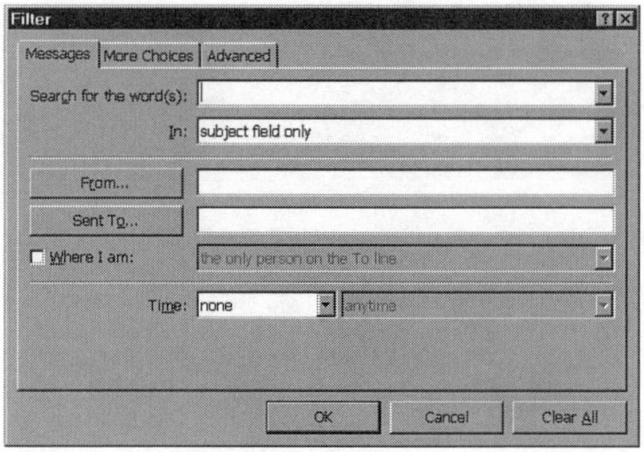

FIGURE 10.26

The number of different criteria on which you can filter messages is quite considerable. This is the same dialog as that which appears with Advanced Find later in the lesson.

9. The More Choices tab lets you filter on Categories, Read or Unread, Attachments, Importance, and Size, as shown in Figure 10.27.

FIGURE 10.27

Filtering on Categories is very useful for contact management.

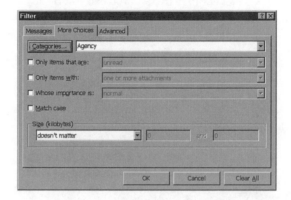

10. The Advanced Tab lets you filter on the contents of any field, and gives the most precise set of criteria. This is particularly useful when filtering with custom fields. Figure 10.28 shows this configured.

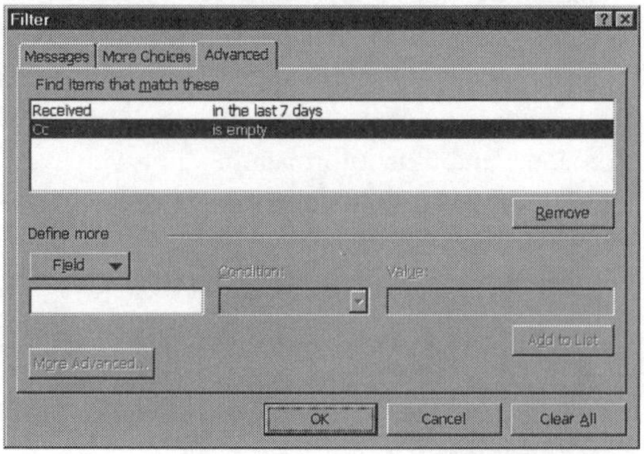

FIGURE 10.28

Here I am filtering for all messages sent in the last seven days that did not have a cc: recipient.

11. Other Settings lets you configure font sizes, column headings, AutoPreview color, grid lines, and Preview pane settings, as shown in Figure 10.29.

FIGURE 10.29

This screen lets you configure the way your information appears.

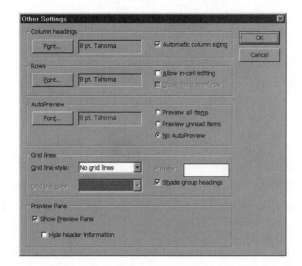

 Tip

The Allow In-Cell Editing setting is very useful when editing contact information. In-Cell Editing means that when your information appears in a table list, you can edit the information just by clicking on a cell. This is not much use for message folders, but if you are updating a database of telephone numbers, it means that you don't have to open each item every time you want to change a number.

12. Automatic Formatting lets you add a further level of formatting to items in the folder, depending on a range of predefined conditions. Click on the Automatic Formatting button, and you will see the screen in Figure 10.30. There are five standard formats already defined, but you can add your own by clicking on the Add button. Give your Automatic Format a name and click on the Format button to define how you want the messages to appear. Then select the Condition button to define the criteria that the messages must fulfill in order to display the chosen formatting. These criteria are identical to the range of settings that you specified using the Filter section.

FIGURE 10.30

Automatic Formatting makes messages that meet certain criteria show up with a specific appearance.

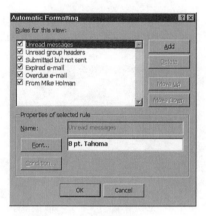

13. After you have finished defining your view, it will now appear in the list of views.

14. Select your view and click the Apply View button. The items in the folder will appear with the new view applied.

Editing Views   After you have defined a view, you can edit that view in three ways.

- Edit the view directly through the Define Views dialog box as in the previous task.

- Apply the view. Then from the View menu, select Current View and choose Customize Current View. You will then see the screen in Figure 10.31.

FIGURE 10.31

You can edit the properties of a specific view directly.

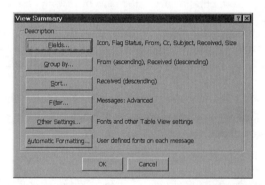

- Apply the view and then change the columns displayed using the Field Chooser or the Group By box in the Advanced toolbar. Any changes that you make remain when you switch to another view.

Field Chooser

The Field Chooser operates in any table view, and lets you select other fields to appear in the view. Click on the Field Chooser button in the Advanced toolbar, and you will see the screen in Figure 10.32.

FIGURE 10.32

The Field Chooser lets you drag-and-drop fields onto your view.

You can drop-down the list to show all fields from all forms in Outlook, or you can create a new field. After you have seen the field that you want to appear in your view, drag it across to the folder and drop into place on the row of headers. A little red arrow will show where the column will appear.

Group By Box

The Group By box gives you the ability to carry out an ad-hoc grouping of your messages. Click on the Group By button in the Advanced toolbar, and you will see an extra gray border appear at the top of your list of messages. You can now drag most of the fields into this border area, and your messages will group by that heading. You can drag subsequent headings onto this area, and create a hierarchy of groupings as with your views.

Note You cannot group by certain columns, such as Categories or Message Size.

Rules Wizard

The Rules Wizard is a very useful feature that gives you the ability to process mail automatically, depending on a number of criteria. The Rules Wizard is more powerful than the Organize feature, and is very useful when you need to be able to forward, copy, or delete mail without any further intervention.

Note The Rules Wizard applies to mail folders only.

10

You can start the Rules Wizard in three ways. Select Rules Wizard from the Tools menu, click on the button in the Advanced toolbar, or select the Rules Wizard option in the Organize window. You will now see the screen in Figure 10.33.

FIGURE 10.33

The Rules Wizard starts with a list of all defined rules.

From here, you can start defining a rule, which involves stepping through the Rules Wizard. There is a vast number of combinations of options here, but for the most part, the process is similar. You select a trigger (a message from a person or contains certain text) and then execute an action (move the message to a folder, forward it, or delete it).

> **Tip**
>
> Wherever you see underlined text in the Rules Wizard, you can click and enter a name, some text, or select a folder. This information will then become part of the Rule.

Rules "fire" in the order that they appear in the Rules Wizard list. To fire, there must have a checkmark next to the rule.

> **Tip**
>
> You can now trigger rules to fire when you send a message. This might include moving the sent message to another folder, thus enabling automatic filing on both incoming and outgoing mail.

If a rule deletes a message, subsequent rules will not apply. In addition, there is a special rule that stops the processing of any subsequent rules.

You can administer rules using the Options button on the Rules Wizard dialog box. Click this button and you will see the screen in Figure 10.34.

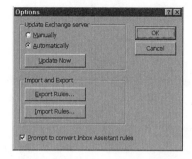

You can import and export rules or update the rules on the Exchange server. Rules are stored on the Exchange server so that if you log on from multiple machines, your rules are preserved. If you create subsequent rules on the client that conflict with rules on the server, there is a mechanism for you to indicate which set of rules you want to override the other.

You can import Inbox Assistant rules from earlier versions of Outlook or from the Exchange client into Outlook 98.

Out of Office Assistant

The Out of Office Assistant is a feature that will automatically reply to messages on your behalf when you are out of the office. The idea of the Out of Office Assistant is that you enter a message and turn the feature on. Thereafter, the first time that someone sends you a message, the sender will receive your message indicating that you are out. In addition, you can then configure rules to forward the incoming message to someone else.

> I find that one of the best uses of this feature is to send mail to my home Internet account when I am out of the office. This means that if I am on site for a few days, I still know what is going on in the office via the Out of Office Assistant.

Let's look at how you would configure the Out of Office Assistant. To start the OOOA, select Out of Office Assistant from the Tools menu. You will now see the screen in Figure 10.35.

FIGURE 10.35

The Out of Office Assistant lets you send a message once and once only to people who email you.

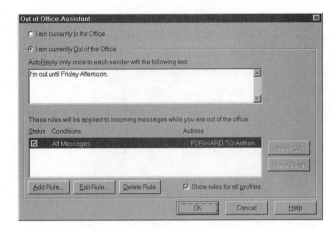

You can specify rules to fire when a message arrives, although configuring Rules in the OOOA is slightly different from the Rules Wizard.

Note

Configuring Rules in the Out of Office Assistant is much like specifying download criteria when using Remote Mail or synchronizing offline folders.

Click on the Add Rule button, and you will now see the screen in Figure 10.36.

FIGURE 10.36

Configuring Rules in the Out of Office Assistant carried out through this dialog box.

The first part of this screen lets you define the criteria that the message must meet in order for the rule to fire. Hence, you can include sender, recipient, subject, items in the message body, or you can use the Advanced tab.

If you click on the Advanced tab, you will see the extra criteria shown in Figure 10.37.

FIGURE 10.37

The Advanced tab lets you specify file sizes, times, and attachments, as well as invert your selection.

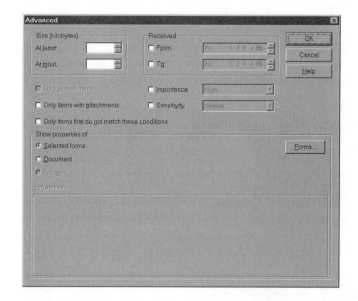

10

> **Note**
>
> The Only Items That Do Not Match These Conditions check box inverts all your search criteria, producing the opposite result to what you have specified.

The second part of the screen lets you specify what will happen to a message that fulfills the criteria. You can send an alert, delete the message, move or copy the message to a folder, forward it to someone else, or reply with a template message.

> **Tip**
>
> To configure a template message, check the Template box and then click the Template button. You will now see a blank message. Type the text of your message into the message body, but do not enter anyone in the To: field. After you have finished your message, select Save and Close from the File menu. Now when the rule fires, the sender of the message will receive the template message.

Add the criteria, select the relevant actions, and then click OK to add your rule to the list. You can now select or deselect rules as required.

 Note | If you configure a rule with no selection criteria, that rule will fire for all messages.

All you need to do now is to remember to switch on your Out of Office Assistant whenever you leave the office. Sadly, there isn't a little reminder that asks you if you want to do this every time you log off Outlook.

Finding Information

After you have put all this information into Outlook, you need to be able to get it out again. There are two main ways of doing this—Find and Advanced Find.

Find

Find provides an easy way to locate information in certain specific fields. For example, if you select the Contacts field, and select Find, you will be searching the Name, Company, and Address fields. With the Message folders, you will be searching the From and Subject fields.

To use the Find window, click on the Find button in the Standard toolbar, or select Find from the Tools menu. Figure 10.38 shows the Find Window.

FIGURE 10.38

Use Find to carry out a quick search on certain preselected fields.

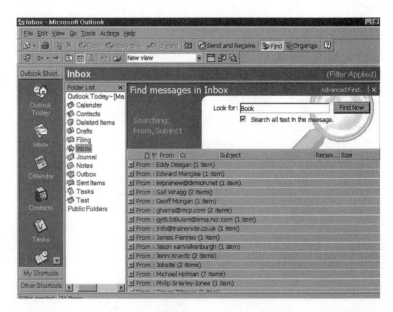

Enter the text or name that you are looking for, check the box if you want to search all the text in the messages, and then click the Find button. Your search results will appear in the normal folder view.

If you have not found what you were looking for, you can go to Advanced Find.

Advanced Find

Advanced Find is more like a mini-application in itself, with its own set of menus and the ability to save and open searches. You can even locate files using Find. However, most of the menu options in Find are the same as those in Outlook.

Advanced Find enables you to be very specific with your search criteria. You can even find normal files throughout your local and network partitions with this utility.

To use the Advanced Find facility, select Advanced Find from the Tools menu. Alternatively, click on the Advanced Find button in the Find window. You will now see the screen in Figure 10.39.

10

FIGURE 10.39

The Find dialog is more like a mini-application.

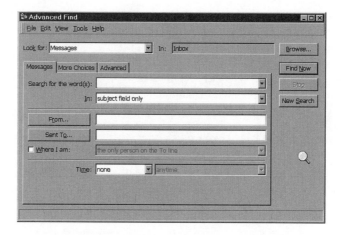

On all tabs, you can select which sort of files you are looking for as well as where you want to look. For example, if you select Look For: Files and then click the Browse button, you will see the screen in Figure 10.40.

You can also look for any type of Outlook item anywhere in a user's mailbox or in the Public folders.

Note Some of the fields displayed in Find change according to your search target.

FIGURE 10.40

Here you can use the Advanced Find utility to find files like Explorer.

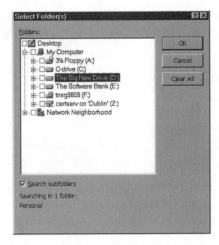

There are three tabs on Advanced Find:

- Messages
- More Choices
- Advanced

On the Messages tab, you can search for a word in specified fields. You can also select a sender or a recipient, and a period in which the message was sent or received. For example, you can look for messages from a particular user received this week.

The More Choices tab lets you select categories to search, read or unread items, items with or without attachments, and items at specified importance level. You can also make the search routine match the letter case exactly, and if you are concerned about size, you can specify lower and upper size ranges. For most searches though, size doesn't matter, which is what they all say.

On the Advanced tab, you can add fields from any of those available to Exchange. For example, if you are trying to find messages changed by a specific person, you would select the Field button, and from All Mail Fields, choose Changed By. Choose the condition Is and then enter the name of the person. Figure 10.41 shows this in action.

After you have finished configuring your search criteria, click Find Now and a list of all items meeting your conditions will appear. You can now double-click on any item to see it in detail.

Categories

Categories are a way of placing your information into user-defined groups. This makes it easy for you to find all your clients, or your prospects, or your suppliers. You can apply categories to most types of Outlook form.

FIGURE 10.41

Here is an example of using the Advanced Find criteria to locate messages changed by a specific person.

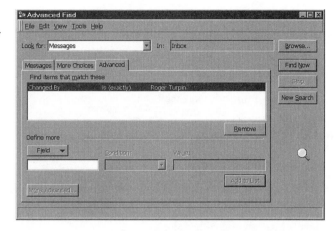

You manage categories through a master category list. However, this Master Category list is not such a master list after all because it is stored on the client and not on the Exchange server. Let's say that you have a public folder, and you add some contacts to this folder. You configure some Categories, and add these contacts to those categories. If you were to go to another client, although the categories would appear, they would not appear as part of the master category list.

To use categories, edit an item such as a contact item. In the bottom-left corner is a Category button. Click on that button to see a list of the categories, and you will now see a screen like that in Figure 10.42.

FIGURE 10.42

The Categories dialog is where you can classify Outlook items according to your own categories.

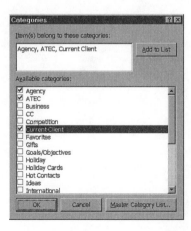

You can add categories to the Master Categories List by selecting the Master Category List button. Adding items to the Master Category List means that this category will be available to all items.

Import and Export

The Import and Export feature gives you the ability to add or extract data to or from your mailbox, public folders, or personal stores. Personally, I think that a good import and export routine is invaluable, and the system on Outlook is good.

You would use the Import/Export facility if you want to:

- Convert from a third-party email or contact management system to Outlook.

- Move data around on floppy disks.

- Take an archive copy of a folder.

- Recover a mailbox as part of your disaster recovery strategy. See Day 16, "Backing Up, Restoring, and Repairing Data," for more information.

- Move a mailbox to another site.

Whatever operations you are carrying out, select the File menu, and then click Import/Export. You will now see the Export and Import Wizard, as in Figure 10.43.

FIGURE 10.43

The first screen on the Export and Import Wizard lets you choose the operation that you want to carry out.

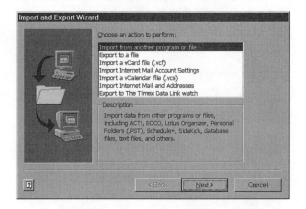

Tip

To get the full benefit of the import and export tool in Outlook, you may need to download an extra component called FIELD98.EXE from the Microsoft Web page. This is the Import/Export Field Mapping add-on for Outlook 98. However, I understand that this component is now included in Office 97 SR-2.

In addition, if you are importing from third-party applications such as ECCO Pro, ACT!, or Sidekick, you should check Microsoft's Web site for any additional converters for these applications.

Additional converters are available from:

`http://officeupdate.microsoft.com/downloadCatalog/dldOutlook.htm`

Exporting   Exporting is far easier than importing as you don't need to carry out any field mapping. There are two main export options—Export to a File or Export to a Timex Data Link Watch. No, I haven't got a Timex Data Link Watch either.

Select the option for Export to a File, and you will see a list of possible file types, including .CSV, .TSV, dBase, Access, Excel, FoxPro, and personal folders. The last option is probably the most useful, for the following reasons:

- Personal folders preserve the structure of the mailbox and support the different form types in Outlook.
- Exporting to .PST files lets you filter the items exported.
- Only .PST files can export an entire mailbox.
- Only .PST files can export from subfolders.
- Only .PST files can export from public folders.
- Personal folder files easily import into another mailbox.

Tip

> If you need to export from a public folder to a .CSV file, export the public folder to a .PST. You can open the .PST file in Outlook and export from there to a .CSV file.

Select your export file type, and click Next. You should now select the export folder, mailbox, or public folder and click Next. Note that there are options to include subfolders, and a Filter button. If you click on the Filter button, you will see a Filter dialog box very similar to that in Advanced Find, with three tabs. This includes More Choices and Advanced, where you can specify fields to match.

Your next choice is where to place the exported file, and what to do with duplicates. Duplicates can occur if the export destination file containing data already exists, or if duplicate records exist in the data that you are exporting.

Click Finish and the export process will run. You can now add the exported .PST to a profile, or import it into a new mailbox.

Import   Importing is more complex because there are a couple of procedures that you must carry out before you start the import process. Firstly, you must clean up the data as much as possible. Remove unnecessary fields and redundant information. Secondly, you need to be able to map your import fields to the fields available in Outlook 98. I find the best tool to use for both of these processes is Excel.

After you have exported from the original database (probably as a .CSV file), you can import this into Excel. Strip out any redundant columns and remove any duplicated data, if possible. Next, you should add a blank row to the top of your data, and in this header row, add the matching field names from Outlook above the relevant columns. For example, if you have a Company name field in your import data, add the word "Company" as a header row to this column. Outlook will then recognize this and map this to the Company field in the Contacts folder. Carry out this field mapping for all the fields in your source data, and then save your file in .CSV format.

 Tip

You can find out the field names in Outlook using the Show Fields tool. Select the form type into which you are importing, and you will now see a list of all the field names in that form. Add the relevant field name to the correct column header on your Excel spreadsheet.

You are now ready to run the Import Wizard. Choose Import from a file, select the file type, choose your import source file, and select what to do with duplicates. You will need to select a folder as the import target.

 Tip

If you are importing from a .CSV, don't import directly into your target folder. This will mean that if you mess up the import, you won't have contaminated your current data with the new (and incorrectly imported) records. Import into a test folder first, and then copy across the records when they import correctly.

When you get to the screen that says, The Following Actions Will Be Performed, click on the button marked Map Custom Fields. You can now see a list of Outlook's fields on the right side of the screen. The fields in your data are on the left side. If Outlook makes a match, there will be an entry on the right-hand list under the Mapped From column.

 Note

If you have carried out the field mapping process in Excel that I outlined earlier, your fields should map immediately.

If Outlook can't match the fields, you can drag-and-drop the fields from the left side (your data) to the right side (the Outlook fields). Figure 10.44 shows what this looks like.

After you have finished mapping the custom fields, select Finish to complete the import. You should now have a new set of records in your Contacts folder.

FIGURE 10.44

Here I am mapping fields from my import data to the relevant fields in my Contacts folder. This example is an easy one because my import data originally came from a contacts folder, hence the field names are the same.

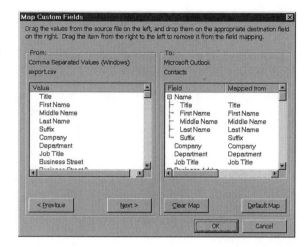

Address Book

The Address Book is something of a relic from the days of the Exchange client. Sadly, it does not reflect the changes in Outlook 98, and now is largely redundant.

The only use that I can find for the Address Book is for storing Personal Distribution lists. To use this feature, you must have added a Personal Address book (.PAB file) to your messaging profile. You can then create a new entry in your Personal Address Book, and add other email addressees from your Exchange directory or your Outlook Address books (Contacts folders).

Make sure that you amend the Addressing tab on your messaging profile to include the new Personal Address Book as a location for checking recipients. When you send a message, you can now add your personal distribution list as an addressee, and Outlook will check your Personal Address Book for a matching address. If your addressee matches your personal distribution list, the message goes to all those in the distribution list.

Configuring Options

Configuring options is what being an Administrator is all about. Whenever I install a new application, the first thing I look for is whether there are any options with which to meddle. Outlook 98 is a gem of an application from that point of view because there are hordes of configuration settings that you can change. The downside is that your users can change them too.

Although this area has changed from previous versions of Outlook, the changes are more in design rather than functionality. The exception to this is Advanced Security, where Outlook 98 can now make use of S/MIME certificates from external Certification Authorities. For more information, see Day 19.

Rather than describe every little option, I will tell you what you can do with the different configurations. I also will not expand on the self-explanatory settings. So now let's get stuck in to some advanced fiddling.

Note

You can set most of these options using Step Five in the Outlook Deployment Kit. This lets you configure User Options. This is the recommended solution for large deployments. You will be able to set Outlook options using the policy configuration tool that will be an integral part of Windows 2000.

Preferences Tab

The Options dialog box is located at the bottom of the Tools menu. The first screen that you will see is the Preferences tab shown in Figure 10.45.

FIGURE 10.45

The Preferences tab lets you configure your folder options.

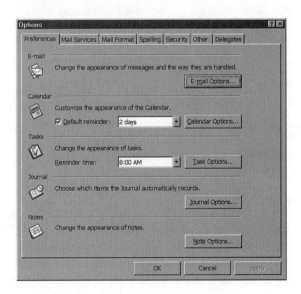

Email Options

This is the most complex of the five buttons. Click here and you will see the screen at Figure 10.46.

FIGURE 10.46

These are only some of the email options.

After I move or delete an email (usually because I've read it), I like to return to my Inbox. I certainly don't want to open the previous item as I've already read that.

Close Original Message on Reply or Forward is useful; otherwise you end up having to close original messages manually after you've sent your reply.

Save Copies of Sent Messages is very useful if you are naturally forgetful or need to cover your back.

> **Tip**
>
> If you are using this option, make sure you AutoArchive your Sent Items folder.

Display a Notification Message When New Mail Arrives is intensely irritating, especially if you're popular.

Automatically Saving Unsent Messages is a good idea.

Replies and Forwards is really a matter of personal taste. The Internet standard is to indent the original text and put a > symbol in front. However, if you do this, the spell checker cannot ignore the original message, and you can't preface your comments with your name.

Advanced Email Options   What, there's more? Yes, as shown in Figure 10.47.

FIGURE 10.47

Advanced email options help with the usability.

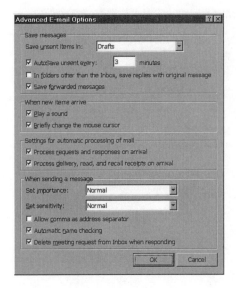

The Save Messages options are a good idea, and can usually be left on the default settings.

When new items arrive, a jolly tune and a flashing cursor always makes my day. As an added bonus, the sounds irritate the heck out of everybody else.

Settings for Automatic Processing of Mail are on by default. You may want to consider turning the top setting off; you may find yourself accepting tasks and meeting requests automatically. Leaving the bottom setting for processing delivery, read, and recall receipts automatically is a good idea.

The When Sending a Message options let you set the importance and sensitivity of *all* your messages. Therefore, if you have an ego the size of a planet, you can set importance to High. Alternatively, if your self-esteem is the size of a raisin that died of thirst in the middle of the Mojave Desert, you could set the importance to Low.

You can set the importance and sensitivity on an individual message through the Message Options button or from Properties in the File menu.

Automatic Name Checking is a good thing, and happens in the background when you are typing in your message.

Deleting meeting requests is fine as long as you check your diary on a regular basis.

Tracking Options   Tracking options apply to all messages. Again, you can set these on a message-by-message basis as with the previous tip. If you want to use either of the first two options, I recommend you switch on the third option as well; otherwise your Inbox will fill up with message receipts.

Calendar Options

Use the Calendar Options dialog box to configure your working week, as shown in Figure 10.48.

FIGURE 10.48

Calendar options include defining a working week, configuring time zones and holidays, and setting up a diary for a resource.

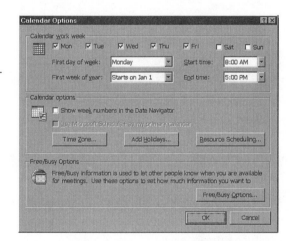

Time Zone   In the Time Zone button, you can configure an additional time zone to show in your Calendar alongside your main time zone. This is very useful if you regularly conduct business with clients from another country, and want to avoid calling them at 3:00 a.m. Figure 10.49 shows this setting configured.

You will now see the additional time zone in your Calendar.

Add Holidays   The Add Holidays dialog box lets you specify which national or religious holidays you would like added to your diary. Check the boxes as appropriate.

Note

Some of these holidays are the same. For example, Christmas is a United States holiday, and it is still a Christian Religious Holiday. Therefore, if you select to add both United States Holidays and Christian Religious Holidays to your diary, you will end up with Christmas as a duplicated entry.

FIGURE 10.49

My editor works in Indiana, but is on Eastern Time without daylight saving.

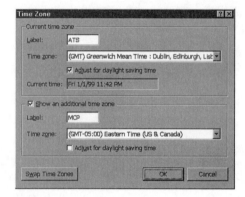

Resource Scheduling

This is a very useful group of settings, which lets you set up a diary for a resource, such as a meeting room. This resource can then be booked, with any conflicts handled automatically. To do this, carry out the following task:

1. Create a mailbox for the resource and give it a descriptive name such as Boardroom.

2. Make yourself the primary owner of that account.

3. Log on to that account, and go to the Advanced EMail options. Check both boxes under Settings for automatic processing of mail.

4. Go to the Calendar options, and click the Resource Scheduling button. Check the three options shown, unless you want to allow people to book recurring meetings. Accept all the Resource Scheduling options and then log out of the resource account.

5. Make the person who is in charge of that room the Primary Windows NT Account owner.

6. The resource will now automatically accept all booking requests (made via the meeting organizer) unless the request conflicts with another booking. The user in charge of that resource handles all conflicts.

Free/Busy Options This governs how much Free/Busy information is available on the Exchange server, and how often this updates. The default settings are usually adequate, unless you need to book meetings more than two months ahead.

Task Options

All that you can change with tasks are the colors for overdue and completed tasks.

Journal Options

Here you can specify which events for which contacts should appear in your Journal, as well as which Office documents. In addition, you can choose what happens when you double-click on an entry in the Journal timeline. Personally, I prefer to open the file that I was working on, but chaqun à son gôut, as they say (unencrypted) in France.

 Caution | You can only create Journal items for your own Contacts folder.
You can only record files for the Office 97 applications installed on your workstation.

10

Note Options

Er, this one you can probably work out for yourself.

Mail Services Tab

On this tab, you can change three main settings.

Profile

This is where you select which messaging profile to use on startup. Alternatively, you can always use the selected profile. You would usually only want advanced or mobile users to be able to choose profiles on startup.

Checking for New Mail

Here you can elect to use specific mail accounts for checking mail. The options that you see here will depend on what mail services you have set up in your profile. Select or deselect mail accounts as appropriate.

Enable Offline Access

This is a new development that enhances the options provided on your messaging profile. You must have configured an offline store (.OST) file for this option to work. If you have not, a prompt will ask you to create an offline store. For more information on offline stores, see Day 7.

Mail Format Tab

The Mail Format tab lets you change interoperability settings, defining how you want to send mail. This is also where the WordMail options and Signatures have ended up. Figure 10.50 shows this screen.

FIGURE 10.50

Configure WordMail and Signature options through the Mail Format tab.

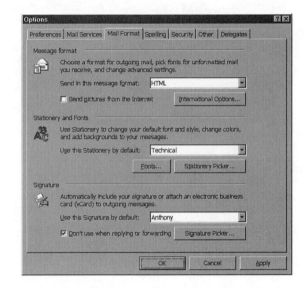

Message Format

There are now four ways in which you can send messages: Plain Text, Outlook Rich Text Format, HTML, or Microsoft Word. If you select Microsoft Word, Word becomes your email editor. If compatibility is an issue, use the plain text option.

WordMail Templates/Stationery Picker

This part of the dialog box will change, depending on which message format you choose. If you select Word, you can then select a template from the installed range of templates. If you select HTML, you can choose a message background from the list of stationery.

Signature

The Signature option does not apply if you use WordMail, as Word supplies its own signature block. However, with the other mail options, you can configure multiple signature blocks. Click on Signature Picker and then click the New button to start the Signature Wizard. You can now step through the process of creating a signature.

> **Tip**
>
> You can create a vCard from your own contact details and send it as part of your signature block. The message recipient can then add the vCard to his Contacts folder.
>
> Also, watch out for word wrapping on your signature block—many email clients wrap text at the 79th character, which can spoil you ASCII artwork!

After you have configured a signature, you can select this as your default signature. When you create a message, the selected signature block will appear at the bottom of your message.

Spelling Tab

I recommend checking all the options on this tab as shown in Figure 10.51. Mind you, that's because my spelling these days is getting wrose and wrose.

10

FIGURE 10.51

Use these settings and save yourself the embarrassment of appearing illiterate.

You can add words to your custom dictionary, or remove words that crept in there by mistake.

Finally, you can choose which dictionary to use to check your spelling. However, this option won't help you with pronunciation quandaries, like the continuing ta-may-to/ta-mah-to controversy.

Security Tab

I will cover these settings on Day 19.

Other Tab

The Other tab is for all the settings that wouldn't fit on any other tab.

Advanced Options

Here you can configure a number of general settings, such as which folder Outlook uses when starting.

Warn Before Permanently Deleting Items only applies to deleting items in the Deleted Items folder.

Feedback With Sound is usually too irritating to have on for long.

Notice the settings for Task Working Hours Per Day and Per Week. These are not set through your Calendar's working hours.

Reminder Options   I find both reminder options useful. The reminder sound is not too intrusive, as it only comes on when you get a reminder of an event.

Add-In Manager   Here you can add a number of different extra components to Outlook. You install add-ins by clicking on the Install button and selecting one of the displayed .ECF files. Sadly, it is very difficult to tell from these files what functionality you are adding.

You will probably want to check that you have loaded the following add-ins:

- Delegate Access (DLGSETP.ECF)
- Deleted Item Recovery (DUMPSTER.ECF)
- Exchange Extensions Commands (EMSUIX.ECF)
- Exchange Extensions Property Pages (EMSUIX2.ECF)
- Rules Wizard (RWIZ1.ECF)
- Server Scripting (SCRPTXTN.ECF)

You may need to load additional add-ins depending on your setup. You can view .ECF files in Notepad to see what function each file installs. To load an add-in, just select Install, double-click on the .ECF file, and a new item should appear on the list of loaded add-ins. You can check and uncheck add-ins to enable and disable functionality.

Advanced Tasks   These settings are best left at their defaults.

Custom Forms   For more information on using the Outlook Forms environment, see Day 18, "Building Exchange Applications".

AutoArchive

AutoArchive enables Outlook to back up your folders to a personal folder file on a regular basis. You can then decide whether to delete your backed up messages or items, as shown in Figure 10.52.

FIGURE 10.52

This is where you can set your overall AutoArchive policy.

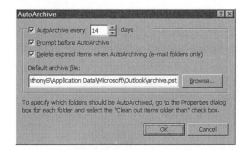

You can set up your general AutoArchive settings here. Note that you can override these settings on a folder-by-folder basis. To configure AutoArchive on an individual folder, right-click on that folder and select properties. Click on the AutoArchive tab, and you will see the screen in Figure 10.53.

FIGURE 10.53

After you have set your general AutoArchive settings, you can then enable or disable AutoArchive on individual folders.

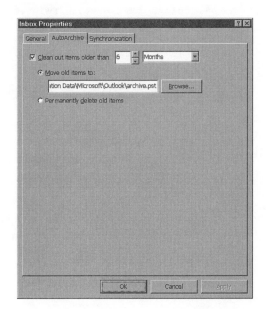

10

Note You can only AutoArchive folders in your mailbox.

Preview Pane

The Preview pane options only come into effect if you have selected to display the Preview pane, as you covered earlier in the chapter. You can either mark items as read after they have been in the Preview pane for a certain number of seconds, or you can mark the item as read when you move to another item. Figure 10.54 shows this configured.

FIGURE 10.54

Preview pane options can be time-based or trigger on moving to another message.

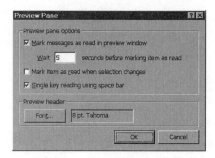

 Caution   If the sender has configured a read receipt on the message, previewing a message will indicate to the sender that you have read the message.

Delegates Tab

For more information on using the Delegates tab, see "Configuring Delegate Access" in Day 19.

Using Outlook Help

Finally, a word about Outlook 98 Help, particularly if you haven't come across the Office Assistants or "Actors" before.

Help technology has come a long way from the days of "Press F1 for an incomprehensible explanation." Help systems today are so much more friendly and interactive, with little cuddly characters to use up all those processor cycles you don't need, and natural language guessing games search routines.

With Outlook 98, if you press F1, you will see a little character pop up, as in Figure 10.55.

FIGURE 10.55

Power Pup to your assistance.

The Search dialog lets you enter a natural language question, such as "How do I format a message"? In Figure 10.56, I have entered this question, and a series of alternative answers have appeared. You could then select the answer closest to what you need to know.

FIGURE 10.56

Outlook uses natural language for help queries.

10

Tip

Dads. Amuse your children for hours with the Office Assistants. Right-click on the assistant and select Animate! This works best with the sound on.

You can download additional actors from the Microsoft Web Site, or you could just switch them off and regain a few processor cycles.

Other options in the Help menu include Contents, Index, and Find. Contents shows the sections of the Help, and Index gives a listing of the headings. Find does a full-text search on all words.

Other sources of Help include TechNet and the Office Resource Kit (included in TechNet). Finally, you can access several preconfigured Web sites direct from the Outlook Help menu.

Summary

As Microsoft's premier Exchange client, Outlook 98 makes the best use of Exchange's features, while adding considerable extra functionality of its own. However, it is a complex product, and does require a structured rollout and support plan for maximum effectiveness.

To summarize the main points of this lesson:

- Outlook 98 can operate as a standalone PIM, an Internet POP3/IMAP4 client, or a full MAPI mail application.
- Outlook can use multiple messaging services and multiple messaging profiles.
- Outlook 98 uses a number of different folder types such as Calendar, Email, Contact information, To-do lists, Journal, and so on.
- You can install Outlook from CD, from the Internet, or using the Outlook Deployment Kit (ODK).
- The Outlook Today feature lets you see your messages, to-dos and appointments at a glance.
- You can organize the way folders display information though views.
- You can arrange meetings and book equipment using the Calendar folder.
- You can telephone, write to, or email people direct from your Contacts folder.
- You can delegate tasks through the Tasks folder.
- You can keep track of files or correspondence with a contact via the Journal folder.
- There is a multitude of configuration possibilities available through Options.

Q&A

Q Our company is currently using the Exchange client on Windows for Workgroups. We cannot upgrade all our hardware, but I would like to deploy Outlook on any new workstations. What issues am I likely to encounter?

A Thankfully, you shouldn't have any great problems here. However, forms created on Outlook (which include Calendar, Journal, Contacts, and so on) won't work on the Exchange client. You also can't use S/MIME security with the Exchange Client. Exchange client forms will work quite happily on Outlook, and both clients can use the Exchange Key Management Service for security.

Q We've deployed Outlook, and we have now started using Schedule+ diaries, but the Outlook users can't seem to get the Free/Busy information from the Schedule+ users.

A Here you need to install the add-on for Schedule+ support. Load the MSSCP.ECF add-in via the Advanced Options button on the Other tab in Options. Alternatively, see if you can migrate your Windows for Workgroups users onto Outlook for Windows 3.x, which is on the Exchange 5.5 SP1 CD.

Q Our department is converting from ACT! 3.0 to Outlook 98, and I have been given the job of transferring all the data. I've tried doing a file import, selected ACT! 3.0, but I get a message saying I haven't got the right converter. What is the problem?

A You need to go to the Microsoft Outlook component download site, and download the additional converters. These are OS-specific—there are converters for NT and 9x, so make sure you use the right ones. After you have downloaded the file, extract and install the converters.

Workshop

The Workshop provides two ways for you to affirm what you've learned in this lesson. The "Quiz" section poses questions to help you solidify your understanding of the material covered and the "Exercise" section provides you with experience in using what you have learned. You can find answers to the quiz questions and exercises in Appendix B, "Answers to Quiz Questions and Exercises."

Quiz

1. How does Outlook 98 normally connect to the Exchange server?
2. What tools does Outlook have for locating information?
3. By default, where are messages currently under composition stored?
4. Where can you find Outlook 98?
5. You have been sent a vCard from a client. How can you use this in Outlook?
6. What is the difference between AutoPreview and the Preview pane?
7. How can you use the Junk Email facility?

Exercise

How would you set up a system to forward all mail to your home Internet account when you are out of the office?

DAY 11

Communication Protocols and the Internet

By Anthony Steven

Chapter Objectives

Today you will look at how Exchange uses messaging protocols to communicate. Although concentrating mainly on the Internet, you will also review Microsoft Exchange's use of the X.400 and X.500 standards.

Today you will learn about the following topics:

- An overview of the Internet
- Key services and protocols
- TCP/IP
- Network services
- SMTP, POP3, IMAP4

- DNS
- NNTP
- LDAP
- Security enhancements—SSL and S/MIME
- X.400
- X.500

Overview of the Internet

The *Internet* is a global routed network of interconnected networks. This network provides a range of core services using a number of standard protocols.

> **INTERNET'N'CHIPS**
>
> These days, almost every magazine article you read has a reference to the Internet. Whether it is being hailed as the savior of humanity or castigated as the scourge of the Nineties (no, not those in their nineties), they'll be a reference to it somewhere. Even my local fish and chip shop is on the Internet (if you don't believe me, take a look at www.harryramsdens.co.uk).
>
> Unfortunately, few people actually have a clear idea what the Internet is, which is why so many training manuals represent it as a cloud. Clouds—they're woolly, undefined, and prevent you from seeing things properly. Just like most people's perception of the Internet!

A Very Brief History

The Internet resulted from an experiment in the late 1960s funded by the US Government's Defense Advanced Research Projects Agency (DARPA). This early version of the Internet was called ARPAnet. The goal of ARPAnet was to show that a routable packet-switched communications network could survive a nuclear missile strike.

 Note

Not knowing your current state of knowledge on the Internet and bearing in mind that you have paid good money for a book on Exchange, I shall keep this section short.

For further reading on the development and technologies behind the Internet, see *Sams Teach Yourself the Internet in 24 Hours*, ISBN: 1-57521-236-6.

ARPAnet's survivability came from having multiple paths that a data packet could take from sender to recipient. Hence if one path failed, whether from a downed server or from a nuclear attack, the packet was re-routed around the failure. By having not just two or three but two or three hundred possible routes from one location to another, this network could lose a large number of links and still function.

The original experiment in 1970 linked four universities (University of California at Los Angeles, University of California at Santa Barbara, Stamford, and Utah) using a packet-switched network. With this elementary system, communications could continue although one link might be down.

For more information on ARPAnet, see `www.arpa.mil`.

NEW TERM In *Packet-Switched Networks*, data travels around in discrete packets. Each packet contains information on where it came from (a source address) and where it is headed (a destination address). In a TCP/IP network, these addresses show as two IP addresses (such as 141.23.1.33 and 132.11.20.10). The packet also contains a data payload (that is, the actual information carried), which will vary from packet to packet.

NEW TERM *Routers* link the parts of a packet-switched network. These devices look at a packet and find out where it wants to go. The router uses a routing table to try to match the destination address of the packet to a delivery route. If the router finds a match, it sends the packet on its way. If the router doesn't find a match, it returns the packet to its sender.

Table 11.1 gives a brief outline of some of the important events in the history of the Internet.

TABLE 11.1 THE HISTORY OF THE INTERNET

Date	Event
1958	Defense Advanced Research Projects Agency (DARPA) is established.
1969	DARPA commissions Bolt, Beranek, and Newman (BBN) to conduct research into survivable networks. BBN designs Network Control Protocol (NCP)—the first packet-switching protocol and hardware to run it on.
1970	ARPAnet links UCLA, UCSB, Stanford, and Utah using NCP.
1972	40 Sites Linked by ARPAnet. FTP used to transfer files, email used for messaging. First remote control of another computer using rlogin.
1974	Vinton Cerf and Robert Kahn release Transmission Control Protocol (TCP) and Internet Protocol (IP). Surprisingly, DARPA releases details of TCP/IP to the world.

continues

TABLE 11.1 CONTINUED

Date	Event
1977	The University of Wisconsin creates Theorynet for science researchers. Other networks are starting to crop up.
1979	Theorynet and other networks meet with ARPA and the National Science Foundation (NSF) and agree to create the Computer Science Research Network (CSnet).
1980	Cerf suggests connecting CSnet and ARPAnet using TCP/IP and a gateway. Cerf also suggests linking several independent networks under CSnet.
1982	Connectivity is achieved between ARPAnet and CSnet. The Internet is born.
1983	The military portion of ARPAnet becomes Milnet and is no longer available to the general public. The Internet Advisory Board (IAB) is founded.
Late 80s	The National Science Foundation Network (NSFnet) is founded. It creates a network of supercomputers linked by a high-speed backbone.
1992	The Internet Society is founded.
1993	InterNIC is created to manage domain registrations. It is managed by AT&T.
1994	The World Wide Web Consortium (W3C) is founded.

EXCHANGE AND THE INTERNET

Exchange 5.0 was notable in the enormous improvement in support for Internet protocols. Rather than just the Internet Mail Connector provided in version 4.0, Exchange 5.0 (and subsequent versions) now supports almost every Internet messaging protocol going.

Policing the Internet

Today the Internet is a vast system linking every country in the world, yet it is strangely intangible. After all, it is just a collection of interconnected networks. No one owns it; no one controls it and no one entity pays for it. Yet there must be some form of policing or else there would be chaos. While there is no centralized Internet authority, a number of organizations joined forces to develop and standardize Internet protocols, policies, and procedures.

The Organizations

Although this is by no means an exhaustive list, I hope to show you the variety of organizations that are involved in policing and controlling the Internet.

Internet Corporation for Assigned Names and Numbers (ICANN) ICANN is a new non-profit corporation created to take over responsibility for the IP address space allocation, protocol parameter assignment, domain name system management, and root server system management functions. These functions were previously under U.S. Government contract by IANA and other entities.

For more information, see www.icann.org.

The InterNIC InterNIC controls the registration of Domain Names. Let's say you run Acme Services Inc. and you would like to register the domain name acme.com. First, you need to check that this particular domain name isn't already in use. Go to www.internic.net; there you can use their WHOIS service to find out if this particular name is already registered. In this case, you would be out of luck, as the name is already registered. So, unless you can persuade the owner to sell you the domain name, you'll have to think of another one. I myself could let you have acmeservices.com for a small consideration (joking, of course).

For more information, see www.internic.net.

The Internet Society The Internet Society is the international organization for global cooperation and coordination of the Internet. It is open to all (as long as you pay your subscription). Its principal purpose is to maintain and extend the development and availability of the Internet and its associated technologies and applications. The goal is to enable organizations, professions, and individuals worldwide to collaborate , cooperate, and innovate in their respective fields and interests.

For more information, see www.isoc.org.

11

Internet Assigned Numbers Authority (IANA) The IANA is the central coordinator for the assignment of unique parameter values for Internet protocols. The Internet Society (ISOC) and the Federal Network Council (FNC) charter IANA to act as the clearinghouse to assign and coordinate the use of numerous Internet protocol parameters.

For more information, see www.iana.org/index2.html.

The World Wide Web Consortium (W3C) The World Wide Web Consortium (W3C) is responsible for the development of the standards behind the World Wide Web.

For more information, see www.w3c.org.

The Telecommunications Companies With their vast investment >in the cabling and communication links that make the Internet function, the telecommunications companies have a great deal of influence on the development of the Internet.

The United States Government   As the sponsor for the original ARPAnet and the government of the country with the largest Internet presence, the United States Government is heavily involved in the direction of the Internet. Not that this involvement is always positive. For example, the U.S. Government's insistence that 128-bit encryption cannot be exported from North America is slowing the acceptance of online retailing.

The United Nations   Through sponsorship of the International Standards Organization (ISO), the United Nations directly influence such areas as messaging standards (X.400 and X.500 are both published by ISO).

Internet Service Providers   There are now so many Internet Service Providers (ISPs) that it is almost impossible to keep track of them all. From one-person-and-a-PC-and-an-ISDN-phone-line to the vast telecommunications companies, ISPs come in a variety of sizes. What they all have in common is a link to the Internet backbone and, usually, some form of dial-up service.

The size of this link to the Internet backbone will depend on the size of the ISP. For example, Demon Internet (my ISP) has a dedicated 45Mbps(T3) connection to the USA as well as a 100MB link to the London Internet Exchange (LINX). At the other end of the scale, some local ISPs have just a 64Kbps ISDN line dialing in to their ISP.

Hence, ISPs tend to piggyback on top of each other. You can set yourself up as an ISP simply by agreeing to an ISDN or leased line connection to one of the bigger ISPs and then providing a Remote Access Service (RAS) server on the end of a telephone line. Chuck in Proxy server, DHCP, and DNS and you're away. Instant money! Well, you will have to market your new service as well, so maybe its back to buying the lottery tickets every week.

> The most important question to ask your ISP is "Do you support Microsoft Exchange Server?" If it doesn't, go somewhere else.

For more information on choosing your ISP, see Day 12, "Exchange on the Internet."

The Standards—Requests for Comments (RFCs)

Before looking at some of the key services and protocols on the Internet, it is important to understand the role of RFCs.

In the early days of the Internet community, there was something of a warm, fuzzy feeling of equality and fraternity amongst the early implementers of this new network. In a bid to avoid any suggestion of imposing standards, Internet "standards" were defined as a series of Request for Comments. Hence if you thought that some key service should be implemented in a certain way, you could publish it as an RFC. Everyone involved in the creation of the Internet could then comment on your proposal. If everyone agreed and that it hadn't been rubbished out of existence, the RFC was adopted and it would be assigned an RFC number.

Note

> Today there are two ways of having an RFC adopted. One method is through the Internet Engineering Task Force (www.ietf.org). Your proposed RFC will then go through a series of working groups before it's published as an Internet Draft. The other approach is to send it directly to the RFC editor on rfc-editor@rfc-editor.org.
>
> If your proposal is already being formulated by a working group, you may be asked to join this. After the Internet draft is accepted, it will be assigned an RTF number by IETF.
>
> For more information, see
>
>   http://www.rfc-editor.org/overview.html

11

RFCs define key services and protocols that run on the Internet, examples of which are shown in the next several pages. RFCs are not all equal, however, as you can see by looking up RFCs 2324—Hyper Text Coffee Pot Control Protocol (HTCPCP/1.0) and 2325—Definitions of Managed Objects for Drip-Type Heated Beverage Hardware Devices using SMIv2. File under J for Joke.

The best RFC links are at http://www.rfc-editor.org/rfc.html.

Internet Services, Applications, Utilities, and Protocols

One of the main problems with the Internet is the confusion that exists in the mind of many people between the Internet itself and the services that it offers. Hence, you will often hear the terms "The Internet" and "The World Wide Web" used interchangeably. As you will see, the World Wide Web is only one of the many services provided by the Internet.

Note A number of protocols run over the backbone of the Internet. These protocols provide support for various services and applications. For example, http, the Hyper Text Transfer Protocol, is the driving force behind the World Wide Web.

Internet Services

The services could be thought of as the top layer of the Internet—these define what facilities you have. The World Wide Web, email, and file transfer are all examples of these services. Now let's look at these in more detail.

Domain Name Service

DNS is without a doubt the most important service on the Internet. Without DNS, there would be no easy World Wide Web (would you like to try typing in—or even remembering —www.143.166.82.35 when you want www.dell.co.uk?) and no user-friendly email. Yet most Internet users are probably blissfully ignorant of the importance of DNS.

What Is DNS?   DNS is a hierarchical distributed database that maps host names to IP addresses and vice-versa. It is the basis of name resolution on the Internet and is growing in popularity. With the expected adoption of the Dynamic DNS standard (combining DNS with Dynamic IP address leasing) and the future implementation of IPv6 (see the IPv6 section later in this chapter), DNS seems like a good bet for the future of both the Internet and intranets.

As you will see in the section on TCP/IP that follows, to connect to a remote host you need its IP address. However, unless your hobby is memorizing telephone directories or train timetables, you probably find that remembering even one IP address difficult enough. Hence, the invention of host names, so that you could refer to a computer by name rather than by number. So much friendlier, don't you think?

Before DNS   In the early days of the Internet, a central hosts file at the University of California at Berkeley kept a list of the host names and matching IP addresses. However, as the number of hosts increased, this solution became impractical. The hosts file became a bottleneck, as all computers on the fledgling Internet needed to download their local host files from there.

Another method was needed and the answer was DNS.

> **WHAT IS AN INTRANET?** Internet, smintranet. So what's the difference?
>
> The *Internet* is the global network over which you can access a number of different services such as WWW, FTP, and so on.
>
> An *intranet* provides the same services as the Internet but on a local network. Hence you can install Microsoft Internet Information Server (IIS) and publish documents or download files from your own Web site. You could then use this for training, distributing telephone lists, and for general dissemination of information.
>
> An *extranet* enables your users or clients to connect to your intranet from the Internet. Confused yet?

How Does DNS Work? DNS uses a hierarchical structure of domains. No, these aren't the same as NT domains—yet. You are undoubtedly familiar with Internet domains already, like microsoft.com or whitehouse.gov.

> **DNS AND WINDOWS 2000**
>
> In Windows NT 4.0, a domain was a group of computers sharing a common security policy. In NT 5.0 or Windows 2000, DNS and NT domains become one. So when you install NT 5.0, a dialog box will ask you to specify a computer name in the form *servername.domainname*.com where *domainname*.com will be your Internet (or intranet) domain name.

11

> Don't put periods in your NT 4.0 domain names. It will cause problems when you try to upgrade to NT 5.0. See the sidebar on DNS and Windows 2000 NT.

So what would you do if you wanted to FTP to `research1.mit.edu`, a fictional computer at the Massachusetts Institute of Technology? To connect to the computer you need its IP address. However, you only have its host name. You can use the procedure illustrated in Figure 11.1 to resolve the address.

Figure 11.1

This is how DNS resolves host IP addresses on the Internet.

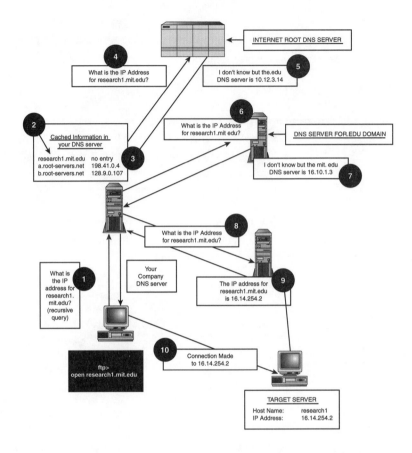

DNS will provide the translation between the host name and IP address. Assume you have set up a Microsoft DNS server on your network and you have a connection to the Internet. You have logged on to a client workstation on your LAN and have started a command-line FTP application. Here's how the request works:

1. Your client makes a recursive request to your DNS server for `research1.mit.edu`.

NEW TERM   A *Recursive Request* occurs when the DNS server must either reply with the IP address of the requested host or that the domain name doesn't exist. The DNS server cannot pass on a recursive request to another DNS server.

2. The DNS server looks in its cache to see if it has an address for `mit.edu`. If not, it will have to make an iterative query to one of the root servers.

NEW TERM   An *interative request* is where a DNS server does not have to fulfill the request but can return the name of another DNS server that can. Most DNS queries on the Internet are of this nature.

3. Your DNS server will select one of the nine world root servers from its cache.

 There are 13 *root servers* in the world and they are authoritative for the . (dot) domain. Not surprisingly, they tend to be somewhat haughty and affect not to know anyone of lower rank than a top-level domain. Microsoft's DNS service (as of Service Pack 3) only knows about nine of them.

The root servers only know about the servers that are authoritative for the top-level domains such as .com, .gov, .org, .mil, .uk, and so on.

4. Your DNS server will then query the selected root server for the IP address of `research1.mit.edu`.

5. The root servers are *far* too grand to be bothered with all the piffling little servers on the Internet. But they do know the IP addresses of the servers that are authoritative for the top-level domains, which includes the .edu domain. So the root server returns the IP address of one of the .edu domain servers.

> **Tip**
>
> You can get the current list of root servers at `ftp://rs.internic.net/netinfo/root-servers.txt`.

11

6. Your DNS server then queries the .edu domain server. This machine is slightly less grand, but still does not deign to know anything about `research1.mit.edu`.

7. However, it does know the IP address of the server that is authoritative for the `mit.edu domain`, which it will return to your DNS server.

8. Your DNS server can now query the DNS server that is authoritative for the `mit.edu domain`.

9. This machine (which is not at all stuffy) will now return the IP address for `research1.mit.edu`.

10. You can ftp to `research1.mit.edu`.

With DNS, each period in a domain name indicates another level in the DNS tree. Hence, even with a very complex domain structure such as `mail.exchange.acme.co.uk`, you only need to go through five iterations to get the IP address for the host "mail".

Seems pretty slow and complex, doesn't it? Just remember, this happens almost every time you connect to an Internet Web site. DNS gives you the ability to resolve *any* host on the Internet, often in less than a second.

The Disadvantage of DNS   Although DNS provides a stable, hierarchical system for host name to IP address resolution, it does suffer from a major disadvantage. DNS, as currently implemented, is a static system, so you must enter DNS entries manually. Although Microsoft offers DNS-WINS integration to circumvent this problem, it is a bit of a kludge. You can also implement Dynamic DNS on UNIX.

Dynamic DNS is a proposed standard that will eventually replace static DNS and hosts will automatically register themselves in the DNS database.

The Internet DNS tables are updated every day at 18:00 GMT.

Exchange and DNS   When integrating Exchange with the Internet, you will need to talk to your ISP about DNS entries. For information on configuring Exchange with DNS, see Day 12.

The World Wide Web

The World Wide Web must be the most famous of the Internet's offspring. Jazzy, graphical, and with a nice, friendly interface, the World Wide Web (WWW) is, for most people, the "face" of the Internet. From global companies to corner shops, a company Web site is becoming de rigeur. Even staid and traditionally technophobic businesses, such as gentlemen's outfitters, are now eagerly plying their wares on the Internet. For the best in Jermyn Street shirts, for example, try `www.thomaspink.co.uk` (a very smart site) or my personal favorite, `www.ctshirts.co.uk`.

The protocol that drives the Web is the Hypertext Transfer Protocol (HTTP). This protocol enables a browser to make a series of commands to an HTTP server, such as the World Wide Web Publishing Service on Microsoft's Internet Information Server. The server returns a Web page that contains Hypertext Markup Language (HTML) code. This HTML code will cause the Browser to display the information in a set format. Depending on the design of the Web page, you can incorporate hypertext links that jump to other Web pages, which gives rise to "browsing."

Several aspects underpin the current success of the WWW. These include

- The ease of developing Web sites.
- The ability to incorporate text, pictures, animations, sounds, video clips, and custom applications.
- The immediate access that it gives to a global market.
- Most Web browsers are free.

I will be discussing this final point in the section on Web browsers later in this lesson.

Email

After the Web, email must be the next best known Internet service, with "email me" taking over from "call me on my mobile" as the cry of the Nineties. With its advantages of almost instant worldwide communication and, unlike faxes, the ability to send files and to reuse the text of a message, it has grown into a very useful means of keeping in touch.

Email requires an email client, like Outlook Express or Outlook 98, with the Internet Email service installed. Alternatively, look at the email client in Netscape Communicator.

Email uses the Simple Mail Transfer Protocol (SMTP) for delivery and collection of mail. However, the use of Post Office Protocol (POP3) servers to carry out the delivery of mail to end users has grown in popularity. This is due to the limitations in SMTP. Interactive Mail Access Protocol (IMAP4) provides an alternate means of overcoming the SMTP limitations but has not yet gained wide acceptance.

One of the problems of SMTP is that it can only deal with 7-bit ASCII text. Therefore, if you want to attach your latest application to an email, you have to find a way of translating it into something that SMTP can handle. The standard ways of doing this are either Multipurpose Internet Mail Extensions (MIME) or uuencode. Both of these encode the file by translating it into ASCII text. The mail client then sends this ASCII text to the recipient and the reverse process is carried out at the other end.

11

 Note

Microsoft Exchange can collect and deliver mail to SMTP servers and can use either MIME or uuencode for attachments. Exchange can also act as a POP3 or IMAP4 server to enable clients to pick up their mail using either of these protocols.

Gopher Service

Gopher is a menu-based information retrieval service. Using a Gopher (go fer this, go fer that) client, you can connect to a Gopher server and retrieve a large number of indexed items. You can search on key words, browse menus, and view a large number of different file formats.

However, Gopher is not as easy to use as the World Wide Web service, nor is it so pretty. Thus, outside the academic world, Gopher has suffered a considerable setback in popularity, especially with the large amount of information indexed and searched through the big search engines on the World Wide Web.

If you would like more information on Gopher and its search interface, Veronica, you will find some useful links at `http://www.screen.com/start/guide/gopher.html`.

The Gopher FAQ is at www.lmb.uni-
muenchen.de/groups/bioinformatics/ch1/gopher_faq.txt.

Internet Newsgroups (Usenet)

Internet Newsgroups are public discussion forums that allow anyone with the right type
of software (a news reader) to read and publish articles on a specific newsgroup. Each
newsgroup has a series of guidelines (often called a Frequently Asked Questions, or
FAQ, file) that lists acceptable use of that particular forum.

 A *FAQ, or Frequently Asked Questions file*, is a text document listing basic questions and answers that crop up most often. They exist throughout the Internet to
give new users a way to bring themselves up to speed on various topics while not inun-
dating channels with redundant queries. If you encounter a FAQ file on a topic you're
interested in, by all means read it.

There are more than 26,000 newsgroups in existence, with dozens more coming online
each week. Whatever you're into, there's a newsgroup for it. And if there isn't, you can
propose one. Get enough support for it and you can start it.

Some newsgroups are moderated—that is, a newsgroup administrator will vet submis-
sions to the newsgroup before allowing them to be posted.

> **Tip**
>
> You can set up Exchange Public Folders as moderated newsgroups. See Day
> 12 for more details.

If you look at ftp://rtfm.mit.edu/pub/usenet, you can view the FAQ documents for
most of the major newsgroups.

Internet Relay Chat (IRC)

Most people tend to see IRC as something of a lightweight service. After all, if you drew
up a list of all the ways to communicate with someone, you would probably find typing
to them would come only marginally above using Morse Code or semaphore.

Microsoft Exchange has a Chat server included, so you can set up a Chat service and an
Internet Locator Server (ILS). To install the Chat service, insert your Exchange 5.5 CD,
select Setup Server and Components, and then select Chat Services.

Internet Explorer 4.0 and Outlook 98 come with the Microsoft Chat client. For more
information on setting up Chat, see Day 13, "Building a Web Site Around Exchange."

SERVICE PACK 1 UPDATE

Service Pack 1 includes enhancements to the Chat service, including Channel Transcription, which enables you to transcribe conversations going on over the Chat service, and an [expletive deleted] profanity filter.

Windows Sockets

Windows Sockets (WinSOCK) is the Windows implementation of the Berkeley Sockets Application Programming Interface (API). This enables applications not using NetBIOS to use TCP/IP services. Sockets applications communicate by connecting to a port number. Table 11.2 shows some of the common port assignments that Exchange uses to communicate in an IP environment, as well as some of the better-known non-Exchange port assignments.

TABLE 11.2 WINSOCK PORT ASSIGNMENTS

Service Name	Port No.	Function	Used by Exchange
ECHO	7/tcp	PING Command	No
FTP-DATA	20/tcp	FTP Data Port	No
FTP	21/tcp	FTP Control Port	No
Telnet	23/tcp	For Normal Telnet Connections	No
SMTP	25/tcp	Internet Mail	Yes
TFTP	69/udp	Trivial File Transfer Protocol	No
HTTP	80/tcp	Web	Yes
X.400	102/tcp	X.400 Connector over TCP	Yes
POP3	110/tcp	POP3 Mailbox Access	Yes
NNTP	119/tcp	NNTP Service	Yes
Location	135/tcp	Exchange RPC Client Server Connections	Yes
IMAP4	143/tcp	IMAP Mailbox and Folder Access	Yes
SNMP	161/udp	Simple Network Management Protocol	No
LDAP	389/tcp	LDAP Directory Access	Yes
LDAP over SSL	636/tcp	Secure LDAP Access	Yes

continues

11

TABLE 11.2 CONTINUED

Service Name	Port No.	Function	Used by Exchange
IMAP over SSL	993/tcp	Secure IMAP Access	Yes
POP3 over SSL	995/tcp	Secure POP3 Mailbox Access	Yes
Chat	6665/tcp	Server-Server Chat Service	Yes
Chat	6667/tcp	Client-Server Chat Service	Yes

> **Tip**
>
> If you are configuring a firewall or proxy server with your Exchange connection, you will need to allow connections across your firewall on the ports shown previously. If you do not, the relevant Exchange services will not work.

NetBIOS over TCP/IP (NBT)

NetBIOS over TCP/IP is the other way in which client-server applications communicate in a TCP/IP environment. Here the connection is not with a host name and a socket number but with a NetBIOS name.

You use NBT when you use a Universal Naming Convention (UNC) path to connect to a server. A UNC path is of the form *servername**sharename*. You add NBT support automatically when you install Microsoft TCP/IP.

Internet Applications

Internet applications are what you need to make use of the Internet services. They are the user-friendly (well, sometimes) front-end to the service.

Web Browsers

The main reason for the popularity of the World Wide Web must surely lie with the availability, cheapness, and relative simplicity of the application you need to access it, the Web browser. Originally developed at the Central European Research Laboratory (CERN) in Switzerland, the Web browser was a tool for accessing research papers. See www.cern.ch for more about the development of the Web browser.

Note

> You can use a Web browser using HTTP to access mail on a Microsoft Exchange server. To do so, you must install IIS and Active Server Pages, and then add support for the Web client when installing Exchange. The browser itself must support JavaScript and Frames. Be sure you have installed the latest service packs for both NT and Exchange, and any hotfixes, or you may have trouble getting it all to work.
>
> See Day 13 for more information.

As far as the commercial browser market goes, there are three rivals for your custom. Or is it two rivals and one that isn't playing?

MICROSOFT AND THE INTERNET

After a false start with the Microsoft Network (MSN), Microsoft carried out one of the most extraordinary corporate realignments of modern times and totally re-orientated their products for integration with the Internet. This has reached such a stage that Internet Explorer 4 is more of a new shell for Windows NT and 9x than just a browser.

This integration resulted in the lawsuit brought by Netscape, alleging that Microsoft was acting in a monopolistic fashion by bundling its browser with the operating system. As they say, this one could run and run...

Note to Microsoft lawyers—I did say "alleging."

11

Microsoft Internet Explorer   Microsoft will try to persuade you that Internet Explorer gives you everything you could possibly want in a browser. It's free, it comes with Windows 98, and it has a little wizzy-wizzy globe that spins round and round while you're waiting.

Some of the other features in IE4 are an Internet Connection Wizard, a POP3/IMAP4 mail client (Outlook Express), an LDAP client (the Windows Address Book), a Chat client, Microsoft NetMeeting, an HTML editor, and the Web Publishing Wizard.

You can obtain Internet Explorer from www.microsoft.com/windows/ie/default.htm. You will only have to answer a few minor questions, and have your hard disk scanned for "registration purposes."

Tip

> If you want to use the Outlook Web client with Microsoft Exchange, you must be using a Java-enabled browser that can deal with frames. This requirement means IE 3.02 or Netscape Navigator 2.0 as a minimum.

Netscape Navigator   More than just a Web browser, Netscape Navigator is now part of a suite of communications programs, snappily titled Netscape Communicator.

Netscape Communicator consists of a POP3/IMAP4 mail client with LDAP address book, a Chat service, a combined HTML editor/Web publishing tool, and an Enterprise Calendar application. I'm not taking bets that IE5 has an Enterprise Calendar as well.

You can download the latest version of Netscape Navigator from `www.netscape.com/download/index.html`.

NCSA Mosaic   One of the first commercially available browsers, you have probably overlooked Mosaic in the great rivalry between Netscape and Microsoft. Although development has now stopped on this browser, you can obtain the latest version of Mosaic for Windows from `www.ncsa.uiuc.edu/SDG/Software/mosaic-w/`.

FTP Applications

FTP applications come in a number of different guises, the simplest of all being the command-line interface on Windows NT. If your taste is for something a bit more graphical, you can download several shareware ftp applications from the Internet. Some look a little like File Manager or Windows Explorer. However, I am still waiting to see a version of Microsoft Windows Explorer that makes the remote site look like my local hard disk.

All these applications use the FTP protocol and communicate over TCP ports 20 and 21.

Telnet

Telnet is a terminal emulator, something of a throwback to the days of mainframe connectivity. It enables you to connect to a server running a Telnet server daemon (UNIX) or the Telnet Server service (NT). After you have connected, you can issue commands to the remote server. As far as the remote server is concerned, you logged on locally.

Telnet is very limited in its support—most Telnet sessions are text-based only. If your telnet client supports ANSI, you may even get to see some text in color. But don't count on it.

You can use Telnet as a troubleshooting tool to see if you can connect to your Exchange server. If you have the Internet Mail Connector installed, try connecting to port 25 (SMTP). You will see a screen like the one shown in Figure 11.2.

FIGURE 11.2

Here Telnet is connected to the Internet Mail Service on port 25, and the Exchange server has responded to the HELO command with a list of supported extensions.

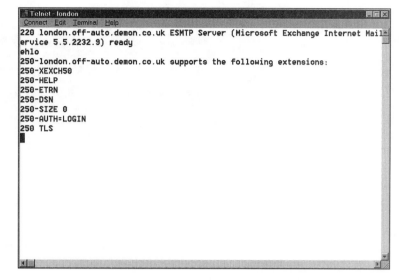

```
Telnet - london
Connect  Edit  Terminal  Help
220 london.off-auto.demon.co.uk ESMTP Server (Microsoft Exchange Internet Mail
ervice 5.5.2232.9) ready
ehlo
250-london.off-auto.demon.co.uk supports the following extensions:
250-XEXCH50
250-HELP
250-ETRN
250-DSN
250-SIZE 0
250-AUTH=LOGIN
250 TLS
```

Chat Programs

Microsoft Chat and NetMeeting are examples of different implementations of a chat program enabling real-time, text-based conversation. NetMeeting is the more serious of the two—it offers video and voice transmission as well, and doesn't offer the small image files or *avatars* some chat programs use to identify users. After all, how many companies do you know that would conduct an online meeting with an alien or a cat in a dressing gown?

There are whole hosts of other freeware and shareware chat programs should you want to try something different.

Internet Utilities

The Internet utilities are down at the less glamorous end of the market. They are the resources you turn to when your latest browser won't browse or your jazzy email client won't speak to anyone. However, they can help you solve most of the everyday problems that make TCP/IP networks such fun to work with.

IPCONFIG

Along with PING, IPCONFIG is probably the most popular TCP/IP utility, and a version comes with Windows NT. IPCONFIG displays the current state of your TCP/IP configuration information, such as IP address, host name, and MAC address, as you can see in Figure 11.3. Note that IPCONFIG is a command line utility.

FIGURE 11.3

Running IPCONFIG with the /ALL switch results in output showing detailed TCP/IP configuration information.

```
Command Prompt                                                    _ □ ×
D:\>ipconfig/all

Windows NT IP Configuration

        Host Name . . . . . . . . . : london.universalexports.com
        DNS Servers . . . . . . . . : 158.152.1.43
                                      158.152.1.58
        Node Type . . . . . . . . . : Broadcast
        NetBIOS Scope ID. . . . . . :
        IP Routing Enabled. . . . . : No
        WINS Proxy Enabled. . . . . : No
        NetBIOS Resolution Uses DNS : Yes

Ethernet adapter PNPNT1:

        Description . . . . . . . . : Novell 2000 Adapter.
        Physical Address. . . . . . : 00-20-18-34-79-56
        DHCP Enabled. . . . . . . . : No
        IP Address. . . . . . . . . : 131.107.2.200
        Subnet Mask . . . . . . . . : 255.255.0.0
        Default Gateway . . . . . . : 131.107.2.200
```

If you are using DHCP to allocate IP addresses, you can use IPCONFIG to release and renew IP addresses.

Tip

A graphical utility called WINIPCFG replaces IPCONFIG under Windows 9x. There is an equivalent utility for Windows NT on the NT 4.0 Resource Kit.

PING

PING stands for Packet Internet Groper. This text-based program is an ICMP Echo command that simply looks for a response from the remote address. You can use PING for two main diagnostic processes.

PING (IP address) will do a simple communications check. The default number of responses is four with Windows NT, as you can see in Figure 11.4. PING (host name) will resolve the host name to an IP address and then check communications with the remote address.

FIGURE 11.4

A normal PING response under Windows NT shows four replies.

```
Command Prompt                                                    _ □ ×
D:\>ping 131.107.2.200

Pinging 131.107.2.200 with 32 bytes of data:

Reply from 131.107.2.200: bytes=32 time<10ms TTL=128
Reply from 131.107.2.200: bytes=32 time<10ms TTL=128
Reply from 131.107.2.200: bytes=32 time<10ms TTL=128
Reply from 131.107.2.200: bytes=32 time<10ms TTL=128

D:\>
```

In either case, if the remote host does not respond, you will receive a `request timed out` notification. In the second case, if the host name cannot be resolved to an IP address, you will receive the message "`Bad IP Address`". If the remote network is not available, you will see a `Network unreachable` message. This could be because of routing problems or an incorrectly configured gateway address.

Tip

You can check IP communications quickly by pinging a machine on a remote subnet by host name. If it responds, everything is hunky-dory. If it doesn't respond but you can ping it by IP address, the problem is name resolution. If it does not respond to pinging its IP address, check default gateways, subnet masks, and so on.

Tip

Type `PING` at a command prompt with no arguments to see the options for this command.

NSLOOKUP

11

NSLOOKUP is probably one of the most annoying TCP/IP utilities to use. It's a great shame because if you can get to grips with it, it is quite useful.

NSLOOKUP is a tool for querying DNS servers. You can use it in two modes: interactive and non-interactive. It is a command-line utility, so you will need to start a command prompt to use it.

You are most likely to use NSLOOKUP to query DNS for MX records for your domain. This would be in the following form:

From a command prompt, type `NSLOOKUP`, and then type `set type=MX` and press Enter. Enter your company's email domain name, such as `universal-exports.com`. If things are set up properly, you should get back the host name of your Exchange server. Here is an example:

```
C:\WINNT> NSLOOKUP
Default server: cache-2.ns.demon.net
Address: 158.152.1.43
>set type=mx
>universal-exports.com
Server: cache-2.ns.demon.net
Address: 158.152.1.43
Non-authoritative answer:
universal-exports.com MX preference = 10, mail
➥exchanger=exchange.universal-exports.com
```

This shows the MX record for the requested domain. If this record is missing, you may have found out the reason why no one is replying to your mail.

Figure 11.5 shows an example of a live trace for my domain, off-auto.demon.co.uk.

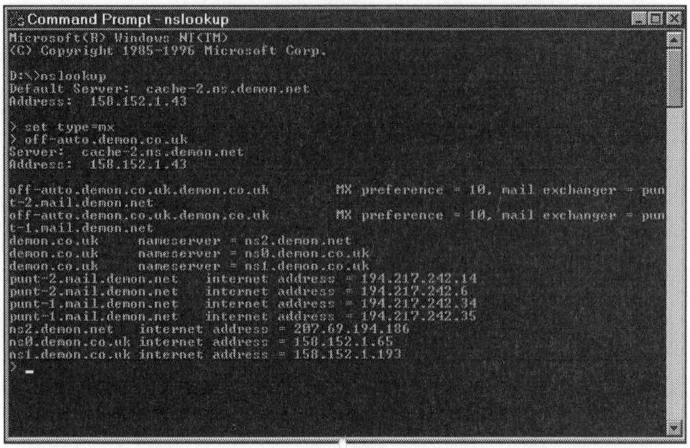

FIGURE 11.5

An NSLOOKUP trace for off-auto.demon.co.uk *on Demon Internet's DNS servers.*

NETSTAT

NETSTAT displays TCP/IP network statistics and connection information. It is a useful advanced TCP/IP troubleshooting tool. For usage options, type NETSTAT /? at a command prompt. Figure 11.6 shows the output from a NETSTAT -s command, which gives per-protocol statistics.

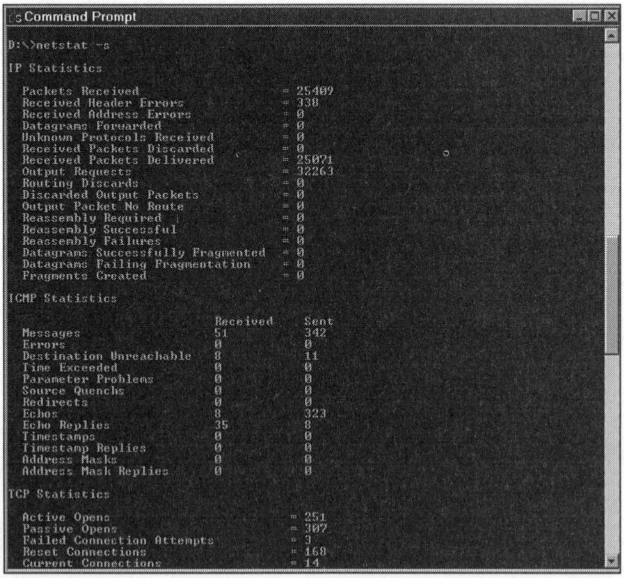

FIGURE 11.6

NETSTAT -s *shows useful statistics on TCP/IP protocol use.*

Tip

> NETSTAT –s gives you your connection statistics by protocol, that is, TCP, UPD, and ICMP.
>
> NETSTAT –a shows you the ports that your server is listening on. Use this command to check that you have enabled the correct ports in a Proxy Server or firewall environment.

NBTSTAT

NBTSTAT provides statistics on connections using the NetBIOS over TCP/IP service. These connections occur when applications use universal naming convention (UNC) paths to connect to remote machines. UNC paths are of the form *servername*\ *sharename*.

TRACERT

TRACERT is a useful diagnostic utility in a routed WAN environment or if you experience routing problems on the Internet. It uses ICMP to trace the hops that your packets make from router to router, displaying the host name or address of each router and the time it takes to connect between the two.

When the Internet is working properly, you should see a trace similar to the one shown in Figure 11.07.

FIGURE 11.7

The TRACERT utility shows all is well with the network.

```
 Command Prompt                                                        _ □ ×

D:\>tracert www.microsoft.co.uk

Tracing route to www.microsoft.co.uk [194.205.207.126]
over a maximum of 30 hops:

  1    150 ms    140 ms    141 ms  finch-216.access.demon.net [194.159.253.216]
  2    140 ms    131 ms    140 ms  trude-access.router.demon.net [194.159.253.9]
  3    141 ms    150 ms    150 ms  finch-core-1-fxp0.router.demon.net [158.152]
  4    150 ms    150 ms    140 ms  ash-fxp0.router.demon.net [194.159.252.252]
  5    160 ms    150 ms    161 ms  fe0.lon2gw2.uk.insnet.net [195.66.225.20]
  6    141 ms    150 ms    150 ms  atm0-2.lon1gw11.uk.insnet.net [194.177.170.1]
  7    151 ms    130 ms    150 ms  atm0-1.lon1gw12.uk.insnet.net [194.177.174.1]
  8    150 ms    150 ms    150 ms  MSUKWWW1 [194.205.207.126]

Trace complete.

D:\>
```

Hopefully, you won't see the trace in Figure 11.08, which indicates a break in the line.

11

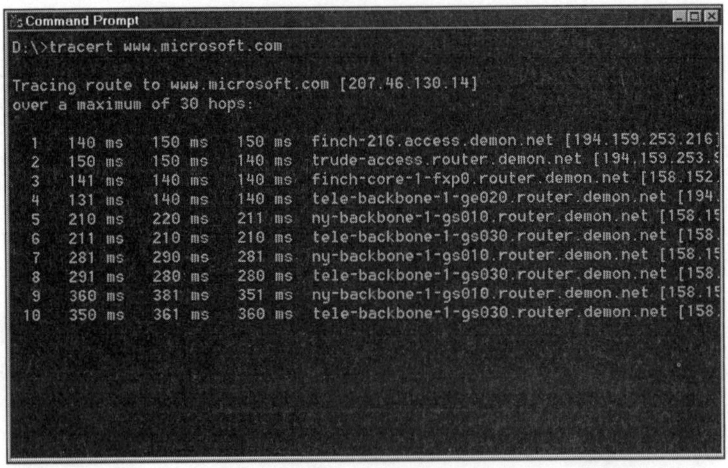

FIGURE 11.8

The TRACERT utility showing a routing failure between New York and New Jersey.

```
Command Prompt                                              _ □ ×
D:\>tracert www.microsoft.com

Tracing route to www.microsoft.com [207.46.130.14]
over a maximum of 30 hops:

  1   140 ms   150 ms   150 ms  finch-216.access.demon.net [194.159.253.216]
  2   150 ms   150 ms   140 ms  trude-access.router.demon.net [194.159.253.
  3   141 ms   140 ms   140 ms  finch-core-1-fxp0.router.demon.net [158.152.
  4   131 ms   140 ms   140 ms  tele-backbone-1-ge020.router.demon.net [194.
  5   210 ms   220 ms   211 ms  ny-backbone-1-gs010.router.demon.net [158.15
  6   211 ms   210 ms   210 ms  tele-backbone-1-gs030.router.demon.net [158.
  7   281 ms   290 ms   281 ms  ny-backbone-1-gs010.router.demon.net [158.15
  8   291 ms   280 ms   280 ms  tele-backbone-1-gs030.router.demon.net [158.
  9   360 ms   381 ms   351 ms  ny-backbone-1-gs010.router.demon.net [158.15
 10   350 ms   361 ms   360 ms  tele-backbone-1-gs030.router.demon.net [158.
```

ROUTE

The ROUTE command is for displaying and amending routing information. Use it for adding static routes to NT servers. If your routers use dynamic routing, such as Routing Information Protocol (RIP) or Open Shortest Path First (OSPF), you will not have to add routes manually.

Internet Protocols

All the services mentioned previously require one or more protocols to work. Hence the protocols are the building blocks that then translate into the services. All these protocols are defined as RFCs and are accepted standards throughout the Internet.

TCP/IP

No discussion of the Internet would be complete without an analysis of the role of TCP/IP. TCP/IP is the foundation and bedrock of the Internet—no TCP/IP, no Internet. In addition, it is rapidly becoming the most popular networking protocol in the world for local area networks.

Although TCP/IP is a standard protocol, individual software vendors tend to have slightly differing implementations of the standard. Hence you will find different TCP/IP suites, such as Microsoft TCP/IP, MacIP, or Novell IP. Although any TCP/IP host can communicate with another, there may be differences in how the protocol is applied.

For example, Microsoft added a proprietary version of the NetBIOS Name Server (NBNS) called WINS (Windows Internet Name Service). DHCP (Dynamic Host Configuration Protocol) is an adaptation of the BOOTP protocol, originally designed to allocate IP addresses to diskless workstations.

Changes OK. —GLH 12/11/98TCP/IP is in fact two parts. Transport Control Protocol (TCP) ensures the delivery of the message while Internet Protocol (IP) takes care of the addressing. I'll describe each of these components separately, starting with IP.

Internet Protocol (IP)   IP requires each host on the Internet to have a unique address, something like 191.34.12.141. With that addressing information, you can now deliver data packets to that address.

An IP address is a 32-bit number, consisting of four 8-bit octets in the form a.b.c.d (such as 131.107.2.200). These can take values (in decimal) ranging from 0 to 255 (2^8). As these are really binary (base 2) numbers, the range of values is from 00000000 to 11111111.

There are a couple of rules about IP addresses. Generally, octets of all ones or all zeros are not allowable, as these tend to indicate broadcast addresses (all ones) or network addresses (all zeros). In addition, you can never have the fourth octet of a host address as either all ones or all zeros.

Note   On an intranet with no direct connection to the Internet, you can use whatever addressing scheme you like. However each host on your network must have a unique IP address or communications will fail.

There are two parts to an IP address—the address itself and the subnet mask. The subnet mask enables a host to tell whether a destination IP address is on a local or a remote subnet. Examples of subnet masks in general use are 255.0.0.0 (Class A), 255.255.0.0 (Class B), or 255.255.255.0 (Class C). There are others, but those are for more specialist situations.

IP is also a routable protocol. To enable this functionality you need to specify a default gateway address. The default gateway is the address to which your client will send any packets that are not for the local subnet.

> **SUBNET MASKS AND CLASSES**
>
> Subnet masks distinguish between a host address and a network address. Class A, Class B, and Class C addresses differ in the number of hosts that each network can support.
>
> For example, with a Class B network, the first two octets are the network ID and the last two octets are the range of host IDs. Hence with a Class B subnet you can have two octets worth of hosts on your network, which is 2^{16}, or more than 65,000 hosts.
>
> On a Class C network, you have three octets as the network ID and only one octet for host IDs. Thus your Class C network can only have 2^8, or 254, hosts (you can't use host IDs with all ones or zeros).
>
> If choosing an addressing scheme for your intranet, make sure your address class will support the number of future hosts and subnets that you want to use on your network.

To find out whether a packet is for a local or a remote subnet, IP will carry out a logical AND operation. Any number AND one is that number and any number AND zero is zero. The result of ANDing the host's IP address and its subnet mask produces the subnet ID. The destination address and the local subnet's subnet mask combine as shown:

Originator's address	131.107.3.101
Subnet mask	255.255.255.0
Destination address	131.107.2.200
Subnet mask	255.255.255.0
Result of AND operation	131.107.3.0
	131.107.2.0

If a destination address is ANDed with the subnet's subnet mask and produces a different subnet ID, the packet is not for the local network. As this is the case in this example, the host then sends this packet to the default gateway.

The default gateway will be some form of router and will again examine the packet. This time the router will look in its routing table and attempt to find a matching route for this packet. If the router finds a match, it sends the packet to the correct interface. If the router can't find a match, it will send the packet to the router's default gateway. The process then continues until the packet is delivered or returned as non-deliverable.

IP is also responsible for routing around any failures in a network.

Transport Control Protocol (TCP)   Although IP will make a best effort at data delivery, TCP is the protocol that guarantees delivery of packets on the Internet. It does this by a sending host establishing a session with the remote host and then transmitting some data. The sender will then wait for acknowledgement of receipt of the data before sending any more. Thus TCP guarantees delivery and any packets that are lost in the routing process are re-sent.

Because TCP must negotiate a session with the remote host and acknowledge each packet, it cannot give ultimate network performance. However, it provides reliable and versatile connection-orientated communication.

Most Internet applications use TCP/IP.

User Datagram Protocol (UDP)

UDP is the alter ego of TCP. While TCP ensures that each packet reaches its destination, UDP has a far more relaxed, laissez-faire attitude and does not carry out any checking to ensure message delivery.

UDP is best with applications that do not want to go through all the palaver of setting up a TCP session. They just need to send off some information *now* and are not too bothered about whether it gets there or not. This is connectionless communication.

Examples of applications that use UDP/IP are Simple Network Management Protocol (SNMP) and TFTP.

Address Resolution Protocol (ARP)

ARP provides the mechanism that matches IP addresses to physical hardware addresses.

Although at the Internet level all that a packet requires is the IP address of its destination, at the physical level there are other requirements. Just as each device on a network must have a unique IP address, each node must also have a unique physical address. This hardware or Media Access Control (MAC) address is the "real" address of the network device.

ARP addresses are 48-bit Base 16 or hexadecimal form—for example, 00-10-a4-fd-ff-07. Every network card manufactured has a unique MAC address. Unless, that is, you brought a lot of dodgy clone Ethernet cards last time you had to save money on the networking budget and you found that they all had the same MAC address.

Windows NT comes with a command line program called ARP that displays current ARP cache and mapping information, as shown in Figure 11.9.

11

FIGURE 11.9

Running ARP -a shows the current state of your ARP cache. Note the mapping of IP address to MAC address

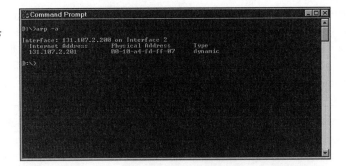

MAC ADDRESSES AND IP

IP Version 4 (the one the world currently uses) can support a theoretical maximum of 2^{32} (4,294,967,296) hosts or separate computers. The practical limit is less than half this number. The result of this limitation and the rapid expansion of the Internet is that the number of available IP addresses is running out. Remember that each host must have a separate IP address.

The pool of addresses will run dry in 2004. Fortunately, by that time, a new version of IP—IPv6—should be in operation. This has a 128-bit address space giving a theoretical maximum of 3.4×10^{38} IP addresses. Apparently, this gives 10,000 IP addresses per square meter of the Earth's surface.

As part of the new implementation of IPv6, a network card's MAC address will be part of the IP address.

Hence ARP provides the translation from IP address to MAC address. This enables one network card to talk directly to another.

Internet Control Message Protocol (ICMP)

ICMP is a troubleshooting protocol and it is the protocol behind the most used TCP/IP diagnostic utility, the PING command. PING (Packet Internet Groper) proves connection between two IP hosts, using either IP addresses or host names. In addition, you can use PING for reverse lookup. Hence PING -a 131.107.2.200 will provide the host name for that IP address.

Other functions of ICMP are as follows:

- Providing routing diagnosis using TRACERT.
- Building and maintaining routing tables.
- Adjusting packet flow to prevent congestion of links or routers.

Internet Group Message Protocol (IGMP)

IGMP is a multicasting protocol that certain types of Internet applications use to deliver a packet to multiple hosts at the same time. Microsoft Exchange does not use IGMP for any of its functions.

 Multicasting is the transmission of a packet to more than one host, but not all hosts. It is more restrictive than broadcasting, which goes to all hosts.

Simple Mail Transfer Protocol (SMTP)

SMTP is the backbone of the Internet's email service. A simple text-based protocol, it handles communication between two SMTP servers. There are several restrictions on SMTP, one being that all SMTP servers expect all other servers to be online all the time. The messages themselves are in ASCII text, which causes problems when you want to send a binary attachment (see the MIME section later in today's lesson).

Microsoft Exchange acts as an SMTP server after you install the Internet Mail Service (see Day 12).

> **Caution**
>
> You cannot use both Exchange's Internet Mail Service and Internet Information Server 4.0's SMTP service on the same computer. Hence, if you are installing IIS 4.0 in order to use the Web Client, you will not be able to install the SMTP server option.
>
> The same restriction applies to the Internet News Service and the NNTP server.

Because SMTP is so simple, it is also lacking in functionality. The next three protocols attempt to overcome some of SMTP's deficiencies.

> **Caution**
>
> SMTP security is not very high and it is possible to fool an SMTP server into accepting forged email. To guard against this, make sure you configure your Internet Mail Connector only to accept mail from specific IP addresses, that is, the address of your ISP's SMTP server.
>
> See Day 12, for more information.

11

Extended Simple Mail Transfer Protocol (ESMTP)

ESMTP is set of add-ons to SMTP that give improved functionality. The implementation of ESMTP varies from computer to computer—you will find that different servers support some parts of the protocol and not others. For a list of the commands supported by an ESMTP server, connect to port 25 on the server and type "EHLO". You will then see a list of the commands that that server supports. See Figure 11.2 earlier in today's lesson for an example.

> **Tip**
>
> One of the most useful ESMTP commands that Exchange Server supports as both client and server is ETRN (extended TURN). This command connects to another SMTP server and strips any queued mail off the server.
>
> Many ISPs now support ETRN, which is the correct way to use Exchange with dial-up access to your ISP. For more information see Day 12.

Post Office Protocol (POP3)

POP3 is the most common client mail retrieval protocol. It overcomes the problem of having to be permanently online for SMTP mail delivery. It also means that you don't have to be running an SMTP server, as you would have to in order to use ESMTP and ETRN.

POP3 is for retrieval only, so a POP3 client (such as Outlook Express) will use SMTP to deliver mail. For example, Demon Internet tells you to use pop3.mail.demon.net for mail collection (the POP3 server) and post.mail.demon.net for delivery (the SMTP server. If you have an Internet account at home, you are probably using POP3 when you collect your mail from your own ISP.

Exchange Server enables POP3 access on all mailboxes by default. You must install the Internet Mail Service to enable your clients to deliver mail back to your Exchange Server via SMTP.

> **Caution**
>
> Do not use Exchange Server as a POP3 client. If your ISP starts talking about having to run a DEQUEUE utility when your server connects to it, you should be thinking about another ISP.

Interactive Mail Access Protocol (IMAP4)

IMAP4 is the latest and most sophisticated attempt to get around the limitations of SMTP. With IMAP4, not only can you receive mail but also download your public folders. However, you still need SMTP to deliver mail. Outlook Express is an IMAP client, shown in Figure 11.10 configured for mail collection.

FIGURE 11.10

Outlook Express as an IMAP4 client showing Public Folders downloaded.

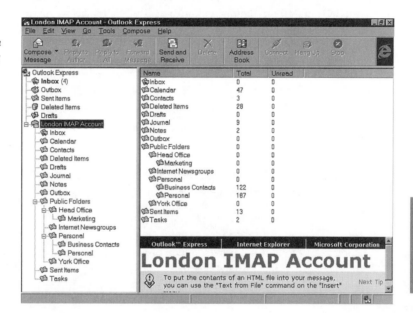

Microsoft Exchange enables IMAP4 access on all mailboxes and public folders by default. See Day 14, "Reading Exchange Mail with Internet Clients," for more information.

Network News Transfer Protocol (NNTP)

NNTP is the protocol that supports the Internet Newsgroups (Usenet) described earlier in this lesson.

Exchange supports NNTP in two ways:

- You can install the Internet News Service, which will enable you to connect to your ISP and download the Usenet newsgroups.
- Your clients can connect to your Exchange server using NNTP and download any public folders you have published as newsgroups.

For more information about Exchange and Internet Newsgroups, see Day 12 and Day 14.

Hypertext Transfer Protocol (HTTP)

HTTP is the basis of the ever more popular World Wide Web (as I described earlier in this lesson). The current implementation of HTTP is HTTP 1.1, which provides better performance and greater functionality than version 1.0.

HTTP enables your Web browser to interpret Hypertext Markup Language (HTML) and respond correctly to the instructions received via the browser's interface. HTTP is the basis of the World Wide Web service as implemented on Microsoft's Internet Information Server.

Microsoft Exchange uses HTTP with the Exchange Web Client when you use Outlook Web client to connect to your Exchange inbox via an HTML-based user interface. See Day 13, "Building a Web Site Around Exchange," for further details.

File Transfer Protocol (FTP)

File Transfer Protocol is the granddaddy of the current Internet protocols—FTP can trace its roots back to ARPAnet. It is even more popular today, given the vast amount of software downloading that happens every day on the Internet.

Although you can use HTTP for downloading files, FTP works better for downloads because it uses multiple ports for uploading and downloading, and is therefore faster. However, FTP does not provide much of an interface. Companies usually design their Internet sites so that you get the pretty Web interface, which uses HTTP. Clicking on a download link will connect you to their FTP server, resulting in better performance.

Note

> FTP uses TCP/IP over ports 20 and 21, plus a randomly assigned port number. Port 20 is the server data port; port 21 is the control port. Then the protocol negotiates a random high order (>1,023) port number to transfer the data. FTP is also more efficient than HTTP for file transfers because its windowing mechanism is more efficient.
>
> Microsoft Exchange does not use FTP.

Trivial File Transfer Protocol (TFTP)

TFTP is a lightweight version of FTP. It uses UDP/IP, not TCP/IP, which means that you have no guarantee of packet delivery. This is a file transfer protocol for all those trivial files you have, like pictures of Cindy Crawford or Leonardo DiCaprio. What, you don't have any?

Serial Line Internet Protocol (SLIP)

SLIP was the first protocol designed to run TCP/IP over serial lines. It is now outdated and very few current systems implement it. Windows NT can act as a SLIP client, but not as a SLIP server.

Point-to-Point Protocol (PPP)

PPP is the replacement for SLIP, supporting authentication (logging on) and other protocols, such as NetBEUI. Its other advantages include error-checking and IP address communication. You can use PPP to make an automated connection to a RAS server or to the Internet.

Microsoft Exchange uses PPP with remote client access over Remote Access Server.

Point-to-Point Tunneling Protocol (PPTP)

PPTP is an extension of PPP that enables you to create a virtual private network (VPN) across a public system such as the Internet. PPTP works by encapsulating PPP packets and then sending them to a PPP server. The PPTP packets are themselves encrypted, using up to 128-bit encryption in the United States and Canada or 40-bit encryption outside North America.

If you use PPTP with Windows 95, you need to update your version of dial-up networking to support PPTP.

Tip

When using PPTP, you can increase security on your network by making sure that your server will only accept PPTP packets. If you do so, your system will only enable access from authenticated users using PPTP.

Security Enhancements

The Internet itself is a fairly insecure network. After all, it has evolved from groups of networks being joined together, and security was never a great consideration. In recent years, however, there has been growing interest in securing messages so that they cannot be read in transit. There are two main standards that provide encryption—SSL and S/MIME.

Secure Sockets Layer (SSL)

Secure Sockets Layer (SSL) is a convenient way of ensuring that no one else can read your data on the Internet. It does this through a series of extensions on your Web browser and WWW server. These extensions encode the data at one end and decode it at the other.

HOW SECURE IS SECURE?

There are two main encryption standards with Windows NT—40-bit and 128-bit.

40-bit encryption gives a total of 2^{40} key combinations. This gives 1×10^{12}, or 1,000,000,000,000 possibilities.

128-bit encryption gives 2^{128} or 3.4×1038 possible combinations. That's 340,000,000,000,000,000,000,000,000,000,000,000,000 combinations!

If you had a computer and wanted to decode a message by brute force (trying every possible key combination), you would quickly become bored or frustrated unless the code was very simple. If your system could decode 10,000 combinations a second, you can decode a 40-bit key in $3\frac{1}{2}$ years.

With 100,000 operations per second, it would take you about 4 months. At 1,000,000 per second, you would be down to just under two weeks and with 100,000,000 operations per second, you would crack the code in three hours.

With 128-bit encoding, even at the currently unachievable rate of 1,000,000,000,000,000,000 (1GGFlop) operations per second, it would take you 100,000,000,000,000,000 years to decrypt *one message*. The next message will use a different key, so you'll have to start all over again.

–A couple of interesting facts regarding the preceding paragraph: First, The fastest computer in the world recently broke the Teraflop (1,000,000,000 operations per second) barrier.– Second, the current estimation of the life of the Universe is 4,500,000,000 years, give or take a couple of weeks.

How Does SSL Work?

SSL works in a similar way to the Advanced Security features of Microsoft Exchange. It uses both secret key and public/private key encryption to combine speed and security.

The browser and the server initiate a handshake procedure to enable a secure TCP/IP connection. The client and server agree on the security level and what method to use to fulfil authentication requests. The client and server can now encrypt their messages and carry out a secure conversation.

11

KEEPING A SECRET

Secret Key Encryption is where both client and server use the same key to encrypt and decrypt the data. It is fast and secure, with only one drawback—How do you get the key from server to client without compromising it? (For example, you might use a courier service to send the key, but you're assuming the service is trustworthy.)

Public/private key encryption uses a different system. Here there are two keys—a public one and a private one. Only the private key can decrypt the public one and vice-versa. The difference here is that you can freely distribute a public key, perhaps to a public key server. Hence, if I want to send a message to you I use your public key to encrypt the message, which you then decrypt with your private key.

The downside with public/private key encryption is that it requires a lot of computation. This makes it unsuitable for large amounts of data.

SSL uses both these systems, except that the public/private key encryption system sends the secret key from one computer to another. This means that you get the computationally efficient secret key encryption to encode the bulk of the message but the transfer of the secret key is also kept secret.

S/MIME

Secure Multipurpose Internet Mail Extensions (S/MIME) is a method for sending encrypting attachments with email. It provides functionality like that in Exchange's Advanced Security but adapted for the Internet.

S/MIME and Digital Signing

S/MIME is of particular use in providing digital signing over the Internet. Digital signing confirms the sender of a message and prevents anyone from altering the text en route.

With digital signing, a hashing algorithm condenses the characters of the message body into a unique message digest, or hash. This hash is then encrypted using S/MIME and sent along with the clear-text message body. At the recipient's end, the message is re-hashed to generate another message digest. The recipient's software then compares this new hash with the decrypted hash that came with the message. If the two are the same then you know that the message has not changed in transit, as any alteration would generate a different hash value.

NEW TERM A *hashing algorithm* is a mathematical computation that calculates a unique number based on the ASCII values of the characters that make up a message. Because of the size of the hash (128 bits is a common value), it is impossible to change any character in the message without altering the hash value. It is like a checksum on a network packet.

Digital signing usually uses public/private key encryption.

Other Exchange Protocols (Non-Internet)

You have been looking at Internet protocols in considerable depth because of their grow-ing importance and the current status of the Internet. But there were messaging protocols before SMTP and its cronies came along, and some of these are also supported by Exchange.

X.400

X.400 is an open standard for messaging connectivity between heterogeneous mail sys-tems. Most telecommunications companies around the world recognize and use the X.400 standard. It gives much greater quality of service and network security than the Internet. While X.400 was once a popular option for international email connectivity (especially in Europe), Internet mail has eclipsed X.400's popularity for new email installations.

The International Consultative Committee on Telephony and Telegraphy (CCITT) are responsible for the X.400 and for a series of updates to the standard that are published every four years.

X.400 is both software- and hardware-independent.

What X.400 Standards Does Exchange Support?

Exchange complies with two main X.400 standards:

- 1984—"Red Book"
- 1988—"Blue Book"

Note

> Exchange is not fully compliant with the 1992 "White Book" standard.

How Is X.400 Implemented in Microsoft Exchange?

Exchange implements connectivity to X.400 systems through the X.400 connector. It is a component of the Exchange 5.5 Enterprise edition.

When Will I Need to Use X.400?

You will need to use X.400 under the following circumstances:

- You want to connect to a foreign X.400 mail system.
- You want to connect to an MS Mail postoffice over X.400.

- You want to connect two Exchange sites over a link that does not support RPC (such as X.25) or has bandwidth restrictions or TCP/IP.
- You want to control which personnel use a specific connection between two sites.
- You need to schedule the connection between two Exchange sites.

The X.400 Connector

The X.400 connector installs as an option on the Enterprise version of Exchange 5.5 server. If you do not have the connector as shown in the install screen in Figure 11.11, you will need to upgrade to the Enterprise version of Exchange.

FIGURE 11.11

Click the check box shown to install the X.400 connector during Exchange Server setup.

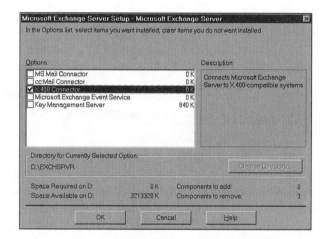

For detailed instructions on setting up the X.400 connector, see Day 5, "Working with Multiple Sites."

X.500

X.500 is a directory service recommendation that is often found in conjunction with X.400. Like X.400, the CCITT and the ISO (International Standards Organization) are responsible for the X.500 standard.

As X.500 is a recommendation for a directory service, its primary function is for storing addressing information.

What X.500 Standards Does Exchange Support?

X.500 differs significantly from X.400 in that it is a recommendation, not a standard. Very few directory systems implement X.500 due to the performance overhead that it imposes.

How Is X.500 Implemented in Microsoft Exchange?

Exchange uses an X.500-based directory structure. It uses a tree and branch structure with leaf and container objects. You can modify the properties of each object through the Exchange Administrator program. When you do so, you modify their X.500 properties as well. However, the Exchange Administrator program shields you from the complexity of the X.500 structure.

You can relate the Exchange directory hierarchy with the X.500 as shown in Table 11.3.

TABLE 11.3 EXCHANGE AND X.500

X.500	Exchange Server
Country	No direct equivalent
Organization	Organization
Organizational Unit	Site
Common Name	Exchange Server Recipient Container
Common Name	Exchange Server Recipient

Because Exchange does not support the Country field, it is not X.500-compliant. This is also why Exchange cannot natively support multiple organizations.

Tip

> If you want to see the true X.500-based structure of Microsoft Exchange, you need to start the Administrator program in RAW mode. Run the ADMIN.EXE program with the /r switch. You can now view the Exchange Directory Information Tree (DIT) in raw mode.
>
> This technique is the equivalent of configuring NT using the Registry instead of using Control Panel. So, beware!

What Is the Connection Between LDAP and X.500?

Lightweight Directory Access Protocol (LDAP) is a stripped-down version on the X.500 Directory Access Protocol. Again, because DAP would put too great a loading on a system, LDAP was developed as a way of making standard queries on an X.500-based Directory Information Tree (DIT). Exchange 5.5 supports LDAP 3.0 by default, enabling you to query an Exchange server's directory using an LDAP client.

The Site Connector and X.500

X.500 is a directory service model, not a messaging protocol. However, when you install a site connector, it creates an X.500 address space of the form that includes the Organization and Site name.

After you have installed this site connector, your Exchange Servers send messages between themselves in Message Database Encoding Format (MDBEF). MDBEF is Exchange's native message format and the MTA routes these messages according to the X.500 address space. Thus, you could say that X.500, in a slightly strange way, is the basis of Exchange's internal messaging format.

Summary

In today's lesson, you had a brief introduction to messaging protocols and the Internet. You have looked at the various services, applications, protocols, and utilities that provide the functionality of the Internet. You have also seen how Exchange uses some of these facilities to extend its range of messaging services. Finally, you looked at two non-Internet standards, the X.400 messaging and X.500 directory service, and how they are implemented within Microsoft Exchange.

To summarize the main points of today's session:

- The Internet is a group of interconnected networks using TCP/IP as its main networking protocol. You could also say that the Internet is a collection of connected intranets.

- TCP/IP is a combination of a transport and an addressing protocol that ensures reliable and timely delivery of data in a heterogeneous routed networking environment. TCP/IP is essential to the functioning of the Internet.

- DNS is a hierarchical, distributed database that maps host names to IP addresses. Without DNS, the Internet would be almost unusable.

- Microsoft Exchange can use a number of Internet protocols and services in order to function in an IP environment. Specifically, Exchange can use SMTP, ESMTP, POP3, IMAP4, LDAP, NNTP, HTTP, MIME, uuencode, SSL, and S/MIME.

- To enable Exchange's Internet options, you must be running TCP/IP. You will also need to install the Internet Mail Service and the Internet News Service, and have Internet Information Server on your network.

- Exchange can communicate with other X.400-compliant messaging systems. Exchange supports the 1984 and 1988 X.400 implementations.

11

• Exchange's internal directory structure is X.500-based and can be queried using an LDAP client. You can view the Exchange Directory Schema directly by starting the Exchange Administrator program in RAW mode.

Q&A

Q I need to connect to a foreign X.400 system but I can't install the X.400 connector. What am I doing wrong?

A You have the Standard version of Exchange 5.5, which does not include the X.400 connector. You will have to upgrade.

Q My manager wants to know if his staff will be able to use Exchange to download Internet Newsgroups. Is this possible?

A It certainly is. See Day 12, "Exchange on the Internet," for a detailed explanation on how to do this.

Q I'm trying to troubleshoot some problems with my Exchange server on a TCP/IP network. What tools can I use to help me?

A You can use utilities like IPCONFIG, PING, NETSTAT and NBTSTAT that all come with Microsoft TCP/IP. In addition, you can use applications such as Telnet to test the correct operation of the ports on the Exchange server.

Q I want to enable my users to connect to their Exchange mailboxes using POP3 over SSL. I am using Microsoft Proxy server as a firewall and I am applying a very restrictive security policy on network access. However, it appears that the users can only connect to the Exchange server using unencrypted POP3.

A In your enthusiasm to secure your system, you have probably disabled communication on port 995. If you enable this for TCP traffic, your clients should be able to connect using SSL.

Q My wife wants to buy a new PC and has seen a really good deal on a Web site. Although she can make a secure connection to the Web site, she is still worried about having her credit card details stolen. What should I tell her?

A If she is in the USA and using 128-bit encryption, you could tell her that the sun would have formed a black hole before anyone could decrypt her credit card number. If she's outside North America and using 40-bit encryption it would still quite difficult to do. If she is worried, she could always ring the company up and give the information in clear speech over the telephone. Now that's *really* secure.

Workshop

The Workshop provides two ways for you to affirm what you've learned in this lesson. The Quiz section poses questions to help you solidify your understanding of the material covered and the Exercise section provides you with experience in using what you have learned. You can find answers to the quiz questions and exercises in Appendix B, "Answers to Quiz Questions and Exercises."

Quiz

1. What is the primary function of DNS?
2. Which Internet protocols use UDP?
3. Which Internet service uses port 25?
4. What is X.400?
5. Name the Internet messaging protocols that Microsoft Exchange supports.
6. If I want to connect to a server using a UNC path (*servername**sharename*) in a TCP/IP environment, what service will I require?
7. How does Exchange use X.500?
8. What is an extranet?
9. What types of applications use ports?

11

DAY **12**

Exchange on the Internet

By Anthony Steven

Chapter Objectives

Yesterday you looked at Exchange's use of messaging protocols and integration with the Internet in general. Today you will examine in detail the components that make this possible. You will cover how to connect your system to the Internet and what to look for when choosing an Internet Service Provider.

Today's lesson covers the following topics:

- The Internet Mail Service (IMS)
- Installing the Internet Mail Service
- Routing tables and registering with DNS
- Choosing your ISP and setting up your Internet connection
- Security and the IMS

- Exchange and newsgroups
- The Internet News Service
- Installing the Internet News Service
- Configuring the Active List
- Push and pull configurations
- Troubleshooting the INS

Exchange and the Internet Mail Service

Whenever I am implementing an Exchange email system, one of the first questions that clients ask me is "Can we send mail to the Internet?" Exchange provides a built-in module that provides this functionality, in the form of the Internet Mail Service.

Basic Concepts

Before you get down to installing the Internet Mail Service (IMS), I will take you through what the IMS is and what is does.

What Is the Internet Mail Service?

The Internet Mail Service (IMS) is an optional component that adds the functionality of an RFC-compliant STMP server to Microsoft Exchange. It comes with both the Standard and Enterprise versions of Exchange 5.5 and installs using a simple wizard-based interface.

What Does It Do?

The IMS enables Exchange to send and receive messages from other SMTP servers over TCP port 25. As SMTP is an Internet standard, the IMS makes it very easy to integrate Exchange and any other SMTP servers, as you can see in Figure 12.1.

The Exchange IMS is optimized for use on the Internet and supports a large range of configuration options, including

- Scheduled dial-up connections to the Internet.
- Security on host connections, including SASL/SSL and Windows NT Challenge/Response Authentication Protocol (CHAP).
- MIME or uuencode support.
- Rich Text formatting of messages (RTF).

- Incoming only, outgoing only or bi-directional mail flow.
- ETRN and ESMTP for mail retrieval.
- Limiting of message sizes.
- Message tracking and configurable diagnostics logging.

Yes, I thought you'd probably want one of these!

FIGURE 12.1

Exchange connecting to other SMTP servers and other Exchange sites over the Internet.

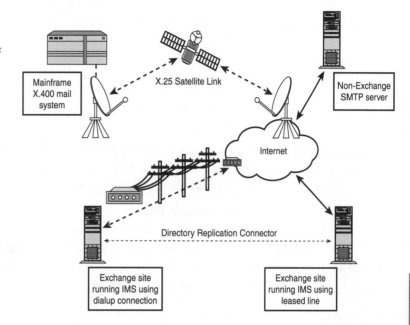

When Would I Use It?

You would use the IMS in the following circumstances:

- You want to send and receive messages from the Internet.
- You want to connect two or more Exchange sites over the Internet.
- You are supporting clients collecting mail from their mailboxes over POP3 or IMAP4.

I will be covering these areas in today's lesson. For more information about the actual process of collecting mail via POP3 or IMAP4, see Day 14, "Reading Exchange Mail with Internet Clients."

12

Installing and Configuring the Internet Mail Service

Before you can start installing the IMS, there are a number of decisions that you need to make. The first and most important question is:

Am I connecting my Exchange Server to the Internet?

If you answer "yes" to this question, you need to work your way through the next section. If you answer "no," that is, you just want to provide POP3 or IMAP4 support in a LAN/WAN environment, skip this section and move straight to the Internet Mail Service Wizard section.

Before You Install

If you are reading this section, you want to connect your Exchange server to the Internet. If this is the case, you will have to do a little bit of legwork before you can run the magical IMS Wizard.

Addressing and Domain Names   The first bit of planning you have to do has very little to do with Exchange. It is more to do with your NT domains and what your company wants to be known as on the Internet.

Choosing Your Internet Domain Name   Your company or organization will require a domain name for others to be able to communicate with you.

Taking my fictional company Universal Exports, I might decide that I would like the domain name universalexports.com. So I can check with InterNIC (www.internic.net) and use their WHOIS service to query for the name universalexports.com.

> I strongly recommend choosing a domain name that is easy to remember and relates directly to your company name. That makes it easier for people who trying to send you mail to get your address right.

Unfortunately, when searching on InterNIC's Web page, I discover that univeralexports.com has already been taken. So I could try the following options:

- universal-exports.com
- universalexports.org
- uex.com

Fortunately, universal-exports.com is not in use, so I could apply to register this for my company.

Tip

You can register domain names directly with InterNIC or via your ISP. Alternatively, companies like NetBenefit will register your domain names and manage DNS entries for you.

Domain name registration with NetBenefit costs $165 plus $83 every two years for the InterNIC charges (January 1999 prices). This includes automatic DNS registration with at least two DNS servers.

For more information, see the NetBenefit Web page on:

    www.netbenefit.com/services

Domain Names and Windows NT As you saw on Day 11, "Communication Protocols and the Internet," Windows NT domains are not yet the same as Internet domains, although this will change with Windows 2000.

Caution

Although they are valid characters in NT 4.0 domain names, don't use full stops. This is because Windows 2000 will interpret these as separate domains.

If you are setting up your NT and Exchange network from scratch with NT 4.0, my recommendation is to make your NT domain names the same as your Exchange site names. This will limit the length of your site names but should not cause any other problems. Don't forget to define your Exchange service account in a central (trusted) domain.

See Day 2, "Planning your Exchange Implementation," for more information on planning an Exchange deployment.

Defining Your Email Names A little bit of thought here really will make your life (and that of your users) significantly easier. Let's say you have decided on and registered the domain universal-exports.com.

1. Make sure that your users' email names are the same as their login names and the same as their Exchange mailbox alias names.

2. If you are integrating Exchange with Novell NetWare, you should also make their NT login names match their Novell login names.

3. If your company policy specifies something different, then change the policy! It will be worth it in the end.

12

Why? Well, for several reasons.

1. Your users only have to remember one thing. The name they log in with in the morning. So if a user logs in to his workstation as fredbloggs, his email address is fredbloggs@universal-exports.com. This is very useful when he passes his email addresses on to clients.

2. When you are creating a new user, Exchange will create an alias name the same as her login name. This alias then becomes her email name. So when you add a new user, her login name becomes her alias name which becomes her email name. This now fits in nicely with your naming convention.

3. If you normally create new users using the Exchange Administrator, you can get a similar result. Configure Exchange to create alias names that match your company's username standards. Do this by configuring Options in Exchange Administrator so that the alias name generation string is (for example) %First%Last (or whatever combination will generate your company's standard login name). Figure 12.2 shows the options screen. Assuming you have already set the site SMTP address (from the Addressing object in the Configuration Container in Exchange Administrator) to be universal-exports.com, when the Exchange Administrator automatically generates a matching NT account this will match the alias name. The email name will now be FredBloggs@universal-exports.com and the new user will log on as FredBloggs. This will apply to all users that you subsequently create.

FIGURE 12.2

The Options dialog in Exchange Administrator lets you configure a custom scheme for auto-generating alias (and hence email) names.

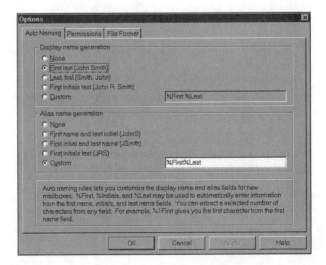

4. It will save time if you are doing a bulk import of users into Exchange from Windows NT, Novell NetWare, or any other system. You don't have to get someone to go through the entire list of imported names and change the aliases to something else. Like one of my clients had to.

Now that you have a company domain name and a policy on email/login names, you are ready to choose an Internet Service Provider.

Setting up Internet Mail with an Internet Service Provider

Note Even if you already have a connection to an ISP, you will need to review this section. Some ISPs, especially the smaller ones or those concentrating in the dial-up (domestic) market are not very good at supporting Exchange. This might be a good time to review your arrangements with your current ISP.

Choosing Your Connection Type If you do not already have a connection to an ISP, you will need to consider the type of link that you want. The options are as shown in Table 12.1.

TABLE 12.1 CONNECTING TO THE INTERNET

Method	Setup Cost	Running Cost	Speed	Usage
Dial-Up (PSTN)	Low	Variable	33.6Kbps	Light
Dial-Up (ISDN)	Medium	Variable	64Kbps	Light–Medium
DOD ISDN	Medium–High	Variable	64/128Kbps	Medium
Cable Modems	Low	Low	Variable	Medium
ADSL	Medium	Variable	up to 5Mbs	Medium–Heavy
Leased Line	High	Fixed	64KB and faster	Heavy

Here it will be a question of looking at the size of your organization and calculating the amount of traffic you are likely to be sending and receiving from the Internet.

Note If you want to host your own Web servers, you will need to have a permanent connection to the Internet. This will also give you the ability to run your own DNS server. Your ISP will be able to advise you on this.

12

For small companies, (fewer than 20 users), you will probably find that a dial-up connection is satisfactory. This is the minimum cost option and your only variable costs will be the price of the (local) phone calls to your ISP. However, if your users need access to the World Wide Web over this dial-up connection, you may need to consider ISDN, or the new kid on the block, ADSL.

If you have cable in your area, you may want to check out your local cable operator's terms and conditions for connection to the Internet as well. Cable connections can vary in speed, as the link speed usually changes, depending on how many users are connected. You will need a cable modem and driver software from your ISP.

For slightly larger sites (10–50 users), a dial-up ISDN line may be the answer. However, your local telephone company will need to install the ISDN line, which may not be possible in rural areas.

Note

> I discussed Multilink (multiple modems using more than one telephone line) with RAS in yesterday's lesson. However, this is normally not an option in this case as very few ISPs support it.

With 25–100 users, some form of ISDN Dial on Demand (DOD) line will be necessary. Here you will rent an ISDN router from your ISP but you will not have the fixed overhead of a permanent connection. However, the variable nature of your ISDN charges will make budgeting difficult. DOD routers give much better response to requests for Web pages by users than dial-up ISDN.

For 50 users and higher or if you have a very heavy Internet usage, you will have to look at a permanent connection. If you choose this option, your budgeting becomes much easier as you will only have the fixed connection charge plus the rental of the ISPs router. You also have the flexibility to host your own Web servers.

Adaptive Digital Subscriber Line (ADSL) is the upstart, threatening to eclipse most other connection methods. Offering speeds of up to 5Mbps, it works by using specialized modems over standard copper wire telephone lines. One modem is at your site, the other at the telephone company's switchboard. The modem at the switchboard then connects to a standard Internet router. Telephone companies like it because it doesn't involve installing new switching equipment. Speak to your local telephone company about the availability of ADSL.

Having decided on your choice of connection method, you are now ready to start interviewing ISPs.

Choosing Your ISP   You have considerable choice when selecting an ISP, so it makes sense to ensure that you find one that will support your organization properly. Here is a list of questions for you to ask your potential ISP. Note that this list is not necessarily exhaustive, depending on your circumstances.

General Questions for Your ISP   The questions you need to ask your ISP are slightly different, depending on whether you have a leased line or not. If you have any form of dial-up access, from a modem over the telephone network to Dial-on-Demand ISDN, your ISP must provide some form of store-and-forward facilities for your email.

There is another handy list in the section "Installing the IMS with a Dialup Connection Checklist" later in the lesson.

- Are you familiar with Microsoft Exchange? If your prospective ISP answers "No" or "What's Microsoft Exchange?" (yes, I've heard this one before), I would recommend that you look elsewhere.
- Can you register my domain name for me, how much will it cost to register, and what is the yearly renewal fee?
- Will you handle the DNS registrations?
- Will you give us at least one fixed Class C IP address?

Questions with Dial-Up Access

- Is your POP (point of presence) a local telephone call?
- Can you provide store-and-forward facilities for my mail?
- Do your SMTP servers support ESMTP and ETRN or TURN? (If they start muttering darkly about "Everyone else uses POP3," they probably aren't right for you.)
- Do your dial-up servers support encryption or authentication? (This isn't essential but is a useful facility if they have it.)

Questions with Leased Lines

- How much will a leased line cost? Does that include renting the hardware?
- How much will it cost to upgrade to the next level of bandwidth?
- How long will it take to have the line put in?
- What are the levels of support that you offer, and do you have a Quality of Service (QOS) guarantee?

Assuming you get satisfactory answers to all these questions and have signed the contract on the dotted line, you will now need to exchange some information with your ISP.

12

You must tell them

- The domain name you want to register (such as `universal-exports.com`).
- The host name of your Exchange Server (such as `exchange.universal.com`).

They will need to tell you the following information. Note that the last two items usually only apply to dial-up connections:

- The IP address(es) and subnet mask that they have assigned to you.
- The IP addresses of their primary and secondary DNS servers.
- The IP address or host names of their SMTP servers, and whether you are to use different IP addresses for sending and receiving mail.
- What form of authentication or encryption (if any) they support on their SMTP hosts.
- With a dial-up connection, the telephone number of their local POP (this may be a national cheap rate number).
- Whether their SMTP servers support ESMTP, ETRN, or TURN.

Registering with DNS   Unless you are managing your own DNS server, you will need to register your Exchange server with the Internet DNS. Your ISP will do this for you and will need to add two or three records.

Let's say your company is universal-exports.com and your Exchange server has the somewhat unimaginative host name of Exchange. Your ISP has issued you with the IP address 195.34.11.2 and a subnet mask of 255.255.255.0. Your ISP's SMTP server offers store-and-forward, its IP address is 195.1.10.2, and its host name is mail.isp.net.

The records your ISP will have to enter in DNS are as follows:

A		`exchange.universal-exports.com`	195.34.11.2
MX	10	`universal-exports.com`	`exchange. univeral -exports.com`
MX	20	`universal-exports.com`	mail.isp.net

The first record is an address or A record for your mail server. This will enable other hosts on the Internet (such as SMTP servers) to resolve the host name for your mail server to its IP address. The next two records are the MX or Mail Exchanger records. These point to the name of the host (or hosts) that receive mail for your domain.

The figures 10 and 20 are preference values. These values indicate in which order to select servers for mail delivery to your domain. In this case, if a user on the Internet sends you an email, her company's SMTP server will look in DNS for an MX record corresponding to your domain. As there are two MX records, it will attempt to send the message to the server with the lowest preference value. In the example here, all mail will go to exchange.universal-exports.com. If the server with the lowest preference value is offline, then the sending SMTP server will attempt to deliver to the server with the next highest preference value. In this case, the mail will go to my ISP's SMTP server.

If you have a dial-up connection, you will not have an MX entry for your Exchange server. This is because the mail for your company will go to your ISP's SMTP server, and your Exchange server will collect it when it dials in.

Installing Remote Access Client   If you are using dial-up access with PSTN or ISDN, you will need to install the RAS client on your network. For details on installing the RAS client, see Appendix A.

After you have installed the RAS client, you will need to create a phone book entry for your ISP's POP, as shown in Figure 12.3.

FIGURE 12.3

Here you see a phone book entry for an ISP's POP using Remote Access Client.

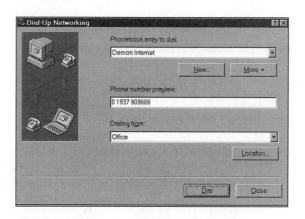

12

The Exchange Server documentation gives useful help on carrying out these tasks.

The Internet Mail Service Wizard

OK, then. You have decided on an Internet domain name, selected a connection method, chosen an ISP, and talked to them about IP addresses, host names, DNS, and so on. Your ISP has installed your routers and the leased line. Alternatively, you have configured and tested dial-up access to your ISP. You are now ready to install the Internet Mail Service.

Starting the Wizard   One of the good things about the Internet Mail Service is that
you don't need the Exchange CD to install it. You do it through the Internet Mail Wizard.

1. Start Exchange Administrator. Select the File menu, choose New Other, and then
   click on Internet Mail Service.

2. You may see a prompt to switch to the Connections Container. Click Yes.

3. The Internet Mail Wizard will start. Select Next to continue.

4. You will see a list of tasks to do as shown in Figure 12.4. If you carried out all the
   previous steps, you should have already done all of these. Select Next to continue.

FIGURE 12.4

*You've done all of
these already!*

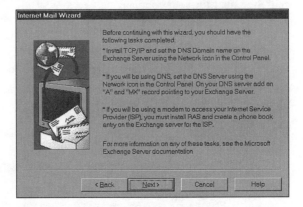

5. The next screen prompts you to select the server that will run the IMS. You have
   the additional option to check the box if you are going through a dial-up
   connection. Figure 12.5 shows this screen.

FIGURE 12.5

*Select the server and
check the box for a
dial-up connection if
necessary.*

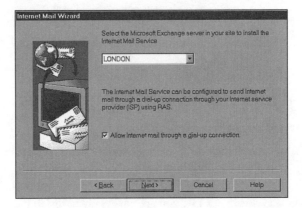

Note

Dial on Demand ISDN acts like a permanent connection—you do not check the box for dial-up access. However, you do select it if you are using an ISDN terminal adapter (modem).

With DOD ISDN, you will still need to have store-and-forward of your mail at your ISP because you will not actually be online permanently. Your Exchange server will dial your ISP when it has mail to deliver.

6. The next screen that you see will depend on whether you checked the box for a dial-up connection. If you did check the box, you will see a screen like Figure 12.6, asking you to select the RAS phone book entry for your ISP.

FIGURE 12.6

If you checked the box for dial-up access, you can now choose your phone book entry for use with the IMS.

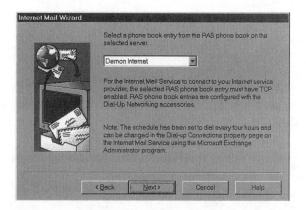

12

Tip

Make sure you define and test your RAS connection to your ISP before you attempt to use it with the IMS. The RAS connection should be capable of automatically dialing up your ISP, connecting and validating without any intervention.

7. The next screen (see Figure 12.7) appears whether you selected the box for dial-up access or not. Here you specify whether you want your system to reroute mail. Select Yes if you want to use your system with POP3 or IMAP4. Select No if you just use Exchange to route mail and your clients do not connect to this host to deliver SMTP mail.

FIGURE 12.7

*Select Yes for
POP3/IMAP4 support,
and No for normal use.*

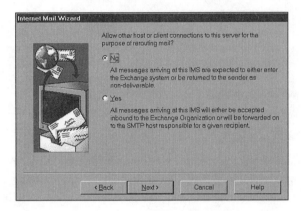

8. Next, you specify where you want to send your outgoing mail. If you have a permanent connection, you will probably use DNS. This means that your Exchange server will use DNS to look up the MX records of the domains to which it wants to deliver mail. If you have a dial-up account, you will usually send mail to your ISP's SMTP server, which will then route your mail. The "typical" option will change, depending on what sort of connection you have chosen. Figure 12.8 shows the options.

FIGURE 12.8

*You can choose DNS to
reroute mail or have it
all delivered to a spe-
cific host.*

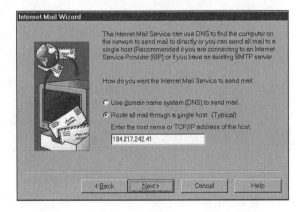

Note   You can enter either a host name or an IP address as a mail delivery destination, for example mail.post.isp.net or 131.109.4.12. It depends on which is less likely to change—IP addresses or host names.

9. The next screen allows you to select which mail addresses this IMS will deliver to. If you want to send mail to the Internet, select all mail addresses. If you only want to use the Internet to send mail to users at another Exchange site, select the "particular set of addresses" option. After you have installed the IMS, you will be able to specify the specific addresses later. See "Installing the IMS with a Dialup Connection Checklist" later in this lesson.

10. Now you can set the SMTP site address that your IMS uses. By default this will be @`site`.`organization`.com. You can change it here or in the Site Addressing tab on the Site Addressing object in your Configuration Container in Exchange Administrator. I will cover this procedure later. Enter your address in the box as shown in Figure 12.9.

FIGURE 12.9

Change this address to the domain name of your site.

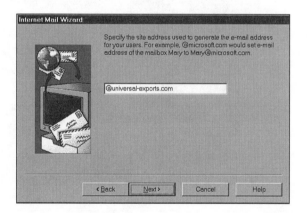

12

11. Bored yet? Only a few more screens to go! Next, you must select a mailbox to receive non-delivery messages. By default, the system will use the Administrator mailbox. However, you can choose another mailbox at this point, as shown in Figure 12.10.

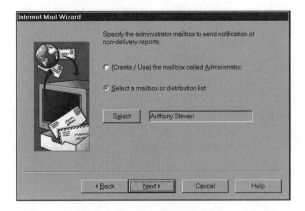

Figure 12.10

Choose a mailbox to receive non-delivery reports.

12. To prevent just anyone adding Internet Mail Services, you have to validate the process by knowing the service account password. Enter the password in the box as per Figure 12.11.

Figure 12.11

Enter the Service Account password to continue.

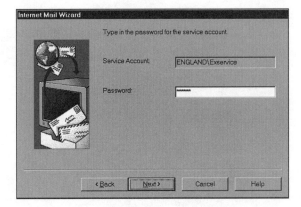

Caution

If you find that the account showing in this box is your Administrator account, you have not set up Exchange properly. You need to create an Exchange service account as described on Day 3, "Setting Up Exchange Server," and then change all the Exchange services (using Control Panel) to start using this new account.

The new account must be a member of Domain Admins and have the following user rights: Log on as a Service, Act as Part of the Operating System, and Restore Files and Directories. It also needs to have Service Account Admin permission at the Organization, Site, and Configuration Container level. Got that?

13. That's it! Click Finish to install and start the Internet Mail Service.

Tip After you have installed the IMS, I recommend that you run Performance Optimizer. In fact, so would Exchange. Which is why it tells you to.

Configuring the Service

Now that you have installed the IMS, you should carry out any further configuration via the Internet Mail Service object. I have limited my comments to the areas that are important for a typical configuration. The Help system provided with Exchange is very detailed should you need further assistance.

Start Exchange Administrator, and select your site in the left pane. Double-click on your site and in the left pane, you should see the Configuration container. Click on this object and now look in the right pane. There you will see an icon labeled Connections. Double-click on the Connections icon and you should now see the Internet Mail Service. Double-click on the IMS icon to see the properties of this object. You will now be able to configure the following items.

General Tab On the General tab (see Figure 12.12) you can limit the message size through this connector. This applies both to incoming and outgoing messages.

FIGURE 12.12

The General tab allows you to limit message sizes.

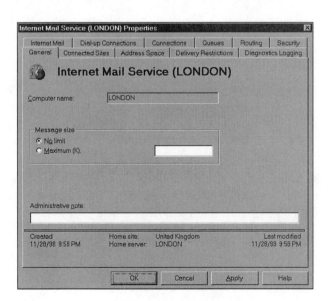

Caution Do not set a message size limit if you are using the IMS to connect two sites across the Internet.

Connected Sites Tab   Use the Connected Sites tab to make your Exchange system aware of other Exchange Sites. You will need to do this if you are connecting sites across the Internet. After you have done this you can then add a Directory Replication Connector as described on Day 5, "Working with Multiple Sites."

To connect your Exchange sites, you need to specify an Organization name (the default is your organization) and a Site name (the other site). On the Routing Address tab you now put the address type (normally SMTP but it could be X.400 or MS Mail) and address of the other site (*othersite*.com). Figure 12.13 shows you how.

FIGURE 12.13

The Connected Sites tab allows you to set up links to other Exchange sites over the Internet Mail Connector.

Address Space Tab   This tab will now show the Address space for this connector. This is of the form SMTP, email domain "*" (such as all addresses) and a cost value of 1. Figure 12.14 shows the Address Space tab.

FIGURE 12.14

You can define additional address spaces such as MS Mail or X.400 using the Address Space tab.

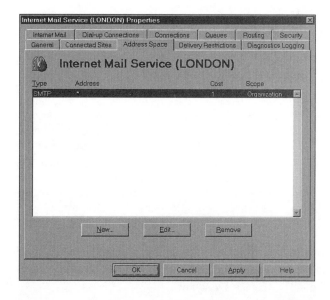

To restrict this IMS connector to delivering mail to a specific set of addresses, edit the default entry and change the * to `deliverysite.com`, where `deliverysite` is the address of the intended delivery site. Figure 12.15 shows this configured for the site `newengland.universal-exports.com`.

FIGURE 12.15

Here I am adding the address of a specified remote Exchange site (`newengland.universal-exports.com`).

12

You can also add new address types such as MS Mail (to connect to an MS Mail postoffice over the Internet) or X.400 (to route to X.400-based systems).

> **Note**
>
> You can edit any of the address spaces when you create them and make them effective for the Organization, Site, or Location through the Restrictions tab. If you define an address space and give it a restriction of "This Site," the address space will only apply to the site in which you created the IMS. Other sites will not be able to route their mail via this connector.
>
> You can use this in complex WAN/LAN environments with multiple connections to the Internet. This will allow you to control costs and to prevent users from sending mail across connectors in other sites.

Delivery Restrictions Tab The Delivery Restrictions tab enables you to specify which users can and can't send mail via this IMS. Any bad boys or girls go on the list on the right. Figure 12.16 shows you how.

FIGURE 12.16

Anyone who annoys you goes on the right-hand list. If everyone has annoyed you, put yourself on the left-hand list.

> **Caution**
>
> If you put someone in the list on the left, *only* that person can send mail over the IMS. Exclude individuals by putting them in the list on the right. The left-hand list is more exclusive!

Note   Delivery restrictions only apply to outgoing mail.

Diagnostics Logging Tab   Use this tab to set up diagnostic logging on the Internet Mail Connector. Increase values to maximum if you are having problems with the IMS, as shown in Figure 12.17. The IMS will now log events in the Applications log in Event Viewer. See "Some Other Troubleshooting Techniques" later in this chapter for more information.

FIGURE 12.17

Increase logging levels to maximum if you are having problems with the IMS.

Caution   You should not leave the diagnostics logging levels at maximum during normal operation; the performance of the IMS will suffer.

Internet Mail Tab   This tab allows you to configure a number of options, including the administrator's mailbox and various messaging features, as shown in Figure 12.18.

Administrator's Mailbox   Change the mailbox and the type of notifications received. If you are having problems, increase the notification levels.

Figure 12.18

The Internet Mail tab gives a range of message configuration options.

Message Content   This allows you to set the type of content in the messages your Exchange server sends. You can select MIME or uuencoded attachments, different character sets, and S/MIME support. The Advanced options enable you to send messages that have Rich Text Formatting (RTF) in them. This is very useful if you are sending messages to another Exchange server, as your users will be able to use different colors and fonts, thus making their messages look prettier. It also saves you from messing around with bold text.

Disabling Automatic Replies to the Internet is generally a good idea. After all, if you send people messages over the Internet, you probably aren't that bothered if they aren't in.

You can set these options by Internet Domain. For example, if you send email to another-company.com and you know that they use Microsoft Exchange, you can add that domain and specify that they will always have RTF formatted mail. All other domains can have normal SMTP mail.

Message Tracking   Check this box if you want to track which users are sending messages over this IMS. See Day 8, "Troubleshooting Exchange," for more information on message tracking.

Dial-Up Connections Tab   The Dial-Up Connections tab specifies which RAS client entry your IMS will use, how often it connects, from where it retrieves mail, and how it logs on. Figure 12.19 shows the Dial-Up Connections tab.

FIGURE 12.19

The Dial-Up Connections tab enables you to config-ure how often you dial into your ISP and specify mail retrieval methods.

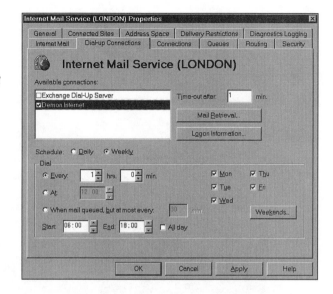

Available Connections Select the RAS phone book entry that you are going to use to connect to your ISP. If you can't see any entries in here, you need to add an address book entry through dial-up networking. See Day 7, "Configuring the Exchange Client," to learn how to add an address book entry.

Tip

Test your RAS connections first to ensure that they can connect without manual intervention and that you are getting the maximum download speed.

12

Mail Retrieval This button gives you access to options for retrieving mail. Here you can specify ETRN, TURN, a custom retrieval command, or not to send a retrieval com-mand. You only need to do this if you are using a dial-up connection because your Exchange SMTP server will not be online all the time.

You can also specify the domain names for which you want to retrieve mail. For exam-ple, if you have just migrated from a previous mail system or Internet domain name, you would want to pick up mail addressed to the old domain name as well as the new. Let's say you used to be prince.com and now you want to be known as squiggle.com, then you could add both prince.com and squiggle.com to your domain names in the dialog box in Figure 12.20. Your IMS would then collect mail for either system when it dials in.

FIGURE 12.20

Here you can specify how you will retrieve your mail.

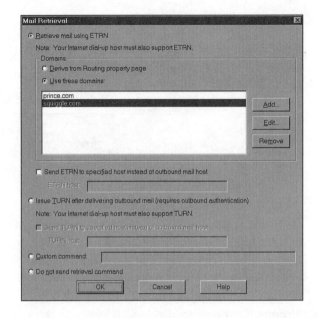

> **Note**
>
> You need to talk to your ISP to find out which method you should use to retrieve mail from its mail servers. You will need this to configure the settings in Figure 12.20. Again, if it expects you to use Exchange as a POP3 client, this could be a good indication that this particular ISP doesn't understand Exchange.

Use the Logon Information tab to enter your logon credentials automatically when your dial-up connection logs onto your ISP. This will include your username and password. You can usually leave the domain name blank and, no, it's not your NT domain. Again, talk to your ISP if you need any help with automating your dial-up logons.

> **Tip**
>
> You can also use a post-connection script to authenticate to your ISP. However, it is slower, less secure, and definitely not sophisticated. You cannot use both logon credentials *and* a post-connection script. You will need to talk to your ISP about connecting via a script.

> **Caution**
>
> If you change your password for your dial-up account to your ISP, don't forget to change it here as well, or else your IMS will stop working.

Dial Dial gives you control over how often your system dials in to collect mail. Your options are as follows:

- Dial every few hours or minutes according to the schedule you set.
- Dial at a specific time every day.
- Dial whenever there is mail waiting, but if you have not dialed up in the last 30 minutes (or however many minutes you specify).
- Whether these settings apply for a complete 24-hour day or only between specific hours.

So what do these all mean and how should you apply them? It really depends on how quickly your company wants to deliver Internet mail balanced against how much it is prepared to pay for the privilege.

SCHEDULING THE INTERNET MAIL SERVICE

One of the problems with using dial-on-demand ISDN is that if anyone sends a message to the Internet, the IMS will kick the DOD link into action. This can mean that your link to your ISP is constantly in use, which can get very expensive.

The solution for this is to use the Scheduler service to start and stop the IMS. You can schedule commands using the AT command, WinAT (comes with the NT Resource Kit) or Command Scheduler.

An example of how to use AT to stop and start the IMS is as follows. Enter each command separately at a command prompt.

```
AT \\SERVERNAME 10:00 "STARTIMS.BAT"
AT \\SERVERNAME 10:10 "STOPIMS.BAT"
```

SERVERNAME is the name of your Exchange server, and STARTIMS.BAT and STOPIMS.BAT have the following line of code:

```
NET START (or STOP) "Microsoft Exchange Internet Mail Service"
```

This example will start the Internet Mail Service at 10:00 and stop it at 10:10. You would set up multiple entries to start and stop the service on a regular basis.

Note

If you have a dedicated link or dial on demand ISDN, these settings do not apply, as your IMS will deliver any queued mail immediately. In this case, you can control message delivery by using the AT command to stop and start the Internet Mail Service. See the sidebar on Scheduling the Internet Mail Service.

If you work for a commercial business, it usually depends who you ask.

12

Ask the CEO how he wants his mail sent to the Internet and my guess is the answer will probably be "Immediately!" If so, you want to use the setting that delivers when mail is waiting, but not more often than every 30 minutes or so. You could make it fewer than 30 minutes, but bear in mind that if you have a lot of Internet traffic your system could be dialing in very frequently. If you use the default 30 minutes setting, Internet mail should reach its recipient on the Internet within an hour of the user clicking the Send button.

If you ask an accountant the same question, she will probably say "As cheaply as possible." Therefore, if you work for an organization that has limited finances, you may want to consider connecting only once a day. You can save some more money by making that connection happen in the evening when the telephone rates are cheaper.

If your outgoing mail is irregular or very low volume, you should look at connecting according to a regular schedule, like every two hours or so. This way you will deliver any mail that is queued to go out and pick up any messages waiting to come in. However, the IMS will still check for incoming mail on a regular basis even if nothing is queued to go out.

 Tip

> If your Internet traffic is very low, don't forget to reduce the connection time to 1 minute. The IMS will still deliver your mail but will wait for one minute after the delivery has finished and then end the connection.

If your organization works 24 hours a day, check the All Day option. Otherwise, it makes sense to limit the hours that the IMS will send mail.

Use the Weekly settings for greater control over when the IMS delivers mail over the weekend. If you select the Weekly option you can select which weekdays you will send mail and how often the IMS sends mail on Saturdays and Sundays. The Weekends button lets you specify a different connection style and frequency during the weekend or even configure Exchange so it doesn't deliver mail at all on Saturdays and Sundays.

Connections Tab   The Connections tab is another important tab that enables you to control how the IMS delivers mail to your ISP. These settings, as shown in Figure 12.21, apply both to dial-up and to leased line connections.

Transfer Mode   These four choices control whether this IMS is set up for two-way traffic (outbound and inbound), mail collection only (inbound), mail delivery only (outbound), or neither. In normal operation, you would use the same IMS for outbound and inbound mail delivery. However, if you have a site where there is very heavy Internet email traffic, you may need to install dedicated IMS connectors to handle inbound and outbound traffic separately.

FIGURE 12.21

The Connections tab allows you to specify transfer modes, delivery, security, and message queue options.

> **Note**
>
> If you want to use separate IMS connectors for incoming and outgoing mail, you must install them on separate servers.

The None (Flush Queues) option is where you just want the IMS to deliver any pending messages, not to collect or receive any.

Message Delivery How you configure this option depends on what type of connection system you are using:

- If you have a permanent connection to your ISP, use DNS.
- If you are using a dial-up connection, you will probably forward all messages to a specific host.

Here you have the option to specify a dial-up connection to deliver mail. Note that this means that you can have a different dial-up connection to deliver mail from the one you use to send mail. Use this in conjunction with an incoming or outgoing only Internet Mail Service, or where your ISP has different SMTP servers for delivery and collection.

Notice the button to specify delivery options by email domain. The options here mean that you can have a different delivery system for a specific domain. You can even get your IMS to hold mail for a particular domain and then the SMTP server for that domain will connect to your Exchange server and use ETRN to retrieve mail.

12

Accept Connections   Here you can control which hosts can connect to your Exchange server. After all, you probably don't want Uncle Tom Cobbleigh and all connecting to port 25 on your server and sending you all sorts of spoof email. Because SMTP is not secure, you will need to control which hosts or clients can connect to your IMS. You can do this in a number of ways:

- Specify which machines can connect by IP address using the Specify by Host button. You will probably use this to restrict incoming connections to your SMTP server to the IP address of your ISP's mail server.

- Prevent hosts from connecting unless they use Authentication, Encryption, or both. This is essential if your clients are using POP3 and SMTP to collect and deliver their mail.

- A combination of both these methods. You might use this if you have a limited number of POP3 clients connecting over the Internet or your ISP supports Microsoft encryption and authentication.

A useful improvement with Exchange Service Pack One is the ability to reject mail by domain or username at the Internet Mail Service level. Click on the Message Filtering button and add the names of the domains or users who are not welcome on your server. An option is to put their mail into a directory called Turf. No, I don't know why it's called "Turf" either. Maybe it's because they are being turfed out, like at a nightclub.

Service Message Queues   This section deals with how often the IMS will attempt to deliver a message. The default retry intervals are fifteen minutes, thirty minutes, and one hour and four hours, after which the IMS will retry every four hours until the message is delivered or returned as undeliverable.

The Time-Outs button is for adjusting the time-out limits for different message types. Exchange has three mail priorities–normal, urgent, and low. If you send a normal priority message the IMS will return the message as non-deliverable after 48 hours of attempted delivery. For urgent messages, this drops to twenty-four hours but low priority messages can hang around for three days before the IMS gives up on them.

During this time, you can configure notifications of non-delivery by email as shown in Figure 12.22. By default, this is active for urgent mail only and the IMS will generate a notification every four hours that the mail remains in the queue. If you want to, you can add notifications for normal and low priority mail as well.

FIGURE 12.22

The time-outs dialog gives you control over when undeliverable mail returns to its originator and whether the IMS sends repeated notifications of non-delivery.

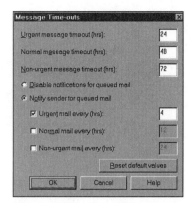

Client Mail Submission   The two final options on this tab are of importance if you have clients using POP3 to connect to their mailboxes. Both these options will only work if you have also specified that hosts must use authentication or encryption to connect in the Accept Connections section.

Clients can only submit if homed on this server restricts incoming SMTP connections to those with mailboxes on this machine. The authentication account matching submission address option checks to see that the client's logon account matches the account in the From: field of their message.

Queues Tab   The Queues tab shows you how many messages are currently queued in four stages of the Internet Mail Service. These four areas are:

- Outbound messages awaiting delivery (the most useful).
- Outbound messages awaiting conversion (not so useful).
- Inbound messages awaiting delivery (not useful).
- Inbound messages awaiting conversion (not at all useful).

The reason behind my assessment of the relative usefulness of the various queues is that you hardly ever see anything in the last three queues. But you will often see messages in the outbound messages queue. If you have a dial-up link to your ISP, you will quite often see messages here between connection attempts. However, if you have a leased line, any messages remaining in this queue normally indicate problems.

Details   The Details button lets you see information about a message in the queue, such as its originator, destination host, recipients, message size, and submit time. Use this if you think there are problems with mail delivery—if the Next Retry Time is not immediate, the message has already failed a delivery attempt.

12

> **Tip**
>
> When you install Microsoft Exchange, you get a set of preconfigured Performance Monitor graphs. One of these is Microsoft Exchange Server IMS Queues and shows you whether any messages are queued up for delivery. Click Start, Programs and click on Microsoft Exchange. You will now see a start menu item called Microsoft Exchange Server IMS Queues. Click on this to run the preconfigured performance monitor graph.

Refresh   This refreshes the queue and removes any recently delivered messages that are still showing in the queue.

Delete   You can delete messages out of any of the queues if you need to clear a backlog or you want to stop a message going out.

Retry Now   This button will force a delivery attempt. You could use this if you have just repaired a failed network connection and you want to accelerate the delivery of messages in the IMS queue.

Routing Tab   The Routing tab enables you to specify what routing your Exchange server will carry out on incoming messages.

If you want to configure support for POP3 or IMAP4 mailboxes you must re-route incoming mail. The normal routing entry is that your site SMTP address (*yoursite.yourcompany*.com) routes to <inbound>.

This means that a message arriving from a POP3 client addressed to a user on that server will not be sent to the Internet but will be re-routed internally by Exchange. The Routing tab is shown in Figure 12.23.

Routing Restrictions   This button gives you control over exactly which clients can connect to your Exchange server via POP3 or IMAP4 and relay messages to users outside your organization. Your choices are

- Users who authenticate successfully.
- Users connecting from a specified IP address.
- Users connecting to a specified internal IP address.

This last option is to cater for multihomed servers with more than one network card. Normally you would enable connections from the network card that is on your internal network.

If you have clients using POP3 or IMAP4 and connecting over the Internet, enter their details in the section on hosts and clients with these IP addresses. By the way, "routing" is pronounced "rooting," not "rowting."

FIGURE 12.23

The Routing tab con-trols the routing of incoming traffic by domain.

FIGURE 12.23

The Routing tab con-trols the routing of incoming traffic by domain.

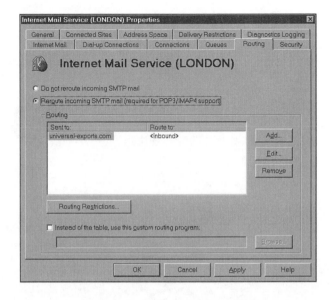

Security Tab   The Security tab, shown in Figure 12.24, gives you control over encryption methods on your outgoing connections to other Exchange or non-Exchange SMTP servers. Use this tab to configure authentication and encryption to another Exchange site. You should definitely do this when you are using the Internet Mail Service as a site connector.

FIGURE 12.24

The Security tab lets you apply encryption or authentication on your connections to remote domains.

12

To get this system working, the server that you are authenticating to must be available on the Internet; otherwise, you will not be able to negotiate the connection.

Click the Add button to add a new Internet domain, and then configure the security settings for that domain. Figure 12.25 shows you how.

FIGURE 12.25

Use this dialog to configure outbound security by domain.

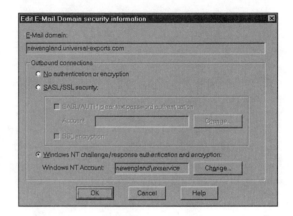

You have a choice of security or authentication methods:

- No security or encryption.
- SASL or SSL encryption with optional authentication to an account on the remote server. This uses ESMTP extensions for logging on.
- Windows NT Challenge/Response. This uses NT's Challenge authentication protocol and data encryption. This should be your choice for Exchange to Exchange connections.

Phew! Have you got all of those? Good. Remember that if you change any settings on the IMS you will probably have to stop and restart the IMS service. A dialog box will prompt you if this is the case.

Configuring Addressing

Configuring Addressing deals with issues like your site SMTP address and regeneration of the routing tables.

The Site Address is the SMTP address that people in other organizations will use when they want to send mail to you. It applies to your Exchange site and you configure this through the Site Addressing Object. Routing tables govern where Exchange sends messages with specific message formats, such as X.400, MS Mail, SMTP, and so on. Let's look at these now.

Site Addressing

When you installed Exchange, the setup routine created a default SMTP site address in the form *@sitename.organizationname.com*. When you add a new mailbox, you will find that this automatically generates an SMTP email address of *aliasname@sitename.organizationname.com*.

However, you may have chosen an Internet domain name that is totally different, such as *cuddlybunnies.co.us*, and will want your email addresses to reflect this. Hence, you may find that you need to change the default SMTP address for your Exchange site.

To do this, start Exchange Administrator and select your site in the left pane. Double-click on the Configuration container in the right pane and you will see a list of the objects in that container. Double-click on the Site Addressing object and then select the Site Addressing tab, as shown in Figure 12.26.

FIGURE 12.26

You can change your organization's SMTP address through the Site Addressing object in Exchange Administrator.

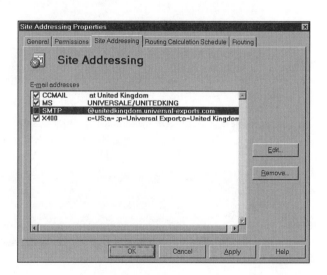

Select the SMTP address and click Edit. You can now change the site address to your Internet domain name (don't forget to keep the @ symbol) and click OK. If you now click Apply or OK on the Site Addressing object, a prompt will appear, informing you that a process will update the SMTP addresses of all your mailboxes. Click Yes to let that go ahead.

Having done this, if you now go to your site recipients container, double-click on a mailbox and select the Email Addresses tab, you will see that the mailbox SMTP address matches the site SMTP address, as shown in Figure 12.27.

12

FIGURE 12.27

Your mailboxes now have the new site SMTP address.

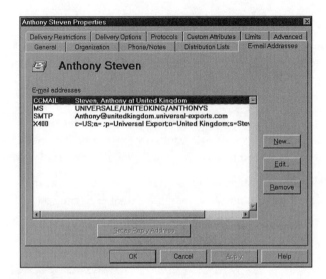

The Routing Tables

After you have installed your IMS, Exchange will update its routing tables to include the new address space for this connector.

To view the routing tables, select the Site Addressing object as you did previously but, this time, click on the Routing tab. You will see the dialog box in Figure 12.28.

FIGURE 12.28

The installation of the IMS has added a route for SMTP mail to this site.

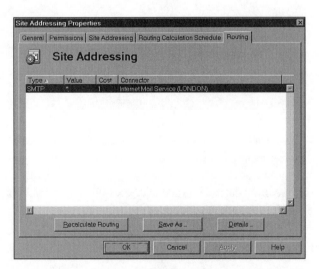

Here you can see a routing address for SMTP mail—in this case, all SMTP mail (*) is routed via the Internet Mail Service. Remember that if you had configured the IMS to route to only one domain, this routing address entry would reflect that. To add other routes to your Internet Mail Service, see the IMS "Routing Tab" section earlier in the lesson.

Note

You can force an update of the routing tables by clicking the Recalculate Routing button. However, if you have several sites, it will take a few minutes for this new routing information to reach all your sites.

Alternate Addressing

You can configure alternate addressing at a mailbox level by adding further SMTP addresses to individual mailboxes. Look back at Figure 12.27. Clicking on the Add button will allow you to select a new address type. Select Internet Address and click OK. You can now enter the new email address.

Configuring a Dial-Up Connection for Internet Mail

You have already looked at some of the requirements for using a dial-up connection. Now I will discuss some of the other considerations that you will need to decide on before you can implement your dial-up solution.

SMTP Server or POP3 Client?

When you choose your ISP, it is very important that it is clear in your own mind exactly what Exchange server is. It is an industry-leading robust scalable messaging platform with the option to add a fully featured SMTP server in the form of the IMS. It is not a client application for collecting mail from ISPs. Thus when you are talking to your prospective ISP, you should leave them in no doubt about the type of connection that you require:

SMTP NOT POP3!

Some ISPs provide SMTP for mail delivery only and require you to use POP3 to collect mail. Avoid these like the plague. You did not spend thousands of dollars on an Exchange messaging system and install a powerful SMTP server to have it behave like a POP3 client. A useful analogy is this—you can hammer in a nail with a Pentax 35mm SLR camera. But you probably wouldn't want to.

See Day 11 for more information on POP3.

12

For further information on configuring your IMS to collect SMTP mail, see the "Connections Tab" section earlier in the lesson.

Store-and-Forward

You need an ISP that can offer some form of store-and-forward facility. Remember that I discussed on Day 11 how SMTP expects instant delivery to other SMTP servers. This is fine if you have a leased line but doesn't work if you are dialing in. If you didn't have some form of store-and-forward facility, you would only receive messages that arrived while you were actually connected.

ESMTP and ETRN

ESMTP was introduced to overcome the limitations of SMTP, offering the facility called store-and-forward, as you saw on Day 11. With ETRN (Extended TURN) you can say to an ESMTP server "I'm here now so can I have my mail please..."

To configure ESMTP and ETRN support, look at the Dial-Up Connections tab covered previously. However, you need to know what ESTMP support your ISP can offer you.

Installing the IMS with a Dialup Connection Checklist

To help you with getting your dial-up connections configured, here is a handy to-do list:

Note | Your ISP should provide you with most of this information automatically.

1. Contact your ISP and obtain the host and IP addresses for its SMTP server(s). You may find that it has different incoming and outgoing SMTP servers.
2. Get a list of its local Point of Presence numbers. Some ISPs have both local numbers for particular areas and countrywide local rate numbers. You should have at least two or three access numbers, as RAS can be configured with alternative phone numbers should one number be engaged.
3. Check with your ISP about how you are going to retrieve remote mail. Do they use ETRN, ESMTP, or TURN? See the section on SMTP Server or POP3 Client for further information.
4. Ask if it can support SSL/SASL or Windows NT authentication or encryption.
5. Install the RAS client as per Appendix A. Add a phone book entry for your ISP and configure your port and modem settings to get the maximum connection speed. Test this RAS connection and make sure that it will dial into and authenticate to your ISP's POP automatically. *This is very important.*

6. After you have the information detailed in steps 1,2,3, and 4 and your dial-up connection is working, you can now install the IMS.

7. On the third screen of the IMS Wizard, check the box marked Allow Internet Mail Through a Dialup Connection.

8. On the fourth screen, select your previously installed and tested phone book entry for your ISP.

9. On the fifth screen, you will probably want to select No for Don't Re-route Mail. Note that this prevents clients from connecting via POP3 or IMAP4.

10. On the sixth screen, select the option for Route All Mail Through a Single Host (Typical). Enter the IP address or host name of your ISP's SMTP receiving server.

11. You can now complete the rest of the wizard accepting the default entries.

12. After the IMS installs itself and starts the IMS service, double-click on the Internet Mail Service object in Exchange Administrator.

13. Click on the Dial-Up Connections tab and adjust the time-out interval to one or two minutes. Click on the Mail Retrieval button and select ETRN, TURN, or Do Not Send Retrieval Command, as you discussed with your ISP. Click on the Logon Information button and specify your username and password (domain is usually not required). Adjust the schedule for when you want mail picked up, either on a daily or weekly basis.

14. Go to the Connections tab and check the transfer mode (inbound and outbound), message delivery (this should show your ISPs inbound SMTP server) and that the Dial Using box shows your address book entry for your ISP.

15. Go to the Diagnostics Logging tab and turn all logging up to Maximum. Don't forget to turn this off later, after you have the IMS working correctly.

16. You can leave all the other settings as they are. Now stop and restart the Internet Mail Service. Click on Start, select Settings, Control Panel and double-click on the Services icon. Scroll down the full list of services until you reach the Microsoft Exchange Server Internet Mail service. Click the Stop button, wait for the service to stop, and then click Start. In a few seconds, you should here the sound of your modem kicking into action as it dials out to connect to your ISP.

Success!

Multiple Internet Mail Services

There are occasions where your Internet traffic could cause a single IMS to become a bottleneck. In this case, you can configure multiple Internet Mail Services. Each server in your site can have one instance of the Internet Mail Service running.

12

Note You only need to do this if your Internet Mail delivery rates are in messages per minute rather than in messages per hour. A typical situation is a company with several hundred users and a leased-line connection to the Internet.

How Do I Configure Multiple Internet Mail Services?

Add an IMS to two or more servers in your site using the Internet Mail Service Wizard, as you covered earlier. After you have installed these services, configure each by double-clicking on the newly created Internet Mail Service object. Select the Connections tab and then select Incoming Only or Outgoing Only. This will result in one IMS collecting incoming mail and the other one delivering outgoing mail, thus reducing the load on each server.

Security Considerations

SMTP is not a secure medium for sending messages. Hence, when using Exchange server across the Internet, you may want to encrypt your transmissions.

Using SSL/SASL to Secure SMTP Connections

You can use SSL/SASL to secure SMTP connections. This is particularly useful if you are using the Internet mail service to connect Exchange sites across the Internet. You could think of this as a virtual private network, similar to that provided by Point-to-Point Tunneling Protocol (PPTP).

If you want to use the Internet mail service to connect two Exchange sites, you will need to add the other site to the Connected Sites tab. Add the organization and site name, and then click on the Routing Address tab to enter any routing information for the remote site.

Now select the Security tab and click on the Add button. If you are using Windows NT and Challenge/Response Authentication and Encryption, you will need to specify a Windows NT account in the remote domain. You will also need an account if you are using SSL/SASL authentication. If you are connecting to another Exchange site using NT Challenge/Response, use the Exchange service account to authenticate.

You will need to get the Administrator in the remote site to add you as a connected site.

Accepting and Rejecting Mail

You can configure Exchange to reject mail from certain users or entire domains. Therefore, if you didn't want to receive mail from people with free email accounts, you could add, say, lukewarmmail.com as a banned domain.

To set up incoming mail filtering, go to the Connections tab on the Internet Mail Service and click on the button marked Message Filtering. You will see the dialog box shown in Figure 12.29.

FIGURE 12.29

Get rid of unwelcome mail at the server level through Message Filtering.

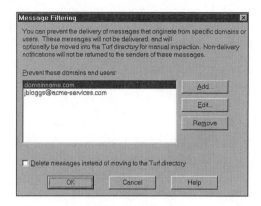

You will now be able to add individual users (*username@domainname*.com) or entire domains (just add *domainname*.com). Additionally, you can specify what happens to the rejected mail. Either delete it immediately you can have it moved into the TURF directory for inspection.

I wish my front door had a similar device—I'd add doubleglazingsalesmen.org and weirdreligiousgroups.net immediately. It would also place them in the \SKIP directory.

Exchange and Internet Newsgroups (Usenet)

Email is not the only service available on the Internet. You may also want give your users access to the global Usenet newsgroups, particularly ones that are relevant to your organization's role.

On Day 11, you looked briefly at what newsgroups are and how they work. You saw that there was a range of newsgroup topics and how some were moderated newsgroups, where a newsgroup moderator decides what should and should not be posted. Today you will be looking at the practical aspects of installing and configuring the Internet News Service.

12

WHAT BENEFITS COULD I GAIN FROM IMPLEMENTING NEWSGROUPS?

A newsgroup is a global discussion forum, allowing a potentially vast number of people to contribute to a particular topic. This gives you a number of potential benefits, which with imagination can greatly benefit your business.

You can use Newsgroups for keeping abreast of innovations, developing new ideas, getting marketing feedback, and providing client support. I am sure that you will find a newsgroup that covers your particular area of expertise. If not, you could always create one and host it, which could give you some extra kudos and possible sales opportunities, especially if potential clients start posting to it.

Installing and Configuring the Internet News Service

Assuming you still are interested in newsgroups, you will now need to look at the Internet News Service.

What Is the Internet News Service?

The Internet News Service is a connector, like the Internet Mail Service, that enables your Exchange server to download Usenet newsgroups from the Internet. It also provides support for NNTP clients. It does this by installing an RFC-compliant NNTP server onto Exchange. After you have installed the INS, you have the following options:

- You can download Usenet newsgroups and publish them as public folders. Exchange can use either a push or pull feed for accepting newsgroups.

- Your users can post to these public folders and thus publish their contributions on the Internet.

- Users with NNTP clients can connect to your Exchange server over TCP/IP and download any public folders that you have published as newsgroups.

For more information on connecting to Exchange using Newsreader (NNTP) clients see Day 14.

Before You Install

Like the Internet Mail Service, you should address several planning issues before you start the wizard.

Which Newsgroups Do I Want?   There are thousands of newsgroups out there; some are useful, some interesting, some slightly strange, some definitely weird, and a small handful contain illegal information. Hence, you will need to exercise caution over which ones you actually publish as public folders on your Exchange server.

Newsgroups fall into several main headings:

- alt—dealing with alternative or "controversial" topics.
- comp—for computing and IT issues.
- misc—miscellaneous topics that defy categorization.
- news—information about Usenet.
- rec—recreational topics such as art and hobbies.
- sci—science and research.
- soc—socializing and social issues.

 A *flame war* is two or more people insulting each other on a Usenet newsgroup.

 A holy War is groups of people insulting each other on a Usenet newsgroup over a period of years. This can go on for so long that no one can remember what it was all about in the first place.

How Will I Connect to My ISP?   You will probably have already decided this, but if you decide to implement newsgroups, this might be a good time to review your connection to your ISP. This could also be a good time to ask for bids from other suppliers for the new service. If you are using a dial-up connection, you might want to upgrade to a leased line. If you are currently connecting at 64KB, you might want to increase that to 128Kbps.

The questions you need to ask your ISP are much simpler than with the Internet Mail Service. You will need to have answers to the following:

- What is your Usenet site name?
- What is the host name or IP address of your Usenet server?
- How can I download your active list?
- Do I need to log onto your newsfeed servers, and what are my logon credentials?
- If you are using a push feed, you need to agree which newsgroups you will receive at your site.

After you have reviewed your connection arrangements with your ISP, you can now answer one of the main planning questions for implementing the INS.

Push or Pull Feed?   Maybe it would be best to take a moment to define what I mean by a push or pull feed:

- A *pull feed* is where you connect to your ISP and pull the requested newsgroups onto your server.
- A *push feed* is where your ISP pushes the newsgroups onto your server.

You would use a pull feed:

- With a dial-up connection

  or

- Where you are only interested in a few newsgroups.

You would use a push feed:

- Where you have a permanent connection to the Internet

  and

- You want to download a large number of newsgroups.

 Note | You will not have to pay extra for a pull feed. However, there may be charges for a push feed, depending on the complexity and amount of information you want replicated to your site.

There. That was easy, wasn't it?

See the section "Push and Pull Configurations" for more information on how you configure the feeds.

The Internet News Service Wizard

Now that you have considered all the planning issues, you can start installing the Internet News Service. Like the IMS, you install this via Exchange Administrator.

1. Start Exchange Administrator, click on the File menu and select New Other. Select Newsfeed from near the bottom of the list. This will start the Newsfeed Wizard.

2. The first screen that you will see will check to see if you have all the necessary information. As long as you have carried out the previous task, you should already have this information in hand. Click Next to proceed.

3. The second screen is where you choose which server to run the INS. You can have multiple newsfeeds just as you can have multiple Internet Mail Services. Give your site a Usenet site name—the default is *sitename.organizationname*.com, as shown in Figure 12.30.

FIGURE 12.30

You can select your server and Usenet site name here.

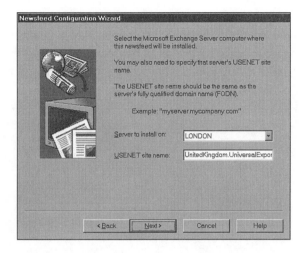

4. The third screen lets you select the type of newsfeed that you want and whether you want it to be a push or a pull feed. You can see the options in Figure 12.31.

FIGURE 12.31

This dialog enables you to choose either an incoming or outgoing newsfeed and whether to use a push or pull feed.

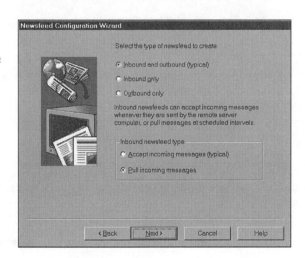

Note

The entry for a push feed is marked as typical. This is only true for larger organizations.

12

5. The forth screen on the wizard lets you specify the connection type. If you have a leased-line or dial-on-demand ISDN, select LAN. If you have dial-up ISDN or PSTN modem (POTS), select the phone book entry. You will need to enter a user account and passwords for the connection. Figure 12.32 shows you how this looks.

FIGURE 12.32

Here you can select a LAN or a dial-up network connection plus any authentication details.

Tip

Just like the IMS, make sure the phone book entry that you select is capable of dialing in and authenticating to your ISP without manual intervention.

6. Screen five sets the connection frequency, from 15 minutes to once every 24 hours.

7. Screen six asks you for your ISP's Usenet site name, which you obtained earlier.

8. Screen seven (there are only another six or so to go!) is where you enter your ISP's newsgroup host name or IP address. You found that out earlier as well, didn't you! You should be up to Figure 12.33.

9. Screen eight lets you specify a connection account for outgoing or incoming connections.

Note

This connection account is a different requirement from the account details that you entered if you specified a dial-up connection earlier.

Usually, you will be able to use an anonymous account to log onto your ISP's NNTP server, so you don't need to enter anything here.

Figure 12.33

This is where you enter your ISP's NNTP server.

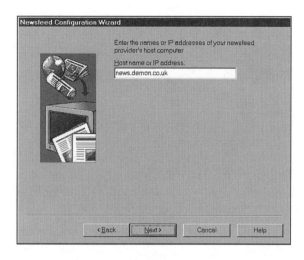

10. If you are using a push feed you should specify an account that your ISP's NNTP server will use to log on to your Exchange server. Note that you will select a mailbox to do this, not a user account. This mailbox can be a normal mailbox or a custom recipient. If required, you can enable SSL security, although your ISP must support this. You will see the options in Figure 12.34.

Figure 12.34

This screen lets you configure incoming and outgoing security, if required.

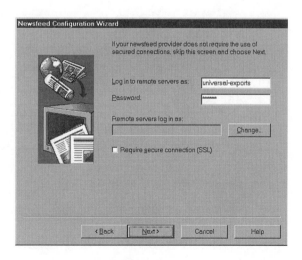

12

11. Screen nine does not require any input; it just informs you that the INS will now start.

12. The Password screen asks you to enter the Exchange service account password, just as with the IMS. Exchange Administrator creates the INS and the service starts.

13. Screen eleven requires you to select an Exchange mailbox to act as the newsfeed administrator. Now that would be you again, wouldn't it?

14. The next dialog box requests your ISP's active file, which is the list of available newsgroups. You have three options on this screen:

    •You have already obtained the active list from your ISP, so you can import it. All you need to do here is to select the relevant file.

    •You want the INS to connect to your ISP and download the active list file.

    •You don't have the active list file, so you will configure this later.

    Connecting to your ISP and downloading the list may not always work, particularly if you have not yet connected your system to the Internet. However, you will probably find that you can download the active list (look for a compressed version) from your ISP's Web page.

15. After the active file is imported, you will see the screen as shown in Figure 12.35.

FIGURE 12.35

After the INS has imported the active file, you can select which newsgroups you want to download.

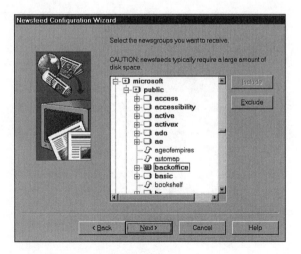

16. You can select entire branches or just individual newsgroups by selecting them and clicking the Include button.

Some newsgroups, particularly those beginning with alt and comp, contain a large number of newsgroups. Check how many newsgroups are contained within a branch before selecting it.

You have now completed the task of adding the Internet News Service. Should you wish to change any of the values, you can do so with Exchange Administrator, which I will cover next.

Configuring the Service

After you have installed the INS, you may find that you want to make changes to its configuration. It is very likely that you will want to adjust the newsgroups you request, particularly after your users have become familiar with Usenet.

To make any configuration changes, start Exchange Administrator, and select your site in the left pane. Double-click on your site and in the left pane, you should see the Configuration container. Click on this object and now look in the right pane. There you will see an icon labeled Connections. Double-click on the Connections icon and you should see the Newsfeed object. Double-click on the Newsfeed icon to see the properties of this object. You will now be able to configure the following items.

General Tab   The General tab has options to enable or disable the newsfeed and to change the Administrator's mailbox. You can also change the display name of the newsfeed to make it something more friendly.

This dialog box also tells you which type of newsfeed you have, that is, push or pull. You cannot change from push to pull feed or vice-versa without removing and reinstalling the INS.

12

Messages Tab   The Messages tab simply limits the outgoing and incoming message sizes. If you want to preserve space on your server and reduce download time, you could specify an incoming message limit. However, Usenet messages are usually text files so a 50K limit would not seriously inconvenience anyone. Usually, it's the unsuitable newsgroups that have large attachments, if you know what I mean!

Figure 12.36 shows some reasonable settings for incoming and outgoing message sizes.

FIGURE 12.36

Adding reasonable values here will help to reduce the bandwidth the newsfeed requires.

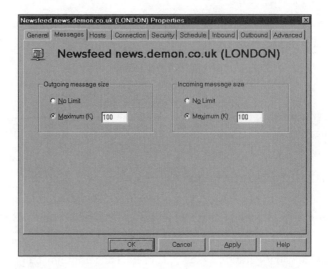

Hosts Tab   The Hosts tab is where you can specify site and host names for the remote Usenet site. You should not normally have to change these values. If you need to add any other remote inbound hosts, you can enter the relevant remote host names in the lower part of the dialog. For most connections, your configuration would look like that in Figure 12.37.

FIGURE 12.37

The Hosts tab is where you can add further incoming hosts to your newsfeed.

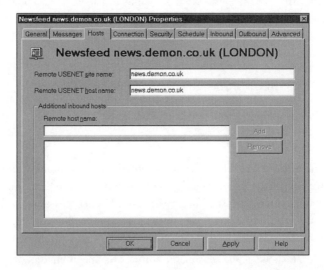

Connection Tab   You can carry out any changes to your dial-up connection through the Connection tab. Enter any new passwords or account names in the boxes, as shown in Figure 12.38.

FIGURE 12.38

The Connection tab is for changing the password on your dial-up networking entry.

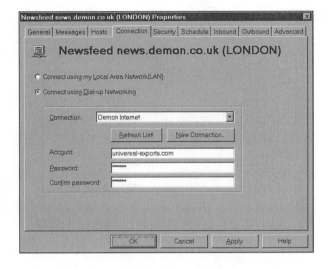

> **Caution**
>
> If you change your password for your dial-up account to your ISP, don't forget to change it here as well, or else your newsfeed will stop working.
>
> The same applies to the IMS.

You can also add a new connection through this dialog box. Click on the New Connection and you will start the dial-up networking client. Click on the New button to create a new phone book entry. See Day 7, "Configuring the Exchange Client," for more information on adding phone book entries.

Security Tab On the Security tab, you have the same range of options as you saw on screen eight of the INS wizard previously. This dialog shows where you can change the authentication account for incoming connections and the account name and password (if required) for any outbound servers.

Use SSL only if your ISP supports it.

Schedule Tab The Schedule tab makes it easy to configure the times that your server will connect to your ISP and download messages. You have the options of Never, Always, and Selected Times. Choose Always if you have a LAN or leased line connecting you to your ISP. Choose Specific Times if you have a dial-up connection. With a dial-up link, you may want to consider connecting during off-peak hours.

Figure 12.39 shows an example of a newsfeed configured to connect at 6:15 a.m. and 6:15 p.m. In this case, these times are set to prevent conflict with the IMS, which dials out every hour.

12

FIGURE 12.39

Control your dial-up costs by only connecting at off-peak times.

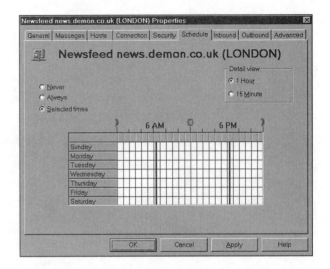

Inbound Tab   The Inbound tab controls the newsgroups that arrive at your site and subsequently appear as part of your public folders. Here you can add or remove newsgroups from your newsfeed. Figure 12.40 shows part of the list of newsgroups, with some groups included and some excluded.

FIGURE 12.40

You will probably need to adjust which newsgroups are included in your newsfeed.

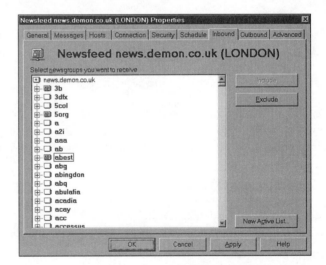

Outbound Tab   The Outbound tab is where you control which newsgroups return to the Internet. Thus you can publish newsgroups on your Exchange server, but your employee's postings don't necessarily return to Usenet. Figure 12.40 shows the configuration of the outbound newsgroups.

FIGURE 12.41

Your incoming and outgoing newsgroups do not have to match

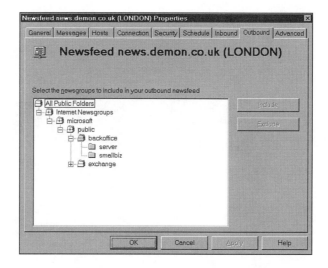

Advanced Tab   The Advanced tab has only one setting—Mark All as Delivered. Click this to flush your newsgroup queues and download new messages. You might want to do this if your connection to your ISP has been down for awhile and you want to clear the old messages out.

Thankfully, configuring a newsfeed is considerably easier than the Internet Mail Service. Having dealt with connecting your organization to the Usenet, I will now take you through some other configuration options with Exchange newsgroups.

Troubleshooting

So what do you do if your newsgroups won't work, no one is receiving any mail, your RAS client doesn't want to connect, or the INS has gobbled all your bandwidth? Well, you can use logging and performance monitor to diagnose and fix any problems.

Configuring Logging

You can set logging levels on several components of your Exchange server. For the IMS, you set logging through the Diagnostics tab on the Internet Mail Connector as described previously.

For troubleshooting newsgroups, you should set logging on the NNTP protocol. You can configure this in two places.

Start Exchange Administrator and select your site in the left pane. Expand this site object and select the Configuration container object. Expand the Configuration object and select the Servers object. Select your server in the left pane and then double-click on the

Protocols object in the right pane. You will now be able to see the server level protocol objects, for example, POP3, NNTP, and so on. Double-click on the NNTP object. This will bring up the properties of the server NNTP object. Click on the Diagnostics Logging tab and you will see the screen in Figure 12.42.

FIGURE 12.42

You can increase or decrease logging levels through the server level Protocols object.

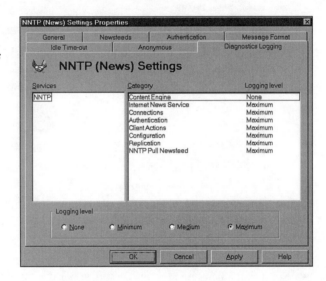

To increase logging on the NNTP protocol, select the relevant components and click the option for Minimum, Medium, or Maximum.

Caution

You should not keep logging levels at Maximum unless you are actively troubleshooting. It will slow the performance of your Exchange server and fill up your Event logs very quickly.

You can configure the same logging options by selecting the properties of your server and selecting the Diagnostics Logging tab, as shown in Figure 12.43.

Event Viewer

With logging switched on, you will see NNTP events in the Application Log in Event Viewer. To do this, Click the Start button, select Programs, Administrative Tools, and click on Event Viewer. Normally, Event Viewer starts with the System Log. Select the Log menu and choose Application to view the Application Log, as shown in Figure 12.44.

FIGURE 12.43

NNTP diagnostics logging can also be configured through the server object in Exchange Administrator.

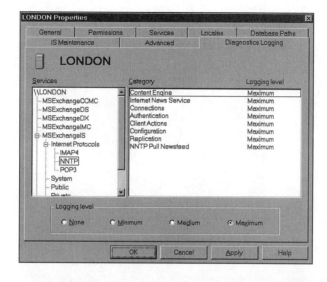

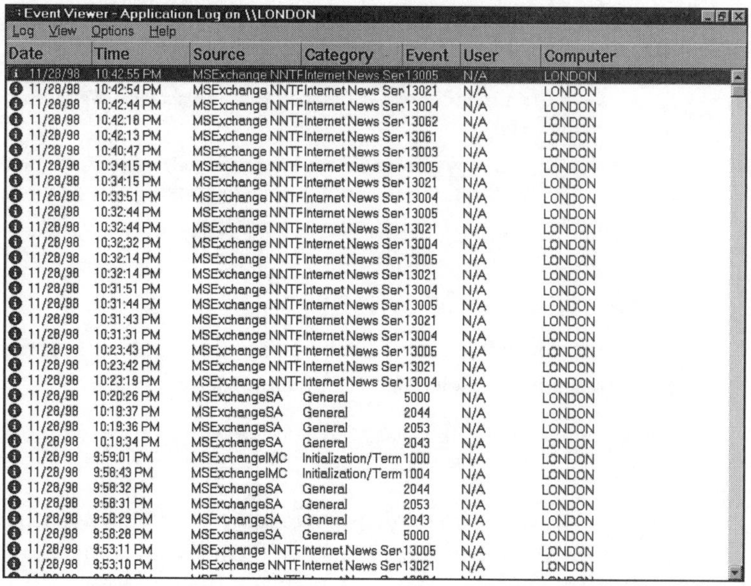

FIGURE 12.44

NNTP events will appear in the Application Log.

If you double-click on an entry in the event log, you will see an explanation of the problem or event. Figure 12.45 shows an NNTP event.

FIGURE **12.45**

Double-click on an
NNTP event to see
more detail.

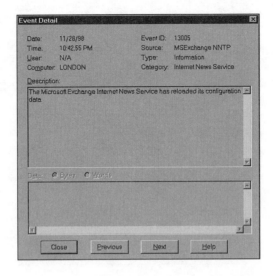

> **Tip**
>
> The Windows NT Server Resource Kit has a help file that explains the various events from the event logs. Install the resource kit and select the Resource Kit menu. Choose Online Docs and click on NT Messages to view this help file.
>
> You may also get more information by searching for the error code in TechNet or the TechNet Knowledge Base.

Performance Monitor

Performance Monitor is a tool that comes with Windows NT. You run it by clicking on Start, Programs and selecting Administrative Tools.

When you install the Internet Mail Service, you get a new set of performance monitor counters specifically for the IMS.

The Internet News Service does not install performance counters like the Internet Mail Service. However, performance monitor counters are available, both from the Process->EXCHINS instance and from the MSExchangeIS object.

> **Tip**
>
> When you install Exchange, you will install a number of preconfigured performance monitor graphs. You will find these in the Microsoft Exchange program group.

Some Other Troubleshooting Techniques

Here are some other tips for what you might try if you still can't get your Exchange server to work with Internet mail and newsgroups. You could try the following:

1. If you are using RAS, start the Dial-Up Networking and dial in to your ISP.

2. Check that you can PING your ISP by IP address and host name, as shown in Figure 12.46.

FIGURE 12.46

You should be able to PING your ISP by IP address and host name.

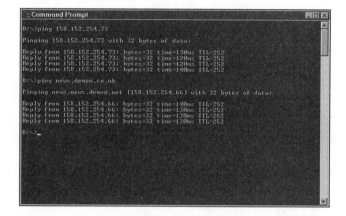

3. For the IMS, run TELNET and connect to port 25. You should get a response similar to that in Figure 12.47.

FIGURE 12.47

Using Telnet, you should be able to connect to your ISP's SMTP server as shown.

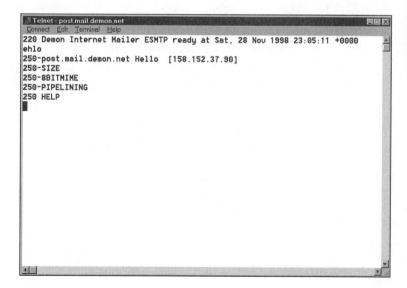

12

4. For the INS, run TELNET and connect to port 119. You should get a response
   similar to that in Figure 12.48.

Figure 12.48

*Using Telnet, you
should be able to con-
nect to your ISP's
news server on port
119.*

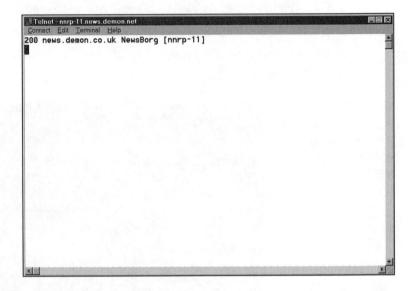

For other problems with Exchange and Newsgroups, see the Exchange online documentation and Exchange Administrator Help.

Summary

In today's lesson, you learned how to install and configure the Internet Mail Service and
the Internet News Service. You looked at the benefits that the IMS and INS can bring and
the capabilities that they add to your Exchange server. You considered some of the
factors behind choosing an ISP and you reviewed the different ways of connecting to the
Internet.

To summarize these points:

- The Internet Mail Service adds an RFC-compliant SMTP server to Microsoft
  Exchange.
- The IMS allows you to connect your Exchange messaging system to the Internet to
  send and receive mail.
- You can use the Internet Mail Service to connect two Exchange sites across the
  Internet. You can then configure directory replication across this connector.

- Installing the IMS provides a delivery mechanism for POP3/IMAP4 clients connecting directly into your server.

- The Internet News Service adds an RFC-compliant NNTP server to Microsoft Exchange.

- The INS allows you to connect your Exchange server to the global Usenet news-groups.

- You can configure push or pull feeds to download newsgroups and publish them as public folders that users can read with Outlook or the Exchange client.

- Installing the INS provides a mechanism whereby NNTP clients can download any public folders that you have published as newsgroups.

Q&A

Q I installed Exchange server a few months ago and now I want to install the Internet Mail Service, but I've lost the Exchange CD in the clutter on my desk. Can I still install the IMS?

A Yes, you can, as you don't actually need the Exchange Server CD to install the IMS. Just start Exchange Administrator, click on the File menu, select New Other, and select Internet Mail Service from the bottom of the list. You will now be able to install the IMS without the Exchange CD.

Q I am configuring dial-up access to my ISP which requires a post-connection script. How do I get the Exchange IMS to use this?

A Just make sure that when you click Dial for your ISP's address book entry on your dial-up networking (RAS) client, you can automatically connect to your ISP. You should see the post-connection script run when your machine dials in. After you have tested that, go to the Internet Mail Service and click on the Dial-Up Connections tab. Your Address Book entry will now appear. Check the box for this entry but do not click on the logon information button or enter any authentication details. Exchange should now dial in and authenticate automatically.

Q I have just successfully set up the IMS today and I can quite happily send mail from Exchange to people in other companies over the Internet. However, when they click Reply the reply never arrives back here. What is the problem?

A Congratulations on getting half your IMS to work. The good news is that problem with the reply mail is probably not your fault at all. It will most likely be because DNS has not updated today and so there is no MX record for your domain yet. When you come back in the morning, everything should work fine.

12

Q **I want to link my two Exchange sites via the IMS but I don't want my users to be able to send or receive mail from the Internet via this link. I also want my messages encrypted while traversing the Internet and I want a secure logon to the remote server. How can I configure this?**

A Easy. Double-click on the Internet Mail Service that you installed and click on the General tab. Make sure you do not have a message size limit. Now click on the Security tab. Add the email domain for your other site and click on the option for Windows NT challenge/response authentication and encryption. Click on the Change button and add details of the Exchange Service account in the remote site. Then go to the Address Space tab and remove the default entry SMTP *. Add a new entry for your remote site domain name and in the Restrictions tab, make this address apply to this site only. Now go to the Connected Sites tab and add a new entry with the same organization name (the default) and the other site name. After you have made these changes, click OK and then start and stop the IMS. Check that you have connectivity by sending a message to *auser@othersite. yourorganization*.com. After you receive a reply to this message, add a directory replication connector. You should then see both sites appearing in Exchange Administrator, although this may take some time.

Workshop

The Workshop provides two ways for you to affirm what you've learned in this lesson. The "Quiz" section poses questions to help you solidify your understanding of the material covered and the "Exercise" section provides you with experience in using what you have learned. You can find answers to the quiz questions and exercises in Appendix B, "Answers to Quiz Questions and Exercises."

Quiz

1. What attachment types can you use when sending messages to Internet addresses?

2. What DNS records are required for Exchange to work on the Internet?

3. Apart from SMTP support, what additional facilities in Exchange require the IMS?

4. What TCP/IP diagnostic utilities can you use to check your Internet Mail Service?

5. What is the difference between a pull and a push newsfeed?

6. Apart from downloading Usenet newsgroups, what else does installation of the INS enable?

7. You have 200 users at your city-center site and you want to connect to the Internet for WWW, email, and Usenet newsgroups. What type of connection to your ISP would you choose?

8. What four mail-retrieval options can the Internet Mail Service use?

9. From where can you obtain a domain name for your organization?

Exercises

1. Your manager has tasked you to track all messages coming from or going to the Internet. How would you carry this out?

2. You have two Exchange administrators and you want them both to be notified of any problems with the INS and IMS. How would you configure this?

12

DAY **13**

Building a Web Site Around Exchange

by Anthony Steven

Chapter Objectives

In version 4.0, Exchange was a messaging system primarily designed for supporting MAPI clients. Today Exchange 5.5 SP1 is a powerful messaging platform supporting multiple access methods. One of these methods is the Outlook Web Access, which lets you connect to Exchange and send messages from a Web browser. Let's look at this and two other new Internet-based features that you can use as components of your organization's Web site.

Today, I will be covering the following topics:

- Operating requirements for the Web Access Client
- Integration with Internet Information Server
- Active Server Pages

- Browser support
- Installing the Web Access Client
- Anonymous and authenticated access
- Exchange chat server
- Configuring chat support

Introduction

You have already looked at accessing your mailbox through the Outlook Client in Day 7, "Configuring the Exchange Client" and Day 10, "Using Microsoft Outlook." This type of access uses MAPI (Messaging API) calls running over RPC (Remote Procedure Calls).

In Day 11, "Communication Protocols and the Internet," I briefly covered how you can use a Web browser to access mail on an Exchange server and I set this in the context of the other Internet-based mail access protocols.

 Note

> Outlook Web Access is not a subset of Outlook 98, but a different method of accessing an Exchange mailbox.

When Would I Use Outlook Web Access?

With previous implementations of the Web Access client, there were mutterings that this was something of a solution looking for a problem. However, with the improvements brought in through Exchange Server 5.5 SP1, Outlook Web Access is a workable client access method.

So why would you want to use this facility? You would consider using Outlook Web Access under the following circumstances:

- Where you have a public Web site, and you want to offer easy Web client-based access to certain public folders to anonymous users.
- You have a private, low-bandwidth WAN, and you want to include support for Calendar and Contacts.
- You have a heterogeneous multiplatform environment with Macintosh and UNIX workstations, and you want a standard messaging front end with support for diaries and addressing information.
- As an alternative for POP3/IMAP4 access when you have clients connecting over the Internet.

You do not need to consider using Outlook Web Access Client in a Windows-based permanent high-bandwidth LAN environment. In this situation, Outlook 98 will make the best use of Exchange's facilities.

Outlook Web Access Client cannot do everything that Outlook 98 can. For example, there is still no support for opening another's diary or for multi-day calendar views. Support for these features is planned in the next release (probably Exchange 5.5 SP3).

Client Connection Types & Security

Outlook Web Access Client supports two types of access: Authenticated or Anonymous.

Authenticated Access

Authenticated access is for users with a mailbox on the Exchange server. They can access all their mailbox folders, look up users in the Exchange Global Address Book, and connect to the Public Folders.

Anonymous Access

Anonymous access is for users who are external to your organization. Anonymous users can access designated public folders, post to those folders, and search for names in the Exchange Global Address List.

You might configure Anonymous access if you are a public service organization, like a City Hall, or a company with a keen eye for PR. This would mean that Joe Public could look up the Mayor's office telephone number, or post to their utility company's suggestions forum.

Support for SSL

You can configure additional security by enabling SSL with Outlook Web Access. This will encrypt information passed between the Web browser and IIS.

What Components Are Required for Web Access?

To use the Outlook Web Access Client, you need to install and configure the following additional components:

- Windows NT Server Service Pack 3 or later.
- TCP/IP with suitable Host Name Resolution.
- Internet Information Server 3.0 or later.
- Collaboration Data Objects (CDO).
- Active Server Pages (ASP) and all hotfixes.
- A Java- and frames-enabled Web browser.

13

Note

Collaboration Data Objects install with Exchange Server 5.5 or IIS 4.0. See the next section for information on CDO.

TCP/IP and Host Name Resolution

Before you can install IIS, you must have installed and configured TCP/IP. You will need a static IP address and subnet mask for your IIS and Exchange servers, and you will need to provide some form of host name resolution.

Note

HOST NAME RESOLUTION MADE EASY

Host name resolution normally means DNS, as local broadcast or hosts files are impractical in all but the smallest networks. The best solution here is to install Microsoft DNS server and WINS server. Configure the DNS server to use WINS lookup. Add the Static IP addresses to the WINS server manually. Configure your clients to use DHCP, and add the DNS server's IP address as a DHCP scope option.

The clients will then attempt to connect to the IIS server by host name, for example

```
http://iisserver/exchange
```

They will attempt host name resolution via the DNS server. The DNS server will call the WINS server, which will reply with the IP address. The DNS server will return this to the client, and the client can then establish a session with the IIS server.

If you are allowing connection from the Internet, you will need to have at least one real Internet IP address for your site. The IP address of your IIS machine must be included in the Internet DNS as an A (Address) record. Note that you do not require an MX (Mail Exchanger) record for OWA to work—MX records are only required when installing the Internet Mail Service on Exchange. When testing a connection to the Internet, PING IISSERVERNAME should return replies from the IP address of your IIS machine.

See Day 11 for more information on the Internet, TCP/IP, and DNS.

Internet Information Server

Outlook Web Access requires Internet Information Server 3.0 or later to function. If you use IIS 3.0, you must add the Active Server Pages component. See the following section on IIS to learn how to add this. IIS 4.0 includes built-in support for Active Server Pages.

The addition of the Outlook Web Access Client means that the browser can make HTTP calls to the Internet Information Server using CDO. IIS translates these to MAPI calls, which it then forwards to the Exchange server. The Exchange server responds by returning the data, which the IIS server then sends back to the client as HTML pages. Figure 13.1 shows this in operation.

Figure 13.1

This diagram shows the integration between IIS and the Exchange server.

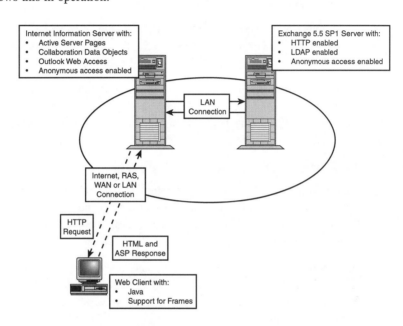

Internet Information Server with:
• Active Server Pages
• Collaboration Data Objects
• Outlook Web Access
• Anonymous access enabled

Exchange 5.5 SP1 Server with:
• HTTP enabled
• LDAP enabled
• Anonymous access enabled

LAN Connection

Internet, RAS, WAN or LAN Connection

HTTP Request

HTML and ASP Response

Web Client with:
• Java
• Support for Frames

The Internet Information Server does not have to be on the same server as Exchange, although this makes the setup easier. I will cover the setup and configuration of IIS in the following section.

Collaboration Data Objects

Outlook Web Access Client uses a feature of Exchange 5.5 called Collaboration Data Objects (CDO). Currently implemented as version 1.2.1, CDO is the new name for Active or OLE Messaging.

CDO is a method of implementing messaging or collaboration applications with the minimum of fuss.

CDO installs when you select the option for Outlook Web Access as part of the Exchange Server setup program. This installs the CDO runtime libraries and DLL files. For more information about Collaboration Data Objects, see the CDO.HLP file in \SERVER\ENG\SERVER\SETUP\I386\BIN.

13

Active Server Pages

Active Server Pages (ASP) is an open non-compiled server side application environment in which you can combine a number of different components into an Active Server Page. Active Server Pages include script or ActiveX modules contained within an HTML framework.

The scripts used in ASP can include VBScript and Microsoft JScript, as well as Perl and REXX via Active Scripting plug-ins. ActiveX modules can be written in any language, for example C++, Java, COBOL, and Visual Basic.

To see an example of an Active Server Page, go to the \EXCHSRVR\WEBDATA\USA folder and open the LOGON.ASP file in Notepad. This page starts with a server-side VBScript module that tests for the browser version. It then goes into a standard HTML page before changing to a JavaScript routine that deals with anonymous logins.

Java and Frames-Enabled Browser

Finally, you need a Java-capable and frames-enabled browser. This means Internet Explorer 3.02 and later or Netscape Navigator 3.0 and later. The Logon page on the Outlook Web Access Client will check the version numbers on your browser, so there is no point in trying to use the incorrect version.

With these components present on your network, you can now install the Outlook Web Access Client onto your IIS machine. With Outlook Web Access Client installed, your Web browser can send and receive messages, view public folders, and query directory service information.

Outlook Web Access and Messaging Profiles

Outlook Web Access Client does away with the requirement to create messaging profiles by creating MAPI profiles dynamically. Thus when a user logs on, an encrypted session is established between the browser and IIS, which authenticates the user. When IIS connects to the Exchange server, Exchange automatically creates a messaging profile for that user, based on his authentication settings.

Outlook Forms Converter

In addition to using the forms available with Outlook Web Access Client, you can convert Outlook 97 or 98 forms into HTML. The application that you need to do this is the Outlook HTML Form Converter. To install this, run FCSETUP.EXE from the \SERVER\ENG\FORMSCNV on the Exchange Server 5.5 SP1 CD. You will then be able to take an Outlook custom form and, subject to certain provisos, convert this into a Web form for use with the Web Access client.

Internet Information Server

To use Outlook Web Access, you must first install Microsoft Internet Information Server 3 or later. You can install IIS on the Exchange server, or on another server. My recommendation is that you install IIS on the same server if you are using Outlook Web Access internally such as when there is no anonymous access via the Internet. If you are configuring your system for anonymous access, you should install IIS and Exchange on separate servers. This is because for Anonymous Access to work, the IUSR_SERVERNAME account must have the Log on Locally right on the Exchange server.

ANONYMOUS ACCESS AND THE INTERNET

If you are enabling Anonymous access from the Internet, there are a number of other security precautions that you should take.

- You should also have all partitions configured with NTFS, and remove the Everyone group from the permissions list.

- Give the IUSR_SERVERNAME anonymous account access only to the \WWW-ROOT directory.

- Install a proxy server or firewall, configured for reverse hosting between the Internet and the IIS. Configure a further firewall between the IIS and your LAN.

- Configure auditing for attempted security violations, like repeated logon attempts. Check your security event logs on a regular basis.

- Rename the Administrator account and give it a 14-character, mixed-case, alphanumeric (that is, a combination of letters and numbers) password. Make sure that all other accounts have passwords.

You can install IIS 3.0 as part of your NT Server setup. To do this, check the box to install IIS 2.0 during NT setup, and then install Service Pack 3 or 4 to upgrade to IIS 3.0. You must be running TCP/IP to install IIS.

Alternatively, you can install IIS 4.0 directly from the Windows NT Server Option Pack. The NT Server Option Pack is available as part of TechNet and comes as an additional disk on recent copies of NT Server.

13

Note

The IIS 4.0 SMTP or NNTP server components cannot coexist on the same server as the Exchange Internet Mail Service or Internet News Service. The IIS setup routine will inform you that the SMTP and NNTP servers did not install.

There are no other particular issues with installing IIS, apart from IIS 4.0 requiring at least 100MB, whereas IIS 3.0 was happy with about 15MB. Mind you, most of this 100MB is documentation.

Installing Active Server Pages

On IIS 3.0, you will need to install Active Server Pages separately. To do this, you need to run ASP.EXE. This is available as part of TechNet on the Server Utilities CD under IIS\IIS30\ASP, with subdirectories for Intel and Alpha.

> Make sure that you have all the patches and hotfixes for Active Server Pages. You can obtain these from:
>
> `ftp://ftp.microsoft.com/bussys/IIS/iis-public/fixes/usa/asp`

If you are installing IIS 4.0, ASP support is built-in.

> If you are installing the Option Pack onto NT Server SP4, a message will warn you that the Option Pack has not been tested on NT 4.0 SP4. However, I haven't discovered any problems yet.

Now that you have installed IIS, you can proceed to install the Outlook Web Access Client.

Outlook Web Access Client

Now it's time to look at the installation of the Outlook Web Access Client onto your Internet Information Server. With IIS and the other required components in place, installing Outlook Web Access Client is reasonably straightforward. However, there are a few extra configuration settings if you are installing OWA on a separate server from Exchange.

Installing Outlook Web Access Client

If your Exchange Server is also your Internet Information Server, the OWA installation is very simple. The Outlook Web Access Client installation routine is part of the Exchange Server setup.

Note

If you have installed IIS on a separate server from Exchange, you will be running this installation routine on the IIS server. See the following section for detailed instructions.

To install this additional component, rerun Exchange Setup from the Exchange Server CD. On the main components page, select Outlook Web Access, as shown in Figure 13.2.

FIGURE 13.2

Rerun Exchange Server setup, and select the option for Outlook Web Access.

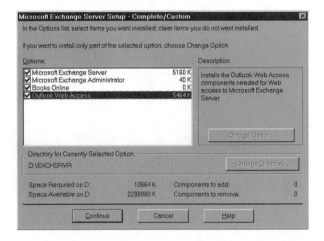

The setup routine will now run. A prompt will warn you that the WWW service will stop during installation. Click OK to continue.

Note

After the setup routine has completed, don't forget to reapply the Exchange Server 5.5 Service Pack 1.

After you have installed the Outlook Web Access, a new virtual directory appears on IIS, with the alias of /Exchange, as shown in Figure 13.3. This /Exchange alias directory now points to the /EXCHSRVR/WEBDATA directory.

As far as the setup of OWA is concerned, that's about it. You can now start using the Outlook Web Access Client.

13

FIGURE 13.3

Here is the new virtual directory with the alias of Exchange in IIS 4.0.

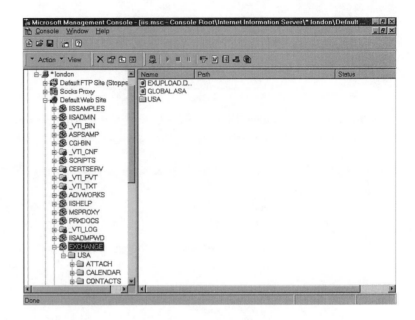

Setting Up Outlook Web Access on a Separate Server

If your Exchange server and your IIS server are not the same machine, you will need to configure Outlook Web Access to point to the Exchange Server.

To install OWA on a separate server, carry out the following task:

1. Install Exchange Server and enable the HTTP protocol at the site level.

2. Install IIS on the separate server.

3. If the IIS server and Exchange server are in separate domains, either create trusts or use the same user accounts and passwords for both domains.

4. Check that you have TCP/IP name resolution working between the two servers.

5. On the IIS server, run Exchange setup. Select only the option for Outlook Web Access, as shown in Figure 13.4.

> **Tip**
>
> You might find it useful to install the Exchange Administrator program on this server as well.

FIGURE 13.4

Select the option for Outlook Web Access on the Exchange Server setup.

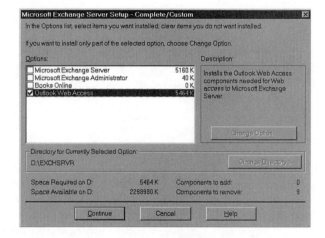

6. A prompt will inform you that the Internet Information Server services will stop temporarily.

7. Enter your Exchange Server license key when requested.

8. You will now see a prompt asking you for the name of your Exchange server. Enter the Exchange server's name and click Continue.

9. Setup will complete. You can now configure Outlook Web Access as in the following section.

Configuring Web Client Access

You configure Web Client Access at three levels:

- Via the properties of the Protocol container object.
- Through the site-level HTTP object in Exchange Administrator.
- Via the HTTP object on the Protocols tab at a mailbox level.

Note

You cannot configure the HTTP protocol at the server level. This is because the Web Access server can be a different server from the Exchange server.

13

Protocol Container Properties

You can configure settings for Outlook Web Access through the Protocol Container Properties screen. The most important setting is the ability to specify the location of the Outlook Web Access server. You will need to configure this setting if you have IIS and

OWA on a different server from Exchange. You can also include and exclude incoming hosts based on IP address.

> **Note** You can override the OWA server setting on a mailbox-by-mailbox basis. I will cover this topic in the following section.

To configure the Protocol Container level options, Start Exchange Administrator, and click on the Configuration button in the toolbar. In the right pane, select the Protocols object and click on the Properties button in the toolbar. You will now see the dialog box shown in Figure 13.5.

FIGURE 13.5

The General tab is where you can specify the Outlook Web Access server.

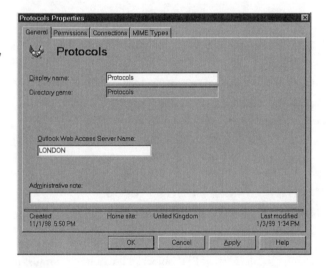

General Tab If you are using a separate IIS and Exchange server, you should enter the name of the IIS server in the box.

Connections Tab The Connections tab is where you can apply restrictions on your incoming connections

Site Level

To configure the HTTP protocol at a Site level, Start Exchange Administrator and click on the Configuration button in the toolbar. Double-click on the Protocols tab and then double-click on the HTTP object.

General Tab The General tab lets you enable and disable Outlook Web Access by checking or unchecking the Enable Protocol check box, as shown in Figure 13.6.

FIGURE 13.6

The HTTP Site level object General tab lets you enable and disable the HTTP protocol, as well as specify the level of anonymous access.

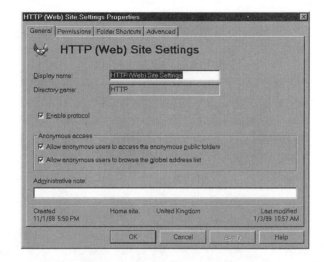

The Anonymous Access section lets you specify the facilities available to Anonymous users. You can enable or disable access to the Global Address List or the public folders by selecting the respective check boxes.

Folder Shortcuts   Use this tab to publish public folders to HTTP clients. Click on the New button, and you will see the dialog box shown in Figure 13.7.

FIGURE 13.7

You can select which public folders you want to publish.

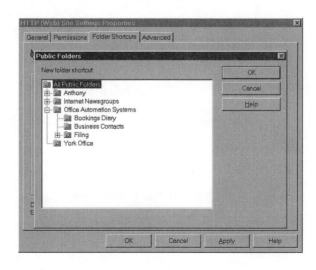

13

Expand the public folders object, and select a folder that you want to publish. After you have finished selecting public folders, your dialog box should look like the one shown in Figure 13.8.

FIGURE **13.8**

Here you can see the anonymous access public folders selected for publishing.

However, anonymous clients will not be able to view the public folders unless they have suitable client permissions. You can configure these in three ways:

- Via the properties of the individual public folder in Outlook.
- Directly on the public folder using Exchange Administrator.
- By clicking on the Properties button in the Folder Shortcuts tab.

Select the relevant folder, and click the Properties button. You will now see the public folder's Properties dialog box, as shown in Figure 13.9.

Note You can propagate public folder permission changes to subfolders by checking the Propagate box.

To check on the current client permissions, click on the Client Permissions button. You will now see the dialog box shown in Figure 13.10.

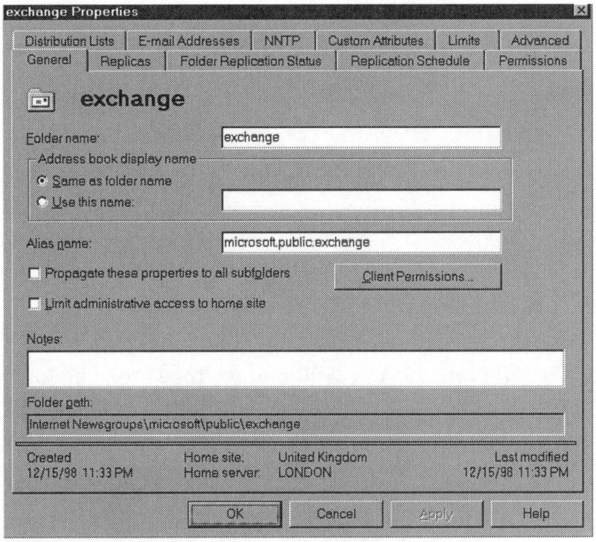

FIGURE 13.9

Click on the Properties button to go the Properties sheet for this public folder.

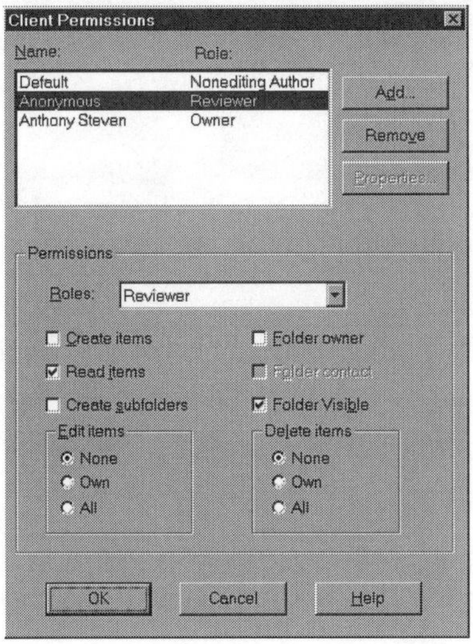

FIGURE 13.10

The anonymous user must have a minimum of Reviewer permission.

For anonymous users to be able to see a public folder, the Anonymous account must have a minimum of role of Reviewer. For anonymous users to be able to post to a public folder, the Anonymous account must have permission to create and read items. There is no implicit requirement for anonymous users to be able to edit or delete their own posts.

Advanced Tab   The Advanced tab simply lets you configure how many address book entries return to a client's query. Usually, there is no reason to change this from the default value.

Mailbox Level

You can make two configuration changes at an individual mailbox level, on the Protocols and Advanced Tab respectively. To change this, go to the Recipients container and double-click on a recipient's mailbox.

Protocols Tab   At the mailbox level, configuration of the HTTP protocol is much simpler. There is only one option—on or off. Click on the Protocols tab and then double-click on the HTTP protocol. You will now see the simple dialog box shown in Figure 13.11.

FIGURE 13.11

There is only one option at the mailbox-level HTTP protocol object.

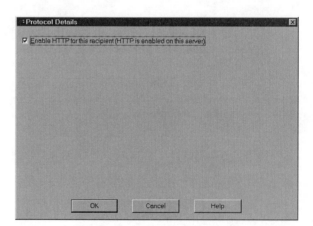

This means that you can enable a site, and then disable specific mailboxes. However, you cannot enable individual mailboxes if you disable HTTP access at the site level.

Advanced Tab   There is an option on the Advanced tab to override the setting for the Outlook Web Access server that you set in the Site level Protocol object in the previous section.

Using Outlook Web Access

To use Outlook Web Access Client, click on the Start button and select Run. Enter the following line:

```
http://IISSERVER/exchange
```

where IISSERVER is the name of your Internet server with Internet Information Server and Outlook Web Access Client installed. You will now see the screen in Figure 13.12.

FIGURE 13.12

The Outlook Web Access Client logon screen gives you the choice of authenticated or anonymous access.

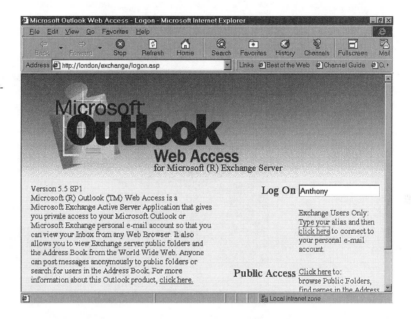

You now can now log on as either as an authenticated user or as anonymous user.

Authenticated Access

For authenticated access, like with a MAPI client, you must have an NT account and a mailbox. You can then type your mailbox alias into the Log On box and press Enter.

In certain situations—if you are logging on from a machine in a separate domain, for example—you may see a prompt asking you for a username and password, as shown in Figure 13.13.

FIGURE 13.13

If you are connecting from a separate domain, you may be required to enter additional security information.

13

You should enter your domain and username in the form `Domainname\Accountname` and your password for that domain. The account information that you should enter should be the primary Windows NT account for your Exchange mailbox.

After you have successfully logged on, you will see a screen similar to the one shown in Figure 13.14.

FIGURE 13.14

Authenticated logon takes you to this screen. The default folder is the Inbox.

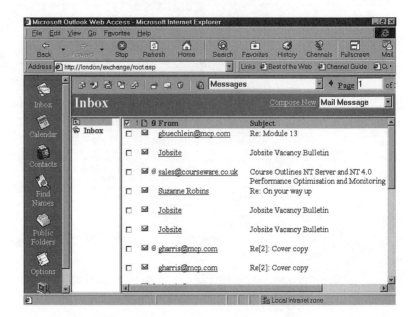

The interface looks something like the Outlook client, with icons along the left side for Calendar, Contacts, and so on. Along the top of the screen below the Web browser's address bar is a list of icons for creating new messages, posting to folders, checking for new mail, and so on. The drop-down list in the center of the toolbar lets you select different views of your mailbox. You can go up a level to show all your mailbox folders, as in Figure 13.15.

Inbox   Your Inbox will show you the messages currently in your Exchange Inbox. To display a message, click on the underlined sender's name. The message will now appear in a separate Internet Explorer window, as shown in Figure 13.16.

FIGURE 13.15

Here you see the root of the mailbox folders.

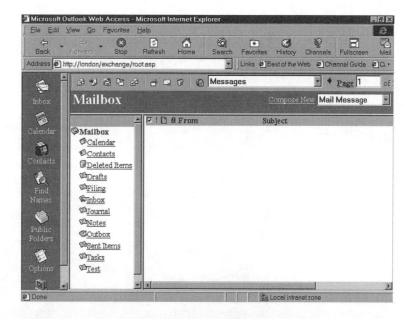

FIGURE 13.16

Click on a sender's name to see the message. You can now click on the Reply button to reply to the message.

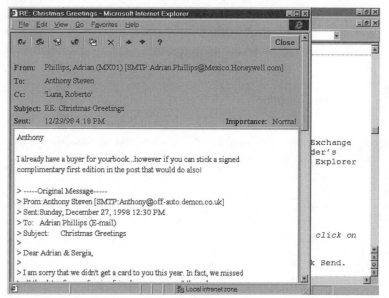

Click on the Reply button, add any attachments, and click Send.

Adding Attachments Adding attachments is a slightly different process than with other clients. Remember that the Outlook Web Access is a server-side process, so you are adding the attachments at the server.

To add an attachment to a message, click on the Create New Message icon. Click on the Attachments tab, and you will see the screen in Figure 13.17.

FIGURE 13.17

Adding attachments to a mail message works at the server level.

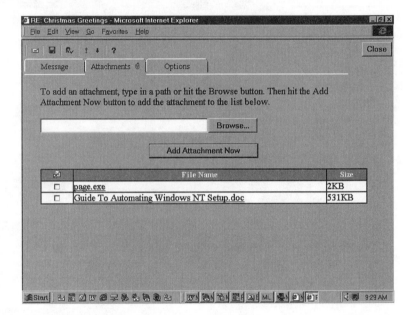

Click on the Browse button, select the file, and then click the Add Attachment Now button. The file will now show on the list of attachments. Repeat this until you have added all the files that you want to attach. Finish adding text to your message, and then click the Send icon.

Checking Addressees To check addresses, enter your addressees into the To: or CC: boxes. Then click the Check Names button. The SMTP addresses for your addressees will appear if all names are resolved. Figure 13.18 shows this in operation.

FIGURE 13.18

The Check Names button resolves names to SMTP addresses.

Options Tab You can specify delivery or read receipts and where to save sent messages through the Options tab. Check the relevant boxes as required.

Calendar Selecting the Calendar icon takes you to the diary module, as shown in Figure 13.19.

FIGURE 13.19

Click the Calendar icon to go to the diary module.

13

You can display the Calendar screen in Daily or Weekly mode.

To create a new appointment, click on the New Appointment button. You will now see the screen in Figure 13.20.

FIGURE 13.20

The New Appointment screen also lets you set up meetings and invite attendees.

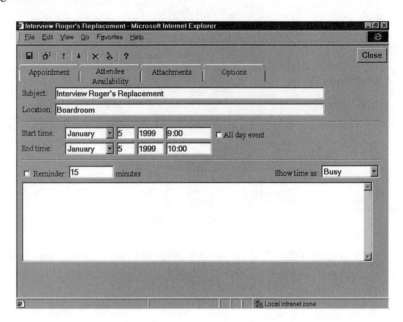

Click on the Recurrence tab to configure repeating appointments.

Contacts   Click on the Contacts button to go to your mailbox contacts folder, as shown in Figure 13.21.

 Note

> The current version of OWA does not support using contact items in any folders other than the mailbox Contacts folder.

Click on a contact's name to add any details on that contact.

Other Folders   Although you can display the contents of other folders in your mailbox, you can only view the items in those folders as if they are mail messages. This is because there is currently no forms support for Tasks, Journal, and Notes. Any message-based folders will display their contents correctly.

FIGURE 13.21

The Contacts icon gives you access to your mailbox contacts folder.

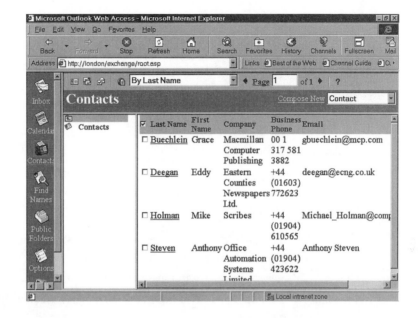

Options Click on the Options icon to see the screen in Figure 13.22.

FIGURE 13.22

The Outlook Web Access Client options screen lets you configure some basic options.

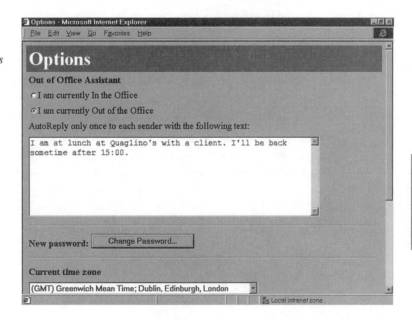

13

You can now configure Out of Office Assistant (but no rules), change your logon password, set a time zone, and change working times.

Anonymous Access

Anonymous access using Outlook Web Access is considerably simpler, as anonymous users do not have a mailbox. Anonymous users can carry out two operations:

- Read and post to published public folders.
- Search for addressing information in the Global Address Book.

Anonymous users cannot mail directly from the Outlook Web Access Client, although they can query the Exchange Directory Service, and then cut and paste an email address into their normal email client.

Enabling Anonymous Access   Before anonymous users can use the Outlook Web Access Client, you must configure the following settings:

- Enable the anonymous user account on the WWW service through IIS.
- Publish any public folders and assign the anonymous account a minimum of reviewer role.
- Configure an anonymous account at the DS Site Level object.
- Enable the LDAP protocol for anonymous access.

Enabling Anonymous Access on Internet Information Server   To enable Anonymous access on the WWW service, you need to configure the /Exchange virtual directory settings. In IIS 4.0, you do this through the Microsoft Management Console.

1. Click on Start, select Programs, and then choose Windows NT 4.0 Option Pack. In the Microsoft Internet Information Server program group, select Internet Service Manager. Microsoft Management Console will now start.

2. Expand the Internet Information Server object and then expand the listing for the default Web site on your server. You should now see the Exchange virtual directory listed.

3. Right-click on the Exchange directory and select Properties. Click on the Directory Security tab and then click on the Edit button in the Anonymous Access and Authentication Control section. You will now see the dialog box shown in Figure 13.23.

4. Select the box for Anonymous Access and then select OK to close the dialog boxes.

FIGURE 13.23

You enable Anonymous Access through the properties of the Exchange directory in IIS 4.0.

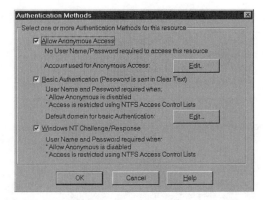

Publishing Public Folders   For anonymous users to be able to read a public folder, you must carry out the following steps:

1. Enable the HTTP protocol on the General tab of the HTTP object in the site-level Protocols container.

2. Enable the option allowing anonymous users to access the anonymous public folders.

3. Publish some public folders via the Folder Shortcuts tab.

4. Give the anonymous account a minimum of reviewer role on these published public folders as I showed in the earlier section.

If you want anonymous users to be able to post to published folders, the anonymous account must have permissions of Create Item, Read Item, and Folder Visible.

Checking Addresses   To enable anonymous users to query the Global Address List in Exchange, you must carry out the following steps in Exchange Administrator:

1. Enable the HTTP protocol on the General tab of the HTTP object in the site-level Protocols container and check the option allowing anonymous users to browse the global address list.

2. Also in the Protocols container, enable the LDAP protocol, and on the Anonymous tab, check the option for Allow Anonymous Access.

3. Add an anonymous account and password to the Anonymous Access section on the General tab of the DS Site Configuration object. This account is usually the IUSR_SERVERNAME account that provides anonymous access to IIS, although you can nominate any guest account.

Logging On as an Anonymous User   To log on as an anonymous user, just enter the same URL in the Run box as before:

```
http://IISSERVER/EXCHANGE
```

From the Login screen that you saw on the section on Authenticated access, click on the Public Access option. You will now see the windows shown in Figure 13.24.

FIGURE 13.24

Anonymous users can view public folders or query the Global Address List.

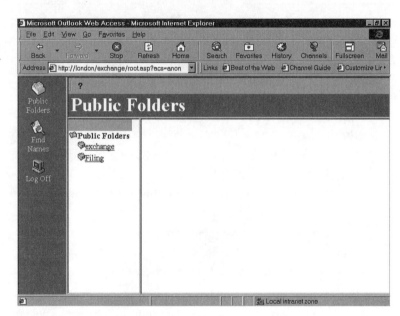

Anonymous users do not have any configurable options.

Browsing Public Folders   Browsing the public folders is identical to the process for Authenticated users, except that anonymous users can use only the public folders that you published.

Checking Addresses   This process is identical for both Anonymous and Authenticated users. Click on the Find Names icon, enter the name of the user you are looking for, and then click the Find button.

Logging Off

After you have finished using the Outlook Web Access Client, you should log off and close your browser. Doing so closes the session with IIS, and prevents another client from attempting to impersonate your connection. This is particularly important with authenticated users.

Having looked at Outlook Web Access, it's now time to take a brief look at two of the new facilities provided with Exchange Server 5.5—the Exchange Chat Service and the Internet Locator Service.

Exchange Chat Server

Exchange 5.5 now comes with a functional Chat Server, which provides support for all the features of an Internet Relay Chat (IRC) server. Exchange 5.5 Service Pack 1 extends these facilities, with support for profanity filters and a transcription service. Profanity filters remind users not to swear at each other, and transcription services generate documented output from the Chat that users can refer to later.

> **Note** This section assumes that you will deploy the Chat service on the Exchange Server 5.5 Service Pack 1 CD. This is found in the \Server\Eng\Chat\Setup\%platform% folder. This version of Chat requires IIS 4.0 and Internet Explorer 4.01.

Terms

Before I start the installation process, I would like to run through a few basic terms first.

Internet Relay Chat

Internet Relay Chat is an Internet protocol that provides a means of conducting text-based conversations between two or more Chat clients. RFC 1459 defines the Internet Relay Chat protocol.

IRCX provides extensions to the original IRC protocol. Microsoft Internet Chat Protocol (MIC) is a further development that allows richer content in Chat messages, such as passing URLs as well as using specialized Chat options, such as whispering.

IRC Server

The Internet Relay Chat server is the machine that hosts the Chat service. This server must run NT Server and Internet Information Server 4.0, and have a similar specification to your Exchange Server.

> **Note** This server does not have to be the Exchange server. However, it does need IIS installed.

13

The Chat service communicates over ports 6667 for client-server traffic, and port 6665 for server-server communication.

Chat Rooms

Chat rooms or Channels are individual areas on the Chat Server where chats are taking place. There are two types of Chat channel—Persistent or Dynamic. The Chat Administrator creates Persistent channels. Users create Dynamic channels, which close when all users have left the room.

Chat rooms can have certain properties such as only authenticated users can enter, or no whispering allowed, or the chat room is Auditorium style.

Chat Clients

A Chat client is an application that can make use of a supported Chat protocol to communicate with the IRC server. I will discuss Chat clients in a later section. However, due to reasons of space, I will not be able to provide a detailed explanation of how to use each Chat client.

Communication and Chat

The very use of the word "Chat" tends to imply trivial gossip, pointless dinner party ramblings, shallow conversations about the weather, or imaginary discussions about what the other party might or might not be wearing. Certainly, if you attempted to demonstrate the Microsoft Chat client at a board meeting, you would at least provoke some amusement. However, you should prepare yourself for comments along the lines of "So you connect to something that looks like a bug-eyed monster and type at them, do you?"

The problem with the Chat concept is that typing is a process for transferring your thoughts accurately into a document. It is not the primary means for conducting real-time conversations. You have probably noticed how your typing errors appear to increase when someone watches you type. There seems to be a similar effect when conducting a Chat conversation, especially at a rapid pace. Therefore, you end up sending out messages such as "How arae yuo?", which doesn't look very professional. In addition, most business users are slow and inaccurate typists, which further reduces the usefulness of this communication method.

Having said that, there are occasions where typing can be a useful method of communication, particularly where you have lots of users online simultaneously. Thus, IRC can be useful in certain situations:

- As a means of hosting a large conference, for example answering support queries from your clients.
- As a means of conducting a conversation across a poor-quality low-bandwidth connection.

- As a cheap form of worldwide communication at local phone call rates.
- When you want to preserve anonymity.
- As a fun hobby.

Of these options, the first is likely to be the most useful in a business environment. I will discuss the considerations for hosting large Chat environments in the following section.

Chat is a poor substitute for a one-on-one conversation, so you could use an Internet Phone to talk to someone at local call rates across the Internet. However, bandwidth restrictions and Internet disruption can prevent Internet Phone services from working acceptably.

Within a company, you are more likely to have an internal phone system, so again Chat on its own is not a particularly useful service. After all, if you want to type something to someone, you would probably use Email, and avoid the embarrassment of making mistakes.

Having said that, many people do use Chat for such activities as brainstorming sessions or for responding quickly to questions. Well, there's nowt so queer as folk, as they say in Yorkshire.

What is useful from a business standpoint is a collaboration application, like Microsoft NetMeeting. This makes use of the Chat service, but can also share applications, enabling multiple users to work on the same document in real-time. NetMeeting supports audio and video conferencing and other collaboration features such as a whiteboard for scribbling on and a Chat window if you really want to use Chat. For more information on Microsoft NetMeeting, see the later section on IRC Clients.

Planning a Chat Service Deployment

When planning a Chat Service Deployment, there are a number of considerations to take into account:

- What hardware and software do I need?
- How many users do I need to support?
- What sort of clients should I deploy or will connect?
- Am I providing public access to the Chat Service?
- What security will I require?

Again, for reasons of space, I cannot give a detailed analysis of all these points, so this next section is more of a summary. For further information, you should look at the Chat Service documentation that installs with the Exchange Chat Service.

13

Hardware Requirements

Your hardware requirements will directly relate to the number of users that you are intending to support. Each Chat server can support a maximum of 4,096 users.

If you need to support more simultaneous users than this, you will need to configure multiple Chat servers. You can configure networks of up to 255 Chat servers. With Chat, it is very easy for you to install a standalone Chat server, and then add servers as your requirements increase.

Typical Configurations   A typical minimum configuration for 1,000 users would be a fast Pentium-class machine with 64MB RAM and 4GB of hard disk space. For a larger network of 5–10,000 users, you should look at three or four servers, each with dual CPUs, 128MB RAM and 8GB hard disks. If you are thinking really big, with up to 50,000 users in over 12,000 channels, then you are looking at 10 servers. Each server would require 4 quad Pentium Pro 200 or dual Xeon processors, 256–512MB RAM and 16GB hard disk space.

Designing Multiserver Chat Deployments   With multiple servers, you must configure Portals from one server to another up to the maximum of 255. This is not particularly complex in itself, as long as you remember that you must not create loops in your portals. Hence if Server A references Server B, which references Server C, then Server C must not reference Server A.

I will cover setting up portals in the section on configuring the Chat Service.

Software Requirements

To install the Exchange Chat Service, your server must be running:

- Windows NT Server 4.0 Service Pack 3 (SP4 recommended)
- Internet Information Server 3.0 (4.0 with the Exchange Server SP1 Chat Service)
- Internet Explorer 4.0 (IE 4.01 SP1 recommended)

Tip

> I recommend that your NT Server is a "clean" installation, not an upgrade from a previous version.

To connect to a Chat server, your clients must be running:

- A network connection to the Chat server, either over a LAN, dial-up link to an ISP, or even over a serial RAS cable.
- A suitable operating system.
- A supported IRC Chat client, such as MIRC, Microsoft Chat, or Microsoft NetMeeting.

Connectivity

Your client and server machines must be running TCP/IP with name resolution support. In most cases, this will mean registering the Chat server with DNS, if you have not already done so. You must be able to PING by computer name from the Chat client to the Chat server, that is, by entering

```
PING CHATSERVER
```

at a command prompt must produce a successful response.

If you are providing a public Chat service, your connectivity requirements to the Internet will be the same as for Internet Information Server.

You can check connectivity using Telnet. To start Telnet, click on the Start button, click on Run, and then type Telnet along with the port number of the machine you're connecting to. Or you can launch the Telnet application, select the Connect menu, and choose Remote System. Enter the host name of the Chat server, and 6667 or 7000 as the port. You will not see any prompt on the screen, but the Telnet title bar will now display the name of the remote server.

Security

Security considerations include authentication, user groups, and Accounts.

Just like IIS, you have three authentication options: NTLM, Basic (Clear Text, and Anonymous. For intranet use, you can disable anonymous access unless you want to provide an anonymous Chat room.

You can create Accounts that you can associate with NT User Groups. Chat Service installation creates certain security roles by default. You can add users to these groups using User Manager for Domains.

The default security roles for managing the Chat Service are:

- Windows NT Administrator
- Chat Sysop Manager
- Chat Sysop
- Channel Owner
- Channel Host
- Channel Member
- Chat User

For more information on these roles, see the Exchange Chat Service Help file installed with Chat.

13

Large Event Considerations

If you are running a large event, like an online conference, you will need to specify an adequate number of servers to support your expected concurrent users. You also may also want to consider making the Chat Room auditorium style and moderating the content. This is a good forum for making a trainer or company executive available to employees in scattered locations.

In an auditorium style Chat Room, questions from the participants can go only to the host, and responses from the host go to everyone. Thus, someone logged into the Chat Room will see the questions from the audience and the replies from the hosts. However, the audience cannot create a background hubbub because they cannot talk to each other. In addition, if the newsgroup is moderated, the postings from the audience are screened for suitability before appearing to all, thus ensuring the discussion stays on-topic.

Installing the Chat Service

Now that you have completed all the prerequisite actions, you can now install the Exchange Chat Service. To install the Chat Service, you must be a Windows NT Administrator.

 Note

> Before you install, you should first review the RELNOTES_CHAT.HTM file from the \Server\Eng\Chat\Setup\%platform% folder on the Exchange Server 5.5 Service Pack 1 CD.

Running the Installation Program

To run the Setup program, carry out the following task:

1. Place the Exchange Server 5.5. SP1 CD into your CD drive. Switch to the \Server\Eng\Chat\Setup\%platform% folder, and run SETUP.EXE.

2. The first screen reminds you to exit all applications before installing the Chat service.

3. You will see a screen asking you to enter your Name and Company Name.

4. You will be able to choose where to install the Chat service. The default is the \Chat subdirectory of your InetPub folder. For maximum security, this folder should be on an NTFS drive.

5. You can now choose the components that you want to install with the Exchange Chat Service. You can also install options like the SDK for server and client, online documentation, and one of the weirdest pieces of software ever, the Visual Chat client. Figure 13.25 shows the Options screen.

FIGURE 13.25

Select the components that you want to install with the Exchange Chat Service.

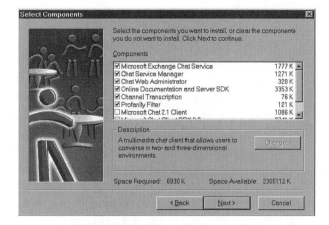

6. The setup routine will stop the WWW service during installation.

7. Setup will now complete.

Configuring the Chat Service

After you have installed the Chat Service, a new program group will appear. Click on Start, select Programs, and choose Microsoft Exchange Chat Service. Click on Chat Service Manager and you will see the screen in Figure 13.26.

FIGURE 13.26

You manage the Exchange Chat Service through Microsoft Management Console.

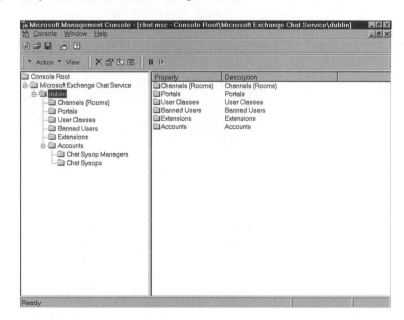

13

You can now configure server properties, Channels, Portals, User Classes, Banned Users, Extensions, and Accounts.

> **Note** Most of the following changes will require you to pause and restart the Chat service. You can do so by selecting the Chat server in the left-hand window and clicking on the Pause button in the toolbar. After a few seconds, click on the Start button.

Chat Service Server Properties

To configure the Chat Service Server properties, right-click on the server name and select Properties. You will now see a screen like that in Figure 13.27.

FIGURE 13.27

The Chat Server service Properties screen lets you configure overall server options.

The service name is the name of the Chat service to which the users connect. This defaults to the Server name, but you can change this for added security.

If you are deploying a Chat server on the Internet, you can specify that there must be a DNS reverse name resolution carried out before the Chat server will accept the connection. This checks that the connecting IP address matches the user's domain name via DNS reverse lookup.

The Channels tab lets you configure ownership of Chat channels.

The Settings tab is where you can configure the port numbers and authentication methods.

The Messages tab lets you set general welcome messages that appear, regardless of the room the user enters.

Channels

The Channels object lets you add, edit, and delete permanent channels. You can also close Channels from the Task menu.

To create channels, right-click on the Channels object and select New. There is now a single option for Create Channel. Selecting this option takes you to the dialog box shown in Figure 13.28.

FIGURE 13.28

This is the dialog box for creating a permanent Channel.

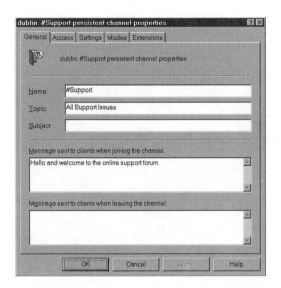

General Tab   You should give your new Channel a name, a chat topic, and a subject. The subject field lets you specify key words for Web-based searches.

Note

> IRC-compatible channels must start with a # or & character and can be up to 200 ANSI characters long. MIC channels can start with any letter and be up to 63 ANSI or Unicode characters long. You can use any characters except for null, bell, carriage return, line feed, space, comma, and backslash.

Access Tab   On the Access tab, you can specify any passwords for this channel. You can include separate or blank passwords for Member, Host, and Owner. You can specify a member account, as per setting up member accounts in the following section. Joining

13

restrictions lets you set options, like only allowing connections from authenticated clients or users running an MIC client.

Settings Tab   On the Settings tab, you can set a member limit that overrides the default setting of 25. However, if this is set to zero, the default setting will apply. You can optionally include client specific data, like identifiers for ActiveX components, PICS content ratings (for use where browsers have been configured to control content), and a country/language code.

Modes Tab   The Modes tab is the most complex of the configuration tabs, and requires you to specify the visibility of your new channel. Options are Public, Private, Hidden, or Secret. You can specify further message settings, for example, preventing external messages going to the channel.

Speaking restrictions let you configure what type of channel you are configuring. Moderated Auditoriums are best for large public discussions. Setting No Whispering (private messages to another user) is good for the paranoid, and checking Only Authenticated Members prevents anonymous users from entering the room.

The Start Channel Automatically setting means that the channel fires up when you restart the Chat service. Other channels only activate if a user enters a room. Cloneable channels reproduce themselves when the number of users in one room exceeds the user limit. This creates a room with an incrementing identification number, but otherwise identical to the first.

Extensions Tab   The Extensions tab shows what extensions (profanity filter and so on) are currently loaded.

Portals

Portals are connections between Chat servers that enable you to increase the number of simultaneous users. You can link up to 255 servers, as long as you have no loops.

To configure a portal, right-click on Portals, select New and choose Create Portal. Enter the Portal name of up to 63 characters, the remote server's IP address, and give the remote server a unique server ID number.

> **Caution**
>
> Server ID numbers must be unique; otherwise the Chat service between the two servers will cease.

After you have configured a portal on one server, you should configure one on the other server pointing back to the one you have just created. Choose which server is to initiate the connection checking the Uplink box.

User Classes

User classes let you create classes for the different types of users that will connect to your chat site. You can specify a Name for the user type, and then configure the settings that this class must use in order to connect to your Chat server. For example, you can use these settings to specify that certain types of user (such as anonymous) cannot log on.

The Settings tab lets you configure defenses against malicious attacks. You can limit the amount of simultaneous connections and the amount of unprocessed incoming data that will disconnect this client.

| **Caution** | Setting the Input Flood Limit to zero can leave your server vulnerable to flooding attacks. |

Enabling IP/DNS masking means that users in the Chat room cannot see the full IP or DNS address of the other users. However, Sysops, hosts, and owners can see the IP addresses of all connected users.

Banned Users

To ban a user from your Chat server, right-click on Banned Users and select New. Choose Create Ban and fill in the details on why you are banning that particular user.

To disconnect a user, choose Task from the menu above and then select Disconnect User. Supply a nickname, username, and domain name, provide a reason, and click Disconnect. The user will be unceremoniously ejected from the Chat room. However, a disconnected user can reconnect.

To get someone off your server and keep them off, ban them first, then disconnect them. They will not be able to reconnect.

Extensions

This is where you can enable, disable, and prioritize extensions. The Chat service currently comes with two extensions—the Profanity Filter and the Transcription Service.

After you have installed the Profanity filter, double-click on the Profanity filter object, and you will now be able to configure your profanity filter. You can have a great time thinking up all the rude words you know, and entering them into a new filter.

The Transcription Service will transcribe a channel conversation into a text file on a Web page. To view the Web page, click Start, choose Run, and click on Programs. From the Microsoft Exchange Chat Service, choose Channel Transcription Log.

13

Accounts

The accounts object lets you define groups of chat users and associate them with Windows NT Accounts. After you have done this, you can go back to the Channels object and on the Access tab, and select an Account that may use the specified channel. All other accounts are barred.

After you have created an account name, you can right-click on the new account, and from the New menu, select Add Member. You can now add Windows NT groups and users, including special groups such as Everyone.

After you have finished configuring the Chat service, close Microsoft Management Console. You will see a prompt asking you if you want to save your settings. If you do, the next time that you configure the Exchange Chat service, the console will appear the way it did when you last closed it down.

Using the Chat Service

Using the Chat service is very simple. As long as you have TCP/IP connectivity and Name Resolution working, you just specify the name of the server to which you want to connect.

Note   For Internet Chat Services, this will be a fully qualified domain name, such as chat.universal-exports.com.

The various Internet Chat clients will have different ways of configuring their settings. However, in the Options section, you should be able to specify the name of your Chat server.

Microsoft Chat

Microsoft Chat 2.1 is an IRC-compatible client that can function in text-only mode or in graphical, comic-book mode. Chat is a component of Internet Explorer 4.0.

To start Chat, select Start, click on Programs, and choose the Internet Explorer. Click on the icon for Chat, and you will see the screen in Figure 13.29.

Enter the name of your Chat server, and a room to enter. Alternatively, you can get a listing of all rooms. You can also change your personal information through the Personal Info tab.

FIGURE 13.29

The Chat startup screen lets you connect to a server and a specified room.

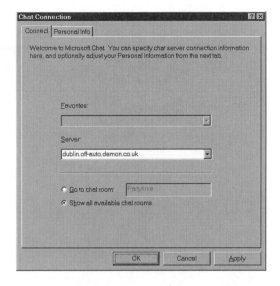

You will now enter your specified room, if it exists.

Microsoft Chat runs in two modes: comic and text-only. In comic mode, you can choose different characters or Avatar ("Av" for short) to represent you, as shown in Figure 13.30.

FIGURE 13.30

Maybe Comic mode doesn't give quite the most businesslike impression.

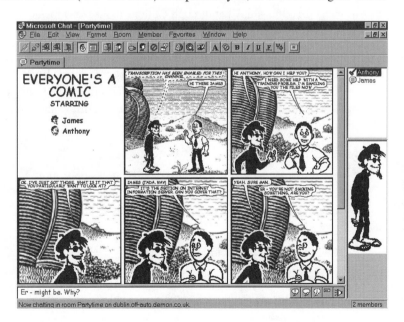

13

Here is the same conversation in text mode in Figure 13.31.

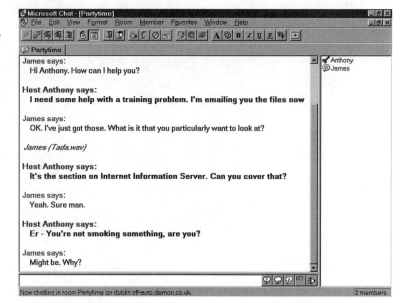

You can set options in Chat through Options in the View menu. This lets you choose your character and a background.

The Room menu is where you have options to create, enter, or leave rooms. You can call up a Room list or view the properties on the current room. If you create a room, you can decide on its properties, like a topic, whether it is moderated, private, and an optional password. After you have finished chatting, you can leave the room and disconnect through the Room menu.

NetMeeting

Microsoft NetMeeting is much more of a business application. However, although it is perfectly capable of functioning as an IRC client, NetMeeting requires the Internet Locator Service (ILS) to function to its full effect. I will cover the ILS in the final section.

NetMeeting gives you the following facilities:

- The ability to locate and call logged on users (requires the ILS to work).
- A Whiteboard for sharing jottings, scribbles, and so on.
- A Chat window, for when the telephone isn't working.

- Application sharing, to let others see what is on your screen.
- Collaboration, to let other users collaborate on the same application.
- Audio (duplex or half duplex, depending on your hardware, and assuming you have a microphone).
- Video (with a suitable camera installed).
- File Transfer.

You can use NetMeeting without the ILS; for example, you can make a NetMeeting call direct from Microsoft Chat. However, you will not get a directory listing without the ILS. Hence, you would not be able to see who was online at any particular time.

The NetMeeting interface has a similar look to Outlook 98, with toolbars and a folder list, as shown in Figure 13.32.

FIGURE 13.32

NetMeeting is much more of a business application, with audio, video, application collaboration, and a whiteboard for scribbling.

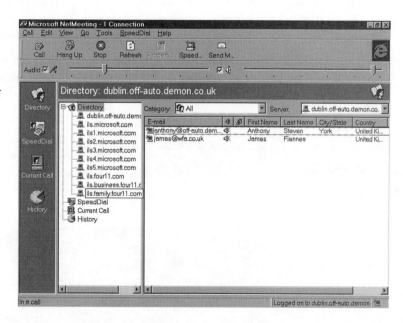

Under the directory servers, you will see certain preconfigured Internet ILS servers, such as ils.microsoft.com. If you have an Internet connection, you can log on to one of these servers, and chat merrily away to anyone listed. If they'll talk to you, that is.

You can configure Options in NetMeeting through the Tools menu, including your identity, the speed of your connection, AutoDial, audio, and video options.

Note If you are sharing applications, the machine receiving the shared application must be running in the same or higher screen resolution to the machine sending. If not, the shared application will not display.

Microsoft Visual Chat

Microsoft Visual Chat is without a doubt the weirdest application that I have ever used. I don't think that you could use it for serious business work—unless you work in a very relaxed company with a fast Internet connection. But it is a lot of fun.

Like Microsoft Chat, you choose an avatar, or image icon, to represent you. Unlike Chat, you can roam around the Chat rooms, which actually look like three-dimensional rooms. People will drift in and out, and may even talk to you. Imagine playing a session of network Doom or Quake in which you converse with, rather than shoot at, the other participants. Mind you, after a few minutes, you'll probably wish you had the option.

You can install Visual Chat 2.0 Beta from the Exchange Server 5.5 SP1 CD. Switch to the Server\Eng\Chat\Setup\i386 folder and run VCHAT2B.EXE. This will create a Microsoft V-Chat icon in Program Files. Start Visual Chat, and you will see the screen in Figure 13.33.

FIGURE 13.33

Stand by for the strangest software experience going. It's even weirder with a sound card.

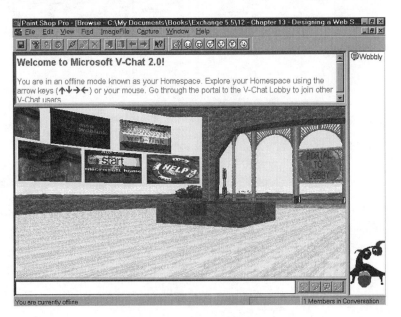

Now click the sign to the right marked Entrance to Portal. After some strange effects, you will arrive in the Lobby, as shown in Figure 13.34.

FIGURE 13.34

Here I am in the Microsoft Lobby.

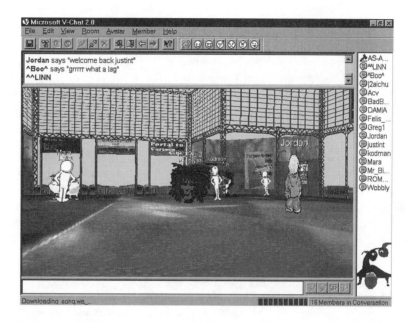

FIGURE 13.34

Here I am in the Microsoft Lobby.

There are various doors off this room, which lead to other rooms. You can wander about using your cursor keys or double-click on a door to go to another room. Various characters enter, make comments, and then leave. It's a bit like being at a party, except you can go home at any time and you don't have to bring a bottle.

Who knows? Maybe in the future, Web pages will be look like this.

Troubleshooting the Chat Service

If you can't connect to the Exchange Chat Service, try the following steps first:

1. Carry out a System Hard Reset on both Server and Client. For details of the System Hard Reset, see Day 8, "Troubleshooting Exchange."

2. On reboot, check that the Chat Service is running via the Services icon in Control Panel.

3. Check for any error messages in Event Viewer.

4. From the client, check that you can PING the name of the Exchange Chat Server.

5. Try connecting to Port 6667 using Telnet.

13

If all these steps work, consult the Chat Service online documentation or search for "Chat" in TechNet or the Knowledge Base.

Internet Locator Service

The Microsoft Internet Locator Server (ILS) is a standards-based solution to the problem of locating users on the Internet. It achieves this by providing a dynamic database of users logged on to an ILS Web site. ILS uses the Lightweight Directory Access Protocol (LDAP) standard as the basis of its directory listings. Microsoft NetMeeting 2.0 and later uses ILS.

ILS runs on Internet Information Server, and maintains a directory database of logged on users in RAM. You can access this database using either an LDAP client (like NetMeeting) or a Web-based interface via Active Server Pages.

ILS replaces the older ULS (User Location Service) that provided similar functionality for earlier versions of NetMeeting. ILS provides legacy support for ULS.

 Note

ILS uses the LDAP protocol on Port 389. This means that for ILS to work on the same machine as Exchange Server, you will have to change the port number for the Exchange LDAP service. See Day 14, "Reading Exchange Mail with Internet Clients" for more information on configuring LDAP.

Installing ILS is separate from installing the Chat service. However, the location service on NetMeeting will not work unless you have the ILS installed.

For further reading on ILS, see the documentation installed with the Internet Locator Service. RFC 1779 defines the Internet directory protocol, and RFCs 1777, 1778, and 1779 define LDAP. For information on obtaining RFCs, see Day 11, "Communication Protocols and the Internet."

Installing the Internet Locator Service

To install the Internet Locator Service, place the Exchange Server 5.5 CD in the CD drive. When the splash screen appears, choose Setup Server and Components. Select Internet Locator Service, and continue. The ILS will install documentation into your \InetPub\ILS directory, create a new LDAP object in Internet Information Server's console, and install the Microsoft LDAP service on the relevant server.

Configuring the Internet Locator Service

You configure the ILS service through Internet Information Server. To do this, choose Start, Programs, NT 4.0 Option Pack, and click Internet Service Manager. Microsoft Management Console will start, and you will now see a program window like the one shown in Figure 13.35.

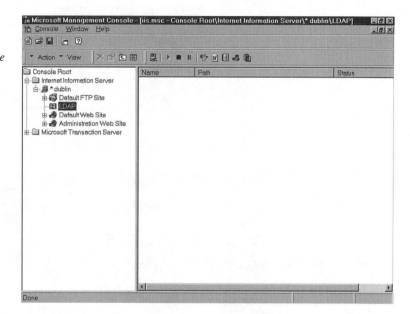

Right-click the new LDAP object and select Properties. The Properties sheet shown in Figure 13.36 will appear.

As far as ILS is concerned, you can specify Anonymous or Authenticated access. On the ILS Server tab, you have settings for the client TTL and the maximum number of users supported (measured in thousands). The Logging and Advanced tabs are standard IIS tabs for configuring logging options and excluding IP addresses.

Using the Internet Locator Service

Microsoft NetMeeting uses the ILS service to locate users.

Start NetMeeting, and connect to the server on which you installed ILS. Click on the Directory icon, and you will now see a listing of all the users connected to that server. Figure 13.37 shows an example taken from one of Microsoft's ILS servers on the Internet.

13

FIGURE **13.36**

The properties of the LDAP service govern ILS settings.

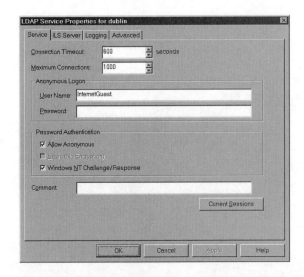

FIGURE **13.37**

The ILS servers on the Internet get pretty busy.

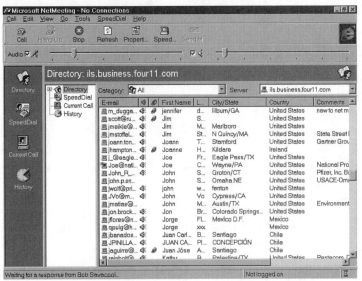

To call a user, double-click on her name. A box will pop up on their screen telling her that someone wants to chat. She can then either accept or reject the call.

Summary

This lesson has covered a number of new or recent additions to Exchange's arsenal of messaging solutions. Doubtless, the next service pack and subsequent releases of the product will add significant functionality to what is already available.

To summarize the main points of this lesson:

- If you have a mailbox on Exchange, you can connect to it using a Web browser. This will give you access to your messages, appointments, and contacts folders.

- Anonymous users can use a Web browser to query Exchange's directory service, and to view and post to public folders.

- Outlook Web Access required Internet Information Server, a frames and Java-enabled browser, and the Outlook Web Access Client installed on the IIS machine.

- You can install IIS on the Exchange server or on a separate server.

- The Exchange Chat service lets you configure a private Chat server supporting IRC, IRCX, or MIC clients.

- Microsoft Chat, Visual Chat, and Microsoft NetMeeting are all IRC clients that will work with the Exchange Chat service.

- The Internet Locator Service provides an LDAP-based listing directory for use with Microsoft NetMeeting.

Q&A

Q I'm installing the Outlook Web Access Client onto IIS, and I want my users to be able to connect to Exchange over the Internet. What are the security considerations here?

A On the Directory Security tab on your Exchange virtual directory on IIS, you must enable NTLM Challenge/Response as the only security method. Also require a secure connection, and restrict incoming connections by IP address. In addition, you should restrict your proxy server or firewall to warn on malformed packets and configure auditing to detect logon failures. Finally, check your security logs on a regular basis.

Q I am responsible for PR at a large multinational oil company. We want to provide a service whereby the public can take part in a forum of question and answer sessions. We want to control the actual questions that people ask and we don't want the process to break down into a shouting match. How could the Exchange Chat service help us?

A This functionality is already present in the Exchange Chat service. After the Chat Service is working, add a permanent Chat channel with Anonymous access. Make this auditorium style and moderated. Hence the people joining the room will only hear the moderated questions to the host, but everyone hears the replies. Users will not be able to chat to each other. Put a marker on your Web site pointing to the Chat room, and after the Chat session is complete, publish the transcript onto the Web.

13

Q I've just installed the Exchange Chat Service and I can connect using Microsoft Chat. However, if I start NetMeeting, I can't see any users listed in the directory. What's the problem?

A The Chat service provides the ability to host IRC conversations. However, NetMeeting uses the Internet Locator Service (ILS) to build its directory information. If you install the ILS component from the Exchange Server 5.5 CD, you should find that your directory is listed correctly.

Workshop

The Workshop provides two ways for you to affirm what you've learned in this lesson. The "Quiz" section poses questions to help you solidify your understanding of the material covered and the "Exercise" section provides you with experience in using what you have learned. You can find answers to the quiz questions and exercises in Appendix B, "Answers to Quiz Questions and Exercises."

Quiz

1. What are the server requirements for installing Outlook Web Access?
2. What are the client requirements for OWA?
3. What are the Connectivity requirements for OWA?
4. What facilities are available to OWA anonymous users?
5. What extra components are required for ASP support on IIS 4.0?
6. What difference will you notice when installing OWA on a separate IIS server from your Exchange server?
7. Which Outlook folders does OWA support?
8. In which areas can you configure OWA in Exchange Administrator?
9. Where can you restrict OWA connections by IP address?
10. What are the server requirements for the Exchange Chat Service?
11. What are the server requirements for the Internet Locator Service?

Exercise

Install a trial Chat service and Internet Location Service, and connect using NetMeeting.

DAY 14

Reading Exchange Mail with Internet Clients

By Anthony Steven

Chapter Objectives

On Day 11, "Communication Protocols and the Internet," you had a general introduction to the Internet messaging protocols that Exchange can use. On Day 12, "Exchange on the Internet," you learned how to add the Internet Mail Service and the Internet News Service. Today you will build upon this knowledge and look at how you can use Internet clients in order to connect to Microsoft Exchange. Using Internet clients, you can read mail, download public folders, and retrieve addressing information.

You will be covering the following topics:

- Retrieving mail using POP3.
- Delivering mail using STMP.

- Downloading and posting to newsgroups using NNTP.
- Using LDAP to query Exchange's address lists.
- Configuring LDAP replication between servers.
- Setting anonymous access permissions for NNTP, LDAP, and IMAP.

Exchange Internet Client Support

One of the major updates that Microsoft brought in with Exchange 5.0 was the increased support for Internet protocols. Exchange 5.5 has increased this level of integration, to the point that you could now run a perfectly functional messaging system based on Microsoft Exchange without using MAPI clients at all.

> **INTERNET CLIENT CAN MEAN INTRANET**
>
> Although I will mainly be talking about using Internet clients, don't forget that everything you cover in this chapter applies equally well to intranet clients.

What Internet Messaging Protocols Are There?

The specific protocols that you will be covering today are as follows:

- POP3
- IMAP4
- SMTP
- LDAP
- NNTP

POP3

Post Office Protocol (POP3) is a message collection protocol that overcomes the problems associated with SMTP. POP3 servers offer store-and-forward facilities, so clients can connect and download their mail and don't have to be online all the time. POP3 also enables you to collect mail from different locations—it doesn't have to be the same machine picking it up. This means that with POP3, you can be anywhere in the world, and you can still dial in and collect your mail from a POP3 server.

POP3 and SMTP   However, POP3 is a message collection protocol, and does not normally perform message delivery. To do this, you have to implement SMTP. As you will now know from Day 12, the Internet Mail Service adds an RFC-compliant SMTP server to Microsoft Exchange.

Hence, to use POP3 clients with Exchange, you have to install a basic configuration of the IMS, as I described in Day 12.

When Would I Use POP3?   You would use POP3 under the following circumstances:

- You have a routed LAN and do not want to support MAPI clients.
- You have a routed WAN which does not support MAPI and you want an alternative to using Remote Mail.
- You have clients accessing their company mailboxes over the Internet.
- You are an ISP and are providing POP3 as a service to your dial-up clients.

I will take you through the configuration of POP3 mailboxes in the next section.

IMAP4

Interactive Mail Access Protocol (IMAP4) is the latest attempt to overcome the limitations of SMTP. It also goes much further than POP3, in that it will handle the downloading of all your Exchange folders, including public folders.

Like POP3, IMAP is a delivery protocol, and it still requires SMTP to deliver mail. Hence, you will need to install the IMS to support these types of clients.

The problem with IMAP is that very few ISPs have adopted it. However, that isn't a problem with your Exchange server.

IMAP and Mailbox Folders   POP3 will only enable you to download messages from your Exchange Inbox. With IMAP, however, you can download any of your mailbox folders, including Contacts and Calendar. However, before you start leaping around with joy, just because you can download the Contacts or Calendar items doesn't mean you can read them. Some folders in Outlook use custom forms, so you won't be able to see any items from these folders properly. Even if you download them into Outlook 98, you still won't be able to use them.

IMAP4 does work quite happily with any folders that you have designated as message folders and it will also download any public folders. Unlike NNTP clients, you do not have to publish these folders as newsgroups.

When Would I Use IMAP?   The big advantage with IMAP is that you can download a consistent mailbox wherever you are located. You can see the same messages and the same public folders at work or at home.

14

> **Note**   If you are carrying out a comparison of Internet-based connection methods, don't forget to include Outlook Web Access. You will cover this on Day 13, "Building a Web Site Around Exchange."

LDAP

Lightweight Directory Access Protocol (LDAP) is not a messaging protocol at all but a means of finding out someone's mail address. Although defined as an RFC, it evolved out of the X.500 CCITT recommendations. See Day 11, "Understanding the Internet," for more information.

LDAP and X.500   X.500 is a CCITT recommendation for implementing directory (addressing) services. X.500 also defined Directory Access Protocol (DAP) as a means of querying an X.500 directory to retrieve addressing information. However, DAP was too resource-hungry and is not widely used.

To overcome this problem, an alternative means of querying an X.500 directory appeared, which was LDAP. Although not X.500-compliant, Exchange supports the use of LDAP clients to query the Exchange Directory Service (DS). This is possible either as an anonymous or as an authenticated user.

Exchange also supports LDAP referrals, which means that if your Exchange server cannot find an address, it can pass the query on to other servers. These servers can be any other type of LDAP server.

When Would I Use LDAP Clients?   You would use LDAP alongside POP3 or IMAP4. With a POP3 or IMAP4 client, you will not have access to the Exchange Global Address List, so LDAP will give you the ability to resolve mail addresses. The Windows Address Book that comes with Internet Explorer is an LDAP client.

Internet LDAP Servers   LDAP clients can also query the LDAP servers on the Internet, such as Whowhere and Bigfoot. See Day 11 for more information.

NNTP

NNTP (Network News Transfer Protocol) is the protocol that underpins the Internet Usenet newsgroups. The Internet News Service that you looked at on Day 11 lets you connect your Exchange server to your ISP's news site. It also enables your clients to download any public folders that you have published as newsgroups.

When Would I Use NNTP Clients?　You would use NNTP clients if you were using POP3 and LDAP for your mail and addressing needs. This means that you are not using Outlook or Exchange Client to connect to Exchange server over MAPI. NNTP provides a way for you to publish public folders so that an NNTP client can read them.

Note

> You do not need to use NNTP with IMAP4. This is because IMAP4 can download all public folders, without you having to publish them as newsgroups.

What Internet Clients Are There?

There are a vast number of Internet clients on the market—Eudora, Netscape, Outlook, and Outlook Express to name but a few. Table 14.1 compares the more common clients. However, as most of them are available for free download, you can try out a few before committing yourself. As I am sure you will find out, there are pages and pages on the Web about how "our client is better than yours—ner-ner-nah-ner-ner." It really depends whose Web page you read.

TABLE 14.1　WHICH CLIENT IS RIGHT FOR YOU?

Name	POP3	IMAP4	NNTP	LDAP
Outlook Express	✓	✓	✓	✓
Outlook 98	✓	✓	✗[f1]	✓[1]
Netscape Messenger	✓	✓	✓	✓
Eudora Pro	✓	✓	✗[f2]	✓

[1]*Uses Outlook Express to read news*
[2]*Add-on from Microsoft Web site*

Generally, the configuration of Internet clients is very similar, regardless of which client you are trying to configure. This is because POP3/IMAP4/LDAP are standards and so the clients tend to require the same standard information.

14

Outlook Express

Outlook Express is a fully featured Internet client, offering support for POP3, IMAP4, SMTP, LDAP, and NNTP. Outlook Express installs as part of Internet Explorer 4.0 and later. It also supports RTF messages with embedded HTML. It seems to work okay, but it's not rocket science. You can obtain IE 4.0 from

```
http://www.microsoft.com/windows/ie/download/default.asp
```

Outlook 98

Outlook 98 is primarily a MAPI client and would therefore normally connect directly to an Exchange server over RPC. However, it can be a POP3/IMAP4 client, using the Internet Email service. There is also a service for LDAP. Personally, I wouldn't recommend Outlook 98 for use as a POP3 client to Exchange, unless you use the dedicated Internet Mail connection option. For an expanded view of the options available with Outlook 98, see Day 10, "Using Microsoft Outlook."

Outlook 98 is available for free download from

```
http://premium.officeupdate.microsoft.com/officeupdate/DistribDownload/
➥outlook98ddl.htm
```

Netscape Messenger

Netscape Messenger is part of the Netscape Communicator suite of Internet tools. It's got a snappy name and it's *not* Microsoft! Personally, I don't think there's that much to choose between the Microsoft and Netscape offerings, although both their marketing departments will probably scratch me off their Christmas card list for saying that. Oh well. You pays your money and you takes your choice. Or rather, you don't pays your money, you takes your choice and *then* you pays your money.

Download Netscape from

```
http://home.netscape.com/browsers/index.htm
```

Eudora Pro

Eudora Pro claims to be the client that uses the most number of features of the IMAP4 standard. If so, it could be a good client to use if you are implementing IMAP4. It doesn't include a newsreader, but if you are using IMAP4, you don't need one.

The shareware version of Eudora Pro, Eudora Lite, is available free from

```
http://www.eudora.com/
```

Note | I will be using Outlook Express for most of this lesson.

Supporting POP3/IMAP Clients

Now I will take you through the process of configuring POP3 or IMAP4 support on your Exchange server. You will then look at configuring clients to use POP3 or IMAP. I have put these two protocols together because the setup for both is almost identical. Any differences I have highlighted in the section on IMAP that follows.

Exchange Server POP3/IMAP4 Configuration

As far as the Exchange Server goes, you have to do very little to install POP3/IMAP4 support. All mailboxes support POP3/IMAP4 access by default. However, you can configure this support at a site, server, or mailbox level, giving you control over which particular mailboxes you select to enable for POP3/IMAP4.

Site Level

You configure POP3/IMAP4 at the site level through the POP3/IMAP4 object in the site level protocols container. Start Exchange Administrator and select your site in the left pane. Click on the site object to expand it and select the Protocols container object. In the right pane, select the POP3 object. Double-click on the POP3 object. You will now see the screen shown in Figure 14.1.

FIGURE 14.1

The site level POP3 object can control all POP3 settings.

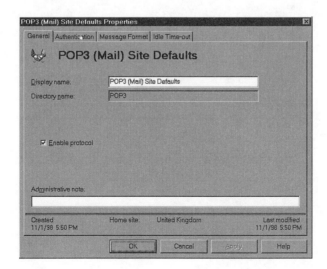

14

> **Tip**
>
> The site level configuration settings will automatically apply to the server and mailbox levels. Wherever possible, you should use the site level object to control POP3 behavior. This also applies to NNTP, IMAP4, and LDAP.

General Tab The General tab lets you do two things: rename the POP3 object and enable the protocol. You can usually enable and disable protocols at a site, server, and mailbox level, as discussed in the sidebar "Enabling and Disabling Protocols."

ENABLING AND DISABLING PROTOCOLS

The POP3, IMAP4, and NNTP objects can all be selectively enabled and disabled at the site, server, and mailbox level. These options really come into play in a multiserver environment, where you have the following options:

- Enable the protocol at a site level but disable it on individual servers.

- Disable the protocol at a site level but enable it on individual servers.

- Enable the protocol at a server level, but disable it at a mailbox level.

- Individual mailboxes can only be enabled if the protocol is enabled at the server level, regardless of whether the protocol is enabled or disabled at the site level.

HTTP and LDAP settings are slightly different. You can enable or disable HTTP at a site and mailbox level but not at a server level. HTTP support at a server level is provided by Internet Information Server (IIS), which is independent of the Exchange server.

You can only configure LDAP at a site and server level. You cannot control which individuals do and don't appear in the LDAP address list in this manner, as this would invalidate the point of the LDAP support.

Authentication Tab Here you specify which types of authentication are acceptable for users to validate to their POP3 mailbox. Figure 14.2 shows the Authentication tab.

Options include the following:

FIGURE 14.2

The Authentication tab enables you to specify which types of encryption and authentication POP3 clients can use.

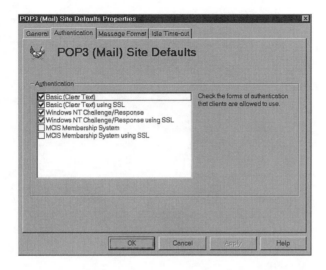

- Basic (Clear Text)—unencrypted text password authentication. Most clients support this method.

- Basic (Clear Text) using SSL—the clear text login sequence is now encrypted using SSL.

- Windows NT Challenge/Response—requires an NT user account and password. The password is encrypted.

- Windows NT Challenge/Response—requires an NT user account and password. The entire login sequence is encrypted using SSL.

- MCIS Membership System—uses Microsoft Commercial Internet Server Membership and Windows NT security.

- MCIS Membership System—uses Microsoft Commercial Internet Server Membership and Windows NT security over SSL.

For more information on SSL, see Day 11.

Message Format Tab   The Message Format tab enables you to set default message encoding types. These will apply to attachments sent with messages. You can select from MIME (most common) or uuencode (only for older mail clients). You can also choose a character set, although I guess most of you will be quite happy with Western European, as shown in Figure 14.3.

14

FIGURE 14.3

The Message Format tab gives you options for attachments, character sets, and Exchange RTF formatting.

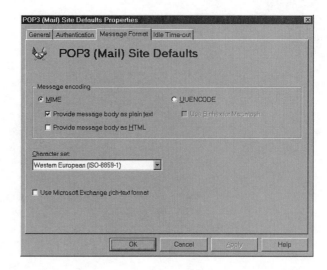

The check box will allow messages to be sent using Microsoft Exchange Rich Text Format (RTF). RTF means that the text of the message displays in color with different font sizes, and so on. Don't use this option if bandwidth is a major consideration, as it does increase the size of the messages somewhat.

Outlook and Outlook Express can both cope with messages using Exchange RTF formatting.

Idle Timeout   This tab simply controls how long a connection to a mailbox can be idle before the server drops it. Keep this value low to reduce the impact of POP3 connections, but not so low that your users keep having to reconnect, which generates additional traffic. Usually the default setting is fine.

Server Level

To configure POP3 settings at the server level, go to the relevant server and select the Protocols object. Again, double-click on the Protocols object and you will see the POP3 object. Double-click on the POP3 object and you will see almost identical tabs to those you saw at the site level.

The two exceptions are as follows:

- The General tab has a new check box for Use Site Defaults For All Properties.
- There is an additional Diagnostics Logging tab.

If you uncheck the option for Use Site Defaults, you will be able to configure the same POP3 options as you could at the site level. Now, the settings will only apply to the particular server that you are configuring. If you leave site defaults option checked, all the settings at the server level will appear grayed out and you cannot change them. However, you can change the settings on the Diagnostics Logging tab.

Diagnostics Logging Tab   The Diagnostics Logging tab is where you can control logging levels on the POP3 object, as shown in Figure 14.4.

After you have changed the logging level, click OK or Apply, and POP3 events will appear in the Application Event Log. See Day 8, "Troubleshooting Exchange," for information on how to use the Event Viewer.

FIGURE 14.4

Use the Diagnostics Logging functions to troubleshoot your POP3 connections. This tab is only present at the server-level POP3 object.

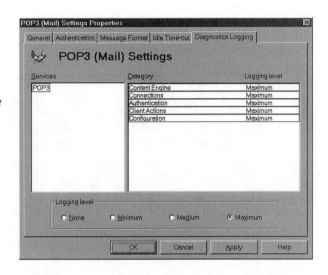

> **Caution**
>
> You should only increase logging levels on the POP3 object when you are troubleshooting. Do not forget to return the levels to Minimum or Off during normal operation. Logging places an extra load on your server and reduces performance.

> **Note**
>
> You can configure POP3 logging from the server object. In Exchange Administrator, click on the name of your server in the left pane. Then select the File menu and click on Properties (keyboard shortcut Alt+Enter). Click on the Diagnostics Logging tab to see the tree of all logging levels on this server. You want to expand the MSExchangeIS tree and look under Internet Protocols. There you will see the POP3, NNTP, and IMAP objects, which you can configure individually.

14

Mailbox Level

You can enable or disable POP3 support at a mailbox level, but only if you enable POP3 support at a server level. The default setting is enabled.

To configure support at a mailbox level, open Exchange Administrator and click on the Recipients container for your site. Select the recipient that you want to change and double-click on their mailbox entry. Click on the Protocols tab and then double-click on the entry for POP3. You will now see the screen at Figure 14.5.

If you uncheck the box for Use Protocol Defaults, you now have the option of changing the message encoding used with attachments, the character set, and whether to use RTF formatting. You would use this if you had a user connecting with a different type of POP3 client from that used by the rest of your users.

FIGURE 14.5

You can now selectively enable POP3 support at a mailbox level.

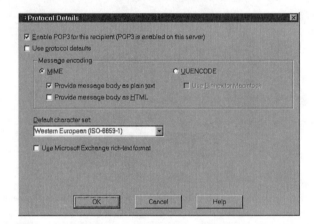

Changing Internet Mail Service Configuration

Having configured the POP3 object, you will need to make some changes to the Internet Mail Service to ensure that your system supports POP3 properly.

If all you are interested in is providing POP3 support, you need to run the Internet Mail Service Wizard, accepting the defaults (typical). For more information on installing the Internet Mail Service, see Day 12. Also, see the section in Day 12 on configuring the IMS for further detail.

If you already have installed the IMS, check the following settings, starting with the Routing tab.

Routing Tab   You must change the configuration of the IMS so that incoming mail for your domain reroutes to <inbound>. This will mean that Exchange will check SMTP mail from your POP3 clients against internal SMTP recipients rather than merely forwarding these messages directly to the Internet.

To do this, start the Exchange Administrator and select your site in the left pane. Click on the site object to expand it and select the Connectors container object. In the right pane, select the Internet Mail Service object. Double-click on the IMS object and click on the Routing tab. You will now see the dialog box shown in Figure 14.6.

Routing Restrictions   You can place restrictions on which clients can reroute via the IMS by clicking on the Routing Restrictions button. See Day 12 for more information on setting restrictions.

FIGURE 14.6

To use the IMS with POP3 clients, you must reroute mail for your domain to <inbound>.

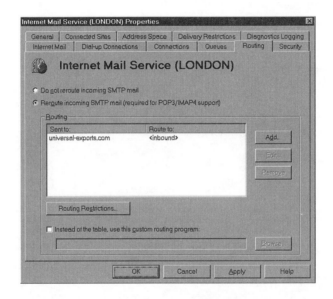

Connections Tab   On the Connections tab you can configure which hosts can connect to this IMS. Select the option for Only From Hosts Using and choose the level of authentication and encryption that you require.

Specify by Host   You can also accept and reject hosts by IP address by using the Specify by Host button. Here you can specify host IP addresses that may connect, and what sort of authentication or encryption they should be using.

Note   You can accept or reject host connections by IP address at the Protocols object level. See the section later in this chapter on how to configure the Protocols object.

14

You should now have successfully configured POP3 from the server end. You have also installed an Internet Mail Service to provide SMTP delivery. Now I will show you how to configure a POP3 client to pick up mail from the Exchange server.

Setting Up a POP3/IMAP4 Client

When setting up a POP3/IMAP4 client, you will normally require the following information:

- Your name and email address.
- Name or IP address of the POP3/IMAP server.
- Name or IP address of the SMTP server.
- Username and password to logon to the server.
- A connection method (LAN/WAN, RAS or via third-party dialer.

I will be using Outlook Express as my client because most of the configuration issues are the same with all Internet clients.

Outlook Express

To install Outlook Express, you need to install Internet Explorer 4.0.

> **Note** The settings for Outlook Express are very similar to those for the Mail and News program that came with Internet Explorer 3.02.

After you have installed Internet Explorer 4.0 and restarted your machine, click on the Outlook Express icon on your desktop. On starting Outlook Express, a prompt will ask you to specify a root directory. Normally, you can just accept the defaults.

Using the Internet Connection Wizard   On first running Outlook Express, you may see a prompt asking you to run the Internet Connection Wizard. This will set up a standard POP3 or IMAP account. Here's how you complete the Wizard.

1. Enter your name in the first dialog box the Wizard presents. This should match your Exchange Mailbox name.

2. Add your email address into the second dialog box in the form *alias@site. organization.com*. This must match the SMTP address on the Email Addresses tab in your mailbox on the Exchange Server.

3. The third dialog box requires you to select whether you want to use a POP3 or IMAP server. Choose the correct configuration from the drop-down list and then add the host name or IP address of the relevant server. With Exchange, this will be something like *exchangeserver.site.organization.com*. The SMTP server will probably be *exchangeserver.site.organization.com* as well, as shown in Figure 14.7.

FIGURE 14.7

With Exchange, you will probably find that your incoming and outgoing servers are the same. You can also use IP addresses.

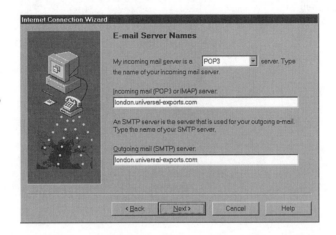

4. The fourth dialog box is where you can configure the client security. You have two options: log on using a particular account, or log on using the account that you logged into Windows NT or 98 with. My recommendation would be to use secure password authentication, as in Figure 14.8.

FIGURE 14.8

This dialog box gives you the option of using a specific logon account or secure password authentication.

14

5. In this dialog box, you should enter a name for your connection that is easy to remember. The default entry is the name of your server. Remember to differentiate between the same type of account on different servers and different types of account on the same server. Figure 14.9 shows an example.

FIGURE 14.9

Pick a friendly name to refer to your connection.

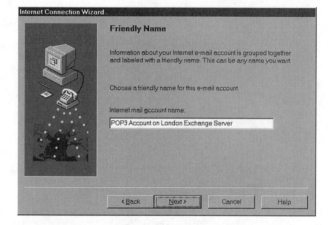

6. The Choose Connection Type dialog box gives you three choices for connecting to your POP3 server—Remote Access, LAN, or a manual connection. If you are using POP3/IMAP4 over a LAN or private WAN, select LAN. If you are using POP3/IMAP4 to connect to your Exchange server over a dial-up connection to the Internet, use the phone line option.

7. If you select the phone line option I just mentioned, now you will need to specify a RAS or dial-up networking connection to connect to your ISP or Exchange server.

Make sure this dial-up connection works and can connect to your ISP or RAS server automatically.

8. That's it! Click Finish to exit the Wizard.

ADDING AN ACCOUNT MANUALLY

To add an account manually to Outlook Express, select the Tools menu and choose Accounts. Click on the Add button and you will see a list of three account types: Mail, News, and Directory Service.

Select the type of account you want to create and the New Account Wizard will start.

To change the properties of an account, select the account and click Properties. Note that the tabs just sort the accounts into their respective types.

Outlook 98

You can use Outlook 98 as a POP3 client by adding the Internet Email service to your messaging profile. To do this, start Outlook, click Tools, and select Services. Select the Add button and then add the Internet Email service.

You can configure Outlook 98 as a Corporate/Workgroup email client, which gives you connectivity to Exchange and POP3 servers, or you can install the full Internet client option. The full Internet client option adds POP3, IMAP, and LDAP support, implemented in a very similar way to Outlook Express. Here I am referring to the Internet Mail POP3 client that comes with Outlook's Corporate/Workgroup client.

You will now have to fill in four tabs' worth of information. These tabs are identical to the General, Servers, Connection, and Advanced tabs I'll discuss in the next section.

If you are using Outlook 98 with just the Internet Email service, that is, you have not added the Exchange server service, you must add a personal folder. See Day 7, "Configuring the Exchange Client," for more information on personal folders.

Configuring a POP3/IMAP4 Client

After you have installed a new POP3 or IMAP4 client, you will find that you can alter some additional settings.

14

Outlook Express

In Outlook Express you configure these by clicking on the Tools menu and selecting
Accounts. Click on the Mail tab and you should see the mail account that you want to
configure. Select this account and click on the Properties button. You will now see a dialog box like the one in Figure 14.10.

FIGURE 14.10

*You can configure your
POP3/IMAP4 accounts
after installation.*

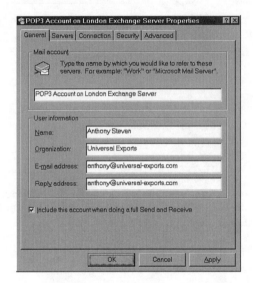

General Tab   The General tab is where you configure any identification settings. You
can change the name of your mail connection, or alter your own name and email address.

Servers Tab   The Servers tab, shown in Figure 14.11, lets you change your outgoing
(SMTP) or incoming (POP3 or IMAP) servers. However, you cannot change an account
from IMAP to POP3 once you have installed it. This screen also enables you to change
your logon settings. In addition to changing these for your POP3/IMPA4 server, you can
also set them for your outgoing SMTP server. You would use this in conjunction with
setting authentication on your Internet Mail Service. See the "Connections Tab" section
in Day 12 for more information about the Accept Connections button.

FIGURE 14.11

The Servers tab lets you change your SMTP or POP3/IMAP4 server, authentication account, and outgoing server authentication settings.

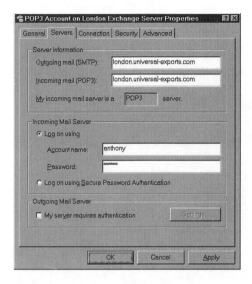

Caution You can run both POP3 and IMAP4 accounts at the same time. So you could have a POP3 connection direct to your private POP3 account and an IMAP4 account to your Exchange server.

Connection Tab   You would use the Connection tab to change how your client connects to the Exchange server. Again, you could have different settings for different accounts, like with my previous tip. Figure 14.12 shows this tab configured to dial into an ISP.

If you are using a private WAN, select the LAN option.

Security Tab   The Security tab gives you the ability to use a digital ID when sending messages. A digital ID includes your public key, which is what someone else requires to send you a message. To obtain a digital ID, you need to apply to a certifying authority, like VeriSign. Click on the More Info button for further reading about Outlook Express and security, or click on Get Digital ID to go to Microsoft's Web site and select a provider of digital IDs. Figure 14.13 shows this screen.

14

FIGURE 14.12

You can change your connection settings via the Connection tab.

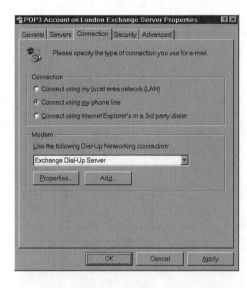

FIGURE 14.13

You may want to configure security if you need to send confidential information over the Internet.

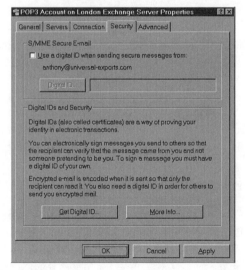

Note

You will probably want to use advanced security only if you are sending sensitive messages onto the Internet. However, if your MAPI clients are using Exchange Advanced security, you may want to enable this feature on your LAN/WAN. In a LAN environment, you would need to set up your own certification server. Internet Information Server 4.0 comes with Certification Server and is available as part of the NT Option pack.

Another option is to use SSL connections on the Advanced tab.

Advanced Tab This is the most useful of Outlook Express's configuration tabs. You can configure SSL encryption between your client and server for either incoming or outgoing mail. This means that your messages are in encrypted form while they are in transit on your network or over the telephone wires. Figure 14.14 shows the Advanced tab.

FIGURE 14.14

The Advanced tab contains a number of useful configuration options.

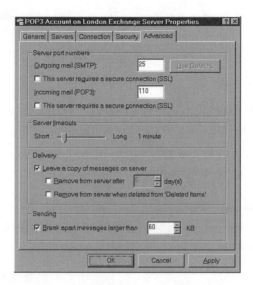

Server Port Numbers Selecting the SSL option on either outgoing or incoming servers will change the port numbers used to talk to these servers. You would use this where you have set up your Exchange Internet Mail Service to accept only encrypted mail. See the "Connections Tab" section on Day 12 to configure your IMS to accept only encrypted connections.

Server Timeouts You would only need to change this value if you have a very slow link or a busy POP3 server. It gives the server more time to respond to the incoming mail request. You should only change this if you are having problems with mail timeouts.

Delivery This section is particularly useful if you are using both a MAPI client and a POP3 client to access your mailbox. One of the problems with POP3 is that it tends to strip your mail off the POP3 server. Now, that's fine when you connect to your ISP. After all, they don't want it on there after you've downloaded it. But with Exchange, this may be undesirable.

So if you are combining POP3 access with MAPI, make sure you leave a copy of the messages on your server. If you don't, you will find yourself constantly having to forward messages back to yourself.

14

Caution   If you do choose to leave your messages on the server, watch out for exceeding your message storage limit.

Sending   This option enables you to let your client and server break up large messages into blocks, which can then be sent and verified separately. Use this option if you are working in a very low bandwidth environment or one where communications are not very reliable.

Outlook 98

To configure the POP3/IMAP4 settings for Outlook 98, start Outlook, click Tools and then select Services. Double-click on the Internet Email service.

Make any changes to the General, Servers, Connection, and Advanced tabs as per the section on Outlook Express previously.

Differences Between POP3 and IMAP4

Having looked at the settings to configure both POP3 and IMAP4 accounts, I will now take you through the areas that differ for IMAP4.

Note   In this next section, I am comparing the IMAP4 settings to the POP3 configuration that you have just covered. All other settings are as per the POP3 settings, which you have already covered.

Exchange Server Protocols Container

With IMAP4, you should make any changes to the IMAP4 object at site, server, and mailbox level. Figure 14.15 shows the IMAP4 site level object.

General Tab   The General tab includes two new check boxes.

The check box Include All Public Folders When a Folder List Is Displayed governs the download of public folders to clients. Disable this if you find that your clients are having problems downloading large numbers of public folders or you don't want your clients to download public folders via IMAP.

FIGURE 14.15

The site level IMAP object allows for download of public folders and anonymous access.

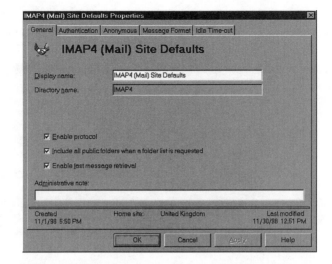

Use the Enable Fast Message Retrieval option if you are using Outlook Express to access your mailbox via IMAP. If you are using other types of client, you may need to uncheck this box. The Fast Message Retrieval option affects the IMAP function of reporting exact message sizes before the client retrieves them. Some clients are happy with an approximate message size whereas others require an exact value.

Anonymous Tab   The Anonymous tab does not exist on the POP3 object and governs anonymous access to public folders. You would use this feature if you have anonymous users from the Internet accessing your public folders over IMAP4.

Having given anonymous access, you must also grant anonymous access permission at a folder level in Exchange. To do this, Start Exchange Administrator and select the Folders object. Expand this object and go into the public folders.

Caution   You can change public folder permissions in Outlook. However, these permissions will not flow down the public folder hierarchy. For this reason, it is better to use Exchange Administrator to configure public folder permissions.

14

Find the folder for which you want to configure anonymous access and press Alt+Enter. This will show you the properties of the selected folder, as shown in Figure 14.16.

FIGURE 14.16

Here you see the properties of a public folder in Exchange Administrator.

> **Note**
>
> If there are subfolders of the folder that you are configuring, check the box to select that you want to propagate any settings to the subfolders. When you click OK or Apply, a prompt will ask you to select which properties you want to propagate, as shown in Figure 14.17. For the configuration changes that we are making, you should check the box for Client permissions. Select OK and continue with the remainder of this procedure.

Click on the Client Permissions button and you will see the dialog box in Figure 14.18.

You must give the anonymous user a minimum of read permission or reviewer role. In Figure 14.18, I have given the anonymous user read and create permission, which is a custom role. The reader will be able to read and post items, but not edit them once posted. Click OK to apply the permission.

If you have configured propagation of client access permissions as shown previously, this permission will now apply to any folders underneath the current one in the hierarchy.

Here you should choose which properties to propagate to subfolders.

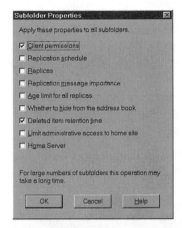

The Client Permissions screen is where you can configure anonymous access.

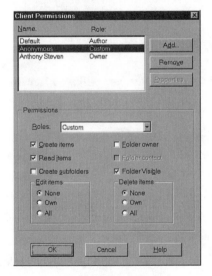

Note

If you want anonymous users to be able to contribute to the newsgroups, the anonymous user must have permission to create and read items.

Message Format Tab This tab is slightly different, as IMAP4 only uses MIME. There is the additional option to provide RTF support by sending the body text in both plain text and in HTML. Use plain text for maximum compatibility, and HTML for clients like Outlook Express that support it.

14

Selecting both these options means that two versions of each message will be sent—one in plain text, the other in HTML. This could affect communications in a low-bandwidth environment. It can also look very ugly when viewed with non-Microsoft clients.

Adding the IMAP4 Mail Service

Adding the mail service for IMAP using the Internet Connection Wizard is identical to that for POP3. However, on completing the wizard, you will see a prompt asking you if you want to download your folders, as shown in Figure 14.19.

FIGURE 14.19

Here you should select Yes to download your list of folders.

After you have downloaded your folder list, you will see a new IMAP account in the left pane of Outlook Express.

Downloading Public Folders

You can now right-click on this new IMAP4 account. You have options to refresh the folder list or subscribe to all folders:

- Subscribing to a Folder means that Outlook Express checks for new messages in that folder.
- Refresh Folder will check for new folders.

After you have refreshed your folder list and subscribed to any relevant folders, your screen will look like that in Figure 14.20.

Figure 14.20

Here Outlook Express has downloaded all the public folders as well as the folders from the user's mailbox.

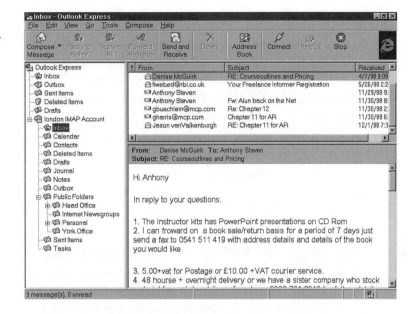

You have now successfully set up an account to use with MAPI.

Configuring the IMAP Client Account with Outlook Express

The configuration settings for the IMAP account at the client end are slightly different from those for POP3. In Outlook Express, select the Tools menu, click on Accounts, and from the Mail tab, choose the IMAP mail account. Click on the Properties button to change the settings for the IMAP account.

General Tab   The General tab has a new check box for Check for New Messages in Subscribed Folders. To do this, you have to subscribe to the folder first.

Advanced Tab   The Advanced tab has different port numbers for the Incoming mail server. There is also a setting for root folder path under Folders. You do not need a folder path if using Outlook Express with Exchange.

The Only Show Subscribed Folders is a way of reducing the number of folders that appear in your folder list in Outlook Express.

You now know how to set up POP3 or IMAP4 accounts using Outlook Express. But if you are using a POP3 or IMAP4 client to send messages, you don't have access to Exchange's global address list. I will cover this deficiency now.

14

Supporting LDAP Clients

So now you are quite happy sending and receiving messages using POP3 or IMAP clients, but you would also like to query Exchange's address lists. Exchange Server 5.5 provides an RFC-compliant LDAP server, which you can use to provide addressing information to LDAP clients. Exchange Server supports both authenticated and anonymous access to the address lists.

An LDAP client provides the means of requesting this addressing information from an LDAP server. The Windows Address Book (WAB) that comes with Outlook Express is an example of an LDAP client.

Before you can download addressing information via LDAP, you must check a few configuration settings.

Exchange Server LDAP Configuration

On the Exchange server, you will need to review your settings on the LDAP object at the site and server levels. To do this, start Exchange Administrator and select your site in the left pane. Click on the site object to expand it and select the Protocols container object. In the right pane, select the LDAP object. Double-click on the LDAP object. You will now see the dialog box shown in Figure 14.21.

FIGURE 14.21

The site level LDAP object enables you to configure LDAP settings for the whole site.

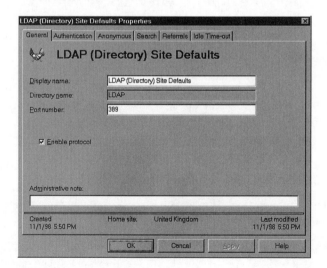

Site Level

As with POP3 and IMAP4, you can configure LDAP settings at a site level and these settings will apply to all servers. Alternatively, you can have different settings for individual servers.

General Tab   The General tab allows you to enable or disable LDAP access and change the port number on which your clients connect to LDAP.

Authentication Tab   The Authentication tab settings are identical to those on POP3 or IMAP4.

Anonymous Tab   The Anonymous tab is simply a check box to enable or disable anonymous access. If you are connecting your Exchange server to the Internet, and you want the public to be able to make addressing requests on your server, check the box. An example of this might be if you are part of a public organization, such as City Hall, and you want members of the public to be able to address email to the Mayor's staff.

Search Tab   This is a new tab that enables you to specify what type of searches are returned by the server. It also governs the maximum number of matches that return from the server. You may want to reduce this number, particularly if you have a high number of concurrent searches. Figure 14.22 shows this tab.

FIGURE 14.22

Use this tab to specify LDAP search behavior.

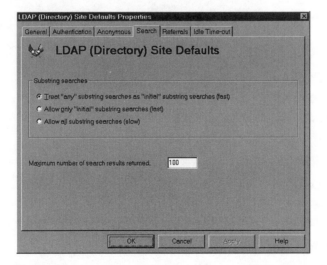

14

Note the comments on performance. My recommendation is to leave this tab on its default settings.

Referrals Use this tab to set up a system of referring clients to other LDAP servers. This means that if a user makes a search on one Exchange server and the search information is not on that server, then the request passes onto another server. As far as the client is concerned, this referral process is completely seamless. Figure 14.23 shows the Referrals tab set up to refer from server London to server Dublin.

FIGURE 14.23

You can configure LDAP referrals to other LDAP servers to provide enterprisewide addressing information.

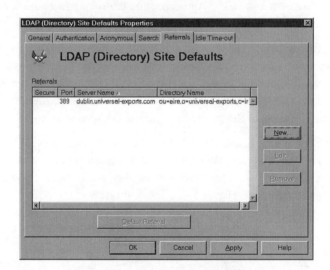

Server Level

The Server Level tab is identical to the Site Level tab, except for the extra check box to use the site level defaults. Uncheck this box if you want to use different LDAP settings for individual servers.

Mailbox Level

You cannot configure LDAP at a mailbox level. This is because you cannot select which addresses appear in the LDAP address list on this basis. To prevent an address from appearing in LDAP, you must hide it, as shown in Figure 14.24.

DS Site Configuration Object

The DS Site Configuration object is where you can control which addressing attributes are available to LDAP searches, depending on whether they are anonymous or authenticated requests.

FIGURE 14.24

Hiding a mailbox also prevents it from appearing in an LDAP search.

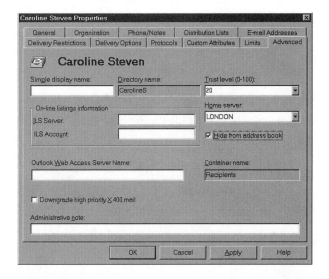

To configure these settings, launch Exchange Administrator and select your site in the left pane. Click on the site object to expand it and select the Configuration container object. In the right pane, select the DS Site Configuration object. Double-click on this object to see its properties and then click on the Attributes tab. A progress bar will appear while the attributes are loading. You will now see the screen shown in Figure 14.25.

FIGURE 14.25

You can change which attributes are available for query via LDAP.

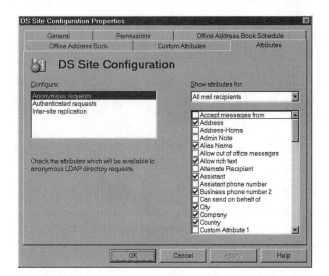

14

If you look at the attributes that are available to an anonymous search by default, you will probably be horrified. My guess is that you will want to reduce the number of attributes sent to anonymous LDAP clients. You may even want to reduce those available to authenticated users as well.

You should not need to change inter-site attributes.

Having configured the LDAP settings on the server side, it's now time to look at the client side.

Setting Up an LDAP Client

Configuration of an LDAP client is considerably simpler than with a mail client. Generally, you only need the following information:

- The IP address or host name of the LDAP server.
- Whether you are going to use Authenticated or Anonymous access.

Outlook Express

In Outlook Express, you add an LDAP account by selecting the Tools menu and choosing Accounts. In the Accounts dialog, select Add and then choose Directory Service.

There are only four screens of the Internet Connection Wizard for directory services.

The first dialog box asks you for your LDAP server host name or IP address and whether you want to use anonymous or authenticated access.

The second dialog box is where you can specify if this address book should be used to resolve addresses, rather like you can add address books to Outlook.

Dialog box number three enables you to specify a friendly name for this account. This must be unique to this LDAP account. I recommend making this something that you can remember.

The final dialog box just needs you to click Finish. Easy peasy!

Outlook 98

To use Outlook as an LDAP client with the Corporate/Workgroup email client, you need to download the LDAP service from the Microsoft Web site:

`http://officeupdate.microsoft.com/downloadCatalog/dldoutlook.htm`

After you have downloaded the Microsoft LDAP Directory Service for Outlook 98 file (O98ldap.exe), double-click on it to install it. You will now have the LDAP service to install on your profile.

To add the new service to Outlook 98, click on Tools and select Services. Click the Add button and the LDAP service should now appear in the list of available services. Select this service and click OK, and you will see a prompt to enter the configuration details as shown in Figure 14.26.

If you are using Outlook 98 with the Internet Mail client, you can set up LDAP client support as an account. The setup procedure is identical to that with Outlook Express.

Configuring LDAP Clients

As LDAP clients are very simple to set up, there is usually little to configure. You might want to change your LDAP server, but that's about it.

Outlook Express

With Outlook Express, select the Tools menu and click on Accounts. Click on the Directory Service tab and then select the LDAP account that you created earlier. Now click on the Properties button to see the General tab, which includes all the information you added previously. Click on the Advanced tab and you will see the options shown in Figure 14.27.

Here you can add SSL encryption to LDAP in a similar way to POP3/IMAP. You can change the search timeout if you are trying to access busy servers over slow links.

The number of matches to return cannot exceed the total number of searches that the Exchange server will return, as you configured in Figure 14.22.

14

FIGURE 14.27

This screen shows the Advanced tab of the LDAP service, which covers all the settings that you couldn't change when you installed the service.

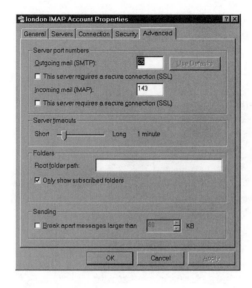

The search base specifies from where you start your search. Normally you only need this if you are searching a public LDAP server.

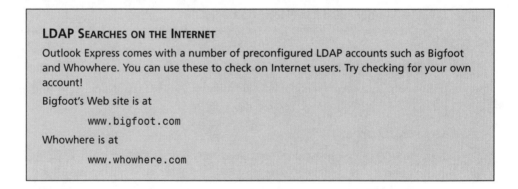

LDAP Searches on the Internet

Outlook Express comes with a number of preconfigured LDAP accounts such as Bigfoot and Whowhere. You can use these to check on Internet users. Try checking for your own account!

Bigfoot's Web site is at

www.bigfoot.com

Whowhere is at

www.whowhere.com

Making LDAP Queries with Outlook Express   After you have added and configured your LDAP account, you probably want to know how to make an LDAP query. The actual LDAP application is part of the search function of the Windows Address Book.

To start the Windows Address Book, select the Start menu, choose Programs, click on Internet Explorer, and select the Address Book. Alternatively, in Outlook Express, click on the Tools menu and then select Address Book. You will now see the screen in Figure 14.28.

FIGURE 14.28

The Search function on the Address Book is the LDAP client.

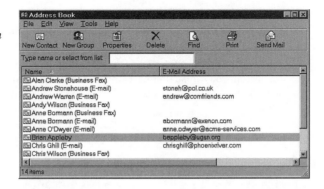

To make an LDAP search, click on the Edit menu and select Find. This will display the Find dialog. Select your LDAP account at the top of the screen and type a name, part of a name, or an email address into the dialog box. The LDAP client will now query the selected LDAP server (and any referred servers), and return any matches found up to the search limit, as shown in Figure 14.29.

FIGURE 14.29

Select a directory service to query via the Find People dialog box.

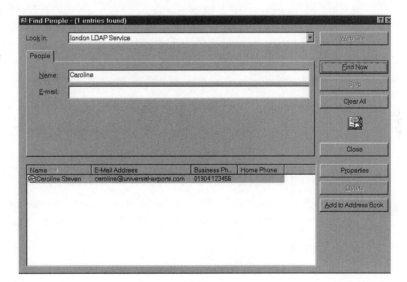

14

> **Tip**
>
> If you have installed IE4, click the Start button, select Find and then choose People. This will also start the LDAP client.
>
> You can also use this when you are addressing mail. When you click the To: button, you can again select Find. When you have found your intended recipients, click the To: or CC: buttons to add their names to the relevant lists.

Outlook 98

With Outlook 98, it's even easier, as there is even less to configure. Start Outlook 98, select the Tools menu, and choose Services. Double-click on the LDAP service you created earlier, and you will see the same configuration screen that you saw in Figure 14.27.

Supporting NNTP Clients

If you have implemented IMAP4 for message delivery and public folder access, you don't need to look at this section. However, if you have implemented POP3 clients with LDAP for addressing, you will need some mechanism by which your users can download public folders. An NNTP client can do this.

However, before an NNTP client can do this, you must publish some of your public folders as newsgroups. Don't worry—this won't suddenly make them appear on the Internet.

You will also have to install the Internet News Service. See Day 12 for detailed instructions on how to install and configure the Internet News Service.

Exchange Server NNTP Configuration

After you have installed the Internet News Service, you can publish Exchange folders as newsgroups. You can also configure the NNTP protocol object at site and server level.

Site Level

Start Exchange Administrator and select your site in the left pane. Click on the site object to expand it and select the Protocols container object. In the right pane, select the NNTP object. Double-click on the NNTP object. You will now see the dialog box shown in Figure 14.30.

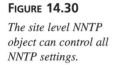

Figure 14.30

The site level NNTP object can control all NNTP settings.

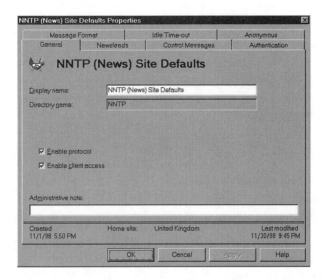

General Tab   The General tab has two check boxes asking you whether you want to enable the protocol and whether you want your clients to use NNTP. Enabling NNTP here enables the protocol for all servers unless you specifically disable it on a particular machine using the server level NNTP object.

Newsfeeds Tab   The Newsfeeds tab shows any installed Internet News Service newsfeeds. Double-clicking on the newsfeed itself in this dialog will bring up the properties of that newsfeed.

Control Messages Tab   The Control Messages tab lets you select which NNTP control messages you accept from other hosts. This would only arise if you had configured a push feed newsfeed from the Internet, and configuration changes are pushed onto your site. You can then decide whether to accept or reject these changes.

Authentication Tab   This tab is identical to the one you saw in the POP3 object (refer to Figure 14.2). The security methods are the same, as well.

Message Format Tab   This tab is almost identical to the one that you saw for POP3. There is no selector for character set, and there is an additional option for supporting S/MIME digital signatures, but that's about it.

Idle Time Out Tab   The Idle Time Out tab is identical to that on the POP3 object.

Anonymous Access   Here you check the box if you want it, uncheck it if you don't. However, you still have to configure anonymous access at the folder level. See the section "Configuring Anonymous Access" later in the lesson.

That's it at the site level.

14

Server Level

At the server level, the settings are almost exactly the same as at the site level, with three exceptions, one of which is *very important*. To configure POP3 settings at the server level, go to the relevant server and select the Protocols object. Again, double-click on the Protocols object and you will see the NNTP object. Double-click on the NNTP object to view its properties.

The General tab has a new check box to accept the site defaults, as you saw in the POP3/IMAP4 objects. Uncheck this to configure this server separately.

There is a Diagnostics Logging tab, as with the POP3/IMAP4 objects. Select the area you want to configure logging for and change the logging levels from minimum to maximum. Don't forget to return them to minimum for normal operation.

The big change comes on the Newsfeeds tab. Here you can specify a Usenet site name for your server and use the Create Active File button to generate an active file for other sites, as shown in Figure 14.31.

FIGURE 14.31

The server-level NNTP object lets you define a Usenet site name and generate an active file.

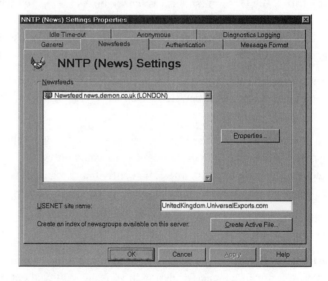

This addition means that Exchange can participate in the global Usenet newsgroups as a newsgroup node server. This configuration would mean that an ISP could use Exchange to provide full newsgroup services to their clients.

Publishing a Public Folder as a Newsgroup

To publish a public folder as a newsgroup (so it can be accessed by readers of newsgroup software), you first need to create a newsgroup hierarchy. A newsgroup hierarchy consists of a public folder and all its subfolders. This hierarchy then appears as a newsgroup.

To create a newsgroup hierarchy (and thus publish your public folders as newsgroups), you should carry out the following task:

1. Start Exchange Administrator and select the Tools menu.
2. Click on Newsgroup Hierarchies. You will see the dialog box in Figure 14.32.

FIGURE 14.32

You can publish public folders as newsgroups through newsgroup hierarchies.

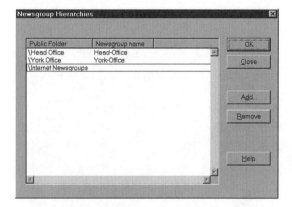

3. Give the newsgroup a name or accept the default choice.
4. You have now added a newsgroup hierarchy. NNTP clients can download this group of public folders.

Note

You can't use full stops (periods, to those who don't live in England) in a newsgroup name, as newsgroup hierarchy levels use full stops to mark the different levels of the hierarchy. Full stops and any other illegal characters are stripped out of newsgroup names.

As an example of newsgroup naming, comp.microsoft is a subfolder of the comp newsgroup, dedicated to things Microsofty. comp.microsoft.exchange is the Exchange forum on the Microsoft newsgroup.

If you want to exclude an individual folder from the newsgroup hierarchy, start Outlook or Exchange client and select the folder that you want to exclude in the folder list.

14

Tip — If you can't see the folder list, select the View menu and then check Folder List.

Now right-click on the folder and select its properties. Click on the Internet Newsgroups tab and uncheck the box for Show This Folder as an Internet Newsgroup. This folder will now not appear in the list of newsgroups downloaded by NNTP clients. Figure 14.33 shows how to configure this.

FIGURE 14.33

You can prevent an individual folder from appearing in your list of public folders.

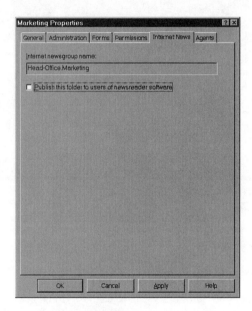

Configuring Anonymous Access

Just because you have published a public folder doesn't mean that anyone can just post to it. They may not even be able to see it. This is due to the two main ways in which NNTP clients can connect to a folder: anonymous or authenticated.

- Authenticated access—requires a valid username and password; that is, your user must identify herself and be validated by Windows NT.

- Anonymous access—has no validation requirements but you do have to give anonymous users permission to access the folders.

You need to enable anonymous access in two areas, both at a protocol level and at a folder level. I'll take you through configuring the protocol level first.

1. Start Exchange Administrator and select your site in the left pane. Click on the site object to expand it and select the Configuration container object. In the right pane, select the Site level Protocols object. Double-click on the Protocols object to see its properties. You will now see the screen in Figure 14.34.

FIGURE 14.34

You must enable the NNTP protocol and grant both client access and anonymous access if you are allowing anonymous access.

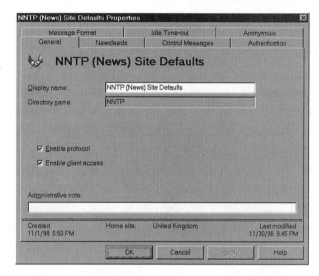

2. Click on the Anonymous tab and check the Allow Anonymous Access box. That's if you want to give it, of course.

Caution	I am assuming at this point that you haven't made any changes to the NNTP object in the Protocols container at the server level. By default, the site properties for the NNTP object apply at the server level as well.

3. Now click OK on the NNTP object.

See Day 19, "Making Exchange Secure," for more information on configuring security permissions on folders.

Setting Up an NNTP Client

Now that you have set up a newsgroup hierarchy, you need to configure your NNTP client to collect newsgroup messages. Before you start, you have to know the following information:

14

- Your name and email address (hopefully no problems there).
- The name of your news server (IP address or host name).
- Whether you want anonymous or authenticated access.
- How you are going to connect (LAN/WAN, RAS, or third-party dialer).

Outlook Express

With Outlook Express, you will be running the Internet Connection Wizard again.

Using the Internet Connection Wizard   As before, start Outlook Express, click on Tools and select the Accounts option. From the Accounts dialog, click the Add button and then select New from the menu. The Internet Connection wizard starts.

1. Enter your name in the wizard's first dialog box. This is the name that you want to appear on your postings to the newsgroup.

2. Add your email address into the second dialog box in the form *alias@site.organization*.com. This is the address used when someone clicks on Reply to Poster in his or her newsgroup client.

> Contributors to the Usenet newsgroups on the Internet often don't put their real email address in here. Instead they might put something like billg@microsoft.nospam.com. Usenet users know to strip out the nospam bit if they want to email someone directly. However, spambots (programs that generate unwelcome mass-mailings from newsgroup postings) generally don't.

3. The third dialog box requires you to enter the NNTP server that you want to connect to. You can use a host name (such as news.isp.net) or an IP address. You can also select whether you are to use authenticated access, which you do by checking the box indicating that you must log on to you news server.

4. The fourth dialog box is where you should enter a name for your news connection that is easy to remember. The default entry is the name of your server. Remember to differentiate between this account and your mail accounts.

5. The Choose Connection Type dialog box gives you three choices for connecting to your NNTP server—Remote Access, LAN, or a manual connection. This screen is identical to the one that you saw when you configured a POP3 account.

6. If you select the Phone Line option in the preceding dialog box, now you will need to specify a RAS or dial-up networking connection to connect to your ISP or Exchange server.

Make sure this dial-up connection works and can connect to your ISP or RAS server automatically.

7. Now click Finish to exit the Wizard.

When you click the Close button, a prompt will ask you if you want to download the folder list from the NNTP server that you have just defined. You will now have a list of downloaded newsgroups as shown in Figure 14.35. Select which newsgroups you want to subscribe to and these will display in Outlook Express.

FIGURE 14.35

Here the Outlook Express client shows the list of downloaded newsgroups (public folders).

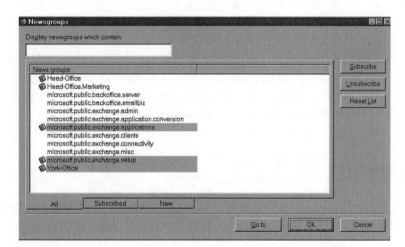

The list of downloaded folders includes the folders that I made newsgroup hierarchies earlier, as well as any newsgroups downloaded from the Internet.

14

Outlook 98

Outlook 98 uses Outlook Newsreader as its newsgroup client, also known as Outlook Express. The configuration settings are exactly as you have just covered.

Configuring an NNTP Client

After you have installed your NNTP client, you may want to change its settings. Normally, this will be to change your subscribed newsgroups.

Outlook Express

The configuration settings for Outlook Express newsgroups are almost identical to the POP3 settings, except there is no Security tab. The only differences are as follows:

- The General tab has an option to include this news account when checking for new messages.
- The Server tab has a check box to enable authenticated access. This enables logon via a specific account and password or using secured password authentication, which uses the current username and password.
- The Connection tab has an extra option for automatic dialing.
- The Advanced tab has only one connection, but still with the option of SSL encryption. A new Descriptions item enables download of newsgroup descriptions from the server, if these have been configured. The option to break up the size of large posted messages is similar to that for the mail accounts.

Outlook 98

Outlook Newsreader is exactly the same as Outlook Express.

Configuring All Internet Protocols

Having looked at the client issues, there are some additional configuration settings that you can change for all protocols. These are set from the properties of the Protocols containers at site and server level.

Site Level

Start Exchange Administrator and select your site in the left pane. Click on the site object to expand it and select the Configuration container object. In the right pane, select the Protocols object. From the File menu, select Properties. You will now see the dialog box shown in Figure 14.36.

FIGURE **14.36**

The site level protocols object has properties too!

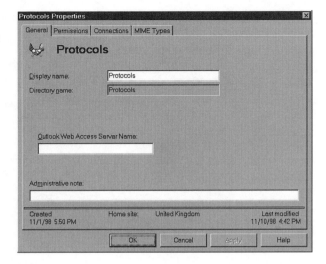

General Tab

The General tab has two options; the display name for the Protocols container and the name of the Outlook Web Access server. This only applies when your Exchange and IIS servers are separate machines. See Day 13, "Building a Web Site Around Exchange," for more information.

Permissions Tab

The Permissions tab lets you configure account permissions for this object. See Day 19 for more details on configuring object security.

Connections Tab

The Connections tab contains a very useful feature—the ability to accept or reject incoming client connections based on IP address. The default setting is to accept all incoming connections. However, if you select the option for Accept/Reject connections, you can click the New button and accept or reject specific IP addresses, as shown in Figure 14.37.

 Note

These settings apply to *all* protocols.

14

FIGURE 14.37

The Protocols tab enables you to accept or reject connections based on IP addresses.

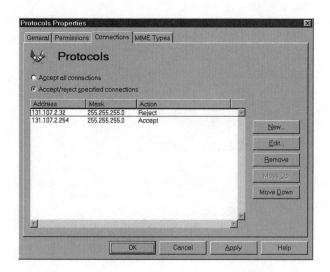

MIME Types Tab

The MIME Types tab enables you to add and edit MIME associations for programs that can use MIME types. Select a MIME type from the list and click Edit to change a value.

Server Level

The Server Level settings are identical to those at the server level, with the addition of the check box on the General tab that propagates the site level settings. Deselect this box to change the server settings individually.

Logging Levels

You configure logging for all the Internet protocols in one place—the Server object. Start Exchange Administrator and select your site in the left pane. Click on the site object to expand it and select the Configuration container object. In the right pane, select the Servers object. Now click on the File menu and select Properties. Choose the Diagnostics Logging tab, and you will see the dialog box shown in Figure 14.38.

When configuring logging for the Internet protocols, you will be interested in the following settings:

- MSExchangeIS—Internet Protocols for POP3, IMAP, and NNTP logging.
- MSExchangeIMC—SMTP events.
- MSExchangeDS—LDAP events.

FIGURE 14.38

You can configure logging for the Internet Protocols from the properties of the Server object.

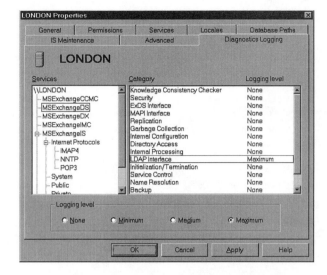

Any events recorded will appear in the Application log in Event Viewer. See Day 8, "Troubleshooting Exchange," for further information on using logging and Event Viewer.

Caution

As I mentioned earlier, you should only increase logging levels when you are troubleshooting. Do not forget to return the levels to minimum or off during normal operation. This is because logging places an extra load on your server and reduces performance.

Summary

In this lesson, you have looked at the various ways in which you can use Internet clients to access Exchange mailboxes, public folders, and address lists. If you are working in a low-bandwidth environment or across the Internet, Exchange's support for Internet protocols gives you a number of alternative configuration options. With a combination of LDAP with IMAP or POP3 and NNTP, you get most of the functionality of a MAPI client, but using less bandwidth.

To summarize the main points of this lesson:

- You can access your Exchange mailbox over POP3 or IMAP4. This gives you the ability to download either your Inbox (POP3) or all your folders (IMAP4).
- IMAP gives the additional ability to download all the public folders.

14

- You can use an LDAP client to query Exchange's directory services. You can then use this to address email messages, find out telephone numbers, and so on.

- Exchange can refer directory queries on to other non-Exchange LDAP servers, enabling you to build up an enterprisewide database of heterogeneous directory services.

- Using an NNTP client, you can download published public folders as newsgroups. If the client permissions have been set, the NNTP clients can post messages back to those same newsgroups.

- Anonymous requests are supported for IMAP, newsgroup folders, and IMAP download of public folders. This lets users from outside your organization have access to certain public folders.

- The Protocols Object enables you to accept and reject connections by IP address. This means that you can control which hosts can connect via POP3, IMAP, LDAP, and NNTP.

Q&A

Q I have a number of mobile clients who need to send and receive mail from their Exchange mailbox. They are often in foreign countries where communications can be somewhat basic. What is the best configuration option for these clients?

A You could use POP3, LDAP, and NNTP to download their mail messages or public folders and to look up addressing details. IMAP4 would probably be a bit bandwidth-hungry.

Q I am also concerned about security. Some of these countries have a reputation for industrial espionage, and I want all electronic communication to be secure.

A You can still use POP3, LDAP, and NNTP, but in this case configure them for advanced security. And don't leave any security loopholes in your company network.

Q My boss has asked me to configure a system where the general public can connect to our Exchange system and look up people's email addresses, telephone numbers, and so on. It also needs to tie in with similar systems in five other cities, but these other systems are non-Exchange servers. Can we do this?

A It depends. It certainly isn't a problem as far as your site is concerned. You can configure LDAP for anonymous access with little difficulty. As for integration with the other systems, as long as they are also RFC-compliant LDAP servers then you don't have a problem.

Q **I am prototyping a POP3/NNTP/LDAP deployment, but I want to prevent other users from connecting to it until it is ready. How can I do this?**

A Go to the site level protocols object and select the Connections tab. Add the IP addresses of the hosts you are using to test the system and reject all others.

Workshop

The Workshop provides two ways for you to affirm what you've learned in this lesson. The "Quiz" section poses questions to help you solidify your understanding of the material covered and the "Exercise" section provides you with experience in using what you have learned. You can find answers to the quiz questions and exercises in Appendix B, "Answers to Quiz Questions and Exercises."

Quiz

1. Which Internet protocols can Exchange use for messaging?
2. What additional component must be installed to support messaging?
3. What do I need to know before I start installing a POP3/IMAP4 client?
4. How do I configure public folders so that they download to authenticated IMAP4 clients?
5. What non-Internet standard is LDAP based on?
6. What is an LDAP referral?
7. What six authentication methods do POP3, IMAP4, LDAP, and NNTP support?
8. What are the considerations when adding support for HTML message bodies to IMAP4?
9. Where can you configure logging on all the Internet protocols at once?

Exercise

1. How would you configure referral between two LDAP servers?

14

Week 3

At A Glance

This week, you'll expand your knowledge of Exchange Server with a discussion of some advanced topics designed to keep the system you set up in the first two weeks running for many more weeks, months, and even years. You'll master vital skills such as system maintenance, data backup and restore procedures, security and disaster preparation.

- Day 15, "Maintaining Exchange" shows you how to take advantage of a variety of maintenance tools Exchange provides, including Server Monitor and Link Monitor. You'll keep track of your message queues, use automated maintenance routines, and review Windows NT maintenance tools.

- Day 16, "Backing Up, Restoring, and Repairing Data" helps you prepare for the failure of all or part of your system by backing up different components of your Exchange system. You'll review different backup strategies, see how to schedule regular backups and consider some third-party utilities that can help.

- Day 17, "Advanced Backup and Recovery Considerations," pauses to consider some advanced disaster recovery concepts. For example, your regular backup scheme can protect you from routine failures, but are you ready for a natural disaster? You'll discover how vital it is to plan ahead and learn proven and prudent preparation strategies.

- Day 18, "Building Exchange Applications," covers the development tools available for creating applications around Exchange.

15

16

17

18

19

20

21

- Day 19, "Making Exchange Secure," teaches how to configure the security properties of your various objects and limit access to multiple mailboxes. You'll also learn to set permissions on shared folders and how to implement a Key Management scheme to provide encryption.

- Day 20, "Building and Exchange Prototype," shows how to prototype a pilot Exchange system to ensure your network can handle the projected load as your organization grows.

- Day 21, "Migrating from Microsoft Mail," shows how to upgrade Microsoft Mail users to the Exchange client and server system. It also provides a review of the differences in the two systems.

DAY **15**

Maintaining Exchange

by Anthony Steven

Chapter Objectives

Today's lesson looks at some of the built-in monitoring facilities that can help you manage your Exchange installation. Exchange provides automated methods for checking that your servers are running and messaging links are functioning correctly. In addition, you can monitor message queues, run scheduled maintenance activities, and control the size of your databases.

This chapter covers the following topics:

- Server Monitors
- Link Monitors
- Warning and escalation levels
- Monitoring message queues
- Using Windows NT Performance Monitor

- Controlling Public and Private Information Store sizes
- Using automated maintenance routines
- Scheduling automated maintenance routines for performance

Server and Link Monitors

After you've installed your Exchange messaging system, you will probably have better things to do than to keep checking it. Thankfully, Exchange comes with two very useful features that can automate the process of checking your servers and links. These are Server Monitors and Link Monitors.

Server Monitors

Server Monitors run periodic checks of the NT services running on your Exchange server. This means that you can set up your system to check periodically that the Microsoft Exchange Internet Mail Service or the Directory Service is still running.

What Can I Monitor?

You can monitor any Windows NT service running on your Exchange servers in any site. Hence, you can monitor all the Exchange services, such as the Microsoft Exchange System Attendant, Microsoft Exchange Directory Service, Microsoft Exchange Event Service, and Microsoft Exchange Message Transfer Agent.

In addition, you can also monitor non-Exchange Windows NT system services, such as the Server Service, Workstation Service, Net Logon, Spooler, and Event Log Service. Server Monitors can also check services installed by other applications, such as DNS Manager, WWW Publishing Service, Lotus Notes Server service, and so on.

However, Server Monitors *are* restricted to monitoring only Exchange servers.

How Does a Server Monitor Work?

Server Monitors operate by checking that the designated services are still running. This happens on a regular basis, by default every 15 minutes. Server Monitors can also check the system clocks to ensure time synchronization.

If a clock is off by more than 15 seconds, the system enters a Warning state. The monitor then readjusts that clock. If a service is not operating, or the clock is off by more than sixty seconds, the monitor will enter an Alert state.

15

If the system enters an Alert state, due to a service not responding, you can configure the monitor to trigger an action. The action can be one of following three options:

- Take no action (just wait—the service might be restarting)
- Restart the service
- Restart the computer

You can cascade these actions so that the first response might be to take no action, the second to attempt to restart the service, and the third to restart the computer. On a system restart, you can add a shutdown message (to warn your users to save their work and log off) and a shutdown delay, so that services have time to close down cleanly.

You can configure both warning and alert states to carry out three forms of notification:

- Sending an NT Alert to a computer
- Sending a mail message
- Running an application

You can configure escalation levels, so that when a server has entered a warning or an alert state, the monitor will check more frequently, typically every five minutes.

Monitoring Non-Exchange Servers

If you need to monitor services running on non-Exchange servers, you need to use a utility from the Windows NT Server Resource kit called Service Monitor. This you can configure to send messages or alerts when services stop running. However, it does not offer the range of configuration options provided by Server Monitors.

The Windows NT Resource Kit is part of TechNet. You can also obtain further information from:

```
http://www.microsoft.com/ntserver/nts/downloads/recommended/ntkit/default.
➥asp
```

Link Monitors

Monitoring servers gives you a useful method of checking the operation of your Exchange site. However, if you have more than one site, you will need to be able to monitor the links between the sites as well.

What Can I Monitor?

You can monitor links between Exchange sites over all connector types and links between Exchange and non-Exchange mail systems.

How Does a Link Monitor Work?

Link Monitors work by bouncing messages off the other site or messaging system. If the messages come back within a reasonable time, the link is operational. If the messages do not come back within 30 minutes, the Link Monitor goes into a Warning state. If the messages do not come back within 60 minutes, the monitor goes into an Alert state. If the link is in either an alert or a warning state, the frequency of the link messages increases from every 15 to every five minutes.

The alerting options on Link Monitors are identical to those on Server Monitors.

Using Link Monitors with Non-Exchange Email Systems

Using Link Monitors with Non-Exchange servers is very simple—you just send a message to a nonexistent user. As long as nondelivery message returns from the remote system in a reasonable time, you know that the link is working. Why? Because the remote system itself is generating the NDR. If the message takes a long time to return, the remote system is unavailable and the message is timing out. I will cover setting this up later in this lesson.

Installing and Configuring Server Monitors

There are two parts to using Server Monitors. The first part is the installation and configuration; the second part is running the monitor. You install Server Monitors from the Exchange Administrator program.

Installing a Server Monitor

To install a Server Monitor, start Exchange Administrator and select the File menu. Choose New Other and then click Server Monitor from the top of the resulting list. A prompt will offer to switch you to the Monitors' container. Select Yes, and you then see the screen in Figure 15.1.

FIGURE 15.1

The General tab on a Server Monitor lets you specify names and polling intervals.

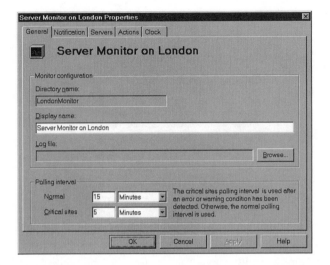

General Tab

Here you should add a unique directory name and a display name for this monitor. You can also choose the escalation levels.

The default setting is that a Server Monitor will check the state of the monitored services every 15 minutes, unless in an alert or a warning state, in which case it will start checking every 5 minutes. When a server resumes operating normally, polling reverts to every 15 minutes.

You can configure an optional log file if you want to log events from this server monitor.

Notification Tab

On the Notification tab, you can define the how and whom. Hence you need to consider whom are you going to notify, and how. As I outlined before, the options are sending a mail message, sending an NT Alert, or running a process.

To add a notification, click New. You can choose one of three notification options.

Launch a Process   The Launch a Process option lets you specify an executable file (such as a paging program) that will alert you to the problem with the server. Figure 15.2 shows this configured.

Figure 15.2

The Launch a Process option lets you run a command routine to alert a pager.

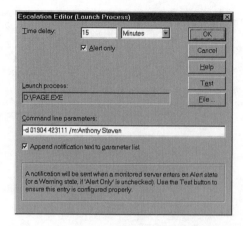

You can specify a time delay. If this process requires you to come into work and disrupt your weekend, I would recommend a reasonably long time delay. Certainly, the time delay should be long enough to let the server reboot itself.

The Alert Only check box means that the specified application will only be run if the system goes into an alert state, that is, a service stops responding. My guess is that you probably won't want a page on Sunday morning to discover that your clock is 16 seconds slow.

Note

The most important button on this dialog is the Test button. Use this to check that your configuration does actually alert you.

Select the application that you want to run by clicking the File button and browsing for the relevant executable. You can add command line parameters, as well as specify that the alerting message appends to the parameter list of that program. This would be very useful with an alphanumeric pager, for example, where you would get to see what the alert actually was. There's no point in spoiling Sunday lunch if one of your replicated WINS servers goes down, but your mission-critical email system might be a different matter.

Caution

With mission-critical systems, you may need to assess the effect on a paging system if the power goes down. If you have a UPS and backup generators, your email servers may continue to run. However, will you still receive notification if there is a total power outage?

In any contingency planning, it is vital to check the effect of a citywide power outage on all services.

One example of this was the company that had spent a considerable amount of money on installing generators on the roof of their building, with UPS support for the main servers. All went fine when the power to the block failed, as the generator kicked in and the UPS system absorbed the changeover. All went fine, that is, for about thirty seconds, after which the generator spluttered and died. It was a pity that the generator's fuel pump in the basement wasn't on the protected part of the electricity supply.

Oops!

After you click OK to accept the new process, a message box notifies you that the next notification will happen during the next polling interval after the notification time has expired.

Mail Message   The mail message option is simpler to configure—you only need to specify a mail recipient to notify.

As it probably won't just be you responsible for the Exchange servers, you may want to configure a distribution list for all the Exchange Administrators and add that distribution list as the notification addressee.

Again, don't forget to use the Test button.

The check box for Alert Only has the same function as in the previous section.

The smart ones among you will have already spotted a potential flaw here. What if one of the failed services is one that is essential to sending messages, like the Exchange System Attendant? In that case, you may need to configure other notification methods.

Windows NT Alert   This option lets you configure alerting on Windows NT machines. For this to work, both the Messenger and Alerter functions must be running on the target NT workstation, and the Messenger service must be running on the Exchange server. Again, this option will not work if the Messenger service stops running on the Exchange server.

I would recommend that you use multiple methods of alerting, and make sure that you aren't the only person on the notification list.

Figure 15.3 shows the Notification tab configured with the various types of notifications.

FIGURE 15.3

Here I have added several notification types to cover for different users not being available.

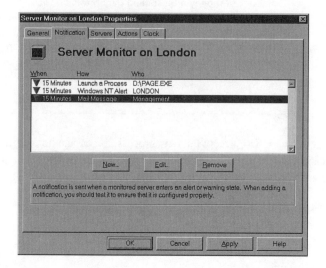

Servers Tab

The Servers tab lets you configure the servers and the individual services that you want to monitor on each server. You can monitor multiple computers with one server monitor, which is easier than configuring multiple monitors, one for each server.

Select the servers to monitor on the left-hand side and click the Add button. If you have directory replication configured, you will be able to select remote sites and add the servers from those sites.

After you have added the servers that you want to monitor to the right-hand list, select each server in this right-hand list and then click the Services button. You will see a list of monitored services, like that in Figure 15.4.

You can add services to be monitored by selecting a service from the list at the top and clicking add.

FIGURE 15.4

This shows the default monitored services.

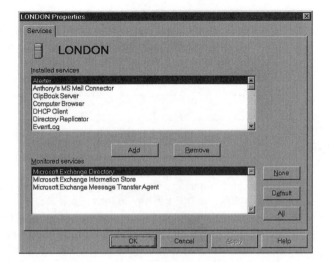

 Tip

You can add services into the default monitored services box by going to the properties of the server object for that server.

After you have added the servers and services that you want to monitor, click the Actions tab to continue.

Actions Tab

The Actions tab lets you specify what actions you want the monitor to take, should it detect that a service has stopped:

- Take No Action does just that. Nothing. You might want the monitor to do this first, so if a service is just restarting, it lets it do so, and checks again in five minutes.

- Restart the Service will try to kick the service back into life, and then checks again in five minutes.

- Restart the Computer will reboot the machine. With this option, you can also specify a message that will appear on logged-on users' screens before the machine shuts down. You can also configure a delay before the machine reboots. This should be long enough to let the services on the server close down gracefully.

Note

> There used to be an issue with Exchange 5.5 about shutdown times. When you tried to shut down an Exchange server, you could be waiting for up to 15 minutes, especially if you had IIS and Active Server Pages installed. Thankfully, NT Service Pack 4 has cured this problem.

Caution

> I had a particular issue with monitoring a server in another site. I set up a server monitor monitoring both the local server and the Exchange server in the remote site. I configured the actions to include a reboot if the monitor still couldn't restart the service. Among other services, I was monitoring the DHCP, WINS, and DNS services on the remote site.
>
> If you start a server monitor and then close Exchange Administrator without stopping the monitor, the monitor will restart the next time you start Exchange Administrator. So a few weeks later, I needed to do some administration on the Exchange Server and I started Exchange Administrator.
>
> About 15 minutes later I got a very irate phone call from the administrator at the other site asking what on earth I was doing rebooting their server. Er, what, me? Yes, you, and so on. I stopped the monitor and the situation calmed down.
>
> What was actually happening was that the administrator had moved the DNS service to another machine. All the monitor could see was that the service wasn't started, so it tried to restart it. As DNS wasn't on this server any more, the service wouldn't start, so the monitor rebooted the machine. The service still didn't start, so the monitor rebooted the machine again, and so on.
>
> The moral of this story is to use server monitoring with care, especially across sites.

Time Tab

The Time tab lets you configure checking and optional synchronization of the server's clock.

Note

> The monitored server will synchronize with the clock on the machine running the monitor. Therefore, the machine running the monitor (which could be an NT Workstation) needs to have the correct time.
>
> I recommend that you keep the clocks on your Exchange servers synchronized.
>
> Another method you can use is to schedule this command:

```
NET SYNC \\SERVERNAME /SET /Y
```

where *servername* is the name of the synchronizing server.

With the introduction of the Active Directory Service in Windows 2000, time synchronization will be much more important than with NT 4.0, so keeping your domain synchronized is good practice for the future.

15

You can set the maximum allowable time difference before the monitor enters a warning or an alert state. Checking the box enables automatic synchronization if the clocks are out.

Starting Monitoring

Now that you have configured a server monitor, you need to start the monitor. Select the monitor in the Monitors container and then click the Tools menu. Select Start Monitor from the list and you get a prompt asking you to connect to a server. Select one of the servers in your site, and you will then see the screen in Figure 15.5.

FIGURE 15.5

After you start the server monitor, you should see this screen.

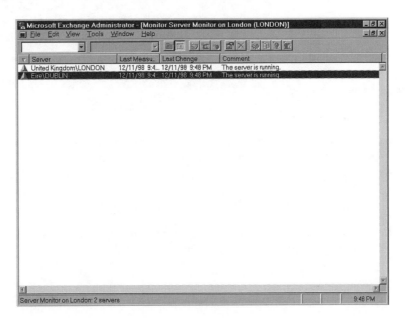

What you want to see is a column of green triangles pointing upward, as shown in Figure 15.5. A question mark indicates that the server's status is not yet available, and a red triangle pointing downward denotes a problem.

Viewing a Server's Status

Double-clicking a server on the screen in Figure 15.5 produces the dialog box shown in Figure 15.6.

FIGURE 15.6

Double-clicking a server shows the status of all monitored services.

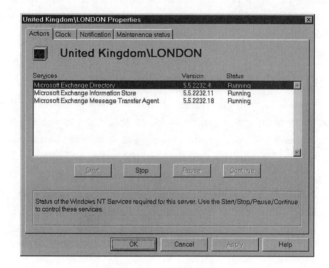

Actions Tab

The Actions tab shows the status of all monitored services and their service version numbers. You can also stop and start services from this dialog box.

Clock Tab

The Clock tab shows the clock synchronization information, as in Figure 15.7.

As Windows NT is time-zone sensitive, you can synchronize servers around the world and their clocks will always be correct to local time.

FIGURE 15.7

The Clock tab shows the last reported time from the server, plus the time zone and any daylight savings time adjustments.

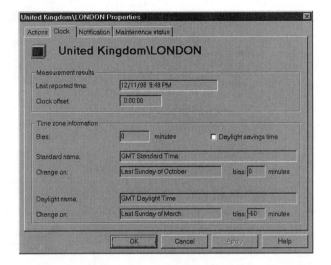

 Note

This is unlike the old Soviet Union, where the State Railway ran to Moscow time, even in Vladivostock, which is seven hours ahead of Moscow time.

Notification Tab

The Notification tab shows a list of any notifications the monitor makes. This list may show warnings and alerts, or only alerts, depending on how you configured your notifications when you configured the monitor. Figure 15.8 shows a list of notification events.

Maintenance Status

The Maintenance Status tab has two check boxes—one to suspend notifications, the other to suspend repairs. You can apply one or both of these when you are carrying out maintenance on a server. Notifications suspended stops the monitor from issuing any notifications when you are repairing a server. The Repairs suspended setting prevents the monitor from attempting to restart any services or reboot the server.

Of course, the other option is just to stop the monitor, but your Server Monitor might be monitoring multiple servers, so you might not want to do this.

Now that you've seen how to install, configure, and start a Server Monitor, let's look at the Link Monitor.

FIGURE 15.8

FIGURE 15.8

Warnings and alerts appear in the Notification tab.

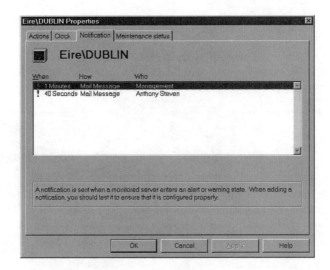

Installing and Configuring Link Monitors

The Server Monitor can run checks on servers throughout the organization and detect any problems. However, the Server Monitor cannot report on the status of the links between sites. For this, you need a Link Monitor.

The Link Monitor is very similar in many ways to the Server Monitor. Hence, for this section I will confine myself to the differences between the two.

Installing a Link Monitor is just like installing a Server Monitor. In Exchange Administrator, select the File menu, choose New Other, and then click Link Monitor.

General Tab

This is almost identical to the Server Monitor. Enter a directory name, display name, and a polling interval.

Note

Depending on the type of connector you are testing, you may need to increase the polling interval times. Obviously, there's no point in having a 15-minute polling interval time on an Internet Mail connection that only delivers every two hours. All that will happen is that the outgoing queue in your IMC will have several Link Monitor messages stacked up.

Notifications Tab

This is identical to that on the Server Monitor. Again, there is no point in sending a mail notification to a user at the far end of the link that you are trying to monitor. The notification probably won't get through!

Servers Tab

This is almost the same as that on the Server Monitor, lacking only the Services button. Here you just specify a server in the remote site. Personally, I can't see much point in putting your own server on here.

Note   You would only use this tab from Exchange site to Exchange site. In addition, if you don't have directory replication configured, you won't be able to see any other sites.

Recipients Tab

This tab is not present in the Server Monitor, and allows you to specify email recipient addresses. This is for use for checking connections to foreign mail systems or Exchange servers in other organizations.

To use this option, you must specify a custom addressee in Exchange Administrator. Start Exchange Administrator, and click the New Custom Addressee icon (the globe on the toolbar). Now configure this custom addressee with an address that matches the address space for the connector to the foreign site. The clever bit is to give the recipient a name that does *not* exist in the foreign site. Add this custom recipient either to the list on the left (Exchange sites in other organizations) or to the list on the right (foreign email systems).

Thus, when the Link Monitor sends the message to this nonexistent user, the remote system returns the message as nondeliverable (NDR). The fact that this nondelivery message returns quickly means that the link is operational. If the NDR does not return, the link is down, as the message would still be in the retry phase.

The difference between the lists is that the list on the left is for connection to systems that will always return the message as it was sent, that is, the message subject is in the subject of the returned message. The right-hand list is for systems that may put the message subject into the body of the NDR. Exchange scans the NDR for a match to the message that it sent out, again guaranteeing that this was a true test of the link.

Bounce Tab

The Bounce tab specifies what is an acceptable delay on a message. Therefore, if a reply doesn't come back within 30 minutes, the monitor enters a warning state. In addition, if a reply doesn't return within 60 minutes, the monitor goes into an alert state.

 Caution | Always use a separate link monitor for dial-up links, like the IMS with a RAS connection. Make sure that the bounce values are long enough to allow for the dial-up connection. So if you are dialing up every hour, you should have the shortest bounce value set to greater than four hours.

Starting a Link Monitor

You start a Link Monitor in exactly the same way as a Server Monitor. The difference with Link Monitors is that after you have started the monitor and double-clicked the link that you are monitoring, you see the screen in Figure 15.9.

FIGURE 15.9

Link Monitors show the time it takes a message to reach its destination and return.

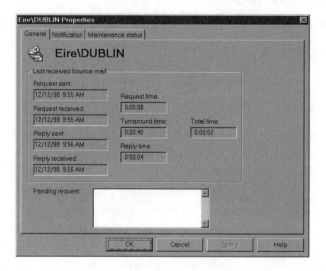

Note the message turnaround times. These indicate how long it takes a message to get to the remote site.

The Notifications tab and Maintenance Status tabs on the Link Monitor are the same as those on the Server Monitor.

So much for installing and configuring the monitors. But what's the use of automatic monitoring if you can't start it automatically?

Starting Monitoring Automatically

So what do you do if you need to implement a monitoring scheme that checks your servers at 10:00 every weekday morning? If you are at work, you could start the monitors manually. Even better, you could get your PFY (Pimply-Faced Youth) to do it for you. If you don't trust your PFY (and few network administrators do), it would probably be much better to get your monitors to start and stop automatically. It's also one less thing to worry about when you are soaking up the rays on some exotic beach.

Using the Scheduling Service

You can start either Server or Link Monitors automatically using the command line options on the Exchange Administrator program. You can run the Administrator program from a command line:

```
ADMIN.EXE /m [Remotesite\]Monitorname\Server
```

This starts the Exchange Administrator program and starts the monitor that you specify in *Monitorname*.

The [*Remotesite*\] variable is optional and is the directory name of the site that contains the monitor that you want to run. *Monitorname* is the directory name of the monitor within the site, and Server is the server to which you want the monitor to connect.

After you are confident that you can use the admin program to start the right monitor, you want to incorporate the command line into a .BAT or .CMD file. Now you can use the AT command to schedule running the .BAT or .CMD file.

You can use either the command line AT command, WinAT (comes with the NT Resource Kit), or Scheduled Tasks (NT Service Pack 4).

An example of how to use the AT command to stop and start the monitor is:

```
AT \\SERVERNAME 10:00 "STARTADM.BAT"
```

SERVERNAME is the name of your Exchange Server, and STARTADM.BAT has your command line switches for starting and stopping the Administrator program.

Tip

If you start a monitor and then close the Exchange Administrator program without stopping the monitor, the monitor will restart the next time the Administrator starts. Thus, instead of mucking about with all those command line switches, just set up the monitors as you want them. Now close down Exchange Administrator without stopping the monitors. Run ADMIN.EXE from the command prompt and, presto, the Exchange Administrator starts along with the monitors.

Monitoring From an NT Workstation

You can carry out all your monitoring from an NT Workstation. This is because you can install the Exchange Administrator on any NT machine. Thus, you could install the Administrator on your own Windows NT box and monitor from there. If you don't have an NT Workstation, you need to get one, as the Exchange Administrator program will not run on Windows 98. When you order it, you will need LOTS of RAM—about 128MB will do. And a big screen—at least 19". And you'll definitely need one of those fancy soundcards as well, so don't forget to specify a speaker system with subwoofers. Don't forget—you need all this to administer the new Exchange system. Honest.

Having dealt with Server and Link Monitors, let's turn our attention to monitoring message queues.

Monitoring Message Queues

Part of the design brief for Microsoft Exchange was the ability to operate under diverse network conditions. Like other messaging systems, it had to be able to cope with sites and servers that were not permanently available. Hence, Exchange must be able to provide storage for messages that are awaiting delivery.

Message queues provide this storage space. These temporary holding spaces let Exchange hold messages until the receiving site or server can accept them. Message queues are incorporated into the MTA, the Internet Mail Service, the cc:Mail connector, and the MS Mail connector.

Hence, when Exchange wants to send a message to another server, site, or even messaging system, it places that message in a message queue. The MTA or relevant connector then holds on to those messages until the remote site can accept them. The messages travel to the remote site.

Where Can I Monitor Them?

There are a number of places to monitor message queues. Where you look depends on whether you want to see all queues or just those on a particular connector.

Message Transfer Agent Object (Server-Level)

The main area where you can monitor message queues is the Site level MTA object. To do this, start Exchange Administrator and click the Servers button in the toolbar. Double-click your server and then double-click the Message Transfer Agent object. Click the Queues tab and you will see the screen in Figure 15.10.

FIGURE 15.10

The Message Transfer Object at the Server level shows the queues within Exchange Server.

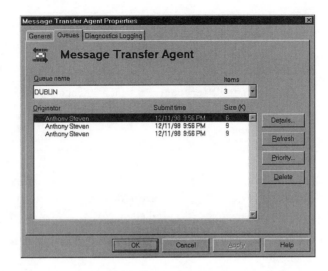

The queues that you see may include:

- Private Information Store
- Public Information Store
- Any Site, X.400, or Dynamic RAS connectors to remote sites
- The Internet Mail Service
- MS Mail Service or other connectors

Messaging Connectors

The following connectors also have their own queues, which can be viewed from the relevant objects in Exchange Administrator.

Internet Mail Service Object   Go to the Site-level Connections container and double-click the Internet Mail Service object. Click the Queues tab to see the incoming, outgoing, and message conversion queues. The important queue is the outgoing message queue—you will rarely see any messages in the other queues.

Note   With a dial-up IMS, it is normal to see messages in the outgoing queue between dial-up sessions. Clicking Retry will not get the system to dial up automatically.

If you want to get all mail delivered immediately on a dial-up IMS, run this batch file:

```
@echo off
net stop "Microsoft Exchange Internet Mail Service"
net start "Microsoft Exchange Internet Mail Service"
```

This will force a dial-up attempt when the IMS restarts, which will then deliver the mail.

MS Mail Connector   If you have an MS Mail connector configured, double-click the MS Mail Connector object in the Site-level Connections container. Click the Queues tab to see the current queues in the MS Mail connector.

cc:Mail Connector   If you have a cc:Mail connector installed, the same applies for the MS Mail connector.

The MTA manages the queues for the Site, X.400, and Dynamic RAS connectors.

Predefined Performance Monitor Graph

Another way to monitor the queues within Exchange Server is to use the preconfigured Performance Monitor graph. Click Start, select Programs, and then choose Microsoft Exchange. From the list displayed, click Microsoft Exchange Server Queues. You will see a graph displaying the size of the current queues as columns, updated every ten seconds.

Operation of the Queues

In normal operation, you should only get messages building up in the queues for the connectors that aren't permanently connected. Hence most queues will be empty most of the time, or occasionally have one or two items, depending on message numbers and server loading.

The messages in queues will only start to build up if you have a break in messaging connectivity or if your servers cannot cope with the volume of traffic. The exception is a dial-up connection, where having messages in queues is part of normal operation. However, if you have a Site connector to another site, and you notice messages building up in this queue, you could have a problem. This is because Site connectors are always available, so queuing will only happen if the link is down or messages are arriving faster than they leave the queue to travel to the other site.

What you need to do at this point is to check the queue and see if the messages are actually leaving the queue. If the messages are leaving the queue, but new ones are arriving faster than the MTA can process them, this is only a cause for concern if the queue becomes too large. What's happening is that the volume of messages in transit is overloading either the bandwidth of the link or the sending server(s). You may need to increase the resources on this server, install additional servers, or, in the case of the X.400 connector, add additional connectors.

If the messages in the queue just keep building up, you probably have a networking problem. Check that you have connectivity to the remote site, and, if your sites are in different domains, that no one has messed around with the passwords, thus preventing the link from authenticating.

USING MTACHECK TO REMOVE LINK MONITOR MESSAGES

One particular messaging problem you may encounter is when you have a Link Monitor running across a failed link. The Link Monitor normally sends a message every 15 minutes, but if something goes wrong, the monitor sends a test message every five minutes. Let's say your link goes down at 6:00 p.m. on Friday, and you don't find out about it until 8:00 a.m. on Monday. In addition to any normal and system site-to-site messages sent over the weekend, there would be more than seven hundred link monitor messages in the queue.

Even if you restore network connectivity, these link monitor messages will be holding up the more important system and user messages. Thus, to remove unwanted link monitor messages, run the MTACHECK.EXE utility with the /RL switch from a command prompt. You will have to change to the Exchange server BIN directory to run this program.

```
D:\EXCHSRVR\BIN>MTACHECK /RL
```

This will remove Link Monitor messages from your MTA queue.

Exchange and the Windows NT Performance Monitor

Performance Monitor is a Windows NT application that installs with both NT Server and NT Workstation. Performance Monitor enables you to monitor and record a large number of Windows NT system criteria, such as processor usage, network utilization, and disk performance. You can even monitor individual processes and threads within applications.

Performance Monitor is a very useful tool, particularly as Microsoft Exchange installs a number of Exchange-specific counters onto your server at installation. These Exchange counters let you look in detail at the actions and performance of your individual Exchange services, such as the Information Stores, the MTA, or the System Attendant.

Using Performance Monitor

If you have already used Performance Monitor, you can skip this bit.

To start Performance Monitor, click Start, select Programs, and from the Administrative Tools (Common) group, choose Performance Monitor. Performance Monitor starts in Chart view.

Performance Monitor runs in four modes:

- Chart view
- Alert view
- Log view
- Report view

Each one has its own specific application. I will cover the detail of using each view later in this section.

What Can I Record in Performance Monitor?

Performance Monitor lets you select items to record at three different levels.

Objects   Objects are physical items, like hard disks, processors, and memory, or services, like the Browser, Server, and Exchange Services. There are other objects, like the Process object, which lets you record performance on individual processes running on your NT computer.

Counter   Each object has one or more counters. These are the actual items that you will be recording. Examples of counters are %Processor Usage (Processor Object), Disk Bytes/sec (Physical Disk Object) or Election Packets/sec (Browser Object). Thus counters are specific to their parent objects.

Some of the standard Objects and counters are shown in Table 15.1.

TABLE 15.1 STANDARD OBJECTS AND COUNTERS IN WINDOWS NT PERFORMANCE MONITOR

Object	Counter	Use For
Processor	%Processor Time	Total load on Processor
Processor	%Privilege Time	System load on Processor
Processor	%User Time	User load on Processor
Physical Disk	%Disk Time	How busy the hard disk is
Physical Disk	%Current Disk Queue Length	Outstanding disk requests
Memory	Page Faults/Second	Checking RAM is adequate

Depending on the counter, either a high or a low level is acceptable. Usually, you want a low loading on the processor (>70% on average), a low value for %Disk Time (>50%) coupled with a low disk queue length (two items or less), and a low level of Memory Page Faults.

Some performance issues are complex; for example, a continuous high level of processor usage usually indicates that you need to upgrade the processor. However, if a large Current Disk Queue Length and a high level of Page Faults accompany this high level of processor usage, the problem is probably excessive paging caused by a lack of RAM. Adding RAM usually solves the problem.

Note

You must enable the performance counters for the Physical Disk and Logical Disk objects manually. This is due to the (mostly historic) reason that they inflicted a 2% performance penalty on a 486-based server. In these days of multi-penti-yummy superchips, you don't need to worry about this performance penalty.

To enable the disk-based counters, run

```
DISKPERF -y
```

at a command prompt. When you reboot your machine, the disk counters will work. If you have a RAID array, then use the –ye switch.

Tip

Adding RAM usually sorts out most performance issues in Windows NT. If you're not sure what the problem is, try bringing some more RAM in there. It certainly won't hurt.

Instances   Instances come into play where you have more than one item to measure. For example, if you have more than one hard disk in your server, you will have two instances for each counter in the Physical Disk Object. In addition, you may have a _Total instance as well. When monitoring multiple processors and network cards you will have an instance for each processor or network card. The Process and Thread objects also give rise to multiple instances.

Chart View

In Chart view, you can create pretty performance charts, showing the instantaneous variation of whichever counter you are monitoring. To add a counter to the chart, click the button with a plus sign (+). You can then select the Object, Counter, and, if necessary, the Instance of the Counter that you want to measure. You can choose a color, line thickness, and style for the measurement line. You can also choose a scale or accept the default setting.

> An optional Explain button attempts to describe the counter that you have selected. So if you want to measure APC Bypasses/sec, the explanation reads:
>
> *"APC Bypasses/sec is the rate kernel APC interrupts were short-circuited."*
>
> Er, thanks, guys. I guess that if you want to measure APC Bypasses/sec, you would have to know what an APC was in the first place. I thought an APC was an Armored Personnel Carrier.

Figure 15.11 shows an example of Performance Monitor in Chart view.

> In Chart view, use Ctrl+H to highlight individual counters.

Chart view is also a good way of showing decision-makers what the problems are. I was trying to get together a business case to replace a Lotus Notes server, but money was proving difficult to come by. So I charted the processor usage on the machine, and demonstrated this to the directors, explaining the problem. As the processor usage was averaging over 85%, and most of the time was at 100%, we had a new machine within a week. Which was a good thing, really, as the old server died rather spectacularly two days after the new one went live.

FIGURE 15.11

Running Performance Monitor in Chart view is good for showing a snapshot of current performance.

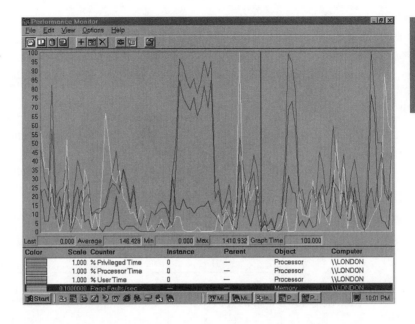

 Caution

Don't ever, ever run OpenGL screensavers on your NT Servers. Just try monitoring processor usage when the screen saver is running. 'Nuff said.

Tip

If you find that the counter you have just added is a flat line at the bottom of the graph, but there are non-zero figures showing in the Last, Average, Max boxes, you need to change the scale. Double-click the counter at the bottom of the graph and change the scale from the default setting.

In the Options menu, you can change settings like the update interval and the scale of your horizontal and vertical grids. Changing to a Histogram shows your counter as a column.

You can use the Chart view to display data gathered from a logging session. The section on Log view later in this lesson tells how to do this.

Alert View

In Alert view, you can configure alerts to fire if a counter exceeds or drops below predefined limits. To do this, click on the Alert View button in Performance Monitor, and then click the button with a plus (+) sign. Again, you can select a counter and, if necessary, an instance of that counter to monitor.

In Alert view, you specify what you want to happen if that counter goes over a certain amount. This will depend on the counter that you have selected, but you might set up an alert if your disk becomes more than 95% full, or your disk queues exceed 10 items. Optionally, you could run an application, like a paging program, that would warn you of the problem.

Initially, the alerts will just stack up in the Alert log in the Alert View window. However, if you want to do something more than this, go to the Options menu and select Alert. If an alert triggers, you can specify to switch the focus to your Alert window, log the alert in the Windows NT Event Log, or send a message to a user or computer. You can also specify the update time.

Note

The messenger and alerting services must be running for the network message functionality to work.

Use Alert view for short- or long-term monitoring of your network.

Tip

If you have problems getting money out of the budget for a new hard disk, and your current hard disk is almost full, why not send the "Disk Full" alerts to the purchasing director? After a morning of being interrupted every five minutes to be told that "The hard disk on ServerX is more than 95% full," you'll have a new hard disk the next day. And if he asks you why he is getting the warning messages, you could tell him that as he signed the purchase order, the software is registered in his name, hence he gets the alerts. And no, you don't know how to stop them. (It is very important *not* to smirk at this point.)

Log View

Log view is best for long-term recording and monitoring. In Log view, you don't get to see anything, but you can record a log file that you can then look at in Chart view.

In Log view, you don't choose individual counters; instead you select an entire object. All the counters within that object are included in the log file.

You can change the log file options through the Options menu. Here you can specify the location of the log file and the update interval.

Log files can grow very large extremely quickly. If you are carrying out long-term logging, keep the logging intervals low.

If you are logging over a day, you will probably want to set the logging interval to every five minutes. If you are logging over a week, you might set it to record every 15 or 30 minutes.

Use log files to build up a long-term picture of the loading on your network and servers. You can then use these figures to predict future expansion requirements, or to isolate and eliminate bottlenecks.

You can view log files in Chart view. After you have saved the log file, switch to Chart view and then select the Options menu. Choose the Data From option, and specify the log file that you want to graph. You can now add counters from the objects that you originally logged, and show them on the chart.

You can export log files to tab-separated variable (.TSV) or comma-separated variable (.CSV) files that you can then chart using Microsoft Excel, or store in Microsoft Access. Again, a long-term logging strategy will pay dividends in helping you to take a more proactive stance to network enhancements.

Report View

Personally, I think that Report view is the least useful option. Report view gives you an average over the reporting period. The only option you can change is the reporting period.

Using the Built-in Performance Charts

When you install Exchange server, you also install a number of preconfigured performance monitor charts. These are in the Microsoft Exchange program group, and measure these settings:

- Server Health
- Server History
- Server Load
- Server Queues
- Server Users
- IMS Queues
- IMS Statistics
- IMS Traffic

Exchange Server Health is the most general chart. It records the demands made on the processor by the core Exchange services, as well as overall processor and memory use.

Use Server Queues if you are having problems with messaging connectivity. Server Users lets you track the number of simultaneous logons.

The preconfigured charts have been set up so that you only see the graph part of the display. Double-click the graph area and the Title bar reappears.

Using Other Exchange Counters

You can manually configure a Performance Monitor Chart, using the Exchange objects. When you install Microsoft Exchange, you get performance counters for the following items:

- Internet Protocols
- cc:Mail Connector
- Directory Service
- Event Service
- Internet Mail Connector
- Information Store (General, Private, and Public)
- Microsoft Mail Interchange
- MTA and MTA Connections
- PC MTA (if MS Mail Connector installed)
- Outlook Web Access

There are more than one hundred counters that install with Exchange.

Remote Monitoring

You can use Performance Monitor to monitor other machines. In fact, this is the recommended configuration because the process of monitoring itself puts a noticeable loading on the server under test. Hence, you should do your monitoring from an NT Workstation, and remotely monitor your servers. Remember that big NT Workstation that I said you should ask for? Well, you'll need it for remote monitoring as well.

To monitor another machine in Chart, Alert, Log, or Report view, select the Add button and then click the ellipsis (...) button to the left of the Computer field and browse for the remote machine. Alternatively, you can enter the computer name in the form \\COMPUTERNAME.

When you connect to a remote machine, you will see all the objects that apply to that machine. Let's say you are monitoring from a workstation and you want to monitor counters on your Exchange server. If you select that server as I have just described, you will find the Exchange objects available to record.

Now that you know how to measure performance and record data on your Exchange server, let's look at a crucial aspect to the management of Exchange—monitoring Exchange's databases.

Managing Database Growth

When I am lecturing about Microsoft Exchange, some people express surprise when I start talking about databases. They seem to associate databases with products like Access and SQL Server, yet Exchange would not be able to function without its own databases.

Exchange's Databases

Exchange maintains a number of databases, depending on the components that you have installed. Most of them function in the same way, so after you understand one, the others are easy.

 Caution | Never tamper with the files in any of the database directories. Unless you like the challenge of restoring Exchange from your backups, that is.

Directory and Information Store Directories

The main databases within Exchange are the Directory and Information Store databases. These make up three databases, one for the Directory Service, one for the Private Information Store, and one for the Public Information Store.

Exchange's directory database is located in D:\EXCHSRVR\DSADATA and the Information Store databases are in D:\EXCHSRVR\MDBDATA. I am assuming D:\EXCHSRVR is where you installed Microsoft Exchange.

Other Databases

There are two other databases that have the same structure as the DS and IS services:

- The Key Management Service database, which holds the data for enabling Advanced Security in \KMSDATA.
- The Directory Synchronization (DX) database, which synchronizes directory information with MS Mail postoffices in \DXADATA.

> **Note** The KMSDATA and DXADATA directories will be empty unless you are using the Key Management or Directory Synchronization Services.

The connectors and the MTA use message queues rather than databases, so the IMCDATA, INSDATA, CCMCDATA, and MTADATA directories have a different structure.

Joint Engine Technology (JET) Database

Microsoft Exchange uses the Microsoft Joint Engine Technology (JET) 3.0 Database engine to store directory and messaging information. This is the database engine behind Microsoft Access and FoxPro. The JET database engine is more suitable than SQL Server for the variable-length fields that you get in a messaging environment.

Transactional Tracking

 JET supports *transactional tracking*, which means that database transactions go first into a transactional tracking log file. During slack periods, the transactions update the database. After this updating happens, a checkpoint file marks the last update.

The advantage of transactional tracking files is this: In the case of the database becoming corrupt, you can recover the data from the last backed up database plus the up-to-date transactional tracking files.

> **Caution** The transactional recovery features of JET databases do not work if you have circular logging enabled. See Day 16, "Backing Up, Restoring, and Repairing Data," for more information.

Key Database Files

The key database files are as follows:

The .EDB file is the JET database itself, containing the directory data, user mailboxes, or Public Folder data. DIR.EDB is the directory, and PRIV.EDB and PUB.EDB are the private and public Information Stores, respectively.

The EDB.LOG and EDBXXXXX.LOG files are the transactional tracking log files. They are numbered and increased sequentially. Transactional tracking log files are always 5,120KB in size. If their size is any different, they are corrupt.

If you have circular logging switched on, you will not have very many .LOG files. If you have circular logging switched off, you may get quite a few as Exchange only deletes these when you make a full backup.

The EDB.CHK file is the checkpoint file, recording the last write to the database.

The TMP.EDB file appears after carrying out sorts and searches.

The RES1.LOG and RES2.LOG files are reserved space. If you load them into Notepad, you will find that they are empty. These are so that if your Exchange server runs out of disk space, the services can close down gracefully, and flush any outstanding transaction data to the database. These files are always 5,120KB in size.

Caution | *Never* delete any of these files manually.

Figure 15.12 shows the files in the MDBDATA directory.

FIGURE 15.12

Here you can see the Information Store files in the MDBDATA directory.

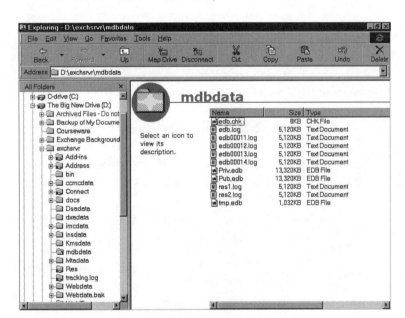

Changes with Exchange 5.5 Enterprise Edition

One of the much-vaunted changes to the Enterprise version of Exchange 5.5 is the removal of the 16GB database limit. You might think that you could now host your entire 10,000-user organization on one server and save lots of money! Unfortunately, this isn't realistically possible, as database size is only one part of the equation.

The reason for this is as follows: Let's say that you are scaling up from 250 users to 2,500 users. Assume each user has an individual mailbox allocation of 50MB, thus requiring 12.5GB of storage space for Mailboxes. Moving to the Enterprise edition might remove the database storage limit, but you will now require 125GB of storage space on your server. That's one big disk array, in anyone's book. Add to that the fact that Microsoft does not recommend that you use more than 70% of your disk capacity, and you are looking at needing a 180GB array. That's seriously chunky!

Moreover, what happens if this server goes down? You have 2,500 users without messaging. Also, what happens when everyone logs on in the morning? I can see this server becoming somewhat overstressed.

Another reason for not having massive databases is the possibility that you may want to run offline compaction. Although improvements to the On-line Compaction utility ESE97 means that offline compactions are required less often, you will still need more free space than your database's current size to carry out the compaction.

The moral is this: Database size is only one factor in calculating the number of users you can host on one Exchange server. What you *can* do with the removal of the limits is to increase everyone's quota. Hence, you could increase the storage limits on your 250 users to 100MB each, thus consuming up to 25GB on your server.

HOW BIG IS TOO BIG?

File this one under H for "How long is a piece of string?"

There are several operational limits on how many users you can have on a server. Among the more obvious ones are:

- Maximum physical partition size
- Maximum server configuration (processors, RAM, and so on)
- Risks from servers failing
- Online backup performance
- Database restore performance
- Acceptable user performance

You will need to consider all these factors.

My personal recommendation is to look at hosting a maximum of about 500 users per server. This gives you a reasonable compromise between too many servers and too many users per server. The hardware to implement this will not be too expensive, as a number of vendors sell such machines. In addition, if one server goes down, the impact will not be too extensive.

A server to support this configuration could have the following configuration: 400MHz Xeon processor, 256MB RAM, 4x9GB disks as a RAID array, plus 4GB FAT disk for transactional logs and a 100MB network card.

See Day 2, "Planning Your Exchange Implementation," for more information on server capacity planning.

Controlling Database Size

Having looked at Exchange's storage facilities, and some of the factors behind sizing the database, I will now show you how to set storage limits on the Information Stores.

Setting Information Store Limits

It is important that you set effective limits on your Information Stores. It is not enough just to look at the file size every so often, as Exchange does not update the file size on an open database until the relevant service closes down. Because your servers could be running for weeks on end, this means that the file size could grow considerably in that time.

You must also manage your Private and Public Information Store limits to ensure you do not run out of disk space. As your maximum database size should be no more than 70% of the available partition size, you can now calculate the total space available for the Information Stores.

You must also consider the relative needs of the Public and Private Information Stores. If you are running a system with a large Usenet newsfeed, you will need a larger Public Information Store. If your users tend to email each other large graphics files, you may need larger Private Information Stores.

 Tip

You could try getting your users to email each other shortcuts to the files rather than the files themselves.

After you have decided on the ratio of allowable sizes between the Public and Private Information Stores, you can calculate a size for the individual mailboxes. Divide the space available for the Private Information Store by the number of users to give you the individual mailbox size.

Limits for the Public Information Store aren't so easy to calculate. The reason is that the Private Information Store sets its limits on a mailbox-by-mailbox level but the Public Information Store does it on a folder-by-folder basis. The creation of mailboxes is quite easy to control, but unless you tie down your Public Folder creation policy very early on, you may find Public Folders springing up all over the place. As each new Public Folder can contain up to the maximum storage space allowed, it is not enough just to limit the space taken up by individual Public Folders. You must also limit the creation of these folders in the first place.

To set a size limit for the Public Information Store, you divide the available space by the total number of Public Folders. You will now have limits for the Public and Private Information Stores.

Public Information Store Limits　　Armed with your limit on the size of a Public Folder, you can now proceed to set this limit. Start Exchange Administrator and click the Servers button on the toolbar. Double-click your server name and then select the Public Information Store object. Click the Properties button or press Alt+Enter. You will see the screen in Figure 15.13.

FIGURE 15.13

This is where you set limits on all Public Folders.

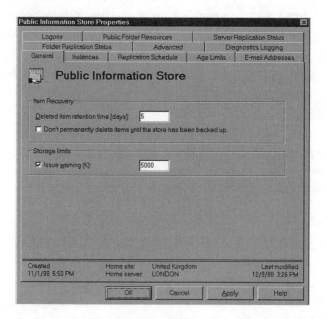

Check the box for Issue Warning and enter a figure for the limit on individual folders in the box. Note that this figure is in Kilobytes.

Caution With Public Folders, you can only issue a warning, which is an email message to the folder contact (usually the owner or creator of the folder). Unlike the Private Information store, you can't prevent any new messages from arriving.

In addition, the owner of the folder may not be particularly bothered that the folder is getting large. Therefore, if you are concerned about monitoring Public Folder usage, make sure that you are either the owner or a contact for all the Public Folders.

15

Individual Folder Limits   Having set an overall limit on Public Folders, you can configure individual limits on particular folders, if necessary. To do this, select the individual Public Folder in the left-hand pane in Exchange Administrator and then click the Properties button on the toolbar. Now click the Limits tab. You will see the screen in Figure 15.14.

FIGURE 15.14

You can also set limits on a folder-by-folder basis.

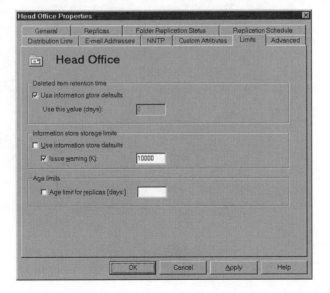

You can either use the Information Store defaults or uncheck the box and set a value for this individual folder.

Note You cannot propagate folder limits down to subfolders.

Click OK to apply the new limit.

Private Information Store Limits   Knowing the limits that you want to put on each mailbox, you can implement these very easily. Start Exchange Administrator and click the Servers button on the toolbar. Double-click your server name and then select the Private Information Store object. Click the Properties button or press Alt+Enter. You will now see the screen in Figure 15.15.

FIGURE 15.15

You can configure mailbox limits at three different levels.

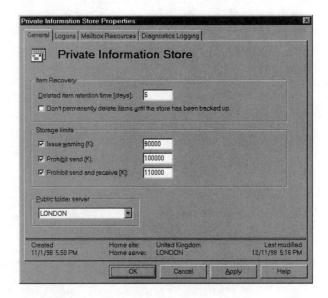

You can set storage limits using a cascaded warning scheme.

The first level is to issue a warning. I would probably make this 90% of the maximum allowable.

The next level prevents users from sending. I would set this at 100% of the individual mailbox limit as previously calculated.

The final level prevents users from sending or receiving any mail. I would set this at 110% of the individual limit.

What happens is that when users exceed the first level, they get a warning to clean out their mailbox, either by Archiving or by emptying the deleted items folder.

If their mailboxes continue to fill up to the next limit, they will be prevented from sending any mail. This usually stings them into purging some mail.

If they are extremely complacent, or haven't logged in for a long time, and they still don't empty their mailboxes, mail delivery will stop. This prevents the mailbox from increasing in size and all messages sent to them return as nondeliverable.

Individual Mailbox Limits   So that's the bulk of your users taken care of. However, there will always be a few users that may need more storage space—like you. I mean, what's the point of being the Administrator if you can't have any perks?

You can cater for users who need larger mailboxes on an individual basis. To do this, select that user in the Recipients container and double-click her mailbox. Click the Limits tab and you will see the screen in Figure 15.16.

FIGURE 15.16

You can configure storage limits at a mailbox level. Alas, poor Roger is not long for this company, but no one has told him yet.

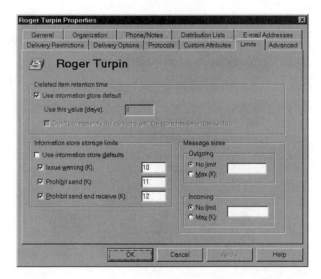

Under Information Store Storage Limits, uncheck the box for using the Information Store Limits. You are now able to enter individual limits for the three levels as you did in the Public Information Store.

Monitoring Mailbox Size

It is very easy to see the users with the largest mailboxes. In Exchange Administrator, go to the relevant server, double-click the Private Information Store, and then double-click the Mailbox Resources object. You will see a listing showing the size of each mailbox.

The good news is that you can sort this list by mailbox size. The bad news is that you can only sort it in ascending order, with the largest at the bottom. To do this, click the column heading labeled Total K.

Now that you know who the main offenders are, you can proceed to do something about it.

Cleaning Mailboxes

What should you do if a few individuals are abusing their mailboxes and keeping them stuffed full of junk? If they are refusing to respond to friendly, stern, or just plain rude emails asking them to clean their mailboxes, you have another weapon in your armory.

To clean a mailbox, select the relevant mailbox in the recipients container, and then select the Tools menu and choose Clean Mailbox. Figure 15.17 shows the Clean Mailbox dialog box.

FIGURE 15.17

With intransigent users, you may have to clean their mailboxes for them.

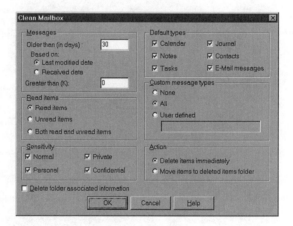

Note

This dialog has changed substantially with Exchange 5.5 Service Pack 1. Now you can clean messages by type. Check the relevant boxes to remove particular message types, such as contact items, journal items, and so on.

Select the age of the messages to clean and their types. You can also choose whether to delete the messages immediately or to put them in the user's Deleted Items folder. After you have set up the required cleaning actions, click OK.

15

Using Personal Folders

Another way of reclaiming storage space in mailboxes is to move the data into personal folders. Personal folders can store any information that you can store in mailboxes, and as the personal folder is usually on the client's local disk, it reduces the size of the mailbox.

You can automate the use of personal folders in Outlook by using the AutoArchive feature. For more information on using AutoArchive, see the section "When Using the AutoArchive Feature of Outlook" in Day 7, "Configuring the Exchange Client."

Day 7 also shows you how to create and use personal folders. To reduce the size of your mailbox, create a personal folder as part of your profile, and just drag messages, contact items, journal items, and so on into folders in the personal folder.

 Caution

The problem with personal folders is that the .PST file only exists on the local hard drive. Hence, if you log on to another machine, you won't be able to access your personal folder. You could always put your personal folders on a shared network drive, but that does somewhat negate the point of having the personal folder in the first place!

Now that you understand how to limit the size of your mailboxes and Public Folders in Exchange, today's final topic is looking at Exchange's automatic maintenance routines.

Understanding Exchange Maintenance Routines

Because of the complexity of Microsoft Exchange and the inherent inconsistencies that arise in all databases, there needs to be a regular maintenance routine. Most of these routine jobs are the responsibility of the System Attendant.

THE SYSTEM ATTENDANT AND MAINTENANCE ROUTINES

When I'm lecturing on Exchange, I try to relate the four core Exchange services to what happens in real life. Thus, the Directory Service is the company 'phone book, and the Information Stores are a combination of your in-tray, filing cabinet and the company notice board. The MTA is the "mail room operative" with the wheelie-trolley and the System Attendant is the janitor, with a big bunch of jangly keys and a plunger for unblocking the sink.

It's the janitor's job to go around at night, closing the windows, switching off the lights, and emptying the rubbish bins. Likewise with Exchange, it's the System Attendant's job to go around (usually at night) and tidy up, get rid of the rubbish, and generally sort your system out.

As I'm sure you're aware, if the janitor goes on strike, the company soon grinds to a halt. Just like Exchange, really.

Routine Operations

There are a number of routine operations that are performed on an hourly, three-hourly, or daily basis. However, you can control when these operations take place, to improve both performance and the service that your users receive.

Note　Generally, your Exchange system will function quite happily without changing any of these schedules. It is only in exceptional cases that you would want to alter the timings of routine operations.

All Settings

You can change all the following settings through Exchange Administrator. All the schedule tabs work in a similar way. Select when you want the routine to run by clicking the boxes, and they will turn blue (On). Click them again to switch off the routine operation. You can switch on whole days by clicking that day's name. Click the gray box at the top of a column, and you can switch that time block on for all days. Some screens allow you to schedule in both 15-minute and one-hour blocks.

Offline Address Book Generation

The Offline Address Book is a copy of the Global Address list that mobile users can download and use on their laptops or at remote locations. Thus, mobile users can address mail to Exchange users although they cannot connect to the Exchange server at the time.

The routing calculation schedule is set on the DS Site Configuration object at Site level. To view or change this schedule, click the Configuration button on the toolbar and then double-click the DS Site Configuration object. Click the Offline Address Book Schedule tab (see Figure 15.18).

By default, the OAB is rebuilt every day at 3:00–4:00 a.m. You can force a manual rebuild by clicking the Offline Address Book tab and selecting the Generate All button. You can also select which Recipients containers will be included in the OAB. You will probably want to do this if you have just added a large number of mailboxes.

FIGURE 15.18

The Offline Address Book Schedule rebuilds the Offline Address Book for download by remote users.

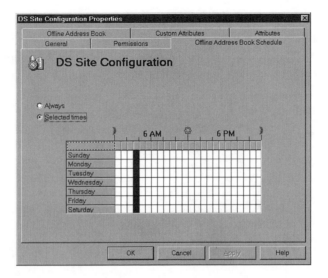

Information Store Warning Generation

The Information Store Warning Generation routine looks at all the mailboxes and Public Folders. It then sends out warning messages according to the values that you set at Information Store, mailbox, or individual folder level. Any other restrictions, such as Prohibit Send, are also applied at this time.

The routing calculation schedule is set on the Information Store Site Configuration object at Site level. To view or change this schedule, click the Configuration button on the toolbar and then double-click the Information Store Site Configuration object. Click the Storage Warnings tab and you will see the screen in Figure 15.19.

By default, storage warnings are issued every day at 8:00 p.m. You cannot force a manual storage warning, but you could click the Always option and select Apply. This will run the storage warnings immediately. You might want to do this if you have just been looking at the size of users' mailboxes and you want people to delete messages immediately.

Routing Calculation

Routing Calculation updates the Gateway Address Routing Table or GWART to reflect any changes to address spaces or connections to other sites. By default, this happens every day at 1:00 a.m. For more information about routing, see Day 6, "Connecting Exchange to Other Sites."

FIGURE 15.19

Storage warnings can apply to Information Stores, mailboxes, and Public Folders.

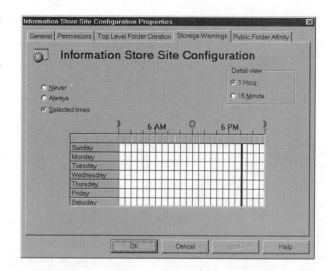

The Routing Calculation schedule is set on the Site Addressing object at Site level. To view or change this schedule, click the Configuration button on the toolbar and then double-click the Site Addressing object. Click the Routing Calculation tab and you will see the screen in Figure 15.20.

FIGURE 15.20

The Routing Calculation Schedule is set to run at 2:00 a.m.

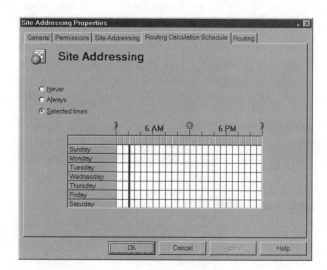

After you have made your changes to the routing calculation schedule, click OK to apply your changes.

You can force a manual update of the routing tables at any time. To do this, click the Routing tab and then select the Recalculate Routing button. You would probably want to do this if you have added a new site or connector to your Organization.

Online Compaction

When a user deletes a message or a Public Folder posting expires, an empty space appears in the file. Although subsequent messages may use that empty space, this can result in fragmentation. Over time, with many deletions and subsequent writes to the database, the resulting fragmentation of messages affects performance. This is similar to the normal file fragmentation that takes place on a disk, except that it is happening with a file. As users are constantly adding and deleting messages from the Information Stores, a defragmentation process is necessary.

Online compaction is the process of defragmenting the JET databases in Exchange. A utility called ESE97 is responsible for this activity, controlled by the System Attendant. ESE97 cleans up databases by collecting any "holes" in the database and placing them as free space at the end of the file.

Online compaction does not make the database file any smaller. It just puts all the free space at the end of the file and defragments messages.

Note

> Exchange 5.5 SP1 has updated ESE97 to include a reporting tool that provides an estimate in the event log of how much free space is available in the Information Store after online defragmentation. You can recover this space using offline compaction.

The online defragmentation routine is set through the properties of the relevant server. In Exchange Administrator, click the Servers button in the toolbar. Select your server in the right pane and then click the Properties button. Select the IS Maintenance tab (see Figure 15.21).

Caution

> Online defragmentation will slow the response of your system. I would not recommend that you run ESE97 during working hours. See the following section for more information.

Figure 15.21

*You control online
defragmentation
through the properties
of the server object.*

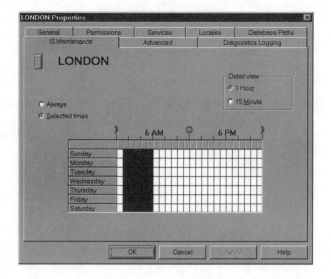

Directory Service

Although ESE97 defragments the Directory Service database as well as the Information
Store, there is an additional process at work. When you set up directory replication,
copies of all mailboxes, distribution lists, and so on replicate throughout the organization.
However, if you delete a mailbox, you need to let the other copies of the directory database know that the deletion has taken place. Hence a tombstone is created, and the tombstone replicates to all the copies of the directory, replacing the original directory object.

The tombstone needs to replicate to all copies of the directory database. To ensure this
happens, a tombstone is given a default lifetime of 30 days. After 30 days, the tombstone
expires. This happens at the next Garbage Collection Interval, by default every 12 hours.
After the expired tombstones are collected, the next time the online compaction runs, the
space from the deleted directory item is reclaimed.

You configure the Tombstone Lifetime and Garbage Collection Interval through the Site
level DS Site Configuration object. In Exchange Administrator, click the Configuration
button and then double-click the DS Site Configuration object. You will now see the
screen in Figure 15.22.

FIGURE 15.22

Use the DS Site Configuration object to change the Tombstone Lifetime and Garbage Collection settings.

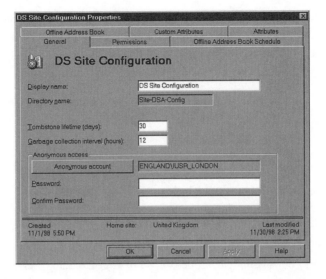

Note

Again, it is unlikely that you will have to change this value.

Offline Compaction

If you examine your Application Log in Event Viewer for ESE97 events, you will see some events of ID Number 1221. Double-click one of these events and you will see the dialog box in Figure 15.23.

FIGURE 15.23

This shows the amount of free space you could reclaim from an offline compaction.

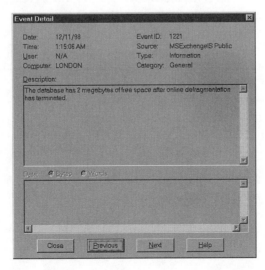

The free space figure shows you by how much your Information Store or directory service database would shrink on running an offline compaction. If this shows a reasonable amount to reclaim, it may be worth running the offline compaction.

 Note

Because of improvements in ESE97 over the earlier version in Exchange 5.0, you do not have to run offline compaction as a matter of course.

When running an offline compaction, you will need to carry out the following steps:

1. Make sure that your free disk space is 10% greater than the size of your database. Hence, if you are defragmenting your Public Information store, which is currently 2.4GB, you will need at least 2.64GB of free disk space. Note that this disk space does not have to be on the same volume.

2. Carry out a complete online backup of your Exchange Server.

3. Stop all Exchange Services.

4. Start a command prompt and enter ESEUTIL /d <databasename>. <databasename> will be either /ispriv, /ispub, or /ds for the Private Information Store, Private Information Store, or Directory Service. For other options, type ESEUTIL/? at a command prompt.

5. Examine the log files to see that the defragmentation was successful.

6. Restart the Exchange services.

7. Carry out a full online backup again.

The second online backup is required because any previous backups will be incompatible with the new database.

 Tip

You can run ESEUTIL to check database integrity by using the /g <databasename> switch.

Scheduling Routine Operations to Maximize Performance

Having looked at the routine operations that Exchange performs, how should you schedule these for maximum performance?

This question only becomes an issue where you have staff working 24 hours. Most companies are not operating between midnight and six o'clock in the morning, so your database defragmentation, offline address book generation and other maintenance routines can run then. In fact, you will probably find that there is an appreciable dip in usage on the system between 7:00 p.m. and 7:00 a.m.

Tip

> Why not use some of the Exchange counters in Performance Monitor to check the usage pattern on your system overnight? You might be surprised.
>
> Use the MSExchangeIS object's Private Active Logons, Messages Sent, and Messages Delivered counters to measure user activity.

The only maintenance routine that you have to worry about is the online defragmentation. All the other maintenance routines have a minimal impact on the performance of your Exchange servers.

Nevertheless, what do you do if your company has true 24-hour working days with three eight-hour shifts? In that case, you have a couple of options.

If you only have one Exchange server, you will need to increase significantly the resources (RAM, processor type, and speed) on that computer. After you have done that, adjust the maintenance schedules to run all the time, except for the times when the shifts change over.

Depending on how often the users change shifts it may be possible to have separate servers for each shift. The servers can then run their maintenance routines when they are not in use. When a user changes shift, you (or preferably, someone in HR) can move her mailbox onto the relevant server for that shift.

You can move groups of mailboxes between servers in the same site using Exchange Administrator. Go to the Recipients container and select the mailboxes that you want to move. From the Tools menu, select Move Mailbox, and then select the destination server.

If this isn't possible, you will have to ensure that all the servers are capable of running the online compaction as well as servicing user requests. Again, it would be best to prevent any maintenance routines running during known times of peak demand, like when a shift logs on.

Caution   However your organization works, you must perform an online defragmentation at least once a day.

A MAINTENANCE ROUTINE

Here is a list of suggested maintenance tasks that you should consider:

Every Day

- Back up your data. Don't forget to store the backups off-site.
- Check the amount of available disk space.
- Run the predefined Performance Monitor counters.
- Check your Server and Link Monitors.
- Monitor the edbxxxxx.log files in the \DSADATA and \MDBDATA directories to see if the transaction log files are building up.
- Check that the Alerter and Messenger services are running on your servers and on the monitoring workstation.
- Check the Application and System Event Logs for errors and warnings. Check that the online defragmentation is running every day when scheduled.

Every Week

- Verify that the Public Folders are replicating correctly.
- Check the TRACKING.LOG directory for build up of message tracking logs.

Every Month

- Validate your backups by restoring your Exchange servers to an alternate server on an isolated network. You need to check the integrity of your backups and you need to practice the procedure before it happens for real!

Every So Often

- Run ISINTEG to check the integrity of the Information Stores.
- Carry out an offline defragmentation of the Directory and Information Stores.
- Check mailbox and Public Folder use by looking at the Mailbox Resources tab and the Public Folder Resources tab to check on use of storage space.
- Clean out any mailboxes that are over the storage limits.
- Check storage limits and adjust as required.

Alternatively, you could always get your sidekick to do it!

Summary

In this lesson, you looked at all the different considerations to take into account when monitoring and maintaining Microsoft Exchange. You learned how to set up Server and Link Monitors, how to manage message queues, and how to schedule routine maintenance.

To summarize the main points of this lesson:

- Microsoft Exchange has a number of built-in tools to help you with monitoring and maintenance.
- Server Monitors let you check on the services running on an Exchange Server.
- Link Monitors can check on the integrity of your links to both Exchange and non-Exchange sites.
- You can schedule monitors to start and stop using the Scheduling service.
- Message Queues are storage areas where messages await delivery to a remote server or site.
- The MTA handles most of the message queues, although certain connectors maintain their own queues.
- Performance Monitor can monitor a large number of Exchange's internal functions.
- Microsoft Exchange comes with a number of preconfigured Performance Monitor Charts, which you can run from the Start menu.
- Exchange uses JET databases for the Directory and Information Stores. These databases use transactional logging to provide recoverability in the case of database corruption.
- You can control database sizes on the Information Stores or on individual mailboxes and Public Folders.
- Exchange runs a number of regular maintenance routines, which you can schedule if required.
- The most important maintenance routine is online defragmentation, which must run once a day. It also has the greatest effect on performance.

Q&A

Q I have five Exchange servers, two in my office, and the other three in remote locations. However, all the servers are in the same Exchange site. I am responsible for administering the entire organization. What tools can I use to make sure that the servers in the remote locations are OK?

A Here you'll need to configure both Server and Link monitors. You can use Link Monitors to check on links within a site. You need to configure a link monitor to all the servers in the remote locations. Then you can configure Server Monitors on the remote servers as well. There is no point in having just Server Monitors on the remote sites, as you won't know if the links go down.

Q **My boss wants to know how many users are logged on to the Exchange system at this moment. How can I do this quickly?**

A This is very easy. Go to the Microsoft Exchange program group and start the pre-configured Performance Monitor chart titled Microsoft Exchange Server Users. Note that some of these users will be Exchange System processes like the System Attendant.

Q **I looked in the Queues tab on my server-level Message Transfer Agent object and I can see several messages in the queue for the Internet Mail Service. Does this indicate a problem?**

A This is only a problem if you have a permanent connection or dial-on-demand link. If you have a dial-up connection, it is quite normal to see messages in your IMS queue between dial-ups.

Q **I need to produce a graph showing the usage of our Exchange system over a whole week. What is the best way to do this?**

A You need to use the Windows NT Performance Monitor in Log view. Make sure that you are only sampling every 10 minutes or so, otherwise the log file will get too large. Add the counters that you want to record, and start the logging.

Q **I need to limit my users to a mailbox size of 50MB per user, except for people in the Design distribution list, who need 100MB each. I have set up the 50MB limit on the Information Store, but is there an easy way to configure the individual limits for the Design users?**

A Sadly, no. You will have to change the limits for the Design users individually. The next release of Exchange, Codename Platinum, should let you do this through the Active Directory Service.

Workshop

The Workshop provides two ways for you to affirm what you've learned in this chapter. The "Quiz" section poses questions to help you solidify your understanding of the material covered and the "Exercise" section provides you with experience in using what you have learned. You can find answers to the quiz questions and exercises in Appendix B, "Answers to Quiz Questions and Exercises."

Quiz

1. What is the job of an Exchange Server Monitor?
2. What is the job of an Exchange Link Monitor?
3. Can Server Monitors check on non-Exchange servers?
4. What three actions can a Server Monitor take?
5. What NT services need to be running in order to use the Alerting function on a remote workstation?
6. Can you use a Server Monitor to synchronize the time between two sites, one in L.A., the other in N.Y.?
7. What utilities can you use to start monitoring automatically?
8. What are Message queues?
9. How do you remove Link Monitor messages from your MTA's message queues?
10. What are the four views in Performance Monitor?
11. Name four Exchange-Specific objects you can record with Performance Monitor.
12. How often does Exchange defragment the Directory Service and Information Stores?
13. By what percentage should your databases shrink during online defragmentation?

Exercise

1. How would you measure the time it takes for your messages to get to a remote site?

DAY 16

Backing up, Restoring, and Repairing Data

By Anthony Steven

Chapter Objectives

After all the work you've done so far to install and configure your Exchange system, it would be a great shame if it all disappeared in a puff of smoke. In this chapter, I am going to look at the vital task of protecting your Exchange data against the various disasters that can and do occur.

You will be covering the following topics:

- Backing up the Exchange Databases
- Online and Offline Backups
- Backup Options
- Scheduling Backups

- Tape Rotation
- 3rd Party Backup Tools
- Restoring Data
- Recovering Corrupt Databases
- Using ISINTEG, EDBUTIL, and MTACHECK

Backing Up Your Data

Now that your Exchange server is up and running, I presume that you are keen to hang onto your data. Backing up your data is an essential component of disaster recovery planning, which I will cover in Day 17, "Advanced Backup and Recovery Considerations.

Backing up an Exchange database is not a straightforward as a simple file-based backup, because the Exchange database files are always open. You are also likely to be dealing with gigabyte file sizes. This makes backing up an Exchange server a challenging prospect.

For most people, mention the word "backup" and they will think of tape. However, back-up is more than just copying files to tape, and here I would like to discuss the concept of backup in its most general form. So, before I start dealing with the nuts and bolts of carrying out a backup, let's look at some of the options.

Backup Options

There are an increasing number of backup solutions on the market. From LS-120 floppy drives to digital tape drives, Zip drives, and DVD-R disks, finding the right solution can be made harder, not easier. I don't intend to discuss every option, but I will look at some of the more common methods.

Backup Methods

With Microsoft Exchange, there are two main backup methods: online and offline. I'll discuss each in turn.

Online Backup   An online backup is done with the respective Exchange services (Information Store or Directory Service) running. It deletes the transactional tracking logs, if appropriate, and messaging activity can continue. Online backups are only available with third-party backup products that have agents that can cope with open Exchange databases. The Exchange-enhanced NT Backup program can also perform online backups, but only onto tape. You can also include the Registry in an online backup.

Offline Backup   An offline backup is file-based, and requires you to stop the Exchange services before commencing the backup. The easiest way to do this is to stop the Exchange System Attendant. You can also back up the registry with a file-based backup, as well as back up an entire server. All backup products can cope with this back-up method.

Tape-Based Backup

Tape-based backup is still the most common. Tape is a mature technology, it is cheap, and can hold large amounts of data. On the down side, it is often slow, gives sequential access, and tapes only have an operational life of 30 passes. Even so, it is still popular.

Tape-based backup is probably one of the easiest to implement in Microsoft Exchange, simply because the enhanced version of Microsoft Backup lets you back up your entire Exchange organization onto tape. In addition, there are a number of third-party tools that will backup an open database, and some even promise individual mailbox recovery.

Tape Backup Hardware   There are a large number of companies producing a bewildering array of different tape backup systems. As no hardware company has yet seen fit to take me on their books as an evangelist for their products, I don't have a particular favorite. I think they call this being impartial.

When you order a new server, you should automatically include a tape streamer in the specification, unless you have some other means of providing access to a backup medium. Whichever tape system you choose, make sure it is on the Windows NT Hardware Compatibility List. Before you buy the latest all-singing, all-dancing auto-loading tape streamer, check that all its features work with NT.

You can find the NT Hardware Compatibility List at:

`http://www.microsoft.com/hwtest/hcl/`

With tape backup hardware, you should be looking for a SCSI (or FireWire if you can afford it) interface and a data transfer rate measured in several GB per hour. After all, if you have 20GB of data to back up overnight, there's no point in trying to do it at 800MB per hour. You'll be there all night (and the next day).

You also will need a large capacity tape format (preferably larger than your hard disk or disk array). Make sure that all your tape streamers need to support this format, as you will certainly need to change tapes from machine to machine.

16

SCSI OPTIONS

It has been said that the best thing about standards is that there are so many to choose from. SCSI is no exception and has now evolved into a plethora of different implem entations. These are:

SCSI-1	Up to 5 MB/sec
SCSI-2 (Narrow)	From under 5 Mbps asynchronous to 5 or 10 Mbps synchronous (Fast SCSI-2)
SCSI-2 Wide (16-bit)	10 Mbps asynchronous, 20 mbps synchronous (Fast-Wide SCSI-2)
SCSI-2 Wide (32-bit	Specified but not implemented
SCSI-3	Various transfer rates, up to and including Fiber Channel at 100 Mbps
Ultra SCSI	20 Mbps Narrow (Fast 20), 40 Mbps (Wide) Ultra2 LVD (Low Voltage Differential) 80Mbps, longer cables.

For the fastest SCSI systems, you should be looking for one with the word "Ultra." However, Ultra-Fast Ultra Wide SCSI can get somewhat ultra-pricey as well.

Backup Types   There are five main backup types used with tape-based backup systems:

- Full
- Copy
- Daily
- Incremental
- Differential

Full Backup   A full backup does just that. It backs up every file just as it is. If you want to perform a restore, then your start point is always a full backup. A full backup also sets the archive bit, indicating that a file has backed up.

With Microsoft Exchange, a full backup commits the transactional logs to the database, writes the database to tape, and then purges the transactional log files. Hence, a full backup will reclaim disk space.

The advantage of a full backup is that a single tape can restore your server. The disadvantage is that full backups are the slowest.

I always recommend that users perform full backups every day. However, you'll need to scale your backup system to cope with this.

16

Copy A Copy backup is like a full backup, but it does not reset the archive bit. Copy backups are useful for taking a snapshot of your system for testing purposes.

Daily Daily backup is like a copy, except it only backs up the files that have changed today, and does not change the Archive bit.

Incremental Backup Incremental backups just back up the files that have changed since the last full or incremental backup.

With Exchange, incremental backups will back up the transactional tracking logs, and then delete them.

The advantage with incremental backups is that they are the quickest to perform. The disadvantage is that to carry out a restore, you need a full backup plus every incremental tape since that full backup. You must then apply those tapes in order, and all the tapes must be working. Only once you have restored the final tape can you restart your services.

Differential Backup A differential backup backs up the files that have changed since the last full backup.

With Exchange, a differential backup will only back up the transactional tracking logs, but this time does not delete them.

Differential backups are quick to begin with, but get longer and longer as the number of days since the last full backup increase. The advantage with a differential backup is that you can restore a server with two tapes - a full backup plus the last differential tape.

You cannot use Differential or Incremental backups with Circular logging enabled.

Tape Rotation Tape rotation schemes come in two guises—manual and automatic.

Ten-Tape Strategy The ten-tape strategy is just one example of a manual tape rotation scheme. Table 16.1 shows how it works.

TABLE 16.1 THE TEN-TAPE STRATEGY.

	Monday	Tuesday	Wednesday	Thursday	Friday
Week 1	Tape 1	Tape 2	Tape 3	Tape 4	Tape 5
Week 2	Tape 1	Tape 2	Tape 3	Tape 4	Tape 6
Week 3	Tape 1	Tape 2	Tape 3	Tape 4	Tape 7
Week 4	Tape 1	Tape 2	Tape 3	Tape 4	Tape 8
Week 5	Tape 1	Tape 2	Tape 3	Tape 4	Tape 5
Week 6	Tape 1	Tape 2	Tape 3	Tape 4	Tape 6
Week 7	Tape 1	Tape 2	Tape 3	Tape 4	Tape 7
Week 8	Tape 1	Tape 2	Tape 3	Tape 4	Tape 9
Week 9	Tape 1	Tape 2	Tape 3	Tape 4	Tape 5
Week 10	Tape 1	Tape 2	Tape 3	Tape 4	Tape 6
Week 11	Tape 1	Tape 2	Tape 3	Tape 4	Tape 7
Week 12	Tape 1	Tape 2	Tape 3	Tape 4	Tape 10

Tapes 1, 2, 3, & 4 are weekly tapes and are used every five days.

Tapes 5, 6, & 7 are monthly tapes and are used every four weeks.

Tapes 8, 9, & 10 are quarterly tapes and are used every 3 months.

The advantages with the ten-tape strategy are that it is easy to implement and does not use an excessive number of tapes. You can combine it with incremental or differential backups, in which case tapes 5 to 10 would be full backups, whilst 1 to 4 would be incremental or differential.

Built-in Tape Rotation Some third-party backup products use built-in tape rotation schemes. This ensures that the tapes rotate on a regular basis, and retires tapes before they become unreliable.

If you are using ARCServe, you will already be familiar with its features, and know how to fathom out the strange sets of serial numbers that it puts on the tape. With this system, you will see a prompt telling you which tape to insert next. At this point, either you won't be able to find it, or if you do find it, then the backup system won't accept it.

Tip

If you are using a product with built-in tape rotation, make sure you have a good stockpile of blank tapes.

Disk-Based Backup

With the continued decline in hard disk prices, disk-based backup is becoming increasingly popular. It is also very simple to implement, especially when using disk mirroring or duplexing under Windows NT.

The simplest form of disk-based backup for Microsoft Exchange would be to copy the EXCHSRVR directory onto another drive. However, you would have to stop the System Attendant service before you did this and your Exchange transactional tracking log files would remain.

Another means of providing a backup would be to use the disk mirroring or duplexing functionality found in NT Server. Here it is very simple to add two hard disks, and make them mirrors of each other. Problems with open databases simply don't occur, and breaking the mirror, replacing the disk and recreating the mirror can easily rectify a failure of one disk.

RAID 5 isn't really a backup system but a more reliable type of hard drive. Hence, I don't really rate this as suitable for backup purposes. Nevertheless, if you implement RAID 10 (mirrored RAID5 sets), then you could consider this a backup method, you well-endowed-with-hardware-person, you.

For more information on disk-based backup, see Day 17, "Advanced Backup and Recovery Considerations".

Removable Hard Disks   Removable hard disks could include cartridge-type Zip drives, proprietary removable hard drives, and Jaz drives.

With the larger sizes of removable hard disks now available, you could use this as a backup option. If you have a smaller Exchange system, then the Jaz 2Gb removable cartridges could be used to back up the information stores or directory services. However, you can't do online backups with Windows NT Backup using Jaz drives, as NT Backup only recognizes tape drives.

Other Options   There are several other backup options, of greater or lesser suitability for use with Exchange. Rewriteable CD-ROM, DVD-R and the like all have particular application, but are often not suitable as a backup method.

Server-Based Backup

Server-based backup uses server mirroring or clustering. As it would be more appropriate to discuss this option as part of a disaster recovery plan, then I will cover this option in tomorrow's lesson.

16

Backing Up the Exchange Database

So, how actually do you back up the Exchange database? You'll learn how to do so right now.

Backups and Circular Logging

As I mentioned earlier, you cannot use circular logging with differential or incremental backups. But what is circular logging?

Circular logging is a configuration setting used with Microsoft Joint Engine Technology (JET) databases. The idea is to reduce the size of the transactional tracking logs. In Exchange, you can configure circular logging for both the Directory Service and the Information store.

 Caution
> If you use circular logging, transactional tracking will not work. Exchange enables circular logging by default.

Let's assume for a moment that you keep your transactional tracking logs on a separate spindle from the Exchange databases. Your hard disk with your directory service and information store fails. You have a full backup, but it is five days old.

If you have circular logging switched off, you will be able to restore your database files using the full backup. Your transactional logs will now contain all the changes made to the database since the last full backup, so you can now restore your server up to the point at which the drive failed.

If you switch circular logging on, Exchange overwrites the transactional tracking logs; consequently, you will not be able to restore any transactions that happened after the full backup.

 Tip
> If you are concerned about data integrity and transactional log sizes, switch circular logging off and do a full backup every day.

To switch circular logging on or off, start Exchange Administrator, and click on the Servers button in the toolbar. Select the relevant server and click on the Properties button. Click on the Advanced tab, and you can now uncheck the circular logging settings as in Figure 16.1.

FIGURE 16.1.

You can configure circular logging through the properties of the Server object.

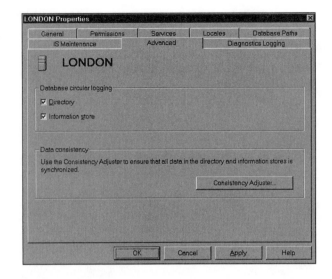

Enhanced Windows NT Backup Utility

The Enhanced Windows NT Backup utility lets you make online backups of Microsoft Exchange. It's just a pity it is so basic, and only works with tape devices.

The enhancement over the standard backup software is the ability to backup individual servers, sites, or your entire Exchange organization.

Note

This facility does not back up all the files on the server, only the Directory Service and Information Stores. However, you can also back up files and the Registry at the same time, to provide a complete server backup.

Figure 16.2 shows the Backup program's extra window that enables you to select a server, a site, or the organization.

Apart from these changes, the Exchange-enhanced backup tool works just like the normal NT version.

FIGURE 16.2.

The Microsoft Exchange window in the enhanced backup program lets you select which part of the Exchange organization you want to back up.

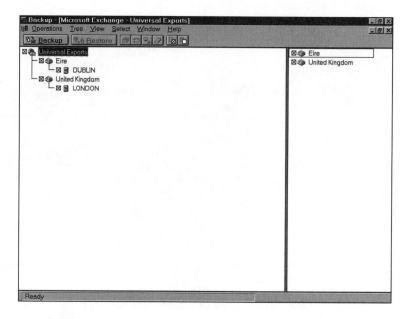

Running NT Backup from the Command Line

You can schedule the Windows NT Backup program using command line options. To view these command line options, enter

```
NTBACKUP /?
```

at a command prompt.

The syntax for this command is as follows:

```
ntbackup operation path [/a][/v][/r][/d "description"][/b][/hc:{on¦off}]
[/t {option}][/l "path/filename"][/e][/tape:{n}]
```

The parameters for this command are as follows:

Operation: Backup or Eject.

Eject will eject the tape (if one is loaded).

You must only use the following switches with the backup parameter.

- Path—Specifies one or more paths of the directories to back up. You can use this parameter with UNC or drive letters.
- /a—Appends this backup to the tape. If not present, the tape is overwritten.
- /v—Verifies the backup (highly recommended)

- /r—Restricts access to administrators (recommended)
- /d "description"—Lets you specify a description of the backup.
- /b—Backs up the Registry (highly recommended).
- /hc on/off—Switches hardware compression on or off.
- /t{option}—Specifies the backup type. The option can be one of the following: normal, copy, incremental, differential or Daily.
- /l "filename"—Specifies a filename & location for the backup log.
- /e—The backup log will include exceptions only i.e. files not backed up.
- /tape:{n}—Specifies a tape drive number to which the files should be backed up. N can take values from 0 to 9. These values are assigned when you install a tape drive through Control Panel.

Online DS/IS Example   Here is an example of a command line entry that will backup the DS and IS on a server.

```
ntbackup backup DS \\EXCHANGESERVER IS \\EXCHANGESERVER /v /d "Exchange
Server IS & DS" /b /t Normal /l d:\exchsrvr\backups\backup.log /e
```

Caution

Although you are taking a backup of the Registry whenever you back up your Exchange server, you should not forget to make regular updates of your Emergency Recovery Disk. Use RDISK /s to do this, which will back up the SAM as well.

Offline File Based Backup Example   In this example, your system will carry out a full backup of the C:, D:, and E: drives as well as the Registry on the Exchange server.

```
NET STOP MSExchangeSA /y
ntbackup backup c:\ d:\ e:\ /a /v /d "Full Server Backup" /b /l
➡D:\Exchsrvr\backups\fullback.log /e
```

Caution

You must have stopped the Exchange Server Services first.

Tip

Microsoft says that you should stop all services in order. I find that stopping the System Attendant service with the /y switch is equally effective.

You will then need to restart the Exchange Services once the backup has completed.

You can put these commands into batch files and schedule them using the AT command. Better still, use WinAT or Scheduled Tasks. Scheduled Tasks is an optional component on Internet Explorer 4.0, and WinAT comes with the NT Server Resource Kit on TechNet. For a list of AT command-line options, type AT/? at a command prompt.

Command Line Backup Program

You can use the BACKUP command line utility to carry out file-based backups of an Exchange server. I wouldn't recommend using it, because it doesn't back up the Registry or the Exchange databases.

Third-Party Tools

There is a range of third party tools to help you with backing up your Exchange servers. Sadly, my experience (and that of everyone I have asked) is that these programs promise more than they can deliver, and double the amount of RAM your Exchange server requires. One of them even managed to get NT to run out of user heap memory after you installed the Exchange Agent. Very Nice!

Adstar Distributed Storage Manager

Adstar is IBM's main backup facility, providing a range of options for distributed backup. It provides an Agent for Exchange Server 5.5. For more information, see:

http://www.storage.ibm.com/storage/software/adsm/adagent.htm#ExchangeNT

ARCServe

The most popular backup utility, which is a bit like being the most conventional member of the Addams family. It has an Exchange Agent, runs on NT, and the Enterprise version will let you back up multiple servers. It also has a somewhat unique method of stamping the backup tapes, which will give you endless hours of fun on a Friday night when you want to go home.

For more information, see:

http://www.cai.com/arcserveit/

BackupExec

Version 7.2 for Windows NT is now out. Again, promises the earth. Exchange agent, Individual mailbox restore, blah blah. Probably the next most popular after ARCServe.

For more information, see

http://www.seagatesoftware.com/bewinnt/

Legato Systems Networker

This one also has an Exchange Agent and all the usual bells and whistles. Catch it on:

```
http://www.legato.com/Products/index.html
```

Yosemite Technologies' TapeWare Universal 6.1

Again, it's an enterprise-level product and it has an Exchange Agent. You can try this one out on:

```
http://www.tapeware.com
```

Restoring / Recovery

With backups, getting the information stored onto tape is only part of the issue. The real test is to get a restore to work.

 Caution

Restores are extremely complicated procedures and can be difficult and time-consuming. Save yourself a lot of grief by practicing your restore procedure, and test it to verify that it has worked correctly. You never know when you will have to do it for real.

Restoring an Individual Mailbox

I'm going to deal with the problem of restoring an individual mailbox first, because it's easier than attempting to restore an entire server. This is because you are only restoring the Information Store, not the Directory Service.

To carry out this restore, you will need a Recovery Server.

 Note

A Recovery Server does not need to attend 12-Step meetings.

This recovery server should be any type of Windows NT server and does not need to have the same name any of your existing Exchange servers. You can even keep this server either running on the network, or have it as a dual boot option on another server.

However, this machine will require a tape drive compatible with the Exchange server. It will also need a disk volume larger than the size of the Information Store that you are restoring. Don't forget to install the same level of NT service packs as on the Exchange servers.

Online Backup

To restore an online backup, carry out the following task:

1. Install Exchange and create a new site. This site should have the same name as the site with the failed mailbox.

2. Install the same Exchange Service Pack as the original server.

3. Install Outlook or the Exchange Client on the recovery server.

4. Insert the full backup tape in the tape drive, and run Backup from the Administrative Tools.

 Caution Do not join the original site. Select Install a new site and enter the original site name.

5. Click the Tapes icon and double-click on the tape name. A catalog status box will appear, stating "Loading...".

6. Select only the Information Store in the right-hand side of the Tapes window. *Do not restore the Directory Service!*

7. Click on the Restore button from toolbar. On the Restore Information screen, enter the name of your recovery server.

8. Select the options for Erase All Existing Data, Private, Public, Verify After Restore, and Start Service After Restore. Click the OK button, and OK the Restore Confirmation message box.

9. Click OK on the Verify Status screen.

 10. Use Control Panel to check that the Exchange services are running.

If you only have a file-based backup, the procedure is a little more complex. I am assuming at this point that you have successfully carried out a file restore of the Exchange Server directory files.

You need to carry out Steps 1 to 3 of the previous task. However, you must then carry out the following task:

1. Start Exchange Administrator, and click on the Servers button. Select your new server, and click on the Properties button. Select the Database Locations tab, and mark down the location of the Information Store Transaction Logs, Private Information Store Database, and Public Information Store Database.

▼   2. Stop all Exchange services.

3. Move all files from the EXCHSRVR\MDBDATA directories (if your server has multiple drives, otherwise there is only be one instance of this directory).

4. Copy PRIV.EDB and PUB.EDB into the database paths that you discovered in Step 1.

5. Copy any information store log files (*.log) into the log path that you recorded in Step 1.

6. Start the Exchange Directory Service.

7. Change to the EXCHSRVR\BIN directory, and run the IS Integrity Checker by entering

```
ISINTEG -PATCH
```

▲   8. Start all the normal Exchange Services.

You haven't finished yet—all that you've done so far is restore the files. You still have to retrieve the mailbox from the Information Store.

For this part, you need to carry out this final task.

1. Start Exchange Administrator, and click on the Servers button. Select your recovery server, and click on the Properties button. Choose the Advanced tab, and then select the Consistency Adjuster.

2. Check all options for the Consistency Adjuster, and check All Inconsistencies. Select OK.

3. Once the DS/IS consistency adjustment has run, go to the Recipients container and double-click on the desired user's mailbox.

4. Add the administrator as the Primary Windows NT Account, and click OK.

5. Create a messaging profile, and add the user's mailbox on the Advanced tab of the Exchange Server Service. For more information on configuring profiles, see Day 7 "Configuring the Exchange Client".

6. Open Outlook and select that user's mailbox. From the File menu, select Import/Export. Export the mailbox to a .PST file.

7. Copy the .PST file over to the production Exchange Server.

8. Create a new mailbox for the user, and log on as that user.

▲   9. Import the PST into the user's mailbox using Outlook.

If you've managed all that without a hitch, then you're a better administrator tech than I am, Gunga Din!

Using an Exchange Agent

If you are using a Third-Party Backup product, then they may well have an Exchange Agent for you to carry mailbox restores direct from tape. However, my experience with these products has been:

- They are very temperamental.
- They have to be patched up to the eyeballs for the Agent service even to start. Even then, the Agent service might stop other services from starting by taking up all user heap memory.
- They gobble up memory and hog the processor.
- Restored mailboxes have no directory information, so no message headers appear. You don't know where the messages came from or went.
- All messages are marked as unread.

Need I go on? Agents for backing up Exchange are rather like Oscar Wilde's remark about dogs walking on their hind legs. It isn't so much that it is done well (as it isn't), but you are amazed that it is done at all…

After all that, let's look at the process of restoring a complete server.

Restoring an Entire Server

Restoring an entire server is not unlike restoring a single mailbox. However, when restoring a single mailbox, you just restored the information store. With a full server restore, you will restore the Directory Service as well. The DS contains references to the computer on which it originally resided, so you have to use the same computer name as the failed machine.

| Tip | If you need to replace your existing Exchange server with more powerful hardware, then this is also the procedure to use. |

Organization, Site and Server Naming

In the case of a server restore, the recovery server must have the same name and exact configuration as the server that went down. This is in addition to giving it the Organization and Site name.

Just like the Mailbox restore, you will give the server the same site and organization name, but you will not join the existing site.

Having a Server Pre-Configured

You could have a server pre-configured, then all you would have to do is to change the name of the server, and then you could start installing Exchange. However, most companies cannot afford to have a server hanging around, doing nothing.

Another option is to have a partially-build or dual boot server that you can pressed into operation as a recovery server if the need arises.

 Ideally, the recovery server should have a hard disk at least as large as the one on the downed server.

Restoring the Server

This is the process for restoring a complete Exchange Server. Let's take a simple case where you have a PDC, a BDC, and your recovery server. The BDC is running Exchange.

Imagine that at 03:14 hours, your Exchange server went to the great workshop in the sky, taking with it your Exchange installation. It is now 08:17 on Monday morning, and you have just arrived at work.

Luckily, you have a recent full backup tape and access to all the NT source files, service packs, and the Exchange CD and service packs. Because you are an organized sort of person, you have also written down the configuration of the crashed server. You have just made yourself a *very* strong cup of coffee—you'll need it!

You will now need to carry out the following task:

1. Remove the computer account for the original BDC from the domain using Server Manager on the PDC.

2. Build the recovery server as a BDC. Give it the same name as the crashed server, and get it to join the domain. Your recovery server will now have the same SAM as the original machine. Add the same level of NT service pack as was on the crashed server.

3. Install the drivers for the tape backup device, and check that the tape system is working. This tape system should be able to read the original tapes from the full backup!

▼ 4. If you don't have any service packs or hotfixes on the server, run the Exchange Server setup program using SETUP /R. This is the Restore option, which lets you restore an Exchange server to a new site.

5. If you do have service packs or hotfixes installed, carry out a normal setup.

6. Select Create New Site (Do not join a new site, even if you have more than one Exchange server in the old site). Use the same organization and site names as before.

7. Use the same Exchange Service account as on the old server, and install the same connectors.

8. Run Performance Optimizer with the same configuration as on the failed machine.

9. Install the same service pack as per the production machine using UPDATE /R.

▲ 10. Check all the services are running.

Restoring the Databases

The next phase has two options, depending on whether there were any changes made to the Exchange server after the full backup tape was made, and if you can then access the transactional tracking log files. Usually, the difference here is that the first set of circumstances is for a planned move to another server, whilst the second set comes about because a server has crashed.

- If there were no significant changes made to the Exchange Server after the full backup, or you *cannot* access the transactional tracking logs for whatever reason, then you should carry out Step 5 in the next task. If you are carrying out an upgrade of your hardware, your latest full backup tape should have all the up-to-date transactions.

- If changes did occur on your old server, and you *can* access the transactional tracking logs from the old machine, then you should skip Step 5 and carry out Steps 6 & 7 instead.

To restore Exchange Data from a backup tape, you need to carry out the following steps.

▼TASK

1. Insert the full backup tape in the tape drive, and run Backup from the Administrative Tools.

2. Click the Tapes icon and double-click on the tape name. A catalog status box will appear, stating "Loading...".

3. This time, select to restore both the Information Store and the Directory Service.

4. Click on the Restore button from toolbar. On the Restore Information screen, enter the name of your recovery server.

▼

▼   5. If you do not have access to the transactional tracking log files, or the backup is
up-to-date, select the options for Erase All Existing Data, Private, Public, Directory
Service, Verify After Restore, and Start Service After Restore. Click the OK button,
and OK the Restore Confirmation message box. Now go straight to Step 8.

6. If you have the transactional tracking log files, then stop the DS and IS Exchange
services, empty the \DSADATA and \MDBDATA directories. Copy just the transactional log files from the old server into the respective \DSADATA and \MDBDA-
TA directories.

7. If you have just copied across the transactional logs, select the options for Private,
Public, Directory Service, Verify After Restore, and Start Service After Restore.
Click the OK button, and OK the Restore Confirmation message box.

▲   8. Click OK on the Verify Status screen.

You will now have restored your old Exchange System on the Recovery Server.

Restoring a Server using a File-Based Backup

If you have a file-based backup, and you are trying to restore a server, the procedure is a
little different.

1. Just install Exchange Server using SETUP without the /R switch on the recovery
server. The server name should be the same as the old server and the Site and
Organization names should be the same as well. Again, Create a New Site as per
the online backup example.

2. Once you have installed Exchange and applied any service packs, run Performance
Optimizer, and note down the new locations of the database and log files for both
the directory service and information store.

3. *Do not restart the services after running Performance Optimizer.*

4. Empty the \DSADATA and \MDBDATA directories on all partitions. The locations
will be as indicated in Step 2.

5. Copy the DIR.EDB file from the backup into the Directory Service database path.

6. Copy the PRIV.EDB and PUB.EDB files from the backup into the respective
Information Stores database path.

7. Copy the Directory Service transaction logs from the backup into the Directory
Service transaction log path.

8. Copy the Information Store transaction logs from the backup into the Information
Store transaction log path.

▼   9. Start the Exchange Directory service, but not the Information Store.

10. From a command prompt, change to the \EXCHSRVR\BIN directory, and run:

    `ISINTEG -patch`

11. Start the Information Service.

12. Reboot the server and check all services are running correctly.

13. CARRY OUT A FULL ON-LINE BACKUP!

> **Note**
>
> You must carry out a full on-line backup as soon as you have verified that the server is working correctly. This is because once you have run `ISINTEG`, your old log files will be out of synchronization with the new database. You can no longer restore onto the new server from the old backups.

Restoring any Options

Some optional components in Exchange must be re-added after you restore a Server. This includes components like the MS Mail or any third-party connectors.

It's time for another task:

1. Reinstall any MS Mail or third party connectors. Site, Dynamic RAS, and X.400 connectors will be restored with Exchange.

2. If the original server had Key Management server installed, add KM server. Select the option to use a startup disk when prompted.

Restoring Key Management Server Data Files

Having installed the Key Management Server service, you must restore the data files from your backup. These files are located in \EXCHSRVR\KMSDATA, and consist of database and transactional tracking files.

To restore the KM database:

1. Stop the KM server service if it is running.

2. Restore the files from the old \EXCHSRVR\KMSDATA directory to the equivalent directory on the recovery server.

3. Start the KM Service, using the old KM Service startup disk.

Testing the Restore

Now that you have restored your server, you need to test it. This testing needs to be more rigorous than with the single mailbox example, because you must ensure full functionality on your Exchange Server.

TASK

To test a restore:

1. Shut down and restart your new Exchange server.

2. Check that all the Exchange services are running, and that no persistent errors are appearing in the Event Logs.

3. Start Exchange Administrator, and look in the Recipients container. Check a number of mailboxes to see if they are associated with the correct Primary Windows NT account.

4. Install Outlook or Exchange client.

5. Log on as yourself and create a messaging profile.

6. See if you can send mail successfully to another user.

7. Log on as that other user, and see if the mail has arrived.

8. Check the messaging functionality on several workstations.

9. Check that the connectors are working correctly.

10. Carry out a full online backup again.

11. That's all, folks!

If everything went well, you should now have a spanking new Exchange server up and running. If you don't, then TechNet has a number of articles to help you on backing up and restoring Exchange Servers.

TechNet is available on:

http://www.microsoft.com/technet

or you can get additional support from

Database Corruption

Although companies tend to get excited about losing a database through disk failure, database corruption is, in fact, a far more likely event. In most cases, you are more likely to recover your data if you try to repair the corruption, rather than restore a backup.

Troubleshooting a Corrupt Database

For this section, I'm assuming that server hasn't gone up in a pile of smoke, or just been taken out of the door by two shifty-looking gentlemen who said they'd come to fix the air-conditioning. However, other less drastic problems do occur to the Exchange databases, and in the first instance, you would attempt a repair rather than a restore.

16

ESEUTIL

ESEUTIL is the replacement for EDBUTIL that came with Exchange 4.0 and 5.0. It is a maintenance utility for Microsoft Exchange Server databases, such as the Information Store and the Directory Service.

ESEUTIL has several modes of operation:

- Defragmentation
- Recovery
- Integrity Checking
- Upgrade
- File Dump
- Repair

From a data security viewpoint, the three options you will be interested in are Recovery, Integrity Checking, and Repair. To obtain a list of all the command line switches, start a command prompt and run:

ESEUTIL /?

You can then get extra help on each option by entering R, D, U, etc.

With each option, you can specify a /IS or /DS switch to check either the Information Store or the Directory Service.

Caution

> Before you use ESEUTIL, you must stop the Exchange services. You should also take a file level backup (even if you just make a copy of the files to another drive).

Recovery   Use the Recovery option when you want to get a database back into a consistent state. You will need to do this before running an Integrity Check. An example command would be:

ESEUTIL /R /ISPRIV

Integrity   Integrity checking verifies the integrity of a database. However, if you have not run the Recovery first, integrity checking may fail. If it continues to fail after Recovery, then you need to run a repair. The syntax for an integrity check would be:

ESEUTIL /g /ispub /x

Figure 16.3 shows a sample output from running an integrity check.

Figure 16.3.

*This is what you want
to see from your
integrity check—no
problems!*

```
Command Prompt                                                    _ □ ×

D:\exchsrvr\bin>ESEUTIL /g /ispub /x

Microsoft(R) Windows NT(TM) Server Database Utilities
Version 5.5
Copyright (C) Microsoft Corporation 1991-1998.  All Rights Reserved.

Initiating INTEGRITY mode...
        Database: D:\exchsrvr\MDBDATA\PUB.EDB
   Temp. Database: INTEG.EDB

checking database integrity

              Scanning Status  ( % complete )

      0    10   20   30   40   50   60   70   80   90  100
      !----!----!----!----!----!----!----!----!----!----!
      .............................................

integrity check completed.
Operation completed successfully in 23.473 seconds.

D:\exchsrvr\bin>_
```

16

Repair   This option (ESEUTIL /P) will attempt a full repair on the relevant database. It
takes parameters of /ispub, /ispriv, or /ds. There is an optional switch of /d, which
just scans for errors without making a repair.

 Caution   You should only use the Repair option if your database is corrupt.

A full ESEUTIL repair would be as follows:

ESEUTIL /P /ISPRIV /V /X

For more information on ESEUTIL, see the command-line help described earlier.

ISINTEG

ISINTEG is an integrity checker for the Information Stores ONLY. It can carry out a number of checks, including checking the integrity of the Public and Private information
stores after an off-line restore. You can also carry out a number of detailed tests on the
Information Store databases.

ISINTEG runs in three modes:

- Patch
- Test
- Fix

Patch   You would use ISINTEG in Patch mode after you have carried out an offline backup and copied across the transactional tracking logs. ISINTEG in patch mode takes no further switches.

```
ISINTEG -patch
```

Test Mode   When running in Test mode, ISINTEG searches the specified information store for any errors. ISINTEG then display any errors and writes them to a log file.

An example syntax might be:

```
isinteg -pri -detailed -verbose -test folder
```

> **Tip**   You must specify –test testname.

The output from this command might look like the information shown in Figure 16.4.

FIGURE 16.4.

This is the output from the ISINTEG *command, with detailed testing and verbose reporting.*

> **Tip**   I would recommend that you always use the –verbose –detailed option when running ISINTEG.

Fix Mode   Microsoft recommends that you do not use Fix mode unless you advised to do so by Microsoft Product Support Services.

ISINTEG in fix mode is exactly like test mode, except for the extra –fix switch. So the test previous test would become:

```
isinteg -pri -fix -verbose -detailed -test folder
```

For additional information on ISINTEG, see the excellent ISINTEG.DOC file on the Exchange Server 5.5 CD. You will find this in the \SERVER\SUPPORT\UTILS directory.

MTACHECK

MTACHECK is slightly different from ESEUTIL and ISINTEG. Firstly, the \MTADATA directory is different from the \DSADATA and \MDBDATA directories. The MTA does not keep messages in a JET database, but as files in the \MTADATA directory.

| Caution | Do not manually delete files from the \MTADATA directory. |

MTADATA has very few command-line switches.

- /v switches on verbose logging.
- /f with a file name logs to that file.
- /rd removes directory replication messages.
- /rp removes public folder replication messages.
- /rl removes link monitor messages (See Day 15, "Maintaining Exchange" for more information.

A typical command would be:

```
MTACHECK /V /F:MTACHECK.LOG
```

MTACHECK.LOG will just contain the same output as is displayed at the command prompt.

Figure 16.5 shows a sample output from MTACHECK.

MTACHECK can also activate automatically if Exchange detects that the last server shutdown did not stop the MTA service cleanly.

16

FIGURE 16.5.

Sample output from MTACHECK *shows verbose logging.*

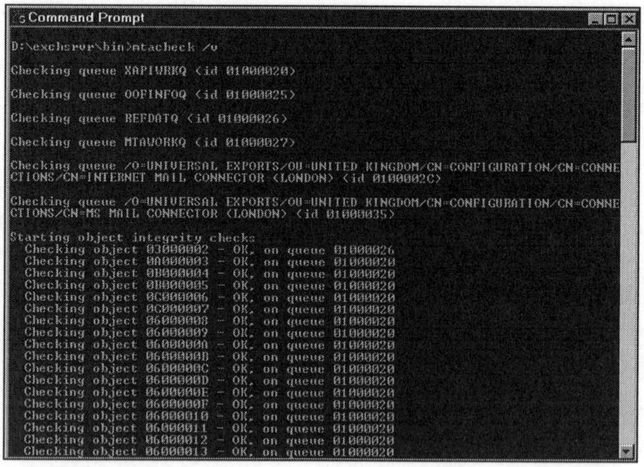

Summary

Backup and restore are essential operations in preserving your Exchange data. However, you should practice these complex procedures before you have to do them for real.

To summarize the main points of this lesson:

- Microsoft Exchange places particular demands on a backup system because of the file size and the fact that the database files are permanently open.

- Microsoft Exchange uses two main types of backup – Online and Offline. Online backups can be made without disrupting messaging traffic, whilst offline backups require stopping the messaging services.

- You can restore individual mailboxes or a complete server using either online or offline backups. Online restores are slightly less complex.

- Full server restores are the most complex, requiring the restore server to use the same name as the faulty server.

- Once you have carried out a restore, you must carry out a full backup again, as your previous backups will no longer be valid.

- Exchange provides ISINTEG, EDBUTIL and MTACHECK to help you maintain your database files. You should always try these utilities before you attempt a restore.

- Make sure you practice your restore procedures on a regular basis.

Q&A

Q. I have just joined a company that currently has no backup plan implemented. There are five Windows NT servers, including two Exchange machines. I'm now a bit worried. What should I do first?

A. Well, if they haven't had a backup system up till now, you're going to be very unlucky if it all goes pear-shaped in the next couple of days. However, you need to draw up a disaster recovery plan, covering your backup requirements, and implement the backup section quickly. You might try installing a tape streamer on the least important machine, and use that to back up all your main servers before you try any serious tinkering with the rest of the servers.

Q. I'm trying to implement a backup system for Exchange, and I'm having trouble deciding which third-party system to use. I want to have the ability to back up and restore a single mailbox, as well as back up an open database. What do you recommend?

A. Actually, I don't always recommend third-party products, mainly because you can provide adequate protection with just the NTBACKUP utility that comes with Microsoft Exchange. Several third-party products promise mailbox-level backup, but the reality falls short of most people's expectations. By all means, investigate the options, but you could save yourself some money by using NTBACKUP.

Workshop

The Workshop provides two ways for you to affirm what you've learnt in this lesson. The Quiz section poses questions to help you solidify your understanding of the material covered and the Exercise section provides you with experience in using what you have learned. You can find answers to the quiz questions and exercises in Appendix B, "Answers to Quiz Questions and Exercises."

16

Quiz

1. What utilities can you use to repair a public information store?

2. What command would you enter as the final part of an offline restore?

3. What must you do to the Directory and Information Store services before an online backup?

4. How does an online incremental backup work with Exchange?

5. When would you use ISINTEG -FIX?

6. What do you need to do to enable differential or incremental backups with Exchange?

7. How can you schedule backups using the Enhanced Windows NT Backup tool?

8. How do you restore an individual mailbox with NT Backup?

9. How must you configure your recovery server if you are carrying out a full server restore?

Exercise

1. Carry out an online or an offline backup and restore of an Exchange server.

DAY 17

Advanced Backup and Recovery Considerations

By Anthony Steven

Chapter Objectives

Many companies are concerned with backing up their data, and rightly so. However, backing up your data is just one component of disaster recovery or business continuity planning. Today you will be bringing together the elements that you covered in yesterday's lesson to produce an effective disaster recovery plan.

You will be covering the following topics:

- Disaster recovery planning
- Calculating the cost
- Assessing the risk

- Planning for disaster
- Implementing high availability solutions
- Server clustering
- Using failover replication systems
- Configuring Exchange for maximum survivability
- Implementing and testing a disaster recovery plan

Disaster Recovery Planning

The morning of Saturday 15th June 1996 was just an ordinary shopping day for the people of Manchester, in the North of England. Trade at the Arndale Center shopping mall in the middle of the city was starting to pick up, as the people of Manchester wandered through the early summer sunshine.

Just after 10:00, a telephone call came through to a local newspaper, together with a codeword used by a terrorist organization. The caller warned that there was a bomb in the area of the Arndale Center, and that it would explode shortly. Within minutes, the Manchester Police were attempting to close off the area while the British Army Bomb Squad teams crashed out from their barracks. The police quickly identified a suspect lorry, parked on the corner of St. Mary's Gate.

While the police continued with the evacuation of the shopping center, the Army team then deployed "Wheelbarrow." This is a remote-controlled tracked robot designed for defusing bombs, equipped with cameras, grappling arms, and a shotgun.

However, as the mechanical device closed in to deal with the vehicle, and with the surrounding streets still not evacuated, the 4,000 pounds of explosive packed onto the lorry exploded.

In the words of Gary O'Neil of the Manchester Fire Brigade, "The Arndale Center, which is the heart of the city shopping area, the whole side, the gable end, has just been blown away."

Luckily, no one was killed. However, about 60 people were injured, mostly by flying glass. The damage to the surrounding streets was intensive, and officials cordoned off the area around the center of the explosion for several days.

By now you might be thinking, I bought an Exchange book, not an espionage thriller. So what's this got to do with Microsoft Exchange?

Imagine you are the Operations Director of an IT training company based three hundred yards from the center of the explosion. Apart from the blast shattering all your windows, you will not regain access to your office for at least another week. You have $75,000 worth of training to deliver during that week and you also want to reassure your clients that you are not out of business.

This very problem faced a Manchester-based company on that Saturday morning in June 1996. Their disaster recovery plan coped. Would yours?

Concepts of Disaster Recovery Planning

Disaster planning is something that people don't really want to consider. I think there might be a denial mechanism going on here, along the lines of "If I don't think about bad things happening, they won't happen."

Sadly, as the example above shows, bad things can and do happen, and always at the most inconvenient time. I hope that none of you will ever come close to a terrorist bomb explosion! But power outages, fire, weather emergencies, vandalism, and theft are all-too-common occurrences, so you need to guard against them and prepare a plan in case they do strike.

How Much Is Your Data Worth?

This is the key question that organizations often never considered. If you were running a ten-million-pound turnover company, the loss of a day's sales records could cost you £50,000 (that's about $85,000, depending of course on the exchange rate). If your profits are 30% of turnover, you are looking at losing 1.7% of your profits from that one day's loss. Would you fancy explaining that to the shareholders at the board meeting?

What if you were a large wholesaler and your entire sales database became corrupt? Data loss can mean more than a small dip in profits—it could threaten the survival of the company.

Tip	If you want to calculate how much downtime would cost your company, look at:
	`http://www.vinca.com/software/downtime.html`

If you are a global banking organization, data loss could be catastrophic. Companies that are heavily dependent on their IT infrastructure and cannot afford a moment's interruption maintain entire offices at alternate locations. Staff members have instructions on what to do in case their main office becomes unusable. Most importantly, companies test their disaster recovery plans on a regular basis, typically three to four times a year.

A good disaster recovery plan is like an insurance policy, where the item insured is your data. So how much should you be paying in premiums to insure your business?

Understanding Your Operational Requirements

Not all companies require the same insurance policies, and so it is with disaster recovery. You could specify a system using server clustering, redundant hardware, and high-speed FireWire optical links to off-site hard drives. However, this might be a bit over the top if you only have a few PCs running WordPerfect for DOS.

The disaster recovery industry speaks in terms of horses for courses. In terms of complexity and cost, disaster recovery plans can include the following range of options:

- Daily backup with off-site tape storage
- Mirrored hard disks
- Prebuilt restore server
- Clustered servers
- Distributed storage and data replication
- Uninterruptable power supplies
- Generator backup
- Mobile offices (mounted on lorries)
- Shared backup office facility
- Mirrored sites

I will discuss some of these options in detail in the latter half of this lesson.

Each of these solutions targets particular areas of a disaster recovery plan and provides a certain level of protection. Nevertheless, there is a huge cost differential between backing up your server every night and taking the tapes home with you the next day, and maintaining a mirrored site at another location with live data replication.

In the first example, it might take you four hours to restore your system and you could lose up to a day's information. In the second instance, data loss would be limited to any uncommitted transactions and measured in seconds. Human downtime would be the time required for the staff to move from one office to the other. System downtime would be minimal, as all that is required is for the outstanding transactions to replicate to the remote site (if possible) and for control to switch to the alternative location. However, the cost of maintaining such a system would typically be similar to the cost of your main office.

The largest provider of disaster recovery services in the world is Comdisco, who provide backup office systems for banks, insurance companies, and share trading organizations. For more information, see the Comdisco Web site on:

```
http://www.comdisco.com/bc/index.html
```

Mission-Critical Systems   It is important to analyze your operational requirements in the light of the effect that systems failure will have on your operation. Many companies have mission-critical systems, and these systems should have a high level of failure protection built in. Nevertheless, how critical is "mission-critical"? If you are trying to negotiate a complex deal using a spreadsheet on your laptop, and the laptop fails, are you going to be able to complete the deal?

Mission criticality is more a question of degree than an absolute term. If you don't believe me, just think about how much work would happen at your company if you switched off all the PCs. Even if you don't have any declared "mission-critical" systems, I think that you will probably find productivity hitting zero in fairly short order. Then think about what would happen if you switched the power off completely.

When I'm training, I always bring a laptop with me with all the presentations and videos for the course. A great advantage of this is that if the power to the building fails, I can continue training with minimal interruption. When my lectures make use of slide-shows, audio, and video, having a presentation system that is proof against power outages means a considerable difference in maintaining the quality of my delivery. How often does this happen? Well, it happened to me in November 1998, and I'm sure it will happen again.

Acceptable Downtime   As part of your analysis of operational requirements, you need to look at your company's level of acceptable downtime. The link here is that the shorter the acceptable downtime, the more expensive the disaster recovery solution will be. For example, a 98% availability system is reasonably cheap to implement. However, if you want to increase availability by less than 2% to 99.8%, the price becomes significantly higher.

You may be in the situation where your acceptable downtime is zero, in which case you will be looking to employ a 7×24×365.25 solution (365.25, because a day every four years might not be acceptable). In which case, your disaster recovery plan will be very expensive.

The important thing with acceptable downtime is to keep it appropriate to the nature of the task. I have worked on military operations where the acceptable downtime was zero. It's called sentry duty. However, we didn't have to pay anyone overtime.

Working Hours   Working hours affect the nature of the protection that your disaster recovery plan must provide. With a normal nine-to-five operation, you can schedule maintenance and backups for times when the building is empty.

However, if your company works 24-hour shifts, you may need to run backup routines when your servers are in use. This may require more in the way of physical resources, such as RAM, hard disk space, network cards, and so on.

If you are working 24-hour shifts, you will need to schedule time to carry out routine maintenance on your Exchange servers, such as installing service packs and new hardware. However, you can transfer users' mailboxes onto other servers, down the server, upgrade any components, and bring it back online again.

Security   Security is a very important aspect of disaster recovery planning. This is true not only because of the threat that disgruntled employees may pose to your equipment, but also the security aspects of storing your backup tapes or hard drives. After all, there's no point in backing up your system if a fire destroys your backups as well as your servers. Moreover, if someone takes the backup tapes home with them and the tapes go missing from their home, sensitive commercial information could be compromised.

The reality is that for all the hype about hackers, most security breaches are from within an organization. Sadly, your disaster recovery plan must take into account the effects of malicious attack from within.

> **Note**
>
> When you create your disaster recovery plan, the section about dealing with the risks from employee sabotage should not form part of the published disaster recovery plan. The exception to this would be the obvious items like physical security on the server room and keeping backups in a secure fireproof safe.
>
> Information on configuring file security, passwords, users, service accounts, and passwords should be in an annex separate from the main disaster recovery plan. The reason for this is that if someone knows how you have configured security, it makes it easier for him or her to mount a more dangerous attack on your system. Even a trusted employee might inadvertently divulge vital information to a hacker posing as a company official.

Access to your data should be restricted with appropriate permissions. Data should be stored on NTFS partitions, and the Everyone—Full Control permission removed. Users should have the lowest level of access that they require to carry out their jobs. You should configure auditing on any sensitive files and folders.

When making backups, you should restrict ownership of backup tapes to the Administrator's group. In addition, you must trust your administrators and backup operators. In a very high security environment, you would not give backup and restore rights to the same person.

Again, you need to find the balance between cost and effective security.

Available Bandwidth   On most networks, all the networking traffic competes for the available bandwidth. So your disaster recovery or backup traffic needs considering in relation to the total network bandwidth. On most 100MB networks, bandwidth is usually not an issue. However, on 10MB Ethernet or 16MB Token Ring layouts, backup traffic between one server and a tape storage unit can easily consume 30 to 40% of your available capacity.

You may need to look at ways of increasing available bandwidth, which doesn't necessarily mean replacing all your cabling, network cards and routers. One simple solution involves two additional 10MB network cards and a UTP cross-over cable. Install the additional cards onto two servers and link them using the cable. You now have a separate backbone that can transfer backup traffic between the servers without affecting the remainder of the network. The total cost is about $50.

Stages in Disaster Recovery Planning

There are several stages in disaster recovery planning. A full planning cycle involves the following steps:

- List the possible risks to your system.
- Make a probability assessment of each risk happening, then rank the risks by probability.
- Predict the results if a particular risk does occur.
- Categorize the results into levels of seriousness.
- Devise a solution that will deal with each particular result.
- Combine these solutions into a cost-effective disaster recovery plan.

However, disaster recovery planning is, by its very nature, a continuing iterative process. Implementing a disaster recovery plan both changes the nature of the risks and affects the possible outcomes. For example, if you install a UPS, the UPS itself brings new risk factors into the equation. In addition, it also affects some of the results, so you will need to review your disaster recovery plan in the light of the changed circumstances.

Risk Assessment

The first stage of disaster recovery planning is the risk assessment. Without a risk assessment, you have no way of knowing that you have considered all potential disasters. Even if you carry out a risk assessment, you still can't guarantee that you've covered every possibility. At least you have a better chance than if you haven't made an assessment.

And if Captain Edward Smith of the *Titanic* had paid more attention to risk management, the fatal collision with the iceberg could have been avoided. In an interview before the maiden voyage, he stated that he couldn't imagine a circumstance that would cause a contemporary ship to sink. Maybe that's why he drove the ship at such great speed when he knew ice was ahead. After the disaster, maritime vessels treated ice fields with more respect, but it was too late for Captain Smith, who also went down with the ship.

There are formal approaches to risk assessment, mainly used by insurance actuaries, and involving fiendishly difficult mathematics with lots of triple integrals. As you are probably not measuring the effectiveness of your recovery plan in terms of profit but in terms of minimizing downtime, you can use a much simpler model.

Risk Types

There are two main categories of risk—foreseen and unforeseen. The only thing you can do with unforeseen risks is to try and make them into foreseen risks.

Foreseen risks might include:

- Electrical surges
- Power failure
- Hardware failure
- Viruses
- Sabotage & vandalism
- Theft
- Terrorist attack
- Fire
- Natural disasters

I'm sure you can think of or have heard about a few others.

Tip

I always find it best to carry out this risk assessment as a brainstorming session. Use a group of people from the company and get them to try to imagine all the things that could possibly happen, from Martians in the server room to marshmallows in the CD drive. If your disaster recovery plan can deal with all these eventualities (foreseen problems), you at least have a fighting chance with the unforeseen problems (like a jumbo jet landing on the company building).

Remember that risks are just probabilities, and all probabilities eventually happen, given enough time. I just thought you'd like to know that.

Assessing the Probabilities

After you have a decent sized list of your risks, you now should sit down and analyze this list. You need to take each risk, and categorize it into how likely it is to occur (high, medium, low, or very low). You then need to rank the risks in order of probability.

Predicting the Results

The next stage is to take each of these risks, starting with the most likely, and attempt to predict the results. Predicting the results uses two very simple questions:

- What if?
- So what?

Examples of these questions include the following:

- What if my server goes down?
- What if the power to the block fails?
- What if we have a fire?
- What if a terrorist bomb blows up the building?

What you are trying to do when predicting the results is to take your list of risks and convert them into results. Working from your list of risks, you should now look at predicting what could happen should a particular risk become reality.

Here's an example of how this works:

- **What if the mains power drops out?**

  The telephones will no longer operate.

- **So what?**

  Clients won't be able to call in, and sales account managers won't be able to call out.

- **So what?**

  We'll lose business.

- **So what?**

  We need to make sure that we have standby power available.

  Or

  We will have to be able to switch operations to another center.

Note that a single "what if" question can produce a number of outcomes via the "so what" process. One approach to this form of analysis uses the concept of branched decision trees, where each level has a set of possible outcomes. However, this approach can get very complex, and you need a really big piece of paper to do it.

Categorizing the Outcomes

Now that you have analyzed the possible outcomes, you should see that many of your solutions are the same. For example, your plan for dealing with a terrorist bomb and gas explosion will be very similar.

Hence, you should end up with between five and ten solutions to the possible results you have analyzed. These then combine into your disaster plan.

Before I move on to the nitty-gritty of producing a disaster recovery plan, let's look at some of the advanced tools and techniques for protecting your data.

Delivering High Availability Solutions

A cornerstone of disaster recovery planning is the ability to keep your servers running. There are many elements to this equation, and a working hard disk is only part of the picture.

Note

> With all disaster recovery solutions, remember that you are dealing with probabilities. You are seeking to make the probability of an event (in this case, the failure of your system) as unlikely as possible. However, as you cannot guarantee that several unlikely events will not happen together, your high availability system can only reduce the probability of a system outage, not remove it.

The key to delivering high availability (HA) solutions is redundancy. Machines developed for particularly hostile environments already implement redundancy, like in the A-10 "Thunderbolt" ground-attack aircraft, where survivability is provided by duplicating or triplicating the control systems. This is particularly important in an aircraft that flies as low and slowly as the A-10, as anyone carrying anything larger than a pistol tends to take a pot-shot at the aircraft.

Managing Hardware Failure

It is impossible to prevent hardware failure because all complex machines eventually stop working. What you can do is to manage the effects of hardware failure, so that your operations are not seriously affected.

Equipment Failure Characteristics

All machines tend to show a characteristic failure probability pattern, as shown in Figure 17.1.

FIGURE 17.1

A graph of the probability of a machine failing (failure rate) against time tends to show a high initial probability of failure then a low followed by a steady increase.

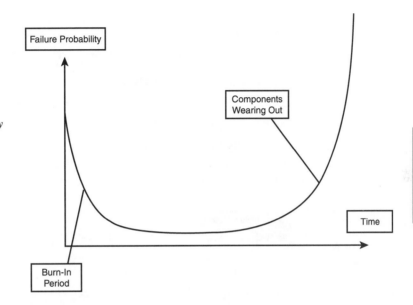

What this shows is that there is a high probability of failure when a machine is new. This higher initial failure rate occurs as the equipment beds in and any manufacturing defects make themselves apparent. Once the possibility of early failure is over, the failure rate decreases until it hits a plateau that typically lasts for 75% of the item's lifetime.

Eventually, the failure rate starts to creep up again as components wear out. There comes a point at which you will consider the machine beyond economic repair.

Burning In

As you have just seen, the problem with a new piece of equipment is that there is an increased likelihood of failure in the first few days of operation. A burn-in program can significantly reduce this effect in that any machines with problems will fail during the burn-in process. Most server manufacturers carry out a 72-hour burn-in before supplying you with a new server.

Caution Do check that this happens!

The burn-in process involves running utilities on the server that carry out repetitive processor, hard disk, memory, network card, and video tests. These tests stress the respective components so that any manufacturing defects will appear before the unit ships to the customer.

In addition, you may want to carry out your own burn-in routine. Most servers come with testing utilities, which will generate results from the burn-in process. You can then save these results and file them with your disaster recovery documentation.

Mean Time Between Failures (MTBF)

Equipment reliability is measured using Mean Time Between Failures (MTBF). This is a statistical concept that requires a little bit of analysis.

If you a take a statistically valid sample of identical machines, some will fail sooner and some later. If you plot how many of these failures occur in a set time period against time, you tend to end up with a graph with a normal distribution, as shown in Figure 17.2.

FIGURE 17.2

Equipment failure tends to show a normal distribution.

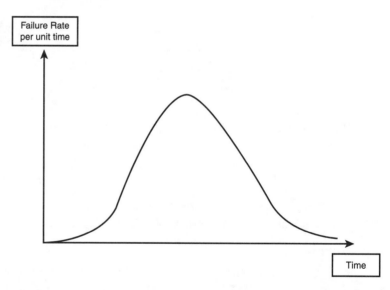

The MTBF is not the highest point on the graph, but is the total measured lifetimes divided by the total number of machines. Let's say that you took one hundred identical components and ran them until they all failed. If you then totted up their lifetimes and then divided that figure by one hundred, that figure would be the MTBF. However, the more symmetrical the failure distribution, the closer the MTBF will be to the highest point on the curve.

MTBF is usually quoted in hours, with 100,000 hours being a typical example for a hard disk. This means that a disk with a MTBF of 100,000 hours will, on average, last 11.4 years before failing.

Choosing equipment with higher MTBF ratings can help in reducing the incidence of breakdown. However, be aware that some manufacturers use different methods of calculating MTBF. Look out for those with ISO manufacturing standards, as they tend to use consistent MTBF tests.

Sadly, the statistical nature of MTBF gives no guarantees. This means that your brand-new wizzy-wizzy hard drive could soldier on for centuries or fall over with its legs in the air tomorrow. It's all up to Ms. Probability (formerly known as Lady Luck).

Redundant Power Supplies

When I refer to redundant power supplies, I am concerned with the internal units that supply 12V, 5V, and 3.3V to a server's motherboard. Like any other electrical component, these are prone to failure. With multiple power supplies, the units work in parallel. There may be some control circuitry to regulate the co-operation between the supplies. If one unit fails, the other takes over immediately.

Some server designs offer the option of hot-swappable power supplies, allowing you to replace a malfunctioning unit without downing the server. Again, these tend to be more expensive.

Uninterruptable Power Supplies (UPS)

The UPS is probably the most popular disaster recovery component, and with good reason. UPS units provide two services—power smoothing and a temporary mains supply.

Irregularities in the mains supply (spikes, surges, brownouts, and so on) are far more common than people realize. Electrical storms can cause havoc, with transient voltages of up to 1,000 volts appearing on a domestic power supply. Enough to make even Agent Mulder lighten up a bit.

The temporary mains supply is required should you have a blackout or a brownout. The UPS then gives you enough time to close down your server cleanly, or if you are using the NT UPS service, the UPS will shut down and switch off your system automatically.

The UPS unit usually consists of a rectifier, a regulator, a battery (the heavy bit), and a converter. Most of them these days have banks of LEDs that show you the state of the UPS and the current charge in the battery.

UPS systems fall into two main types, although hybrid versions do exist. These are online or offline (Standby). With online systems, the server receives its supply from the converter fitted in the UPS. Hence, the UPS takes the mains supply, converts it to 12 or 24 volts DC, and uses this to keep the battery topped up. The converter then takes that 12 or 24 volt DC supply and changes it back to 240 or 115 volts AC for use by the server. If the mains supply fails, the electrical power then comes from the battery until the battery is exhausted.

Offline UPS systems monitor the mains voltage but only switch in their converters when this voltage dips below acceptable levels. Generally, online UPS systems offer better power management and changeover times than offline models.

UPS models are capable of providing a certain power (VA or watts) output. Depending on the amount of equipment that you are trying to protect and its power consumption, you can then calculate the size of the UPS that you need.

 Caution Don't forget to use the UPS to power any peripheral components that you require during a power outage, like the server's monitor. Otherwise, when your power goes down, you won't be able to see anything on the screen. Remember that CRTs tend to use quite a lot of power, so scale your UPS accordingly.

Most UPS systems come with a communication port that you can connect to your NT server. Before you buy your UPS, check with the manufacturer that their model is compatible with NT's UPS service. You must also check that the UPS comes with a suitable connecting cable and that you have a free COM port.

The UPS should have instructions on how to connect it to your Exchange server. The UPS may come with its own software, or may use the NT interface directly. If you are using the NT UPS service, you will run the UPS applet in Control Panel. You will now see the dialog box in Figure 17.3.

From this dialog box, you can specify the COM port on which the UPS communicates and the type of signal (positive or negative) that the UPS uses to talk to the server.

If necessary, you can have the UPS run a program that calls your pager, or sets of some other form of alarm. This is fine if you are not operating around the clock, and you just want notification during non-working hours. If you are on 24-hour working, you should have someone on-site at all times to react to a power outage.

You can also configure the amount of emergency power available, the time it takes to recharge the battery, and the time between the power failing and the first warning. You should not configure this to zero, or a minor power outage will trigger the alarm.

FIGURE 17.3

The Windows NT UPS service lets you configure the amount of standby power available.

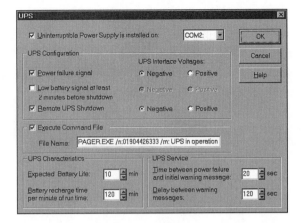

17

Caution

It is very important to test the operation of your UPS when NT boots. This is because NT sends a hardware detection signal to all COM ports on startup. Some UPS systems misinterpret this signal and switch off. If you find this is a problem, you need to add the line

```
NOSERIALMICE=COMx
```

to your BOOT.INI file where COMx is the COM port connected to the UPS. Hence the startup line in BOOT.INI will look like this:

```
multi(0)disk(0)rdisk(0)partition(1)\WINNT="Windows NT Server"
➥/NoSerialMice:COM2
```

Redundant Disks (RAID)

You have already seen how one way of improving reliability is to have redundant components. Redundant Arrays of Inexpensive Disks (RAID) uses several relatively cheap hard drives to increase the overall reliability of the array.

Note

Most RAID systems (except RAID Level 10) can only deal with one hard disk failure at a time.

RAID systems are either hardware- or software-based. Windows NT Server offers software-based RAID, but I would only recommend this if you are seriously strapped for cash.

NEW TERM **RAID Level 1** RAID Level 1 is *disk mirroring* or *duplexing*. *Mirroring* is two disks configured so that changes to one disk occur simultaneously on the second. Each disk is an exact mirror of the other.

Mirroring uses two disks on one controller whereas duplexing uses two disks on separate controller cards. Figure 17.4 shows this in operation.

FIGURE 17.4

With disk mirroring and duplexing, each disk or partition is an identical copy of the other.

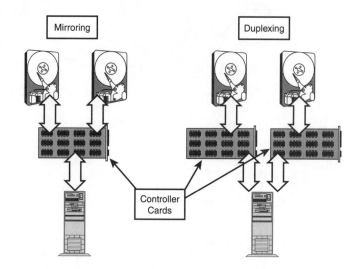

Windows NT Server offers disk mirroring as an integral part of the operating system. With disk mirroring, NT writes data first to one disk and then to the other, using the fault-tolerant driver, FTDISK.SYS.

The advantages of mirroring are that it is simple to implement and can mirror the system and boot partitions. The disadvantage is that you waste 50% of the available storage space. I would only recommend software RAID Level 1 where you are looking for a very simple RAID solution.

RAID Level 5 RAID Level 5 (Striping with Parity) is the most widely used form of RAID, and is usually hardware-based, implemented via a RAID controller card. With hardware RAID Level 5, the disk controller generates parity information from the incoming data. The controller then writes the original data and the generated parity data in stripes across all the disks, instead of just one disk. RAID Level 5 requires a minimum of three disks, although most arrays have between four and six disks.

> **Note**
>
> With RAID Level 5, your array's total capacity will be one drive less than the total number of drives. Hence Array Capacity = (n-1)*C, where n is the number of disks and C is the capacity of the disks.
>
> If you have five 4GB disks in a RAID 5 array, your total storage space will be (5-1)*4 = 16GB.

If a disk in a RAID 5 array fails, the controller will automatically regenerate the missing data using the remaining data and the parity information.

Generally, RAID 5 arrays use hot-swappable disks. This means that you can remove and replace a disk without downing the server. However, performance will decrease while the RAID array rebuilds the missing data.

17

WHAT HAPPENED TO RAID 2, 3, AND 4?

RAID levels 2, 3, and 4 were evolutionary developments in RAID technology.

RAID 2 uses bit striping, with extra check disks. RAID 2 is good for reading and writing large blocks of data at high transfer rates, but performance becomes very poor when reading smaller amounts of data. Windows NT does not implement software RAID 2.

RAID 3 has a single redundant disk, on which all the parity information resides. RAID 3 has a limitation on the minimum amount of data in a single read operation, which also makes it unsuitable for small data transfers. Windows NT does not implement software RAID 3.

RAID 4 works better with transaction processing operations and is particularly effective in read operations. RAID 4 also dedicates a single disk for check data, which becomes a bottleneck on write operations. Windows NT does not implement software RAID 4.

If you implement Cluster Server, you would normally use a RAID 5 array as the shared disk resource.

Windows NT can implement software RAID 5, accommodating from three to 32 disks in a stripe set. I would only recommend using software RAID 5 if you are short of money.

> **Note**
>
> To implement RAID 5, you may need to triple the amount of RAM installed in the server. If there is a disk failure, NT must use RAM to recalculate the missing data on the fly. In addition, Windows NT does not support hot swapping of disks in a RAID array, so you must power down the server before replacing the disk.

RAID Level 10   RAID Level 10 is for people with loads of money. In RAID 10, two RAID 5 arrays combine to form a mirror set. Hence the minimum number of disks is six and your effective storage space is $((n/2-1)*C)$, where n is the number of disks (always an even number) and C is the capacity of the drives. Hence if you have 6*4GB drives in a RAID 10 array, your effective storage space is $(6/2-1)+4GB = 8GB$. That's not a lot, considering that you started with 6*4 = 24GB of hard disk space!

RAID 10 implementations are all hardware-based. There is no support for RAID 10 under Windows NT.

Multiple Components and Failure Probabilities

The idea behind RAID and redundant power supplies is to increase reliability. What many people don't realize is that implementing RAID actually *increases* the likelihood of component failure. How does this come about?

This apparent conflict arises because in a RAID array, for example, you have multiple disks. Although the probability of failure of any one disk stays the same, the fact that you have several of them running at the same time means that overall, the likelihood of a failure increases. However, the array itself will be more reliable than a single disk on its own.

Hence, the most reliable RAID 5 array would be one with three disks. However, other factors come into play at this point. The more disks you have in an array, the higher the performance. In addition, more disks in an array means a greater overall storage capacity.

Maintenance Contracts

All reputable server manufacturers offer some form of maintenance contract. Depending on how much you pay, you can specify a certain maximum response time such as four-hour, eight-hour, or 24-hour. Maintenance contracts can provide a useful component of your disaster recovery plan in that you can arrange for the replacement of broken items. However, if that item was your hard disk, a maintenance contract won't get your data back. In addition, four hours can seem a long time if the boss is tearing a strip off you for not having the servers running.

Although maintenance contracts are a good way of providing second and third-line support, they do not provide continuity service levels.

Data Recovery

If you have to recover your data from a failed hard disk, there are a number of specialist companies that can do that for you. Many operate on a no-fix, no-fee basis and use a number of different tools to recover the data. For example, the Data Recovery Centre UK offers this type of service. You can locate them on:

```
http://www.recovery-uk.com/index.htm
```

If the failure is mechanical, the recovery company may need to open the disk unit. This takes place in a clean room, and is a highly specialized operation.

One of the leading companies for data recovery is Ontrack (http://www.ontrack.com), which operates clean rooms for recovering failed disks. According to Ontrack's figures, the causes of data loss are as shown in Table 17.1. This table shows the main causes of data loss and the relative likelihood of each occurring.

TABLE 17.1 LEADING CAUSES OF DATA LOSS

Cause	Percentage
Hardware or system malfunction	44%
Human error	32%
Software corruption or program malfunction	14%
Computer viruses	7%
Natural disasters	3%

17

Data Replication

Data replication provides a higher level of protection than backing up a server. With data replication, you keep a separate copy of your data at another location. Data replication systems usually mirror all committed data, whereas a backup is normally at least 24 hours out of date.

Data replication can span a range of different implementations, including linked sites, FireWire disk systems, and Storage Area Networks. Data replication is appropriate where ensuring the survival of the data is more important than reducing downtime. However, pure data replication tends to be rare, on the basis that if your data is that important, you probably don't want much downtime either. Hence, a data replication with failover solution would be more appropriate.

All the products reviewed in the section on replication with failover later in this lesson can provide simple replication-only services.

Linked Sites

In its simplest form, linking sites using a leased line simply provides a path by which data can replicate from one site to another. In case of system failure, you would have a copy of your data at the remote site.

However, you will need software that can replicate open files. Most of the products in the next section will provide this functionality.

Note The Windows NT Replication service is not suitable for providing this type of replication. The NT Replication Service cannot copy open files like the Exchange Directory and Information Stores.

FireWire Disks

FireWire, or the IEEE 1394 bus, is a new technology that offers exceptionally fast bus speeds, with up to 400Mbps for the S400 implementation. Based on optical fiber technology, FireWire provides the ability to create a SAN or Storage Area Network, with disk drives, tape devices, CD-ROM jukeboxes, and DVD-R writers all connected on a separate network. This SAN would provide a storage solution for all network users, and would appear as a large collection of shares. As far as the users are concerned, the SAN would be like a very large, very fast set of disk drives. Figure 17.5 shows an example of a SAN.

FIGURE 17.5

The SAN or Storage Area Network is a new concept that depends on the speed of the FireWire standard. Look out for these coming to a server room near you soon.

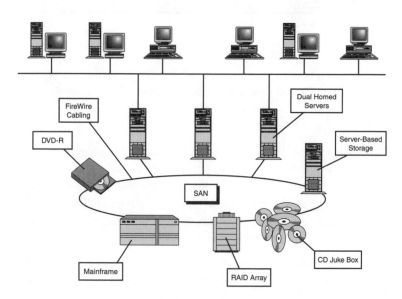

The other enormous benefit of FireWire is that it can run using optical links between the server and the hard disks. This means that the cable connecting the two is not limited to a couple of meters as in SCSI, but can extend to several miles. Hence, your disaster plan can allow for the fact that an office could cease to exist, but its data would be safe in another location. However, don't forget to allow for what happens if the location where the FireWire drives are located burns down. In addition, what happens if they both burn down together?

One possible disaster recovery solution might be to use a FireWire implementation with mirrored disks. You could have a server in one location, a FireWire disk in another, and the mirrored FireWire disk at a third. This system would be possible using nothing more complex than an NT Server, a FireWire Controller, and two FireWire disks. Oh yes, you'll probably need a lot of fiber-optic cable as well.

Implementing High Availability Systems

High Availability (HA) Systems are appropriate for situations where both your data and continuity of service is of paramount importance. Here you are looking at 24-7 systems where you might measure downtime in minutes per year.

As companies realize the value of their data, there has been a noticeable increase in interest in HA systems. The introduction of Microsoft Cluster Server has generated further attention, although Cluster Server has not been as successful as Microsoft hoped.

There are two main methods of implementing HA systems. These are as follows:

- Mirrored systems
- Clustering
- Data replication with failover

Mirrored Systems

Mirrored systems require you to have two identical servers, one online, the other offline (its Exchange services would be stopped). You would mirror the data between the two systems using a data replication product. On failure of the primary server, you would close down the first server and change the name on the second to match the original machine. On reboot, you would start the Exchange services. Because the information in the Exchange databases is up-to-date, thanks to the replication product, the new server is identical to the old one.

The disadvantage with a mirrored system is that this failover process is not automatic, and you cannot use the mirrored server for anything else, which is wasteful. Clustered systems overcome this disadvantage and make better use of resources.

Clustering

NEW TERM   Clustering is a term used to describe systems that provide fault-tolerance through sharing resources. The cluster itself behaves as a single system, although it might consist of several nodes. A *node* is in fact a server, acting as part of a cluster.

Digital first introduced clustering in the mid-eighties with the VMSCluster product. Clustering is not the same as mirroring or redundant servers because with clustering, both servers can provide primary services. In case of failover, the cluster management software switches operation of the cluster-aware applications to the other server. Hence cluster implementations represent a better use of resources and scale better than redundant servers.

There are two main clustering models:

- Shared disk
- Shared nothing

With a shared disk system, a Distributed Lock Manager (DLM) prevents both nodes from accessing the same data simultaneously.

With shared nothing systems, only one node accesses the clustered application and data files at any one time. In the case of failure of the primary node, the secondary node takes over ownership of the clustered data and continues the service.

Cluster Server   Microsoft entered the clustering world with Cluster Server (codename Wolfpack), now known as Windows NT Server Enterprise Edition. Microsoft Cluster Server implements "Shared Nothing" clustering, with maximum support for two nodes per cluster. Both your nodes must have identical hardware configurations and must be on the Windows NT Enterprise Edition Hardware Compatibility List.

Each server will have its own system and boot partition, containing the Windows NT Enterprise Edition system files and the startup environment. In addition, you will require a (probably hardware RAID5) disk array on a shared SCSI bus. This disk array will contain the Exchange server files. Finally, two NIC cards on a private network separate from the main LAN forms a backbone between the two servers.

If you are using clustering to support Microsoft Exchange, the idea is that one node is the active node and carries out all the processing during normal operation. However, if that node fails, the other node can take over, with your users experiencing minimal disruption, as shown in Figure 17.6.

Not all components on Microsoft Exchange support clustering; for example, some of the connectors (excluding the Site Connector) don't, neither do the dial-up connectors, such as RAS, dial-up IMS, and so on. For clustering to work, you must install all the latest service packs and patches to both NT and Exchange.

Windows 2000 will take support for clustering even further, with the introduction of Windows 2000 Advanced Server (formerly Windows 5.0 Enterprise Edition) and Windows 2000 Datacenter Server (a new product).

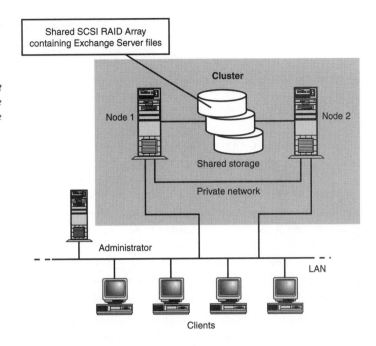

FIGURE 17.6

Cluster Server places the Exchange server files on a shared hard disk, which means that control can pass to the other node in case one server fails.

For more information on setting up Exchange 5.5 with Cluster Server, see Chapter 2 of the Exchange Server 5.5 Resource Guide and the MS Cluster Server documentation on TechNet.

Data Replication with Failover

The next stage up from clustering is Data Replication with Failover. Here you are not just concerned with preserving your data, but getting your system up and running again as soon as possible.

Data replication with failover is different from clustering. With clustering, there is a degree of symbiosis between the servers. For example, Cluster Server requires identical servers to form a cluster. With data replication with failover, the integration between the servers is not so encompassing, so some implementations allow for different server types and configurations.

Rather than take a snapshot of the information on your Exchange databases as a backup does, data replication systems continuously update your backup copy. In the event of a failure, control is passed in its entirety to the second server. Examples of this type of system include Octopus, Co-Standby Server, Double-Take from NSI Software, and ARCserve Replication for Windows NT.

Most of these products have downloadable evaluation copies that you can test out. I would recommend that you don't try doing this on your production Exchange servers.

> **Note** For more information on a competitive comparison between these products, check out the following Web page. However, I can give no assurances for its impartiality.
>
> `http://www.sunbelt-software.com/dt_competitive_compar.htm`

Octopus for Windows NT 3.2   Octopus for Windows NT from FullTime Software is both a replication and a replication with failover product. As a file replication product, it can replicate open files. With Super Automatic Switch-Over (Super ASO), you can set up failover between Windows NT Servers. Because Octopus supports many-to-one relationships, one failover server can service several operational servers, as well as provide primary services. This means that you are not restricted to duplicating all your operational servers, with the extra costs that this would entail.

Octopus is not hardware-dependent and does not need dedicated network cards. However, it can use dedicated cards if these are present, thus removing your Octopus-related network traffic from your LAN.

For more information on Octopus, see the Qualix Web page at:

`http://www.qualix.com/java/solutions/other.html`

Co-Standby Server   Co-Standby Server for NT 4.0 from Vinca is a similar product to Octopus. It can also use a dedicated link to mirror data between two servers. You can configure two machines to act as backups for each other and in case of failure, services running on the failed machine can restart on the running server. You can then repair the downed server, restart it, and re-mirror the running data back to the newly repaired machine.

For the full picture, see:

`http://www.vinca.com/products/sbsnt/`

Double-Take for Windows NT   Double-Take 3.0 for Windows NT from NSI Software appears to offer the largest feature set of all the products reviewed here. Data encryption, file-delta (changes) transfer only, and automatic rebuilds seem to be more fully represented in this release. Doubtless, the competition will catch up, but you could always download the trial version and see for yourself.

Double-Take 3.0 and 1.5 are available from:

`http://www.nsisw.com/`

ARCserve Replication for Windows NT   ARCserve Replication for Windows NT
from Computer Associates does not appear to offer all the features of the other products.
However, if you are already using ARCserve's backup product, you may be able to
obtain a better price on the replication software.

Find out more from:

`http://www.cai.com/products/arcserve_replication/`

Configuring Exchange for Maximum Resilience

When considering all the factors that go towards configuring Exchange for maximum
resilience, I ended up with a big list of dos and don'ts. Although this list is not exhaustive, I hope that it will give you an insight into some of the more common configuration
settings that will make Exchange more robust.

- Have more than one Exchange server, if possible.
- Don't attempt to host too many users on one Exchange server.
- Replicate your public folders onto more than one server.
- Don't make your Exchange server the PDC.
- If you configure your Exchange server as a member server, make sure you have at
  least one BDC in your domain.
- If you have a very large number of accounts in your primary domain, either put
  your Exchange servers into another domain that trusts your primary domain or
  install the Exchange servers as member servers. This will reduce the size of the
  SAM that the Exchange servers will need to load into RAM.
- Check your event logs daily.
- Locate your transaction logs on separate physical disks.
- Disable Circular Logging.
- Standardize your backup format (tape type).
- Take full online backups every day.
- Take regular file-based offline backups, including the Registry. You will need to
  stop the Exchange services to do this.
- Run RDISK/s on a regular basis on your Exchange server.
- Keep accurate configuration records in a safe location alongside your backups and
  your emergency recovery disks.

17

- If you have SCSI disks, disable the SCSI Controller Write Cache.
- Locate your information stores on hardware RAID 5 disks.
- Use mirroring or hardware RAID 5 on the boot and system partitions.
- Check disk space usage on a regular basis. Configure alerting to warn you if this exceeds 75%.
- Carry out regular monitoring of disk space. Clean mailboxes or archive information to control the size of your message store.
- Use Microsoft Cluster Server for increased reliability. Where an Exchange component does not support clustering, use multiple instances of that component (IMS, X.400 connector, and so on).
- Use a Replication with failover product if you require greater reliability than Cluster Server. Configure many-to-many replication and failover support.
- As a minimum, make sure your Exchange server is protected from mains spikes and surges.
- Use a suitable UPS with a serial connection to the server.
- Configure alerting on the UPS service as appropriate.
- Test the UPS regularly.
- If you have a generator backup, make sure you protect all your machines against surges and momentary loss of power, particularly any spikes generated when the generator kicks in.
- Again, if you have a generator backup, make sure that all the components necessary for running the generator (such as the fuel pump) are on the protected supply. This is particularly important if the generator is on the roof and the fuel tank in the basement.
- Publish an Exchange Maintenance Schedule. This is particularly important in a 24-hour working environment, where there is no natural downtime.
- Build a disaster recovery toolkit as detailed in Day 16, "Backing Up, Restoring, and Repairing Data."
- Produce a full disaster recovery plan and test it regularly.
- Don't *ever* get complacent about disaster recovery!

Now that you are familiar with the concepts of disaster recovery planning and know about some of the techniques to protect your data, let's put this all together into the disaster recovery plan.

BUILDING A RECOVERY TOOLKIT

You should specify a recovery toolkit as part of your disaster recovery plan. I'm sure you can think of a few more items to add, but these will do as a start:

- A partially built NT Server with a supported tape drive.
- NT Server source files (on the server).
- NT Service Pack 4 source files (on the server).
- Microsoft Exchange 5.5 source files (on the server).
- Microsoft Exchange 5.5 SP1 source files (on the server).
- The CDs for the above with license keys.
- A recently updated Emergency Recovery Disk.
- The three installation disks for Windows NT Server.
- An NT Emergency Boot disk.
- A copy of the Key Management service startup floppy disk (this needs to located in a secure place).
- The latest full online and file-based backup tape.
- Up-to-date documentation on the current Exchange installation, including the location of the database and transactional logging files.
- TechNet and the Knowledge Base CDs.
- Access to the Internet.
- A computer toolkit.
- Plenty of spare cables.
- A torch (flashlight, to my American readers)

With access to these items, you should be able to carry out any of the tasks in this lesson.

17

A Disaster Recovery Plan

A disaster recovery plan is a formal statement of how your company intends to recover from possible disasters. It will require proposing, drafting, funding, and implementation. It will need management approval and must include the consequences of disciplinary action for failure to carry out the procedures. Remember that failing to follow the requirements of the disaster recovery plan could (in extremis) lead to the failure of the company and everyone losing their jobs.

Your disaster recovery plan is your insurance policy. Should the unthinkable happen, it could make the difference between a small interruption and bankruptcy. A comprehensive and well-executed plan will also be a reflection of your own professional standards.

Creating Your Disaster Recovery Plan

Let's put all these elements together to make the plan. To create an effective disaster recovery plan, you must have the following ingredients:

- Management support.
- A defined level of service or acceptable downtime.
- A list of possible risks to your enterprise.

DISASTER RECOVERY AND MANAGEMENT SUPPORT

There is no point in proceeding with a disaster recovery plan unless you have management support.

If your senior management is unwilling or unable to appreciate the risk to the business, my recommendation is that you document this. You should prepare a business case that details the cost of equipment or system failure and the damage that it could do to the business. Keep the focus on the bottom line cost to the business and avoid any technical jargon.

Make sure that the decision-makers get to read your business case and understand the implications. You may need to back this up with a presentation to get your point across.

If this approach results in no further action, I would recommend looking for another job. Because I can guarantee that if everything goes pear-shaped (as it eventually will), guess who will get the blame? You.

From this information, you will be able to deduce the following:

- Relative probabilities of each risk occurring.
- Solutions for coping with each risk.
- The respective costs involved.

Armed with your analysis of risk probabilities, the solutions, and costs involved, you can then formulate your disaster recovery plan. Once you have approval for your plan and you have secured the necessary budget, you will be able to document your solutions.

A typical disaster recovery plan might have the following structure. The sections in *italics* are my comments; the parts in normal script would appear in the plan.

UNIVERSAL EXPORTS

DISASTER RECOVERY PLAN

MARCH 1999

1. INTRODUCTION

   Brief introductory paragraph, something along the lines of:

   Universal Exports recognizes the vulnerability of the company to data loss. A disaster recovery plan is required and all relevant employees are to be aware of this process.

2. AIM

   This would be a concise (one sentence only) statement of the aim of this document.

   The aim of this document is to record the disaster recovery plan for Universal Exports.

3. BACKGROUND

   This section should detail general information on why your disaster recovery plan is important.

4. DISASTER RECORD

   This section would brief the reader on events that have happened to the company. Examples of previous failures that the company has experienced will appear in Annex A.

5. DISCIPLINARY WARNING

   You need to include a section on the disciplinary consequences of failure to follow the disaster recovery plan.

6. THREAT ANALYSIS

   Annex B would list the probable threats to the company. The section on internal threats to the company from employees would be confidential and restricted to senior management only.

7. ACCEPTABLE DOWNTIME

   Here you define what level of service is required. With this example, you would be looking at a data replication solution with failover or clustering. The building would need a generator and every workstation and server would require a UPS.

   Universal Exports defines the following levels of downtime as acceptable:

Effect	Operational Disruption	Data Loss
Total Destruction	1 Day	>10 Seconds
Power Cut	Nil	Nil
Server Outage	Not noticeable	>10 Seconds

17

8. STANDARD OPERATING PROCEDURES

Again, a short paragraph as all the detail will be in the annexes.

In order to provide this level of service and prevent equipment failure or data loss from disrupting the operations of Universal Exports, the Standard Operating Procedures detailed in Annex C will apply with effect from (date).

9. RESPONSIBILITES

Here you set out who is responsible for ensuring recovery of the system.

In case of system failure, operational responsibility will be as listed in Annex D.

10. CONTACT INFORMATION

Again, this paragraph would be a pointer to an Annex.

Contact information is as listed in Annex E. It is the responsibility of (blank) (named in Annex D) to ensure that this information is kept up to date at all times. All personnel named in Annex D are to notify (blank) of any changes to their contact information within 24 hours.

11. SUMMARY

A brief summary paragraph.

12. ANNEXES

You would probably want to include the following annexes:

13. Annex A—Previous Events

Continuously updated list of "events" that have invoked the disaster recovery plan including actions taken and outcomes.

14. Annex B—Risk Analysis

A list of possible risks to the company's data.

15. Annex C—Standard Operating Procedures

This is the important one. This annex and its appendixes would give the details behind, of course, standard operating procedures for disaster recovery.

16. Annex D—Responsibilities

This annex would contain a list of names and areas of responsibility. There should be a primary and a secondary name for each area to cover holidays, sickness, and so on.

17. Annex E—Contact Details

Names of all people named in Annex D, with home telephone numbers, mobile numbers, pagers, golf club number, and so on.

Your disaster recovery plan will doubtless be more complex than this simplified example.

Testing Your Disaster Recovery Plan

Without testing, the most detailed disaster recovery plan is worthless. If you are not going to test your procedures, you might as well not bother to write them down.

Testing Components

You can test a disaster recovery plan in a number of ways. My recommendation is that you test the components as you implement them. So, if you deploy a recovery server, try seeing how long it takes you to build it into a working Exchange server. If you implement a cluster, try stopping one of the nodes.

Live Exercises

After you have tested all the components in your disaster recovery plan, you can start testing it in its entirety.

The best way to test a plan is as a live exercise. On a quiet day (the first day after you start work on the New Year is usually quiet), just come in and take your Exchange server offline. Then try to implement your disaster recovery plan, and see how long it takes to get up and running again. Also, notice the effect that this has on the network, and you may find that people's perception of how "mission-critical" your IT system is will change.

	By the way, it helps if the directors of the company know and have agreed to you doing this.

If your disaster recovery plan requires your office to be operational in another location within an hour of the destruction of the building, you need to test this. One morning, (again with approval), just lock everyone out of the building, and see if you can be up and running again at your backup location within sixty minutes. If you can't, the plan needs reworking.

	Don't try this as your first exercise in disaster recovery. You need to work up to such a scenario; otherwise there will be chaos.

17

The Scenario

At the beginning of the chapter, I gave you the example of the IT training company in Manchester that had its offices partially destroyed by a terrorist bomb. In this case, they had configured replication of their SQL database to a remote location, so they could still work with their data. On Monday morning, they took the opportunity to ring round all their clients and tell them that no, they weren't out of business, and, by the way, would they like some IT training?

Summary

Disaster recovery is a subject that often only gets attention when it's too late. Every organization will require a differing level of protection from its disaster recovery plan. A simple backup and restore system may be adequate, or you may need to implement High Availability servers if you cannot tolerate any downtime or data loss. With care, a properly formulated disaster recovery plan can save a company from ruin.

To summarize the main points of this lesson:

- Disaster recovery planning requires you to analyze your operational requirement in terms of acceptable downtime, cost, available bandwidth, and potential outcomes.

- Risk analysis allows you to convert unforeseen risks into foreseen risks, and then plan to prevent the consequences of those risks disrupting your operations.

- Risk analysis involves asking the questions "what if" and "so what," until you have extracted all the relevant factors. This will produce a range of results.

- You then combine the different results and produce a smaller number of solutions that cope with all the possible outcomes. You can then rank the Solutions according to probability and cost. These solutions become the basis of your action plan.

- Microsoft Exchange can work in a clustered environment like Windows NT Enterprise Edition. This currently supports two nodes in one cluster.

- Several third-party tools can work with Exchange to provide replication or replication with failover services.

- You must document your disaster recovery plan and ensure you have the full support of management.

Q&A

Q **I am currently producing a risk analysis for our company backup system. We are thinking of installing a fire safe in which to keep our backup tapes. Are there any implications of which we should be aware?**

A Yes. Where are you going to put your fire safe? If it's higher than one story up, then it might split open on hitting the ground if the floor collapses during a fire. If it's on the ground floor, it might end up buried under the falling masonry from the floors above. So how about putting it in a one-story building, like your Security Guard's hut?

Q **I've just bought a new UPS for my Exchange server and connected up the UPS cable. I've configured the UPS service correctly and the server and UPS are talking quite happily. However, I've just rebooted the server, and the UPS switches off. I've had to disconnect the UPS again.**

A The problem is that the hardware detection routine on the Exchange server switches off the UPS. You need to put the line /noserialmice:COMx into BOOT.INI at the end of the startup line for NT Server. Replace COMx with your UPS's COM port. Don't forget to back up BOOT.INI first!

17

Workshop

The Workshop provides two ways for you to affirm what you've learned in this lesson. The "Quiz" section poses questions to help you solidify your understanding of the material covered and the "Exercise" section provides you with experience in using what you have learned. You can find answers to the quiz questions and exercises in Appendix B, "Answers to Quiz Questions and Exercises."

Quiz

1. What are some of the risks to a computer network?
2. What two questions help you analyze risk factors?
3. How can you configure your transactional tracking logs to maximize survivability?
4. What components of Microsoft Exchange does Microsoft Cluster Server not support?
5. How does replication with failover differ from clustering?
6. What fault-tolerant RAID levels does Windows NT Server support?
7. How much effective storage space will you end up with in a RAID 10 Array with 10 disks, each of 9GB?

Exercise

1. Produce a disaster recovery plan for your organization.

DAY **18**

Building Exchange Applications

by Patrick Grote

Chapter Objectives

In this lesson, you'll learn what development solutions exist for Microsoft Exchange 5.5. You'll also see examples of each solution and learn what the benefits are for each type of development solution.

Microsoft Exchange 5.5 application development is a specialized, if not arcane, field of knowledge. There is not one definitive resource for Microsoft Exchange 5.5 development, but many resources that contribute. You may use a little bit of this, toss in some of that and shake liberally. Before you know it you have an application for Microsoft Exchange 5.5.

What we're going to do is expose the many methods in which you can develop applications for Microsoft Exchange 5.5.

Before development begins, you need to qualify the type of application you'd like to create. The following list of application types can help you narrow your list:

What's Your Goal?

When you develop an application it is usually because you need to solve a problem or simplify a process. Developing applications for Microsoft Exchange 5.5 isn't any different.

By using the available Microsoft Exchange 5.5 development tools you can design applications that meet the following goals:

- Information Gathering. Typical examples of information gathering would include surveys, feedback, commentary, or status reports. An Employee Satisfaction Survey, Beta Product Feedback, or Project Status Report are great examples of information gathering applications. You can store the information gathered in public folders or route to a specific person or distribution list.

- Mobile Workers. Microsoft Exchange 5.5, through the Outlook 98 client, offers a superior advantage over other email and Web-based systems for mobile users. Users can work offline and when they return to the office or home, synchronize and consolidate their data with the Microsoft Exchange 5.5 server. Database front ends and onsite reports for the medical industry are super examples of mobile worker-based applications. Because Outlook 98 and Microsoft Exchange 5.5 handle the synchronization and consolidation automatically, very little user intervention is necessary.

- Information Distribution. Ensuring certain information is disseminated to the proper individuals or distribution lists is easy with Microsoft Exchange 5.5. Users do not have to remember where to route certain types of information. Example applications for information distribution include news updates, new program features, or contact distribution. Users are free to manipulate information and leave the distribution to Microsoft Exchange 5.5.

- Information Sharing. An organization based on information needs to share the information at one point or another. Microsoft Exchange 5.5 and Outlook 98 can be used to develop applications that ensure automatic information sharing. For instance, a sales organization may want to develop a New Contact folder where new leads are shared. Instead of placing the onus of entering and sharing the information on the user, an application can be developed to ensure after the user creates new contact information it is automatically shared among all users.

- Process Automation. Microsoft Exchange 5.5 and Outlook 98 support the automation of processes through routing. As a developer, you can move the old, paper-based processes onto the Microsoft Exchange 5.5 infrastructure. Not only can you ensure the process is automated, but you can also build in controls. Examples of controls would be to ensure certain users respond by a deadline, ensure the process routes to users who are in the office, and using digital signatures. Process automation is a good development option for vacation requests, expense report approval, purchase orders, and new product approval.

- Information Organization. Information is only as good as its presentation and organization. What good is a public folder with a list of approved vendors if the information isn't organized properly? By using Microsoft Exchange 5.5 and Outlook 98 the public folder can be organized so the user can search the public folder, realign data, and ensure the proper decision is made.

- Information Collaboration. In today's age of electronic communication, information very rarely is static. One person will interpret information and change it and then pass it along. Microsoft Exchange 5.5 and Outlook 98 make sharing information with others and incorporating their changes much easier. Applications you can develop allow users to share the information with the proper resources and then incorporate their changes while tracking the who, what, and where of each change. An audit trail can be developed showing the necessary information. Excellent examples of information collaboration applications are New Product Development areas, Project Tracking, and New Process Development.

Development Choices Available

The application development methods we'll look at include the following:

- Forms. Each component of Outlook 98 used to accept and display information to the user is a form. You can create formatted data documents that accept user input and display data. Forms created by a developer can offer more control and information than standard Outlook 98 forms.

- VBScript. Based on a subset of the Visual Basic programming language, VBScript can be used with Outlook 98 and the World Wide Web. VBScript enables a developer to add controls and additional functions to Outlook 98 forms. You can see an example of a simple VBScript program's output in Figure 18.2.

- Collaboration Data Objects. Otherwise known as CDOs, Collaboration Data Objects are the building blocks for integrating Web-based applications and

18

Microsoft Exchange 5.5. CDOs allow developers to combine HTML and core Microsoft Exchange 5.5 technologies such as collaboration, scheduling, and messaging. Taking advantage of the entire Microsoft Active Platform, CDOs leverage all the services of Microsoft Exchange 5.5 through a Web-based front end.

FIGURE 18.1

Forms are the most common component of Outlook 98.

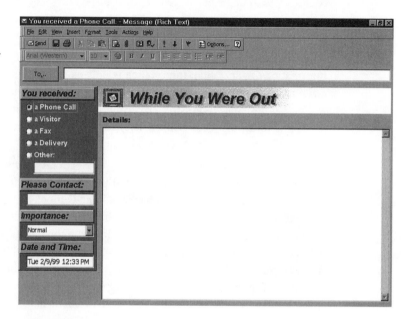

FIGURE 18.2

Here's the World's Standard Example Program (the one that says "Hello World) done in VBScript.

- Exchange Scripting Agents. Relying on triggers, these server-side scripts can be used to implement a custom action based on a user's action. Triggers can be anything from posting, editing, or deleting messages and much more. This tool is best used when automating processes.

Each of these choices has unique features and can accomplish and development goal.

Developing for the Client, Web, or the Server

Microsoft Exchange 5.5 supports application development for the following platforms:

- Outlook 98 client
- Outlook Web Access
- Microsoft Exchange 5.5 Server

Depending on your development goals, you may find yourself exclusively developing Outlook 98–based applications, Outlook Web Access–, or Microsoft Exchange 5.5–based applications.

Outlook 98–based applications work with client data. This includes Inbox, Outbox, personal folders, contacts, notes, journal, calendar, or deleted items objects. Outlook 98 applications are typically run on the local machine where Outlook 98 is located and sometimes require user intervention.

Outlook Web Access applications move the functionality of the Outlook 98 client to a Web-based interface. These applications typically improve upon the functionality offered through Outlook Web Access.

Microsoft Exchange 5.5 server applications work with public folders, mailboxes, distribution lists, and other server-based objects. Microsoft Exchange 5.5 applications typically manipulate data before it is presented to the Outlook 98 client. These applications run on the server and do not require user intervention.

Table 18.1 details which application development solution is best suited for client or server based applications.

TABLE 18.1 APPLICATION DEVELOPMENT OPTIONS

Application Development Solution	Client Based	Web Based	Server Based
Forms	X	X	
VBScript	X	X	
Collaboration Data Objects	X	X	X
Exchange Server Scripting			X

Forms Development

The most basic method of developing applications for Microsoft Exchange 5.5 and Outlook 98 is forms. Forms allow you to create a new method of displaying or receiving information for Microsoft Exchange 5.5 through Outlook 98.

Being client based, Outlook 98 form development is easy for end users and advanced enough for developers.

Outlook 98 forms have many features that position them as strong application development tools. Some of these features include:

- Forms can be linked from Web Pages. Because Outlook 98 uses a standard, simple file format, forms can be linked from Web pages and inside other Office documents. This allows organizations to ensure their collaborative efforts are available across the organization.

- Forms are not compiled. Instead of having to track down source and compiled code, Outlook 98 forms do not need to be compiled. They are ready to use. This makes it easier for users to track their forms and for developers to make changes.

- Forms are 32-Bit. Outlook 98 forms benefit from a 32-bit design. This allows Outlook 98 forms to be execute quickly and consume a small amount of resources.

- Forms Provide Inherent Functionality. Each beginning development effort starts with a form that already has functionality built into it. Developers do not need to spend time redeveloping the wheel.

The Outlook Forms Designer——The Heart of It All

Outlook 98 provides an integrated, 32-bit Forms Designer for designing forms.

To designs forms using Windows 95/98, you'll need 12MB of available memory. For Windows NT designers, you'll need 16MB.

Windows 95/98 clients running your forms will need 8MB of available memory, while Windows NT clients will need 16MB.

To begin using the Outlook 98 Forms Designer, open your Outlook 98 application and then select the Tools menu, click Forms, and then select Design Forms, as shown in Figure 18.3.

After the Outlook 98 Forms Designer loads, you'll need to choose which type of form you would like to begin with as shown in Figure 18.4. Remember, Forms Designer begins with already developed forms that you add functionality to.

FIGURE 18.3

Issue this menu command to enter the Outlook Forms Designer.

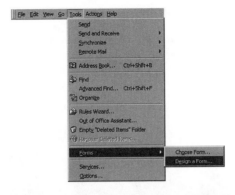

FIGURE 18.4

Select the base Outlook 98 form type.

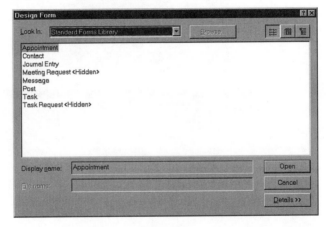

18

You can also look at the details for each form. This may help you determine which form to use. Select a form to use, such as the Task Request form. At the Design Form window select Details and you will see more information about the selected form, as shown in Figure 18.5.

One of the more structured features of the Outlook 98 Form Designer is the ability to store your forms in a Library. Think of the Library as a collection or book of forms. By selecting the drop-down list box next to Standard Forms, you will see the available options, as shown in Figure 18.6.

Select the Message form to begin our walk-through. After you have double-clicked on message you will see Figure 18.7.

When the Outlook 98 Forms Designer is in Design mode, the following editing components are available:

FIGURE 18.5

You can review the details of an Outlook 98 form.

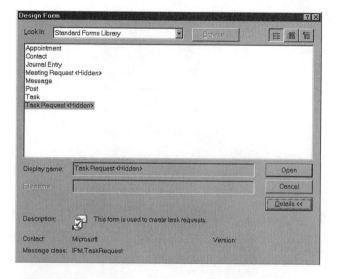

FIGURE 18.6

Select a different library from this pop-up list.

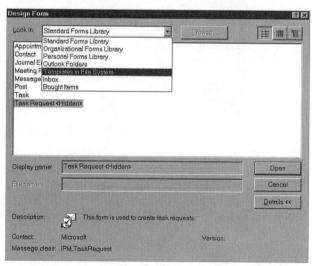

- Form Design window. The Form Design window is the component that controls actions and commands. Notice in Figure 18.8 the method of accessing the other components.

- Field Chooser. Outlook 98 forms support the use of fields for displaying or accepting data. Figure 18.9 shows the Field Chooser component.

FIGURE 18.7

The main design view of the Outlook 98 Forms Designer lets you select, place, and resize data fields.

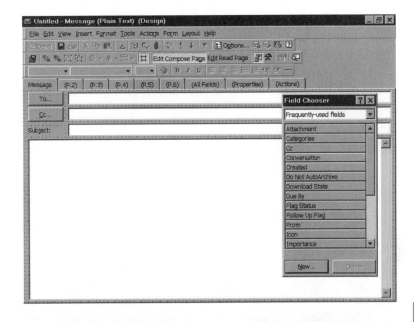

FIGURE 18.8

The Form Design window controls the development components.

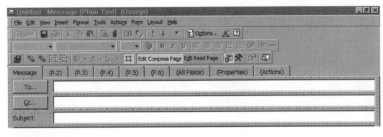

FIGURE 18.9

The Field Chooser component supports drag-and-drop.

18

- Script Editor. Outlook 98 Form Designer supports the VBScript programming language to automate forms. By using the Script Editor you can add programming objects. Figure 18.10 shows the text editor look and feel of Script Editor.

FIGURE 18.10

The script editor allows you to enter VBScript.

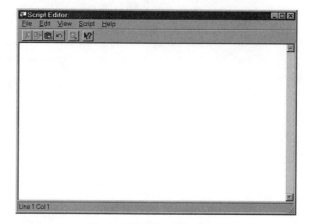

- Control toolbox. Controls are objects that bring functionality to an Outlook 98 form. As shown in Figure 18.11, examples include buttons, combo boxes, and text boxes.

FIGURE 18.11

The Control toolbox features controls for your forms.

- Properties dialog box. Depending on which object you select, the Properties dialog box allows you to control various display and control settings. As you can see in Figure 18.12, the Message control's properties can be modified. If you were to select the To field and open the Properties dialog box, you would see the properties for the To field.

Selecting a Form Type

Depending on the goal of your development effort, you'll need to choose an appropriate form type as the basis of your application.

Outlook 98 Forms Designer provides four basic types of forms for you to begin developing with.

FIGURE 18.12

The Properties dialog box in the Outlook 98 Forms Designer lets you modify a control's properties.

The Message Form

When you are developing forms with the goal of sending information to users, distribution lists, or public folders, you should start with the Message Form. Message Forms follow the normal transport process when being sent to a recipient. Examples of applications that are based on Message Forms include While You Were Out forms and Company News forms.

To begin your development effort with a Message Form, select Actions from the Outlook 98 menu and then click New Mail Message, as shown in Figure 18.13

FIGURE 18.13

Select New Mail Message to begin working with your form.

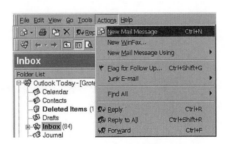

After the Mail Message form is open, you need to select Tools, Forms, and Design This Form as shown in Figure 18.14.

18

FIGURE 18.14

Once you've selected a message form, issue this command to edit it.

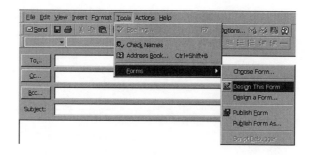

After you have selected the Design command, the Message Form opens in Design mode, as shown in Figure 18.15.

FIGURE 18.15

You've opened the Message Form in Design mode.

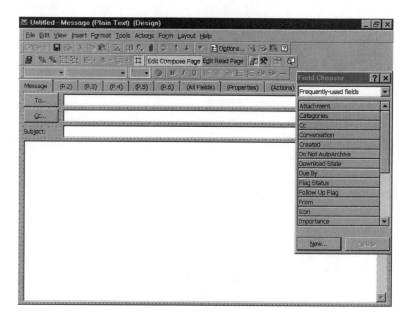

The Post Form

If the goal of your development effort is to enable users to post and respond to information in personal or public folders, you'll need to start with the Post form. Post forms are connected to folders in a very detailed way, so when information is entered through a Post form it is added to the active folder immediately. Examples of applications using Post forms as a basis for development are employee feedback forms and group collaboration forms.

To begin your development effort with a Post form, select the Outlook 98 File menu, choose New, and then click Post In This Folder, as shown in Figure 18.16.

FIGURE 18.16

This menu command selects a Post form.

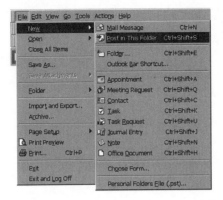

To create a Post form you must be in a folder that contains mail items such as an Inbox or a personal folder.

After the Post form is open, you need to select Tools, Forms, and Design This Form as shown in Figure 18.17.

FIGURE 18.17

Choose this command to enter Design mode with a Post Form

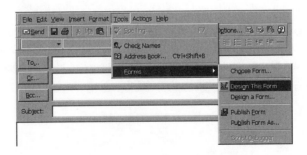

After you have selected the Design command the Post form is in Design mode as shown in Figure 18.18.

The Built-In Forms

Outlook 98 may already have some of the functionality you need to develop. You can use the Calendar, Contact, Journal, and Task forms built into Outlook 98. You can start with the basic functionality of the form that Outlook 98 gives you and add additional functionality.

FIGURE 18.18

Post form Design mode looks like this.

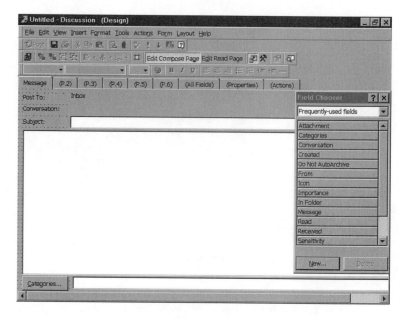

If your organization needs to modify the Contact form to handle custom fields or push data to different users, you can modify the default Contact form.

To begin your development effort with a built-in form, decide which built-in function you need. Choose Calendar, Contact, Journal and Task. Based on your selection choose File from the main menu of Outlook 98, select New, and then select the function you would like. New Contact is chosen in Figure 18.19.

FIGURE 18.19

Select the contact built-in form.

After the New Contact form is open, you need to select Tools, Forms, and Design This Form as shown in Figure 18.20.

FIGURE 18.20

Choose this menu command to enter Design mode with a new contact form.

After you have selected the Design command the New Contact Form is in Design mode as shown in Figure 18.21.

FIGURE 18.21

Design mode for a new contact form looks like this.

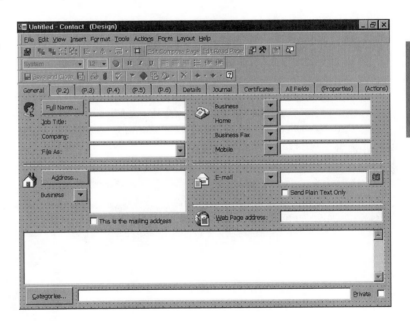

18

Microsoft Office Forms

If you have Microsoft Office 97 installed, you will have access to Microsoft Office forms. Microsoft Office forms are based on Microsoft Office documents from Microsoft Word, Microsoft Excel Worksheet, Microsoft Excel Chart, and Microsoft PowerPoint.

Rather than modifying the structure of the Microsoft Office document, your form can only send or post the information contained within. Online expense reports or collaboration on a sales presentation are excellent examples of applications that use Microsoft Office forms.

To begin your development effort with a Microsoft Office form select File from the main menu of Outlook 98, select New, and select Office Document as shown in Figure 18.22.

FIGURE 18.22

Select a Microsoft Office form from Outlook's menu.

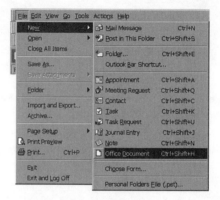

You will then see the dialog box to choose which type of Microsoft Office form you would like. You can select Microsoft Word, Microsoft Excel Worksheet, Microsoft Excel Chart, or Microsoft PowerPoint as shown in Figure 18.23. For the purpose of this example, choose Microsoft Word.

FIGURE 18.23

You choose the type of document you want to create.

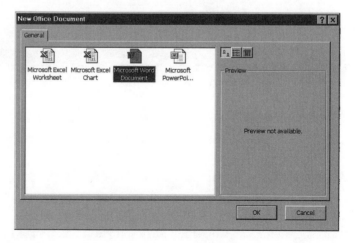

After you select the Microsoft Word type you will have to select whether you will post the document in this folder or send the document to someone. Choose Post the Document In this Folder, as shown in Figure 18.24.

FIGURE 18.24

Select the Post the Document In This Folder radio button.

After the Microsoft Office form is open, you need to select Tools, Forms, and Design This Form as shown in Figure 18.25.

FIGURE 18.25

Enter Design mode with a Microsoft Office form selected.

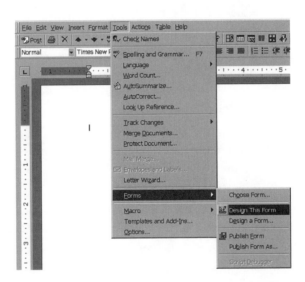

18

After you have selected the Design command the Microsoft Office Form is in Design mode as shown in Figure 18.26.

Publishing Your Forms

After you have created your Outlook 98 form, you need to publish it for other users to access. Depending on your situation, the developer may publish the forms directly to users or submit them to the Microsoft Exchange 5.5 administrator for distribution. In either case there are multiple methods of distributing the forms to the necessary users.

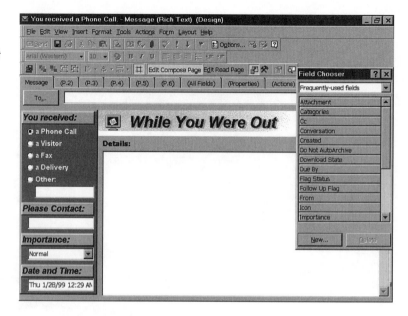

FIGURE 18.26

You're now in Design mode for the Microsoft Office form.

Form Distribution Methods

There are four methods of distributing forms to users. The distinction among methods is based on user access. Questions such as which users need access to the forms and what is the purpose of the form dictate which method should be selected. The four distribution methods are as follows:

- Forms library. Add the forms to a forms library. This includes the Organizational Forms Library, the Personal Forms Library, or the Folder Forms Library.

- User distribution. Distribute the form directly to another user.

- Personal folder distribution. Distribute the forms via a personal folder file under Outlook 98.

- Offline forms distribution. Distribute the forms for offline access.

Forms Library Distribution

Microsoft Exchange 5.5 supports forms distribution in libraries. Forms libraries should be thought of as a directory for forms. Microsoft Exchange 5.5 administrators can control access to different forms libraries. Three types of libraries are supported:

- Organizational library. This library allows the entire organization to access available forms. The forms are stored on the Microsoft Exchange 5.5 server, thereby allowing centralized access.

- Personal forms library. In the case where access should be limited to certain users or just yourself, a personal forms library should be selected.

- Folder forms library. For storage or development purposes, forms can be stored in a user-defined folder forms library.

Organizational Forms Library   Located on the Microsoft Exchange 5.5 server, the Organizational Forms Library should be used for Message forms the entire organization needs access to.

There are two primary types of Message forms that are typically stored in the Organizational Forms Library:

- General purpose forms. Examples of these include the While You Were Out form, user support request forms, or other forms that allow users to send messages to each other.

- Public information forms. Examples of these include user feedback forms, new product idea forms, or any other forms that allow users to post information to a public folder.

Caution

In a typical corporate environment, developers are not the administrators for the Microsoft Exchange 5.5 installation. If you are the developer and administrator for your company, you do not have to complete the following steps. You should begin with the "Publishing the Form" section.

18

As a developer you will need to submit your form for distribution in the Organizational Forms Library to the Microsoft Exchange 5.5 administrator.

To send the completed form to your administrator, you should complete the following steps from inside the Outlook Forms Designer:

1. Ensure the form you would like to publish is loaded in the Outlook Forms Designer. To publish a form you need to ensure the Outlook Forms Designer is in Design mode, as you saw earlier in Figure 18.28.

2. Select Save As from the File menu. Select a name for the form (I used EXAMPLE) and ensure the file type selected is Outlook Template (.oft) as shown in Figure 18.27. Select OK.

3. After the form is saved you may need to send it to the Microsoft Exchange 5.5 administrator. Select New Mail Message from the Action menu. Address the message to your Microsoft Exchange 5.5 administrator. Attach the form you would like

published and note in the message you would like the form published under the Organizational Forms Library as shown in Figure 18.28. Select Send.

FIGURE **18.27**

Be sure to save the form as an Outlook template.

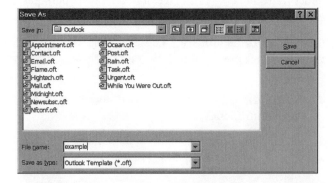

FIGURE **18.28**

If necessary, you can send the form to the administrator.

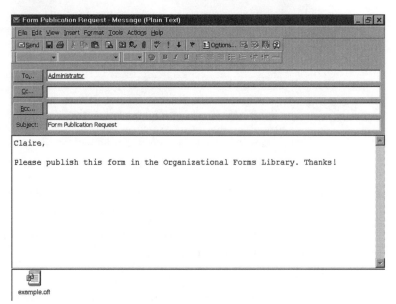

After the form is sent to the Administrator, he or she will publish the form. The Administrator follows these steps:

4. Using Outlook 98, open the new message, open the attached form, and select Tools, Forms, Publish As (see Figure 18.29).

5. When prompted for the form name, enter something descriptive so other users can access the form. In our example we used the common acronym WYWO to signify While You Were Out, as shown in Figure 18.30.

FIGURE 18.29

Select the Publish Form As command in Outlook 98.

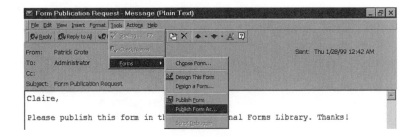

FIGURE 18.30

Enter a descriptive name for the form.

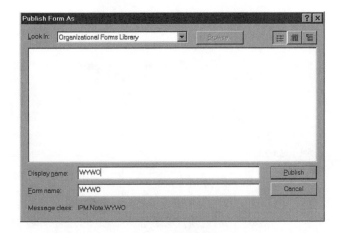

The form you just published is now available to all users through the Organizational Forms Library. To test the form's functionality, follow these steps:

1. Load Outlook 98 and select the File menu, click New, and select Choose Form, as shown in Figure 18.31.

FIGURE 18.31

The Choose Form command lets you select your newly published form.

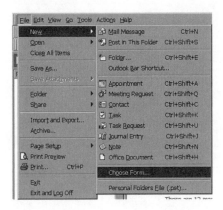

18

2. From the Choose Form dialog box, ensure the Organizational Forms Library is selected from the Look In drop-down list, as shown in Figure 18.32.

FIGURE 18.32

Ensuring the Organizational Forms Library is Selected

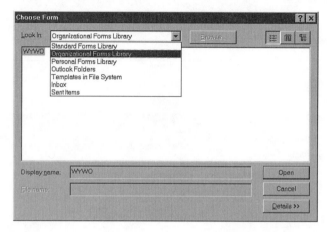

3. Select the name of your form—our example is WYWO—and click Open. You will then see your form, which you can use immediately to send a message to another user, as shown in Figure 18.33.

FIGURE 18.33

You're now using the WYWO form to send a message.

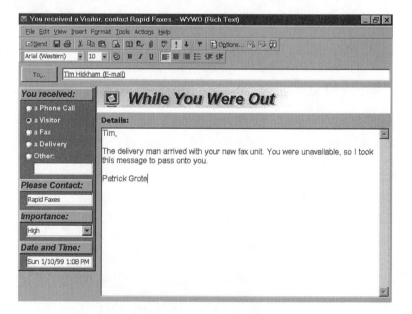

Tip

Sometimes your administrator may not be able to publish forms to the Organizational Forms Library. This is probably due to the fact he does not have the necessary permissions.

To ensure the proper permissions are set, load the Microsoft Exchange Administrator and select Forms Administrator from the Tools menu. You will see a dialog box similar to the one in Figure 18.34.

FIGURE 18.34

The Forms Administrator dialog box lets you assign permissions.

Select New, and you will see a dialog box similar to the one in Figure 18.35.

18

FIGURE 18.35

Select a new library to modify.

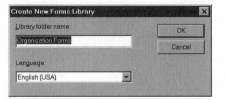

Accept the default settings and click on OK. You will then be placed at the main menu of the Organization Forms Library Administrator. Select the Organization Forms and click on Modify. The Forms Library Permissions screen shown in Figure 18.36 will appear.

Select the Add button on the Forms Library Permissions screen and add the Administrator or other user ID using the dialog box shown in Figure 18.37.

Select the Administrator user ID and modify the permissions by selecting a new role, as shown in Figure 18.38.

FIGURE 18.36

This dialog box lets you set forms library permissions.

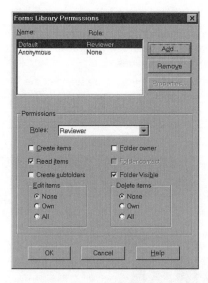

FIGURE 18.37

Add the forms administrator to the forms permissions list.

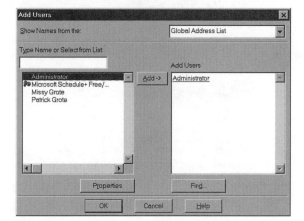

Personal Forms Library   Personal forms libraries should be used when you are developing for three reasons:

- Limiting User Access. If you are developing forms for a certain group of people you may need to control access to the form.
- Personal Use. Sometimes you need to use the form you are developing for yourself only.
- Forms Testing. Eventually the form will be available to all users, but you need an area in which you can test the form.

FIGURE 18.38

Modifying the role of the administrator lets him or her publish forms.

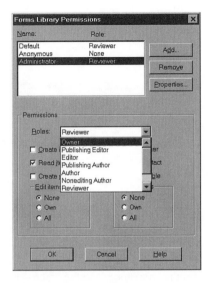

You will need to complete the following steps from the Outlook Forms Designer to publish the form to a personal forms library.

1. Ensure the form you would like to publish is loaded in the Outlook Forms Designer. To publish a form you need to ensure the Outlook Forms Designer is in Design mode as shown in Figure 18.39.

18

FIGURE 18.39

Ensure Outlook Forms Designer is in Design mode.

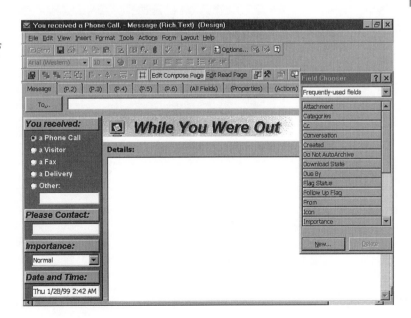

2. Select Save As from the File menu. Select a name for the form (for example, PERSONAL) and ensure the file type selected is Outlook Template (.oft) as shown in Figure 18.40. Click OK.

FIGURE 18.40

Save the form as a template.

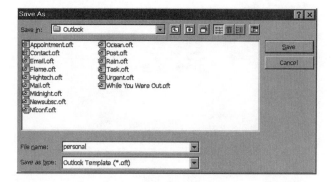

3. After the form is saved you need to send it to the Microsoft Exchange 5.5 users who you would like to give access to, including yourself. Select New Mail Message from the Action Menu. Address the message to the Microsoft Exchange 5.5 users. Attach the form you would like published. Note in the message that you would like the form published under the personal forms library, as shown in Figure 18.41. Select Send.

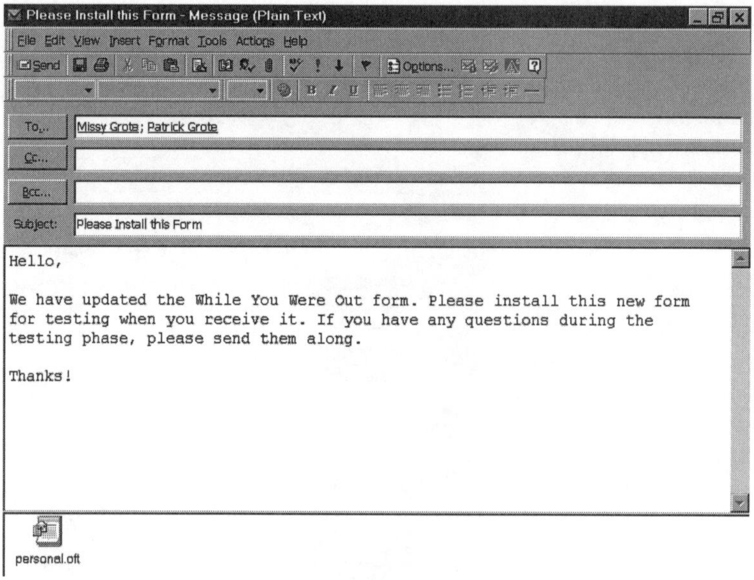

FIGURE 18.41

Send the form to the users for access so they can use it too.

After the form is sent to the users, they will need to publish the form. The user should follow these steps:

4. Using Outlook 98, open the new message, open the attached form and select Tools, Forms, Publish As as shown in Figure 18.42.

FIGURE 18.42

Select the Outlook 98 Publish Form As command.

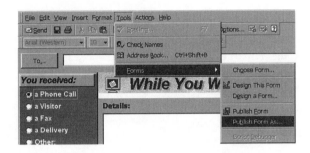

5. Change the value of the Look In field to Personal Forms Library. When prompted for the form name, enter something descriptive so other users can access the form. In this example, I used While Out to signify While You Were Out, as shown in Figure 18.43.

FIGURE 18.43

Select a forms library and name for the form to publish.

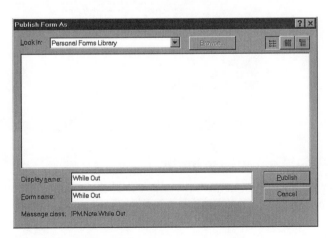

Folder Forms Library Folder forms libraries are typically used to either store custom Post, Contact, or Task forms for use by users. They are published in the same method as Personal Folder forms, but the library selected is different.

Direct User Distribution

In some cases you may want to send a form directly to a user without worrying about the end user installing the form in a library for future use. This is an excellent method for distributing a form for collecting customer information or company pre-sales information.

When publishing a form in this manner you first publish the form to a personal forms library as explained previously, but ensure that the Send Form Information with Item check box on the properties page is enabled as displayed in Figure 18.44.

FIGURE 18.44

Be sure the Send Form Definition With Item check box is selected.

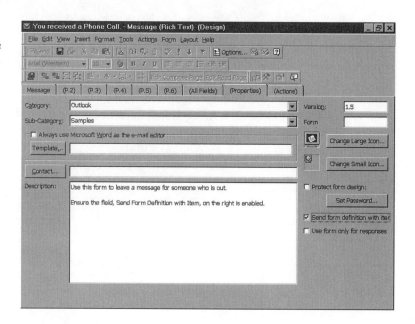

Personal Folder Distribution

Personal folder distribution of forms is a good strategy if you need to install or move multiple forms from one location to another. You may also need to use this if your organization uses forms remotely.

To use this function you should create an Outlook 98 personal folder file (.PST) through the Services section of the Mail control panel applet.

After the personal folder is created, you can copy your forms into the folder. Copy the .PST file from the original location to a new location and then install the personal folder into a new copy of Outlook 98. After the personal folder is accessible in Outlook 98, the forms you migrated will also be available.

Offline Forms Distribution

Forms are part of the Outlook 98 offline processing system. When a user has configured Outlook 98 to work offline, the synchronization process is used to ensure the latest mail is on the user's remote drive.

After a user installs a form in her offline folder (.OST), the synchronization process will control new updates and so on.

VBScript—Making Forms Come to Life

With forms, Microsoft took a good step in helping bring new functionality to Microsoft Exchange 5.5 and Outlook 98. It has taken this a step further by adding VBScript to the lineup.

VBScript is an abbreviation for Visual Basic Scripting Edition. VBScript is a subset of Visual Basic for Applications, which is the scripting language used for Microsoft Office. Both of these are subsets of Visual Basic, the programming language from Microsoft.

By using VBScript you can program extra functionality in your forms that is compatible with other Microsoft products.

You can use VBScript to accomplish the following:

- Use Outlook 98 forms to collect information for a database.
- Manipulate a collection of folders for data reporting or storage.
- Modify field values and properties depending on conditions.
- Declare and control events as they happen using Outlook 98.
- Control fonts and other associated display characteristics of a folder.
- Interface Outlook 98 forms and data with other applications.

The key to using VBScript is the Script Editor. The Script Editor allows you to add code to an Outlook 98 form.

To see the Script Editor in action, load Outlook 98 and complete the following steps:

1. Under Inbox, select Actions, New Mail Message.
2. Select Tools, Forms, Design this Form.
3. While in Design mode, select Forms and then View Code as shown in Figure 18.45.

18

FIGURE 18.45

Select View Code to enter the script editor for Outlook 98 forms.

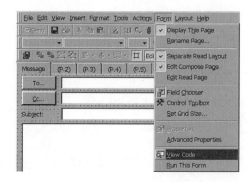

4. After the Script Editor is active it will appear as a simple blank text box, as shown in Figure 18.46.

FIGURE 18.46

The VBScript Editor appears as a simple window.

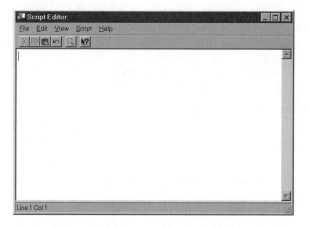

VBScript can run as straight code or it can be event-based. By running as straight code the VBScript executes its commands without regard to the form.

An event is an action concerning the form as specific as someone using the Send button to changing any property on the form. By controlling events you can modify user interaction with the form as well as behind the scenes computations. Most of the VBScript used in Outlook 98 forms is event driven.

As with other programming languages, VBScript provides a script debugger. As you can see in Figure 18.47, the script debugger runs as the form is being used.

FIGURE **18.47**

The VBScript Debugger runs as the form is in use.

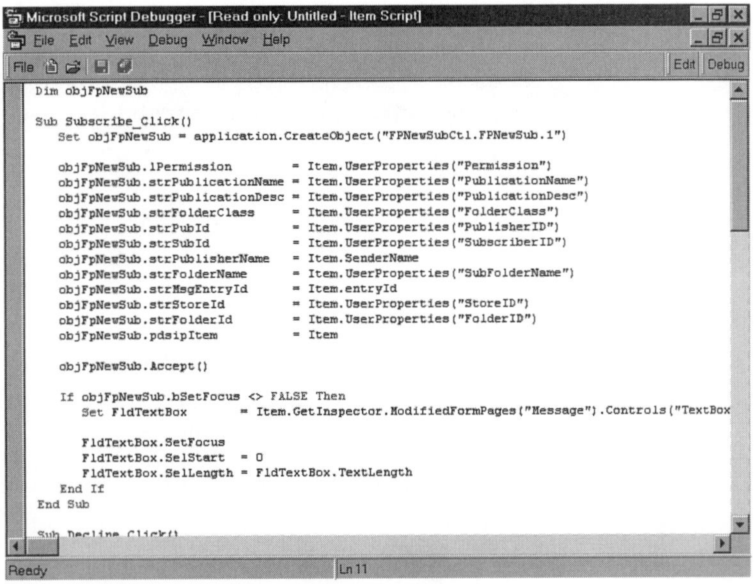

```
Dim objFpNewSub

Sub Subscribe_Click()
    Set objFpNewSub = application.CreateObject("FPNewSubCtl.FPNewSub.1")

    objFpNewSub.lPermission       = Item.UserProperties("Permission")
    objFpNewSub.strPublicationName = Item.UserProperties("PublicationName")
    objFpNewSub.strPublicationDesc = Item.UserProperties("PublicationDesc")
    objFpNewSub.strFolderClass    = Item.UserProperties("FolderClass")
    objFpNewSub.strPubId          = Item.UserProperties("PublisherID")
    objFpNewSub.strSubId          = Item.UserProperties("SubscriberID")
    objFpNewSub.strPublisherName  = Item.SenderName
    objFpNewSub.strFolderName     = Item.UserProperties("SubFolderName")
    objFpNewSub.strMsgEntryId     = Item.entryId
    objFpNewSub.strStoreId        = Item.UserProperties("StoreID")
    objFpNewSub.strFolderId       = Item.UserProperties("FolderID")
    objFpNewSub.pdsipItem         = Item


    objFpNewSub.Accept()

    If objFpNewSub.bSetFocus <> FALSE Then
        Set FldTextBox     = Item.GetInspector.ModifiedFormPages("Message").Controls("TextBox

        FldTextBox.SetFocus
        FldTextBox.SelStart  = 0
        FldTextBox.SelLength = FldTextBox.TextLength
    End If
End Sub

Sub Decline_Click()
```

Collaboration Data Objects

18

What if there was a way to bring the functionality and features of Microsoft Exchange 5.5 to the Web? Could you imagine developing applications for Microsoft Exchange 5.5 that worked for local clients as well as your Web users? What would that do for your development costs? What would that do for your business? This technology is here today and new with Microsoft Exchange 5.5.

Collaboration Data Objects (CDO) is the key piece for allowing a developer to develop Web-based applications with the functionality and features of Microsoft Exchange 5.5. CDO is the next generation of Active Messaging. By using Active Server Pages and CDO you can add the following functionality to Web pages:

- Creating messages
- Sending and receiving messages
- Address book access
- Attachment distribution
- Group discussions
- Forms
- Public Folders

Tip

CDO is not a new messaging model. It is a scripting interface for MAPI. Messaging Application Programming Interface (MAPI) is the programming interface used for sending email under the Microsoft Windows family.

To fully utilize CDO you'll need to have Outlook 98 on your system and Microsoft Exchange 5.5 on your network installed.

Active Server Principles

Beginning with Microsoft's Internet Information Server Version 3.0, the active environment was brought to the Windows NT environment. The active environment allows developers to create server- and Web-based applications.

The Active Server Platform from Microsoft is best visualized as in Figure 18.48.

FIGURE 18.48

Here's how the Active Server Platform from Microsoft works.

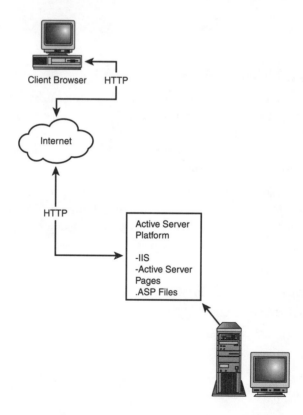

There are two components of the Microsoft Exchange 5.5 Active Server platform:

- Outlook Web Access
- Collaborative Data Objects

When the Microsoft Exchange 5.5 Active Server platform objects are added to the environment, the platform shifts to the diagram shown in Figure 18.49.

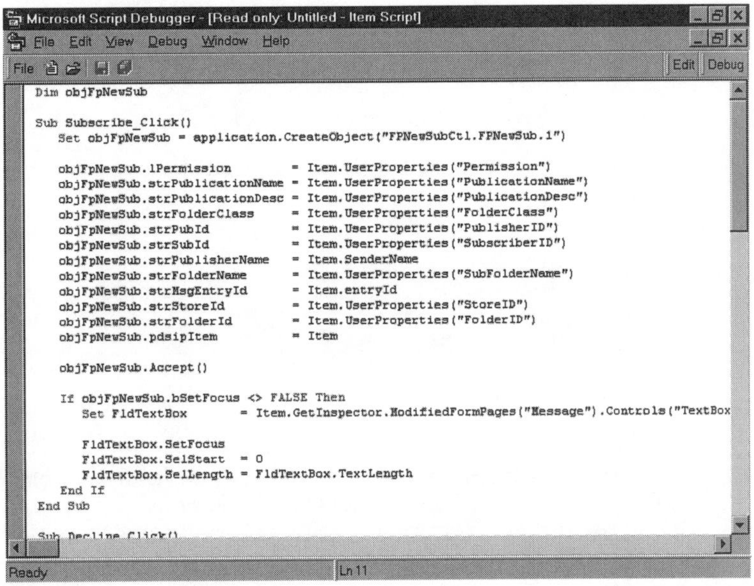

FIGURE 18.49

The Active Server Platform with Microsoft Exchange 5.5 from Microsoft works like this.

The final piece of the Active Server platform is Active Server Pages. Active Server Pages are indicated by the .ASP extension on Web servers and combine HTML and scripts to create Web-based applications.

Active Server Pages (.ASP) files are standard HTML documents interlaced with ActiveX script code that calls specific Active Server components, such as CDO.

The Microsoft Exchange 5.5 Active Server Page components include a number of server-side scripts in .ASP files.

CDO Libraries

There are two CDO libraries used to create Web-based applications:

- CDO Library. This library allows you to add messaging functionality such as creating, sending, and receiving email, and access to address books and public folders. This library is client based.

- CDO Rendering Library. This library is used to render the CDO objects in HTML. This library is server-based.

CDO libraries can be called from the following development languages:

- Microsoft Visual Basic
- VBScript
- JScript
- JavaScript
- Java
- Visual Basic for Applications

The following is a sample program using CDO to send a test message:

```
' This sample uses Visual Basic 3.0 error handling.
'
Function QuickStart()
Dim objSession As MAPI.Session ' use early binding for more efficient
Dim objMessage As Message      '                code and type checking
Dim objOneRecip As Recipient

On Error GoTo error_olemsg


' create a session and log on -- username and password in profile
Set objSession = CreateObject("MAPI.Session")
' change the parameters to valid values for your configuration
objSession.Logon profileName:="Sender Name"

' create a message and fill in its properties
Set objMessage = objSession.Outbox.Messages.Add
objMessage.Subject = "Sample Message"
objMessage.Text = "This is sample message text."

' create the recipient
Set objOneRecip = objMessage.Recipients.Add
objOneRecip.Name = "Recipient Name"
objOneRecip.Type = CdoTo
objOneRecip.Resolve ' get MAPI to determine complete email address

' send the message and log off
objMessage.Send showDialog:=False
MsgBox "The message has been sent"
objSession.Logoff

Exit Function

error_olemsg:
```

```
    MsgBox "Error " & Str(Err) & ": " & Error$(Err)
    Exit Function

End Function
```

CDO is the newest tool in the Microsoft Exchange 5.5 armory. It brings the promise of allowing developers to code once and run locally or on the Internet. Because it is so new there aren't many resources for help, so expect more trial-and-error programming than normal.

Exchange Scripting Agents

Could you imagine a world where your server controls business processes? What about a world where you could control the flow of information in your organization? Imagine no more, as Exchange Scripting Agents give you the control you need.

Exchange Scripting Agents work on the Microsoft Exchange 5.5 server waiting to be triggered when a certain event occurs. The event could be something as simple as a message sent to a folder or as complex as a certain message being deleted.

Sample applications that use Microsoft Scripting Agents well are conference room schedule programs, expense report routing, and help desk applications.

Instead of working on the client side as most scripts do, the Exchange Scripting Agent runs on the Microsoft Exchange 5.5 server.

Putting Scripting Agents to Work

The first step in using Exchange Scripting Agents is to ensure the service is installed on your Microsoft Exchange 5.5 server. To do this, follow these instructions:

1. Select Control Panel.
2. Select Services.
3. Verify the Microsoft Exchange Event Service is running.

If the service is successfully installed and running you will see a screen similar to Figure 18.50.

If the service is not installed, follow these directions:

1. Insert the Microsoft Exchange 5.5 CD-ROM and run the setup program.
2. Select Add/Remove Components.
3. Select Microsoft Exchange Server then select Change Options.

18

4. Select Microsoft Exchange Event Services.

5. Select OK twice when prompted.

6. Restart the server if needed.

FIGURE 18.50

You can see the Microsoft Exchange Event Service available.

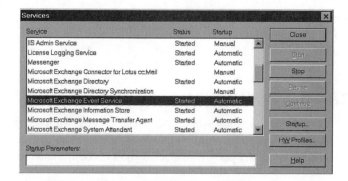

Benefits of Exchange Scripting Agent

The following are several benefits of using Exchange Scripting Agents:

- Data validation. The server could be used to verify that completed forms had all the information necessary for processing before forwarding them.

- Routing determination. Depending on the content of the form or message, the agent can determine which recipient to route the message to.

- Status verification. Agents can verify the status of each form submitted.

- Exception handling. If a routing group has been created, the server agent can ensure that approvals are not delayed by people outside the office.

Issues With Exchange Scripting Agent

The following issues exist when using Exchange Scripting Agents:

- Scalability. The scripting agents are not designed to handle multiple server interactions.

- Performance. Piping too many messages through an agent could affect Microsoft Exchange 5.5 server performance.

- Security. Because Exchange Scripting Agents use the Exchange service account, changes can be made to users' mailboxes without their knowledge.

Exchange Scripting Agents are extremely powerful when used properly. Look for specific, niche areas where server-based, centralized control of a process is necessary.

Development with Microsoft Exchange 5.5 ranges from as simple as designing a form to as complex and designing an entire server-based application using Exchange Scripting Agents. The bottom line is Microsoft Exchange 5.5 supports any level of development. You can modify the environment to satisfy your business needs today.

Summary

Microsoft Exchange 5.5 Server is the platform best suited for today's groupware development efforts. Forms are just the beginning. By adding the ability to code Microsoft Exchange 5.5 functionality into Web sites and standalone applications, your entire organization can harness the information that already exists.

You've learned that there are four methods of developing applications for Microsoft Exchange 5.5 including:

- Forms
- VBScript
- Collaborative Data Objects
- Exchange Scripting Agents.

You've also learned the advantages and disadvantages of each development solution, so you can determine which solution is best for your organization.

Q&A

Q As I am developing forms for use in our organization, what is the best method of testing the functionality?

A As the developer, you should test the form initially and ensure it performs as you expect. After it passes muster, you should make it available to a small group of beta testers. Ensure each of the users have a different computer configuration if possible. Publishing the form to a public forms library that is configured with access rights for the beta test team is the best way of accomplishing this.

Q I've just completed work on a great form that will revolutionize our sales process. I want to be able to offer access to this form to our salesforce, but they are all remote users. They use their laptops to dial in and access the network to retrieve and send Microsoft Exchange 5.5 email messages. Is there a method I can use to provide access to the forms to them?

A Yes, you can use the Offline Forms Folder Library to distribute the forms and offer access. The remote users can use the forms as if they were directly connected to the Microsoft Exchange 5.5 server. A synchronization process occurs when Outlook 98 contacts the Microsoft Exchange 5.5 server.

Q Our organization has embraced Java as our standard Web-based development language. Can we utilize Collaborative Data Objects (CDOs) in our Java applets?

A Yes. You can use the CDO libraries when developing applets under Java.

Workshop

The Workshop provides two ways for you to affirm what you've learned in this lesson. The "Quiz" section poses questions to help you solidify your understanding of the material covered and the "Exercise" section provides you with experience in using what you have learned. You can find answers to the quiz questions and exercises in Appendix B, "Answers to Quiz Questions and Exercises."

Quiz

1. VBScript is a subset of what development language?
2. What is the primary advantage of using Collaborative Data Objects?
3. Which two development methods support server-side development?
4. What is the minimum amount of memory needed to develop forms on a Windows 95 workstation? What about a Windows NT 4.0 workstation?
5. Can I use Microsoft Office 97 templates as forms?
6. Can Personal Folder Files be used to store and distribute developed forms?
7. Is VBScript compatible with VBA?
8. CDOs are a scripting agent for what messaging interface?
9. What are the software requirements for using CDOs?
10. Which Windows NT 4.0 Server service must be running to take advantage of Exchange Scripting Agents?

Exercise

Modify the existing While You Were Out form for your organization. Add your logo and a new notes section.

DAY 19

Making Exchange Secure

by Anthony Steven

Chapter Objectives

You now know enough to implement a perfectly functional Microsoft Exchange messaging system. However, if your company works with classified, confidential, or commercially sensitive information, you may want to implement the security features of Exchange.

Today, I will be covering the following topics:

- Configuring object security
- Enabling access to multiple mailboxes
- Managing distribution lists
- Setting permissions on public and system folders
- Implementing advanced security
- Configuring Key Management Server

- Enabling mailboxes for advanced security
- Implementing advanced security on the client

Exchange Object Security

In Microsoft Exchange, everything is an object. Mailboxes are objects, distribution lists are objects, public folders are objects, and servers are objects. So are Recipients containers, Connectors, Address Books, and Information Stores. They are all objects.

All objects maintain a permissions list, and that permissions list defines exactly which users or groups of users are allowed to do what with the object. Hence, object security is the ability to define exactly who can or can't access an object.

Object security is a pervasive and tightly controlled feature of Microsoft Exchange, and integrates fully with the Windows NT security model. You manage Exchange object security through the Exchange Administrator program.

Defining Who Can Access an Object

In order to be able to specify permissions on all objects, you need to be able to define users and groups of users, and then assign them the relevant permissions. Here the operating system comes to our aid, as we already have a means of defining users and groups.

Integration with Windows NT

In Windows NT, you must identify yourself to the operating system before you can log on. Thus, to use Windows NT, you must have an account and a password. Your account can have certain rights and permissions by assigning the account to one of the local groups within NT. Alternatively, you can assign the user accounts into a global group, and then add the global group to a local group.

The recommended method is that accounts go into global groups, which go into local groups, which get the permissions. AGLP, as Microsoft say. Which is really easy to remember.

Exchange makes full use of the security model built into Windows NT. However, one of the changes to the normal AGLP way of assigning permissions is that in Exchange, you can assign permissions direct to global groups, instead of assigning them to local groups.

Discretionary Access Control

Discretionary Access Control means that you can configure specific permissions on individual objects.

Within the Exchange Administrator program, you can configure permissions on three main levels. These are as follows:

- Organization
- Site
- Configuration container

The permissions applied to each level only flow down as far as the next level.

Organization If you set permissions at the organizational level, these settings only affect the Organization object. These permissions do not flow down to any other objects at the organizational level. You only need to set permissions on the Organization object if you want to give a user or group permission to manage the entire organization.

Note | Permissions on the Address Book Views object are set at site level.

Site   Site level permissions flow down to all site-level objects, including the Recipients container. Site-level permissions do not affect the Configuration container.

Users must have at least View-Only Admin permissions at a site level. This allows them to connect to a server in that site when they run Exchange Administrator.

Users with Admin permission or Add Child right at the Site or recipients container level can add recipients to that site.

19

WHEN SOMEONE JOINS YOUR COMPANY

When someone joins your company, which department is responsible for taking him through the induction process? That's right—the Personnel or Human Resources department. So why is it an IT job to set up their user account and mailbox? The answer is usually because it has to do with computers. So, why not try this approach to reduce your workload.

Train one or two people in the HR department to use User Manager for Domains. Add them to the Account Operators group and put User Manager for Domains (from the Client utilities on the NT Server CD) and the Exchange Administrator onto their workstations. Note that they would need to have access to an NT Workstation. Give your account operators local group Admin role at the site level in Exchange Administrator.

Now, when someone joins the company, part of his induction process would be that the account operators in the HR department add his name as a new Windows NT account. Exchange Administrator will then prompt the account operator to create a new mailbox, and add all the necessary detail. As soon as the new employee joins, he can log on to the network and send mail. The department that the new employee joins can then add his name to the departmental distribution list.

You don't have to be involved in this at all.

Configuration Container   The Configuration Container permissions are the most widespread, as permissions given at this level spread down to all the servers in the selected site. Hence, if you give a user Admin permission at the Configuration Container level, that permission will apply to, say, the Directory Service Object at server level.

Let's assume you have an apprentice working for you, and because you don't want (or trust) her to be a Network god like yourself, you have made her a server operator. However, if you want this person to administer your Exchange servers in one site only, you can give the server operators group Admin permission in the Configuration container of that site.

However, to use Exchange Administrator for a particular site, users must be able to log on to the site. To do this, she must have at least the View Only Admin role at the site level.

Using Exchange Administrator to Change Permissions

The tool that you use to manage Exchange permissions is Exchange Administrator. Start Exchange Administrator, and connect to your server. (I'm guessing that by now you probably know how to do this.)

The first thing you need to do to be able to manage permissions is to configure a couple of options. Select the Tools menu and then choose Options. Click on the Permissions tab, check the boxes for Show Permissions Page For All Objects, and Display Rights for Roles on the Permissions page.

Showing the Permissions Page on All Objects

After you have checked the box to show the Permissions page (or tab) on all objects, every container and object that displays properties will have a Permissions tab. Some objects don't have any associated properties, like the Folders object at organizational level.

Showing Rights for Roles

Checking the box to Show Rights for Roles will add a small list of check boxes to the bottom right corner of each Permissions page. Figure 19.1 shows an example of this.

FIGURE 19.1

The list on the bottom left shows which rights apply to the selected role.

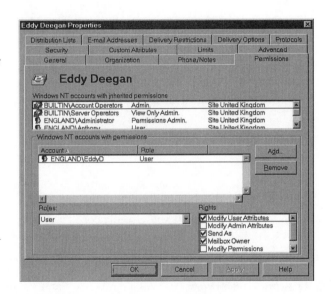

You can then specify additional rights that do not fit into the standard roles offered. The role type will then change to custom.

Selecting Roles

You can now start to configure permissions for your organization. You do this by adding a user, global, or local group, and then assigning them a role. If required, you can then customize this role by allocating additional rights.

It is important to understand that roles are preconfigured sets of rights. The roles that you can select depend on whether you are at the Organization, Site, or Configuration container level.

19

Service Account Admin   The Exchange Site Service Account automatically takes on the Service Account Admin role. The Site Service Account is the one that you used when you installed Exchange. This gives the Exchange Service account the ability to start services, log in to Exchange, and make any necessary configuration changes.

 Caution   The Exchange Service Account is a very powerful account, and you must take appropriate security measures to protect it.

The Service Account Admin role operates at Organizational, Site, and Configuration Container Level.

Permissions Admin   The Permissions Admin role is the one that you should have allocated to yourself or to your Exchange Administrators global group. This role lets you administer carry out any action on an object (except search), including modify permissions.

The Permissions Admin role operates at Organizational, Site, and Configuration Container Level.

Admin   You would probably allocate the Admin role to your sidekick. Admin role has exactly the same rights as Permissions Admin, except that a user with Admin role cannot configure permissions. Therefore, if you give someone the Admin role, you know that they can't then start giving themselves or anyone else any extra rights.

The Admin role operates at Organizational, Site, and Configuration Container level.

View Only Admin   The View Only Admin role lets a user log on to a server in a site, but does not let them do anything else. If you want to give one of your users the ability to configure servers, you must give them View Only Admin role at the site level.

The View Only Admin role only operates at the Site level.

User   When you create a mailbox, and select a Windows NT account, that account automatically takes on the User role. You can add subsequent accounts and give them the User role, in which case the newly added account will be able to open and use that mailbox.

> **Caution**   If you give an NT account the user role at the site level, then the Recipients container inherits that permission. This means that this NT account can open any mailbox in the site. Use with care!

The User role operates at Site and Configuration Container level.

Send As   I will explain the Send As role in the relevant section later in the lesson.

The Send As role operates at Site and Configuration Container level.

Search   The Search role is something of a special role that you use in conjunction with Address Book views. See the section "Address Book Views Container" later in this lesson for more information.

Custom   The Custom role is any combination of rights that does not fit into one of the roles listed previously. The Custom role operates at all levels.

Rights

As roles are a combination of rights, let's have a look at the individual rights. Remember that to view rights, you must have selected the option to View Rights for Roles in Exchange Administrator Options.

- The Modify User Attributes right lets you modify the user-level attributes of a mailbox.
- The Modify Admin Attributes right lets you change the administrator-level attributes of a mailbox. In other words, this would let you modify the Title or Department fields in a mailbox.
- The Send As right lets you send messages with the sender's return address; that is, the real sender can impersonate the owner of the mailbox. Server objects receive this permission so that directory service processes can send messages to each other on behalf of the server objects.
- A Mailbox Owner can log on to this mailbox and use it to send and receive messages. Accounts with Mailbox Owner permission do not automatically have to be the Primary NT Account of that mailbox.
- The Logon Rights role enables the selected account to log on to any server in the site using the Exchange Administrator program.

19

- The Add Child right lets you add objects to a container, such as other mailboxes or recipient containers.

- The Delete right lets you, like, delete an object.

- The Replication right lets an account replicate information to other sites. The Site Service Account can do this.

- The Modify Permissions right lets users modify permissions on objects that already exist. This right does not apply to new objects.

- The Search right is used in conjunction with Address Book views. See the section "Address Book Views Container" later in this lesson.

With rights and roles, the important things to understand is that the roles are a preset group of rights, and that these roles and rights flow down through the Exchange hierarchy to the next level.

Using Other Mailboxes

Having looked at the general topic of rights and roles, let's address the issues of configuring mailboxes for multiple access. Remember that for a mailbox, the default setting is that only the user logging on using the Primary Windows NT Account can open that mailbox.

There are six ways of using mailboxes other than your own:

- Using a Group Account
- Send As
- Send On Behalf Of
- Delegate Access
- Configuring Permissions at Mailbox Level
- Mailbox Owner Permission

Using a Group Account

Instead of using a Windows NT account as the primary account for a mailbox, you can select a group account. You could then use this as a mailbox for a group of users or a jobshare partnership. To do this, follow these steps:

1. Add both jobshare partners to the domain via User Manager for Domains. Do *not* create new mailboxes for these users.

2. Create a global group, and add the jobshare users as members.

3. Switch to Exchange Administrator, and click on the New Mailbox button.

4. Create a new mailbox, giving the mailbox a descriptive name so that other users know that it is a shared mailbox.

5. Click on the Primary Windows NT Account, and select the Global account that you created earlier. The mailbox will now look like that in Figure 19.2.

FIGURE 19.2

In this example, I have configured a mailbox called Julia & Elizabeth (Job Share).

6. Now either jobshare partner will be able to log on to the mailbox and answer mail.

Send As

Send As is one of the two methods of delegating access to a mailbox, the other being Send on Behalf Of. Send As is by far the more powerful of the two.

With Send on Behalf of, the message that you receive says `From: Mrs. Robinson of behalf of Mr. Hoffman`. With Send As permission, the recipient cannot tell that the message was not actually sent by the person named as the sender.

> **Caution**   Use Send As permission with great care, as it delegates executive authority to someone else.

In this example, Roger (who irretrievably blotted his copybook last week) is going to be "let go." However, I don't actually want be around when the deed is done, and, conveniently, I'm on holiday next week. As firing people is an HR thing, I'll make sure that everyone thinks Geoff did it. Here's what I'm going to do:

19

1. First, I give myself Send As permission on Geoff's mailbox, as shown in
   Figure 19.3.

FIGURE 19.3

Here I have Send As permission on Geoff's mailbox.

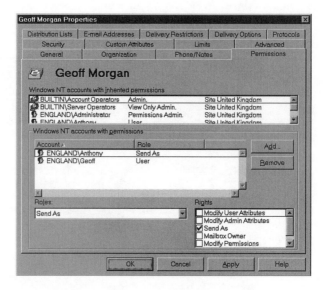

2. I am already an alternate recipient on Roger's mailbox because I've been monitoring his mail. Figure 19.4 shows this in action.

FIGURE 19.4

Of course, I'm monitoring Roger's mail as well.

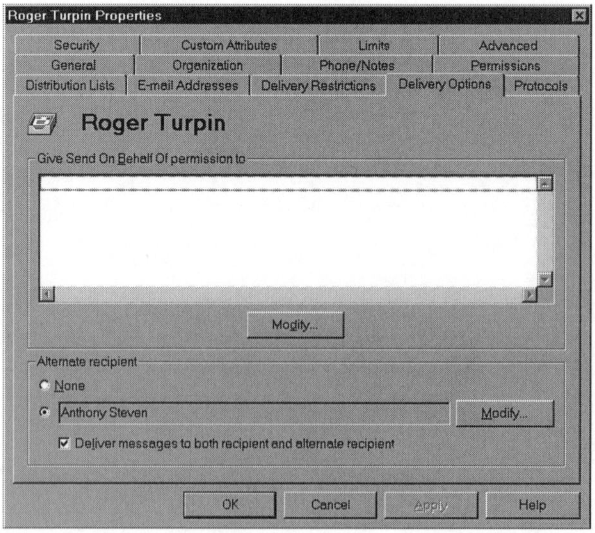

3. Next, I log on to Outlook and compose a suitable message. However, I click the View menu and select From. This adds a From box to my message headers.

4. Having composed a suitably sensitive message, I select the From box and add Geoff's name, as shown in Figure 19.5.

FIGURE 19.5

Getting the message ready to go.

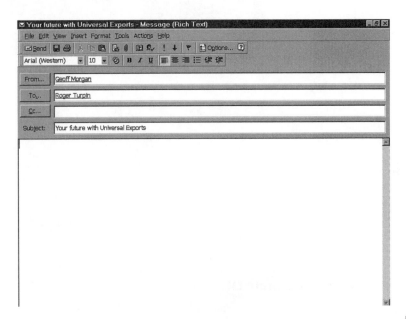

5. I go to the properties of the message, and delay sending until next week, as shown in Figure 19.6.

19

FIGURE 19.6

Now I am delaying sending the message until I'm on holiday.

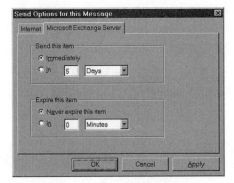

6. The message remains in my Outbox until the due time.

7. Figure 19.7 is what Roger will see. Bye-bye, Roger!

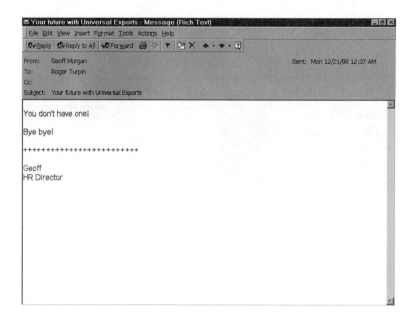

FIGURE 19.7

Roger gets the good news.

Machiavelli would have approved of that one!

Send on Behalf Of

As you have just seen, Send As is a very powerful role to give to someone. Most of the time, all you will need is the ability for one user to send mail on behalf of another. This might happen where you have a secretary reading and replying to his boss's mail on her behalf.

You configure Send On Behalf Of permissions through Exchange Administrator. To do this, follow this next procedure:

1. Start Exchange Administrator, and click on the Recipients button.
2. Select the Recipient whose mailbox you want another user to Send On Behalf Of.
3. Double-click on that mailbox, and then select the Delivery Options tab.
4. Click the Modify button, and select the user or distribution list that will be sending on behalf of this mailbox.
5. Your screen will now look something like Figure 19.8.
6. Click OK.

FIGURE 19.8

Here I have configured Send On Behalf Of access.

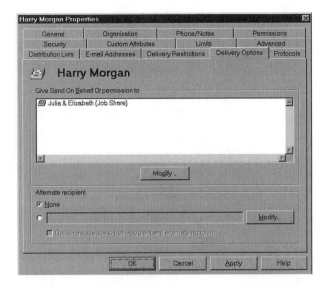

Using Send On Behalf Of permission is just like using Send As. You use the From button to select the name of the person on whose behalf you are sending the message. However, when the message arrives in the recipient's mailbox, it will be headed From: Elizabeth Mayo on behalf of Anthony Steven.

Users can also give Send On Behalf As permission using Outlook. To do this, they need to follow the procedure in the next section on Configuring Delegate access, but they must give the other person a minimum of Author role on their (the person doing the delegating) own mailbox.

Configuring Delegate Access

Delegate Access is the fourth option for giving other people permission to open mailboxes other than their own. You configure Delegate Access through Outlook or the Exchange Client.

To do this, follow this procedure:

1. Start Outlook and select the Tools menu. Click on Options.

2. In the Options dialog, click on Delegates tab.

3. To add a delegate, click on the Add button.

4. Delegates can be mailboxes or distribution lists. Add the mailbox that you want to be a delegate.

5. You will now see the dialog box in Figure 19.9. Here you set up the exact level of delegation you require.

FIGURE 19.9

From this dialog, you can configure delegate access.

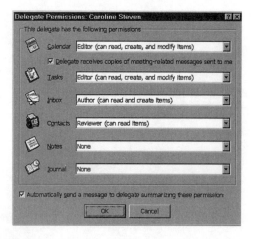

  Note

If you give another user Author or Editor role on your Inbox, that is the same as giving him the Send On Behalf Of role through Exchange Administrator.

6. After you have set up the level of access you require them to have, check the box to inform your delegates of their access levels automatically.

7. Your delegate now needs to start Outlook. On starting Outlook, they will see the message informing them of their current access permissions.

8. The delegates should then click on the File menu, select Open, and click on Other User's Folder. The dialog box in Figure 19.10 will appear.

FIGURE 19.10

Enter the name of the user and select which folder you want to open.

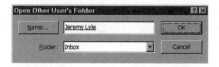

9. The delegates will now be able to choose from the Calendar, Tasks, Journal, Inbox, Contacts, or Notes folders. After they have entered a name and chosen a folder, if they click OK, that folder will open in a separate window.

10. If they attempt to open a folder that they do not have permission to access, they will see the message in Figure 19.11.

FIGURE 19.11

This message means you do not have access to a folder.

You can change delegate access options, and arrange to send a message to the other user each time you make a change.

Giving Permission at the Mailbox Level

A further development of Delegate Access lets you configure your mailbox so that someone else can open it. The way to do this is to give that user a minimum of Reviewer role at the Mailbox level. To do this you should

1. Start Outlook, and make sure you can see the folder list in the left pane.

2. Right-click on the [Mailbox—Your Name] folder at the top of your mailbox tree.

3. Select Properties and click on the Permissions tab. You will now see the screen in Figure 19.12.

FIGURE 19.12

You can let someone access your entire mailbox through Outlook.

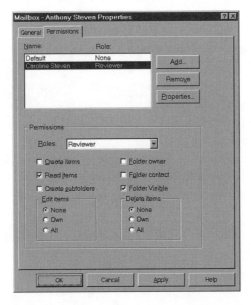

4. Add the user that you want be able to open your mailbox and give her a role of Reviewer. If you want her to be able to create subfolders in your mailbox, check the relevant box.

5. You can use the Delegate Access tab in options to give her access to any other folders below the Mailbox level, or you can configure permissions directly on each individual folder.

6. The other user will now be able to open your mailbox as an additional mailbox in their messaging profile. I will cover this procedure in the next section.

Note that you must give the other user at least reviewer permission at the mailbox level. Delegate Access alone will not do this—it only configures permissions for the second level folders.

Using the Mailbox Owner Permission

The final method is using the Mailbox Owner permission. Here you need to go back to the Exchange Administrator:

1. Start Exchange Administrator, and click on the Recipients button.

2. Select the Recipient whose mailbox you want another user to open.

3. Double-click on that mailbox, and then select the Permissions tab.

4. Click Add to add the relevant account from the NT domain, as shown in Figure 19.13.

FIGURE 19.13

Here I have added another account with the User role.

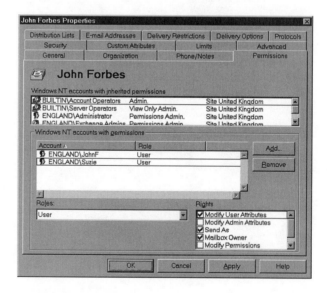

5. The new account will appear with the role of User. If you want this account to be able to open the mailbox, but not to send mail as the other person (in the User role

they can do both), uncheck the box for Send As. The role will then change to Custom.

6. That's it as far as Exchange Administrator is concerned. You now need to carry out the next set of steps as well.

For the next phase, you need to configure the messaging profile. You can do this through Outlook. This is also the procedure to carry out if you are giving another user permission at the mailbox level as per the last section.

1. Start Outlook, select the Tools menu, and click on Services. The properties of the current messaging profile will appear. Double-click on the Exchange Server service and then click on the Advanced tab.

2. Click on the Add button and type in the display name or alias name for the other mailbox.

3. Select OK and you will see a screen like that in Figure 19.14.

FIGURE 19.14

Here the other mailbox is now part of the messaging profile.

4. Select OK, and then OK to accept the changes to the profile.

5. The other mailbox will now appear in your folder list.

If you have Mailbox Owner permission on the mailbox that you have just added, you will see all the folders. If the other user has configured delegate access permissions, and then given you permission at the folder level, you will only see those folders for which you have a minimum of reviewer permission.

Having covered the issues involved in opening other folders, let's look at configuring distribution lists.

19

Distribution Lists

Distribution lists display both the best and the worst aspects of email. They're the best because you can keep in touch with a group of people via one address. They're the worst, because you're bombarded with more junk than ever before.

> **Tip**
>
> Distribution lists can contain distribution lists. The easiest way to create a company distribution list is to add a distribution list that contains all the departmental distribution lists. Then your users can send loads of vital messages to everyone, like "Has anyone seen my handbag" or "What's on at the canteen today?" Remember that any complaints directed at someone misusing the "all employees distribution list" address should also go to everyone for maximum annoyance.
>
> To prevent this, you can stop users or groups of users from sending mail to distribution lists by configuring the Delivery Restrictions tab on that distribution list.

The first thing to do with distribution lists is to plan them. You should already have done this in Day 4, "Server Configuration."

Delegating Ownership of a Distribution List

Part of the planning of your distribution lists should be to assign owners. You need to consider the owner of a distribution list carefully. After all, he or she will be the person who maintains the list.

> **WHY DELEGATE THE OWNERSHIP OF DISTRIBUTION LISTS?**
>
> Maintaining a distribution list is really a people thing. After all, distribution lists are groups of people, organized by department, project, building, company, and so on. Groups of people are, in turn, managed by managers, and managers seem to delight in rearranging the organizational tree on a whim. Your main job is to sort out computers, not people. Just because this month has an "R" in it, (R for Reorganization) is no reason why you should have to stay at work late sorting out the departmental distribution lists.
>
> Hence, delegate the ownership of the distribution list to the manager in charge of the department. Better than that, give it to his secretary. The job will probably get done then.
>
> The best thing is that now, if anybody doesn't get included in a distribution list and misses important mail, you can shrug your shoulders and do your "Is this the face of concern?" look.

An owner of a distribution list can add and remove people from the list. You can do this through the Address Book in Outlook.

1. Start Outlook and select the Tools menu. Choose Address Book and then double-click on the distribution list that you own. You will see a dialog box like that in Figure 19.15.

FIGURE 19.15

You can modify a distribution list that you own.

2. Click on the Modify Members button.

3. Click on the Add or Remove button and select mailboxes or distribution lists as required.

4. Click OK twice to accept the changes.

Tip

Distribution lists cannot own distribution lists. Only mailboxes can own distribution lists.

Having dealt with distribution lists, let's look at the issues involved in administering public folders.

Public Folders

Applying public folder permissions is very much like giving other users permission to access a mailbox. The difference with public folders is that the default settings allow access by all authenticated users.

However, before I get any further into this topic, there is something which, if you haven't yet done it, you must do *now*.

Restricting Top-Level Folder Creation

You must, must, and must restrict permissions on who can create top-level folders. If you don't, you will end up with a veritable cat's cradle of proliferating folders, over which you will only regain control by some very savage pruning.

1. To restrict top level folder creation, start Exchange Administrator, and click on the Configuration button in the toolbar.

2. Double-click on the Information Store Site Configuration object, and then click on the Top Level Folder Creation tab.

3. This is one of the few times that you will use the left-hand list. Add yourself to this list.

4. You are now the only person who can create top-level folders.

Now you have that under control, you can look at public folder permissions.

Permissions and Roles

As part of your Exchange deployment, you should have considered the layout and areas covered by your public folders. As part of that planning process, you need to consider public folder permissions.

Generally, I would recommend a system whereby you are the only person who can create top-level public folders. That means that the departments have to come to you, cap-in-hand, to request a new top-level folder. Heh heh heh.

> **Note**
>
> There is an important issue here. Remember the public folder storage limits you set in Day 15, "Maintaining Exchange"? Well, they were per folder, weren't they? So what happens if everyone starts creating new public folders? That's right, you can end up with a Public Information Store database considerably larger than you planned.

You then need to plan the permissions on those top-level folders. Again, I would recommend that you define your top-level folders by department or by project, and you restrict the users that can create subfolders to the managers of those departments.

Permissions   There are a number of standard permissions that combine into standard roles. Public folder permissions include:

- Read
- Create

- Edit items (none, your own, or all)
- Delete items (none, your own, or all)
- Create Subfolders
- Folder Owner
- Folder Contact
- Folder Visible

The first five items are self-explanatory.

The Folder Owner is the initial folder contact and has full permissions to do anything with the folder. Every folder must have an owner, which can be a distribution list.

Folder Contacts are additional users or distribution lists whom will receive replication conflict messages, and requests for additional permissions on the folder.

If the Folder Visible box isn't checked, users won't be able to see the folder. This is particularly useful if you are developing a folder-based form, and don't want users messing about until you have finished testing your folder. All that you do is uncheck the Folder Visible box for the default user, and then only the users that you specify will be able to see the folder.

Roles   The roles that you can assign to a folder are as follows:
- None—No access to the folder.
- Reviewer—Can see but can't contribute.
- Contributor—Can contribute, but can't read.
- Author—Users can contribute, read, edit, and delete messages that they have posted.
- Publishing Author—can do everything an author can do, plus create subfolders.
- Editor—Can edit and delete other people's postings.
- Publishing Editor—Can also create subfolders.
- Owner—Can do everything.
- Custom—Any combination of individual permissions that does not fit the categories above.

Accounts   The list of accounts and their respective roles is at the top of the Permissions tab. Here you will see any accounts that have permissions on this folder. You can then add individual accounts or distribution lists, and configure their role.

19

The Anonymous and Default accounts are special cases, as it's the role of the Owner.

You always have a folder owner. If you delete the folder owner, when you re-examine the properties of the folder again, the owner will still be there.

The Anonymous account permissions apply to all users attempting to connect to a folder using anonymous authentication. This could be via NNTP, IMAP4, or HTTP. For more information, see the section on Anonymous Access in Day 8, "Troubleshooting Exchange".

The default entry applies to all users not specifically named in the permissions list. The default value is also that applied when you add another user to the Permissions list. However, you can modify this default value after you have added a user or distribution list.

Note

Permissions combine like NT permissions—your effective permission is the best combination of all your permissions. Let's say you have Reviewer role on a folder, and you are a member of a distribution list that can contribute to the same folder. Your effective role will be a custom role that lets you post and read but not edit your own posts.

The exception is that unlike NTFS permissions, the None role applied to a specific mailbox or distribution list does not override any other roles. So if the default role is None, this only applies if the user is not listed with a specific role or is a member of a DL.

Setting via Client

To set the permissions on a folder using Outlook or Exchange Client, select the View menu and choose Folder list, so that you can see the list of public folders in the left pane. Right-click on a folder, and select Properties. Now click on the Permissions tab, and you will see a dialog box like the one in Figure 19.16.

Change the permissions and then click OK.

For more information, see the section "Configuring Permissions" in Day 8.

Setting via Exchange Administrator

To set public folder permissions via the Exchange Administrator, you need to select the relevant public folder in the left pane of Exchange Administrator. After you have selected the folder, click on the Properties button on the toolbar. You will see a dialog box like that in Figure 19.17.

FIGURE 19.16

You can configure permissions via Outlook or the Exchange client.

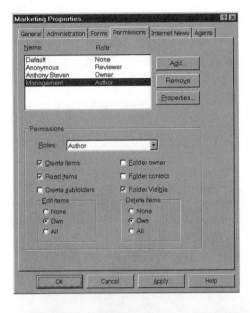

FIGURE 19.17

You can propagate client permissions down a Public Folder tree.

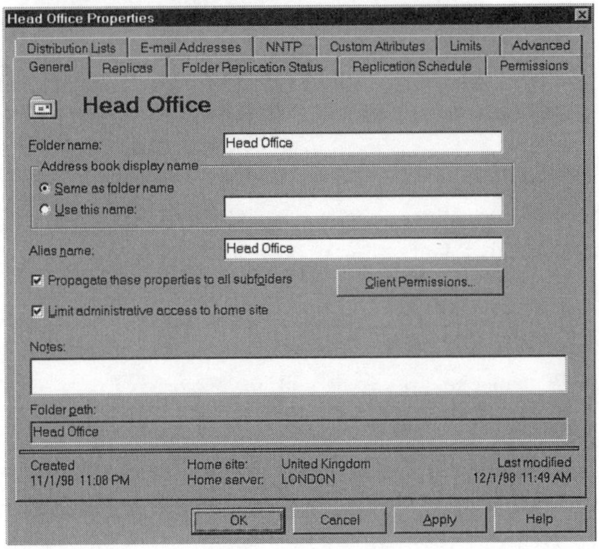

19

Select the button marked Client Permissions and change the access settings as you did using Outlook.

Cascading Permissions Down the Folder Tree

When you change a folder's permissions in Outlook, subfolders are unaffected. However, in Exchange Administrator, you can specify that these permissions should cascade down the folder tree to all subfolders.

Before you click OK on the folder's general page, check the check box marked Propagate These Properties to All Subfolders. When you click OK on the folder properties, this brings up a dialog box asking you which properties you want to propagate, as shown in Figure 19.18.

FIGURE 19.18

Check the option for client permissions to propagate the new permissions down the folder tree.

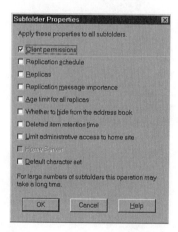

Select the option for client permissions and any changes that you made to client permissions on this folder will now flow down the folder tree. All subfolders will inherit the permissions that you defined at the top level.

Use of the Favorites Folder

There is a particular security issue with the Favorites folder. This folder is just a shortcut, not a copy of the original folder.

After a user has added a folder as a favorite, the link to that folder bypasses any file permissions assigned at a higher level, unless you propagate these permissions down the folder tree. Hence, if you want to change permissions on a hierarchy of folders, you cannot just change the permission on the root folder, using Outlook. You need to change the permission using the Exchange Administrator program, and propagate the permissions throughout the folder tree, as described previously.

Having looked at security issues on public folders, you need to be aware of some particular aspects of the System folders.

System Folders

As well as the public folders, Exchange has a few system folders that provide special functions within Exchange. These folders behave just like any other, except that they are dedicated to a particular function, rather than posting messages. These system folders are as follows:

- The Organizational Forms Library
- The Address Book views Container
- The Events folder
- The Offline Address Book
- The Schedule+ Free Busy Connector

The Schedule+ Free Busy Connector will only concern you if you are connecting to MS Mail postoffices and you want to provide diary scheduling with Schedule+ users. See Day 21, "Migrating from Microsoft Mail" for more information on integrating Exchange with MS Mail.

Let's look at the issues on the remaining system folders.

Organization Forms Library

The Organizational Forms Library is where you can store forms, and any user in the organization can then use these forms. You can then replicate the Organizational Forms Library to all sites, and thus provide a single point for storing forms.

Developers will need to publish their forms to the Organizational Forms Library, and thus will need a minimum of Author role. Users will need to have at least Reviewer permission, or Author role if you want them to be able to copy personal forms into the Organizational Forms Library.

As creator of an Organizational Forms Library, you should give yourself the Owner role.

For more information on the Organizational Forms library, see Day 18, "Building Exchange Applications."

Event Service System Folder

The Event Service System Folder is similar in some ways to the Organizational Forms Library, and stores scripts that run when an event occurs in a folder. Events can be new messages arriving, timers expiring, message deletions, or message changes.

Again, similar permissions apply. All users need to have reviewer role, and developers need to have a minimum of Author role.

19

Note | If you want your developers to be able to edit each other's scripts, they need to have the Editor or Owner role on the Organizational Forms library.

Address Book Views Container

The Address Book views container lets you create address book views that can categorize your users into offices, departments, cities, and countries, as well as custom categories. You can also use Address Book views to create virtual organizations, where users in one virtual organization cannot see users from another, even though they are hosted on the same Exchange server.

The security issues on Address Book views really come into play when you are using virtual organizations. To implement Address Book views using virtual organizations, you must carry out the following changes to permissions:

- You must give the Exchange Service Account the Search right at Organization and Site level. This will change the Service Account's role to Custom.
- You must give the search right to each Windows NT Global group that you define as part of setting up Address Book views. You apply this search right to each virtual organization container generated by the Address Book view.

However, you do not need to do this if you are just using Address Book views to help with the categorization of your users.

For more information on Address Book views, see Day 4. See also the section on Address Books in the Operations Chapter in Exchange Server Books Online.

Offline Address Book

Permissions on the Offline Address Book only come into play when you define Address Book Views. In this case, when users attempt to download the Offline Address Book, they will see the subset of the address book that they would be able to see if connected to Exchange. The exception to this is if a user downloaded a copy of the OAB before the creation of the address book views. In this case, that user will still be able to download the complete Offline Address Book.

There are no additional configuration requirements here, as the Address Book view controls the permissions.

Now that I've covered permissions on mailboxes and public folders, let's look at the topic of Advanced Security.

Advanced Security

In most organizations, the normal levels of security provided with Microsoft Exchange should be sufficient. Nevertheless, what do you do if you want to prevent the possibility of anyone intercepting your messages in transit, either on your network or on the Internet? Or if you need to be able to guarantee that a message has come from the person indicated on the message?

Advanced Security provides both these options.

Introduction

After covering the first half of this lesson, you should have no doubt that Exchange is a secure messaging platform. Normally, to open a mailbox, you have to log in as the Primary Windows NT account of that mailbox. You can only open other mailboxes if you have permission to do so, either through Exchange Administrator, or by the owner of that mailbox, using Outlook or the Exchange client. So what is the point of Advanced Security?

Advanced Security provides two extra facilities on top of the discretionary access control and integration with Windows NT security that you have just covered. These facilities are Signing and Sealing. But before I discuss these facilities, I need to explain a couple of concepts.

Cryptography

Cryptography as a subject has a very long history. Examples of codes used by the Ancient Greeks and Romans show that the peoples of the classical world were aware of the importance of keeping information secret. Children find codes fascinating, and a Master Spy kit, with one-time pads and letter substitution codes, is a perennial favorite as a Christmas or birthday present.

During the Second World War, code-breaking played a major component of the Allies' success in defeating the menace to the Atlantic convoys posed by German U-boats. Under the direction of Dr. Turing and with the assistance of Colossus, one of the first electronic computers, the code-breakers of Bletchley Park cracked the codes generated by the Nazi's Enigma machine.

Today, there are two main types of computer-based coding systems in operation. One is Secret Key Encryption, where both sender and recipient use the same code. Enigma was a mechanical variant of this type. The other is Public/Private Key Encryption, as used by software packages such as PGP (Pretty Good Privacy).

19

Secret Key Encryption

Secret Key encryption is like the one-time pad. Both sender and recipient know the transposition codes that can encrypt or decrypt the message. It is very efficient, and good for encrypting large amounts of text. The downside is that you must ensure that both parties have the same secret key. In addition, if you pass the secret key from one to the other, the key is vulnerable to interception. The one-time pad gets around this problem, but then both parties must work from the same one-time pad, and the pad itself is prone to compromise.

Public/Private Key Encryption

Public/private key encryption uses intensive computations based on large prime numbers to generate two keys—a public and a private key pair. After you encrypt a message with the public key, only the private key can decrypt it, and vice-versa. The advantage with public/private key encryption is that this system does not require the passage of a secret key between the parties. Public keys can be widely published, residing on public key servers, attached to messages, or incorporated into an email signature block.

The disadvantage with public/private key encryption is that it requires considerable computing power to work. Hence, it is unsuitable for bulk encryption of messages.

Key Lengths

Whichever encryption type you are using, the key length is a measure of how secure the code is. For a discussion on key lengths and security, see the sidebar "How Secure is Secure?" in Day 11, "Communication Protocols and the Internet."

Now let's look at how these encryption methods are used by Exchange.

Signing

Digital signing provides the ability for a recipient to verify that a message came from a particular person, and that the message was unaltered in transit. For example, when I regrettably had to let Roger go earlier in this chapter, I did this by sending him an email purporting to come from Geoff, the HR Director. (I did come in for a lot of criticism over this approach. A few people were asking why I didn't just use the time-honored approach of a black bin-liner on the desk – so much more personal.)

However, as the security guards escorted Roger out of the building immediately, he didn't have time to realize that the message wasn't signed. Therefore, the message could have come from anyone.

Digital signing not only guarantees that a message came from the person recorded as the sender, but that the message was unaltered in transit. It works by generating a hash or message digest, which is a unique 128-bit number, computed from the ASCII values of the text of the message. The client software then encodes this hash value with the private key of the sender and sends it with the original message. On receipt of the message, the remote client software then regenerates a hash value for the received message. It also decrypts the transmitted hash value using the public key of the sender. If, on comparing the two hash values, they are the same the message has not changed in transit.

Exchange generates its unique signature or checksum by applying the 128-bit Rivest-Shamir-Adelman (RSA) algorithm called Message Digest 5 (MD5) to the text of the message.

Note that with signing, the message is in clear text. The *sender* uses her private key to encrypt the message digest, and the recipient uses the *sender's* public key to decrypt the digest. As the message uses the *sender's* private key, this is the guarantee that the message came from the sender.

Sealing

Sealing encrypts the entire message, so that it is not readable while it is in transit. One method to do this is for the sender to encrypt the message using the recipient's public key and then send the message. The recipient can then decrypt the message using her own private key.

> **Note**
>
> The *sender* of a sealed message uses the *recipient's* public key to encrypt the message, and the recipient uses her private key to decrypt it.

19

As I mentioned earlier, public/private key encryption is inefficient for bulk encryption. Therefore, Exchange reduces the computational overhead by combining elements of secret key and public/private key encryption to provide Sealing.

How Does Microsoft Exchange Implement Advanced Security?

Microsoft Exchange implements Advanced Security in two ways. You can use either the Exchange Key Management Service, or S/MIME encryption, with certificates provided by a third-party Certification Authority or from Microsoft's Certificate Server.

What Services Does Exchange Advanced Security Offer?

Microsoft Exchange implements both signing and sealing in Advanced Security. Signing works as I described previously, using the sender's private key to encrypt, and the sender's public key to decrypt.

With sealing, Exchange uses a combination of public/private key and secret key encryption. When you send a sealed message in Exchange, the Exchange client collects the recipient's public key from the Global Address List. The bulk of the message is then encrypted using secret key encryption. The secret key goes into a lockbox and is encrypted using the recipient's public key. The encrypted message and the lockbox travel to the recipient.

The recipient's client then decrypts the lockbox using the recipient's private key, and extracts the secret key. The secret key will then decrypt the bulk of the message. By implementing sealing in this manner, Exchange gains the advantages of both secret key and public/private Key encryption.

Which Operating Systems Are Supported?

Advanced Security supports 16–bit Windows, 32-bit Windows and, er, that's it. No DOS, and no Macintosh.

Encryption Standards

Exchange supports X.509 certificates, which are the most widely used standard for defining digital security. However, X.509 is still an ITU Recommendation, which means that it does not have official definition or approval.

Exchange can use both the original X.509 V1 certificates for backward compatibility, and the X.509 V3 certificates with S/MIME.

For more information on X.509, see the following (pay) Web site:

```
http://www.itu.int/itudoc/itu-t/rec/x/x500up/x509_27505.html
```

Key Management Server

The component that regulates encryption on Microsoft Exchange is the Key Management Server. The Key Management Server performs the following functions:

- Generates the public/private key pairs.
- Acts as a Certification Authority (CA) by creating X.509 and public signing certificates.
- Maintains copies of user's private encryption keys.
- Maintains and distributes a Certificate Revocation List (CRL).

Signing and sealing uses the public/private key pairs.

A Certification Authority is an authority trusted to generate X.509 or sealing certificates.

Exchange's Key Management Server maintains a copy of each user's private keys. This is in case that user leaves the company, and the company needs to recover their encrypted messages. The public keys are stored in the Directory Service and made available through the Global Address List.

The Certificate Revocation List is a central listing of all compromised, expired, or revoked keys.

S/MIME Support

If you have deployed Exchange 5.5 Service Pack 1 and Outlook 98 from the Service Pack CD, you now have the option to use Secure MIME encryption instead of Key Management Server. S/MIME is becoming increasingly popular on the Internet, which means that your users will be able to send secure email to Internet addressees.

However, to use S/MIME exclusively, you need to have all your clients running on Outlook 98. Otherwise you will need to operate in Compatibility mode, and your S/MIME clients will not be able to send S/MIME mail to non-S/MIME users.

To use S/MIME, you require a X.509 V3 certificate from an external Certifying Authority. Examples of external Certification Authorities are VeriSign or Microsoft Certificate Server, which is part of Internet Information Server 4.0.

Using an External Certification Authority   If you want to use S/MIME with Internet clients outside your organization, you will need to use a certificate from an external Certification Authority, like VeriSign. In this case, you will need to purchase a multiuser key.

You can contact VeriSign on:

```
http://www.verisign.com
```

Certificate Server   If you are using Microsoft Certificate Server, you must generate a certificate. You specify where to place this certificate when you install Certificate Server. Usually, you install certificates onto a read-only share on an NTFS partition.

After you have created your certificates, you can use the CA object to specify where your certificates are located. See the section on setting up Exchange to use Certificate Server later in this lesson for more information.

Encryption Algorithms and Key Lengths

With the Introduction of S/MIME, Exchange now supports a number of encryption standards.

19

Key Management Server   Key Management Server in North America supports CAST–64, CAST-40, and Data Encryption Standard (DES). All other countries are limited to CAST-40, except for France, which forbids the import of encryption technology.

S/MIME   If you are using S/MIME in North America instead of KM Server, you have the option to use 3DES, DES, RC2-128, RC2-64, and RC2-40. If you are using S/MIME in other countries, you can only use RC2-40.

Security Components

The security components on Exchange include both client and server DLLs, and X.509 certificates.

Key Manager Service   The Key Manager Service is the core component of Advanced Security. This service runs on the server that you have designated as the Key Management Server, and provides all the functionality listed previously. The service itself does not have to be running all the time, and the KM service starts manually. The Key Manager Service requires a password when started, which you can type in or supply on a floppy disk.

Key Management Server Database   The Key Management Server files reside in \EXCHSRVR\KMSDATA. This directory is empty until you install Key Management Server. It is an encrypted database, with 512-bit encryption strength. The Key Management Server database has a master encryption key, which uses the KM Service password.

The KM Service Database, like the directory service and information stores, uses the Microsoft JET database engine, with transaction tracking logs and checkpoint files to provide recoverability.

Security DLLs   dvanced Security uses three main types of security DLL:

- The KM Service uses the SECKM.DLL library. Clients make calls to this library, which either deals with the request, or, if necessary, forwards the request to the KM Service. Hence, the KM Service does always have to be running.
- The Exchange Administrator program uses SECADMIN.DLL. When you install Key Management Server, the setup program places this DLL into \EXCHSRVR\BIN.

- The Client uses either ETECH.DLL (16-bit) or ETECH32.DLL (32-bit). This DLL provides the main security functions on the client.

Now that you have an understanding of what is involved in Advanced Security, let's look at how you would actually deploy Key Management Server.

Deploying Key Management Server

A Key Management Server deployment is more a political than a technical issue. If your company is planning to implement encryption technology, it is probably for a good reason. Hence, you need to make sure that you have properly thought through your deployment of encryption technology.

Planning Key Management Server Deployment

Not surprisingly, you can't just chuck in a few Key Management Servers and expect everything to work. I'm afraid you're going to have to do a bit of planning.

How Many Key Management Servers Will I Need?

I used to tell my training delegates that Key Management Servers are like the Immortals in the film *Highlander*—There Can Be Only One. However, with the new S/MIME facility, it should be possible to configure multiple Key Management Servers. However, my advice would still be to stick with one Key Management Server. This means that you will avoid any possible problems with recovering keys and so on.

Where Should I Site the Key Management Server?

You would normally want to site your Key Management Server in your central site or headquarters. This will probably be where you are located, and you will have RPC connectivity to the server. Ideally, the KMS location should have good communication links with all other sites. Other considerations are

- The server must be physically secure.
- The server's file system should be NTFS.
- You must be able to back up the Key Management database regularly.
- You will be using Exchange Administrator to connect to the key Management Server, so you must be able to connect to the KM Server using RPCs.

How Many Key Management Administrators Should I Have?

This depends on the level of security you want to implement. Key Management Server not only allows you to specify more than one KMS administrator, but also how many of these administrators are required to make changes to the Key Management Server.

19

In a normal commercial environment, one KM Administrator should be sufficient. In a high-security or government agency environment, you may want to have three or four Key Management Administrators. You would then set a policy so that at least two or even three administrators must be present when you recover security keys, revoke privileges, and so on.

Installing Key Management Server

Now you've selected the site where you are going to install your KM server, and you have appointed a suitable number of KM administrators. You can now proceed to install the KM server.

The setup program for installing the Key Management server is now part of the Exchange Server Setup.

> In Exchange 5.0, the KM Setup program is in the \EXCHKM directory.

Before You Start

Before you start, it is worth thinking about how you want to start the KM service. You start this service manually, and you must supply a password. The password is a 15-character random string that the KM service requires to start, for example, QVMEDHVCWEJNUSD. You have the choice of entering this in the service startup parameters, or you can have the setup program write the password onto a floppy disk. You will then have to provide the disk every time you start the service.

> I would strongly recommend using the floppy disk option. If you choose the manual option, you only get one chance to write the password down correctly.

Installing the Service

To install the Key Management Server, carry out the following task:

1. Carry out a full backup of your Exchange server.

2. Prepare two blank formatted floppy disks.

3. Run the setup program from the Exchange Server CD. This should Autorun when you insert the CD in the CD drive.

4. Select Setup Server and Components, and then choose Microsoft Exchange Server 5.5. The Setup routine will run.

5. Select the Add/Remove button.

6. On the option for Exchange Server, and click on the Change Option button. You will now see the screen in Figure 19.19.

FIGURE 19.19

Select the option for Key Management Server.

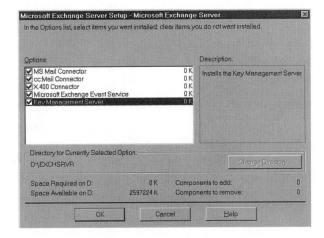

7. Check the box for Key Management Server, and select OK.

8. Select Continue. A dialog box will ask you for the Exchange Service Account password. Enter this and select OK to proceed.

9. You now have the choice for how you want to start the Key Management Service. If you select the manual option, you will see a prompt like that in Figure 19.20.

FIGURE 19.20

This is the password that you must write down!

Caution | Don't forget to write this password down!

19

10. If you choose the floppy disk option, you should insert the two floppy disks one after the other. (Don't forget to take the first one out before you put the second one in. I've heard of it happening....)

11. The setup routine will now complete. You should now re-install Exchange Server Service Pack 1.

Apart from the floppy disks, there isn't a lot to the installation of the Key Management Server.

The two floppy disks that the setup routine created should have just one file on it. The name of this file is kmserver.pwd, and contains only the 15-character string required to start the KM server.

Key Management Server Administrator Password

When you install KM Server, you become the first KM Server Administrator. The setup routine creates a default password, which is "password." You will need this password to access the Certification Authority object, as I will describe in the next section. You will also need to change this password as soon as possible.

Changes After Installation

After you have installed KM Server, you will notice three changes to your Exchange Administrator.

Certification Authority Object   There is now a new site-level object, called CA. This is the Certification Authority object. I will come back to this object shortly.

Site Encryption Object   If you double-click on the Site Encryption Configuration object, you will notice that the Primary KM Server location now displays the name of your site, as shown in
Figure 19.21.

Again, I will come back to this shortly.

Mailboxes   All individual mailboxes will have a new Security tab. Distribution lists are unaffected, as you cannot have a security key for a distribution list.

Enabling Advanced Security

Having installed your KM server, you need to enable Advanced Security. This involves a number of steps.

First, you need to start the KM Service and configure the CA object. After you have done this, you can enable your users' mailboxes.

FIGURE 19.21

*The Site Encryption
object is now aware of
your KM Server.*

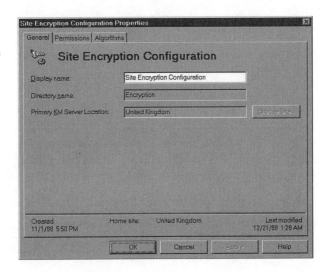

Starting the Service

You start the Key Management Server Service from the Control Panel. You will need to have one of your floppy disks or the 15-character password that you noted down earlier.

1. Click on the Start button, select Settings, and then choose Control Panel. Double-click on the Services icon.

2. Scroll down the list until you find the Microsoft Exchange Key Management Server. Note that this service is a manual start.

> **Caution**
>
> You should not change this value to automatic. The KM Service does not have to run all the time, and you should only start it when you need to administer the KM Server.

3. Ensure you have the floppy disk with the KMSERVER.PWD file in the floppy drive.

4. Click the Start button and the Key Management Service will now start.

Now that the KM Service is running, switch to Exchange Administrator for the next procedure.

Replication to Other Sites

You need to ensure that the other sites are aware of the location of your newly installed server. You do this through the Site Encryption Configuration object. To do this:

 Note

> You must have replication configured between sites for the next procedure to work. If you haven't configured replication, sites won't be aware of the KM Server. Remember that replication takes a few minutes, unless you force an update of the remote site.

1. Start Exchange Administrator, and connect to a server in the other site.
2. Click on the Configuration button in the taskbar.
3. Double-click on the Site Encryption Configuration object.
4. Click on the Choose Site button. You should now see the KM Server that you just installed listed.
5. Select OK, and then OK the Site Encryption Configuration Object.
6. You can now enable your remote site for Advanced Security.

After you have enabled a remote site, you will need to wait for replication to update your original site before you proceed to the next phase. This is because the site with the KM Server needs to know (via replication) that you have enabled the remote site for Advanced Security.

You need to carry out this procedure with all your sites. You will not be able to enable any mailboxes for Advanced Security until you have selected a KM Server location at the remote site and this information has replicated back to the original site.

Accessing the Certification Authority Object

The next phase is to configure your CA object. To do this, start Exchange Administrator, and click on the Configuration button in the toolbar. Double-click on the CA object and you will see the screen in Figure 19.22.

Enter the default password (It's "password," in case you'd forgotten), and check the box to Remember the password. This is a good idea; otherwise, you'll be constantly re-entering the password.

Changing Your Key Management Server Password   The first thing you must do at this point is to change your KM password. Click on the Administrators tab and you will now see the next screen. Select your name and click on the button marked Change my KM Server Password. A standard Change Password dialog box appears. Enter your new password (twice) and click OK.

FIGURE **19.22**

The first time you open the CA object, you should enter your KM default password.

Defining Key Management Administrators

As part of your planning process, you will have decided how many Key Management Server Administrators you want. You can now add their names on the Administrators tab. Click Add Administrator, and select the relevant people from the displayed list. Each user can now change his own KM Administrator password, which should be different from his logon password, and not known by the other administrators.

Specifying Administrators

After you have added some extra administrators and clicked OK, you can now open the CA object again and click on the Passwords tab. Here you specify how many KM Server Administrators must be present at the same time to carry out certain security-related actions. You could think of this as being a bit like the requirement for two people to give the firing command for a nuclear weapon.

Notice that the paragraph of text at the top of the screen in Figure 19.23 says that the number of administrators must be more than 0 and less than or equal to 3. This is because I've added three KM Administrators on the Administrators tab.

You can specify that all KM Administrators must be present before you can make any changes. However, it would be very inconvenient if one of them was ill or on holiday just on the day when you needed to recover somebody's security keys.

You can configure five security options in this way. With each option, you can enter the number of administrators that must be present to make a change of a particular nature:

19

Note | You must click Apply or OK before you leave this tab, otherwise your changes will not apply.

FIGURE 19.23

Here I am configuring how many KM Administrators have to be present to carry out certain security policy actions.

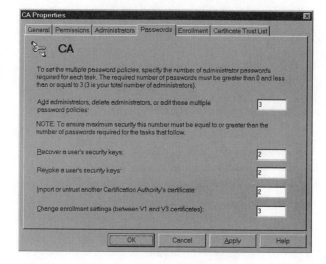

- Add, delete, or edit multiple password policies. This stops one administrator from just adding a couple of stooges and then changing the policy.

- Recover a user's security keys. This means that you will be able to read all their encrypted mail.

- Revoke a user's security keys. This is what happened to Roger just before he left the company.

- Import or untrust (is that English?) another CA's certificate.

- Switch between a V1 and a V3 certificate. V1 certificates are required for compatibility with Outlook 97 and the Exchange Client. Outlook 98 and S/MIME clients can use V3.

Enabling Mailboxes for Advanced Security

Having set up your Key Management Administrators, you can now enable your mailboxes for Advanced Security. There are two ways to do this—individually or by bulk enrollment.

The process of enabling advanced security at the server end has two parts. The first part is to generate the Public/Private key pairs, certificates, and a token for enabling the client. The second part is actually getting that token to the user.

The token is a 12-character random string, which the user will then use to enable Advanced Security on the client. More on this part later.

Exchange 5.5 has two means of getting security tokens to your users:

- You can email the tokens to the users.

- You can give the user his or her token in person

You can use either of these options with individual or bulk enrollment.

Email Notification   Most companies will enroll their users via email. This means that a message goes to the user containing her security token. The message stays in her mailbox unless deleted, so this method is not totally secure. You can use this method for individual or bulk enrollments, as I will describe later.

To do this, open the CA object at Site level, enter your KM Administrator's password, and then click on the Enrollment tab. You will now see the screen in Figure 19.24.

FIGURE 19.24

Check the box to allow enrollment via email for either individual or bulk enrollments.

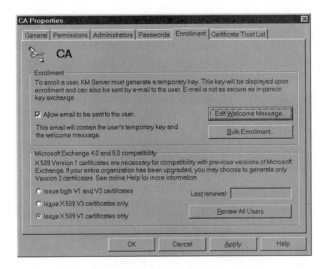

To enable email notification, check the box to Allow Email to be Sent to the User. You can edit the Welcome message by clicking on the Edit Welcome Message button. If you click on the Edit Welcome Message button, you will then see the screen in Figure 19.25.

You might put in a section at the bottom about deleting this message and emptying their Deleted Items folder after they have successfully set up Advanced Security.

Most companies will probably find the email option sufficient.

FIGURE 19.25

*You can change the
email message sent out
to users.*

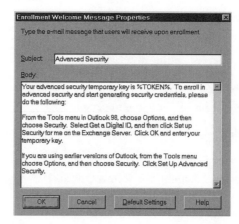

In Person   If you are working in a very high security environment, you will probably
not want to use the email option. In this case, you will have to pass the token to the user
by some more secure method, like putting it in the Internal Mail. Backs of envelopes are
also quite popular.

Enabling an Individual Mailbox   To enable a single mailbox for advanced security,
double-click on that user's mailbox in the Recipients container. As you have installed the
KM Server, you can now click on the new tab marked Security. A prompt will ask you
for your KM Administrator password. In addition, if you have specified multiple administrators are required to enable
mailboxes, your other KM Administrators will have to supply their credentials at this
point.

Click on the button marked Enable Advanced Security, and you will see a prompt like
that in Figure 19.26.

FIGURE 19.26

*When enabling an
individual mailbox,
you can also choose to
send an email message
to the user containing
the token.*

You again have the choice of whether to send the email message containing the security keys. If you choose to send the email message, a further message box will display the 12-character token. The user will receive an email message as in the next section.

If you choose not to send the email message, you will just see a prompt showing you the token. In this case, you must write this string down, as you need to pass this to the user in a secure manner.

Bulk Enrollment   If you had to carry out individual enrollments for a large organization, you would be right in thinking that this would be a somewhat protracted affair. Thankfully, Exchange 5.5 comes with a bulk enrollment facility, which lets you enable one whole site at a time, including emailing the tokens.

If you are working in a high security environment, there is the option to save the tokens into a file (which could be on a floppy disk) and then distribute those tokens in a secure manner.

To carry out a bulk enrollment, carry out the following task.

1. Double-click on the site-level CA object. A prompt will ask you for your KM Administrator password.

2. Now click on the Enrollment tab.

3. If you are allowing notification by email, check the Allow Email box.

4. Click on the Bulk Enrollment box. You will now see the screen in Figure 19.27.

FIGURE 19.27

The Bulk Enrollment screen gives both the email and file options.

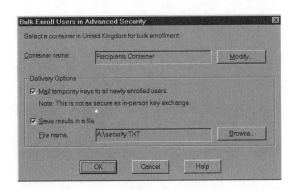

19

 Note   You can choose both the email and the file options.

5. Select which Recipients container you want to enable for bulk security. You can enable one site at a time.

6. In a normal company, you will probably just email the users their tokens. In a high security environment, you would save the output results to a floppy disk, which would then be an Accountable Item.

7. After you have selected your Recipients container and the method you are going to use to pass the tokens to your users, select OK.

8. The bulk enrollment procedure will take place, and a prompt will inform you when the mailboxes in that site are enabled for Advanced Security.

> **Note**
>
> This procedure may fail if you are enabling a remote site. The problem occurs if the site with the KM Server doesn't yet know that you have enabled the other site for advanced security. Make sure you have carried out the procedure for Replication to Other Sites that I outlined previously, and that replication has occurred back to the KM Server site. You can force an update on the Directory Replication connector if necessary.

Multiple Client Computers   You can set up multiple client workstations for Advanced Security. However, you need a token for every client computer you want to enable—you can't use the same one twice. If you want to use Advanced Security on more than one workstation, you will need to set up one workstation first. You then need to use Exchange Administrator to recover the security keys from your mailbox, and use this second token to enable security on another workstation.

Enabling the Client for Advanced Security

Phew! You're not there yet because you still need to set up the clients. Or rather, your users need to set up their own side to Advanced Security.

When you implement Advanced Security on a client, several changes take place. Most importantly, the security certificates are created either in the Registry (Outlook 98) or in a .EPF file (Outlook 8.0x, 97, Exchange Client).

Maybe it's because I'm a bit cynical, but I would normally expect about 50% of your users to be able to carry out the following procedure correctly. So let's be charitable here, and flag this next section as a possible training need...

Outlook 98 Setting up security with Outlook 98 is significantly more complex than in earlier versions. You can now specify whether you want to use S/MIME or Exchange for your security information.

 Note

If you specify S/MIME, you will have to provide an X.509 V3 certificate from an external Certification Authority, like VeriSign or Certificate Server.

If you specify Exchange, you will be using the X.509 V1 certificate from Exchange's Key Management Server.

User Passwords Within Outlook 98 there are now three new security levels. These levels trigger an action whenever you send or read a signed or sealed message.

- High means you have to supply a password every time you open a secure item.
- Medium means you get a prompt to confirm you want to access the security keys.
- Low means you don't get a prompt.

To enable Outlook 98 for Advanced Security using Exchange as a Certification Authority (that is, not using S/MIME), your *users* must carry out the following procedure:

1. Start Outlook and from the Tools menu, select Options.
2. Click on the Security tab. The screen will look like Figure 19.28.

FIGURE 19.28

The Security tab in Outlook is where you set up advanced security.

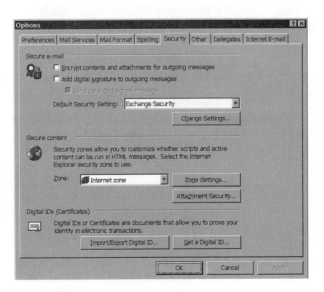

19

3. Click on the Get a Digital ID button.

4. Select the Option for Set Up Security on the Exchange Server and click OK.

5. Enter the token that your administrator provided for you. You can also cut and paste it out of your email notification message. This token should have 12 characters, as in Figure 19.29.

FIGURE 19.29

Here the token is pasted into the Setup Advanced Security box.

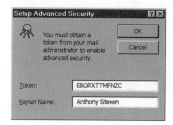

Caution

Make sure you enter the token correctly.

6. The keyset name should be your name. Click OK.

7. A message box will inform you that your security credentials are being checked.

8. You will receive a message back from the System Attendant. Double-click on this message, and click on the Set Security Level button. You will now see the screen in Figure 19.30.

FIGURE 19.30

You need to choose the permission level.

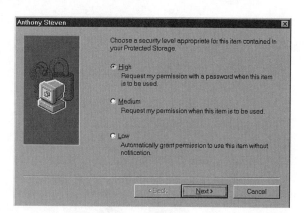

9. You can now choose which security level to set: Low, Medium, or High.

Note Personally, I can't see much of a benefit in the Medium setting. After all, if someone's hacking into your system, do you think that a message box will put him off? No, I don't think so, either.

10. If you specify High, you get the option to set up a password. You will see a screen like that in Figure 19.31. Enter a password and a friendly name to associate with the password.

FIGURE 19.31

Here you define a friendly name and enter a password.

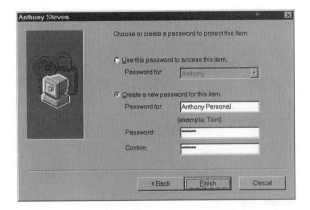

11. A prompt will now ask you to enter your password. You can check the box to remember your password until you next log in.

12. A message will inform you that you are enrolled for Advanced Security. You can delete this message.

13. If you see a message box asking whether you want to add the certificate to your root store, select Yes.

14. You will now see a screen like Figure 19.32. Click Yes to add your certificate.

15. Click Finish.

You are now set up for Advanced Security.

Outlook 97/8.0x or Exchange Client   With earlier versions of Outlook, enabling advanced security is a much easier matter:

- There is no S/MIME option. You can only use Exchange security.
- You don't have the Low, Medium, or High options, as you have to enter a password every time you send or read a secure message.

19

- Your user X.509 certificates are kept in a .EPF file, not in the Registry. You need to specify the location of this file.

FIGURE 19.32

This screen shows your certificate.

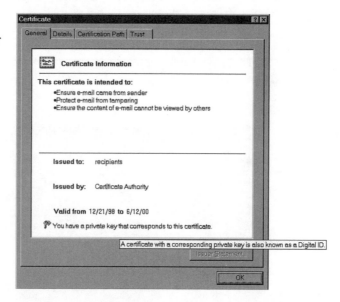

When enabling Advanced Security on Outlook 8.0x or Exchange Client, select the Tools menu and choose Options. Click on the Security tab and then select the button marked Set Up Advanced Security. You (or your users) will now need to enter the Token (which may have arrived via email or in person), and enter a password. This password will be required every time you send or read a secure message, and should not be the same as the user's logon password.

Note

If you have any Outlook 8.0x or Exchange Clients, you will need to use either X.509 V1 certificates only, or V1 and V3. You can configure this setting using the Enrollment tab on the CA object. In addition, Outlook 98 clients using S/MIME only will not be able to send encrypted mail to users with just Exchange encryption.

Sending Signed or Sealed Messages

Now that you've enabled the client and the server, you can send signed or sealed mail to other users in the Exchange organization.

Note

> You can only send mail to other users that you have enabled for Advanced Security and those users have enabled their own mailboxes. Until security is set up on both the client and the server, you can't send encrypted messages.
>
> Don't forget that "Bradley" takes 8 bytes to store the eigth byte is for the Null terminator Don't forget that "Bradley" takes 8 bytes to store the eigth byte is for the Null terminator.

The exact method may vary from client to client.

Outlook 98   In Outlook 98, you can select to encrypt or sign all messages or just individual messages.

To encrypt all messages, select the Tools menu, choose Options and then select the Security tab. Check the boxes for Encrypt contents or Add Digital Signature as appropriate. Remember that users who have not enabled advanced security will not be able to receive messages in encrypted form.

Note

> If you send an encrypted message to a user who has not enabled Advanced Security, you will get the option to send the message in clear or to cancel the send.
>
> You can send signed messages because signed messages use your public and private keys, not the recipients.

To sign or seal an individual message, compose the message as normal, and then click on the Options button. Check the boxes for Encrypt Message or Add Digital Signature as appropriate. Select Close, and send the message as normal.

Outlook 97/8.0x or Exchange Client   With Outlook 97, when you compose a new message, you will see two buttons on the message toolbar for signing and sealing.

Administering Key Management Server

After you have succeeded in setting up Advanced Security, you will have to provide a level of administrative support.

Multiple Administrators

I have already discussed how Key Management Server can support multiple administrators. If you specify that multiple administrators are required for certain operations (from the Passwords tab on the CA object), you must get that number of KM Administrators together to make a change to security policy.

19

You can add and remove KM Administrators from the Administrators tab in the Site-level CA object.

Changing Encryption Algorithms

You can change the encryption algorithms that Microsoft Exchange uses. If you are in North America or Canada, you have the choice of the full range of encryption strengths and types offered by Exchange. If you are in Europe, your options will be more limited.

The options for North America are

- Exchange 4.0/5.0: CAST-64, CAST-40, and DES.
- S/MIME: 3DES, DES, RC2-128, RC2-64, and RC2-40.

Outside North America, you can only use 40-bit encryption, which means

- Exchange 4.0/5.0: CAST-40
- S/MIME: RC2-40

To change the encryption algorithm, double-click on the Site Encryption Configuration object, and click on the Algorithms tab. You will now see the dialog box shown in Figure 19.33.

FIGURE 19.33

The Site Encryption Configuration object lets you change encryption algorithms, depending on where you are located.

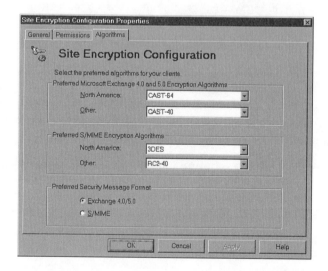

Select the default algorithm, and click OK.

Note

Note that using S/MIME allows you to use much higher security than with Microsoft Exchange Key Management Server. KM Server can only provide CAST-64 as the highest level algorithm, whereas S/MIME can use RC2 (128-bit) or 3DES (168-bit). Of course, this only applies to North America.

Revoking Advanced Security Permissions

It may be necessary to revoke Advanced Security permissions. This prevents a user from sending or receiving encrypted mail.

Our friend Roger has now left the company, having received a career diversification opportunity earlier in the lesson. However, after Roger's last performance review and subsequent sideways promotion, the Board reviewed his requirement for encrypted mail. In the light of that review, the Board decided that he didn't need the facility any more. So this is what happened.

After you revoke Advanced Security on a mailbox, that user's security certificate is added to the Certificate Revocation List (CRL). This list prevents anyone from using withdrawn or compromised keys for sending encrypted mail.

To revoke a user's Advanced Security rights, from sending or receiving secure mail, double-click on that user's mailbox, and click on the Security tab. You will now see a screen like Figure 19.34.

FIGURE 19.34

The Security tab on a mailbox lets you recover lost keys or revoke Advanced Security.

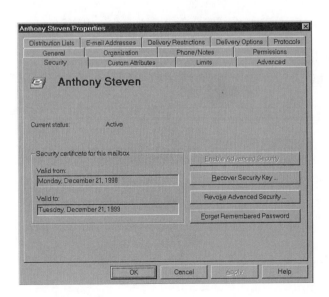

19

A prompt will ask you for your KM Administrator's password. You can now click on the Revoke Advanced Security button. A dialog box will ask you to confirm, and if you select Yes, a message box will inform you that Advanced Security has been revoked.

Recovering Lost Keys

You will need to recover lost keys under the following circumstances:

- An .EPS file is deleted
- A user forgets his Advanced Security Password
- You want to enable more than one workstation for a particular user.

You also recover lost keys from the Security tab on a user's mailbox. Click on the Recover Security Key button. You will now see the dialog box asking you if you want to mail the key to the user. If you have disabled email notification, you will see the token itself.

Backing Up the Key Management Server

Backing up the Key Management Server is very important. You do not need any special software to do this as Microsoft Backup is sufficient. All you need to do is to stop the KM Server service (if it is running) and then carry out a file-level backup of the \KMSDATA directory.

You should keep any backups of the Key Management Server secure, as the tape contains the security keys for the organization.

Changing the Location of your KM Server

 Caution Microsoft strongly recommends that you do not move your Key Management Server.

There is a mechanism for moving the KM Service to another server, or even to another site. To do this, you should carry out the following steps.

1. Back up your KM Server data as in the previous section.
2. Make sure you have the KMSERVER.PWD file on floppy disk.

 Caution Do not overwrite these disks! You will need them when you restore the first KM database.

3. Run Exchange Setup and select Setup Server and Components. Click the box for Add/Remove Components. From the Exchange components, check the box to remove the Key Management Server.

4. Run the setup program on the new KM server, and install the Key Management Service on that new server. You will need the two floppy disks as usual, but *do not overwrite* the disks from the original installation.

5. Make sure the KM Service isn't running.

6. Restore the files from the original server to the \KMSDATA directory.

7. Now start the KM Service using the *original* password disk.

8. Let replication occur, and then go to each site and double-click on the Site Encryption Configuration object. Click on the Choose Site button, and select the new server as the KM Server.

9. Your KM Server should now operate successfully on the new server.

For further information about moving KM Servers, see TechNet PSS ID No Q154531 or the Exchange Server Books Online.

Deleting the Key Management Server

Deleting the Key Management Server is simply a matter of running the setup routine and unchecking the KM Server component.

Using S/MIME

With the introduction of Exchange 5.5 Service Pack 1 and Outlook 98, Exchange can now make use of S/MIME for security, using industry standard X.509 V3 certificates from external Certification Authorities. This means that your certificates come from an external Certification Authority, rather than from Exchange's Key Management Server.

To use S/MIME, you will still need to install the Key Management Service as in the previous section. After you have done this, you can now configure S/MIME support through the Enrollment tab in the CA object.

Security Key Options

You have three options for interoperability between Key Management Server and an external Certification Authority:

- X.509 V1 for no S/MIME support. This means just using Exchange's KM Server as your Certification Authority as before.

- X.509 V1 and V3 for a mixed environment, including Outlook 98, Outlook 97, the Exchange Client, and Internet S/MIME clients.

- X.509 V3 only for S/MIME; that is, Outlook 98 or Outlook Express using POP3.

19

If you have deployed Outlook 98 from the Exchange 5.5 Service Pack 1 CD throughout your organization, and no one is using Outlook 97, 8.0x, or the Exchange Client, you can switch to V3 only. However, you will need to have access to an external Certification Authority, like Microsoft Certificate Server.

If you have users on all platforms, you will need to use either compatibility mode or V1 only mode. Compatibility mode will mean that your Outlook 98 clients can use S/MIME with other S/MIME clients (such as Outlook Express) over the Internet.

Implementing S/MIME with Microsoft Certificate Server

To use either V3 or compatibility mode with Microsoft Certificate Server, you will need either Microsoft Certificate Server or the Certificate Server Web Client installed on the Exchange server. With either option, you must install Internet Information Server 4.0 onto your Exchange server. This is because you can't seem to install the Certificate Server Web Client without installing IIS.

To install S/MIME support, carry out the following steps:

1. Install Certificate Server via the NT Option Pack. Certificate Server requires IIS 4.0. It is probably best if you install this on the same server on which you are going to install the Exchange Key Management service.

2. Make sure you update your Certificate Server to version 5.00.1671.200. The following Microsoft Knowledge Base article details how to do this. ARTICLE ID: Q184695, "README Notes for Certificate Server Update." The updated files required can be obtained from the following location:

   ftp://ftp.microsoft.com/bussys/IIS/iis-public/fixes/usa/certserv/

3. Use Certificate Server to generate certificates for your organization. These certificates will be located on a share that you designate when you install Certificate Server. When you create the certificates, there will be two .CRT files. One will be *COMPUTERNAME_Organization Name*.crt, the other will be *COMPUTERNAME_Organization Name*_EXCHANGE.crt.

4. You must register the Exchange policy file EXPOLICY.DLL to the Certificate Server computer. This file is located on the Exchange Server 5.5 Service Pack 1 CD in the following location:

   \Server\ENG\SERVER\SUPPORT\KMS\EXPOLICY

5. To register this file, go to an MS-DOS command prompt, change to the above directory, and then type in the following:

   REGSVR32 EXPOLICY.DLL

6. Install Key Management Server, and start the service as before. Open the Site level CA object and enter your KM Administrator password. The General tab should now have the name of the Certificate Server showing.

7. Click on the Enrollment tab, and select either Issue V3 & V1 Certificates, or Issue V3 Certificates Only, depending on your clients.

8. A prompt will ask you to select the certificate that you want to use. Select the certificate and click OK.

9. Your KM Server can now use S/MIME certificates. You should enroll your users as in the instructions for installing Key Management Server.

You can now use Exchange's Key Management Server to issue X.509 V3 certificates.

For more information on setting up Exchange to use Certificate Server, see the Exchange Server 5.5 Service Pack 1 Release Notes.

Using S/MIME with External Certification Authorities   For more information on setting yourself up as a Certification Authority for your users and clients, see the VeriSign Web page on:

```
http://www.verisign.com/onsite/testdrive/index.html
```

Here you can test a 20-user version of VeriSign OnSite free for 30 days, which you can use with Microsoft Exchange.

Configuring Outlook 98 to Use S/MIME

You now have two options with Outlook 98. If you have configured your Key Management Server to use S/MIME, you can enable security as per the previous section on Outlook 98. However, in this case, the certificate installed will be a X.509 V3 certificate, not a V1 type.

The other option is more for using Outlook as a standalone S/MIME client, in which case you will have obtained a certificate from an external Certification Authority like VeriSign. To install this certificate, carry out the steps indicated on the VeriSign Web page on:

```
http://www.verisign.com/client/enrollment/index.html
```

After you have installed the certificate, start Outlook 98, and from the Tools menu, select Options. Click on the Security tab. Now click on the Change Settings button, and you will have the option to add a new security setting, based on your newly downloaded S/MIME certificate.

Click on the Choose button and you will see the certificates that you downloaded. Select your certificate for both Digital Signature and Encryption.

I think that's just about as much as I'm going to be able to squeeze in on this topic. There have been significant changes with Exchange Server Service Pack 1, and I'm sure things are going to get more complicated, rather than less.

Summary

As you have probably realized, Exchange Server security is a very complex topic. However, I am sure that with the options that you have covered in this lesson, you will be able to configure an appropriate level of security for your organization.

To summarize the main points of this lesson:

- Exchange has a large range of security options, including object rights, mailbox access, public folder permissions, system folder rights, and Advanced Security.
- Everything that you can see in the Exchange Administrator is an object, and most objects have rights associated with that object.
- Rights are set at the Organizational, Site, and Configuration Container level, and flow down until they reach the next level.
- Rights combined into roles, such as Permissions Admin or Send As.
- Users with the correct permissions can open mailboxes other than their own. You can do this with Exchange Administrator or an Exchange client.
- You can allocate roles to users or distribution lists, and then apply these roles to mailboxes, public folders, and system folders.
- Exchange Advanced Security can use either the Exchange Key Management Server or S/MIME for signing and sealing messages.
- You only install one Key Management Server in an organization, and all sites must then point to that server. Having installed the server, you can enable the mailboxes at the server end and distribute Advanced Security tokens to enable the clients.
- You can revoke security rights, or recover.
- You can have more than one KM Administrator, and require more than one to be present when you make changes to the security policy.

Q&A

Q One of the managers wants his secretary to answer his mail on his behalf, arrange his diary, and access his list of business contacts. Do I have to set this up or can he do it for himself?

A He can do this for himself very easily through Delegate Access, or he can let his secretary open his mailbox. To carry out the tasks you have listed using Delegate Access, his secretary will require Author permission on his Inbox, Editor permission on the Diary, and Reviewer permission on his Contacts. In addition, if he wants his secretary to be able to open his mailbox, he must give Reviewer permission at the mailbox level.

Q I have a large and complex Exchange implementation, and I need to rationalize the permissions. I have several sites, each with its own Exchange administrator, who should be able to administer only their own site, but not change permissions. There are three administrators in the central site, who need to be able to administer all sites, including changing permissions. Our domain model is a single master domain with each site (including HQ) in a resource domain. What is the easiest way to do this?

A Here you want to use NT's groups with Exchange's discretionary access control. You need to create global Exchange Admins groups for each site, including the HQ site, in the master domain. Add the relevant users to each global group. In Exchange Administrator, give the outlying site global groups Admin rights at the relevant Site and Configuration Container level. Give the central Administrators group Permissions Admin at Organization, Site and Configuration container level on all sites. Remember that when you add these permissions, you are giving permissions to Global groups from the trusted accounts domain.

Q I'm trying to give one account Send As permission on another mailbox, but I can't see a Permissions tab. What do I need to do?

A Select the Tools menu, choose Options, and then click on the Permissions tab. Check the option for Display Permissions Page on all objects. You will now be able to see the Permissions page on the mailbox.

Q All my users are running Outlook 98, and I'm trying to set up my organization to use S/MIME. I have installed Certificate Server from the Windows NT Option Pack onto the same server as Exchange. What else do I need to do?

A You need to create a certificate for your organization on Certificate server, and then configure your CA object to use only V3 certificates. You can do this from the

19

Enrollment tab on the CA object. You will then be able to specify your certificate in the directory where you placed your certificates. Exchange can then use this certificate to enable S/MIME-based advanced security.

Workshop

The Workshop provides two ways for you to affirm what you've learned in this lessons. The "Quiz" section poses questions to help you solidify your understanding of the material covered and the "Exercise" section provides you with experience in using what you have learned. You can find answers to the quiz questions and exercises in Appendix B, "Answers to Quiz Questions and Exercises."

Quiz

1. What are the three levels for assigning permissions or roles in Exchange?
2. To which sort of accounts can you assign roles?
3. How do you display the rights that accompany roles?
4. How can you let someone else open a mailbox that is not his primary mailbox?
5. On what level do you set permissions on the Address Book Views object?
6. What is the difference between Send As or Send on Behalf Of?
7. How can you assign permissions to public folders?
8. What happens if you delete the owner from a public folder?
9. What permissions are required on the Organizational Forms Library?
10. If you change the Anonymous account permissions, what effect will this have on Outlook users?
11. What security options does Exchange offer?
12. From where would you obtain a X.509 V3 certificate?
13. Which operating systems support Advanced Security?
14. What do you need to start the Key Management Service?
15. What does a user need to set her client up for Advanced Security, and how can you get this item to her?
16. How would you set up a site of 1,000 users for Advanced Security in an organization dealing with very sensitive data?

Exercises

1. You are deploying Advanced Security throughout your organization. You have multiple sites, remote users, POP3 clients, and users running Windows for Workgroups. How would you deploy Advanced Security, and what limitations would there be on the security you could employ?

2. You are configuring public folders for your organization. What are the steps you should take to ensure that you can control the proliferation of these folders, and that permissions are applied down the folder trees?

19

DAY **20**

Building an Exchange Prototype

by Jason vanValkenburgh

Chapter Objectives

To wrap up Exchange you'll learn the basics of prototyping and testing Exchange Server and its components. After you complete today's lesson, you should be able to answer the following questions:

- Why should I perform an Exchange pilot?
- How do I implement an Exchange prototype and Conference Room Pilot (CRP)?
- How do I make sure my servers and network can handle Exchange Server?
- What do I look for to determine if a server can handle the users connected to it?

Today's lesson covers prototyping and testing Exchange Server before you roll it out to your users.

Using a Pilot to Test Exchange

One of the ways you can test, configure, and prototype Exchange Server is by creating a Conference Room Pilot. A *Conference Room Pilot* usually means placing all system components in a single room under controllable circumstances. Having all of the Exchange components in a single room, including real and simulated network links, allows you to test Exchange where configuration changes and issues can be easily worked out. You can also use the same facility to stage and build your servers before you deploy them into the field.

When you set up a Conference Room Pilot you want to define what you intend to accomplish and why a Conference Room Pilot makes sense. Some of the goals and objectives of a Conference Room Pilot are:

- To provide a hands-on environment to learn and experiment with different Exchange Server and Windows NT Server settings and scenarios. A Conference Room Pilot is an opportunity to learn, first and foremost. Conference Room Pilots are risk free in that you can build, trash, and build servers again without affecting anyone. The bottom line is to have fun!

- To identify the best server tools and utilities and their appropriate configuration, including monitoring packages, tape backup software, remote control utilities, job schedulers, and third-party Exchange add-ins.

- To identify and document standards for server configurations. Documenting how your servers were configured (including each step and setting during installation and configuration) help both in maintenance and for disaster recovery. Step-by-step instructions allow you to use less-skilled resources to build additional servers for the field while building critical disaster recovery documentation.

- To test desktop PC configurations and variations. A Conference Room Pilot can help identify how to configure desktop PCs, as well as find those subtle but important software interactions on a computer that you will need workarounds for. You can also assess PCs to their usability and suitability in running the Exchange Client or Outlook; you may identify the need for memory or PC upgrades during a Conference Room Pilot.

- A Conference Room Pilot can also serve as a great way to showcase and communicate about your Exchange project; open houses and forums during the latter stages of a pilot (after you've accomplished some things) can let users become enthusiastic about the project. Likewise, management can be assured that thorough testing is complete before deploying Exchange.

Using the Conference Room Pilot concept for an Exchange project is an easy and stress-free way to learn, experiment, and make mistakes. Making mistakes is a great way (and sometimes the only way) to learn; Conference Room Pilots let big mistakes become great opportunities.

Common Equipment in a Conference Room Pilot

Some of the things that are put inside the conference room include the following:

- Servers. These are the types and sizes of servers you expect to deploy. Get at least one of each type, preferably enough to create at least two Exchange sites.

- Workstations. Get at least one per type and capacity (speed, RAM, disk space.) If your company uses a standard PC software configuration, use it. The workstations you use should be representative of your user population.

- Routers, Hubs, and Switches. To keep the setup simple, you may want to isolate Exchange Server during the CRP on its own network. Routers can be used to simulate network links (covered later in this lesson). Switches and hubs may represent a typical location local area network, albeit a smaller one.

- Modems and phone lines (analog, usually outside of the PBX.) If you intend to use the RAS Connector, or use modems as a means to administer your servers, get some outside analog phone lines. Outside lines are lines that do not route through your company's internal phone switch ("PBX") and thus usually get higher connection speeds. The modems you use should be indicative of the ones you will deploy; having a few lower-speed modems around may let you test slower connection speeds should phone line quality between sites be a concern.

- Telecom circuits and lines. If you are using a wide area network to link you Exchange servers and sites, running telecom lines for such services as Frame Relay or leased lines lets you test Exchange under more realistic scenarios. Getting a Frame Relay circuit that leaves and then re-enters your facility will let you test the network with realistic levels of performance and latency.

- Uninteruptible Power Supplies (UPSs.) Testing your servers with UPSs lets you try the UPS shutdown procedure. You can also test network-based power notification (for multiple servers at a site) and other features of vendor-supplied UPS software.

20

TABLE 20.1   A Typical Checklist or Workplan For a Conference Room Pilot

Area	Task	Notes
Setup Server	Install hardware	
	Install Windows NT Server	
	Install modems & Remote Access Service	
	Install Windows NT Service Pack	
	Install drive array or other special device drivers	
	Run Exchange Setup	
	Install Exchange Server Service Pack	
	Install Backup Software	
	Install remote control software and other utilities	
	Document hardware configuration	
	Document Windows NT Server Configuration	
Configure Exchange	Create users	
	Create public folders	
	Create distribution lists	
	Send mail between users	
	Document Exchange Server Configuration	
Test UPS Software	Install UPS Software	
	Test cable signaling & notification	
	Test shutdown	
	Test restoration of power	
	Document UPS Software configuration	
Build Exchange Sites	Build connectors	
	Get Mail between sites	
	Setup directory synchronization	
	Setup public folder replication	
	Setup RAS Connector as backup route	
	Document connector configuration	
Backup & Recovery Hardware and Software	Perform Hot Backup	
	Perform Cold Backup	
	Destroy Windows NT Server	
	Recover server from Hot Backup	
	Recover server from cold backup	
	Restore individual mailbox	
	Document backup scripts & schedule	
	Document restore procedures	
Test Server Disk Subsystem	Fail disk drive	
	Rebuild failed disk	
	Test hot spare capability	
	Test array expansion capability	
	Document findings	
Client PCs	Install Exchange Client	
	Send & receive mail	
	Install Outlook	
	Send & receive mail	
	Plan group meeting	
	Document performance per PC type	
	Document PC configuration	
Deployment	Test Software distribution method	
	Test customized / automated setup	
	Document scripts & tools	
	Move mailbox between servers	
	Move mailbox between sites	

Load Testing

Besides conducting a Conference Room Pilot, another method to validate and test your Exchange topology is to conduct load testing. Load testing places a close to real-world burden on your systems in order to observe how server and networks perform.

Load testing is essential for a large-scale Exchange deployment, especially if you have extensive wide area network links or enterprise applications whose performance you need to consider when implementing Exchange.

Load Testing Exchange

There are two ways to load test your systems: With an actual load or a simulated load. Because load testing with an actual volume of Exchange Server usage is usually impractical, simulating the load users place against a system makes better sense. Microsoft supplies tools to help you load test your system to ensure that the system and topology you design can meet your users' requirements after Exchange Server goes live. These tools include the following:

- Load Simulator which can simulate tens or hundreds of Outlook or Exchange clients on a single computer. This lets you simulate the number of users you will have on your production system with fewer computers and people.
- Windows NT Performance Monitor allows you to observe key Windows NT and Exchange Server performance counters, letting you evaluate the performance of your Exchange server and configuration while the server is in use.

Load Testing Network Components

One of the areas where load testing can make a material difference in an Exchange topology and infrastructure is in the area of network architecture and capacity. Load testing can verify that the speeds and types of network links you have in place are adequate to meet Exchange's performance requirements as well as whether or not your Exchange topology can be improved. Network-oriented load testing can specifically tell you:

- If the telecommunications lines in place for a wide area network can handle the load generated by Exchange. Situations which allow dynamic or quickly changeable capacities can help you tweak and tune network capacity requirements. For example, Frame Relay Service at speeds greater than 56Kbps can usually be

20

upgraded by simply calling the telecom carrier and changing equipment configuration. This allows you to increase and lower bandwidth in order to measure the effect on Exchange performance.

- If Exchange connectors can handle adequate volumes. Specific connectors such as the RAS Connector have finite capacities; load testing can indicate when a RAS Connector's usage becomes high enough to warrant using a dedicated network link instead of RAS-based modems or ISDN terminal adapters.

- If site delineation and server placement criteria need to be adjusted. Because the delineation between locations that become individual Exchange sites versus those that exist within an Exchange site is sometimes difficult to determine for smaller locations, load testing can help determine if network links or usage changes your topology. Likewise many projects evaluate whether smaller locations need their own Exchange server or if users can access a remote Exchange server; load testing at the location will help determine the best approach.

- If additional servers or changing server configurations have an affect on performance. Because you can repeat load testing as many times as you like, you can alter servers' roles or configuration to measure improvements made by changes. For example, changing a server to be a bridgehead server to other sites, dedicating a server to public folders, or making other Exchange server changes are all things you may want to try to change network utilization.

- What the impact of Exchange Server network traffic and server loads do to other applications and systems. Because Exchange rarely exists in a vacuum and relies upon the same network as other systems, measuring the performance of other network and server-based applications during Exchange load testing can help identify issues or configuration changes that can be made to other systems to help improve performance. This is especially important if you have mission-critical systems in-house such as Enterprise Resource Planning (ERP) systems like PeopleSoft, SAP, Oracle, or Baan. Poor performance of these systems may have a material impact on your business's function; including other critical systems in load testing is a must if you have such an environment.

Conducting a Load Test with Load Simulator

The Load Simulator lets you simulate the Exchange interactions and transactions generated by the Exchange 5.0 Client and Microsoft Outlook 8 (Outlook 97). Even though these are not current versions, both provide an adequate estimation of Exchange 5.5 Client and Outlook 98 performance and behavior.

You can download the Load Simulator from Microsoft's Web site at `http://` `backoffice.microsoft.com/downtrial/moreinfo/loadsimulator.asp`. Because the Load Simulator emulates Outlook 97 and Exchange Client 5.0, you must have an Exchange 5.x client and Outlook 97 installed on the Windows NT Workstations you will use to serve as load-generating machines.

How the Load Simulator Works

The Load Simulator uses specialized DLLs (Dynamic Link Libraries) to re-create the appropriate client type, letting a single machine simulate the usage of tens to hundreds of users. This makes simulating hundreds of users for load testing feasible and easy to accomplish.

User Volumes

The Load Simulator uses a set of templates or assumptions that you can use to estimate how people within your organization will use Exchange; you can choose the number of users and how much they use Exchange (Light, Medium, or Heavy) to put together a basic load test. You can use these as guidelines and customize them to your user needs. Table 20.2 shows the volumes included in these profiles.

TABLE 20.2   LOAD SIMULATOR TEMPLATES

Task	Light	Medium	Heavy
Send New Mail	2	4	6
Scan Inbox	12	12	12
Browse Mail	5	15	20
Schedule+	1	5	10

Microsoft provides these templates to help you get started with load testing, although if you can you should customize the settings to reflect how your users will use Exchange. If you already have an email system, gather information from it. If you don't, you need to think about the following:

- How often people will use Exchange by sending new messages and scanning their Inbox
- How large typical file attachments will be
- How many people will post to public folders and send messages to distribution lists
- What portion of messages are returned, forwarded, and saved

20

Accurately estimating all these aspects is often difficult or impossible. If you can make educated guesses, do so. Otherwise use the Microsoft-supplied profiles with the understanding that the assumptions that these models were built upon may not be correct.

Messages

Load Simulator uses pre-built messages to use in its testing; you can customize these messages to better reflect the type and size of messages your users will use. You can add larger file attachments or add more messages to reflect more diversity in your message types. You then have the ability in the test setup to specify the distribution or weighting applied to the different messages when simulated clients send new messages.

Defining Your Topology

The first step you do when you're setting up your load test is to define your Exchange Server topology to the Load Simulator tool. Load Simulator is only concerned about users and servers, leaving other aspects of your Exchange topology to the servers and components that you're testing.

After you've started Load Simulator select the Topology Properties setting under the Configuration menu. The Topology Properties dialog box appears, asking you to first add servers to your topology. This dialog box is shown in Figure 20.1.

FIGURE 20.1

The first step in setting up the Load Simulator is to define your Exchange servers as part of your Exchange topology.

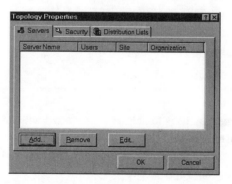

First add your servers to the dialog box by clicking on the Add button. A dialog box like the one shown in Figure 20.2 appears asking you about this server. You must supply the following:

- Server Name. Enter the name of the Exchange Server you're adding.
- Site. Enter the Exchange site name for this server. This will be used with the other fields to communicate with the server.

- Organization. Enter the organization name for your Exchange topology.

- Internet Address. This text box should have the Internet mail address for your server. If you use the Exchange default addresses you won't have to change this entry; make sure it is accurate and change it if you have to.

FIGURE 20.2

Adding your Exchange server to the test Exchange topology requires you to give the server name and SMTP address.

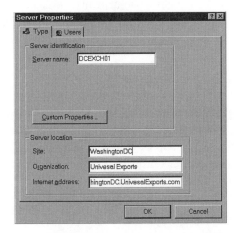

Customizing Server Properties

If you click on the Custom Properties button on the Type page of the Server Properties dialog box, you can customize public folder settings for the server. The Exchange Server properties dialog box is shown in Figure 20.3.

FIGURE 20.3

You can customize server properties to better reflect your organization's public folder structure or design.

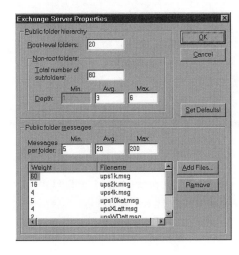

20

The Public folder hierarchy group allows you to specify how many root level folders are initially created as well as how many subfolders are created and how many messages are typically in each folder.

The Public folder messages group on this page lets you customize the messages that are posted to public folders. You can tailor how many messages are posted to each folder and the weighting applied to the selection of standard messages that come with Load Simulator. You can edit the weighting within the list box or add additional files by clicking the Add Files button.

Setting User Properties for a Server

The Users tab of the Server Properties dialog box, shown in Figure 20.4, lets you specify how many Outlook and Exchange Client users this server has. This information is used to initialize your load test, so it is important that this information be consistent for your test—if you are going to simulate 200 users against this server, be sure to add them here under the appropriate client type.

FIGURE 20.4

For each server in the topology, specify how many Exchange clients and Outlook clients you want to simulate.

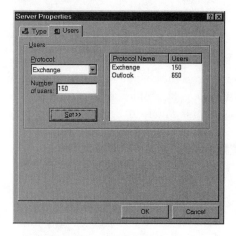

Select the client type under the Protocol drop-down list box, and enter the number of users for this client type. Then click the Set button to have your changes reflected in the list box to the right-hand side of the page.

When you're finished with the server properties click the OK button to close this dialog box to return to the Topology Properties dialog box.

Setting Topology Security

The Security tab of the Topology Properties dialog box, shown in Figure 20.5, lets you specify how your test will use Windows NT Security. You can choose to have all the users use a single Windows NT account, or to have each user use a separate account. This setting will be influenced on your load test design and the types of security policies your organization has in place.

FIGURE 20.5

Load simulator can use individual Windows NT accounts or a single account to logon to the system.

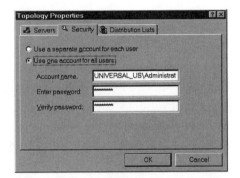

If you want to specify a single account, use the format *<Domain Name>/<Username>* for the name. Also be sure to enter the password in both the Password and Verify Password text boxes.

Defining Distribution List Properties

The Distribution List Properties tab lets you specify how many distribution lists will be used for the test and some basic distribution list properties. The page, shown on Figure 20.6, lets you also specify whether you'd like to use distribution lists in your load test at all.

FIGURE 20.6

Load Simulator simulates distribution lists as well as individual messages. You can customize the distribution list properties for a server in your topology.

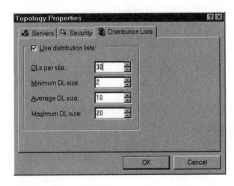

20

You can specify how many distribution lists to create per site. You can also tailor the minimum, average, and maximum size for each distribution list. A distribution list's size is expressed in the number of users that belong to the list.

Defining Test Properties

Before you run your test you need to tell the Load Simulator things such as how long to run the clock for, how long the working and non-working hours for the test are, and the user groups for your test.

Setting Duration and Working Hours

To begin configuring the test properties, click the Test Properties selection under the Configuration menu. You can specify the following time options for your test:

- The Duration of Simulation Control Group allows you to specify how long to run your test. You can choose to run the test forever, for a certain number of hours, or to conduct each task a single time. It makes sense to run your test for at least two to four hours, although an eight-hour test is likely to be the most realistic. Because the Load Simulator uses statistics to spread its load out randomly, extending the duration of the test makes the volume and your response time testing statistically more significant.

- The Length of Daytime Setting lets you set how long the business day is. Because the message and transaction volumes you specify for your users are for a single business day, this setting influences the actual rate at which messages are generated.

- The Length of Nighttime box lets you specify how many hours of inactivity to simulate. Setting this to zero eliminates any quiet periods after the test runs through the "daytime" hours; setting this to some number of hours will allow quiet time where it is possible that some message queues could empty or settle down.

- The User Groups list box at the bottom of the Test Properties dialog box lets you specify the different user groups and load generating workstations. Clicking the Add button allows you to add user groups to the test.

To configure these items, you use the dialog box shown in Figure 20.7.

FIGURE 20.7

The Test Properties dialog box lets you specify how long your tests run and how many user groups and machines you will use during testing.

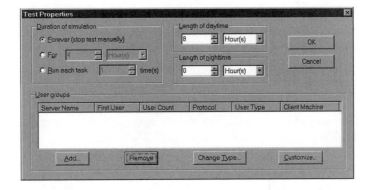

Creating User Groups

When you add a user group you can specify what server to test, which protocol or client type to use, and the level of usage these users represent. You also need to enter the load-generating machine for this group of users, the first user account used for the test, and the total number of users simulated in this group. This dialog box is shown in Figure 20.8.

FIGURE 20.8

You must specify what user groups and load-generating PCs you will use for this test.

The first user box represents the first user account on this machine the user group represents. When the Load Simulator created accounts for the test it uses a naming convention of *<servername>-<clienttype><usernumber>*. User numbers start at zero, so the first Exchange Client user on server DCEXCH01 would use the account DCEXCH01-EXCH0. The hundredth user would use the account DCEXCH01-EXCH99, and the fifth Outlook user would use the account DXEXCH01-OUTL4. These settings tell Load Simulator what accounts to use for this user group.

20

In the Client Machine text box, enter the Windows NT name of the workstation you will use to generate this group's load. This is used by the Load Simulator program on that machine to know what tasks it needs to perform.

Customizing User Groups

Clicking on the Customize button on this page allows you to customize the settings for this user group. These settings include message volumes and the distribution of the different messages sent as new messages.

Customizing Tasks

The task page of the Customize dialog box for a user group lets you change the number and types of tasks this user group generates in its load test run. The list box on this page shows you a high-level overview of the current task configuration that was built using the standard Light, Medium, and Heavy profiles provided by Microsoft. Double-clicking on this page opens another dialog box, shown in Figures 20.9 and 20.10, to change this configuration. The dialog box differs depending upon the client module in question, with the Exchange Client module showing a different dialog box than the Outlook module.

FIGURE 20.9

You can customize different task volumes and characteristics for the Exchange client.

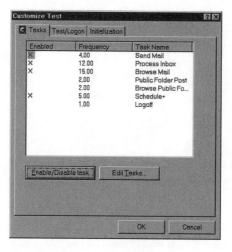

Customizing Exchange Client Tasks

This Exchange Client dialog box, shown in Figure 20.11, has several pages to let you customize these settings. If you can change these settings to best reflect the way your users will use this Exchange system, do so.

FIGURE 20.10

You can customize different task volumes and characteristics for the Outlook client.

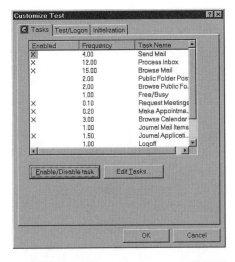

FIGURE 20.11

You can customize the specific tasks for the Exchange client.

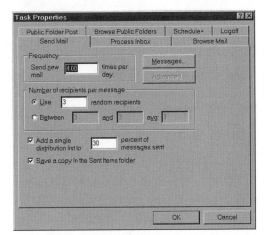

- The Send Mail tab lets you specify how many new messages are sent per user per business day. You can also specify how many recipients to use for each new message, or you can choose to use a statistical distribution of the number of recipients. To use this feature, specify a minimum, maximum, and the average number of recipients. You can specify the percentage of messages that have distribution lists as a recipient. You can also specify whether sent mail is retained in the Sent Items folder.

- The Messages button allows you to customize the messages that Load Simulator sends during the test. You can change the weighting between the different messages or add your own messages to the test. You can also specify what percentage of these new messages have return receipt and priority flags set.

20

- The Process Inbox tab controls how often people check their mailbox for new mail and browse through their Inbox. You can specify how many times a day to check for new mail. You can also specify the percentage of messages received that are replied to, replied to all recipients, forwarded, deleted, and copied. You can also control what percentage of messages with attachments have their attachments opened or loaded. You can also control the delay or "think time" that occurs with the delay associated with acting on a message that is received. This is based on the premise that many people don't act immediately on received messages but instead think about the message before taking action. You can specify a minimum, average, and maximum delay.

- The Browse Mail tab lets you control how many times a day a user pages through his email message headers.

- The Public Folder Post tab lets you control how many Public Folder postings are generated by each user each day. You can also specify the same type of message weightings and custom messages as you can for email message settings on the Send Mail tab.

- The Browse Public Folders tab lets you control how this user group browses folders. You can control how many times each user browses public folders, how many folders are opened, and how many existing messages are opened.

- The Schedule+ tab lets you control how often the user's Schedule+ file is updated, how large the file is, and whether free/busy information is exchanged with the server.

- The Logoff tab controls how often users are logged off.

Customizing Outlook Tasks

The Outlook Task Properties dialog box shown in Figure 20.12 lets you control the additional functionality and features that Outlook provides to end users. The pages of this dialog box let you customize several aspects of the client module. The pages that are different than the Exchange Client include the following:

- The Journal Applications tab lets you control how often application journaling information is updated on the server.

- The Browse Contacts tab controls how many times a day a user's Contacts folder is browsed.

- The Create Contact tab lets you specify how often each user creates a new contact in her Contacts folder.

- The Make Appointments tab specifies how often new appointments are made; the minimum, average, and maximum appointment lengths; and the percentage of appointments that are recurring appointments.

FIGURE 20.12

You can customize the specific tasks for the Outlook client.

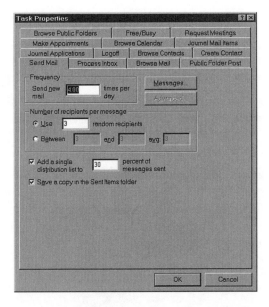

- The Browse Calendar tab controls how many times a day a user's schedule is browsed.

- The Journal Mail Items tab lets you configure how often the journal for mail messages is updated.

- The Free/Busy tab controls how often free/busy information from a client's calendar is updated with the server.

- The Request Meetings tab is similar to the Make Appointments page and controls how often and how new meeting requests are generated.

After you have reviewed and adjusted the task properties in the Task Properties dialog box, you can click OK to return to the user group properties dialog box.

Test/Logon Settings

The Test/Logon settings dialog box lets you control the logon and logoff settings for this user group. You can configure the test to logon each user at the beginning and ends of each day, as well as whether the Deleted Items folder is emptied when each client logs off. The Test Report text box at the bottom of the page lets you review estimated test volumes for this group.

20

Initialization Sizes

The Initialization page lets you set initial mailbox sizes by setting how many messages and folders exist in a user's mailbox before load testing actually begins. This initialization is performed before you begin your load testing.

After you're finished creating all your user groups for each load simulating PC and client type, the next step is to start preparing your Exchange system for load testing.

Creating the Topology

With all the user groups defined, the next step is to create the user accounts and logons for each of these simulated users to use during testing. This is done through the Create Topology setting under the Run menu. This process, shown in Figure 20.13, will take your user groups and create accounts for them on the different servers defined in your testing Exchange topology.

FIGURE 20.13

Before you run your test you need to create the user accounts and Exchange objects for the Exchange topology you created.

Initializing Your Test

Selecting the Initialize command from the Run menu will pre-populate user mailboxes, distribution lists, and public folders as shown in Figure 20.14. This process uses the same mechanisms that the load test itself uses to send messages in order to fill individual mailboxes and public folders.

After you have completed initializing you're ready to start your load test.

Running the Test

The next step is to actually run your test. Before you actually start the process it makes sense to take a breather and make sure that everything is ready for your test. Install the Load Simulator on each machine and define the topology on the PC (or load a saved .SIM file from your setup.)

FIGURE 20.14

Before you run your test you need to pre-populate mailboxes and public folders with messages.

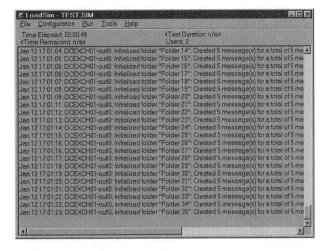

Setting Up Remote Load Generators

If you're testing remote connectivity you will want to place load-generating computers out in the field where your users will actually be. Preconfiguring machines and shipping them to remote locations often works well; loading remote control software on the PC lets you control Load Simulator on the machine remotely. This makes larger-scale load testing more realistic because you can set up machines days or weeks in advance of your test, or have less skilled people plug your machines into the local area networks at remote locations.

Synchronizing Clocks

Because the Load Simulator time-stamps its performance logs, it is important for analysis purposes that the load-generating machines have the same time. That way references to performance at certain times or when specific configuration changes are made can be properly analyzed by you and Microsoft tools. You can do this a variety of ways, although the easiest is to enter the net use command from the Windows NT command prompt on each workstation:

```
net time \\<servername> /set
```

where *<servername>* is the name of a single machine you are using as the time source.

Organize Your Team

Make sure that you have the staff available that you'll want to observe the load testing. Exchange administrators, network administrators, and network engineers are all people you'll want to be available, if not actively involved. These people can make sure that the necessary measurements are being gathered and analyzed.

20

Notify Users

If your load test uses networks or servers that are also being used by normal users you'll want to warn them that you're conducting load testing. The last thing you want is to interrupt or interfere with your business's operations—after all, load testing is designed to prevent that once your system is live! Tell users about the test, its objectives, and how they can report problems when the test is going on. If you're testing email you'll probably want to give them another way to contact you.

Setting Target Performance Levels

The hardest part of load testing and capacity planning is answering the question, "How fast should it be"? This question is difficult to answer, but you should have some general guidelines that you can pull together. One key way to set your target is to gauge user expectations; if your current email system takes two seconds to send a new email, you'll probably want Exchange Server to respond as quickly. You'll want to set target guidelines for the following:

- Initial logon to Exchange Server
- Sending a message
- Checking for new mail
- Sending mail within a site
- Sending mail between sites

Some of these factors, such as sending mail between sites, will be determined by your connector configuration. Others will be directly related to server configuration, horsepower, and network capacity. Also, not all of these events will be captured by Load Simulator. However you can use Exchange yourself while the load test is going to log on to the system and send mail to another person involved in the test. In this fashion the Load Simulator is a great way to artificially slow down your system so that you can interact and experience server and connector performance with your own eyes.

Running the Test

Start the test by clicking the Run Test selection under the Run menu. Each workstation will begin to simulate the user groups defined in Load Simulator's configuration. Status messages and activity will appear on the screen as shown in Figure 20.15 as well as go to the file lsperf.log on the machine's local hard disk drive.

FIGURE 20.15

Running the load test looks like this.

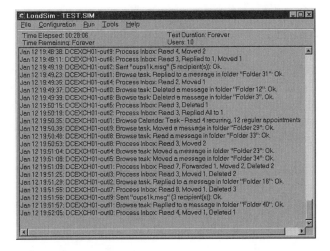

Shutting Down the Test

To stop the test, select the Shut Down command from the Run menu. This will gracefully stop the test.

Analyzing Testing Results

After you've completed a cycle of load testing you need to sit down, take a breather, and analyze your results. Although you can do this to some extent while the test is going on, the truth is that you'll probably want to wait until the test is over, sift through the reports, screens, and files, and then re-run the test. These reports will include the Load Simulator's output files, Windows NT performance monitor charts, other logs from router or switch tools, and anecdotal observations you make along the way.

Using LSLOG

Microsoft supplies a tool to help analyze and consolidate the log files generated by the Load Simulator. The LSLOG tool allows you to merge log files together to help you analyze a single set of results collected from multiple load simulation machines.

The LSLOG command's arguments and usage can be shown by simply typing **LSLOG** at the command prompt; the key things you will use LSLOG for are for grooming your log files prior to analyzing them and then actually performing the analysis.

20

Preparing Log Files

If you're preparing a widely distributed load simulation you will want to determine the groups of servers and load-generating PCs you want to evaluate. For example, because the network is more likely to play a role in performance, you may want to analyze local area users differently than users who access an Exchange server across a slower network link. The network is a variable you want to consider, so keeping the log files separate makes sense. After you know what machines you will analyze together, you need to consolidate their log files together.

After your test is finished, gather all the relevant log files together and consolidate them. Use the LSLOG command:

```
Lslog merge <logfile1> <logfile2> <logfile3> > <newlogfile>
```

The LSLOG command sends the new file to "standard output," so the > symbol on the command line sends the command's output to a file. The > sign only includes log results; if you want to see error messages you can use the 2> to get errors sent to a file as well.

Analyzing the Log Files

After the log files you want to analyze are in a single file, you use the LSLOG command again to calculate specific performance percentiles for the different Exchange actions (for example, Send Message or Reply to All). Load Simulator uses percentiles as measures of performance because users don't notice great performance and you're concerned about the slowest response time for a given percentage of transactions. For example, if the 95th percentile Reply All response time was 500 milliseconds, this means that 95% of the transactions took 500 milliseconds or less. A 50th percentile means that 50% of the transactions took a certain time or less. The LSLOG command uses the 95th and 50th percentiles as standard measurements; you can use different percentiles if you like, although I find these work fine.

To calculate the performance percentiles for a log file, run the LSLOG command:

```
Lslog answer <logfile>
```

You can also use command-line parameters to override the percentiles; typing **LSLOG** at the command line provides all of the commands that LSLOG performs. A typical analysis from LSLOG is shown in Figure 20.16.

FIGURE 20.16

Results from the LSLOG *analyze command for a load test.*

Results for "Outlook" module:						
Category	Weight	Hits	50th Pctile	95th Pctile	Mean	Std. Dev.
SEND	1	28	190	410	210	97
READ	10	428	71	331	115	148
REPLY	1	28	100	200	120	54
REPLY ALL	1	18	130	461	164	105
FORWARD	1	22	180	370	195	111
MOVE	1	66	100	201	116	55
DELETE	3	119	71	260	111	149
DELIVER	0	301	140	1402	581	1480
LOAD IMSG	0	28	0	60	16	41
RESOLVE NAME	0	50	30	31	26	7
SUBMIT	0	96	121	320	145	84
LOAD ATTACH	0	8	10	151	32	49
OPEN MSG STORE	0	20	490	1312	463	492
LOGON	0	10	8332	8642	7276	2092
BROWSE CALENDAR	1	23	20	280	132	173
MAKE APPOINTMENT	1	2	200	200	190	10
JOURNAL APPLICATIONS	0	9	230	891	307	214
Weighted Avg	20	1256	92	310	116	126
<--"score"						

Re-running Your Test

Load testing is rarely a single occurrence; you will want to run and rerun your load test as you change and configure your Exchange topology. For the best load testing results, follow these guidelines:

- Run your test for at least two hours. Load Simulator uses statistics and random numbers to generate its load at random intervals; extending the load testing time will maximize the effectiveness of the test in achieving the load you really want.

- Don't change more than one thing at a time. Load testing, like troubleshooting, is a game of variables: analyze each variable, change one, and then observe the changed results. Changing too many things either while your test is going on or between tests will prevent you from really measuring the effect of an individual performance change . You can miss opportunities to improve things by making one change that speeds up the system while making a change that also slows the system down a little. While the net effect is positive, not making the second change could make things even faster.

- Use beefy Windows NT Workstation or Server PCs to simulate your users. Load Simulator is a memory-intensive application because it needs to simulate so many client connections and sessions. A good feel for memory is that a 200Mhz Pentium machine with 256MB of RAM can support 400 moderate Exchange Client users.

20

Outlook users will use more resources, as will users who have higher usage patterns. Windows NT Performance Monitor can help you determine if a client's CPU or memory can't support the number of users you want to test. Removing the load-generating PC as a bottleneck is important for accurate testing results.

Looking at Servers

The Load Simulator can tell you if your client-side performance is unacceptable or not up to your targeted levels; the next step is to look at your servers and Exchange system, to understand where Exchange users are using the resources you've provided. Because performance is influenced not only by Exchange but by Windows NT and the hardware Windows NT uses, your analysis needs to look at both your Exchange Server topology and configuration and Windows NT itself.

Analyzing Exchange

Microsoft Exchange Server provides some basic performance information through the Exchange Administrator interface and the Windows NT Performance Monitor. We'll focus on examining the Exchange and Windows NT performance counters through Performance Monitor because it's one place to find the information you need.

Using the Performance Monitor

Day 8, "Troubleshooting Exchange," introduced you to the Windows NT Performance Monitor. The Performance Monitor is Windows NT's standard performance measurement tool; it can gather, display, and log all of the important performance information about your server. Exchange Server adds Exchange-specific performance metrics that you can monitor to see how healthy your Exchange system is.

You can use either the Chart or Alert views to monitor performance; Figure 20.17 shows using the Alert view to set thresholds for our test. Alerts show up in the log if a counter's value is exceeded.

Key Performance Counters

While you are performing the load testing you'll want to see how your Exchange server can keep up with the load that is being generated. This means that the message queues within Exchange rise and fall as opposed to rising and never falling. However it is important not to place too much emphasis on an "unbounded" or never-dropping queue; load testing, unlike the real world, rarely has quiet periods and valleys of activity where a server can catch up. The key is to use common sense.

The key counters you will want to monitor during your test include the following:

- MSExchangeISPrivate "Send Queue Size," which should average less that 1% of the total number of simulated users for this server.

FIGURE 20.17

The Performance Monitor's Alert view lets you notice when a problem occurs while you're load testing.

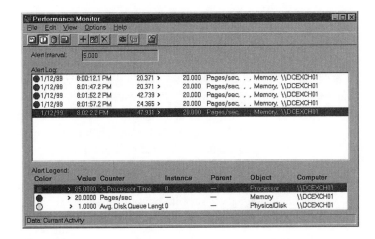

- MSExchangeMTA "Work Queue Length," which should average less that 1% of the total number of users on this server.

After your test you'll want to review the total transaction volume and statistics to make sure that your test gave you the expected volume. Often the parameters you can give the Load Simulator can multiply into volumes you don't anticipate. Reviewing some statistics can help ensure your test is reasonable:

- MSExchangeISPrivate "Message Recipients Delivered," "Messages Submitted," and "Messages Sent."

- MSExchangeMTA "Total Recipients Inbound," "Total Recipients Outbound," and "Inbound Messages Total."

Analyzing Windows NT Server

Problems or issues that you observe in the Exchange Server performance, either in terms of interactive response time or server-based queuing, can usually also be seen within Windows NT Server. Exchange Server uses Windows NT Server, which uses your machine's hardware. Windows NT provides basic hardware performance information that is critical to seeing how a server is behaving.

There will always be bottlenecks on a server; if you believe performance to be an issue you need to address the most significant bottleneck. A step-by-step process of eliminating major bottlenecks can greatly improve performance. While tuning Windows NT is an art and merits an entire book, there are some basic indicators you can use to guide your analysis of Windows NT.

20

The areas that you need to examine are the processor, memory, network card, and hard disk drives. The key things to look for with these components are

- Processor Utilization. While a machine may have peaks and valleys of processor utilization, sustained utilization above 70% usually indicates the need for more or faster processors. You can also lower Exchange Server's processor requirements by limiting message attachment encoding and decoding for Internet mail.

- Physical Memory. There needs to be enough memory for Exchange and its client load. If the server is low on physical memory the server will start to "page" or swap memory to disk as part of virtual memory. Excessive paging while a server is under load indicates the need for more physical RAM. Another alternative is to lower Exchange Server's memory requirements by running the Exchange Optimizer.

- Disk Drives. An Exchange server that is always sending and receiving mail needs quick access to the Private and Public Information Stores. Likewise the server needs to write transaction logs to keep databases recoverable in the event of a server failure. Observing queued disk transactions through Performance Monitor indicates that you may want more separate, independent-acting disk drives to keep transaction logs and databases on separate disks. The Exchange Optimizer can move Exchange files to take advantage of a new disk drive configuration.

- Network Interface. Occasionally a network card can become the bottleneck on a server. Observing queued transactions waiting at the network card indicates the need for either a faster card (100Mbps versus 10Mbps) or additional cards.

Monitoring Your Network

During load testing you will want to monitor your network and its components to see if Exchange Server is putting too great a burden on your infrastructure. The best Exchange Server design will fail without adequate networks, and Exchange topology decisions can influence a network's ability to meet application requirements.

When your Exchange Server load testing is going on you need to monitor the different network components used by Exchange users and servers. These components usually include the following:

- Routers, which link different networks together. If you use any networks to link your Exchange Sites it will be key to monitor intersite traffic flowing between routers at each site.

- Switches and hubs, which connect workstations and servers on a local area network. Network traffic within a location will go through these components, although hubs share network connections between devices on the same hub while switches allow each device to have a dedicated connection (or "segment") into a local area network.

- Wide area network links. Reviewing performance data from a telecom line or service can help you properly size your lines. Likewise, performance on a line could be fine but your service agreement or pricing is designed around a set of volume assumptions that Exchange will render invalid; changing line speeds or settings to be closer to the expected volume could save money.

Tools To Use

When you're looking at the network during load testing you'll want a standard toolbox of things to help give you insight to how Exchange is affecting the network. Some of the tools you'll want are as follows:

- Protocol Analyzer. The protocol analyzer is a network engineer's best friend; an analyzer can go unused for months at a time, but when you need one you really appreciate having one. Every network should have one. A protocol analyzer allows you to look at network traffic at a physical level. Protocol analyzers tell you what's happening on a network, letting you see what's causing problems on a network link. Some protocol analyzers can also replay network traffic that was previously captured onto the same or another network, letting you add traffic to an otherwise quiet network. This lets you add non-Exchange traffic to your load test so that your results take into account other systems as well.

- Router and Switch Management Tools. These tools will vary depending upon your network management system and the vendor of your equipment. These tools will give you utilization and other performance metrics for these devices, as well as letting you see the errors they observe on the network. If you don't have dedicated tools, these devices usually have a console port or telnet feature that allows you to manually gather relevant information.

- Modeling and Analysis Tools. If your network and Exchange Server implementation is particularly complex you may want to acquire network modeling applications from companies such as Optimal Networks or CACI. These tools help you predict application response times based on network topologies, and can be useful in environments with performance critical applications such as ERP systems.

Measurement Points

While the load testing is going on you'll want to look at different aspects of the network to determine what impact Exchange is having on your network.

20

Local Area Networks

On routers be sure to observe CPU utilization and forwarding rates. Use your protocol analyzer to look for transmission retries that indicate that the router can't keep up and is dropping packets. High CPU utilization or dropped packets may indicate the need for a larger router. While Exchange alone may not require more router horsepower, adding Exchange to an existing network may push you into more powerful equipment.

With hubs and switches, look for any indication of physical problems such as CRC or alignment errors. These kinds of problems are often indicative of bad cabling or interference, but they may not appear in significant or noticeable amounts until a load is placed on the network. With switches, look at CPU utilization and any indication of switch overload; with hubs, look at bandwidth utilization as an indication of the need for further network segmentation or switching.

Wide Area Network Lines

On any telecom lines you will need either a specialized management tool or management reports from the telecom vendor. You want to look at overall utilization, as well as any indication of poor performance. On Frame Relay links look for lengthy bursts above the Committed Information Rate (CIR) and any indication of dropped frames. You'll also want to see that any centralized ports (places where multiple sites' PVCs aggregate to a single location) are not overloaded. You can usually get detailed management reports from your vendor to help you determine this, provided that their tool's sampling time is equal to the duration of your load test. Extending the sampling before or past your load testing period will lower key counters.

Server Network Connections

On the server itself the key is to observe network transactions queuing on the network interface. With Windows NT Performance Monitor look at the Current Commands counter for the Redirector or look at the queue length for the network interface. Counts of either variable above the number of network cards is an indication that you may want to add another network interface.

Other Load Testing Tools

While Load Simulator is a useful tool, some organizations may want to use other load testing tools, either to perform the same functions as Load Simulator or in conjunction with Load Simulator. These tools include the following:

- Microsoft InetLoad, which can simulate Internet protocols just like Load Simulator can simulate Exchange Clients and Microsoft Outlook. InetLoad would be a better load testing tool if your Exchange topology relies heavily on POP3 and NNTP

clients. InetLoad is available from the Microsoft Web site at
`http://www.microsoft.com/msdownload/inetload/inetload.htm`.

- Mercury LoadRunner and WinRunner are popular general-purpose client/server load testing tools. These tools are more often used for enterprise-quality client/server applications such as SAP or PeopleSoft, although they can work well with Exchange. These tools can also be useful to generate non-Exchange application loads on servers during a test with Load Simulator.

Summary

Today's lesson showed you how to conduct an Exchange pilot and how to load test your Exchange topology. Doing this provides several benefits:

- Using the concept of a controlled yet experimental Conference Room Pilot allows you to learn about Exchange before you go into production.

- Building a pilot of Exchange involves testing and configuring all the Exchange components and infrastructure where you can observe the impact of your changes.

- Load testing with the Load Simulator can help determine if your servers and network links can handle the additional requirements of Exchange Server.

- Observing a server that is handling a high number of clients allows you to observe bottlenecks and constraints in your hardware.

Q&A

Q We're using Load Simulator and get a lot of MAPI logon failures. We can create the testing topology but we can't initialize it.

A Make sure you have the Exchange Client and Outlook 97 installed on the PC. If you have Outlook 98 installed instead, you will have this problem.

Q My load tests show a lot of unbounded queues (queues that continue to grow and never shrink down). Is this a problem, and can I fix it?

A This may or may not be a real problem. Load Simulator uses statistics to generate a load that is constant in the big picture of things, even though individual transactions are randomly generated. This is great for testing a maximum load a system can handle, but doesn't take into account that email and other systems have peaks and valleys in their usage: People use mail in the morning and the afternoon, with a lull around lunch time. So the answer depends upon the sensitivity of the queue: Does a slightly lower load resolve the issue, or does even a light load leave the queue unbounded? If even a light load causes the problem, you'll probably want to check it out.

20

Q **One of the challenges my project team faces during a Conference Room Pilot is the fact that our organization's networks are too complex to test out in a single room. Can we use the real production network that's already in place for testing?**

A Sure, if the production network can take a performance hit. Just to be on the safe side pick a low-usage time for the initial runs of your test. Sad for us technical folks, three-day holiday weekends are great for this.

Q **When I try to run the load test on a PC, nothing happens when I click Run. What's going on?**

A Chances are the machine name is set incorrectly on the user group setup for the test's properties.

Q **How can I tell how big a load-generating PC we need?**

A For simulating Outlook users, figure at least 4MB of RAM per user, plus enough for the operating system and other tools you will use. Also monitor the CPU utilization to make sure the PC is not overloaded. Another technique is to configure another similar machine to generate a load with 1/4th the users and measure the different response times; if they're different you'll want to cut back on the users on the slower PC.

Workshop

The Workshop provides two ways for you to affirm what you've learned in this lesson. The "Quiz" section poses questions to help you solidify your understanding of the material covered and the "Exercise" section provides you with experience in using what you have learned. You can find answers to the quiz questions and exercises in Appendix B, "Answers to Quiz Questions and Exercises."

Quiz

1. You've been tasked with load testing your Exchange servers for your company, which is migrating to Exchange Server from another email system. Because estimating the load you see in production is important, where would you look to find indications of your current email system's usage?

2. You've requested the equipment and facilities to perform a Conference Room Pilot. Your boss says that the money spent on such an effort would be better spent on production equipment, not "throw-away" equipment to simulate site conditions. How would you respond this argument?

3. You are performing load simulations against an Exchange Server using Load Simulator on a Pentium 200Mhz machine with 64MB of RAM, generating the load of 10 users. You have another PC running Load Simulator with 100 users, this one a Pentium II workstation with 512MB of RAM. Assume that each machine is capable of handling the number of clients being simulated. Which machine should generate better performance statistics?

Exercise

1. Review the output lslog.exe created from a Load Simulator performance log (see Figure 20.18). Under this scenario, what's the longest amount of time that almost all users can expect to wait to open Microsoft Outlook?

FIGURE 20.18

The analysis from a load simulation log file.

D:\Program Files\Load Simulator>lslog answer lsperf.log
Loadsim log file version 5.5.2187.0 (flags: 0x00000000).

Perf: Parsed data: 0.067 s.
Perf: Sorted data: 0.000 s.

Results for "Outlook" module:						
Category	Weight	Hits	50th Pctile	95th Pctile	Mean	Std. Dev.
SEND	1	35	240	781	388	571
READ	10	446	130	761	241	394
REPLY	1	26	161	1091	281	306
REPLY ALL	1	14	221	530	237	126
FORWARD	1	37	260	2503	459	630
MOVE	1	66	241	4006	787	1191
DELETE	3	121	150	621	234	285
DELIVER	0	298	181	10064	1169	4050
LOAD IMSG	0	35	0	150	28	65
RESOLVE NAME	0	78	20	50	29	28
SUBMIT	0	112	200	1071	312	444
LOAD ATTACH	0	9	10	250	55	85
EMPTY FOLDER	0	10	2664	5888	3001	1379
CREATE PROFILE	0	10	621	4617	1305	1579
OPEN MSG STORE	0	20	2684	13249	3228	3562
LOGON	0	10	25697	30504	23472	4187
BROWSE CALENDAR	1	36	70	1182	227	360
MAKE APPOINTMENT	1	1	160	160	160	0
REQUEST MEETING	1	3	1442	1933	1439	404
HANDLE MEETING REQUEST	0	9	541	991	602	271
HANDLE MEETING RESPONSE	0	6	20	60	30	15
JOURNAL APPLICATIONS	0	18	401	4356	728	995
Weighted Avg	21	1400	216	1031	251	399
<--"score"						

20

DAY 21

Migrating from Microsoft Mail

by Patrick Grote

Chapter Objectives

You've accepted the challenge of moving your company from Microsoft Mail to Microsoft Exchange 5.5. I guess a few words are in order before you start:

- You've made a great decision to move your organization forward! Microsoft Exchange 5.5 is the latest generation of messaging software.

- There are many decisions that have to be made before you can use Microsoft Exchange 5.5. Don't worry, though, we'll walk you through them.

- Keep in mind that Microsoft Exchange 5.5 is as different from MS Mail as an 8088 CPU is to a Pentium III. They both do the same job, but the performance, features, and benefits are much different.

The goal of this section is to walk you through the process of migrating your email infra-structure from MS Mail to Microsoft Exchange 5.5.

By using the ideas and knowledge presented in this lesson, you'll be armed and ready to decide the following:

- Migration method. There are three different strategies you could implement. Which should you choose?

- Wizard usage. Microsoft Exchange 5.5 provides a very powerful Migration Wizard. Do you want to use it? Should you use it?

- User impact. Migrating from MS Mail to Microsoft Exchange 5.5 affects users. You'll learn how to minimize the impact.

There are several steps you'll need to follow to prepare and then actually migrate your MS Mail system to Microsoft Exchange 5.5:

1. Establish a migration team. A team representing the various IT skills in your organization needs to be established with a project manager.

2. Choosing a migration strategy. Priority needs to be assigned to features and staging of the migration. From the priority list an appropriate migration must be chosen.

3. Planning the migration. After the migration strategy is chosen, a comprehensive project plan must be developed.

4. Completing the migration. The actual migration will be completed according to the project plan.

5. Migration follow-up. There are follow-up issues after any project. These include backups and documentation.

Good luck with your migration project. The rewards for moving from MS Mail to Microsoft Exchange 5.5 are many, including the following:

- Client functionality. Instead of the very basic MS Mail clients, Microsoft Exchange 5.5 features the cutting edge Outlook 98 client. You can say the difference between the Model T and today's Lexus cars is similar to the difference between the MS Mail client and Outlook 98.

- Server functionality. MS Mail wasn't a server-based product. Microsoft Exchange 5.5 is server-based, which offers a rich set of features.

- Server performance. Being a store-and-forward email system, MS Mail relied on clients to perform message distribution. Microsoft Exchange 5.5 uses the server to handle these tasks, thereby improving performance and reliability.

- System stability. Instead of relying on late '80s, early '90s technology, which MS Mail is based on, Microsoft Exchange 5.5 is this generation technology.

The single most important task you have to complete at this point is planning. Without an adequate plan, you are actually planning for disaster—or rather, courting it.

Establishing a Migration Team

Depending on the size of your organization, you'll need to develop a migration team. A migration team could include anywhere from one to one hundred people. Each person should have a role on the team. Some people will have multiple roles and some roles will have multiple people. For example, the Mail Infrastructure Architect might also have the role of Microsoft Exchange 5.5 Administrator, whereas there may be ten Help Desk people on the team. The following describes each team member and includes the typical or standard number of these players on a migration team:

- Project manager. The project manager's focus includes assembling the migration team, developing a project plan, assigning tasks, and keeping the project on track through management of priorities.

    Per Team.   Small Organizations—1.

    Medium Organizations—1.

    Large Organizations—1.

- Mail infrastructure architect. The mail infrastructure architect is responsible for designing the mail flow including MTA, gateway, and application design.

    Per Team.   Small Organizations—1.

    Medium Organizations—1.

    Large Organizations—2.

- MS Mail Administrator. The current MS Mail administrator is included on the migration team for guidance on current configuration and support.

    Per Team.   Small Organizations—1.

    Medium Organizations—2.

    Large Organizations—2.

- Microsoft Exchange 5.5 Administrator. The new Microsoft Exchange 5.5 administrator is included to help with design and user support issues.

    Per Team.   Small Organizations—1.

    Medium Organizations—2.

    Large Organizations—3.

- Help desk staff. User support is a very important concern during an email migration. Help desk staff are used to provide end user support before, during, and after the migration.

21

Per Team.   Small Organizations—2.

Medium Organizations—5.

Large Organizations—8.

- Trainer. End users and administrators need to complete training for the client and server portions of Microsoft Exchange 5.5 respectively. Trainers complete programs to help facilitate the transition. A close working relationship with the team is necessary to ensure the training program represents the final Microsoft Exchange 5.5 implementation.

Per Team.   Small Organizations—1.

Medium Organizations—2.

Large Organizations—4.

- Beta testers. To test the new system, you'll need to recruit users to help. Do not select only power users. You should select power users, capable users, and new users. The goal is to gain perspective from every level of user comfort.

Per Team.   Small Organizations—2 per type.

Medium Organizations—4 per type.

Large Organizations—6 per type.

- Consultant. If this is your first migration or the company's first experience with a migration, it is a good idea to secure the efforts of a consultant. You should ensure the consultant has experience with MS Mail and Microsoft Exchange 5.5 server in a migration role. This person should not be the project manager, but should work as a technical liaison.

Per Team.   Small Organizations. 1.

Medium Organizations. 1.

Large Organizations. 2.

- Business Representatives. A migration from MS Mail to Microsoft Exchange 5.5 is not a purely technical project. Business impacts will occur, so to minimize and manage the issues that occur during the transition business, representative should be involved. Business representatives should be mid-level managers that can communicate impending changes to departments and offer input and guidance to the team concerning the business impact of changes made.

Per Team.   Small Organizations. Depends on structure of the company.

Medium Organizations. Depends on structure of the company.

Large Organizations. Depends on structure of the company.

The migration team should have a kick off meeting to discuss the migration project and discuss and agree to roles. A contact sheet should be completed that has the following information:

- Team member name. The full name and title of the team member. This is important for ensuring proper spelling and recognition.

- Role designation. You should designate each team member's role so he can easily scan and find help when needed.

- Phone numbers. The business and home phone numbers for each team member should be supplied for contact purposes.

- Pager numbers. Each team member should have a pager for emergency contact.

- Mobile numbers. Not a necessity, but it is a good idea to note these numbers for team members who have them.

- Building or location. In enterprise situations not every member of the team will be located in the same area. You should note the building or mail stop number of each team member.

- Supervisor name. The supervisor name for each team member. This is important in case there are issues with contacting the team member or for recognition after the project.

An example contact form is shown in Figure 22.1. This form shows just a few of the team members.

FIGURE 21.1

Here is a sample contact form for the migration project team.

MSMail to Microsoft Exchange 5.5 Server Migration Project
Team Members

Team Member	Role	Business Phone	Home Phone	Pager	Mobile	Location	Supervisor
Patrick Grote	Project Manager	xt. 92068	314-555-1911	314-555-0922	314-555-1297	MS. 22	Missy Hickham
Dave Schrader	Help Desk	xt. 66442	314-555-0123	314-555-2211		MS. 66	John Bloom
Alvin Tyler	Trainer	xt. 51223	314-555-9032	314-555-3011	314-555-9102	MS. 32	Josh Goodwin
Roger Klein	Consultant	xt. 41233	314-555-3751	314-555-9206	314-555-6712	MS. 22	Patrick Grote

After the initial meeting, weekly status meetings should be held until the actual migration is implemented. At that point daily status meetings should be held. Remember, a successful migration takes a team of people working together. It is important to solicit ideas and feedback from each team member, so she feels like part of the process.

Choosing a Migration Strategy

The most important decision you have to make when migrating from MS Mail to Microsoft Exchange 5.5 is which migration strategy to employ. Choosing a migration strategy should be accomplished based on the following criteria:

21

- Business model. The method in which your business works is an important consideration when choosing a migration strategy. Pay particular attention to remote users and branch offices.

- User impact. A critical goal of any migration is minimizing user impact. Your organization may have a higher threshold for disrupting an end user's computing experience than other organizations. For instance, in a data-entry business desktop interruptions aren't critical, but in an order-processing center they are critical.

- Business saves. Your business justification for moving to Microsoft Exchange 5.5 should be expressed in dollars. The business unit that provides the highest cost savings should be a priority.

- Technology inventory. The equipment you'll use for the migration must be in place. Your migration choice must take into account whether you are using new or existing equipment.

- Human resources. The strategy you choose shouldn't impact your human resources negatively. You'll need the proper amount of staff to continue business as usual activities and support while completing the migration plan.

Based on the criteria you establish, you can choose from one of three migration methods. Each one has advantages and disadvantages. You need to apply your criteria to each and justify the choice.

The Total Cut Over Migration

The most drastic and quickest method of migrating from MS Mail to Microsoft Exchange 5.5 is the total cut over method. The *total cut over method* involves simply creating existing MS Mail users in Microsoft Exchange 5.5, deleting the Microsoft Mail client, pushing an installation of Outlook 98, and shutting down the MS Mail implementation.

The advantages of this method are as follows:

- Speed. This is the quickest method of migration available.

- It's clean. Due to the fact that you aren't migrating user information or data, you're starting with a brand new installation of Microsoft Exchange 5.5.

- Mail transfer issues. Because you'll only be using one email system you won't have to connect MS Mail to Microsoft Exchange 5.5.

- Less human resource intensive. Each user is handled in the same manner as the next. Support is minimal, so support staff can be minimal as well.

There are several disadvantages to this migration strategy as well:

- User data loss. Because the migration to Microsoft Exchange 5.5 is done without migrating user data, all user data is lost. For users who do not keep copies of their email or utilize personal distribution lists, this isn't a problem. For users who do keep their email and utilize personal distribution lists, this is not a good choice.

- Possible application issues. When a cut over occurs you are totally replacing one system with another. Applications that are mail-enabled may not work when moving from MS Mail to Microsoft Exchange 5.5.

- Software distribution. Unless your organization has a good software distribution system in place, you will have trouble or won't be able to push Outlook 98 down to the clients. As a last resort, or for those with a small amount of users, you can visit each desktop and install the software. You also have to consider software distribution to remote users. Are they capable of installing Outlook 98 on their own? How will you physically send them the software?

- Post implementation administration. Because the MS Mail system is being replaced, you will have to re-create any distribution lists by hand that existed on the MS Mail system.

User Data Location

During a total cut over migration, your users will lose their data, depending on the client they are using and the configuration. Several MS Mail clients can store data locally. Table 21.1 demonstrates where client data can be stored:

TABLE 21.1—CLIENT DATA STORAGE OPTIONS

Client Type	Server Based	Client Based	Depends on Configuration
MSDOS	X		
Windows 3.1x		X	
Macintosh	X		
Windows 95/ NT Inbox			X
Exchange Client for Windows			X
Outlook Client for Windows		X	

21

Verifying where the client data is stored is critical to understanding the impact on users. For example, you can see in Figure 21.2 the option of storing data locally on a Windows 3.1x client. You can access this by choosing Mail, Options, Server from the main menu. In the figure you can see the option for server storage is enabled.

FIGURE 21.2

You need to verify the location of the mail data file.

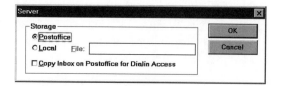

If the client you are migrating stores his mail locally, you can import the mail by using Outlook 98. Typically, mail stored locally will have an .MMF extension. To import this mail into Outlook 98 follow these instructions:

1. Find the .MMF mail file on the local computer by using the Start, Find command. Note the location.

2. Load Outlook 98.

3. Select File, Import and Export as shown in Figure 21.3.

FIGURE 21.3

The import and export is the key to managing external mail data files.

4. Select the Import from Another Program or File option and select Next as shown in Figure 21.4.

FIGURE 21.4

It's important to select the proper file type.

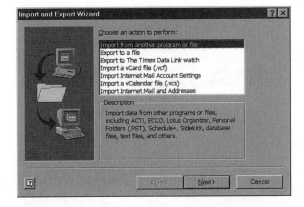

5. Select Microsoft Mail File (.MMF) from the menu selection and click Next as shown in Figure 21.5.

FIGURE 21.5

The Microsoft Mail file type is a standard choice.

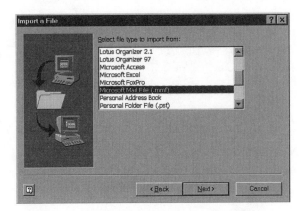

21

6. At this point you may see an error message similar to the one in Figure 21.6. If so, follow the instructions and add the necessary component. If you didn't receive an error message, continue with the next instruction.

FIGURE 21.6

You may receive an error message if the proper component is not installed.

7. You will need to specify the location and select the file you would like to import as shown in Figure 21.7. Click Open to confirm and continue.

FIGURE 21.7

You can import one MS Mail data file at a time.

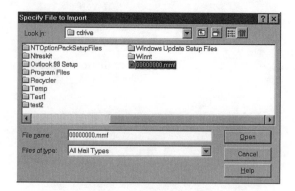

8. You'll need to supply the password of the mailbox you are importing as well as select whether you would like the messages and/or personal address book entries imported. Figure 21.8 shows the selections.

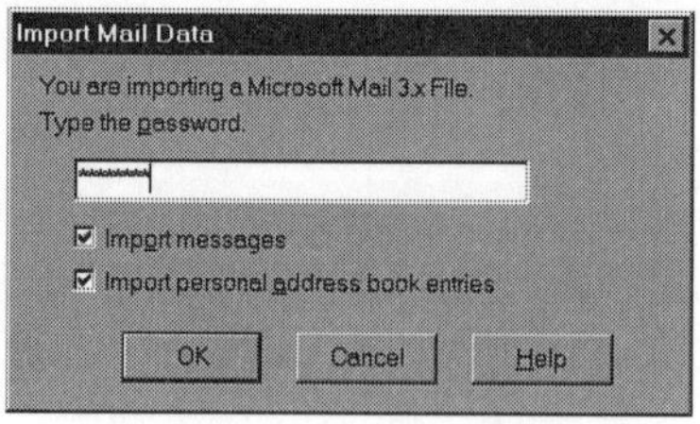

FIGURE 21.8

If the Mail Data file has a password you must enter it.

9. Selecting the personal folder to use as a container for the imported messages is shown in Figure 21.9. Select the personal folder you would like and click OK.

FIGURE 21.9

MS Mail data files are stored in personal folders.

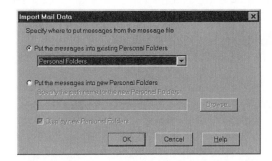

10. After the personal folder selection is made, Outlook 98 begins to process the MS Mail mailbox. A status indicator, shown in Figure 21.10, appears while the import is taking place.

FIGURE 21.10

The import process will display a status bar.

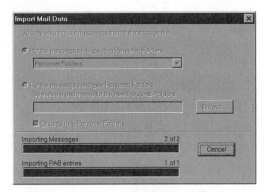

11. After the import is completed a status page similar to Figure 21.11 is shown. Select OK and your MS Mail messages and personal address book entries will now be in Outlook.

FIGURE 21.11

When the import process is complete you are notified.

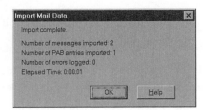

21

The term *push* relates to a software distribution/installation method. Instead of the user at a network workstation using original disks and loading (pulling) the information the software is copied (pushed) to their local workstation when they log onto the network.

It sounds like a total cut over migration is a nightmare, right? Yes, it is. You should really only consider a total cut over migration if you find yourself in one of the following situations:

- Very small organization. If you have a very small organization, ten or fewer users, and they are located at the same office, a total cut over may be used. Remember, though, user data is not migrated to Microsoft Exchange 5.5.

- Disaster recovery. The worst has happened. The server housing the MS Mail data files has crashed and there is no backup. If you have been planning a migration to Microsoft Exchange 5.5, you might as well implement the new software. You should also purchase and use a tape backup at this time.

> **Caution**
>
> Do not choose the total cut over migration strategy without first thinking through all the issues. User perception is paramount in technical support. If the user base feels you can't competently handle the task they will not work with you.

Pre-Planned Cut Over Migration

Hopefully your migration from MS Mail to Microsoft Exchange 5.5 isn't being forced by a disaster. If not, a pre-planned cut over migration might be for you.

A pre-planned cut over migration involves extensive preplanning, but does not maintain the use of the MS Mail infrastructure. When the migration is completed, Microsoft Exchange 5.5 handles all mail transfer and client functions.

The difference between a total cut over migration and a pre-planned cut over migration is the amount of planning involved.

The advantages of a pre-planned cut over migration include the following:

- Speed. This is the second quickest method of migration available.

- User comfort. Because the migration is comprehensively pre-planned, the user community will have an opportunity to attend training and understand the process.

- Mail transfer issues. Because you'll only be using one email system, you won't have to connect MS Mail to Microsoft Exchange 5.5.

- No surprise issues. Yes, I understand that every installation has a surprise or two, but if you pre-plan your migration the surprises will be limited.

- MS Mail support. No more MS Mail, no more support.

There are several disadvantages to this migration strategy as well:

- Software distribution. Unless your organization has a good software distribution system in place, you will have trouble or won't be able to push Outlook 98 down to the clients. As a last resort, or for those with a small amount of users, you can visit each desktop and install the software. You also have to consider software distribution to remote users. Are they capable of installing Outlook 98 on their own? How will you physically send them the software?

- Post-implementation support. Because there will be an entirely new email system in production, support calls will be heavy due to user and administrator unfamiliarity.

A pre-planned cut over migration is a good choice when the following conditions are met:

- Test environment. Because you are preplanning the migration, you should install a test environment so you can test the functionality of various tools. A test environment also allows you to test mail enabled applications under the new Microsoft Exchange 5.5 system to ensure compatibility.

- Small- to medium-sized organization. If you have a small- or medium-sized organization this strategy can work for you. You should not attempt this strategy if you have more than 200 users or if the users are remotely located.

- Consultant availability. Because deadlines are of the essence in a pre-planned cut over migration, you should avail yourself of the services of a consultant. Ensure the consultant has the appropriate experience for your organization.

The timing of a pre-planned cut over migration should be coordinated over a weekend at least. At best, try to select a three-day weekend such as Memorial Day or Labor Day.

Phased Migration

Do you like being as close to perfect as you can? Does the idea of shutting down your MS Mail infrastructure make you cringe? Do you have a large organization? Very important users? If so, the phased migration is for you.

A phased migration is similar to the pre-planned cut over migration in that you pre-plan every aspect of the impending migration. The difference is that the MS Mail infrastructure is not shut down when the users are moved to Microsoft Exchange 5.5. Users are moved in phases onto the Microsoft Exchange 5.5 system with complete access to the users still on the MS Mail system.

21

For large organizations, or organizations with multiple sites, this is the only strategy you should employ. Medium-sized businesses would benefit from this approach. Small businesses should use the pre-planned cut over migration strategy, as it offers the best use of resources.

The advantages of a phased migration include:

- Correctable installation. Because users will be migrated in phases, you will have the opportunity to correct migration issues experienced. By the end of the migration there shouldn't be any migration issues.

- User comfort. Because the migration is comprehensively pre-planned, the user community will have an opportunity to attend training and understand the process.

- No surprise issues. Again, every installation has a surprise or two, but pre-planning will cut down on surprises.

- Flexible scheduling. MS Mail and Microsoft Exchange 5.5 will coexist, so there isn't a rush to move users from MS Mail to Microsoft Exchange 5.5. If you experience a resource crunch or another project takes priority, you can leave the remaining users on MS Mail until you can complete the project.

There are several disadvantages to this migration strategy as well:

- Resource intensive. To carry out a phased migration properly requires the effort of many staff members. For large organizations they should be dedicated to this single project.

- MS Mail support. This is the single largest issue when choosing a phased migration. You must continued to support the MS Mail environment. This doubles your administration chores and can be very touchy to work with.

If managed properly, a phased migration offers the best opportunity for success. You should only consider a phased migration if the following conditions are met:

- MS Mail postoffices. The MS Mail infrastructure is operating correctly or close to correctly. You need to ensure the MS Mail infrastructure is transferring mail and that directory synchronization is working. If either of those are not working you'll need to fix them. If you cannot fix them you should consider either a total cut over migration or a pre-planned cut over migration.

- Upper-management support. The project should have the backing and dedication of business upper management. The migration from one email system to another is the largest project you will experience outside of migrating network operating systems. The business upper management needs to buy into the benefits and back your efforts.

Planning the Migration

Regardless of the migration strategy you choose to employ, planning should be a part of every effort. Even in the total cut over migration, some preplanning should be accomplished.

For the pre-planned cut over migration and phased migration, a detailed project plan should be completed to serve as a roadmap for the migration and to help discover any potential issues.

You can use a formal project management software package to track your project plan or you can use something as simple as Microsoft Excel or Microsoft Access. The important thing to remember is that the effort you put into planning will show in the migration.

The following fields should appear on your project plan at a minimum:

- Task. This field should detail what needs to be accomplished. For example, read *Sams Teach Yourself Microsoft Exchange 5.5 in 21 Days*.
- Due date. This is the date on which the task should be completed.
- Resource requirement. You should use this field to indicate how much time a specified task should take.
- Responsibility. This field details who or what group is responsible for completing the task.
- Status. Of course, this field is to denote whether the task is complete. You can also use this field to log comments.

After you have the form fleshed out and ready to use, you'll need to add the meat. Again, the idea is to plan your migration to avoid any issues during implementation.

Pre-Planned Cut Over Migration Tasks

We'll cover some of the tasks associated with a pre-planned cut over migration. You may have additional tasks based on your organizational structure. These tasks also serve as the basis for a phased migration.

For the best effect the tasks should be grouped into five subject areas:

- Configuration. You should configure the new environment in a test area.
- Microsoft Exchange 5.5 environment preparation. This includes creating new mailboxes and more.
- Testing. You should test all areas of the migration to ensure no hidden issues appear.

21

- Implementation. All tasks associated with the implementation should be noted.

- Post-implementation. There will be housekeeping and production issues you will need to complete.

Configuration

The following tasks are associated with the configuration subject:

- Microsoft Exchange 5.5 Server. Ensure the server is configured properly, both hardware and software.

- Client software. Ensure the client software is configured for the new installation.

- Network administration. Any network administration consoles should be upgraded to handle the Microsoft Exchange Administrator program and other diagnostic utilities.

- Gateways. Ensure the proper gateways are configured.

Microsoft Exchange 5.5 Environment Preparation

The following tasks are associated with preparing the Microsoft Exchange 5.5 environment:

- Create Windows NT accounts. Create the Windows NT accounts you'll need for the migration. Verify Microsoft Exchange 5.5 accounts are created.

- Create test addresses and distribution lists. You're testing process should test any connectors installed.

Testing

You should test the following system components:

- Message sending. Test the message sending functions of Microsoft Exchange 5.5.

- Message reception. Test the message reception functions of Microsoft Exchange 5.5.

- Verify public folders. Verify the proper public folders and security are valid.

- Gateway function. Test the various connectors and gateways installed by sending and receiving messages to and from them.

Training

The importance of training cannot be overstated. The more comfortable and familiar your users and administrators feel with Microsoft Exchange 5.5, the smoother the migration will go.

The following training tasks should be completed:

- Train support staff. Support staff should be trained to handle the calls from new Outlook 98 users.
- Train administrators. Administrators need to learn to use the administration programs that came with Microsoft Exchange 5.5.
- Train end-users. End users should have every opportunity to become comfortable and familiar with Outlook 98 and the new administrative procedures. This could include classroom and self-study options.

Implementation

The most taxing phase of the migration is the implementation phase. You should pay particular attention to client issues. As they arise you should document them so as the migration continues you won't repeat the same mistakes.

The following implementation tasks should be completed:

- Ensure outbound messages are delivered. To ensure there is no mail loss, you should ensure all mail has been delivered. This includes any gateway mail.
- Disable the MS Mail postoffice. To ensure there is no mail loss, disable access to the MS Mail postoffice.
- Migrate mailboxes to Microsoft Exchange 5.5. Use the Microsoft Exchange Migration Wizard to move the mailboxes.
- Install Outlook 98 on workstations. Push or install the Outlook 98 software on to the workstations.
- Test workstations. Test the workstation functionality by sending and receiving a message.
- Complete distribution list creation. Finish creating the systemwide distribution lists such as the Everyone group.
- Complete public folders creation. Finish creating the initial public folders and assigning proper permissions.

Post-Implementation

Post-implementation tasks ensure the hard work you just finished isn't wasted. You'll need to clean up and help the users and administrators understand what to do next.

The following post-implementation tasks should be completed:

- Shut down the MS Mail infrastructure. Ensure you shut down the MS Mail infrastructure so users cannot access the server. Make a final full backup of the server before you take it offline.

21

- Back-up Microsoft Exchange 5.5 Server. After the user's have been migrated and tested, back up the Microsoft Exchange 5.5 server.

- Leave information package on user's desk. A neat way to cut down initial support calls from users is to leave an information package. This package should detail and document an initial logon. The package should also have a FAQ on common support issues.

> NEW TERM   FAQ is an acronym for Frequently Asked Questions. A FAQ details common information about a particular subject. For instance, a FAQ on Outlook 98 would include how to change views, how to send a new message, how to read a message, and much more.

Phased Migration Tasks

To plan the phased migration you should include the tasks associated with a pre-planned cut over migration in addition to the following tasks.

Configuration

The following tasks should be added to the phased migration project plan:

- Configure foreign email addresses. Some MS Mail systems will have foreign email addresses for fax server software or a unique mail gateway.

- Configure remote connectivity. If your organization has remote users you'll need to configure their email addresses.

- Configure custom recipients. If users need to add mobile phone or pager numbers to Microsoft Exchange 5.5, you should add them as custom recipients.

Testing

The following tasks should be added to the phased migration project plan:

- Directory synchronization. You need to ensure the directory synchronization between MS Mail and Microsoft Exchange 5.5 works properly.

- Mail transfer. Proper mail distribution is critical during a phased migration. Test the MTA functions between MS Mail and Microsoft Exchange 5.5.

Training

The following task should be added to the phased migration project plan:

- Training the network infrastructure help desk. In larger organizations a different group handles the network infrastructure management and support. A representative from their help desk staff should be involved in Microsoft Exchange 5.5 training. This will help circumvent issues of responsibility when support is needed.

Implementation

The following tasks should be added to the phased migration project plan:

- Notify business groups of migrations. Your business representative team member should work with a scheduled business unit to ensure the migration schedule is acceptable. The business unit may be gearing up for a busy time, such as tax season, so migration may actually hinder productivity.
- Disable existing MS Mail addresses. After the migration you should disable the user's account on the MS Mail postoffice.

Post Implementation

The following task should be added to the phased migration project plan:

- Gateways/connectors functionality. Ensure the gateways or connectors installed on the system are working properly.

Completing the Migration

Now that all the pre-planning has been completed and the users are prepared, it's time for implementation.

There are two utilities used in implementation that are vital. The first is the MS Mail Connector and the second is the Migration Wizard.

The MS Mail Connector is used to transfer mail to and among MS Mail postoffices.

The Migration Wizard is used to move MS Mail mailboxes to Microsoft Exchange 5.5.

Each of these utilities is extremely reliable under most circumstances.

The MS Mail Connector

The MS Mail connector is used for exchanging messages with an MS Mail postoffice. The Microsoft Exchange 5.5 server can act as the main mail backbone for MS Mail after installation.

The MS Mail connector allows the MS Mail postoffices to appear like Microsoft Exchange 5.5 sites. In addition, the Microsoft Exchange 5.5 sites appear as MS Mail postoffices.

By default, the MS Mail connector is installed when a Complete installation of Microsoft Exchange 5.5 occurs.

To access the MS Mail connector, open the Microsoft Exchange Administrator and select the server you would like to enable the connector on and select Configuration, Connections as shown in Figure 21.12.

21

FIGURE 21.12

*Choose the MS
Mail Connector
for configuration.*

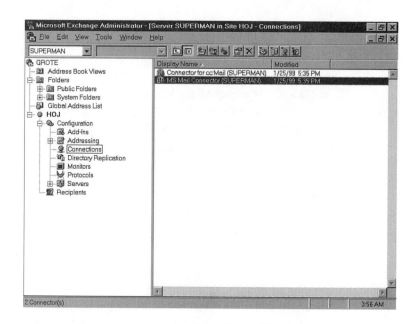

After the correct server has been selected, double-click on the MS Mail Connector. You
will see a screen as shown in Figure 21.13.

FIGURE 21.13

*The MS Mail
Connector Properties
screen has many
options.*

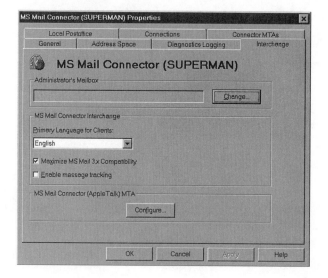

There are seven configuration tabs you will need to review and possibly modify to begin transferring mail with the MS Mail system:

- Interchange.
- Diagnostics Logging.
- Address Space.
- General.
- Local Postoffice.
- Connections.
- Connector MTAs.

To connect to the MS Mail postoffice you'll need to modify certain fields on each of the configuration tabs. In the next few sections we'll walk through the changes that are required.

The Interchange Tab

The Interchange tab has the following fields:

- Administrator's Mailbox. This is the mailbox to which updates are sent. You need to modify this with the name of your local administrator.
- Primary Language for Clients. The language you choose here will be used for administrative email messages.
- Maximize MS Mail 3.x Compatibility. Select this option to ensure OLE works between the email systems.
- Enable Message Tracking. Use this feature for tracking messages if there are issues.
- MS Mail Connector (AppleTalk) MTA. This option is used for connecting to the Macintosh version of MS Mail.

To configure this tab you should modify the Administrator's Mailbox field, ensure the proper language is set, and enable the Maximize MS Mail 3.x Compatibility. After you have completed these choices you will see a screen similar to Figure 21.14.

21

FIGURE 21.14

The MS Mail Connector Configuration Interchange tab is used for configuring transfer options.

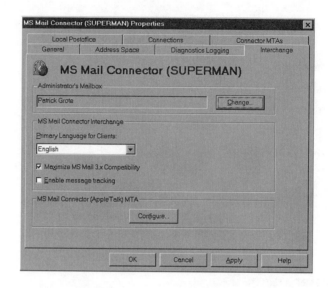

FIGURE 21.14

The MS Mail Connector Configuration Interchange tab is used for configuring transfer options.

The Diagnostics Logging Tab

The Diagnostics Logging tab should only be modified if you are interested in troubleshooting a recurring issue with your MS Mail connector.

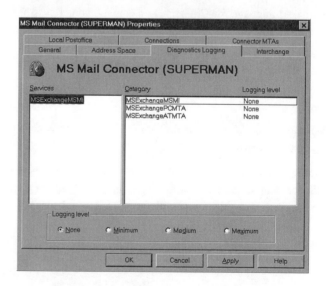

FIGURE 21.15

The MS Mail Connector Configuration Diagnostics Logging tab is used to enable message tracking.

The Address Space Tab

The Address Space tab is used to route messages among multiple sites. In most cases, you won't have to modify this configuration.

FIGURE 21.16

The MS Mail Connector Configuration Address Space tab is used to specify addressing information.

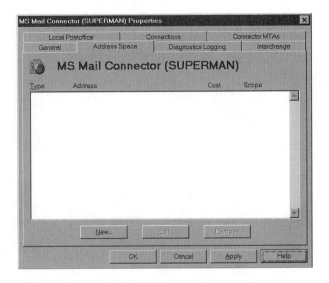

The General Tab

The General tab displays the Microsoft Exchange 5.5 server name on which the MS Mail connector is running. You can also configure the following information:

- Message Size. You can limit the size of messages traveling through the connector. The size limit is in K.

- Administrative Note. Making a note concerning the installation is a good idea. You can do that here.

To configure this tab you need to add a comment and possibly limit the size of email as shown in Figure 21.17.

The Local Postoffice Tab

The Local Postoffice tab allows you to specify the settings for the shadow postoffice on the Microsoft Exchange 5.5 server. Because MS Mail needs to transfer mail with another MS Mail server, Microsoft Exchange 5.5 attempts to dupe the MS Mail server.

You can configure the following information:

- Network. This is the name of the MS Mail postoffice network on the shadow system.

- Postoffice. Notice the name of the postoffice is the same as the Microsoft Exchange 5.5 site.

- Sign-on Password. The password to gain access to the server.

To complete configuration of this section, you need to note the Network, Postoffice, and Password fields.

21

FIGURE 21.17

The MS Mail Connector Configuration General tab allows you to limit message sizes.

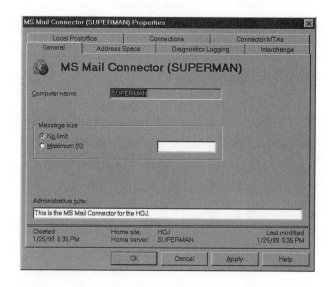

The Connections Tab

The Connections tab controls the method in which a connection is made from the Microsoft Exchange 5.5 server to the MS Mail postoffice.

To create a new method select Create from the main menu followed by Change. You will be prompted for the path to the postoffice. Enter the proper path along with the connecting username and password as shown in Figure 21.18.

FIGURE 21.18

Creating a new connection for the MS Mail Connector is simple using this option.

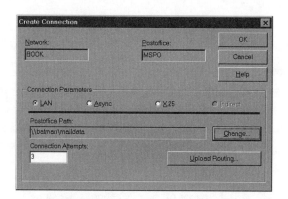

Tip

When specifying the location of the postoffice, you can either designate a network connected local drive such as M: or you can use a UNC such as //BATMAN/MAILDATA.

After you select OK to confirm your changes to the new connection, your Connections tab should look similar to Figure 21.19.

FIGURE 21.19

The MS Mail Connector Configuration Connections tab allows you to administer the various connections.

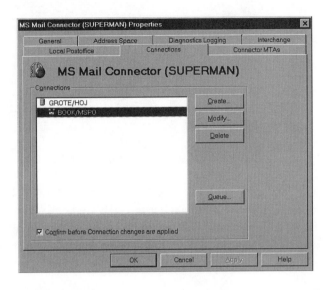

The Connector MTAs Tab

The Connector MTAs tab controls the mail transfer function between Microsoft Exchange 5.5 and the MS Mail postoffice. You can use Microsoft Exchange 5.5 to replace the existing EXTERNAL based MS Mail transfer infrastructure.

From the Connector MTAs configuration tab you need to select New. This will allow you to configure a new MS Mail MTA for the Microsoft Exchange 5.5 server. After selecting New you will need to complete the following fields:

- Service Name. This is the name of the actual MTA service that will run on your Microsoft Exchange 5.5 server. In our example we use MY MTA.

- Logging. You can enable logging on Sent and Received email. Our example enables logging for each type of message.

- Polling Frequency. This field controls how often the MTA Service will Update Configuration and Check for New Mail. Our example looks for configuration updates every 60 minutes, while transferring mail every 5 minutes.

- Connection Parameters. You define the connection method used for connecting the Microsoft Exchange 5.5 server and the MS Mail postoffices. Your choices are LAN, Async and LAN, and X.25 and LAN. Our example uses a LAN connection.

After the fields are configured you will see a screen similar to Figure 21.20.

21

FIGURE 21.20

Creating a new MS Mail Connector MTA Service is important for transferring mail between systems.

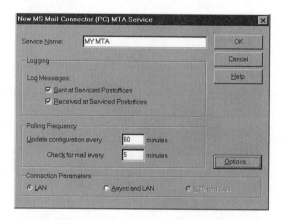

After you have created a new MS Mail Connector MTA Service, select OK and you will be back at the Connectors MTA configuration tab. Under the Postoffices Serviced section, select Edit. This command allows you to control which postoffices are used for this Connector MTA. When the Serviced LAN Postoffices window appears, select the correct MS Mail postoffices and click on Add. You will then see a screen similar to Figure 21.21.

FIGURE 21.21

Selecting postoffices to use with the Connector MTA is a vital part of the migration process.

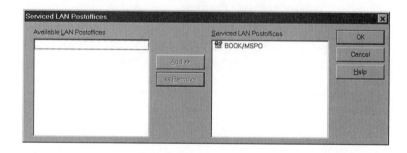

After you have finished selecting MS Mail postoffices, click on OK and you will be presented with a completed MS Mail Connector MTAs configuration tab as shown in Figure 22.22.

Testing the Connection Between MS Mail and Microsoft Exchange 5.5

After the configuration is complete, you'll need to test the functionality of the connector. To do this you should send a message from Microsoft Exchange 5.5 to the MS Mail postoffice and then from the MS Mail postoffice to the Microsoft Exchange 5.5 server.

You can send a message from Outlook 98 to the MS Mail postoffice by specifying the MS Mail address of a user of the MS Mail postoffice. For someone whose mailbox is CGROTE on the MSPO MS Mail postoffice in the network BOOK the specific address would be BOOK/MSPO/CGROTE. After the message is sent open an MS Mail client and check for delivery.

Sending a message from the MS Mail client to Microsoft Exchange 5.5 is handled just as previously noted, but you'll need to specify the ghost postoffice and network information of the Microsoft Exchange 5.5 server.

FIGURE 21.22

Completing the MS Mail Connector MTAs Configuration tab is accomplished after a few options are detailed.

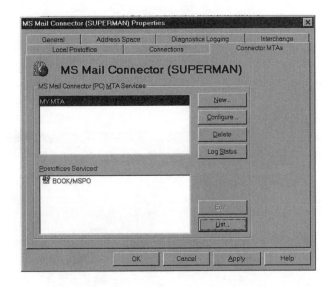

Caution

If email is not transferred between the systems, ensure the connector MTA you configured as a service is started under Start, Control Panel, Services.

The Microsoft Exchange Migration Wizard

Moving users from an MS Mail postoffice to a Microsoft Exchange 5.5 server is easy if you use the Microsoft Exchange Migration Wizard.

To load the Migration Wizard select Start, Programs, Microsoft Exchange, Microsoft Exchange Wizard. You will be presented with the opening screen as shown in Figure 21.23.

21

FIGURE 21.23

The Microsoft
Exchange Migration
Wizard opening
screen is the first step
in the migration
process.

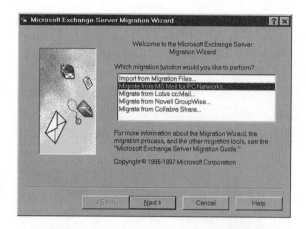

Select the option Migrate from MS Mail for PC Networks and click on Next. You will
then see a screen of information concerning your choice as shown in Figure 21.24.

FIGURE 21.24

This is important
information concern-
ing the Microsoft
Exchange Migration
Wizard.

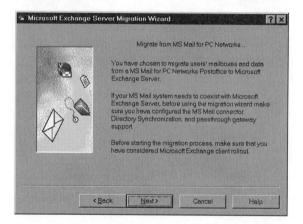

Select Next and you will be presented with the Microsoft Exchange Migration Wizard
MS Mail Postoffice configuration window. You'll need to specify the location of the MS
Mail data files and the MS Mail administrator name and password. Figure 21.25 shows
the screen with our example data.

At this point you need to decide whether you will blindly migrate the MS Mail postoffice
or base the migration on a data file. The Microsoft Exchange Migration Wizard labels
these as a one-step or a two-step migration.

The difference between the two methods lies in what is migrated. With the one-step
migration all data is migrated from the MS Mail postoffice to the Microsoft Exchange

5.5 server. Under the two-step process a list of users is created, the administrator can edit the list deleting users who shouldn't be moved, and then use the list to migrate users.

FIGURE 21.25

The Microsoft Exchange Migration Wizard MS Mail PostOffice Configuration Information allows you to enter important information.

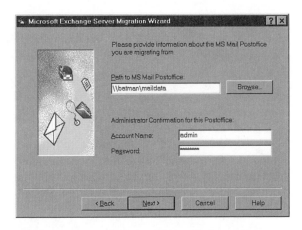

You should almost always select a one-step migration unless your MS Mail postoffice is in horrible shape from an administrative point of view.

As shown in Figure 21.26, the one-step method has been chosen.

FIGURE 21.26

Choosing a migration method should be a planned step.

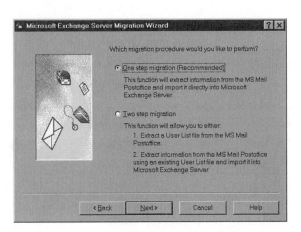

After you have selected the one-step method, click on Next. You now have the option of specifying whether you would like the user's mail data migrated to a Microsoft Exchange 5.5 server or personal folders (.PST). In most cases you'll need to migrate the data directly to the Microsoft Exchange 5.5 server. You'd want to choose personal folders if that is your default configuration for end users or you are migrating remote users.

21

For our example we'll look at migrating all the data to the Microsoft Exchange 5.5 server. Select the Migrate to Microsoft Exchange Server Computer option as shown in Figure 21.27.

FIGURE 21.27

Choosing the migration data destination is important depending on your migration strategy.

After selecting the destination, click Next and you will be presented with a screen where you need to decide which information to import.

The following choices need to be enabled per your wishes:

- Information to Create Mailboxes. This is a double-edged choice. The Microsoft Exchange Migration Wizard will create the new mailbox, but the mailbox needs to exist if you would like personal messages.

- Personal Email Messages. Personal email messages can be migrated if you would like. Further, you can limit which mail messages are imported by specifying a date restriction.

- Shared Folders. If a user has shared folders, these will be migrated if this option is enabled.

- Personal Address Books. User personal address books will be imported if this option is enabled.

- Schedule Information. If users use Schedule+ their schedule information will be imported.

For purposes of example, we've enabled all the choices except personal email messages as shown in Figure 21.28.

FIGURE 21.28

You can choose which MSMail information to migrate.

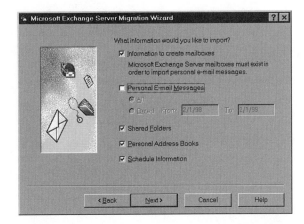

After selecting your choices and clicking on Next, you'll be presented with the user selection screen. You can select which mailboxes you would like to migrate. Our selection will migrate all users except the administrator as shown in Figure 21.29.

FIGURE 21.29

You are not forced to select all mailboxes for migration.

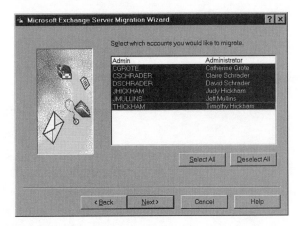

After the mailboxes are selected and you click Next, you are asked to verify which Microsoft Exchange 5.5 server should be used as the destination server. Input the server name as shown in Figure 21.30.

21

FIGURE 21.30

Ensure you select the proper destination Microsoft Exchange 5.5 server.

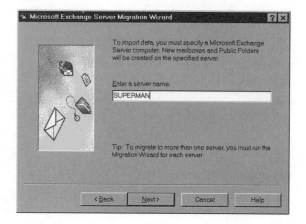

After the server name has been entered click on Next. The public folder migration security option appears. You need to select the default security for all users of the public folders created after the shared folders are migrated. Your choices are as follows:

- No Access.
- Author Access.
- Publishing Editor.

Select the level of access as shown in Figure 21.31.

FIGURE 21.31

Selecting public folder default access level of migrated personal folders is important for security reasons.

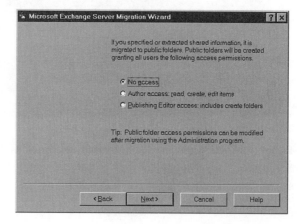

Select Next and you will be asked for a default owner of the new public folders. Select Administrator as shown in Figure 21.32.

FIGURE 21.32

The owner of migrated public folders should be the Administrator by default.

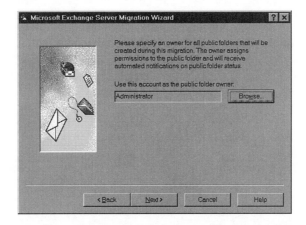

After specifying the default owner and clicking on Next, you will be asked to choose which container to import the mailboxes to. Select the default RECIPIENTS container. You can also specify a template to use when mailboxes are created. Enter your information as shown in Figure 21.33.

FIGURE 21.33

Selecting a default container and templates requires pre-planning.

21

Clicking Next will display the Windows NT Account Creation screen. You can choose to create Windows NT accounts with random passwords, with aliases as passwords, or the option of not creating Windows NT accounts. You can also specify the domain in which they should be created.

By default you should select new user with a random password. This is for ultimate security. Generated passwords are stored in the \EXCHSRVR\BIN\ACCOUNT.PASSWORD file. You can see these options selected in Figure 21.34.

FIGURE 21.34

Ensure you choose whether to create Windows NT Server accounts.

Hold on to your chair, because as soon as you click Next the migration begins! You will see a status screen similar to Figure 21.35 as the migration continues.

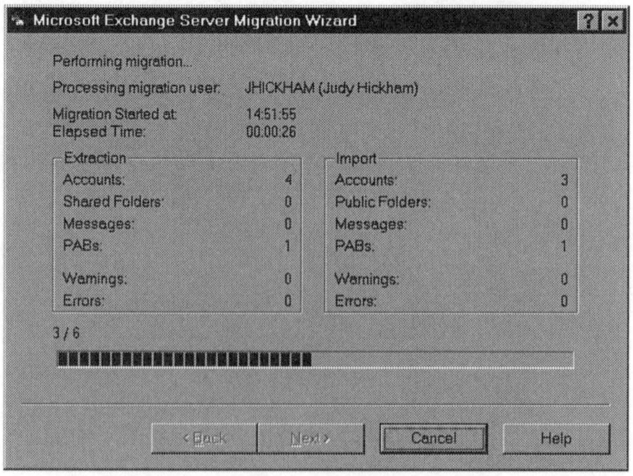

FIGURE 21.35

The Migration Status screen displays the migration in process.

After the migration is complete you can click on Finish. The Microsoft Exchange Migration Wizard informs you the migration is complete as shown in Figure 21.36.

FIGURE 21.36

The Migration Complete dialog box alerts you when the migration is complete.

You can use the Windows NT Event Viewer to review a detailed status of the migration process. You need to change to the Application Log to view messages. A sample message is shown in Figure 21.37.

FIGURE 21.37

A detailed application event log entry for the migration is created when the migration is finished.

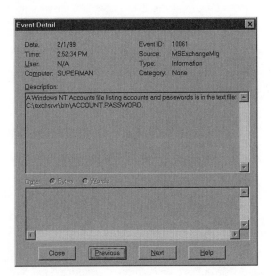

Migration Follow-Up

Congratulations on completing a successful migration. At this point your teams should follow-up and complete a backup of the new Microsoft Exchange 5.5 server and the old MS Mail postoffice.

You should assemble all documentation related to the project and archive a copy for future reference.

21

In this lesson you learned how to migrate an MS Mail postoffice and mailboxes to a Microsoft Exchange 5.5 server. This included planning and implementation.

Summary

You've now learned how to prepare and execute an MS Mail to Microsoft Exchange 5.5 server. The key to a successful migration is preplanning.

To summarize the main points of this lesson:

- The importance of establishing a good, well prepared migration team.
- The benefits on moving from MS Mail to Microsoft Exchange 5.5 far outweigh the time and effort necessary to migrate.
- The proper process for preparing the clients and servers for migration.
- The correct method of installing and configuring the MS Mail Connector.
- How to manage a MS Mail and Microsoft Exchange 5.5 hybrid system.
- The steps to ensure an issue-free migration from MS Mail to Microsoft Exchange 5.5.

Q&A

Q Do we really need to have a project manager on our migration team?

A Yes! The project manager is responsible for ensuring the tasks associated with the MS Mail to Microsoft Exchange 5.5 migration are completed.

Q OK, I can understand that migrating to Microsoft Exchange 5.5 is something we'd like to do, but do we need to do it?

A Yes! Even though your users might be happy with the functionality that MS Mail provides them, MS Mail is a discontinued product. This means there will be no support for you if you come across an issue.

Q We've installed the MS Mail Connector and have configured Microsoft Exchange 5.5 properly. When we send test messages they seem to disappear. What can we do to troubleshoot this?

A On the Microsoft Exchange 5.5 server, you can enable diagnostics logging on the MS Mail connector. Set the level of diagnostic to high. Microsoft Exchange 5.5 will track each message for you. You can then see where the messages are going.

Workshop

The Workshop provides a way for you to affirm what you've learned in this lesson. The "Quiz" section poses questions to help you solidify your understanding of the material covered. You can find answers to the quiz questions in Appendix B, "Answers to Quiz Questions and Exercises."

Quiz

1. What role should a consultant play in your migration from MS Mail to Microsoft Exchange 5.5?

2. You don't want to worry about converting user data when you migrate. Which migration method should you choose?

3. You currently use the standard Windows 3.11 MS Mail client for access. Where are the mail data files stored?

4. Which migration strategy is the most human-resource intensive?

5. Does a phased migration support Directory Synchronization?

6. How can you ensure users don't have issues with attachments through the MS Mail connector?

7. When random passwords are chosen where are the passwords stored for your use?

21

Appendixes

A

B

APPENDIX A

Exchange Server Service Pack 2

by Anthony Steven

Introduction

One of the exciting (or frustrating) things about technical writing is that software manufacturers will insist on improving their products. While Jason and I were writing this book, Microsoft produced Exchange 5.5 Service Pack 1. This service pack made several changes to the Exchange Administrator interface, as well as adding many new features.

It was only a month after SP1 came out that Service Pack 2 also made an entrance, so I eagerly checked this product out to see what other goodies were in store. However, although there are a couple of useful changes, the additions with Service Pack 2 are, in fact, minor.

The following appendix covers only the features that appeared with Service Pack 2. However, Service Pack 2 also includes all changes from Service Pack 1.

 Note

> For information on the changes included in Service Pack 1, see the Exchange web page at:
>
> `http://backoffice.microsoft.com/downtrial/moreinfo/ex55sp1.asp`

Downloading Service Pack 2

Service Pack 2 is now available on TechNet, or you can order it from the Microsoft Web site. You can also download it from the following location:

`ftp://ftp.microsoft.com/bussys/exchange/exchange-`
`➡public/fixes/Eng/Exchg5.5/SP2`

The file sizes are quite large, and I would only recommend downloading the service pack if you have a fast connection and don't have access to the CD. It took me 10 hours at 28.8Kbps to download all the files!

There are two subdirectories, one for the server and one for the client. These are the files that you need to download from the /Server directory:

- SP2_550I.EXE—Server update for Intel
- SP2_55CI.EXE—Chat server update for Intel
- SP2_55DC.EXE—Documentation
- SP2_55FO.EXE—HTML form converter
- SP2_55SS.EXE—Server support files (cluster, KMS, and so on)
- SP2_55XI.EXE—Exchange connector installation (Intel)
- SP2_55RE.EXE—Readme and HTML file

You will require the following files for Outlook 98 and Outlook for Windows 3.x from the Client directory:

- Sp2_55su.EXE
- SP2_55WI.EXE

If you are running Exchange server on an Alpha, you will also require:

- SP2_550A.EXE—Server update for Alpha
- SP2_55CA.EXE—Chat server update for Alpha
- SP2_55XA.EXE—Exchange connector installation (Alpha)

A

Finally, if you want to carry out debugging sessions, you will need the updated symbol files:

- SP2S550I.EXE—Server symbols for Intel
- SP2S55CI.EXE—Chat server symbols for Intel
- SP2S550A.EXE—Server symbols for Alpha
- SP2S55CA.EXE—Chat server symbols for Alpha

After you have downloaded the files, you should double-click the relevant .EXE files. You will see a prompt asking you where to place the decompressed files. I recommend that you place these files into a new folder, not into the default \temp directory.

Service Pack Documentation

After you have expanded these files, change to the Exchange\Eng\Docs\Relnotes\Misc and open DEFAULT.HTM. This documentation describes all the components available in Service Pack 2.

New Features

The following tools and utilities are unique to Service Pack 2.

Move Server Wizard

The Move Server Wizard was available as part of Exchange Server Service Pack 1, but only as an extra download from the Microsoft Web site. With Service Pack 2, this component is now included on the CD and as part of the download.

 Caution   Do not attempt to run the Move Server Wizard until you have read the documentation and carried out the necessary steps for both the Administrator and the User.

The Move Server Wizard gives you the ability to carry out the following tasks:

- Move a Microsoft Exchange server between existing sites and organizations.
- Move a Microsoft Exchange server to create a new site or organization.
- Move a Microsoft Exchange server to a new site in an existing organization.
- Merge existing Microsoft Exchange server sites and organizations.

However, moving an Exchange server is not a trivial task and there is a large checklist of tasks that you need to complete both before and after the move server process.

To install the Move Server Wizard, change to the \Eng\Server\Support\Movesrvr folder created by the Service Pack 2 extraction process and run SETUPMVI.EXE (for Intel) or SETUPMVA.EXE (for Alpha). If you have the CD, the folder will probably be Server\Eng\Server\Support\Movesrvr. Running this executable will install the Move Server Wizard files into the EXCHSRVR\BIN\MOVESRVR directory.

After you have run the setup program, change to the newly created \EXCHSRVR\BIN\MOVESRVR directory and read the README.HTM file. Having read this file, you can now review the documentation. You can access this information in three ways:

- Run the MVEXSRVR.HLP file.
- Open the MVEXSRVR.RTF file in Word.
- Change to the \MISC folder and open DEFAULT.HTM.

After you have reviewed the information, and assuming you still want to go ahead with the move server process, you can start the wizard by running the MVEXSRVR.EXE file. Good luck.

Replicating Public Folder and Free/Busy Information Between Organizations

One of the main disadvantages of Microsoft Exchange has always been the lack of support for sharing information between organizations. The Public Folder Replication tool goes someway towards resolving this shortfall, and enables you to configure data sharing and collaboration between two Exchange organizations.

The Inter-organizational Replication Utility works by using two mailboxes, one in each organization. These mailboxes then communicate across a suitable connector, that is, the X.400, Internet Mail Service, or Dynamic RAS connectors. The public folder replication messages then pass from one mailbox to the other, and hence to the other organization.

 Note Whichever connector you are using will require a "connected sites" entry for the other Exchange Organization.

The Inter-organizational Replication Utility comes as two files—a configuration file (EXSCFG.EXE) and an installable service (EXSSRV.EXE). These are both located in the \Exchange\Eng\Server\Support\Exchsync*Platform* directory.

You can use the EXSCFG utility in two modes—one mode sets up sharing of free/busy data, and the other you use to configure which public folders you want to replicate.

Using EXSCFG, you create a session, which includes the mailboxes that will take part in the replication. You save that session as a file, which you then install and run as a Windows NT service using the EXSSRV.EXE utility.

For more information on using the Inter-organizational Replication Utility, see the Service Pack 2 release notes in Exchange\Eng\Docs\Relnotes\Misc\DEFAULT.HTM.

Migrating Lotus Notes Applications

If you are migrating from Lotus Notes to Microsoft Exchange, you will definitely want to look at the Application Services for Lotus Notes. This suite of utilities includes:

- Microsoft Exchange Application Analyzer for Lotus Notes
- Microsoft Exchange Application Conversion Assistant for Lotus Notes
- Microsoft Exchange Application Connector for Lotus Notes.

These tools are not included in the download version of the service pack—the documentation only gives a link to the Microsoft Web site as shown:

```
http://www.microsoft.com/exchange/support/deployment/migrate/tools.asp
```

If you have both Notes and Exchange on your site, I recommend you review the material on this site, as there are several tools and utilities to help you configure your Exchange server to work with Notes.

Disabling Read/Unread Message Tracking in Public Folders

This is a MAPI call that you implement to prevent a public folder from indicating to users when they have read a message. This is only important where you have very large public folders with thousands of messages, where such indication slows performance. If you implement this, it will confuse your users because when they read a message, the message will still show as unread in the folder.

Preventing Recovery of Deleted Data

If you are working in a high-security environment, you are probably aware that you don't just delete files, but you have to erase them by overwriting the data. Exchange can now do this for you by overwriting zeros onto any deleted messages in the information stores.

To set this on the Public and Private information stores, configure the following setting in the Registry:

[HKEY_LOCAL_MACHINE\SYSTEM\CurrentControlSet\Services\
MSExchangeIS\ParametersSystem]"Zero Database During Backup"=dword:00000001

The usual provisos about tinkering with the Registry apply. If you goof it up, you're on your own. So, don't forget to run a full backup and to update your Emergency Recovery Disk.

After you have changed this setting, you should carry out a full backup, which will change the information held in deleted messages to zeros. However, the backup that you take at this point will still have the original deleted messages on it, so you may want to destroy this tape.

Connector Feature Enhancements

If you are using the Lotus Notes, OfficeVision\VM or SNADS connectors, you should extract and install the relevant files. These are located in separate folders under the Exchange\Eng\Exchconn\Setup\i386 directory. NTSCONN holds the updated Notes connector, OVVCONN is for OfficeVision, and SNACONN contains the SNADS connector file.

After you have extracted the relevant files, see the README.RTF file in the EXCHSRVR\CONNECT\EXCHCONN directory for details on the enhancements to each connector.

Known Issues

This section deals with known issues specific to Service Pack 2.

Clustering Services

If you are installing SP2 onto Exchange that operates as part of a cluster, you need to read the relevant section in the SP2 documentation. This just tells you the order in which to upgrade the nodes in the cluster.

Using IMAP4 Fast Message Retrieval

If you do not have any IMAP4 clients, you can ignore this section.

This issue relates to the problem of IMAP4 clients that require exact message sizes from the IMAP4 server. Examples are Netscape Messenger v4.5 and any version of Pine from the University of Washington.

Exchange has the facility to respond to IMAP4 queries with a rough estimate of message size, which means that the Exchange server saves time by not calculating exact message sizes. Some IMAP4 clients take this message size reading too literally, and will truncate the message at the size given should the client select that message for downloading. This can lead to loss of data.

When you upgrade to Service Pack 2, the site and server level settings for Fast Message Retrieval on the IMAP object are set to off. If you are using Outlook Express or Eudora Pro V4.0 as your LDAP client, you can switch Fast Message Retrieval on again.

Update Does Not Upgrade Some Connectors

If you have the Lotus Notes, OfficeVision/VM, or SNADS connector, you've probably worked out that these have separate upgrade files in the respective subfolders under Exchange\Eng\Exchconn\Setup\i386. The main SP2 update process does not upgrade these connectors.

Do Not Install Beta Version of Internet Explorer 5.0 with Outlook Web Access and Internet Information Server 3.0

If you are using the Beta version of Internet Explorer 5.0, then you should be using Internet Information Server V4.0 to host the Outlook Web Access Client.

Appendix B

Answers to Quiz Questions and Exercises

Day 1

Quiz Answers

1. The Information Store. Because the mailboxes are on the same server, the message does not need the Mail Transfer Agent.

2. The Mail Transfer Agent (MTA) is responsible for delivering and accepting mail between servers.

3. Public folders are managed at the organization level because they are shared for an entire organization.

4. Public Folder affinity, which allows you to connect with remote public folders. Remember that this approach only works if the user has network connectivity to the server containing the public folder.

Exercise Answer

1. The "best" route is A to C, C to D. When the link between A and C fails the best route is from A to B, B to C, and then C to D. The ability to reroute mail is a key Exchange feature. In this example the most direct route would have a lower cost than a less direct one, although the second route can be used when a lower-cost route fails.

Day 2

Quiz Answers

1. No. Domain trusts are only required if your Exchange server users reside in different domains than the Exchange server itself. Sites connected using the Exchange Site Connector do not have to belong to the same domain or have domain trusts; you simply supply the credentials for a valid account when you're configuring the connector.

2. Don't install the product (this is a trick question!) Before you install Exchange, define your requirements and plan your project. Spending the time up-front will make your installation go smoother. Besides, you'll probably end up installing and re-installing Exchange Server several times as part of your testing and configuration effort.

3. You lose security as well as the ability to schedule delivery. The Exchange Site Connector is more configurable and integrates with Windows NT security; use the Internet Mail Service for inter-site mail only if you have to.

Exercise Answer

1. There is no right answer to this question (there are as many possible solutions as dollars in Bill Gates' bank account.) The connections between the permanent business locations are best accomplished by creating an Exchange site per business location using the Exchange Site Connector. The remote connectivity can be accomplished in several ways, using either traditional dial-up modems, Internet firewalls and Virtual Private Networks, or Outlook Web Access. Quite often the best approach is to combine newer Internet technologies with more traditional technologies as backup mechanisms should Internet connections fail. Figure B.1 shows a possible Exchange topology combining all of these elements.

FIGURE 2.15

A potential Exchange Topology for the situation described in Day 2's Exercise.

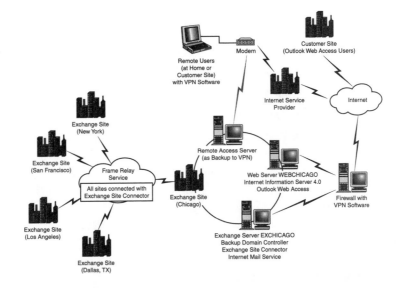

Day 3

Quiz Answers

1. Service Pack 3, with some hotfixes applied to use Outlook Web Access. You should now use Service Pack 4 to take advantage of new security fixes and Year 2000 compliance.

2. Applications running on Windows NT machines cannot connect to each other unless you use an account that has valid user credentials on each machine. For that reason servers within the same Exchange site must run using the same domain-wide Windows NT account.

3. You will want to run the Exchange Optimizer whenever you make a system change, including adding additional users or applications. You should also run the Optimizer whenever your base assumptions about your Exchange topology change. Remember to always back up your system before running the Exchange Optimizer!

4. Use TCP/IP, and only TCP/IP if you can. You will get better performance that Novell IPX/SPX and routability, something NetBEUI can't offer. You may want to consider using NetBEUI for dial-in users only, but disable the NetBEUI binding to your network cards to keep unnecessary NetBEUI broadcasts from entering your network.

Day 4

Quiz Answers

1.
   - ClintWiJ
   - McCarPa
   - LoJaG

2. You are probably logged in to your Exchange Server, so any account creation messages actually have to be sent to the Exchange server at the other site. Waiting for email to be delivered to the other site and acted upon should fix the problem; the amount of time you wait will depends on your Exchange site connector configuration.

3. Go to the Addresses tab in the Properties dialog box for the user. Click the Set as Reply Address button.

Exercise Answer

1. The trust level is set higher that the trust level of the DirSync requestor for this container. Lower the trust level to equal or less than the setting for the container.

Day 5

Quiz Answers

1. Remote Procedure Calls

2. Site, X.400, Internet Mail Service, and Dynamic RAS.

3. The Internet Mail Service at both sites.

4. The Directory Service and the MTA.

5. The MTA and the messaging connectors.

6. A directory replication bridgehead server is one running a directory replication connector.

7. A Star topology.

8. The Public Folder Replication Agent (PFRA).

Exercise Answers

1. Start Exchange Administrator and select Folders in the left pane. Now select Public Folders, and continue expanding the public folders until you find the folder you

want to replicate. Select this folder and then press Alt+Enter. You will now see the properties of the public folder.

Click on the Replicas tab, and in the left-hand column, select the sites and servers that you want to receive a copy of this folder.

2. Start Exchange Administrator and select your site in the left pane. Click on the site object to expand it and select the Configuration container object. In the right pane, double-click on the server's object. Double-click on the server you want to configure, and then select the public information store object. From the File menu, select Properties and click on the Instances tab.

You can now select the folders that you want to pull onto this instance of the public information store.

B

Day 6

Quiz Answers

1. Site, X.400, Internet Mail Service, and Dynamic RAS.

2. Site connector or Dynamic RAS connector.

3. X.400, Dynamic RAS, and Internet Mail Service.

4. X.400, Dynamic RAS.

5. The Gateway Address Routing Table. This holds Exchange's routing information and is maintained by the System Attendant.

6. Distinguished Name (DN), Domain Defined Attribute (DDA), and X.400.

7. A cost is an arbitrary value attached to a connection used to control routing. Costs are cumulative and range from 1 to 100.

8. Exchange will choose either route at random, thus providing load-balancing.

9. You could define an address space as only applying to a site or server location. This address will then not replicate to other sites.

Exercise Answers

1. You only need to resynchronize your site.

    1. On the server where you installed the connector, click on the Recalculate Routing button on the server level MTA object.

    2. Go to the Site Addressing object and click on the Recalculate Routing button on the Routing tab.

3. On any other servers in the site, click on the Update Now button on the General tab on the server level Directory Service object.

2.
1. Add the Internet Mail Service at one site. (See Day 12, "Exchange on the Internet," to learn how to do this.)

2. Check that you can Telnet into this Exchange server on Port 25.

3. Configure each IMS to deliver and collect mail from each other. Use the Connections tab on the IMS to specify the other Exchange server's IP address as the delivery address.

4. In the Connected Sites tab, add the details of the other Exchange site in both sites.

5. Add a directory replication connector, specifying that the remote site is not available.

Day 7

Quiz Answers

1. A messaging profile is a set of addressing, information, transport, and messaging services configured for a specific user.

2. As many as you want.

3. In Outlook, select Tools, Options. Click on the Mail Services tab and select the radio button for Prompt For a Profile to be Used. Log out of Outlook. When you restart Outlook, you will now be prompted to select a profile.

4. Depending on your client operating system, you can add Exchange Server service, Internet Email service, Microsoft Mail service, LDAP service, CompuServe mail, MSN mail, Fax service, Fax address books, Outlook address book, Personal address book, or Personal folders.

5. Remote Procedure Calls (RPC).

6. Multilink enables you to combine two or more modems connecting over multiple phone lines to a RAS server and multiply the speed of a RAS dial-up connection. You would use Multilink if you want to increase bandwidth on a dial-up connection from a remote site but ISDN or a leased line is impractical.

7. NetBEUI. It's fast, easy to configure, and you can use your RAS server as a gateway to translate NetBEUI to TCP/IP or IPX/SPX on your internal network.

8. RAS Manager or User Manager for Domains

9. 16,000 items or 2GB.

10. You can't. It's gone for good.

11. It lets you designate folders with contact items in Address books. When you type a recipient's name into your email message, Outlook will check these folders to try and find a match.

Exercise Answers

1. Start Control Panel and double-click on the Network icon. Click on the Services tab and double-click on the Remote Access Service. Click the Add button and either select the new RAS device from the list displayed or install another modem or X.25 PAD by clicking on the relevant button.

2. Start Control Panel and double-click on the Mail icon. Double-click on the Exchange Server service to see its properties and then click on the Advanced tab. Check the box to encrypt information when using the network.

3. Make the users members of a new global group. Start User Manager for Domains and select the Users Menu. Click New Global Group. Give the group a name and an optional description. Select the Add or Remove buttons to add the relevant users to this group. Then start Exchange Administrator and click on the New Mailbox button. Add the information on the new mailbox and click OK. You will now be prompted to associate the mailbox with an NT user account or to create a new account. Choose the option to select an existing account and then double-click on the new global account that you have just created. Now any member of the global group will be able to log in and open the mailbox.

Day 8

Quiz Answers

1. User, Network, Application, Operating System, Hardware.

2. Identify the Problem, Define the Limits, Find a Solution, Implement the Change, Monitor the Result, Problem Solved?, Record the Actions, Continue to Monitor.

3.
   1. Close all applications and save any current work.
   2. Close the system down using the Shut Down option on the Start menu.
   3. Once the system has closed down, power the system off at the power switch.
   4. Switch off the processor unit at the mains or pull the power lead out.
   5. Wait 5 seconds.
   6. Reconnect the power.

B

      7. Switch on.

      8. Log on and check the User's logon credentials.

4. Application Level.

5. The Exchange Administrator because you can get the permissions to flow down the tree.

6. SCANPST.EXE

7. IP Addresses and Host Name Resolution.

8. The MTA service could have stopped.

9. cc:Mail Connector, Directory Service, Information Stores, Message Transfer Agent, Internet Mail Service, MS Mail Connector, and Directory Synchronization Service.

10. The Diagnostics Logging tab on the properties of the server object.

11. Diagnostics logging messages appear in the Application log in Event Viewer.

12. The System Attendant.

13. You can monitor message queues trough the Queues tab on the Server Level Message Transfer Agent object or via Performance Monitor.

14. Start Task Manager, click on the Processes tab, and click the header for the column labeled CPU. The processes will now be in order of CPU usage.

Exercise Answers

1.
    1. On the client open REGEDT32 and find the `KEY_LOCAL_MACHINE/` `SOFTWARE/Microsoft/Exchange/Exchange Provider/RPC_Binding_Order` key.

    2. Start Outlook, and enter a partly complete name in the To: box. Click on the Check Names button and time how long it takes to resolve the partially completed name.

    3. Now change the binding order on the `RPC_Binding_Order` key. Select OK to commit the values to the Registry. Try the name resolution exercise again, and note the change in response time.

2.
    • The MTA has more than 25 items in the queue.

    • The IMS has more than 50 items in the queue.

    • The Exchange server has more than 100 connected users.

    • Any Exchange services stop running on the Exchange servers.

    • Any links to other sites stop working.

3. You would do this through a combination of Performance Monitor in Alert view, a Server Monitor, and a Link Monitor:

    1. Start Performance Monitor, and switch to Alert view. Add the following Counters:

       MSExchangeMTA: Work Queue Length—alert if over 25.

       MSExchangeIMC: Queued Outbound—alert if over 50.

       MSExchangeIS: Active User Count—alert if over 100.

    5. From the Options dialog box, select Log Event in Application Log and Send Network Message, entering your name in the box.

    6. Configure a Server Monitor and a Link Monitor as per Day 15, "Maintaining Exchange."

Day 9

Quiz Answers

1. Make sure that all of the components you want to install on end-users' machines are installed on the workstation where you're running the Outlook Deployment Wizard.

2. A CD-ROM–based installation would make the most sense. A great addition would be to use the Connection Manager Administration Kit that comes with the Windows NT 4.0 Option Pack. That would allow you to provide a simple way to configure the necessary connections to your corporate network.

3. The dialog box shown in Figure 9.13 shows the version number and configuration identifier. These two items are combined with the company name you specified early in the wizard to combine a way to identify your package. For this version feature to work you must use the same company name and configuration identifier for subsequent versions of the same package.

Exercise Answer

1. No. You need to select Personal Folders as the default store, instead of Exchange Server. This will download mail messages to the Personal Folders configured in the profile.

B

Day 10

Quiz Answers

1. Using MAPI over RPCs.

2. Find and Advanced Find.

3. The Drafts folder.

4. On the Exchange Server 5.5 SP1 CD, or on the Internet.

5. You can import the vCard information into your Contacts folder using Import/Export.

6. AutoPreview only applies to unread messages. The Preview pane displays one selected message at a time.

7. You must first switch the facility on using Organize. You can then mark senders as Junk senders using the Action menu or by right-clicking on the message and selecting Junk Email.

Exercise Answers

1. 1. Create a custom recipient in Exchange, using your home email address. Start Exchange Administrator and click on the New Custom Recipient button. Select Internet Address, and enter your home SMTP address. You must give this custom recipient a different display name and alias name from your Exchange mailbox. Click OK, and then add any further detail to the custom recipient as necessary.

    2. Start the Out of Office Assistant, and enter the text that you want people to receive.

    3. Click on the Add Rule button, and check the box for Forward Mail To. Add the new custom recipient as the destination address. Click OK.

    4. A message will remind you that this rule will fire for all incoming messages. Select OK.

    5. Finally, don't forget to switch on the Out of Office Assistant when you leave the office!

Day 11

Quiz Answers

1. DNS maps Host Names to IP addresses on the Internet.
2. Two examples are TFTP and SNMP.
3. SMTP.
4. X.400 is a global non-Internet messaging standard defined by the International Standards Organization.
5. SMTP, ESMTP, POP3, IMAP4, SSL, MIME, S/MIME.
6. The NBT (NetBIOS over TCP) service.
7. Exchange has an X.500-based directory structure that can be queried using LDAP.
8. An extranet means users on the Internet can access your intranet. Intentionally, that is.
9. Winsock Applications.

Day 12

Quiz Answers

1. MIME and uuencode.
2. MX (Mail Exchanger) and A (Address) records pointing to your Exchange Server.
3. POP3 and IMAP4.
4. PING, IPCONFIG and Telnet.
5. A pull feed is where you pull the relevant newsgroups onto your Exchange server. A push feed is where the ISP pushes the newsgroups onto your server.
6. It enables NNTP clients to connect to your server and download any public folders that you have published as newsgroups.
7. With that number of users, you will be looking at a minimum of a 64kbps leased line. Depending on the overall level of usage, you may even need to consider a 128kbps line. Alternatively, if your telecommunications company supports it, you could look at ADSL.
8. ETRN, TURN, a custom retrieval program, or do not send retrieval command.
9. From InterNIC or from your ISP.

B

Exercise Answers

1. You will configure this through message tracking.

   Start Exchange Administrator and select your site in the left pane. Click on the site object to expand it and select the Configuration container object. In the right pane, select the Connections object. Double-click on the Connections object and then double-click on the Internet Mail Service object. On the General tab, check the box marked Enable Message Tracking.

2. First, you need to create a distribution list that contains your two Exchange Administrators. Then, on the Internet Mail Service object, click on the General tab and change the administrator's mailbox to this new distribution list. Adjust the notification levels if necessary. Then go to the Internet News Service (newsfeed) object and select the General tab. Again, change the newsfeed administrator to the new distribution list that you have just defined. Messages generated by the IMS and the INS will now go to your Exchange administrators.

Day 13

Quiz Answers

1. NT 4.0 SP3, IIS 3.0, and Active Server Pages.

2. Java-enabled frames-capable browser such as Netscape 3.0 and later or MSIE 3.02 and later.

3. TCP/IP and Name Resolution.

4. Access to published public folders and the Address book.

5. None. IIS 3.0 needs an add-in.

6. You will see an extra prompt asking you for the name of the Exchange Server.

7. Calendar, Contacts, and any mail-based folders.

8. Site Level—properties of the Protocols Container and properties of the HTTP object. Mailbox level—HTTP object on the Protocols tab and OWA server on the Advanced tab.

9. In Exchange Administrator—Properties of the Protocols Container or through IIS—Properties of the Exchange virtual directory.

10. Pentium or Alpha processor, 64MB RAM, 4GB HDD.

11. NT Server 4,0 + SP3, IIS 3.0 or later.

Exercise Answers

1. Your procedure will vary depending on your system.

Day 14

Quiz Answers

1. POP3 and IMAP4.

2. The Internet Mail Service.

3. Host or IP address for SMTP and POP3/IMAP servers, username, email address, connection type (LAN, RAS), authentication method.

4. You don't. They will all download by default.

5. X.500 DAP.

6. Where one server cannot resolve an LDAP request, and so passes it onto another server.

7.
   - Basic (Clear Text).
   - NT Challenge/Response.
   - Microsoft Commercial Internet Server Membership System.
   - All three methods can also have SSL encryption.

8. It increases bandwidth use, as the messages are sent twice.

9. On the Diagnostics Logging tab on the properties of the Servername object.

Exercise Answers

1. Start Exchange Administrator and select your site in the left pane. Click on the site object to expand it and select the Configuration container object. In the right pane, double-click on the Protocols container. Double-click the LDAP object and select the Referrals Tab. Click on the New button, and then enter a full server host name, a directory name, and a port number.

   The host name should be a Fully Qualified Domain Name (FQDN), such as *hostname.domainname*.com. The directory name should be in the format specified in RFC 1779, for example, ou=sitename,o=organization,c=us.

Day 15

Quiz Answers

1. A Server Monitor can check that certain services are running on Exchange Servers. You can also use them to synchronize the clocks throughout an organization.

2. A Link Monitor checks that messaging links are operational.

3. Yes, by sending messages to a non-existent user, thus generating a non-delivery report. The NTR is proof that the link is working.

4. No Action, Restart the Service, and Restart the Computer.

5. Alerter and Messenger.

6. Yes, because Windows NT is aware of time zones.

7. The AT command, WinAT, and the Command Scheduler.

8. Message queues are temporary storage areas that hold messages until the destination server is able to accept the messages.

9. `MTACHECK /RL`.

10. Chart view, Alert view, Log view, and Report view.

11. Exchange DS, Exchange Public IS, Exchange MTA, and Exchange IMS, among others.

12. Every 24 hours.

13. They don't. Databases only shrink when you carry out an offline compaction.

Exercise Answer

1. Install a Link Monitor, connecting a server to the remote site. Start the Link Monitor and, when the link is operational, double-click on the monitored link in the Link Monitor window. The General tab will show you the time it is taking messages to get to the remote site.

Day 16

Quiz Answers

1. `ESEUTIL` and `ISINTEG`.

2. `ISINTEG -patch` to restore the transactional tracking logs.

3. Check that they are running.

4. An incremental backup backs up and then deletes the transactional tracking logs.

5. Only if instructed to do so by Microsoft Product Support Services.

6. Disable circular logging in Exchange Administrator using the Advanced tab on the relevant Server object.

7. With the AT command, WinAT utility, or Scheduled Tasks from IE 4.0.

8. Restore the Information store onto a recovery server, associate the mailbox with the Administrator's NT account, log on to the mailbox, and export its contents to a personal folder.

9. The new server's storage capacity should be more than the size of the data you are going to restore onto it. It must have the same name as the old server, must join the same domain, and must have the same organization and site name when you install Exchange. When you have installed NT and Exchange, you should apply the same service packs as on the original server.

B

Exercise Answers

1. Exercise Answers will vary depending on system configuration and procedure.

Day 17

Quiz Answers

1. Fire, viruses, theft, vandalism, electrical strike, power outages, terrorist bombs, rats and mice, and so on.

2. "What if" and "So What."

3. Put the Transactional Tracking logs on separate disks from the Exchange databases.

4. X.400 Connector, Dynamic RAS Connector, INS, MS Mail, and cc:Mail connectors.

5. With clustering, you have two servers accessing the same data. With replication and with failover, the two servers have a mirrored set of data.

6. RAID 1 (Mirroring or Duplexing) and RAID 5 (Striping with Parity).

7. $(10/2-1)*9 = 36GB$.

Exercise Answers

1. Exercise Answers will vary.

Day 18

Quiz Answers

1. Visual Basic for Windows.

2. Collaborative Data Objects allow Microsoft Exchange 5.5 functionality to be brought to a Web-based environment.

3. Collaborative Data Objects and Exchange Scripting Agents.

4. Windows 95 workstations require 12MB, while Windows NT 4.0 workstations require 16MB.

5. Yes. Outlook 98's Form Designer supports Microsoft Office 97 templates.

6. Yes. The Personal Folder Files (.PST) work well with distributing and testing new forms.

7. VBA (Visual Basic for Applications) is used for bringing new functionality to Microsoft Office 97 applications. With minor coding revisions VBScript is compatible with VBA.

8. CDOs are a scripting agent for MAPI.

9. You need Outlook 98, Microsoft Exchange 5.5, and a development environment such as Visual Basic for Windows or Java.

10. The Event service must be active and running.

Exercise Answers

1. Exercise Answers will vary.

Day 19

Quiz Answers

1. Organization, Site, and Configuration Container.

2. NT User accounts, Global Groups, and Local Groups.

3. Check the box for Display Rights for Roles in the Permissions tab on in Exchange Administrator options.

4. Give them Mailbox Owner right through Exchange Administrator.

5. At the Site level.

6. With Send on Behalf Of permission, the recipient knows that the message was sent on somebody else's behalf. With Send As permission, there is no immediate way of knowing that the message is not from the person named in the message.

7. Through Outlook/Exchange Client or Exchange Administrator.

8. The Owner reappears the next time you view the folder's properties.

9. Developers—Author, Editor, or even Owner. Users—Reviewer.

10. None. It only affects users logging on via NNTP, LDAP, or HTTP.

11. From Microsoft Certificate Server or from Certification Authorities such as VeriSign.

12. Windows 3.x, 95, 98, and NT.

13. A 15-character password. Normally this is written to a floppy disk when you install the KM Server.

14. They need a token. You can email this to them or pass it to them in person.

15. You would use the bulk enabling option, and then write the output file to a floppy disk. You would then distribute the tokens to your users by secure means.

Exercise Answers

1. With the combination of clients given in the question, you will need to use a combination of S/MIME and Exchange KM Server, that is, both V1 and V3 X.509 certificates.

   The POP3 clients and Outlook 98 will be able to use S/MIME, and the earlier Exchange clients will be able to use Exchange security. You will need to configure an external Certification Authority for your S/MIME certificates. Either use Microsoft Certification Server to generate your certificates, or obtain them from a third-party Certification Authority.

   You will install the Exchange KM Server, and configure the CA object. Click on the Enrollment tab and select the option for V1 and V3 support. If you are using Microsoft Certificate Server (or Certificate Server Web Client), you will now see a listing of all the certificates on your Certificate Server share. Choose the certificate that you want to use with Exchange.

   If you are using an External Certification Authority (that is, not your own Certificate Server), you should obtain a certificate from the Certification Authority.

   You will now need to generate security tokens for the Outlook and Exchange clients. For efficiency over security, do this through bulk enrolling and distribute the tokens by email. The users then need to enable their clients.

You should enable the POP3 clients through Options. The Security tab lets you connect either to your Certificate Server share or to VeriSign and obtain a certificate.

The limitations are that the S/MIME only POP3 clients (such as Outlook Express) cannot communicate securely with the Outlook 97/Exchange Clients. Outlook 98 can use both types of encryption, so can talk to both.

2. Before you do anything else, you must restrict the creation of top-level folders. Start Exchange Administrator, and click on the Configuration button. Double-click on the Information Store Site Configuration object. Click on the Top Level Folder Creation tab, and then add yourself as the only person allowed to create top-level folders on the list on the left.

Next, create top-level folders for each Department, and configure permissions so that the Head of Department has Publishing Editor rights for his own folder. If you are publishing folders to Anonymous users, change the anonymous role to at least Reviewer.

To make sure that any changes to the rights flow down the folder tree, use Exchange Administrator to make changes, and then select the option to propagate the changes down the folder tree.

Day 20

Quiz Answers

1. If your email system provides MTA logs or performance statistics, these are your best bet. Some estimations of capacity may be gathered indirectly: postoffice or database size divided by the number of users. Daily or weekly growth can give a rough (but highly unscientific) estimate of volume. Regardless, estimating current system usage can often be a difficult task.

2. Often the equipment used in a Conference Room Pilot doesn't go to waste: Equipment can often be re-deployed or maintained as spare inventory. Likewise, money spent up-front on equipment can save costly mistakes and downtime

3. Both machines should provide similar performance numbers, again assuming that they are capable of handling the number of clients that Load Simulator is generating. One indication of a Load Simulator machine's inability to handle a certain number of clients is differences in performance numbers between workstations with high numbers of users and workstations with few simulated clients.

Exercise Answer

1. The process of opening Outlook involved two actions: logging into Exchange and then opening your personal message store. Combining the 95th percentile performance numbers for logging on and opening a message store (23472 + 13249) yields a score of 36721 milliseconds, or up to 36 seconds.

Day 21

Quiz Answers

1. A consultant should be used as a sounding board for your migration strategy and plan. You should also confer with the consultant when technical issues exist that you cannot handle.

2. The total cutover migration doesn't involve any existing user data.

3. Mail data files for the Windows 3.11 MS Mail client can be stored on the local workstation, network share, or on the ostoffice.

4. The Phased Migration is the most human-resource intensive.

5. Yes. Microsoft Exchange 5.5 will support MS Mail Directory Synchronization.

6. You need to ensure the Maximize MS Mail 3.x Compatibility option is enabled on the MSMail connector.

7. The passwords are stored in \EXCHSRVR\BIN\ACCOUNT.PASSWORD.

B

INDEX

SAMS
Teach Yourself
in 21 Days

Sams Teach Yourself in 21 Days teaches you all the skills you need to master the basics and then moves on to the more advanced features and concepts. This series is designed for the way you learn. Go chapter by chapter through the step-by-step lessons or just choose those lessons that interest you the most.

TCP/IP Network Administration

Brian Komar
ISBN: 0-672-31250-6
$29.99 US/$42.95 CAN

Other Sams Teach Yourself in 21 Days Titles

Access 97
Craig Eddy,
Paul Cassel
ISBN: 0-672-31298-0
$34.99 US/$46.99 CAN

Windows 98
Paul Cassel
ISBN: 0-672-31216-6
$29.99 US/$42.95 CAN

SQL, Second Edition
Bryan Morgan
ISBN: 0-672-31110-0
$39.99 US/$57.95 CAN

Web Publishing With HTML 4
Laura Lemay,
Denise Tyler
ISBN: 0-672-31345-6
$29.99 US/$42.95 CAN

Internet Programming with Visual Basic 6
Peter Aitken
ISBN: 0-672-31459-2
$29.99 US/$42.95 CAN

Visual Basic 6
Greg Perry
ISBN: 0-672-31310-3
$29.99 US/$42.95 CAN

More Visual Basic 6
Lowell Mauer
ISBN: 0-672-31307-3
$29.99 US/$42.95 CAN

Active Server Pages 2.0
Sanjaya Hettihewa
ISBN: 0-672-31333-2
$34.99 US/$46.99 CAN

Windows NT Server 4

Peter Davis
ISBN: 0-672-31555-6
$29.99 USA/$42.95 CAN

Microsoft SQL Server 7

*Rick Sawtell,
Richard Waymire*
ISBN: 0-672-31290-5
$39.99 US/$57.95 CAN

SAMS

www.samspublishing.com

All prices are subject to change.

Disclaimer